17 <u>00</u>

PETER HALL'S DIARIES

PETER HALL'S DIARIES

The Story of a Dramatic Battle

EDITED BY

JOHN GOODWIN

HAMISH HAMILTON
LONDON

First published in Great Britain 1983
by Hamish Hamilton Ltd
Garden House 57–59 Long Acre London WC2E 9JZ

The quotation from *Collected Poems* by W. B. Yeats is reproduced by permission of
Michael and Anne Yeats, Macmillan, London Ltd.

British Library Cataloguing in Publication Data

Hall, Peter, *1930–*
    Peter Hall's diaries.
    1. Hall, Peter   2. Theatrical producers and directors – Great Britain – Biography
    I. Title   II. Goodwin, John
    792'.0233'0924   PN2598.H/
    ISBN 0-241-11047-5

Filmset by Computape (Pickering) Ltd, North Yorkshire
Printed in Great Britain by
St Edmundsbury Press Ltd, Bury St Edmunds, Suffolk

CONTENTS

ILLUSTRATIONS

FOREWORD

This book is condensed from the diaries I kept between March 1972, when I was asked to launch the National Theatre on the South Bank, and January 1980. I kept them, not for publication, but as source material for another kind of book which I thought I might one day write. When I resigned from the Royal Shakespeare Company in 1968, after ten years of effort in founding and developing that company, I had no notes, no diaries. Since then, I have often been asked about that time. My memory is quite good, yet I found I could not recapture much of what happened. I felt I must not, at the National, make the same mistake of preserving nothing.

Once started, these diaries quickly became a part of my life. I would dictate into a small tape recorder each morning between 6 and 6.30. I found this helped me to sort out my ideas, and to get things in perspective. It was, in a way, a daily confessional to myself.

I told things as I saw them. But I tried to do so as honestly and factually as possible. I did not want to perform for the diaries, correct them for inconsistences, or change them with hindsight. So I did not read or go over them during the eight years I was keeping them.

I ended up at the beginning of 1980 with more than a million words, which had been typed out day by day by two wonderful people—Sue Higginson, who was my assistant at the National and who often encouraged me to carry on when I wondered whether my daily record was of any use at all; and earlier by Philippa Chadwyck-Healey, who was my secretary before and during my first years there. Only these two knew the material. The typescripts were locked away to await the time, many years hence I thought, when I might try to write a book.

But a few years ago I told John Goodwin, a friend and colleague from the years at the RSC and now at the National, of the existence of the diaries. He was very intrigued by them. I had always been certain they could never be published as they were because I did not write them in a considered way, by hand; and if I had done so, I suppose this could have been a different sort of book. For the act of writing necessarily slows down—and can alter—one's thoughts. By dictating into a machine every morning, my entries were, it's true, as immediate as a newspaper but, I suspected, as ephemeral, and only of value to me. John Goodwin asked to read them.

He then told me he thought a shortened version could make a good story, and perhaps interest those who would like to know how it was to work in a large, highly-subsidised arts organisation in the seventies, involved in politics and management as well as making theatre. I asked him if he would condense the diaries for me, and two years later I was able to read the result of his enormous and careful labour.

What did I think? Well, I was as confused as when I see myself on television or hear myself on the radio. Another person is there whom I only half know, full of contradictions. I had intended, for instance, that these would only be professional diaries—that I would keep all reference to my personal life out of them. I was therefore su prised to find that my children were constantly bounding across the pages. They would not be kept out. Another aspect was one which disturbed me. I come from the working class, and my family are country people from Suffolk. I was brought up by my railwayman father to believe fervently in trades unions. I believe, as well, in the equal opportunities and social justice fought for by the old Labour party. So I was depressed to read of myself as a son of the seventies fighting unions and voting Conservative for the first time in my life, as a protest.

I discovered, too, a fair amount in the diaries about the press. It was certainly very painful, having been a young lion of the sixties, generally encouraged by the media, to find myself an abused figure of the seventies. Don't ever believe anyone who says that a bad press doesn't really hurt. You just have to find ways of coping with it.

Most of all, the diaries revealed to me what a frenzied life I'd been living. Much of what is recorded is of course the dramatic and bad side. But there were enormous compensations: the good rehearsals, the good working relationships with actors, the satisfaction I found in fighting and winning the battle to open the National, the comradeship of those who fought with me.

The question of whether to take the risk of publishing now, while I am still in the job, while the diaries are still warm, or whether to publish them much later as a piece of bygone theatre history, was a problem. In the end I felt that for them to come out after I had left the National could look like an attempt merely to set the record straight. Also, by then, any interest in them would, in my view, largely be gone.

Because this book is a much shortened version of what I actually recorded, some of my colleagues who have supported me so marvellously are barely, or not at all, mentioned in its pages. I hope they will forgive me and know how grateful I am to them.

I would, as well, like to say thank you to John Higgins who, with great kindness and care, read the proofs.

*   *   *   *   *   *

Let me now briefly set the scene as it was at the point where the diaries begin.

In May 1971 I resigned from Covent Garden just before I was due to become co-director with Colin Davis of the Royal Opera. I had been working there for a year and a half, also freelancing as a theatre and film director. But when it was actually time to take up the appointment I was convinced I had not been right to accept it. I was enervated by the prospect of constantly reviving my own productions, with less and less rehearsal because of the demands on stage-time of a large-scale international repertoire. I had thought something could be done about this. I was wrong. It was nobody's fault but my own. I had miscalculated the possibilities.

Soon after, I was asked by the then chairman of the Arts Council, Lord Goodman, to lunch at his flat to meet Sir Max—later Lord—Rayne, the new chairman of the National Theatre. The NT was in its eighth year of 'temporary' occupation of the Old Vic, under Olivier, and looking forward to the move to the new South Bank building, expected at that time to be at the end of 1973. But in the summer of 1971 the National was in trouble. The season had been a poor one, money was short, and despite the fact that Olivier had made a miraculous recovery from his illness, his health was still · very uncertain and there was a feeling that he was finding it difficult to continue as director.

At the lunch I was asked if I would consider succeeding Olivier. He had indicated, though vaguely I gathered, that he was thinking of stepping down. He is the supreme man of the theatre of our time, and a colleague whom I had loved working with. I had no wish to be cast in the role of the usurper by the profession which he headed. It was also, I thought, vital that it was he who launched the National on the South Bank.

I therefore said that I would be happy to talk further only if Olivier was really determined to resign; and it was agreed that if there were to be more conversations he must be brought into them. I was asked to do nothing for the time being because things were unclear. Olivier was saying he was going one day and thinking of staying the next.

That more or less remained the position for the next nine months, so I kept my own council, except for some confidential conversations with my colleagues at the RSC: Trevor Nunn who had succeeded me there, Peggy Ashcroft, David Brierley, John Goodwin, John Barton and Peter Brook. Though I had resigned from running the RSC four years before, I had stayed an associate director and was still part of the company. The RSC is in my blood. The idea of starting another family in rivalry to my own was rather bizarre.

Peggy Ashcroft felt that if I made the move it would be like changing one's political party, crossing the floor. Trevor's reaction was to ask me to return to the RSC—proposing that we could together lead them into their own new London home in the Barbican when it was ready. By standing in for each other now and again, we could give ourselves some free time and some easing of the perpetual pressures of running a big theatre. Only Peter Brook advised me to go to the National if I wanted to, though at this point I wasn't sure I did.

Just before the first entry in these diaries, I was told by Max Rayne that he had now talked things over fully with Olivier, and mentioned me as his successor. This meant I was able to talk to Olivier myself. Though his response to Max Rayne's news apparently could not have been more generous, I suspected it was rather a bitter pill for him to swallow. I came from the RSC—the opposition.

The next months were not going to be easy. I was desperate that things were handled properly. I telephoned Olivier and arranged a meeting...

PETER HALL
Bayreuth, 1983

EDITOR'S NOTE

To condense these diaries to book length I had to cut them to less than a sixth of their original 1,020,000 or more words. In selecting the material, my main guidelines were two—what interested me personally; and the need to try and make a coherent narrative that covered all the main events.

Because I was working from a transcript of tapes, often dictated at speed, some shaping and clarifying were necessary. But changes of this kind have not, I believe, altered the meaning or, I hope, the immediacy of the original.

I did not think it was part of my job to edit material for diplomatic reasons. This was the concern of Peter Hall who, in the event, left my shortened manuscript very much as I presented it to him. Changes or deletions suggested by the lawyers we felt bound to make.

My thanks especially to my son, Tim Goodwin, who put aside his own writing in order to help me with the initial cutting, and who wrote the footnotes and compiled the index. My warmest thanks also to Helen Greenwood, Lyn Haill, and Colin Simon. All three, in ways too many to list, simplified my work on this book.

JOHN GOODWIN
London, 1983

1972

Monday 27 March

The morning with Larry[1]. I felt our old friendship again. But he is clearly upset, and his feelings are very ambiguous. He wants to retire as director of the National and can't wait to get out of the theatre. He also does *not* want to retire. I think one small part of him is pleased I may be his successor; he talked about 1959, when he was trying to amalgamate Stratford and the Old Vic[2] and get me to come in with him as his number two. Another part of him doesn't want me to be his successor. I am Royal Shakespeare, not National. I have not been Larry's man ever.

He was hoping it could all be squared up and announced this week. I said that was impossible. He wants me to join by the beginning of '73 at the latest. I stressed that I must have time: time to negotiate the contract; time to discuss the whole matter and inform my RSC colleagues properly. Larry is scared stiff of the press getting on to it. I told him it was too big a decision for me to make under pressure and that if I am asked by the press I shall tell them the truth—that discussions are going on with him and with Max Rayne[3] but that nothing has been concluded.

There were four hours of conversation. They took no form but ranged all over the place. Larry still has heroic energy, but he strays from the subject, forgets names, muddles up attitudes. You have the impression of a great and splendid animal constantly being deflected by the fight with some stronger power.

He brought with him a list of all who work at the National. At this point there is only one person whom I categorically said I could not work with— Kenneth Tynan[4].

It was a good morning although I don't kid myself that life will be simple if all goes well and I go to the National. The interregnum period will be very difficult, and even thereafter, Larry will never be an easy man to have around. He is to be made honorary life president of the National or some

---

[1] Laurence Olivier was appointed director of the National Theatre company at the Old Vic in 1962 and held the post until November 1973—two and a half years before the company's move from there to the South Bank. The National Theatre company officially came into being in 1963 and lodged at the Old Vic for all the twelve years up to the move. Sir Laurence was created a baron in 1970.

[2] In 1959 Olivier was already involved in setting up the National Theatre company.

[3] Chairman of the National Theatre Board from 1971.

[4] Writer and critic. Literary adviser to the National Theatre company 1963–73.

damn thing. He wants this and doesn't want this. He seems to have a love-hate relationship with practically everybody—directors, actors, writers.

Then to Max Rayne. He is clear, watchful, economical, and gives you the feeling he is listening to what you are thinking rather than to what you are saying. I told him how things had gone with Larry and that I was now ready to negotiate the contract. I sketched out the general terms. Rayne is a business man and understands the realities of the situation. Civil servants, treasury officials and cabinet ministers still believe one should work in the arts for honour. I think Rayne appreciates that bread is also needed.

To the Aldwych to see *All Over*[1]. The performance has held wonderfully, and I think it a superb play. Here I know the critics are wrong.

Today Edward[2] asked me if I believed in God. I told him I didn't but I was still trying to find out. He replied confidently that he did. He told me God was a tall man with a long red scarf, a red cloak and a beard. He had a silver crown on his head. But because he lived up in the air, he did not need shoes, he walked around barefoot. My own five-year-old idea of God was the old Ovaltine poster of a large peasant earth-mother with a sheaf of corn.

Tuesday 28 March
The phone is buzzing all day. Pinter wonders if there is any news on the *Homecoming* film[3]. There isn't. David Warner[4] rings to ask what I think of him playing in John Mortimer's stage adaptation of *I Claudius*, directed by Tony Richardson. I say the obvious: it must be a good part. People only ring for advice when they have already made up their minds.

Wednesday 29 March
Lunch with Otto Pleschkes, the film producer. He liked my script, *The Last of Summer*[5], and has a book he wants to give me hoping I might write a script of that. I told him I would be delighted but what I really wanted was to direct another film. There was something unreal about talking to him with the National Theatre situation hanging over my head. I told him of it in confidence. He thought it a splendid idea, but worries for me that I then shouldn't be able to do films. But you can't do everything. I wish I could stop trying.

---

[1] Play by Edward Albee which Hall had just directed for the RSC and which received cool reviews.
[2] Hall's son by his second wife, Jacky. Then aged five.
[3] Attempts were being made to set up a film of Harold Pinter's play, *The Homecoming*, which Hall had directed at the Aldwych for the RSC in 1965.
[4] Acted a wide variety of roles at the RSC in the 1960s, including Hamlet and Henry VI in, respectively, Hall's productions of *Hamlet* (1965), and *The Wars of the Roses* (1963/4). Most of his subsequent work has been in films.
[5] Based on a short story by H. E. Bates.

To the Arts Council[1] for a fairly boring meeting. Private words afterwards with Hugh Willatt[2] and Arnold Goodman[3]. They both expressed satisfaction at the way the National Theatre situation is developing. Goodman rather floored me by saying, 'I shall inform the Minister[4] and the Prime Minister at a little dinner party tonight for William Walton's 70th birthday.' I said I hoped they would be pleased. Goodman brushed the question aside.

Late at night I am still rambling in my mind on the major problem. Do I tell Trevor Nunn[5], Peggy Ashcroft[6], David Brierley[7] now about my decision to move towards the National? Or when the deal has actually been negotiated? They know I have not entirely made up my mind, although Trevor, being a natural optimist, is convinced I am returning to the RSC. I have not said I will.

I don't want to upset them until the position is clear. Yet I am terrified that they should hear from another source that I am negotiating. I fear I must wait and run the risk, yet I know I am glad to be a coward at this moment. I don't want to tell Trevor.

Thursday 30 March

A day of idiocy in the film world. MGM had seen the film I made last year, *Perfect Friday*, and liked it. It had apparently expunged the reservations they felt after seeing another film of mine, *Three Into Two Won't Go*. So it was almost certain we would be going ahead with the script I've done, *The Last of Summer*. We would know at 9 pm. I have learnt from experience to take nothing that happens in the film world seriously. Nonetheless, my spirits rose. How wonderful to do a film before locking myself up again in a theatre.

At 11 pm MGM turned the project down. Some new vice-president in charge of something or other, whose existence we had not even known of, had decided that the script was not 'viable commercially'.

To put it bluntly, it seems I cannot get a job in films. My start in them came at a moment when the industry collapsed. Also, considerable things were expected of me, and because I was learning the trade, they didn't happen. I have so far made no really good films—at least not at the level of quality of my best theatre work. But I know I can make them now. I have served my

[1] Hall was a member of the Arts Council 1969–73.
[2] Secretary-General of the Arts Council 1968–75.
[3] Outgoing Chairman of the Arts Council 1965–72; and, among much else, member of the South Bank Theatre Board from 1968, and Governor of the Royal Shakespeare Theatre from 1972.
[4] Lord Eccles. Paymaster-General with responsibility for the Arts 1970–73.
[5] Artistic Director of the Royal Shakespeare Company from 1968; Hall's successor.
[6] A Co-Director of the RSC from 1968.
[7] General Manager of the RSC from 1969.

apprenticeship. And I wonder if I would be going to the National if my film career was flourishing? Yet the National is an enormous challenge and in no sense second best. I have to run theatres. I have an ability for that which I have proved to myself. You must do the things that you do best.

Tuesday 4 April and Wednesday 5 April
Meeting with Laurie Evans[1], my agent; also Larry's. He is now beginning the negotiation with the NT on my contract. He told me what Larry's artistic control is. His contract is worded precisely the wrong way round. The Board can require him to do anything they want. More horrendous, they can appoint, after consultation with him (although he has no right of approval), any associate directors they see fit. I would not sign a contract like this, so I foresee trouble.

Leave for New York on the 5 pm plane[2].

Sunday 9 April
New York: I am getting increasingly nervous about the National Theatre negotiations. It is a very bad week to be out of the country and out of touch. *The Observer* ran a story this morning saying that I'm to succeed Larry and an announcement is expected soon. So for the rest of the day and night I have been bombarded by the English press. I have not been able to say it is not true. Or that I am going to the National. Or use that stale old comment, 'No comment'. I have said: 'It would be stupid to deny discussions are going on. I hope they work out for both sides.'

A comment on acting. Humphrey Bogart talking about Spencer Tracy. 'Spencer does it, that's all. Feels it. Says it. Talks. Listens. He means what he says when he says it, and if you think that's easy, try it.'

Tuesday 11 April
New York: Ran smack into Edward Albee in Sardi's who purred his disapproval of the fact that I had not phoned him. He told me he had nearly finished a new play, a comedy. And that the only directors for it were either me or himself. He asked me if I could rehearse it as soon as *Via Galactica* had opened. I said I was flattered and fled into the night. Life sometimes contains too many stimulations.

I have a feeling the National Theatre is going to go wrong. It makes me think one can only make small decisions from day to day, from hour to hour. The big decisions are somehow made for one. And yet I resent that thought.

[1] Laurence Evans, Chairman of International Creative Management.
[2] To hold auditions for a science fiction musical, *Via Galactica*, which Hall was to direct on Broadway later in the year, with music by Galt MacDermot, the composer of the music for *Hair*.

I have always believed passionately that one makes one's own luck. I have tried to make mine all my life. The truth is that at this moment I don't know whether I want to go to the National Theatre or not. It is flattering to be asked. The status is enormous. The possibility of doing good work is boundless. The impression it makes on people is ridiculous. But I grasp eagerly at every possibility that it may go wrong. What will be the outcome?

To bed late, more dead than alive. And with the melancholy prospect of getting up early to take the plane back to England where the National Theatre crisis awaits me. Then I must go to Stratford on Saturday to say something to my colleagues, and then on Sunday to Vienna to begin directing Pinter's *Old Times* for Vienna's Burgtheater, my first play in German.

Wednesday 12 April
New York: A phone call from John Goodwin[1] in England to warn me he had heard that Larry had talked to the National Theatre company last night, had become emotional, and under the dramatic circumstances of the meeting had made the company feel that he had not been consulted about the appointment, and was going to 'fight on' in order to open the new building. Who is he fighting?

On getting home from America this evening, a message from Kenneth Tynan asking me to ring him the following morning 'to discuss something to our mutual advantage'.

Thursday 13 April
Spent most of the morning on the telephone. There is a fine old rumpus developing. Tynan has indicated publicly that he is unhappy about me succeeding Larry. I rang him as requested. He said whatever I might read in the papers, none of his chagrin was directed against me personally. 'It never crossed my mind for a moment that it was directed against me personally,' I replied.

He told me that feelings were now so inflamed at the National Theatre (by him, no doubt) that the only proper thing was a cooling-off period during which no decisions were taken. I made no comment. He asked me what was happening. I asked *him* what was happening. I said I had been in America, and only knew what I read in the papers.

Meeting with Max Rayne, Laurie Evans and myself. All the points in the contract are tidied up.

A good meeting with the Board. They asked tough questions; so did I. I told them that if I wanted to do a play I regarded as controversial, in any sense of the word, I would warn them about it and discuss it with them. If

---

[1] Head of the RSC Press Office from the creation of the company in 1960 until 1974. Head of the National Theatre Press Office from 1974. Is an NT Associate.

they wanted, they could of course read it. I appreciated they had the right to overrule my decision and stop me doing such a play. But I wanted them to understand that if they did it twice, I would resign. There was acceptance of all this, though with much banging of the table and head shaking.

But I am very worried about the Larry situation, and how everything will be handled. The Board will meet again next Tuesday, to confirm their decision.

Friday 14 April
The brouhaha continues. The Sunday papers are apparently printing full insight 'probes' into the National Theatre 'scandal', following the line that Larry was not kept properly informed of the Board's intentions. *24 Hours* are trying to do a television piece with Tynan rumoured as appearing. I talked to Rayne, warning him.

To supper at Peggy Ashcroft's. She understands what is driving me to the National. Is glad that I am going back to running a theatre, as it is what she thinks I have to do. But she is very sad I am moving away from the RSC. Is this the end of fifteen years work together? It can't be.

Saturday 15 April
The 'scandal' is now growing so large that Tynan may achieve what I guess is his objective and either get a mass resignation from the company or one from Olivier or both. Or so much of a public hoo-ha that a cooling-off period becomes essential.

An extraordinary meeting with Trevor Nunn and David Brierley. There were tears in everybody's eyes. Very un-English. One of the low points in my life. There is no reproach, no anger—in fact, a great understanding.

Trevor said he felt he could not in the circumstances go on with the RSC for much longer. It was not a criticism of my action but a recognition of the fact that the RSC could not go on as it was anyway. Slowly the conviction began to grow in the room that we had to amalgamate in order to make a strong National Theatre. The suggestion came from Trevor and was eagerly supported by David. We became very excited and euphoric. All our problems seemed solved. It will take time and it will take skilful politicking, but I believe that in two or three years it could be in everybody's interest.

Sunday 16 April
More stories in the newspapers. I am angry that the idea of a 'scandal' should be perpetuated. Late at night I finally got in touch with Olivier. I am most eager that when the announcement of my appointment to the National — planned for Tuesday—is made, he and I should be seen to stand together. The Larry who wants me to join supports this view. The Larry who wants to keep the National Theatre until his death doesn't support it at all. The conversation therefore reflected the ambiguity. Larry welcomes my coming,

he says, and will support me in everything and co-operate in every way possible. But he won't do anything in public at this moment to show he is glad—have a press conference or a picture with me, or any interviews. That, he says, would be endorsing the bad behaviour of the Board in keeping him in the dark.

Monday 17 April
Jenny and Christopher[1] returned from Los Angeles where they were seeing their mother, and Lucy[2] had her third birthday party. I spent a minute with my children before returning to the telephone.

Tuesday 18 April
The last day of the farce. Or is it merely Act I? The press release goes between Rayne, Olivier and myself all day. Apart from weeding out Larry's purple prose (why is it that actors are so addicted to over-writing?) the whole statement is now moving subtly away from the concrete to the vague. I am to join some time in 1973 and take over after Olivier has opened the new building at the beginning of 1974.

The whole of the press has been told an announcement is expected tonight. This gave an unnecessary drama to the Board Meeting this evening. I arrive at the National's offices at Aquinas Street at 7 pm. Tynan is still complaining to the Board, but I do not see him or meet him. When I am called in, celebrations are already in progress and the drinks are out. The Board examines the press release. Craig Macdonald, the press chief at the Old Vic, prepares to put it out to Press Association. He is stopped three times while John Mortimer[3] corrects the words for better English, or Larry makes sure there is enough reference to Oliver Lyttelton's[4] mother, who campaigned for the National Theatre movement many, many years ago. Professor Spencer, from the Shakespeare Institute at Stratford, who is on the Board, shakes his head gravely and quotes that if this were seen upon a stage now, it would be condemned as an improbable fiction.

The atmosphere is euphoric and crazy.

Wednesday 19 April
The press on the phone all day following yesterday's announcement, but I avoid most of the calls. Jenny and Christopher pack and leave for school in the afternoon. Meantime, I am trying to catch up on all my work and pack

---

[1] Hall's children by his first wife, Leslie Caron. Christopher was then 15, Jenny 13.
[2] Hall's daughter by his second wife, Jacky.
[3] The writer and barrister. Member of the NT Board from 1968.
[4] Oliver Lyttelton, Lord Chandos, was first Chairman of the NT Board, to 1971. He died January 1972.

and leave for Vienna in the evening. A rehearsal room will seem a peaceful place after all this.

Tuesday 25 April

Vienna: I was amazed this afternoon to get a letter from Kenneth Tynan. 'I trust you suffered no lasting wounds from being caught in that flurry of crossfire between the Board and the Executive. As I told the Board on Tuesday (and you last week) none of us had anything against you personally. What we deplored about the whole exercise was the total lack of consultation. . . . So: Congratulations—and I needn't warn as wary a bird as you to keep a sharp eye on the Board and its doings.' There was much more in similar vein. Perhaps I will just write a charming letter back.

Sunday 21 May

Days and days without a diary. The time has been too full rehearsing *Ulisse* at Glyndebourne[1] and Pinter's *Old Times* in Vienna to snatch even a few moments. In the four weeks I've had of rehearsals, I have ended up with two evenings off and two days free—and they have been filled with visiting Jennifer's school, and the christening of John Bury's[2] smallest daughter. The compensation for all the work has been the wonder of *Ulisse*: one of the best things I've ever done, I think. I took the metaphors of the baroque stage seriously—a heaven with gods, man on the stage, and the devils beneath him—and it worked. So (again) did working with Janet Baker[3].

Tuesday 13 June

Vienna: An interesting thing comes from rehearsing *Old Times* here. When the actors' *intention* is right, the inflection is virtually the same in German as it is in English. How can this be? There is a human truth which transcends language and is the one thing common to all humanity. This is why we can understand plays in languages that we are ignorant of—always assuming the work is sufficiently realised to reveal the truth.

Sunday 18 June

Vienna: A press conference in the Burgtheater. What does Pinter mean? How do you work with Pinter? Are German actors different from English actors? Are you, for Vienna, changing the way you did the production in London? What are your plans for the National Theatre? I made the usual

---

[1] Hall's production of Monteverdi's *Il ritorno d'Ulisse in patria*, which opened at Glyndebourne on 25 May 1972 to an excellent critical reception.

[2] Head of Design at the RSC 1965–68. Head of Design at the National Theatre from 1973. Is an NT Associate.

[3] Penelope in *Ulisse*. Hall previously worked with Janet Baker in 1970 when he directed Cavalli's *La Calisto* at Glyndebourne, in which she played Diana.

replies and as usual they were slightly misquoted. Headline: 'I don't work for the public.' Well, I don't. Sometimes what I do pleases the public. But I really work for the author and a good rehearsal—something which extends the actors and myself.

Tuesday 20 June
Vienna: First night of *Old Times*. The family leave first thing in the morning for the long drive to Calais and then home. I am looking forward to getting back to my own house so much. What with Glyndebourne and Vienna, this has been nine weeks away. Too long for someone as bourgeois as me. I need my possessions. They reassure me.

Wednesday 21 June
Vienna: Last night appeared to be a triumph. The house was snobbish and attentive and didn't dare laugh much. But they were held. The performance was the best we have given. It disturbed the audience. My friend Maximilian Schell, Annemarie Düringer, and Erika Pluhar acted with passion and precision.

I must remind myself to think twice before working abroad again, though. The whole operation is so organised, so much in the hands of the bureaucrats, that there would be very little chance of anything startling or original.

Now we begin our long journey home. By Sunday we shall be back in Wallingford[1].

I can't wait.

Monday 3 July
Board Meeting of the National Theatre. The agenda was enormous; the bumph shoulder high. I am picking up all sorts of useful bits and pieces. The financial position is much healthier. Business is good and they have paid back some of the colossal debts they incurred a year ago; but then they now have a small company and a small, carefully considered repertory.

The subject of Ken Tynan came up. He had asked for his contract to be extended for another three years, to be present at Board meetings, and that a deputy director should be appointed forthwith. He suggested Michael Blakemore[2]. Tynan may be thinking that he could develop a caucus of power within the organization.

I asked for it to be minuted that a condition of my accepting the job was that Tynan should go. I also said I wanted to tell him myself as soon as Larry and the Board thought it fit. I think I went a little far in being forthright, but I was fed up with everyone pussy-footing round the subject.

---

[1] The Thameside village of Hall's country home.
[2] An Associate Director of the National Theatre company at the Old Vic 1971–76.

Larry looked worried. He has a love/hate for Tynan and considers, rightly, that he owes a lot to him. He wants him got rid of but obviously feels he ought to be defending him. Larry doesn't like hurting people. Though how you run an organisation without sometimes causing emotional bruises is beyond me. I believe the only rule is to be as truthful as possible. People never thank you for softening blows by lying.

Tuesday 4 July
I rode home with Larry from a meeting at Max Rayne's and talked about *The Tempest* as the one play I wanted to do and the need for him to play Prospero. I pointed out that Prospero was acted traditionally by a remote old man—an aesthetic schoolmaster who was thinking of higher things, whereas Prospero should really be a man of power, of intelligence, as shrewd and cunning and egocentric as Churchill.

Larry listened. I think he was interested. He said he wanted to play the part for comedy, and that Prospero should lecture his daughter in the first scene while shaving. He said he couldn't wear all those whiskers and wigs Prosperos always wore. I love the fact that actors always go straight to their appearance. When Bully Bottom is given the part of Pyramus in *A Midsummer Night's Dream*, the first question he asks director Quince is: 'What beard were I best play it in?' There speaks the actor.

I don't think Larry *will* play Prospero. I believe he will open the National with *King Lear* directed by Michael Blakemore. I shall let him do exactly what he wants.

Wednesday 5 July
A fascinating meeting with Ken Tynan. Before I could deliver my blow, he told me he was thinking that after ten years at the National the time had come to move on, and that Larry had always needed him, but possibly I wouldn't. I wonder who had warned him. This though gave me my opening and I said gently that I didn't think he and I would get on. He hotly denied this. I told him I thought it best to resolve matters now in case he should hear rumour. I said I was fed up with reading in the press that when I arrived at the National Theatre, he would leave. He remarked he had planted so many stories in the press himself, he no longer believed anything he read.

I am sorry about this situation, but at least it is now clear and in the open. Ken will certainly be gone before I am fully involved with the National[2].

Sunday 16 July
A lunch and afternoon meeting of the directors of the RSC. It was a happy meeting because Ashcroft, Brook[1], Nunn, Brierley and I were really

[1] Peter Brook, stage and film director. A Co-Director of the RSC from 1962.
[2] Tynan's appointment to the NT ended officially on 31 December 1973.

12

discussing the ways and means by which a future amalgamation could happen. It makes sense in terms of artistic resources and finance. My proposition is that the RSC should leave the Aldwych[1] and run the NT's proscenium theatre, the Lyttelton, on the South Bank as the first step in a fusion. Then, when the RSC moves to the Barbican, it would offer continuous major Shakespeare productions and there would be no Shakespeare on the South Bank. This was an idea I had already sketched out with David Brierley and with Trevor. But it was encouraging now to find Peter Brook also thinking of it as the only sensible rationalisation.

Wednesday 19 July

Ulisse tonight at Glyndebourne. Although Raymond Leppard[2] had fever and was full of antibiotics, it was a superb performance. This is the first time I have been able to look at the production absolutely objectively, and I enjoyed myself. I normally detest seeing my own work. I liked this. Technically it was effortless and looked as if there were no problems at all. The piece floated. Tonight I actually felt like a good director. A rare feeling.

Thursday 20 July

Lunch with John Schlesinger[3]. I asked him if he would join me at the National, coming in as an associate director with responsibility for doing a minimum of two productions in three years. He agreed. He just said 'Yes'. It was a heart-warming moment.

Friday 21 July

I gave lunch to Arnold Goodman, who arrived late and went early. In 1960, it was Goodman's job, as a relatively unknown solicitor, to come down to Stratford at the behest of Lord Chandos to try to get the Shakespeare Memorial Theatre and the Old Vic to amalgamate to form the National Theatre. I made it my business then to send him packing—a fact which he often makes jokes about. He says he had to leave Stratford like Toad disguised as a washerwoman.

This present lunch was a first step in the amalgamation plan of the National and the RSC. I let Goodman come to the idea of the plan himself. It wasn't very hard. I am not even sure that he didn't know I was letting him think of it. I did it by recounting some of my present anxieties for the future of the National—shortage of staff, management, money, directors. He said

---

[1] The Aldwych was taken over by Hall in 1960 as a London home for the Stratford company, whose work before then had been mainly confined to Shakespeare seasons by the Avon. The addition of the Aldwych made it possible to add modern and other plays to the repertoire. This widened the actors' range and brought about the creation of the RSC, a flexible ensemble of artists under long-term contract.

[2] The conductor; and the editor of Monteverdi's score.

[3] The film and stage director.

it was entirely reasonable and sensible that the two organisations should now get together. But he feared it could never happen because of the people involved. After all, it was me that had stopped it happening once before. What was Trevor Nunn's view? I said I happened to know that nothing could be closer to Trevor's heart than an amalgamation. Goodman was overjoyed. He said I could certainly count on his support and what I must do now was win over Max Rayne, then Patrick Gibson[1] and then Hugh Willatt. He advised caution and slowness, but said he would certainly support the scheme and if Pat Gibson rang him up, he would tell him what a wise move it could be.

Dinner with Jonathan Miller[2]. I have known him slightly for years. A long time ago he asked me for help and advice, and I helped get him some productions at Nottingham. He told me then his great ambition was to be a director. Well now he is one and a very successful one too.

I was pretty blunt, said I admired the clarity of his work, but did not admire his habit of directing plays as if he were advancing a theory for the New York Review of books. He pushes home his points so strongly that he makes the play a very simple shape, with little ambiguity. It is an interesting example of a dazzling intellectual turning out rather simplistic work. Like Marx writing *Das Kapital*. Miller accepted my observations with good grace. The burden of my song was that he needed to trust his instincts. Plays, because they are human, are more complex than theses. He agreed.

Our evening was heartening. He said he would like to join me at the National as an associate director. I now think this should happen, because it would give continuity with the past.

Saturday 22 July
A little seed begins to root in my mind. I wonder why it is I still bother with the ideal of a theatre company. This year could hardly be better for varied and interesting work—*All Over* at the Aldwych, *Ulisse* at Glyndebourne, *Old Times* in Vienna, *Via Galactica* to come in New York, *The Homecoming* film to be made. Yet still I look forward with great excitement to the creation of that living company at the National Theatre.

I don't believe in the theatre for aesthetic reasons. I don't believe in it for political propaganda: good politics always make bad art. And a lot of the ideas that sustained me at Stratford—among them the belief in finding somehow a wider audience of young people, poor people, working class people, which was I suppose a reflection of my own background—now seem curiously naive, because anyone who wants to go to the theatre is today well able to do so. I believe in the theatre as a community form. If the actors

[1] Chairman of the Arts Council 1972–77, succeeding Lord Goodman. Created Baron in 1975.
[2] An Associate Director of the National Theatre company at the Old Vic 1973–75.

have enjoyed, then the audience will enjoy. There is communication.

Tuesday 25 July
Denys Lasdun[1] showed me round the South Bank building. Architectur-ally it is going to be wonderful. It is not palatial, but human. The roof is not yet on and the concrete is raw and rude. But one can feel the intimacy of the place. On the Olivier stage one man could play Beckett, or a hundred men could fight the Wars of the Roses. I was agreeably surprised too with the proscenium theatre. We also heard this morning that the Minister has got the extra money to make possible the Studio theatre which had been cut from the plans for economy. It seems I'm winning a first battle.

I begin to understand how it could all work. I am tremendously excited.

Friday 28 July
I went in the evening to see *Front Page*—the American play by Hecht and McArthur at the Old Vic. This was a simply magnificent production: well balanced, well presented and meticulous. It is the first time I have felt Michael Blakemore is a great, as opposed to a good, director.

Saturday 29 July
I have been reading again bits of David Addenbrooke's enormous thesis *The Royal Shakespeare Company 1960–68*. Trevor Nunn talks in it about the differences between him and me as directors. He says that I am a 'political' director—not in the sense of political commitment, but because from the beginning I know what I want the play to mean and how I want the actors to do it, and by persuasion and diplomacy I nudge them into doing just that, whereas he doesn't know where he's going and undertakes a voyage of discovery with the cast.

It is an interesting comparison. But I think it's too simple. And it is not true. I go on voyages of discovery too. He cons and wheedles too. We both often find things we didn't know were there and which we certainly weren't looking for.

Monday 31 July
A meeting with Michael Blakemore at the National. There was much in the air between us—but the tensions gradually relaxed. Blakemore wants to stay, and having seen *Front Page*, I certainly want him to.

He was the man Tynan was running as the successor to Larry. He referred to this obliquely and said what he wanted out of life was to direct plays and films, not run theatres. I wonder.

[1] The architect, and designer of the National Theatre building on the South Bank. Knighted 1976.

15

Peter Hall's Diaries

Thursday 3 August

A day's trout fishing on the Lambourn and the Kennet with Michael Hordern. Christopher and I went last year and were eager to repeat the experience. It was a perfect day. Beautiful countryside, beautiful water, England at its best. I caught nothing. But it didn't matter.

Christopher fished from 9.30 am until 10 pm with fanaticism and application. He was rewarded with two trout and three grayling. It was a marvellous day.

Monday 7 August

Harold Pinter and I had a long talk in a pub. He wanted to question me more about the future of the National and my invitation to him to become an associate director. He is always a cautious man. He wanted to know precisely what it would involve all over again. And he wanted to know who his colleagues would be. I told him at this moment Schlesinger, Blakemore, and probably Miller. He said his disposition was to say yes.

He commented on how well I looked and how alive I seemed now I had recommitted myself to running a theatre. That is the way I feel.

Tuesday 8 August

Lunch at Prunier's with Nicholas Tomalin. He is an old friend from Cambridge. I have always respected his intelligence and his ability as a journalist. In any issue, his heart is in the right place.

He is interested in doing a book on the National Theatre because he finds it, he says, a metaphor of our society. He thinks the living organism of a theatre company is subject to all the pressures and all the illnesses of society at large. And this metaphor also has in Larry the most superb heroic leading part.

He made one thing quite clear. He was prepared to show the Board what he had written and listen to their comments and if he thought them correct, adjust his text accordingly. But the final arbiter must be him, not them. I think this is very reasonable. I hope the Board and Larry will see it the same way.

Home fairly early. Jean Mallandaine, our friend from Glyndebourne, is staying. She is a member of Ray Leppard's continuo group—plays the pipe organ in our Baroque operas. We played the Schubert Fantasia in F minor for four hands. My fingers creaked and ached. The result was not bad. I showed musicianship but no craft. That is lost for ever.

Wednesday 9 August

South Bank Board[1] meeting. I immediately ran up hard against Desmond

---

[1] The South Bank Theatre Board (abbreviated in the diaries as the South Bank Board) was appointed by the government to be responsible for the building of the National Theatre and, on completion, to hand it over to the NT Board.

Plummer[1]. He doesn't want the Studio theatre finished. Nor indeed does Eccles, the Minister, for in his letter to the South Bank Board he tells them the good news of the extra money to finish the building to the highest standard, but then drops in one of those ministerial sentences which is meant to be taken note of by civil servants for many years to come. It was, he observed, hardly necessary to reopen the question of the Studio theatre.

I made a fighting speech about the need for it. Most of the members looked pained. Artists, it seemed, should not be allowed in when art is being discussed.

The joke is that the South Bank Board cannot avoid having the Studio. Denys Lasdun has built it as the cornerstone of the building. The space has been created by the structure that actually holds up the two other theatres. Even if we can do nothing except put a wooden floor in this space and paint the brickwork of the walls white, it is there. So they have had it.

Friday 11 August
Slept late and then sadly took Jenny and Christopher to the airport where they go to Sardinia for a month's holiday with their mother. I shall not see them now until November. The longest break ever. I am sad.

Thursday 24 August
To London for a long session with Larry. I did most of the talking, though. He listened in that familiar pose I remember from years ago when I was trying to persuade him *not* to cut every morsel of text in *Coriolanus* that referred to pride, arrogance and mock modesty. Eyebrows down, some suspicion on the face, trying to find the catches.

I brought him up to date with all my meetings. But mainly I outlined the whole scheme of how I want to use the three theatres within the National. This is fairly far away from Larry's plans—he always saw Shakespeare and large-scale work only on the open stage; Chekhov, Feydeau, and the like in the proscenium theatre; experimental work and new writing in the Studio. Quite apart from the enormous strain this would put on the organisation in terms of output, it does not make aesthetic sense to me to divide the repertoire in such a way. Each home would become a ghetto. I don't think you can have three separate companies in three separate theatres. Nor do I think one company can run in three theatres. Ideally, we should have three separate companies, each with at least one play in each theatre. Then all the actors would have the benefit of all three spaces.

Larry heard these ideas and despite his own views, I think he liked them.

---

[1] Leader of the GLC under its Conservative administration 1967–73. Member of the South Bank Theatre Board 1967–74. Knighted 1971.

We talked about the opening of the building, and how I could take over from him immediately after it is opened, and with the minimum of fuss and bother.

We discussed the possibility of me doing *Lear* with him. I am not sure that I want to. I am not sure I am ready to do *Lear* yet—even if I found a conception for it, I think it would be unlikely to fit with Larry's. He needs someone who will make the play work smoothly around him and accept his performance as it is. And I suspect he himself is torn between wanting me to do it, and wanting me not to do it. I raised again the question of *The Tempest*. This I do want to do.

He wondered. So we are both going on wondering.

Friday 25 August

To London early. A very great deal to do. The pressure is now going to mount. Only one week is left before the family—Jacky, Edward, Lucy, and the indispensable Jae who looks after us—leave for three months in New York, where I'm to direct *Via Galactica*. It will be the longest time I have spent out of England since National Service over twenty years ago.

At the end of the day, off for a weekend in Suffolk to talk about a much longed-for project: to make a film based on Ronald Blythe's book, *Akenfield*, which draws a haunting portrait of an East Anglian village. The determination of a talented film editor, Rex Pyke, somehow to set up the film has revivified the idea, and he and Blythe wanted me to see how near to reality it could now be. I had spent three years trying to get the money to make this film and it is so near to my heart and so upsetting that I almost didn't want to go this weekend.

Rex and I are staying with Ronald Blythe who lives on the outskirts of Charsfield—the Akenfield of the book—in two knocked-together Tudor cottages on a Roman road. The arrival by night is mysterious and powerful. He is nervous and jumpy but very hospitable. It is one of those houses where I walk around with my head permanently folded down, the ceilings are so low. But it is a beautiful place and the silence is extraordinary.

Saturday 26 August

We went to visit Benjamin Britten to try to get him to write the music for *Akenfield*[1]. Then three Suffolk men—author, composer, and director — would do the film.

I have not had a proper long conversation with Britten since 1960 when he and Peter Pears came to Stratford to stay in my house for a night (though we had a later flirtation about me directing his opera, *A Midsummer Night's*

---

[1] Britten agreed, but became ill and could not do it. The music used was Michael Tippett's *Fantasia Concertante on a Theme of Corelli*.

Dream[1]). They had been to the first performance of *The Winter's Tale* because it had music by their friend Lennox Berkeley.

Britten hasn't changed much. There is something thoughtful about him —like a precise headmaster who is going to stand no nonsense. But he has infinite charm and a great sense of humour. He has a reputation for gathering a court around him so that he can play the wilful emperor. But he is already a living legend.

It must be difficult for him to protect himself against pressures from the outside world. Artists may be respected more in our day and age than they were, and they may be elevated more into the rare creatures that they are, but they are also eaten alive: privacy is impossible, and I would suspect even work is a luxury in which it is sometimes difficult to indulge.

Britten has now taken a secret cottage in the middle of the cornfields where he is composing his next opera, *Death in Venice*. It is the only way to get peace. He told me he used to enjoy living in Aldeburgh until so many people stood on the garden wall to take pictures of him. Then he moved inland. But now, even there, the noise of American bombers is disturbing. So among the cornfields he writes his operas. He said it was a new experience for him—he had always been a man who lived by the sea. Now he is much more aware of the land—and of rabbits.

Wednesday 30 August
A last desperate day in England, which started early in the morning and went on till very late—dictating letters, clearing up papers, and attempting to reach a finished state in order to go away for the three months in New York.

Thursday 31 August
Up very early to get on paper a memorandum setting out my policy for the National Theatre. This had been left as I had thought I would do it once I got to New York. But who knows what complications and problems await me there? By the time the house was stirring at 8.00, the memorandum was done. I am not sure what it is like. No doubt, it is too colloquial and too optimistic. But it gave me a great feeling of peace to know that two months' work had reached some conclusion.

I am of course nervous that the Board, the Arts Council, and all, will start tearing my rough observations[2] to pieces in my absence. Certain aspects of the policy will not be popular. Too many people think the National Theatre

---

[1] Hall eventually did this at Glyndebourne in 1981.
[2] The main points were that the Olivier Theatre should continue the work of the National Theatre company at the Old Vic; the Lyttelton concentrate on new writing, touring and retrospective seasons; and the Cottesloe be mainly used as a workshop. This was all provisional on the NT grant being set at an adequate level.

should be a kind of dramatic national gallery, packed all the time with many masterpieces. They don't realise that to stage constantly such a large repertoire is the most expensive and exhausting work. And if you try to keep too many productions going for too long they quickly become dreadful and routine. One has only to look at many Continental theatres.

Sunday 24 September
New York: Letter from Trevor Nunn in England. It would appear that the financial position of the RSC is going to help us achieve our Grand Design of some form of amalgamation between the NT and RSC. Trevor writes that their losses this year and the projected losses next must lead the Arts Council to do something.

Thursday 12 October
New York: David Brierley phoned from Stratford. He has just discovered that the RSC's chairman, George Farmer, has had a secret meeting of the finance committee of the RSC and has discussed the Grand Design. It didn't go down at all well. The inner governors—or most of them—simply thought that I was at my old empire-building tactics. I'm not.

Tuesday 24 October
New York: Another early morning call from David Brierley. He had a good meeting with Paddy Donnell[1], who said little about the desirability or the undesirability of the merger. He did, however, say he thought Larry would welcome it, as Larry had often spoken with regret that he failed to make me merge with him back in 1959 when I was first going to Stratford. I hope this is a true evaluation, but I think Paddy is being naive.

Friday 24 November
New York: I have now been for one solid month and more in the grip of a rehearsal nightmare which is the same each and every day. *Via Galactica*, though getting better technically, is getting thinner and less worthwhile in its heart. It is dying, as shows can. And there is nothing much I can do about it. There is life there, but it is life of the wrong kind. A director knows by this stage of rehearsal whether something is good or bad. This is bad—but I have to go on pretending to the cast.

Wednesday 29 November
New York: The notices of *Via Galactica* are universally terrible. The show closes on Saturday. Galt MacDermot, its composer, doesn't seem too disturbed. He liked what we ended up with.

---

[1] Administrative Director of the National Theatre 1971–74.

I didn't. I am not ashamed of the production as it now stands. But it is far away from the dream I dreamed. The script was never right and still isn't. It was and is a fine score. However, if you can't have a monumental success, I suppose you may as well have a monumental failure. This is it.

Thursday 30 November
On a Jumbo jet which showed, appropriately after my flop with a space show, a *Planet of the Apes* film. I did not watch. Edward was entranced. I began reading a wonderful book, *The Imperial Animal* by Lionel Tiger and Robin Fox. It is something of a shock to realise that it is the first book I have read in three months. A reporter from the *Daily Express* was at the airport and asked me if I would like to say a few words about New York critics. I declined. He asked me why I was about to do a Pinter film—of *The Homecoming*—as the last two Pinter films had been commercial flops. I asked him to ask the backers. He looked like a vulture, but he was a timid one.

Friday 1 December
Spent the day at Wallingford in bed in a daze. Very tired. Very dispirited. Not yet able to pick myself up. Read a great deal.

Saturday 2 December
Was driven to London to look at the location for *The Homecoming* film. No problems. Then down to Shepperton to look at the sets. No problems. Had a long and helpful talk about the way we are going to shoot the picture, and then came back to Wallingford. I can't quite face anyone at the moment. The air is too thick with commiseration. Why do I find sympathy so hard to bear? Arrogance I suppose.

Tuesday 5 December
A meeting at the Arts Council with Patrick Gibson and Hugh Willatt. I told them the feelings Trevor Nunn and I had of the future of the National and the RSC. Willatt pointed out (and rightly) that he and I had spent a good deal of the last ten years maintaining the necessity for independence and competition between the two theatres. I said the identities of the RSC and the National in the sixties were now an historical fact which should not be confused with what their identities should be in the future. For one thing, the existence of the new South Bank buildings must mean that many of the functions of the RSC would be taken over by the National.

I also stressed how much the RSC personnel wanted the merger, and how much it would help the sudden expansion of the National. Gibson observed that I was saying that if the Arts Council didn't let the merger take place, there was a danger that the RSC would be destroyed—by me. That is not true.

The meeting was genial, ironic, and cryptic. All options were kept open. It was obvious from the attitude of Willatt and also of Gibson that the Arts Council must have serious reservations about the idea of two great companies being turned into one.

Gibson nevertheless said the suggestion made a lot of rational sense: it was a marriage of compatibles.

I left the meeting not quite sure how I had done. But at least the ball is now rolling.

To the National for the last night of Jonathan Miller's production of *School for Scandal*. I have never understood Sheridan's reputation for classic wit and eloquent comedy. I hate this play. It is tepid and tame and unexceptional. I don't know how one would do it. The only eighteenth- century comedy I have ever liked is *She Stoops to Conquer*—and that is because of the reality of the characters. There is a naturalism in it that is poetic.

At the end of the performance, went across to the Aldwych and crept into the back of the Circle to see the last fifteen minutes of John Arden's *The Island of the Mighty*. It started at 6.30 and was over four hours long. I wanted to be there as I'd heard that David Jones[1], who directed it, had invited Arden to address the audience from the stage at the end of the evening and tell them why he disagreed with the production. Arden and Margaretta D'Arcy, his wife, had caused a storm during rehearsals. They had publicly accused the RSC of an 'Imperialist' attitude to their play, of changing its political slant, and had paraded outside the Aldwych carrying placards and forming a picket line. The audience was attentive but tired. I saw fifteen minutes of strange rhetoric, full of stamping and roaring. John Arden did not appear. Brief talk with Trevor backstage. I told him of the Arts Council meeting. John Goodwin told me the hot news of the evening. Angus Maude, the right-wing Tory MP for Stratford-upon-Avon, has resigned from the governors of the RSC because of a letter in *The Times* today from Trevor and David Jones. In it, as part of a defence against the Arden attack, they say the RSC is 'basically a left-wing organisation'. Johnny, who drafted the letter, says he is mortified: he should never have written the phrase; it was far too provoking. I think it is highly comical Maude should react in this way. He is at the moment a right-wing irritant to Edward Heath. He writes indignant articles in the *Sunday Express* pulling Heath back from his increasingly left-wing stance. There couldn't be a better man to criticise the company because he is so extreme. But this will give fuel to *Daily Telegraph* leader writers and to others who think subsidy for the arts should be reduced or even stopped.

Home late but happy. I am a fish who is glad to be back in my own pool.

[1] An Associate Director of the RSC from 1966.

Wednesday 6 December

The papers are full of Angus Maude's resignation. The text of a letter from him in *The Times* is quoted at some length. He of course tries to have it both ways. He says he would be just as opposed to Government money being spent on a predominantly right-wing organisation.

To the National, where I was to have met Paddy Donnell but found Larry holding court. He was very funny about Trevor's boob and the RSC being called a left-wing organisation. His exuberance was indeed triumphant. We are often not very pretty to each other in adversity.

At home in the evening, Derek Bowman of the *Sunday Telegraph* rang me. A classic journalist conversation. He explained he had been briefed by his editor to do a piece about the political affiliations of the RSC and its predominantly left-wing bias. He explained to me that he was himself a Labour Party supporter but, as I knew, the *Sunday Telegraph* was resolutely Tory. I offered no comment.

He said the list of plays David Jones had done at the Aldwych did seem to be extremely left-wing—Gorky, Gunter Grass, and now this. I said we[1] were even contemplating Chekhov.

He also told me that it was well-known that Dame Peggy canvassed for the Labour Party, and she was, after all, a director of the RSC. I said that is why I thought it had been a very good idea for her to appear in a very right-wing play by William Douglas-Home at the Savoy Theatre[2]. He asked me to take him seriously. I asked him if it was a witch hunt. He said of course not. He begged me to get Trevor Nunn to speak to him.

I should not have been so facetious. But sometimes it becomes impossible to allow journalists to have it all ways.

Saturday 9 December

Very worried about how I can find the time to do *Akenfield*. Shall I leave it to chance—to good or bad fortune? Or shall I not do it and so disappoint Rex Pyke and all those people in Suffolk? The problem is simple. I must make a good *Homecoming* film. And then I must organise and think clearly at the National. Can I also be rushing down to Suffolk to shoot? I don't know.

A brief chat to Trevor. Norman St John Stevas[3] has told him he is worried about the Angus Maude business and the left-wing, right-wing nonsense which has continued in the papers all week. He warned Trevor that a question will be asked in the House—an ugly question. He urged Trevor to make his position clear by another letter to *The Times*.

---

[1] Hall remained with the RSC as a Co-Director from 1968 to 1973.
[2] As Lady Boothroyd in *Lloyd George Knew My Father*, in 1972.
[3] Minister for the Arts 1973–74. Shadow spokesman on Science and the Arts 1975–79. Minister for the Arts 1979–81.

It seems to me Trevor should write a letter, taking the heat out of the present situation by humorously suggesting that a function of the RSC is to irritate extremists—whether of right or left. The notion of the RSC as a left-wing organisation would arouse hoots of derision in Marxist circles. They are just as anti-RSC as Angus Maude and the extreme right-wingers.

Sunday 17 December

Casting for *Akenfield*, which we did at Woodbridge in a school[1]. I believe that in any forty or fifty people there are two or three who have not lost the ability to 'play'—as children play. They are not actors but they can improvise, lose themselves in their own fantasies. After eliminating many, I did tests with the best dozen.

Yesterday I had a long talk with David Brierley. The Stratford season has ended and Trevor was leaving for two weeks holiday. The rumblings about Angus Maude's resignation continue, though there was an RSC governors' meeting last week which passed a total vote of confidence in Trevor, and he was advised not to make any further statement. I still believe this is wrong. He ought to say *what* he means by the RSC being a left-wing organisation. It is not a party label but an aesthetic attitude.

This little storm in a teacup has to some extent affected the Grand Design of a merger. We have now given a stick to our enemies and they will unhesitatingly beat us with it. A merger between the RSC and the National will be seen as the left-wing clique all getting together. David advises that the next steps are for me to try to get Rayne, George Farmer, Trevor and myself together. But first I must talk to Larry. We will have to go slower until this present heat has cooled.

I spent the night reading Harold Pinter's film script of *A la Recherche du temps perdu*. It is an extraordinary achievement. He has managed to condense those complex volumes into 221 pages of precise images and precise dialogue. Yet there seems to be nothing lost, no simplification.

I do not know Proust very well. In 1955, after I had finished directing *Mourning Becomes Electra* at the Arts Theatre[2], I went to Spain to read all twelve volumes. I was at the end of volume nine when a telegram arrived saying 'Business failing come at once'. I returned to London, then immediately directed *Waiting for Godot*, and never read the rest. But I remember the atmosphere of the book vividly. This is what is in Pinter's screenplay. A fastidious compassion and precision.

Tuesday 19 December

To the Garrick Club for Patrick Gibson's Arts Council dinner—an informal evening designed to give the Council the opportunity to assess the future in

---

[1] The film was cast with non-actors, Suffolk country people. It was also entirely improvised.
[2] Hall was Director of the Arts Theatre, London, 1955–56.

relaxed terms. It was my last meeting as a Council member: my four years are up.

There was a certain amount of criticism of the way the Council operated, a general feeling that it should rely more on its panels—Drama, Art, Literature, etc.—so that the Council itself is more free to consider strategy. There was some discussion too about the increasing government pressure that is bound to be applied—and I believe this will be so whichever party is in—now that the Council is dispensing upwards of £15m[1] a year and becoming, like the BBC, another estate of the realm. It is therefore resented fiercely by some politicians and civil servants. It has too much money for it to be out of their immediate control.

C. P. Snow and I had a passage of arms. There was the inevitable discussion on censorship, and the curious idea was floated that if a seditious play was being done by a well-established, long-established company, then the Arts Council was in the clear. If, however, it was an ad hoc group, it might not be. The John Arden play about Northern Ireland[2], which apparently offended the sensibilities of the C-in-C there, was mentioned. I said surely the Arts Council was backing the talent of John Arden and if it at this moment was seditious and critical of British policy, that would not invalidate the talent.

Snow attacked me for being a lefty, a liberal talking humanitarian cant. I said if he could write for me a right-wing play which was against the Race Relations Act, or which gave a sympathetic study of the Afrikaans point of view in South Africa, I would be delighted to put it on. We got so fiery that in the end we agreed. He went right, I went left, and I suspect we met round the back. Our combat was diverting to the members of the dinner table but hardly, I think, constructive to Pat Gibson, whom I like more and more.

Thursday 21 December
The news on the National building is very depressing. The latest projected plans are for an opening in the spring of 1975 instead of in the early part of 1974 as forecast. I have two years of inactivity—at least as far as the National is concerned.

---

[1] In 1983, the year these diaries went to press, the Arts Council was dispensing a total of nearly £100 million.
[2] *The Ballygombeen Bequest*, co-written with Margaretta D'Arcy.

1973

Wednesday 3 January
After a day's filming on *The Homecoming*, a quick change into the ridiculous panoply of the past: tails, white tie and my dangling CBE. It is the sheer discomfort of starch and stud which distresses me, quite apart from the unwilling feeling that I am now part of the Establishment and don't want to be.

The grand occasion was the Gala at Covent Garden to mark Britain's entry into the EEC. It was a Fanfare for Europe.

The Establishment—political, artistic, and commercial—were out in force. On one side of the Queen's box, the Archbishop of Canterbury, on the other Lord Goodman. Outside the Opera House noisy protestors jeered and jostled, surrounded by the largest collection of policemen I have ever seen in London. An effigy of Edward Heath was hanging at the gallows and the crowd chanted 'traitors, traitors, traitors' as we all disembarked in our finery.

Saturday 6 January
A gathering at the Savoy after the National Theatre's *Twelfth Night* at the Old Vic. Max and Jane Rayne were hosts. I had a giggle with Norman St John Stevas, an old acquaintance from television and radio panel games, and now Under-Secretary and spokesman for the Arts in the Commons. He is an extraordinary man: irreverent, very funny, very Catholic, and he can sometimes be delightfully indiscreet. I have always felt that his heart is in the right place. We were speaking of the energy of the Prime Minister in a very crowded week, which included Fanfare for Europe, Boat Shows, and battling with the TUC and CBI over a wage policy. Norman said that celibacy was a great aid to energy, didn't I find? I said I didn't. He remarked that since he had become a minister, all sexual desire had faded. Celibacy, he said, was the secret of Heath.

Friday 12 January
Phone call from Larry this morning. He urgently wanted to see me. I arrived at his flat early and had a talk with Joan[1] who told me the situation. Now

---

[1] Plowright (Lady Olivier). Frequently worked with the National Theatre company at the Old Vic 1963–74.

the opening of the National Theatre has been postponed by a year, until spring 1975, because of building delays Larry feels he cannot soldier on until after then before handing over to me. He is fed up with the load and the worry and the burden and wants to leave at the end of this year and relax.

He arrived looking as fresh and vigorous as a baby and we talked until nearly 4 am. We agree that I should take over the reins as director this autumn. But I was adamant that he had to come back in 1975 to lead the company into the new building.

I was expecting two years of thinking and writing and taking stock for the future. Now I shall be thrown in almost immediately at the deep end. At least it will have the advantage of keeping the pressure on me. I might have become very bored with waiting.

Larry and I discussed everything. Plays he would do. His desire to direct. The current staffing of the National Theatre. And then, because the opportunity was ideal, I went into the idea of a merger with the RSC. By the end of the evening, he said he would push to make it all happen.

Thursday 18 January
Meeting with Trevor. He told me a horrifying story. On Monday he was taken to lunch by Hugh Willatt who seemed nervous and uneasy. Trevor thought it was something to do with our amalgamation plans. After the soup, the truth came out. Lord Eccles had been informed that there were three or four people in the RSC who were political activists far to the left. He had asked Hugh to ask gently if Trevor could do something about it. Trevor said do you mean fire them? Hugh said he was merely passing on what he had been asked to pass on.

This really is the Establishment at work. There are a couple of extreme lefties in both the RSC theatres. One of them, I discover, is predictably Corin Redgrave[1]. They are boring and cranky and constantly seeking confrontations with the management. But they do their job professionally and well, and while this continues there is no earthly reason why in a democratic situation they should be removed.

Trevor was amazed. So was I.

Friday 19 January
Spoke to Rayne. Larry had told him of his decision to leave at the end of this year. Rayne said Larry was now convinced the merger was a good thing. He had replied he thought so too but we must wait until we were established on the South Bank. I said that was dangerous. The National faces in 1974 the responsibility of more than doubling its company. Rayne seemed to

---

[1] The actor. Son of Sir Michael Redgrave and brother of Vanessa.

respond, and when I reached Wallingford this afternoon there was a message that he had set up a meeting for Monday at Arnold Goodman's office with Larry, George Farmer, Trevor Nunn, myself and Patrick Donnell all there.

Saturday 20 January

Read a new book by Michael Billington[1]: *The Modern Actor.* There was something in it which pleased me.

If I were asked what I have done which was original or significant, I would answer that I have brought back a standard of speaking and of understanding Shakespeare by actors. When I went to Stratford I was very worried by the absence of any tangible tradition of speaking Shakespeare. Nobody agreed on how Shakespeare should be spoken. What I and my colleagues did to change this has been accepted. That, far more than the creation of an ensemble company, is what so far I am proudest of having done.

Billington recognises this achievement.

Monday 22 January

At the National Theatre offices by 10 am and discussed tactics with Paddy Donnell for the meeting at Goodman's this afternoon.

Larry did not come until late morning after a session at his gym. He was in a devilish mood and was changing ground on everything that had been said previously. He first of all told me he wasn't sure that he would leave at the end of the year. I said it was his decision and he must do what he wanted; I would stand by in any way that was necessary.

He also said he was very unhappy about the idea of Trevor becoming number two of the merged organisation, because this, with me at the head, would look like an RSC takeover and be received badly in the National; Michael Blakemore would leave. I told Larry I wanted Michael to stay, thought highly of him, and believed he would stay. But if the coming of Trevor meant that Michael would go, then Michael would have to go.

As a result of all this, Paddy and I, in some confusion, rushed across the river and took Trevor out to lunch to warn him we were on shifting sands. After lunch, I had an hour with Larry in which I got him back to some sort of order for the Goodman meeting. He was suspicious and changeable but said he would still support the merger.

We all then went like the conspirators in *Julius Caesar* to Goodman's office off Fleet Street. It was thought it would be secret and secure—though how Arnold Goodman, Max Rayne, George Farmer, Laurence Olivier, Trevor Nunn, Paddy Donnell, and Peter Hall could all meet in the middle of

---

[1] Drama critic of *The Guardian* from 1971.

Fleet Street and expect not to be noticed is past my understanding. Particularly as Larry arrived in his well-known purple taxi.

The meeting was depressing. The air was thick with pomposity. I said there might not be sufficient money, or writing, directing, and managerial talent enough for two large organisations. George Farmer asked me why, therefore, I had persuaded the Stratford governors to form the RSC and take the Aldwych in 1959. I said the National Theatre did not at that time exist and was only a gleam in Larry's eye.

George Farmer then asked Trevor whether he would take on the job if I fell under a passing bus (I have been threatened by this bus at all important decisions in the RSC's history since 1959—always by George Farmer). Trevor said he would, providing he could have the right number two.

Larry at this point jumped in to say that although Trevor was a delightful chap and fantastically talented etc he hoped that he, Trevor, realised that if I *was* under that bus, it did not guarantee Trevor the job. The decision was the Board's. Trevor said of course, of course, of course.

That was the nearest we got to Larry's obsessional anxiety—the succession. But his support in general was good and he had moved some of the way since this morning.

What is clear is that on one hand we have an RSC chairman who is convinced the RSC is being taken over by the National, and on the other hand, we have Larry who is convinced that the National is being taken over by the RSC. I wish they could see they are both wrong.

In good English fashion we were asked to prepare a paper on behalf of the two managements and meet again at the end of February.

Wednesday 24 January
As I was listening to Michael Blakemore telling me he thought Larry *should* go at the end of the year, and announce it publicly so that he couldn't go back on it, then all of us could get on with planning 1974, Larry strolled in. We were like children caught with our hands in the jam pot.

Thursday 25 January
Sneaked off to Munich on the 2.30 plane. I am going to act in a film of Maximilian Schell's over the weekend[1]. I was met and conducted rapidly to my hotel and then to Max's for supper. His house—filled with wonderful paintings (he has the best Ben Nicholson I have ever seen)—was in uproar. Production assistants and secretaries were rushing round yelling at each other. Max was trying to cast the scene for tomorrow. He had suddenly decided that the newspaper conference at which I, playing the Editor, am to

---

[1] *Der Fussgänger* (*The Pedestrian*).

32

preside should be peopled by all the Intendants[1] of Germany. Accordingly, people were ringing up Schuh, Liebermann, Rennert, Meisel, etc, etc. Not surprisingly, none of them was free.

To bed early, trying to learn my lines. It is the first time I have memorised a script for twenty years.

Friday 26 January and Saturday 27 January
Munich: We shot in a beautiful, modern newspaper office on top of a high building. I was very bad. Max kept saying he needed a fast, light, funny scene. He was right. But I fell into the silliest trap an actor can fall into. I achieved the right tempo before I had achieved the scene. I don't like acting—mainly I suppose because I am not an actor. But it is of the greatest worth to be the wrong side of the camera, for me, for a while. It teaches any director humility.

Back to London tomorrow afternoon.

Wednesday 31 January
It is clear we shall need a subsidy of about £1.2 million to run the new building in its first year. We are currently in expectation of only £800,000. Here we go. The familiar switchback. I shall once more be asked to cut according to my cloth, while others feel bound to criticise the style of the coat.

Meeting with Larry in the afternoon. He was most insistent that he saw me. He started off by saying it was a pity he could not reach me at the weekend as he was going to tell me he had decided to do *Lear*. Now he had decided against it. The implication was that if I had been available at the weekend I would have been doing *Lear* with him; now it was lost for ever.

One thing, however, is settling. He confirmed that he wanted me to take total control of the National Theatre in the autumn, and before that to assume joint direction with him from the spring.

Friday 9 February
Larry rang me twice today. He tries to talk to me most days now. I can't quite make out what is going on. I think he wants me as part of the court. If I could be with him at lunch and dinner and sit up drinking with him all night he would be happy. But I can't do that.

Wednesday 14 February
Went to have a cup of coffee with Harold Pinter and he told me, to my great surprise and pleasure, that he had decided to accept my invitation to join the National Theatre as an associate director. I never doubted that he would

---

[1] The name given to those who run theatres in Germany.

direct the odd play, and that he would give me his new plays to direct, as he did at the RSC. But to my pleasure, he is in, heart and soul, though pointing out that he can only do what he can do.

Wednesday 21 February
Our paper on the NT/RSC merger idea is drafted. Meeting with Larry at the National offices to take him through it. He liked it. I said that I thought it should be signed by Trevor and myself; we had, after all, done most of the work on it. He insisted on signing it too. I didn't have to persuade.

Thursday 22 February
First night of *The Misanthrope*[1]. The audience at Old Vic first nights are horrendous. I suppose as there are only just over 700 seats, the proportion of professional knockers, agents, gossips, scandal-mongers, establishment figures, Arts Council men, ministers of the arts, etc is ridiculously high. I am going to do something about this. The critics and the ordinary public should constitute the first night audience. The regular 'first nighters' should come at another time.

Monday 26 February
Rode with Larry in his purple taxi to the next secret meeting at Lord Goodman's on the NT/RSC merger idea. Larry said he did not now feel his name should be on the paper. He had, after all, not written it. He had only written three paragraphs and I had changed one of them. I reminded him it had been his suggestion for him to sign, not mine. He agreed, and said how awful it was, but what was he to do? I said he had better tell the meeting the truth—ie that he had volunteered his name and was now having second thoughts. He thought this might take most of the meeting.

He was right. But as neither Goodman, Rayne, Farmer, nor obviously Brierley, Nunn, or Donnell take Larry's contortions very seriously, not much harm was done. When he announced that his name should not be on the paper, George Farmer solemnly took out his Biro and crossed his name out. That was all.

It's very difficult to know what motivates Larry's vacillations. Certainly in some cases—and this is one of them—a Machiavellian love of intrigue. He loves being naughty.

Saturday 3 March
First day's filming on *Akenfield*[2]. Our sequence is the school at the turn of the century. Sixty local children in period costumes. I explained that we

---

[1] By Molière. Directed by John Dexter in an English version by Tony Harrison.
[2] From now until the end of August, Hall spent most weekends, and occasional weekdays, shooting *Akenfield*, in Suffolk.

were going to shoot their arrival at the school. They were very dutiful and obedient, though private. All very East Anglian. But the children didn't understand why their school mistress should be such a termagant, demanding silence, discipline and total stillness. The first take lasted eight minutes. The children looked horrified. They thought they had come for a giggly day's filming and found themselves instead in this movie about some prehistoric time. One little boy cried, was reassured, and then on the next take cried again.

The right people in the right circumstances can say and do amazingly true things on film, but they cannot repeat to order. Yet a scene has to be covered from a number of different angles, so some amount of repetition is essential. It will work, but editing will be a nightmare.

Thursday 27 February
To the South Bank for over two hours of walking round the building. I haven't been since last August. Progress. I think Lasdun's work is triumphant. He has divested concrete of its brutality. It is slender, delicate and in beautiful geometric patterns. I think the theatre is a masterpiece.

Tuesday 6 March
Larry suddenly produced an appalling press release for next week about his going. He wants it to be a personal statement, and it is exactly like the great actor-manager saying farewell to his public—with the proviso that if they insist he will be appearing again next week.

I asked that we attach it to a fact sheet which speaks constructively—of the new associates joining, some of the plays we are going to do, the continuing of John Dexter, Michael Blakemore, and Jonathan Miller. Larry obviously doesn't want that though he agreed to it. It is a curious duality in him. He wants this to be his farewell performance, yet he wants to be seen to be generous to me. He wants it to be thought he is going of his own free will, and yet in some curious way to have the benefit of the supposition that he is being forced out. I wonder whether he will ever appear at the new building? It will depend on what is more dramatic—the National Theatre opening without him, or he in the centre of the stage. I am sure whatever I do, he will take umbrage.

Thursday 8 March
Journeyed with Pinter down to the National offices for the first meeting of our group of associates: Pinter, Schlesinger, Miller, Blakemore, Olivier, myself. A great deal of Guinness and champagne was drunk as a celebrating ritual. Larry was very pleasant, if a little over-humble; and the baroque fantasies of Miller's conversational style were occasionally checked by

Harold Pinter saying 'What do you mean?' or 'Would you mind saying that again?'.

I am getting very neurotic about my first play for the National at the Old Vic. I want it to be *The Tempest*. But can I do it without Larry?

Tuesday 13 March
We all met the press at midday. Very urbane and jokey. There was a good deal of sub-text but nothing horrible emerged.

Thursday 15 March
To Wallingford on the 8 am train for a talk to my parents at their cottage, just built near my house. The cottage is beautiful but my mother was deciding not to like anything. The daffodils are out, spring is in the air, and I was angry at never being there.

Meeting with Peter Nichols on the George Orwell play he is writing. I have urged him to start again, to make his own interpretation of Orwell, rather than hide behind a documentary format.

The extraordinary thing about Orwell was that he had a journalist's ability to be in the place where history was happening. As the Empire was collapsing, he was in Burma. At the time of the great thirties depression he was among the workers in the north. At the time of the Civil War, he was in Spain. He was an Etonian socialist who hated authority. He wanted there to be a revolution, yet hated the totalitarian government which was apparently the only way of maintaining it.

All this is tremendous stuff for a play. My point with Peter Nichols was that Sonia Orwell[1] will be offended whatever he does. And I believe she is less likely to object if the play is Peter Nichols's view of Orwell and does not masquerade as a documentary.

Monday 19 March
Lunch at *Time* Magazine to meet the Managing Editor, Henry Grunwald. One of my very favourite men, George Steiner, was there. With the possible exception of Isaiah Berlin, he is the most educated, lucid man I know. He had read everything, speaks all langauges, and glitters with provocative thought. He talked about what was going to happen in the future to satisfy people's need for savagery. If we are to have ritualised wars, where will desire for conquest go? Into greater urban violence? Into some Roman-like contests where human life is at stake? Will sport in fact become more violent?

[1] Orwell's widow. Died 1980.

Tuesday 20 March
Trevor, David Brierley, John Goodwin and I met at my flat. One point has been worrying me: by this coming autumn I have to have an experienced press office chief on the South Bank. With a big scandal undoubtedly ahead of us on the expense of the building, the sooner we start projecting the facts the better. I want John Goodwin, but Trevor and David were very resistant. They kept saying there was no need for John to be seconded from the RSC to the NT, I would have him anyway because of the merger. I said I hoped their feelings about the merger were true but regarded them as optimistic. The meeting was inconclusive, but showed me how very easily the present very cordial and intimate relations between all us old RSC friends could become poisoned and suspicious. If the merger doesn't occur, we could be daggers drawn in a few months.

Wednesday 21 March
To the revival of Coward's *Private Lives* at the Queen's Theatre. Brilliant play. Strange how yesterday's commercial plays and films become un-disputed artworks of today. A lesson for the over-serious—particularly the over-serious critic who naturally suspects the successful.

Thursday 22 March
This morning was the end of an era. Binkie Beaumont[1] is dead. His housekeeper brought his breakfast and found he had died in his sleep. Consternation in the theatre. He was undisputed king of the forties, fifties and early sixties. Indeed, if you didn't work for Binkie, you didn't work for anybody. I admired him, and enjoyed the glee he had over any kind of intrigue, but I never really enjoyed working for him. His priorities were not mine.

There is a possibly apocryphal story which concerns Binkie's advice on how to handle a recalcitrant actor: 'If the worst comes to the worst we can always tell him the truth'.

Binkie leaves no one to carry on. No heir, no relatives, no means of continuing his immensely successful business. He began as a box office boy in Cardiff and was apparently illegitimate. Nothing else is known about him.

Monday 26 March
First meeting of the National Theatre's dauntingly named Protocol Commit-tee—members from the NT Board, South Bank Board, the GLC, the DES[2], Uncle Tom Cobley and all bureaucrats. The committee met to consider trivia—like who should be allowed to strike a medal to commemo-rate the opening of the NT, or promote some ghastly pot. But we moved on

---

[1] Hugh Beaumont, the impresario.   [2] Department of Education and Science.

to how you open the new theatre. From the South Bank Board came the view that there should be a gala night of a new production with a royal personage, presumably the Queen, there and that Shakespeare would be the best dramatist for the occasion, naturally.

I dropped my spanner into the works. I said I thought the National Theatre stood a good chance of being a scandal. It had cost much and was going to cost more. And it could well look like another pompous institution built for the elite. If we opened grandly with a new production for the Queen, we could have a mass demonstration outside, and slogans daubed all over Denys Lasdun's nice clean concrete. I suggested that the opening of the theatre—as a building—should be a celebration, *not* a play; and that the launching of the theatre—as a playhouse—should be spread over the subsequent season.

After a good deal of amazement and debate and some good support by Larry, my ideas were accepted.

Thursday 29 March
I find myself getting more and more worried about the NT/RSC merger. Will Trevor push it enough? And will it happen in time to support all the important work we at the National have to do in the next eighteen months in order to get the building open?

Also, now I am getting to grips with the needs of the South Bank, I am appalled by the size of that operation alone.

Friday 30 March
Paddy Donnell and Tony Easterbrook[1] in some consternation as late last night Larry decreed that he was handing over his office to me, and moving into smaller, more modest accommodation further down the passage. He is Lear-like, divesting himself of position and grandeur in a great hurry. The two lieutenants didn't know what to do. I hope I settled it by saying that of course Larry could do what he liked about his office, but I was certainly not moving into his until 1 November, when I actually take over. . . .

Meeting with the heads of departments. I did a re-run of my policy for the South Bank. It didn't go very well. Watchful eyes, a lot of suspicion, and not much understanding. There were almost no questions.

Christopher's birthday. Family lunch: all four children, and Jacky, plus Jae who looks after us. Very pleasant. Sixteen years since Christopher was born between the run-through and the dress rehearsal of a production I did of Tennessee Williams's *Camino Real* . . . .

---

[1] General Manager of National Theatre at the Old Vic 1968–74.

To Cambridge for the Ramsden dinner[1]. I made the mistake of travelling in the rush hour and though armed with a first class ticket, had to stand all the way. Infuriating because I couldn't work.

I travelled in a taxi to St Catharine's with an ecclesiastical gentleman who said he was up with me, and was surprised to see such a busy man at such a function. I said I could hardly miss the quatercentenary. He said it was a good job I wasn't making a speech as it was the quincentenary.

Tuesday 3 April

To a performance of *Hello and Goodbye* by the brilliant South African Athol Fugard, a born dramatist with a gift for poetic story-telling. He maintained a hold over the audience the entire evening. Beautiful performances from Janet Suzman and Ben Kingsley. I don't think I have ever seen Janet better—the South African accent, the root of her own voice, released a boldness in her which has sometimes been absent from her classical acting. I have often found a restriction in the work of actors from the Commonwealth who have manufactured special accents and voices for themselves over here. Because of that, acting for them often remains imitation and not revelation.

Wednesday 4 April

Morning at home play-reading. I have read *Heartbreak House* again. Magnificent: the Shaw I like best. It is ambiguous and unschematic. I am getting through about three plays a day. Most of them are rubbish.

A wine-soaked lunch with Sonia Orwell on the subject of Peter Nichols's play. It is clear she is miserable about the draft. She kept acidly referring to Nichols as a middlebrow playwright. She is now a widow protecting the interests of a husband whose preoccupations she probably didn't even know. What writer shares his myths with his wife? She is the worst professional widow I have met since Arnold Schoenberg's widow, who so far leads the field. I could never imagine Arnold sharing some jolly inversion of his tone-row over the afternoon tea[2]. But she tried to make you feel he did.

I was so rapidly bored by Sonia Orwell that on impulse I agreed with her that we shouldn't go on with the play. Nichols isn't that keen to continue anyway. But if in five or six months he returns to the subject, I shall return to Sonia Orwell and attack her.

Friday 6 April

Outside Liverpool St Station I met Arnold Goodman, he on his way to lecture, I on my way back to Ipswich to film *Akenfield*. He said the chance

[1] For the Fellows of St Catharine's College and their guests—a dinner held annually for over 200 years. Hall was made an Honorary Fellow of St Catharine's in 1964.
[2] Hall directed Schoenberg's *Moses and Aaron* at the Royal Opera House in 1965.

was a happy one as he was wanting to get hold of me. He looked a very Dickensian figure among that beautiful nineteenth-century cast iron.

Blinking among the rush hour crowds, he launched into a tactical consideration of our whole position. He said he remained for the merger, but had been taking other soundings and thought the political difficulties were extreme at this moment. With carefully weighted irony he pointed out that I was a man well known for my modesty and lack of empire-building instinct. If there was now a public outcry and enquiry into the desirability of the merger I would undoubtedly be presented in a bad light. Larry was the only person who could push public opinion towards the merger—and that he was not about to do. He would be far more likely to turn against it at the last moment. Arnold reminded me that Larry had consistently suggested Joan Plowright should succeed him and that she had apparently supported the idea.

He therefore advised me to forget the whole notion for the next three years and to placate Trevor and my colleagues at Stratford. He said I needed to take over a very difficult job, move into the new building, and get it running before I heaped further difficulties upon myself.

This encounter was depressing, but it clarified all the fears of the last weeks. I don't know what to do next. I shall think.

Tuesday 10 April
Supper with Stuart Burge[1] and Jonathan Miller. Stuart as nice and modest as ever. Jonathan, ebullient, charming and alarmingly full of confidence. He is the only director I know who always likes his own work. He is fascinated by it. He is also one of the funniest men that I have met in my life, and regaled us with cockney sexual slang which he collected from hospital porters during his period as a doctor.

Wednesday 11 April
Day off. I wanted time to think through Goodman's advice of last week. What is to be done? It can only be a matter of time before the press reveals our talks—probably in a bad, intriguing way. So John Goodwin and I secretly decided, this evening, that the best course was to leak to the press what was happening. The object of this plot will be to draw the fire of the opposition by getting the whole thing out into the open. In my present pessimistic mood, I hope it is a way of stopping it. For I am now unconvinced of its wisdom. But I would like at least to know how it stands up to public scrutiny.

Friday 13 April
Easter. The start of some blessed time at home. Despite this, an uneasy day. Is it the date?

[1] Director of Nottingham Playhouse 1968–74.

The *Daily Telegraph*, to whom John gave the merger story, carried it somewhat truncated, but the emphasis was correct and the tone factual. The initial reaction of the press, on the phone to John, is of amazement and some hostility to the idea. John tried to make them see the economic problems facing the two companies if something was not done.

Monday 16 April
To the National offices. Much whispering in corridors. Kenneth Rea[1] asked me when it was I had lunched with Fordham Flower[2] and Larry at Notley Abbey to discuss the earlier idea of an NT/RSC merger. I said it was in March or April 1960: the last day that Larry lived at Notley. He was moving out the next day, in the process of divorcing Vivien and marrying Joan. He gave me a pot of jasmine.

Flying the kite has had this effect. It has shown that the strength of the opposition is not very great. But it has also polarised the feelings of my own associate directors, and they are against the merger.

During Easter, despite alarms and excursions, I have read *All For Love*, *The Tempest*, *Heartbreak House* again, *John Gabriel Borkman*, *Spring Awakening*[3], and *The Traitor* and *Hyde Park*, both by James Shirley. No rest, but at least I have caught up.

Tuesday 17 April
I have the glimmerings of an idea. Suppose there were an association which meant that until the Barbican is ready the RSC, and only the RSC, provides Shakespeare on the South Bank? Trevor would join the National's Board, I would remain on the RSC's. The National's directors or actors wanting to do Shakespeare would have to do it with the RSC. The actual managements of the two organisations could merge, and the actors would have the free choice of *what* they wanted to do with either organisation.

I think it could gain the support of all the outside factions. It is not a merger. But it can lead naturally into a merger in a few years time if that is what is needed.

I floated the plan with Larry and with Paddy. Paddy greeted it with acclamation; Larry embraced it eagerly too. Now we will see.

Wednesday 18 April
An inscrutable letter from Larry in *The Times* this morning about the merger. Yesterday he had shown me the draft and I had commented favourably on one particular paragraph. It said that whatever the rights and

[1] Secretary to the National Theatre Board from its incorporation in 1963, until 1974.
[2] Sir Fordham Flower, Chairman of the Governors of the RSC from 1944 up to his death in 1966.
[3] By, respectively, Dryden, Shakespeare, Shaw, Ibsen, Wedekind.

wrongs of the idea, the country had to answer one question: 'Who was going to pay to keep the RSC and the NT apart?' I thought this a crucial point to make; a main reason for the proposal to join us together was that it would be cheaper. That paragraph was not, though, in *The Times*. Larry had cut it out. . . .

Friday 20 April

Long chat with Peter Brook, here from Paris. We discussed the NT/RSC situation. Talking of how press comment had polarised views, he giggled and said 'You obviously leaked it.' 'Why do you think that?' I said.

Tuesday 24 April

Read *Tamburlaine The Great*, a play I much want to do. Emblematic, medieval, and something that would work very well at this moment.

Wednesday 25 April

Depressing evening with Trevor and David. I went through the association plan and Trevor looked worried. He doesn't want it. He remains optimistic about the merger, and kept on affirming that all that has changed was that the news had leaked, there had been little antagonistic press comment, and the elder statesmen were getting frightened. I suppose what has changed is that faced with the reality of the situation, most of us have begun to draw back from the total merger as something schematically wrong, though I still believe it might happen, given time. I just don't know. . . .

I asked Trevor if we could try an exercise. I wrote down the fifteen or sixteen projects that I was enthusiastic about and I asked him to do the same. Ten of my sixteen projects also figured on his list. Who, therefore, is to legislate which company, if they stay separate, does which? Chance? Or who gets up the earliest? And where is the money for two big separate companies?

Friday 27 April

Long meeting with Larry. We spoke of *Lear*. I reiterated that I would direct it either publicly or privately, as an assistant or as an associate, or not at all. My main concern was to get him to play Lear. He appeared to accept the offer. I also told him that I wanted to do *The Tempest* if there was any possible casting of Prospero.

Tuesday 1 May

Trevor rang. He has moved a little. He said it is a question of working out *what* is possible in an NT/RSC association. I said that if each side only protected its own interests we would get nowhere. It is certainly worrying for the RSC to give up all its repertoire except Shakespeare. It is, though, equally worrying for the NT not to do any Shakespeare, But if we both believe that out of the association could come a creative combination — which at this moment we may not even be able to imagine—then we should do it. If we don't, we should leave it alone.

Private meeting between Rayne, Olivier and myself. When I said that the association meant the RSC would provide six to seven months of Shakespeare on the South Bank, Larry stopped me and said 'Six or seven? I thought it was only three.' Rayne immediately said: 'Are you not keen on this, Larry?' and Larry looked worried and muttered. If I bring Trevor and Larry together now, I am wasting my time.

Many phone calls tonight. Larry rang to see if I could see his lights flashing on and off on his balcony high up in Victoria from my top floor flat in the Barbican. Said he didn't want to talk about work.

Wednesday 2 May
The 'topping out' ceremony of the National's new theatre. A fine spring day. The last bit of the roof was ceremonially filled in by the Lords Olivier and Cottesloe[1], and Larry made a vintage speech about Pagan Ritual, Wotan's Day and Thor's Day. Then we all had drinks and tramped round the building. It is looking magnificent. The world and his wife were there. Tynan in pink-trimmed blazer. Jennie Lee[2], who greeted me warmly and said she would like to gossip about the NT some day, as she didn't trust me at all. She used to call me her tame Maverick when I ran the RSC, which infuriated me keenly. She is like a reproving aunt of a naughty nephew.

Thursday 3 May
Bad news from Alec Guinness whom I had asked to do Prospero, a part he has never played. He has decided he dare not in such an exposed situation as the NT. Funny, everyone always agrees the propositions, and then gets out of them. At least in the theatre. I do it myself. Perhaps we are too anxious to be loved, or perhaps the basic insecurity about our work makes us agree to every possibility as something too reassuring to refuse. Perhaps we only contemplate something seriously *after* we have agreed to do it.

Feel I must persevere with *The Tempest*. I shall ask Gielgud, who I know wants to do the part again. He is perhaps too gentle and too nice. But I think I know him well enough to push him into a harsher area of reality.

Monday 7 May
Telephoned John Gielgud who sounded delighted at *The Tempest* idea. We are to lunch on Thursday.

[1] Chairman of the South Bank Theatre Board 1962–77.
[2] Minister for the Arts 1965–70.

To see *Last Tango in Paris*. Paradox: why are moralities always castigated for their immorality? It is a sad, moving, heavy film, analysing very sensitively the danger and the pain of unthinking promiscuity, and also the loneliness of lust. I have never seen Brando better, even though the plot is frequently ridiculous. The erotic scenes are interesting. They are elegant and beautifully shot and achieve a new formalism, a stylisation of the sexual act, which involves the audience's emotions rather than exciting their sexuality. I cannot understand why the busybodies were so against the film. I suppose it deals with sexual practices, sexual behaviour, they would prefer to pretend do not exist.

Thursday 10 May
Lunch with John Gielgud. Excellent meeting. John in an expansive and gossipy mood. He liked my ideas for *The Tempest* and accepted the challenge of doing the part as a William Blake-like figure going through the purgatory of the play. I want the play to happen *to* Prospero, rather than have a sweet, well-spoken old retired vicar meditating on it from the outside.

Monday 14 May
Very plodding NT Board meeting going over all the agenda already covered by the finance committee.

I was asked to give the history of the NT/RSC negotiations, and the reasons behind them, which I believe I did in fair style. Larry tried to torpedo matters by saying that in his view the RSC could only be on the South Bank for a month or two. Rayne came to my rescue, saying that if Stratford were not given a decent share, they obviously were not going to participate. He then smartly asked the meeting to pass a resolution that talks should continue and that I should examine with Trevor Nunn in detail how we could associate and help each other. He is working on my side.

Sunday 16 May
Spring has come at last. *Akenfield* takes place during the course of one day, the day of Old Tom Rouse's funeral, a spring day with big clouds, fitful sunlight, changing light, young corn rippling. Cold wind, unfixed patterns, uneasiness, youth. Today was that sort of day. We shot Young Tom Rouse walking home to breakfast. He sees his grandfather's grave being dug in the churchyard; earth is thrown out on to the fresh young cow-parsley. Overhead the American aeroplanes roar. Every image that Ronnie Blythe had imagined in the book was there for the taking.

Friday 1 June
To the Arts Council for a chat with Patrick Gibson. I outlined to him again the need for an RSC/NT association, and then Hugh Willatt came in so I outlined it all again.

I think Gibson is rather for it. Willatt not. He kept saying that as he and I had sweated blood to make two great national institutions, we couldn't stand by and let one of them be reduced. I said we were doing no such thing — merely making sure the two organisations used each other constructively, and that there was competition as opposed to duplication. I don't think it washed with Hugh.

I ended by saying that even if this was not the answer I wanted to urge on the two of them that an answer had to be found. There *was* a problem. Trevor and I were two very worried men. There were insufficient resources —financial and human.

Sunday 3 June
Spoke to Ralph Richardson yesterday, who sounded bubbling with excitement about the proposal for him to play *John Gabriel Borkman*, and wishing a meeting with me today before he leaves for Australia.

I was a little late. Ralph was mooning round the exterior of his beautiful house in Regent's Park looking vaguely for me. There followed two hours filled with whisky and enthusiasm. I don't drink whisky, but he had nothing else.

In 1945 he was the greatest Falstaff I ever hope to see. I am convinced that in 1963 I failed to persuade him to play Falstaff at Stratford because I fell off his Norton motor bike on a private road on Hampstead Heath. I had been riding on his pillion and he asked me to try to ride the bike. I have always thought he concluded from this failure that I was no fellow to be entrusted with his talents.

Ralph stamped up and down reading notes he had made on Borkman. He said it must be a whirlwind, a volcano, a typhoon—go straight through with no stop. Be cataclysmic.

He also said he had had a chat with John[1] and he thought all of them should get behind me at the National. It was, he said, an exciting idea that next year at the Old Vic I was going to, as he put it, stack up productions in the air, like aeroplanes awaiting a landing on the South Bank.

Tuesday 5 June
Glyndebourne: Yesterday I started *Figaro*[2] rehearsals, and today we roughed out the first act in the morning. It is extremely difficult: all the

[1] Gielgud.   [2] *Le nozze di Figaro* by Mozart.

performers resist the pain that is there in order to keep up a false effervescence. Moved into Act II in the afternoon, the deeply erotic scenes of Susanna and the Countess playing around with Cherubino[1]. It is a highly sexy scene. The women unconsciously resisted it. Heterosexual men never have the slightest problem in making love to each other on the stage. But women always recoil from it. I have found it in Shakespeare comedy as well as in opera. Women have a deep repugnance about showing passion for each other. They prefer convention.

Monday 18 June

Glyndebourne: Spoke to Larry and he invited me to Brighton for dinner. Long, unsettling drinks with Joan, skirting around subjects before he arrived. She was trying to pump me about the future of the National, and also—or so it seemed—trying to sow unrest in me. She told me of all the suspicion and worry there was in the profession about large theatres, how there was a fear of institutions etc, etc. She said she wanted to form an independent company, and so did lots of other actors.

Larry arrived and we ate well and gossiped. Apparently the front of his house, a beautiful Regency one, is falling down, and he is committed to a fortune for rebuilding.

I had booked a taxi at 10.15 to take me back to Glyndebourne. It duly arrived, the doorbell rang, and the Oliviers looked at each other with surprise. I explained it was my taxi. Larry said I was expected to stay the night—that I had been asked, and had indeed accepted. I had done no such thing: I hadn't been asked. So I sent the taxi away again and went on gossiping until 1 am. As far as Joan is concerned, I sense an antipathy to me which she very nearly masks. From many remarks she made tonight about her need to do more than act, her need to direct, her need to manage, her need to make atmospheres where people could work, I am convinced that she *did* want the succession at the NT. To bed surrounded by mementoes of great actors, the sea beating outside.

Tuesday 19 June

Larry had promised to wake me just before 8 am so that I could set off early for Glyndebourne. He appeared brightly in sweatshirt and running shorts and woke me. My watch said 6.45. I thought it had stopped, put it forward to 8, and then began to get up. Some five minutes later, Larry re-entered, full of apologies. He had mistaken the hour and it actually was only 6.45. I went back to bed and slept for another half hour.

---

[1] Played respectively by: Ileana Cotrubas, later Britta Möllerström; Elizabeth Harwood, later Kiri Te Kanawa; and Frederica von Stade. (Figaro was played by Knut Skram and the Count by Benjamin Luxon.)

Wednesday 20 June
Spoke to Antonioni this morning. Two days ago a bewildering message arrived asking me if I would be in his new film called *The Passenger* starring Jack Nicholson. I would be appearing as the third lead. Comically, he has seen Maximilian Schell's film and thinks I am just right. He was extremely courteous and I was extremely non-committal. It would be wonderful to watch Antonioni working, but I can't see how I can fit everything in—editing *Akenfield*, finishing *The Homecoming* film, setting up the National, etc, etc.
I left it open with Antonioni. I said I would like to read the script.

Tuesday 26 June
Am out of touch with everything else except *Figaro*. Had a message that John Gielgud's contract for Prospero in *The Tempest* is agreed.

Sunday 1 July
Glyndebourne: The first night of *Figaro*. Very hot. John Pritchard[1] did wonderfully. The cast were very variable, each one ranging from brilliant to an off night, from scene to scene. Audience wildly enthusiastic. Hugs, kisses, and congratulations. George Christie[2] announces at the end that I have now given Glyndebourne three successes in a row[3]. But *Figaro* is only just all right. We have in some sense got away with it. But we have not achieved our objectives. The heart of the matter is true and good, but not the details.

Monday 2 July
Had to do an interview for American TV on the lawns of Shepperton to promote *The Homecoming* film. 'Who would you like to be if you weren't Peter Hall?' said the interviewer. I have never considered this before. I had to be honest and say that I had no desire to be anybody else at all. I'd like to be a better me, a cleverer me, a more organised me. And wouldn't mind being a me of twenty-eight knowing what I knew at forty. But the thought of being somebody else is inconceivable. Not because I'm particularly pleased with myself—I just can't imagine *being* somebody else. Perhaps you only want to be somebody else when you are very much in love. You want to become the other person.

Thursday 5 July
To the Arts Council for a meeting with its drama panel. I was assailed for two hours with questions and observations. I recognised, know and like

[1] Principal Conductor 1967–77 and Musical Director 1969–77 of Glyndebourne Opera. Knighted 1983.
[2] Chairman of Glyndebourne Productions Ltd from 1956.
[3] Hall's production of *Figaro* was an immense success, with revivals at Glyndebourne in 1974, 1976, 1981 and 1984 (for the fiftieth anniversary season). It was also televised.

Peter Cheeseman[1], Oscar Lewenstein[2], Albert Hunt[3], Michael Elliott[4]. But there were 20 or so young people of both sexes I didn't know. These were the new radicals.

An ironic situation: for a hundred and fifty years, the radicals of the theatre have been fighting for a National Theatre: they have collected money for it, given up their careers for it, and spent their energies in a most prodigal and altruistic way for it. But now we *have* a National Theatre—or nearly—the whole attitude has changed. At the end of my two hours cross-examination, it was perfectly clear that the drama panel—the new radicals —*didn't* want a National Theatre. But as we now had one, they were going to make the best of it without enthusiasm and with a great deal of suspicion because they were going to see to it that the National's position did not hurt their own theatres. Repeatedly I was asked: Why should you have such wonderful rehearsal conditions? Why should you have so much money? What did I mean by standards of excellence? What was excellence? Whose excellence?

And to my point that the National Theatre was the nation's theatre and that any company of standard should be invited to play in it, there was just resentment at the unfair discrimination against those who were *not* going to be invited.

The panel were hotly antagonistic to any association or link with the RSC. Several said that if Trevor and I were not so close, there would be no problem. Nobody said that the building was nice or that my paper on my plans for the NT had any qualities whatever. Everything was suspicion and caution. Truly, I have now joined the Establishment.

Here is a perfect metaphor of how the radical dreams of yesterday become the institutions of today, to be fought and despised. The end of my two hours found me exhausted. I had to bat all the time. They kept on bringing in fresh bowlers. It was a profoundly depressing evening. George Bernard Shaw should be writing about it. But Bernard Levin would do just as well.

Saturday 7 July, Sunday 8 July
Had some wonderful thoughts about *The Tempest*. Ferdinand and Miranda should of course be very young—16 and 14. But so should Ariel, and sexless. Opening image of the play—Gielgud aloft, head some sixteen feet high. From his shoulders a vast cloak which surrounds the stage. In his hands a huge staff. He dreams. He places the staff in the centre of the stage and it begins to sway from side to side. It becomes the mast of the ship. Within his cloak are shapes, spirits, children. They sing. All the music is vocal.

---

[1] Artistic Director of the Victoria Theatre, Stoke-on-Trent since its opening in 1962.
[2] Artistic Director of the English Stage Company 1972–75.   [3] The writer and critic.
[4] Resident Artistic Director of the Royal Exchange Theatre Company, Manchester, since 1973.

The question is not *how* do we do the masque—if we need to ask the question, the style of the rest of the production is not correct. The whole play must be a masque, Inigo Jones, a piece of early Baroque theatre.

The above was the best thing that happened to me this weekend. A great treat from *Figaro*.

Many phone calls. Nothing of much interest. I am worried by certain aspects of a talk I had with John Barton. He is now actively engaged on the Greeks as the centre of his work. So am I; *The Oresteia* is cooking. I said it seemed pretty daft that we didn't do it together.

The sun has been shining and the grass is green. I caught four trout and worked and worked and worked.

Wednesday 11 July
To the Old Vic for the *Equus* run-through. Very fine. Dexter has done a wonderful job in cutting out the over-writing which Peter Shaffer is prone to, and which I signally failed to do on the play of his I directed, *The Battle of Shrivings*[1].

To the Royal Court to see *Magnificence* by the new writer Howard Brenton. This is bursting with talent although not fully achieved. He has no sense of overall form yet. But there is a great imagination at work and a wonderful power of speech and character. I also like the way he uses time: following a long first act when a group of young revolutionaries occupy a deserted house, there is an electrifying five minutes of action, a tumult of disaster, which overwhelms the audience after the naturalistic rhythm of what preceded it. Brenton is a writer worth watching. He is also very funny. He deals in caricature, but his voice is assured.

Thursday 12 July
Alan MacNaughtan to see me first thing in the morning. He is one of the actors in the company who is already becoming insecure about his position next year. There is going to be a lot of this. I have deliberately kept away from the company as far as is possible because I did not want to get over-involved for the time being. But now they are all beginning to realise that the future is very near; and that the future is me. Over forty actors are therefore beginning to wonder what I think of them.

Friday 13 July
By car to Alveston, near Stratford, to see Jack Priestley. For a man of 79 he is very vigorous and hearty; very cordial too. We used to meet regularly in the sixties because we were almost next door neighbours. He would insult me about the modern theatre with great glee and I would shout back.

---

[1] At the Lyric Theatre, Shaftesbury Avenue, in 1970.

We had tea and too many cakes and he spoke most of old times. That is what he enjoys. I suppose old men do. How can one stop oneself reminiscing? I detect it in myself already.

I came as the bearer of good news. 'Can I do *Eden End*?' I asked. 'I don't really want you to do *Eden End*,' said J.B. 'The play to do is *Time and the Conways*.' But, I indicated, *Eden End* is a jewel, has perfection, is an extraordinary evocation of period, etc etc. 'And what's more,' said I, producing my trump card, 'Larry has at last agreed to direct it.' There was a long pause. Priestley pulled on his pipe. 'I've never really got on with Larry,' he said. I was aware of walking through a minefield.

To the Stratford theatre to see Eileen Atkins in *As You Like It*. It was modish and awful. I have rarely been so upset in the theatre I regard as my home. Eileen could have done something with Rosalind. I went to see her afterwards. 'Well?' she said. I wondered whether to tell the truth, something which is always dangerous in dressing rooms. 'I'm afraid I absolutely hated it,' I said. Eileen was overjoyed. 'I couldn't have borne it if you had pretended,' she answered.

Saturday 14 July
Preparations for the two-week holiday in Scotland. Many phone calls. Dashed to Oxford with Christopher to buy various texts on *The Tempest*.

Saturday 28 July
During the holiday my tension never went. And I put off writing to Glyndebourne to say I couldn't do *Idomeneo* in 1974. It is madness to do it because of the responsibilities and problems of next year, with the opening of the new building getting ever nearer. But I could not bring myself to make the decision. Mozart exerts a great pull. I wandered about like a sulky child who wants his cake as well as eating it. And did nothing. And became more worried by doing nothing.

Friday 3 August
Today, John Russell Brown[1] came to Wallingford and we talked about *The Tempest*. Our concentration throughout was interrupted by telephone calls (the modern Shakespearean messenger) giving the latest news on an Aldwych drama. Trevor, apparently, is in a state of complete exhaustion. Having previewed *Titus Andronicus* at the Aldwych tonight (which I thought quite wonderful last year at Stratford), he has to begin rehearsing *Coriolanus* with Nicol Williamson next week. Then he has to go straight into *Antony and Cleopatra*. Additional to this are the financial problems of the

---

[1] Scripts Adviser and Associate of the NT from 1973. Author of several works on the theatre.

RSC, my action in going to the NT, and apparently his personal life is stormy. It is clear that Trevor is boxed in as I was in 1963. One can only take so much.

I remember George Devine saying to me in 1961: 'It's splendid what you are doing at Stratford, but can I give you a word of advice? The day you feel that the walls are coming in on you, get out. No matter what the price or the difficulty. Get out.'

Well, George didn't. He died instead. This work is a killer.

Saturday 4 August

To bed early. Began reading Mrs Gaskell's *North and South*. I have never read it before. I began with a great feeling of relief; I was reading something which had nothing to do with work. Within four chapters, I caught myself thinking of it as a film. . . .

Sunday 5 August

The Trevor crisis has continued all day. They now hope to postpone the start of the *Coriolanus* rehearsals by some five weeks. This would give Trevor a holiday, and rest the company which is near mutinous. I wish I could do something. . . . I feel partly responsible.

The parallel is uncanny with ten years ago when I too was boxed in: by *The Wars of the Roses*[1]; by Larry starting the National Theatre and its attendant competition; by complications about the custody of the children after the break-up of my first marriage.

Monday 6 August

The Homecoming titles cut in a dingy viewing theatre in Soho. They work. The film is finished, at last. Later this week should see the final print.

A carefully worded letter from Hugh Willatt in which he expresses his concern, and the Arts Council chairman's, that several people have been lured into our top management lately by considerably increased wages. This is rumour. John Goodwin will be paid little more than he gets at the RSC. Peter Stevens[2] is to get virtually what he gets at present at the Haymarket Theatre, Leicester. And Gillian Diamond[3] has had a tiny increase, but this is certainly not the reason she left the Royal Court.

There is also a sub-text to the letter which indicates that if the work is exciting and splendid, people should be prepared to work for *less*. British puritanism dies hard.

I have no doubt that the letter has been produced by fears and by gossip. I shall enjoy replying.

[1] Peter Hall and John Barton's famous production of their adaptation into two plays of Shakespeare's three parts of *Henry VI* which, with *Richard III*, were first seen at Stratford in 1963 and later in London at the Aldwych.

[2] About to join the NT as Hall's assistant. In September 1974 he was promoted to General Administrator.

[3] Recently appointed to the NT to be in charge of casting. Is an NT Associate.

Wednesday 8 August

To the Coliseum to see *Siegfried*. Took Jonathan Miller with me. It was his first Wagner. *Siegfried* is not the best of baptisms. He said to me afterwards that he had had an absolutely fascinating experience, and he could say without hesitation that he would never do it again. . . .

My love/hate relationship with Wagner continues. I still feel that the possibility of revealing these works is something no director could refuse, given the chance. Yet there was a moment in the second act of *Siegfried* when the sheer pomposity and slowness of the proceedings nearly drove me screaming from the theatre. My overall feeling was of great relief that the three temptations I have had to do *The Ring*—one with Solti at Covent Garden, one with Colin Davis at Covent Garden, and one tentatively discussed for Bayreuth, have so far been resisted. But I'll do it one day I know.[1]

Lord Goodman and his brother at the performance. Many a chat in the interval. We spoke of Trevor's collapse and the anxiety everyone was feeling about him and his overwork. Goodman said we had been a year too early on our NT/RSC merger plans. But the merger now seems to me one of the silliest ideas I have ever been seduced by. The reasons I once wanted it are obvious—it would have been wonderful to work again with my old RSC colleagues, and it would have saved them and the NT from our present money difficulties. But the size of the resulting organization would have induced artistic paralysis.

Thursday 9 August

I am worried about the music for *The Tempest*. Shakespeare's obsession with music deals with its harmony, its order, its symmetry, its powers of resolution. Modern music is about the opposite of all these qualities. It would be like asking Jackson Pollock to design Prospero's magic island.

A letter in today from Max Rayne enclosing a copy of a letter from George Farmer to him. All is now explained about Hugh Willatt's recent rum letter saying there are growing rumours that I am poaching people with financial bait. Farmer had written complaining to Rayne that I have poached Goodwin from the RSC for a considerably greater salary. This is wrong: Goodwin will end up £300 better off by coming to the National. Not much inducement.

Sunday 12 August

John Bury to the flat in the morning. We worked on the designs for *The Tempest*. John had done the idea of a huge figure with its arms outstretched creating the storm. But it is too potent and too mechanical. It was cut.

After lunch to Glyndebourne. We were on the opera special: a compartment crammed with dinner-jacketed people who have been going to Glyn-

---

[1] A Hall/Solti production of *The Ring* opened at Bayreuth in July 1983.

debourne for the last 25 years. One lady informed the other that she had been to *Figaro* the night before. It was, she remarked, quite different: 'Different clothes, different sets. All quite, quite different.' The other lady was appalled. 'It can't be quite different.' she exclaimed. 'That's terrible!' To which the first lady said, 'Oh, it's just the same. Quite different, but just the same.' I felt complimented and hid more carefully behind my *Sunday Times*.

Great welcomes. And they want me back even though I have turned down *Idomeneo*. *Don Giovanni* is now being spoken of for 1976.

Monday 13 August
Larry phoned me last Friday to beg me to come with Jacky to his hideout in Sussex. The directions were worthy of James Bond. I practically expected to be asked to eat them when we arrived. The cottage has a pleasant garden which Larry made himself, a swimming pool, and secret peace. We found him cleaning out the goldfish pond, covered in mud, and in blue shorts.

He was as relaxed as I have known him during the last three years. Much less suspicious. Joan too was very pleasant. Their children are a handful. But other people's children always are. He let slip at lunch that he'd wanted to be an actor from the age of nine. He suppressed it for years because he felt he should be a clergyman, like his father.

We sat in the sun among his carefully planted hedges and chatted of this and that. He is enjoying his holiday. He was fairly cutting about Trevor's collapse, and about Trevor, who has not, in Larry's view, had the outside experience to do his present job. He has been too insulated from the harsh world—by school, by Cambridge, by Coventry, and then by me at Stratford. I fought back.

Wednesday 15 August
Had a talk with Janet[1] about Trevor. She was very forthcoming. She believes he should either leave the RSC or recognise that the future would need not a war with me but a duel—a duel in which points would be won and lost, and there would be pleasure in the match.

To bed depressed about Trevor's situation. In one respect, it is not the same as mine was in 1963. I never had any doubt that I was in the right job for my own happiness, at Stratford. It seems that Trevor has doubts for himself now. But how can you know another man's doubts?

Saturday 18 August
A marvellous day in the harvest field filming *Akenfield*. We bought this field from the farmer last winter, and now are to harvest it in the old way. Everybody in 1912 costume. An old reaper has been rebuilt and reconditioned by the wheelwright and clattered all day harvesting the field. The old

[1] Suzman, Trevor Nunn's wife.

men worked with a will on tasks still remembered from long ago. The young joined in, rapidly learning the skills. It was as if the collective memory was operating. Nothing was staged, nothing was phoney. The people were actually working.

Wednesday 22 August
The print of *The Homecoming* film was splendid. So was the sound. All the difficulties are resolved. It therefore went to America tonight[1].

Saturday 25 August
The last day of shooting *Akenfield*. We filmed the baptism of Barbara in the Baptist Church at Woodbridge. Most of the congregation were genuine Baptists. This is the most solemn ceremony of their life so I had to be careful.

The church is a beautiful building of around 1770, but now painted a bright blue and fitted with neon lighting.

The act of immersion was very moving. A ritual that meant something to those present, and even stirred some of the camera crew.

Richard Dobson, our production manager, who has appeared in the film as an undertaker, a naked swimmer, and various other things, was baptised. He is a strict Baptist. His voice took on the quaver of emotional religion as he made his affirmation.

The minister resented my authority and kept on telling me from 9.45 am onwards that we must finish: the organist had to go, the congregation had to go, his wife had to go, he had to go etc etc etc. I smiled and went on filming.

We finished at 6 pm, the slate reading No 777 take 3.

I can't believe it is over. Tearful goodbyes, for many of the Suffolk people have become fond of us and we of them. These were real tears, not like the affected farewells that you normally get in show business.

Monday 27 August
A severe feeling of anti-climax after *Akenfield*. I always get uneasy when I emerge from a piece of work. It's as if the world had been going on without me, and possibly stealing a march or conspiring against me. Tiredness inevitably produces paranoia.

Tuesday 28 August
Another letter from Hugh Willatt awaiting me in the office substantiating his accusations of poaching. The whole situation is now getting out of hand. The chairman of the Haymarket Theatre, Leicester, is apparently upset that I have stolen Peter Stevens. But as Peter wrote to me asking for a job, there isn't much stealing about it.

[1] *The Homecoming* film was shown first in America because it was produced by an American—Eli Landau.

Saw Alan Ayckbourn's *Absurd Person Singular*. It is a hard, beautifully constructed play. But because it is commercial, it tends to be unregarded. I think Ayckbourn is much more likely to be in the repertoire of the National Theatre in fifty years' time than most of the current Royal Court dramatists.

I love farce. It is so merciless. I have never directed one as cruel as this and would dearly love to.

Monday 17 September
Back to work after two weeks in Corsica which should have been three. Half the day working, half the day swimming and playing with the children. My ideal holiday. I went nowhere.

Tuesday 18 September
Read documents and dictated for most of the day. Marvellous letter in from Sybil Thorndyke about an article of mine in the *Observer* about my plans for the new NT. Quote: 'Oh! I wish I were young again and with Lewis could be working in this splendid forward-looking theatre you speak of.' I was very touched. Though I don't like my article.

Rayne is now moving in with a vengeance on the building, gingering contractors all over the place. He is the perfect man for doing this.

Long phone talk to David Brierley. Our estimates for 1975/6 show we will be more than £400,000 short of what we need to run for that year on the South Bank. By then the RSC will be over £200,000 short. The Arts Council certainly hasn't got that kind of money. I wonder if the powers-that-be are now turning back to the idea of the two of us merging? There was a call tonight from *The Guardian* saying they had on good authority that a merger was going to take place. I said it wasn't, to my knowledge. Straws in the wind?

Thursday 20 September
Evening with Trevor Nunn and David. I put some possibilities to them: the total merger—suspect because of size and perhaps politically not on at the moment; or going on as we are—thinking of the future as a duel, rather than a war to the death; or an association—where until the Barbican is ready the RSC has an explosion of theatre of all kinds at Stratford in the summer, and the use of the Lyttelton Theatre for London seasons of Shakespeare only.

Another possibility was more difficult to mention. Trevor has said to me repeatedly that he doesn't want to direct any more Shakespeare plays for years. So the question is, does he want to run a Shakespeare company at all? I said he must make himself sure; be more selfish, less dutiful; and run the company, if that is what he wants, more for his pleasure than out of a firm, East Anglian, sense of obligation.

We came to some decisions. I proposed that with Trevor unclear about the future policy of the RSC, we couldn't really judge whether an association was a good or bad thing. We therefore agreed that Trevor and I should together write a letter to the Arts Council saying we didn't think either a merger or an association was on, but we hoped the need would be recognised for subsidising both organisations in a way that made it possible for them to maintain their independence in a healthy fashion. We can then duel on.

Not a sad evening, or a bad evening, as I had feared. David and Trevor know well that our relationship will continue. So do I. But the hopeful optimism about some future marriage between the two companies, which we tried to bring to a point of decision or achievement so many times in the last year, is now no more. We have moved out of unreality. A great feeling of relief.

Friday 21 September

To George Street for a morning with the building contractors. Rayne in the chair; Joseph Lockwood[1] in attendance. Incredible revelations. Each contractor, under pressure, admits he is behind—but it is because of other contractors, who have let him down. Of course. After a while I wondered how anything ever gets finished, or how any firm ever shows a profit.

But this new pressure group of Rayne's first met only last week, and already it has started to show some results. The technique is very simple. Having discovered which supplier is holding up the contract, Rayne looks up the chairman of the company and then either he or Joseph Lockwood or Goodman or some other heavy-weight rings him up and says, surely the firm doesn't want to be the one that stops the National Theatre opening as planned, on Shakespeare's birthday[2] 1975? After all, the Queen is booked and you can't put off a royal personage.

Our orders are leap-frogging to the top of the queue.

Thursday 27 September

A good and lively associates' meeting. Fascinating tensions. Gradually Larry is realising that a director has taken over his job, rather than an actor. A lot of talk about the actor's lot, and the actor's instinct. And a lot of talk against young directors.

Larry is battered and weak from his encounter with a burglar last Sunday in his Brighton home. The shock has affected the actors' most vulnerable part: the voice.

---

[1] Sir Joseph Lockwood. Member of the South Bank Theatre Board from 1968, and Chairman from 1977.
[2] April 23.

56

Saturday 29 September
A marvellous day spent reading from cover to cover the two-volume book on Inigo Jones by Roy Strong and Stephen Orgel[1]. This is theatre scholarship at its best. No mad speculation, or unsupported theory. Just facts, facts, facts. You feel very near to the working life of Inigo Jones, the fury and the frenzy and the *speed* of it. Many of the designs, it is noted, are covered with scene painter's distemper—spotted with it. And design after design is cribbed from Callot or some Italian artist Jones encountered on his grand tour: there wasn't time for anything else.

After this book one understands the masque—and that it is a very different form to the drama. It is a wonderful study for *The Tempest*.

Sunday 30 September
An offer from Munich: a film immediately, in Hamburg, for £5,000. My acting career is big in Germany!

Robert Graves' definition of poetry: 'heartrending sense.' I found it in one of the Sunday colour comics.

Tuesday 2 October
Morning with Peter Daubeny, discussing his future and the future of the World Theatre Season now it has completed ten years[2]. Michael Kustow is to be the man who books foreign companies for the NT[3], but it is foolish to think he can do it without the brilliant help of Daubeny. Although Daubeny needs a year off, he has every intention of working again.

He was flattered at the prospect of being involved with the new NT. And what it came down to was that he would help us on occasional visits by special companies.

He seemed in better health, though he still moves from subject to subject anxiously. He is very unstable about the future. He continued the song I've heard many times before. Nobody helps; nobody cares; you can never get hold of anybody. But as his courage against his terrible illnesses is indomitable, we all get swept into this mixture of enormous charm, and paranoia.

I had to make a decision today about the film in Germany. £5,000 and all expenses can't be turned down. It is not many days work, and I am fairly up to date. I've said I'll do it.   •

Wednesday 3 October
Up at 4 am for a real onslaught on back correspondence.

[1] *Inigo Jones: the theatre of the Stuart court.*
[2] Sir Peter Daubeny's annual World Theatre Season at the Aldwych was started in 1964 during Hall's regime at the RSC. After a successful decade, its continuation was in doubt because of Daubeny's failing health. He was knighted in 1973.
[3] Kustow, an NT Associate 1973–80, was also to be in charge of the short, early evening platform performances, and of exhibitions.

An off-the-record lunch with Hugh Willatt. He said the chairman and he were quite disturbed to receive the letter Trevor and I have written saying there was no prospect of any NT/RSC links at this time. It's possible an association of some sort now becomes an economic necessity to the Arts Council, and they are thinking out how they can effect it.

Thursday 4 October
Associates' meeting. Larry asked Harold and me if we would have a private word with him afterwards on a most urgent matter. He began with one of his classic gambits: 'There is great unease in the profession.' This time it was about the fact that I was still a director of the RSC and that Harold had 'come over'. Could he beg us both to resign from the RSC forthwith. Harold icily pointed out that he was not a member of the RSC, nor had he ever been; he had therefore not 'come over'. That dealt with that. Larry went on about actors not knowing when they came to see me, whether they were seeking a job at the National or the RSC. I answered that I had resigned some time ago as a full RSC director. He was delighted. . . .

Monday 8 October
Jonathan Miller to see me. Apparently, Ken Tynan is going through a crisis. He is a very sick man. I knew he was not well, but Miller startled me by telling me that Ken had not too long to live, and must know it. His lungs are in a terrible state and hardly support him. I had no idea of this.

Saturday 13 October
The script of the film I'm to act in in Hamburg arrived last night. I read it early this morning. It is an amiable, inane family comedy, about the day when the wife of a famous author (me) has had enough of being a slave to the household and walks out for two months. The film is the father's attempts to look after his two daughters and small son. The title translated is *When Mother Went On Strike*. It will not, I'm told, be shown anywhere but Germany. I hope that's right. I think I can honestly say this is the first thing I have ever done entirely for money. But working in art needs occasional support.

Wednesday 17 October
To Edward's school to collaborate on a project. In a small room half a dozen children aged 8 to 9 were waiting for me. They had a camera on a tripod, a tape recorder, notebooks and pencils. There was no staff supervision. They switched on the tape recorder and began to interview me. 'If you had all the money you wanted would you still work?' 'Yes.' 'Would you work as much as you do now?' 'Yes, I wouldn't do anything different.' A small boy thought about this: 'That's very interesting,' he said, making a note. . . .

Jonathan Miller told me Nick Tomalin has been killed on the Golan Heights by an Arab missile. It had dropped on his car. He was covering the Israeli war as part of the *Sunday Times* Insight team.

Wherever there was trouble, whether it was the adulteration of French wine, or burning the crops in South East Asia, Nick was there. He had an indignant social conscience and a caustic attitude to the pretensions of the world. A wife and three children are left. Jonathan said to me, 'This is the first of our Cambridge generation to go.'

I wonder how much he had done on his book on the National Theatre? I wonder if anyone could take it on?

Sunday 21 October
Four hours with John Bury on *The Tempest*. We make progress. But I must confess to terror. Terror because *The Tempest* is such a difficult play to do. How I would like to work for a month with the actors before designing it.

Monday 22 October
At 9 am the phone rang: Larry in full flow. Last night after rehearsal Franco Zeffirelli had insulted him and the company[1], called them amateurs, incompetents etc, and in fine Italian rage had walked out. Larry is playing Henry V rallying the troops, and is to take over the production. I listened, heart sinking. How am I to go to Germany on Wednesday to pursue my secret life as a film actor?

After an afternoon at the office I went to see if Larry and Zeffirelli were at blows. The dress rehearsal was proceeding and Franco was back. Apparently he has apologised all round and thinks there is nothing odd that he should have had a screaming match; he is, after all, Italian.

Tuesday 23 October
Breakfast at the Savoy Grill with John Dexter to talk about his wish to go on with us as an associate director. He wants a stronger commitment, and to do a lot of studio work. He also, of course, needs to be outside the organisation from time to time earning money. Somehow we must keep him. I am very pleased at the meeting and the news.

Then on to Max Rayne's ginger group where we insult all the building contractors and they give alibis and complain about each other. Very depressing morning.

[1] Of Eduardo De Filippo's *Saturday, Sunday, Monday,* translated by Keith Waterhouse and Willis Hall, which was being directed by Zeffirelli, and soon to open at the Old Vic with Olivier and Joan Plowright in the cast.

A meeting with David Warner. He looked haunted yet calm. He said he didn't want to act at all at the moment. And he is breaking up with his wife Harriet. A sad meeting. This boy was potentially one of the greatest of stage actors. Will he ever work in the theatre again?

Wednesday 24 October

To Hamburg on the 9.45 plane. I plunged straight into some stupid scenes. And enjoyed it. I am trying not to imitate, not to be technical, but to reveal. To sleep, not too contented with my double life.

Friday 26 October

Agreeable surprise. The Arts Council are offering us £1,133,000 for the first year of full operation on the South Bank. As long as we go against proper practice by putting no money into a depreciation or repairs fund, we can just make out. Somehow or other we have to get the Ministry of Works to take over the maintenance of the building, as is done at Covent Garden.

Tuesday 30 October

Junia Birkett's[2] funeral. Jacky and I left London for Winchester. The drive was a nightmare. Dreadful fog, so we got lost. And then nearly at Winchester there was an enormous traffic jam. We arrived just before everybody returned from the cemetery. We were very upset.

The funeral took place from a tiny but exquisite late seventeenth-century stately home. The owners were friends of the Birketts. Michael was haggard, but somehow achieving a concern for his friends who were there.

The lady of the house begged me to have a talk with Michael soon. She apparently has been seeing him through these terrible days, and says that now he needs some of my time, for he feels closer to me than anybody. I am flattered but amazed. Jacky remarked in the car going back that I never get close to anybody in friendship. I suppose that is true.

Wednesday 31 October

The last night of Larry's ten year reign as director of the National Theatre company at the Old Vic. I didn't mention it because he didn't mention it. There were no speeches, no sense of occasion. But tomorrow, legally, I ascend the throne.

Thursday 1 November

So this was my first day . . . a little toast which Larry very sweetly made at 1 am at an associates' meeting was all that marked it.

[1] Wife of Michael (Lord) Birkett.

There was a good deal of talk at the meeting about the tendency of the theatre today to move away from the cathedrals of art to small rooms. The concept of the Studio in the new building actually functioning as a studio was totally demolished. It is now to be thought of as our third theatre—the Cottesloe Theatre: a small space. And we will regard our three theatres as three separate and different statements rather than as steps up a ladder towards the ultimate standards of the largest theatre.

To the Arts Council this afternoon for a meeting of the drama panel: my chance to get back at them after the battering they gave me on July 5. I was very tough and very outspoken. But I felt it did little good. Those who were against remained against. But how can one expect a lot of people who are begging for another £1,000 or £2,000 to keep their theatres alive, to sympathise with a vast new organisation that is going to eat a million or a million and a half?

So, little was achieved. But the resentment and antagonism that I had felt in the summer were at least brought into the open. And that, I suppose, is something. I am going to have to be very careful of the drama panel.

Wednesday 7 November
The main thing in today's piles of office work was the news that Equity[1] will not allow our actors to be stood off without payment while we put productions into cold storage, waiting for the new building to be finished. But the fact is that to pay them over this indefinite period is not possible.

Larry told me on the phone that he was very sorry about this as he presumed it meant the ruination of all my plans for the South Bank because I wouldn't be able to hold the build-up of productions together. I said I was sure we could find a way.

The way I have decided is to let the actors go if we have to. It's no real risk, as I believe most of them will want to be with us on the South Bank—at least at first.

Monday 12 November
This morning the Gryphon arrived—a talented pop group who specialise in medieval and renaissance music. They have their generation's curious ability to sit and say nothing. My generation seem uneasy if silence falls, and chatter like magpies. Not so the young. They sit silent, unconcerned. Waiting for something.

The meeting was to talk about them composing the music for *The Tempest*. The interview got off to a bad start because one of the group was walking on this cold November day in bare feet. And I planted my boots firmly on them as I sat down at the tiny conference table in my office.

[1] British Actors' Equity Association, the actors' trade union.

61

Then all afternoon at a Board meeting. Meetings, meetings, meetings. Much talk about our likely deficit for 1974/75 but sympathy, enthusiasm and determination were expressed. Most of the time was spent discussing catering. It is a basic rule of subsidised theatres that as long as you have catering to discuss with the Board, the directorate can always get on with their job of running the art of the theatre without too much interference.

Tuesday 13 November
Phone call late afternoon from the States to tell me that *The Homecoming* film has been hailed by the critics. There were many other superlatives which embarrassed me. I become very English at times like this. I am also uncomfortably aware that if the film had been a hideous disaster in America, no one would have phoned to commiserate. But clearly the film has been well received and it was a courtesy to tell me so. But it won't be a success unless it makes money.

Wednesday 14 November
The South Bank Board meeting was bad. There were imprecise answers to questions about the finishing date of the building and cost. Just an atmosphere of impotent gloom. Lord Goodman made one of the best entrances of all time. He arrived, as usual, late. The double doors burst open and he announced: 'I bring tidings of national importance.' Whereupon he trundled towards the conference table and sat down gravely, holding the pause very well: 'Both parties said "I will."' He had been, as he always is, arbitrating some differences. Who knows with whom?

Thursday 15 November
In the evening, to RADA for a seminar with the staff. A discussion on training. I said that my objection to most young actors was that they were too ready to *act*—whereas acting was revelation, not imitation. They must learn technique, but they then should throw it away or transcend it. The teachers took another view. The young were, they said, reluctant to learn technique and only concerned with honesty and self-expression—being true to themselves. We argued.

The most interesting happening was a conversation with Hugh Crutwell, the Principal of RADA, after the talk. He was disturbed that, because of shortage of funds in drama schools, drama training was liable to become more educational and less vocational. To go to a drama school backed by an educational authority you have to have two A-levels. A-levels have never been any proof of an actor's ability. I can think of several great actors who are certainly not natural A-level material.

62

Friday 16 November
Today Gielgud suddenly asked me if I had seen *Julius Caesar* at the Aldwych. I said no. He said it was awful, ugly, the men were clothed in odious black leather pants, they shouted and screamed and had no idea of character. It was terrible and if this was *avant garde* Shakespeare, he really felt it would be better if he didn't play Prospero. After all, he said, how did he know that I wasn't going to get up to such things? I blinked and asked him how he knew I *was*? He behaves like an extremely nervous race-horse.

Monday 19 November
At the South Bank ginger group. The chief man on site for McAlpine's was once more giving his gleeful Richard Widmark performance: the heavy who brings bad news with an exaggerated smile. As usual all the contractors fell to blaming each other. The truth is they are building a theatre, not a quick block of offices, and it is a very complex activity where co-operation and a willingness to improvise and solve problems collectively is absolutely essential. Of this there is little sign.

Tuesday 20 November
Meeting on an actors' salary policy. Clearly the maximums must be pushed up. I very much doubt if we are going to get Ralph Richardson for less than £300 a week. And this will mean a similar salary for John Gielgud and Olivier. But it is still, actually, too little.

I am only concerned about a philosophy for salaries. We cannot pay anything like commercial rates—nor should we. But the rewards for leading actors should not be ludicrously low. They should not be doing us a favour.

Thursday 22 November
To Bury St Edmunds to see the NT's *Measure for Measure*, directed by Jonathan as a small Mobile production[1].

Because of the fuel crisis and the 50 mph speed limit it took us an age to get there. We drove past 24 Avenue Approach, the little terraced house where I was born, which has just sprouted a sun-lounge-cum-porch on its front. Jacky and I tried to make it seem right that we should be visiting my birthplace on my birthday. It wasn't so, though: I was there to see a play.

To the Theatre Royal for the performance. I last stood in this theatre when I was about 17. I broke in to see what a Regency theatre was actually like. It was then a barrel store for the local brewery. Now it has been lovingly restored to something like its 1817 splendour.

---

[1] Simply staged touring productions.

A very good production, set in Freud's Vienna. I don't really approve in my puritan soul of moving Shakespeare into a modern period in order to illuminate him. You merely illuminate some things and obscure others, though this often compels admiration in critics more than it irritates. In the present instance, the Dionysian side of life—the sensual, the gleeful, the vigorous—are entirely discounted. There is no joy in sin in this city.

More rewarding is the level on which the company play. A tiny theatre, and the closeness of positions on stage, enable them to use conversational tone. The speaking is therefore rapid and human, with none of the gloss of rhetoric or the inflation of emotion. Emotion is the most obscuring thing to great poetry in the theatre. The emotion should be suppressed so that the words are a necessary expression. But there should be true music in the speaking as well. It wasn't there tonight.

It is the best production of Miller's that I have seen. But it raises a question. Shouldn't we now, if we want to do Shakespeare out of period, re-write it? It would be absurd, but at least it's logical. There is something pathetically stupid about Renaissance language in 1920s Vienna. Why didn't Jonathan modernise the text as well?

Angus Wilson[1] was at a dinner party afterwards. He lives near Bury and has been a prime mover in the restoration of the theatre. He was as entertaining as ever. The voice and the love of gossip is now positively female. He is very shrewd, very quick, and has enormous exuberance.

Friday 23 November

Messages that Larry urgently wanted to see me. I know from past experience that the only thing to do in these circumstances is to see him quickly.

I had to invite him over to the flat because I was collecting the children from school. I was uneasy about this as I always vowed I would never let him see the flat. He makes many remarks about it being higher off the ground than his[2]! So I whisked him in fast, waved a vague hand in the direction of the main room, and then rushed him into my study.

He had many little points, among them that it was a mistake to tour *Eden End*. I heard the voice of Joan in Brighton, who hates touring anything anywhere. I then told him that John Dexter was to do a Mobile of *Romeo and Juliet* next year. The eyebrows shut down. He reminded me that he wants to direct a *Romeo and Juliet*. I said there was no clash. When would he do it? We looked at the NT production plans and he said he would direct it early in 1976 after our *Lear*. I pounced, pointing out that by saying that, he had just committed himself to do *Lear*. He said he had done no such thing.

---

[1] The novelist.

[2] Hall's flat was at the very top of the Cromwell Tower in the Barbican, on the 39th and 40th floors.

He *thought* he was going to do *Lear*. Perhaps he wasn't. But he *thought* he was. He just wanted to contemplate it. I poured vast quantities of whisky down him and he became quite expansive. He is in good form.

To the Rainbow, the derelict, monstrous Egyptian picture palace of the thirties in Finsbury, to hear a group called *Yes*. Their piece, *Tales from Topographic Oceans*, is too long, but it's extremely sophisticated musically, and rewarding. Five awesome young men make a thunderous noise which would completely eradicate the London Symphony Orchestra. I went backstage afterwards to meet the group and their manager. He also manages the Gryphon and there were little talks about *The Tempest*.

Interesting evening. I certainly got more out of the sensuality of this music than I would out of the dryness of John Cage[1], for instance.

Monday 26 November
To the South Bank in the freezing cold to show a group from the GLC around the new building. A general feeling of chaos on the site. And very little is happening. Few workmen about. I now become depressed with each visit. I cannot believe it will be ready as scheduled—or even approximately.

Quick dash to the Old Vic to try the speed of Ariel in flight. Instead of him, a sandbag was hauled up and down in five seconds—the required speed for the fastest exits and entrances. I stressed it must be quiet. The technicians made one of their usual speeches: it was as quiet as it could be, considering the pulleys, winches etc. I stressed it must be quiet.

Thursday 29 November
Two angry telegrams:

One from Trevor Nunn reading: SHOCKED AND UPSET THAT MY LEADING LADY HAS BEEN APPROACHED BY YOU WITH NO CONTACT BETWEEN US STOP WHY STOP CANNOT UNDERSTAND BREAKDOWN OF ALL KNOWN RULES OF CONDUCT STOP WAIT ANXIOUSLY TO HEAR FROM YOU—TREVOR.

And one from John Barton reading: AM NOT SURPRISED AT HOW YOU GO TO IT AS ALWAYS THOUGHT YOU WOULD BUT AM WRYLY DISGUSTED AT HOW SOON AND CRUDELY YOU SET ABOUT IT STOP THERE ARE STILL TELEPHONES AND I HAD HOPED MANNERS STOP IN THE MEANTIME STOP IT—JOHN

What caused these was that John Hopkins had met Susan Fleetwood at a party and had decided she was the answer to his prayer for the part of Barbara in his new play, *Next of Kin*, which we are doing[2]. Pinter, who is directing, agreed but was concerned, as I was, about her position with the

---

[1] The avant-garde American composer.
[2] In the event the part was played by Lynn Dearth.

RSC[1]. We checked with her agent, were told she was available when we wanted her, so made an offer.

It would appear from the telegrams that the agent's view of Susan Fleetwood's availability does not tally with the RSC's. I was disturbed. But more amused than disturbed by John Barton, though little flurries of indignation rose in me during the evening.

Friday 30 November

I answered the Stratfordians this morning, deciding to be tough. Harold Pinter is furious about the situation. Steam is coming out of his ears. He considers we have behaved impeccably. So do I.

Paddy Donnell has had a meeting on what we pay top actors, at which Larry indicated that unless Knights, Dames, and other superstars get between £400 and £500 per week there will be great unhappiness. I think this sum is about right. But if we pay it, it will cause great unhappiness in the Arts Council—and at the RSC as well.

The country is running down. The trains are late. Petrol is short. Electricity cuts are imminent. The stock market is jittery. Everyone forecasts a big slump in the West.

Saturday 1 December

David Brierley rang. He says the reason Trevor has taken the Sue Fleetwood situation so badly is because we didn't inform the RSC of our offer. I don't see why they should be informed when her agent says she is free. In any case, individual actors have to have the right to decide their own futures.

It was not a happy conversation with David. In a small way the war clouds are already gathering. This makes him unhappy, and me too.

Sunday 2 December

Mr Heath has finally reshuffled, and Lord Eccles has stepped down to the accompaniment, in the arts world, of muffled cheers. He is succeeded by Norman St John Stevas, the Catholic dandy and socialiser who sports a harp in his bathroom. I suppose I can talk to him, which was hardly possible with Eccles, but is he to be the man I fight with? I can hardly imagine it.

Monday 3 December

An incredible afternoon with John Gielgud and John and Liz Bury[2] on *The Tempest* set. JG began the afternoon by announcing that he didn't want to wear a beard or hat or be in grey or black as Prospero, who was a boring man, and it was a boring part, and he didn't want to look boring. He questioned practically everything that I proposed, told John Bury that he

---

[1] With whom she was then playing.   [2] John Bury's wife, also a designer.

drew more and more like Gerald Scarfe, and whirled away with suggestions, about twelve per minute, most of them contradictory. John Bury showed one or two signs of losing his temper, but kept it.

JG remembered that when he first played *The Tempest*, it was all divinely Eastern and he wore a turban. In a later production, he recalled, he wore a long grey beard and glasses. Then in Peter Brook's he had some kind of ragged, hermity shift with sandals.

At the end of three hours, I had gently but firmly ridden John to a standstill and managed to get him to listen to why I was doing the play in a Jacobean masque-like way. He then announced that he loved the set, and perhaps he had better wear a buttoned, belted, scholar's coat after all. And a beard (should he grow it or have a false one?). And he agreed to wear a scholar's hat.

JG runs around in circles with huge charm and energy. He keeps making self-deprecating remarks, reminding us we shouldn't listen to him, and that he is a romantic who loves the old-fashioned theatre.

I walked him off down the road to the wardrobe to be measured. He summed up the three hours by announcing again that I should ignore all he had said. He really thought our notions very fascinating although he himself had never considered doing the play like that. He strode off into the dark, beaming.

John Bury and I sharpened a number of our ideas because of the opposition we had been given.

Wednesday 5 December

I usually go to work expecting a bombshell. Years at the RSC taught me that the news which comes to the director's office is mostly bad: that's what it's for. So the mail nearly always contains a nasty surprise.

I walked in today and found a note that Joan Plowright refuses to tour[1]. I counted ten. It is all to do with the children, Larry going away, the recent robbery etc. We must play this calmly.

A hurt and wounded letter from Trevor about the Sue Fleetwood situation. I don't know what will come of all this. I'm very upset.

Thursday 6 December

Had a conversation with Larry about the Joan position. I said if she couldn't tour, it was perfectly understandable. But equally we would have to re-cast, because unless the NT toured, it was not going to justify its subsidy. Larry didn't argue this, because he can't. But he was gloomy.

[1] In *Eden End*.

Friday 7 December
By the time we met this morning, everything was very amicable and Joan was sitting down with Michael Hallifax[1], Larry and I to see if we could rearrange the *Eden End* tour in any way to fit in with Larry's dates and the children's holidays. Quite a different atmosphere.

Monday 10 December
To a running of *The Homecoming* film: our first try on our own people. All the cast and crew were there, plus a formidable array from John Gielgud to Joe Losey, from Edna O'Brien to Simon Gray.

It was a tough audience, but the picture actually involved them. Many congratulations afterwards. Only David Mercer[2] was hostile. 'It's not a film, it's an archive,' he announced to me. 'You are a fucking archivist.' He went on and on that though it was inhumanly well acted and directed it wasn't a film.

Harold Pinter remarked to me that there was only one person that David Mercer, when he was drunk as he was today, bored more than Harold and that was David Mercer himself.

Wednesday 12 December
At the barber's first thing; usual resentment for wasting an hour, and being in the hands of somebody else.

South Bank Board at 11.30. Still no clear information about progress on the building. The quantity surveyor talked lightly and gloomily, like a sad Lewis Carroll walrus, of possible over-spending of half a million to three quarters or even a million. Max Rayne sat next to me doodling furiously and muttering that it would be a million and a half. Lord Cottesloe, the perfect English chairman, smiled optimistically at all the bad news, while the members of the Establishment nodded their heads and clucked and tutted about the grave economic crisis facing us and how this would affect our theatre. They then all left early for a large Christmas lunch with some tycoon or other.

Thursday 13 December
To Prunier's for my annual lunch with Harold Hobson[3]. Much talk about the national crisis—Hobson maintaining a progressive Tory position. Things are very grave. It is the first time the have-nots have been able to say to the

---

[1] Executive Company Manager, then Company Administrator, for the NT from 1966. Is an NT Associate.
[2] The playwright. Died 1980, aged 52.
[3] Drama critic of *The Sunday Times* 1947–76. Member of the National Theatre Board 1976–80. Knighted 1977.

haves 'You can't have it'. And there is nothing that the haves can do about it. We are, I think, moving into a new future, where the old structure of class is completely revalued. Those who do rotten jobs are going to be paid high wages, and I can't say that is a bad thing. What worries me is that out of the chaos we are going into, some simple and extremist group of the far right or the far left may very well break up our society and take over. God preserve us from extremes. Humanity and compassion are immediately forgotten. Intelligence also.

Back to the Barbican late where I just missed Edward's school singing carols at the bottom of the Cromwell Tower. I did not miss, however, their arrival in our flat. Jacky had invited home what she had been informed were a dozen children, for Ribena, fruit punch and mince pies as an end to their carol singing round the City. But 37 children were streaming into the flat and bouncing on the furniture. I had to shout. Three quarters of an hour was spent rushing round restraining children.

Friday 14 December
Lunch with Trevor to make peace after the Sue Fleetwood storm. Peace was made. I said it was not possible that the NT is all black and the RSC all white. Or vice versa.

To the television centre for another awful evening taking part in a BBC 2 special on 'the state of the English theatre.' A series of flippant and trendy films were set up and then various groups discussed them with no time to develop proper arguments. The programme showed television's desperate reluctance to take anything seriously or do anything at length. I would have thought anyone interested in the theatre would have been enraged by the programme, and those who were not interested would have switched off. Why does television consistently underestimate its audience, and only allow them the concentration span of a few seconds?

As I left, I am afraid I said to the people who made the programme that I thought it was awful. They smiled apologetically and agreed.

Thursday 20 December
First night of Trevor Griffiths' *The Party* at the Old Vic. It went quite well and Larry[1] was superb. Jacky and the family had all left for Wallingford for Christmas, so I was alone in the first night audience, something I hate. Much waving, smiling and nodding to acquaintances. Horrendous.

Victor Mishcon[2] made a long speech to me in the interval. He had two points to make, and he hoped I would not take them amiss.

---

[1] Olivier played John Tagg. The production was directed by John Dexter.
[2] Member of the National Theatre Board from 1965 and of the South Bank Theatre Board from 1977. Created Baron 1978.

Was it right, he said he asked himself, that the National Theatre should be in the vanguard of developments in the theatre relating to sexual frankness, nudity, etc. etc? I answered very charmingly that he must lead a rather sheltered life if he was referring to *The Party* because it was way behind many plays in London today.

And then was it right, he asked himself again, that the National Theatre should, as in this play, deal with subjects which are critical of politics and of the British way of life and in some sense are revolutionary, even anarchist? I said I thought it was essential for the National Theatre to deal with such subjects if good dramatists dealt with them. To apply any other criterion would have resulted in a National Theatre of Shaw's time not presenting his works. Wasn't it, I said, a sign of a mature society that its theatre should ask questions?

Victor was not comforted.

Saturday 22 December

Christmas preparations continue. John Mortimer and his wife and baby came over to lunch. All jolly. And tonight we in turn all drove across to the Mortimers' for a Christmas party. Most of the theatre seemed to be present including the impossible but very funny Robert Morley. He was taking the position that directors were unnecessary fellows; actors were the important chaps. I gave him a going over by being less insistent than he. I nearly cracked though when he began to praise the present Russian regime, saying they were quite right to suppress their intellectuals and their writers. He would argue with anybody just to be contrary.

Monday 24 December

Bad news all the time. An economic slump threatens. The bomb scares go on. The miners continue their go-slow. The trains are in chaos. Meantime, the nation is on a prodigal pre-Christmas spending spree.

Sunday 30 December

Jenny and Christopher to Paris to see their mother. The holidays feel over. Back into the world of telegrams and anger. Had long telephone conversations with Jonathan Miller, Blakemore, John Russell Brown. We are amassing the repertoire for 75/76 on the South Bank.

Monday 31 December

I thought this was going to be a day at home working on *The Tempest* before rehearsals start on Wednesday. Things began to go wrong early. Ron Bryden[1] brought Matthew, his son, to play with Edward and asked if he

---

[1] Drama critic of *The Observer* 1967–71. Play adviser to the RSC 1972–75. A neighbour of Hall's at Wallingford.

could come in for a moment. That moment was an hour: RSC problems and our clashes of repertoire.

Then, just as Ron was going, Larry rang from Brighton to tell me he could not play in *The Party* tonight as his voice had gone. It is not like him to be off. What I think has happened is this: Larry indeed has a cold and his voice is strained, but I also believe he wants to see if the play will work with Paul Curran in his part so we can continue it after Larry has left. He was very insistent that I see Paul Curran play. So I had to leave for London mid-afternoon, having hurriedly packed and sorted out all my myriad papers.

Some money was given back at the box office. The disappointment of people coming into the theatre when they found Olivier was not playing was almost unbearable. Many of them looked and behaved like heart-breakingly deprived children.

Back late to the London flat and a long sauna bath to ease the sinus. Thus I saw in 1974.

1974

1974

Tuesday 1 January
We took Edward and Lucy to the Palladium to see *Jack and the Beanstalk*. They enjoyed it, but not extravagantly. Frankie Howerd looked as if he wished he was telling blue jokes at a working men's club. I admire him greatly, but he wasn't entirely at ease this afternoon.

I yearn to see a properly written, properly directed magic play. A pantomine without television jokes.

I felt happy today for the first time in months. The excitement of imminent work?

Thursday 2 January
First day of rehearsal of *The Tempest*, my first NT production.

I talked for an hour about the play. The heat was so intense from the television lights[1] that I wilted and began to bore myself on occasion. But I believe it went fairly well and interested the company.

Larry was in earnest attendance. This upset John Gielgud, though he masked it, perfectly mannered Edwardian that he is. Larry had asked if he could come to the first rehearsal and really I felt in no position to say no. He busied himself by wandering round shaking hands with everybody.

Took John Gielgud off to my office for lunch and we had only been seated for two minutes when Larry re-appeared. He sat and chatted, making Gielgud feel uneasy. It is extraordinary to watch these two giants. Gielgud obviously is disturbed by Larry, and Larry knows it.

Back at rehearsal after lunch, we began reading the play. Larry reappeared again. So the poor new members of the company (and especially the young ones) had the hideous experience of reading with Sir L's beetle brows watching them.

We read half the text. John was singing, and though it is beautiful singing I must try and make him concrete and specific. Jenny Agutter as Miranda hid rather—as did Michael Feast as Ariel. But the Court were magnificent: particularly David Markham and Cyril Cusack. And Arthur Lowe[2] was just naturally funny as soon as he opened his mouth. It is a joy to have a clown as a clown. No artificial work is required.

---

[1] London Weekend Television were making a documentary on the National Theatre, for showing when it opened.
[2] As Stephano.

I was very excited, but, by the evening, so entirely exhausted that I fell into a deep depression. There is nothing worse for a director than the first day. Much worse than the first night.

Thursday 3 January

Gielgud was more restrained at rehearsal today. After my conversation yesterday urging him not to sing or emote, he had cooled down. But he is now wrinkling his nose and wondering if he is not being boring.

A problem on *The Tempest* now is the music. The Gryphon delivered one dirty folded sheet of manuscript paper with a rather conventional-looking setting of 'Come unto these yellow sands' scribbled on it in pencil. I have asked that we look out Purcell's music to *The Enchanted Island*—Dryden and Davenant's version of *The Tempest*. We will cannibalise this if necessary. The Gryphon are in the Cotswolds making their new album. It doesn't sound as if we are going to get much of their attention[1].

Friday 11 January

A run-through rehearsal of *The Tempest*. A shambles with nothing precise, nothing fixed. But it gave me the possibility of seeing how the play was working, or could work, and gave everybody concerned with it the opportunity of getting to know it.

The play is monstrously difficult and I realise with a shudder that five weeks from now we are actually out of the rehearsal room and on the stage.

Gielgud worries me. Prospero is a man who is contained and careful. He does not reveal himself to the audience. He can hardly reveal himself to himself. He is controlled. His passion for revenge is not emotional but puritanical. John shows the agony that Prospero is going through from the very beginning of the play. He should wait until the end. Macbeth has to be played by an actor who is content to act dangerously little for the first half of the play. The technique is the same with Prospero. Except that Prospero must wait until three-quarters of the play is over until he gets emotional—in the masque.

But I am very hopeful.

Lunch with Norman St John Stevas, our new Minister for the Arts. He asked me if I were still a Labour man. I said I was. He also asked me whom I would vote for at the next election. I said I could not vote for Wilson because he would obviously land us in a worse mess than we are in now. I would find it hard though to vote Tory. I believe politics are more a matter of instinct and conditioning than reason, like religion.

Monday 14 January

Farewells: Jenny and Christopher back to school[2].

[1] In the event, the Gryphon did a very successful score for *The Tempest*.   [2] Bedales.

The morning spent on the first scene of *The Tempest*: shouting lords, pulling ropes. A lot of enthusiasm and will to work in the company, but I felt at something of a loss. I couldn't get it happening. I don't actually *like* the scene. It is a naturalistic presentation of a shipwreck, with little opportunity to establish any of the people. I was struggling.

Ran the rough-cut of *Akenfield* with Cyril Bennett[1]. Without his faith, it would never have happened. He gave me the money to make it on the strength of an 18-page synopsis, and allowed me to go off and shoot it without actors and without script, just real people improvising.

But the film seemed appalling to me at today's running: too rich and too indulgent. I was very low when I returned home. But I must not get too obsessed with the problems of *Akenfield* at the moment or I shall mess up *The Tempest*. With a shiver my thoughts returned to 1968 when I was editing *Work is a Four Letter Word*[2] and rehearsing the RSC's *Macbeth*[3] at the same time. The result was catastrophe for both. And shingles.

I should think there is still three months of editing and cutting work to do on *Akenfield*.

I have been skimming through Geoffrey Whitworth's book, *The Making of a National Theatre*: a record of a century of misunderstandings, intrigue and ludicrous heartbreak. It was published in 1951. But nothing has changed.

Thursday 15 January
A wonderful afternoon's rehearsal. We went from Prospero's first scene through to the end of the meeting of Ferdinand and Miranda: the great arc of exposition. Gielgud is becoming contained and strong. A great leap forward by Michael Feast. I am happy and free. One of those afternoons when the scene comes into one's head without any beating of the brains.

Wednesday 16 January
Early with Max Rayne for a session on many matters. I was there promptly at 9.30 having already worked for a couple of hours. Rayne arrived at ten. I was furious because I was then made late for rehearsal.

He was in one of his provocative moods, behaving like a featherweight boxer. He teemed with ideas, seeming to dance from foot to foot, jabbing small challenging punches to see if I would fight back. I did.

Thursday 17 January
Rehearsed 'Come unto these yellow sands' and 'Full fathom five', Gielgud getting on beautifully with the young Miranda and Ferdinand[4]. He is like a

---

[1] Programme Controller for London Weekend Television from 1969 to his death in 1976.
[2] A film directed by Hall. His first.   [3] With Paul Scofield in the name part.
[4] Rupert Frazer.

giggly and outrageous uncle. Most of the humour of his behaviour comes from the delight and amazement of the young that the great Sir John can send himself up so much, can be so funny.

Monday 21 January

I am very pleased with *The Tempest*. I feel it is pointing the right way. We have not yet achieved a lot of it but we know what we need. Disquieting rumours though that the three-day week[1] may be applied to theatre workshops, and that therefore *The Tempest* scenery will be late. I cannot stand another *Via Galactica* or *Figaro*. Both these productions were endangered by the ludicrously late arrival of the settings. *Figaro* survived; *Via Galactica* didn't.

Tuesday 22 January

Dashed to the Savoy at lunchtime for the *Evening Standard* drama awards. Sat with Lauren Bacall on one side and Maggie Smith on the other: two ladies who do not, as they say, let very much go by. Norman St John Stevas spoke, and spoke for too long. To try to get a politician to make a short speech is like trying to make a habitual drunkard stop at one drink.

I made a fool of myself. I was to present the award to Janet Suzman as the best actress[2], but they took things out of order and I was deep in conversation with Lauren Bacall when I heard my name called. I was therefore catapulted into the speech without having organised my head.

Larry got a special award for his ten years at the Old Vic with the National and made a beautiful, dignified and sincere speech, with no purple excesses. I admired him greatly. But most of the other speeches went on and on. The best was Rex Harrison, who said one sentence when he presented the trophy for the best actor to Alec McCowen[3].

Friday 25 January

Up at 6 am. Mountains of correspondence. Breakfast at the Savoy with a gentleman from the Post Office who is in charge of the commemorative stamps issues. What stamp should be issued for the National Theatre opening? I suggested three ideas. First, the building. Second, the building as part of the nation rather than as part of the metropolis. Third, Olivier. The man said they had great trouble in putting living persons on stamps unless they were members of the Royal Family.

---

[1] Ordered by Edward Heath to save power during industrial action by the miners.
[2] For her performance as Cleopatra in *Antony and Cleopatra* at the Aldwych.
[3] For his performance as Alceste in *The Misanthrope* at the Old Vic.

Did a run-through the *The Tempest.* Terrible. We have hit the bottom. From now on the work can only go up. I think it's the usual problem: I now know what needs to be done, but have to find the time and energy to do it. It is no longer a question of exploration but of execution.

Saturday 26 January
This afternoon took Edward to a football match: 42,000 people watching Arsenal v. Queens's Park Rangers. I am frightened by so many people in a mass. I haven't seen a major football game for over 20 years. In those days I thought, perhaps mistakenly, that players played fair. But this was all aggression, pushing, shoving, kicking—hoping to foul without being seen. Free kicks abounded. It was a draw, to Edward's disappointment, 1–1, but he still absolutely adored it.

Tuesday 20 January
Early morning start. Then Sally Beauman arrived to interview me for the *Telegraph* colour mag. All the usual questions: 'You have a reputation for being ruthless....' 'You like power....' 'Why do you work so hard....?'
  She had been right through my cuttings in the press association library. She said I had one of the fattest files there.
  These files are self-perpetuating. I was described as being ruthless and power-loving by Peter Lewis in *Nova* magazine in about 1962. I have been ruthless and power-loving ever since.

Wednesday 30 January
Victor Mishcon's party at the Old Vic. He had invited Olivier, myself, and some of the Board to accompany Harold Wilson and his wife to *The Front Page* which the Wilsons wanted to see. But Larry remained in Brighton, giggling no doubt. He has been opposed to the evening for weeks. He thinks it shows bad taste for the NT to entertain the leader of the opposition who might shortly be Prime Minister. Arse-licking he calls it.
  I find Harold Wilson difficult to talk to and spoke mainly to Mrs Wilson, whom I have chatted to before, in Covent Garden days. A homely cheerful lady, very likeable and intelligent.
  Appalling experience tonight. *Work is a Four Letter Word*, my first film, was on BBC 2. I made it in 1968 when I didn't know how to direct films and was anyway going through a very bad patch. Excuses? I suppose so. I watched with glazed horror. I was trying to make a modern farce, and was over-influenced by my love for the silent movie, Buster Keaton, etc. etc. But my film had words....
  I know sometimes I do very good work. How therefore can I do things that are so very, very bad? I think it's because I take enormous risks. Sometimes they open new doors; sometimes they are just failures.

Thursday 31 January

Could hardly wake this morning, I was so tired. A great feeling of oppression in the head all day.

Finished rehearsals at 5.15 and dashed to the Collegiate Theatre where Frances Yates was lecturing on *The Tempest*. She is one of the great scholars of the world: extremely erudite. But if you had not read her books you wouldn't have had the least idea of what she was talking about.

I was depressed as usual by the scholar's habit of imputing motives to artists. This evening, Shakespeare, in writing his plays, was apparently referring to the Rosicrucian doctrine and to the Hermetic tradition.

I know Samuel Beckett and Harold Pinter well. I think I know how they write and why they write: instinctively. Yet already, the world is full of scholars discovering their motives with all the exuberance of Sherlock Holmes solving a case. It just isn't like this.

Dashed back to the flat where Peter and Natasha Brook came for dinner. There was the usual hot news from the cultural front. Had I heard of the American, Robert Wilson? No I hadn't. I am told who Robert Wilson is—a painter/dancer/director who makes expensive shows which are like slow-motion Magritte paintings. I listen, amazed and inferior. This always happens to me with Peter. I remember him in 1955 asking me if I knew Francis Bacon, and shouldn't he design *Waiting for Godot*? I remember him in 1960 asking me if I had read the works of Antonin Artaud; and in 1963, the work of Jan Kott. I must now look into Robert Wilson!

He asked me a good deal about *The Tempest* and looked unimpressed at my ideas. Or was it that I was too tired to see things straight?

Sunday 3 February

Talked to David Brierley who is full of despair about the economic situation of the RSC and the NT. So am I. The miners are about to strike and we are about to go into a deep, deep recession. A fine time to be asking for money for the arts.

Thursday 7 February

Very long and demanding associates' meeting. We talked about Jonathan Miller's idea to do *The Importance of Being Earnest* with an all-male cast.

There was a sharp division between Jonathan and Harold Pinter. Pinter's position is clear: an author has certain clear intentions, and Wilde's intentions were not that the women should be played by men. Jonathan asserted repeatedly that it was a director's right to reinterpret a play in any way that seemed significant to him, once the play was no longer new. He was making a fool of nobody but himself, and the play was still there at the end of the day. Harold feels one has a greater responsibility to a dead dramatist than to a living one.

It was quite a tense meeting. Michael Blakemore, John Bury and I were for allowing Jonathan to do what he wanted. Pinter, John Dexter, Larry and Paddy Donnell were for him not doing it with all-male cast.

I summed up by saying I hoped Jonathan would feel he did not need to do the play with an all-male cast—but that if he decided he must, I and everybody else would back his right to do so. That was agreed.

This meeting could have entirely split our group. Larry, no doubt, was thinking that a lot of intellectuals were running on about a perfectly obvious issue. I was carefully trying to preserve the strength of both Pinter and Miller.

Thursday 14 February
Lunch with John Russell Brown and Peter Stevens. Discussed the repertoire for 1975/76. I mentioned what a shock in many ways *The Tempest* rehearsals were being for me. It was the first time since the beginning of the RSC that I had done a Shakespeare play without a group of actors most of whom were familiar with my approach to the text, and who had a shared attitude towards speaking Shakespeare. Peter Stevens said my most common stance in rehearsals had been that of a teacher. I said I was aware of it and did not at all think that that was what a director should be. This is basically what's wrong with the production at the moment. It is too didactic, not freely creative enough.

Friday 15 February
An interview with me by Sydney Edwards[1] has appeared in the *Evening Standard*, illustrated by a Quasimodo-like picture where my resemblance to Charles Laughton becomes stronger. It is very strange how one never looks as one feels. I don't feel as fat or as puffy—or as sly.

Saturday 16 February
This morning *Tempest* rehearsals were for the first time on the Old Vic stage. We were on the bare set of *Saturday, Sunday, Monday*—without props, without costumes, and without sound effects. But the company went through the play in two hours and a half with a great deal of expertise.

John talked to me afterwards with the kind of modesty and frankness which make him a great man. He said he knew that in some sense he had become old fashioned—all actors do. He remembered in his youth how wonderfully immediate Baliol Holloway and Dorothy Green had been—the new actors of that age. Yet, by the end of their lives, even they seemed to him rhetorical old hams. He felt he was the same, which is why he wanted to do *The Tempest* the way I wanted. And, said he, the stage always went to his

[1] Arts columnist and later Arts Editor of the *Evening Standard*, from 1966 to his death in 1979.

head anyway. He loved to wander around swinging his cloak and dominating the audience. It was a romantic style of acting which had served him well all his life and his public loved it. But, added John, I want to get rid of my easy solutions.

Sunday 24 February
Walked from the Barbican to the Old Vic in the spring sunshine. Incredibly mild. I wish I was in the country. And I certainly wish I wasn't dress-rehearsing.

The afternoon spent on the storm, and the evening on the second part of the play. Slow and difficult progress. I finished at 3 am.

At 1 am we were trying the trapdoor for bringing up the chess game scene. To my incredulous eyes, Sir John dropped through the trap apparently in slow motion. There ensued a long silence. I ran and looked down. John was smiling amiably as he picked himself up from the pile of chess pieces and the entangled limbs of Miranda and Ferdinand who were waiting below to come up. Miraculously no-one was hurt.

Monday 25 February
Unable to sleep after the 3 am finish of *The Tempest* technical rehearsal. Run of Act II this afternoon. Then this evening's dress rehearsal. I found it dreadful: slow, heavy and over-rich. Every moment was illustrated and jammed with effects. Certain things just have to be simplified. We have created a production for presenting later on the South Bank. It is too heavy for the Old Vic. The stage can't cope with it.

So in the night I looked failure in the face again. This is a very expensive piece of work, and I am in a vulnerable position because it's my first production as the NT's new director.

Some of this feeling is paranoia produced by physical fatigue. I have allowed myself to get much, much too tired. I disguise it from the cast (I hope). But it shrivels my instincts, and my instincts are what I work on.

By the end of the night I had come through it. Suppose it is a failure. They have happened before and will happen again. What I have mainly to find is the strength to go on and improve the production. Failure is something far more inside yourself than in the eyes of the outside world.

Tuesday 26 February
John Gielgud in good spirits and launched himself merrily into the first public preview tonight. He is an amazing man, and my debt to him is enormous. He has never complained, never been restless. He has led the company and helped me every inch of the way.

The preview went quite well and made me slightly more optimistic. Larry gave me a few constructive notes afterwards. Whether he liked the proceedings or not, I don't know. I was polite and so was he.

Dreadful feeling of loneliness at the moment. I would like colleagues around as in Stratford days. Here they don't offer help because of shyness. And I don't ask for it because of shyness. I am not quite sure what I am doing.

Thursday 28 February

General election day. I shall not be able to vote. I have been too lazy to get a postal vote and Jacky and I do not have the energy to travel down to Wallingford.

I feel bad about it. But I am relieved too because I would have had to face voting Tory. Could I have done it? I don't think so. It would have been a little like a Catholic leaving the religion he was born to. I dislike Heath's dogmatic attitude and the brutality of his party. But Wilson's contortions over the Common Market have lost him my support.

Tuesday 5 March

Harold Wilson is again Prime Minister. Labour have a minute majority over the Conservative Party but no working majority. We must surely have another general election before the end of the year.

Day of *The Tempest* first night. Uneasy. I lay in bed worrying from an early hour. Then went to the office and fiddled about. A short rehearsal to key everybody up—and the usual mounting excitement, thank-yous, good wishes, telegrams, flowers etc.

But the performance was the best we have so far given. The production *just* floated. The text came on to the top and there were the beginnings of a lightness and ease.

I am not easily deceived by first night euphoria, but too many people came up to me and wrung me by the hand for me to think that we had not achieved something. The reception at the end was absolutely wild.

I myself thought we had succeeded—just. Gielgud was a little woolly. Michael Feast and Denis Quilley[1] were magnificent; Julian Orchard[2] and Arthur Lowe, wonderful. I still though have a deep sense of disappointment that I have not done the play the way I wanted to. While the new stage on the South Bank could have created a masque, the Old Vic can't.

But I went home in enormous relief and with some elation. At 1.15 am Harold Pinter woke me up by telephoning. He was most anxious because neither he nor Peggy[3] had seen me afterwards, and they had loved it. He

---

[1] As Caliban.   [2] As Trinculo.   [3] Ashcroft.

said John Bury and I should feel very proud. I think I heard him say we should 'dance down Piccadilly with a lily in one hand and a rose in the other'. . . .

Wednesday 6 March

Usual stunned feeling after an opening. Then the adrenalin begins to run again from the notices. They are what is known as mixed. The truth is, the play has not achieved the level of mastery and certainty that silences criticism. If you like the approach, you like it. But if you resist it, there is plenty to quibble with.

To the theatre for the second night. Then twenty-five minutes before the start, an authentic nightmare begins. Micky Feast is not there, and nobody knows where he is. Julie Covington[1], his girlfriend, has not seen him since early afternoon.

The house is full of the second night press, the Arts Council, Max Rayne etc. The unfortunate understudy Steven Williams who has been on the flying stirrup only once, is on at a few minutes notice. I urged him not to fly and meant it. I pointed out that it was only a play. He insisted he had to fly— otherwise he would not feel he was playing the part.

So the second night was rough technically, low in impact and concentration, and vibrant with nerves. All the cast were thrown.

Steven Williams did very well. But he is not an Ariel and he can't sing. The audience were not too disappointed, although one or two of our official friends looked tight-lipped.

The evening was an experience that none of us—certainly not the cast and certainly not me—is fresh enough or courageous enough to cope with at this moment. A play's worst moment is always its second night. Even if the notices are good, it requires an enormous effort to make the thing live again. Micky could not have chosen a worse night for his aberration, whatever it is; by the end of the evening, we still had no news of him.

Friday 8 March

The Times diary carries a piece today about Steven Williams, the triumphant understudy. It also says that at one point, the equipment on which he flies crashed up to the roof of the theatre without warning leaving him without transport. This is not true.

Michael Feast came in to see me this afternoon. He is now out of the strange depression that hit him after his great success on the first night, and is back with us again.

Saturday 9 March

I am home at Wallingford, dead tired, and quite unhappy. And with me I

[1] Playing Iris in *The Tempest*.

have an enormous suitcase full of unanswered correspondence and undigested memoranda.

It highlights a dilemma which has been confronting me for the last two months. How can I ever run the National Theatre and at the same time direct plays without going mad? The organisation is at present small, contained, and the problems are nothing like as vast as they will be on the South Bank. And yet I am at breaking point: very near the abyss which is all too familiar from Stratford days—an abyss which everybody faces who manages a theatre and tries as well to be an artist.

Sunday 10 March

The Sunday notices for *The Tempest*: Harold Hobson in *The Sunday Times* is awful and Robert Cushman[1] in *The Observer* is wonderful. The *Telegraph* is dismissive. What do I think? Well, the production does not have the physical grace and clarity that I would have liked. Also, I have taxed myself and the organisation too far too early.

Wednesday 13 March

South Bank Board. New target dates for the handing-over of the new building from them to us are the three months from the end of August. Richard Pilbrow[2] came up to me after the meeting and said that from the completion of hand-over at the end of November, his people needed four months before we could even begin rehearsing[3]. This could be a night-mare. My brain begins to tick. I smell a crisis.

Thursday 14 March

A difficult lunch with Paddy[4], Gillian Diamond, Peter Stevens and Michael Hallifax on the salaries for knights, dames, and superstars. I'd had a private conversation earlier with Laurie Evans who reiterated that none of *his* clients would come to the National for less than £500 per week, and that Larry was behind him. So at our lunch I said we simply had to decide whether we needed Ralph, Peggy, John, and Larry on the South Bank during the opening period or not. In actual terms of money we are speaking of only about £7,500 to £10,000 over the year. It is worth much more than that to have their names associated with the launch of the new building. It's true that if we have the stars we shall be accused of being square and predictable, and if we don't we shall be accused of not attracting the best

---

[1] Drama critic of *The Observer* from 1973.
[2] Chairman of Theatre Projects, responsible for the mechanical and electrical installations in the new building.
[3] This meant rehearsals could not start until the end of March 1975 for an opening scheduled for 23 April.
[4] Donnell.

talent—there is no way of winning. But there is one way of losing—not having them at all.

Friday 15 March

It is spring. And raining. But very beautiful. I walked to Wallingford village and back before lunch. Calm is coming.

The rest of the day I worked on the text of *John Gabriel Borkman*[1]. I wish I was a writer. The quiet solitary life suits me much better than working in theatre. But it's a bit late now. . . .

Tuesday 19 March

A great event. I took Ralph Richardson and John Gielgud for a tour of the South Bank. It was very funny. John, who is nearly seventy, treated Ralph, who is seventy-one, as if he were an extremely aged and endearing relative up from the country, unused to city ways: 'Mind those holes. . . .' 'Don't trip over those wires.' They were both in long coats and large trilbys, Ralph sporting a stick. They could have been nothing but actors. And great ones too. Both sleek with success.

Thursday 21 March

Larry's last performance at the Old Vic. As his last bow on stage with his fellow actors ended, I sneaked in behind and tapped him on the shoulder. He turned and looked at me, horrified. For about a hundredth of a second I saw the natural reaction: 'What are *you* doing here? Get off the bloody stage.' It was then replaced by the actor's mask, looking surprised, amazed. I made a speech which I hope covered the situation and the audience rose to its feet.

Larry began acting at the Old Vic in 1936 and has given many of his greatest performances there. Without him, the Vic would not have continued as it did, and there certainly would be no National Theatre.

After the performance, in that dreadful rehearsal room, Denis Quilley played the piano while the actors had a singsong and Larry imitated Noel Coward.

Monday 25 March

To a meeting at County Hall[2]. Illtyd Harrington, the firebrand Welshman who is deputy leader of the GLC and who I think sees himself as the reincarnation of Aneurin Bevan, expressed concern in a speech about the new National Theatre. 'We don't want monuments,' he said, 'either for

---

[1] Hall's next production at the Old Vic. The English version was by Inga-Stina Ewbank and Hall.
[2] Of the Theatres' Advisory Council.

Peter Hall to play in, or as a memorial to Lord Olivier.' I asked him afterwards why he was so against the National. He explained he wasn't but that he had difficulties with the people on his back, and so speaks out the new dogma. Twenty years ago Labour dogma was that we must have beautiful municipal theatres and a beautiful National Theatre; that is why the GLC gave the site. The new dogma is that you don't need buildings, but when nine or ten people are gathered together in a space in Brixton or Fulham or Poplar, there is art. It is all balls.

Tuesday 26 March
Private dinner of some of the NT Board: Rayne, Victor Mishcon, Ronald Leach[1], and Leslie O'Brien[2], at Mishcon's flat. I got them to agree the new top artists' salaries. It is, after all, less than a third of what the great talents could earn in the commercial theatre.

Wednesday 27 March
Early morning meeting with Richard Pilbrow. Horrifying news. It emerged that it would now be impossible to depend on previews of our productions until the beginning of June '75. So our plans are in ruins. Our build-up of plays and actors at the Old Vic to a size large enough to occupy the three auditoriums on the South Bank, a build-up already seven months old, is a farce. I was staggered. We shall have to prepare a broadside. I asked for an early morning meeting with Denys Lasdun tomorrow. Why didn't he speak at the South Bank Board meeting the week before last when he heard them and me say that even with the new dates, showing the building now being delivered to us in the autumn, we could still just make a royal opening in April '75?

I had only one immediate thought. We shall have to continue our build-up plans for the rest of this year—it is too late to get out of them: contracts have been made with artists. Then we will stop and start to run down our programme until we are given an absolutely guaranteed date for the completion of the building.

Thursday 28 March
Nine o'clock at Denys Lasdun's. Richard Pilbrow and all my gang present. We wanted to get clear news before today's NT Board meeting. Lasdun tried to put all the blame on us. We should not have made our plans, not have started our build-up. Cheek. . . .

---

[1] Member of the NT Board 1972–80. Knighted 1970.
[2] Member of the NT Board 1973–78. Governor of the Bank of England 1966–73. Created Baron 1973.

Anyway I left some very frightened gentlemen—frightened because they see what I aim to do, which is to disassociate the NT from the architect and from the builders. If there is a national scandal—which I believe there will be—let it rest on the shoulders of those who have produced it. Not on the theatre company.

I made all these points later to the NT Board who were flabbergasted by the news of a further set-back. They were alarmed too at my proposition that we should run down at the end of this year and await a definite signal of completion. For from that time it would take us months to run up again. But they saw the wisdom of it.

Thursday 4 April

First night of *Eden End*, Olivier's last production of his regime. Priestley made a little speech at the end praising Larry's production, and this pleased the audience keenly.

Then there was a party in the dress circle bar where I said a few words and presented Larry with a silver model of the Olivier Theatre, mounted on a hideous green ormolu base, and a cheque for £500 from the staff of the Old Vic. Ghastly show business atmosphere.

On to a small party at the Priestleys' flat in the romantic Albany. Jacquetta[1] told us it was a great place to creep out of as the milkman arrived. Memories of the romance with J.B. all those years ago, I suppose.

Home late. I do not believe that *Eden End* is a success. It is beautifully done but tonight the audience did not trust it. So the actors didn't either.

Friday 5 April

Eden End notices are moderate. Respect for the production, reservations about the play. Not much impact.

Tuesday 9 April

The South Bank Board met today. Lord Cottesloe, in the smoothest English establishment way, said he quite saw the difficulties of the National Theatre, and if the NT Board in their wisdom decided they had to run down their present programme, of course they would have to. But he did hope that somehow or other they would maintain their programme in order to keep the pressure on the builders.

He would not admit to the architects or the contractors that the 23 April opening date was off, although in private session he read a letter he is drafting to the Palace to warn the Queen. He pointed out cosily that in fact the Queen had never had a firm date fixed—only 'the spring of 1975'. There

---

[1] Hawkes, Priestley's wife.

was a good deal of talk about Ascot. For if she is at Ascot, she won't open the theatre in June, should that become the first possible date.

Wednesday 10 April

The big surprise of the morning was some 4,000 dollars from the film of *The Homecoming*. This is the result of the box office take in America. I never expected to see any part of my percentage.

Meeting with John Russell Brown. I warned him I was getting a certain amount of feed-back about him as an over-rigorous academic. All my life I have encountered the theatre's deep suspicion of the academic. I had it myself in my early years, and I'm not entirely free of it now. And I had it for years at the RSC with John Barton. I told JRB not to alter what he was doing but just exercise great care and tact. He took it very well.

The first associates' dinner. We have decided to dine together once a month in order to have a freer exchange of opinions. Unfortunately, John Dexter did not turn up, and Jonathan Miller cancelled at the last moment. He is not talking to me, and is obviously estranged, it seems, since *The Importance* discussion. I suspect he doesn't like open talk about his ideas. If he is not happy, he should say what he's unhappy about.

Saturday 13 April

John Gielgud's surprise seventieth birthday celebration. I went up from Wallingford on the 8.30 pm train and arrived just in time for the end of *The Tempest*. I stood at the back. There in the Vic audience were Sir Ralph, nodding, Sir Laurence smiling, and Dame Peggy rapt in the play.

The last moments went very well, John doing the epilogue beautifully. I bounded on at the finish and said three sentences. I introduced Larry, who introduced Ralph, who said Happy Birthday to John.

Ralph is like an old soldier scenting battle when the audience is there. Suddenly he came to life and stamped round the stage joking and shouting.

John cried, which is appropriate, and was genuinely surprised.

We had a short party upstairs in the rehearsal room afterwards. There was a cake with seventy candles, and the presentation of the Doulton figure of Ellen Terry which the company had subscribed to.

I sneaked away and caught the eleven o'clock train back. At home and in bed at one o'clock.

Sunday 14 April

Better weather today. Blazing sunshine this morning. Michael Tippett over this morning and stayed for lunch. He was in marvellous form. Although his sight is troubling him badly, he is lively and energetic. He said he had got to the end of Act I of *The Ice Break*[1] and it would take him some two years

[1] At the time, there was talk of Hall directing this. He had directed Tippett's *The Knot Garden* at the Royal Opera House in 1970.

more to complete the score. Wonderful to have such definite objectives, such optimism at an advanced time of life.

He left after lunch. A happy and stimulating morning even though those intense blue eyes do not burn brightly any longer.

Domestic afternoon: the Brydens with us, Ron and his wife plus children. Much swimming, splashing, and hunts for Easter Eggs.

Wednesday 17 April

Lucy's fifth birthday, so I stayed at Wallingford. About thirty-five kids to the party. The day was cold, grey and cheerless, but the children swam, had pony rides, played football, and fought. Everybody seemed happy except Lucy, who was overwhelmed by the numbers, and Edward who was resentful at not winning anything. I tried to explain to him that the host always has to be modest. . . .

Thursday 18 April

The situation the South Bank Board has put us into, by not absolutely settling for the fact that a seriously delayed opening is now inevitable, is a perfect illustration of how difficult it is for non-theatre people to comprehend a working theatre's problems. We cannot be too flexible. We cannot keep changing plans. If you promise an actor a part, you have to see to it that he or she plays it. Any repertoire is a house of cards. Pull one production away and the whole thing collapses.

Today came my confrontation with Jonathan. He explained he was depressed, had been working hard, and had been shattered by the controversy at the associates' meeting two months ago when his idea of doing an all-male *Importance* was debated. But he did not want to go, and did not want to be difficult. It was a much better meeting than I had anticipated and all is healed for the moment. I think I recognise in Jonathan something that is in myself—a desire to be an outsider in any organisation, to be the victim of authority, and to use that victimisation to collect sympathy and to go one's own way.

Saturday 20 April

To Stratford with all the family for the Shakespeare birthday celebrations.

The usual rather boring lunch. Jack Priestley told me that in his speech he was going to 'Have a go' at the directors. In the event he didn't have much of a go at all—merely a nostalgic longing for the old fit-up days at Bradford when the strolling players came round doing Shakespeare on a shoestring. I in my speech had a go back.

There were the usual gracious and overlong orations from the Ambassadors—Guyana told us about Shakespeare in Guyana, and Hungary about Shakespeare in Hungary. We all slumped afterwards in Trevor's office. Too much wine and too much chat.

Supper with the Nunns, and I sat up chatting with Trevor until 3.30 am. Once again our anxieties about the future raised themselves. How are we both to run two enormous theatres at full tilt? There is insufficient money. Sometimes there seem insufficient people. Trevor once more raised the ghost of amalgamation.

Sunday 21 April
Peggy and I crept out of the Nunns' house at quarter to ten, leaving Trevor and Janet still fast asleep. We collected Jenny and Christopher, who were staying with a friend, and then Peggy drove us back to Wallingford.

Peggy is one of those ladies who cannot talk and drive. She makes extravagant gestures and her hands disconcertingly leave the wheel. When I told her that she was a potato in Leicester—that the theatre bar there had a 'Spud Ashcroft' stuffed with prawns, she took both hands off the wheel and waved them about with pleasure and amazement. We nearly hit a lorry.

Jenny and Christopher got us lunch back at Wallingford, then we sat in the sun for the afternoon. Jenny talked a good deal to Peggy about Avoncliffe[1], for Peggy remembers the house well and lived in it for long periods before we did. I am still amazed by Jenny's inaccuracies. She says, in the childhood memories section, that when Leslie and I split up she did not see her mother for two years and didn't recognise her when she met her. In fact it was two months.

Wednesday 24 April
To County Hall where the Leader of the GLC and all the various chairmen of the significant committees were giving lunch to the arts and crafts. Joan Littlewood fell on me and humorously said she didn't expect to be sitting opposite her enemy. I asked her why she was my enemy. 'You are the Establishment,' she replied. I told her she was the Establishment too.

Hugh Jenkins[2] took me aside and whispered that all was going to be well for the money to complete the theatre.

---

[1] The house at Stratford where Hall and his family lived while he ran the RSC. Jenny was working on a history of the house as an A-Level project.
[2] Minister for the Arts in the new Labour Government, 1974–76.

Monday 20 April

Lunch with David Hare[1]. I asked him where his interest lay as a director. He said only with modern plays. Old plays irritated him because he wasn't able to carry on a dialogue with the writer. I know what he means.

Sometimes I feel that the desperate turning over the past that all theatre directors do is only a search for accidental resonances which would surprise the original author and would mean nothing to his original audience. In a sense we are all making new art objects out of old plays, almost as if we were writers. A dangerous activity.

Tuesday 30 April

Lunch with Huw Wheldon[2] who gets more Dickensian than ever: bellowing guffaws, army metaphors, and with a lively, very Welsh, mind.

We discussed future tie-ups with the National and the BBC. Wheldon said his chaps were not really for any relationship—they would sooner do the plays themselves. I said my chaps were not really for such a relationship — they would sooner work for Lew Grade and earn a fortune. But we both agreed that a situation which allowed the National to make films its own way and the BBC to distribute them in England by television would be advantageous.

Jonathan Miller was at the Vic tonight for the preview of *Next of Kin*, looking all strange and unhappy. I took him out to supper afterwards. He went on talking until one o'clock about play after play. At this moment in his life he wants to direct everything. He said with engaging frankness, 'Only time stops me from doing ten productions a year.'

He also said that just before he went to France some ten days ago, he'd had a phone call from Joan Plowright. She told him how worried she was because the National company were so unhappy, so fragmented. I had, she said, split up the beautiful company of the past and now all the actors felt no identity with the proceedings, no leadership. They were just doing jobs etc. She was accordingly, with Larry's help, going to start a new company working in another theatre and would Jonathan direct for it? Jonathan seemed surprised that I was not more surprised.

It is all going to be very lively.

Wednesday 1 May

A horrible afternoon at the office: a series of classic disasters. The first news was that Michael Feast had walked through a window, injured his arm, was in plaster, and might not be able to play for a fortnight. Lovely. Then came news that Ralph Richardson had refused our latest offer because the new

---

[1] The playwright and director.
[2] Managing Director of the BBC 1968–75. Knighted 1976.

dates for the South Bank did not work for him. Almost at the same moment a messenger arrived from the Old Vic telling me that all the little children in *Next of Kin* were lying in serried ranks with food poisoning—something they'd eaten in the canteen. And this was followed by some rude poems Edward Bond has written for the programme for *Spring Awakening*[1] and which he wants printed in it.

This afternoon was a perfect example of what it is like to run a theatre. Quite like old times.

Friday 3 May

Mixed notices for *Next of Kin*. The worst is Michael Billington's, who takes the opportunity to give *The Tempest* and *Eden End* further bad notices and call in question the whole new regime. History repeats itself. In 1961, when I was beginning the RSC, Tynan wrote a big article in *The Observer* saying he was fed up with the new regime and the sooner it went the better. Billington's notice brought my paranoia up several points.

I made the usual ritualistic phone calls that I make after a first night. Never mind, never mind, I said.

Monday 6 May

The Old Vic's Lilian Baylis celebration, *Tribute to the Lady*. I had viewed it with foreboding. In the event, it was a very good evening. By far the best item, the achievement, was Lilian Baylis herself, amazingly portrayed by Peggy Ashcroft. It was one of the finest performances I have seen her give. You can always tell when an actor is absolutely creating. Conventional timing, normality, is broken. The rhythm of speech, the rhythm of the body, become something different. This happened to Peggy tonight.

She presented that strange, Cockney, busybodying, straight-laced, crooked-mouthed eternal mother, bossing everybody about—and created a genuine eccentric. And what a mystery it all is. There would be no Royal Ballet, no National Theatre, and I shouldn't think much Royal Opera, and certainly no Sadler's Wells, without the dotty, single-minded, good works of Miss Lilian Baylis. Joan Littlewood, though less the do-gooder and more the revolutionary, is in the same tradition.

The world and his wife were there, and the Queen Mum. I had to play the courtier. But she is very funny, and well informed about the theatre.

I reminded her of an occasion in 1959 or 1960 but not in much detail. The story is this. She came to open the new BBC Television Centre at Shepherd's Bush and, as part of the programme that was being televised in her presence, Ralph Richardson, Arnold Wesker, and I had a discussion on whether or not

---

[1] Bond had adapted Wedekind's play, which was being directed by Bill Bryden.

we should have a National Theatre. Before we began Ralph had produced an aging newsclip from his pocket and told me it was 'the speech that Her Majesty had made' when she had laid the foundation stone in the early fifties for the National Theatre. He asked me if I, as chairman of the discussion, would give him the cue so that he could read it out. I said I would, making a mental note to do no such thing. It was rather purple palace-ese.

We had our discussion. I wound up speedily, giving Ralph no chance to read the Queen Mum's speech. We then lined up to be presented. While we were waiting he told me how disappointed he was that I had not given him his cue. I muttered that it had not seemed appropriate.

When, though, the Queen Mum talked to Ralph, she mused 'I wonder if we shall ever have a National Theatre?' 'Ah, Ma'am,' said he, 'I still remember with pleasure that fine speech you made when you laid the foundation stone. I remember every word of it.'

'Do you really?' said the Queen Mum. 'Can you say some of it for me now?'

Ralph made noises like an expiring fish. He could hardly pull his newsclip out of his pocket. Then, superb actor that he is, he began to make it up. It was much better than the original. He rolled out fine phrases about the National being a sounding-board of English drama for generations to come etc. The Queen Mother looked pleased. 'Ah yes,' she said, 'it's coming back to me.'

Ralph looked at me sheepishly afterwards. 'That was a close one, cocky,' he said.

Wednesday 8 May

I was suddenly called to the office early this morning for a quick meeting with John Dexter. Now he is going to the Met[1] etc, etc, he wants to fade out from being an NT associate. But I shook hands with him on doing one production each summer in the new building. This was fervently done, though it may mean nothing to him. But I will try to keep him to it.

Thursday 9 May

Some forty members of the Fringe—or as they now call themselves, the Alternative Theatre—visited the South Bank and came afterwards to the NT offices so that we could talk about how they could play from time to time on the South Bank.

The going was heavy, and we opened to some hostility, but not as much as I had expected. Various community group leaders made forthright speeches, saying they had no interest in playing in any sort of space except

---

[1] The Metropolitan Opera House, New York. Dexter had just been appointed Director of Production there.

their own communities. There were various ritualistic insults directed at the building: concrete mausoleum, fit for Mussolini, etc, etc. But I felt this aspect of things rather lacked conviction. I thought the building had actually impressed them, although none of them was about to say so.

Groups with exotic names, like The Bubble and The John Bull Tyre Repair Outfit, took me on happily. Actually it was quite moving and very English. There was a desire to make contact, yet a desire to keep the difference. And it is impossible for them to *like* an institution swallowing millions of pounds, when a few hundred can mean the life and death of their own enterprises. I would be the same.

I believe the hand I have extended to the Fringe will almost certainly get badly bitten, bruised and shat upon. But it is a gesture which had to be made. Otherwise I will be running a greedy institution which is out of touch.

Yet I think of Jean-Louis Barrault in Paris in 1968. He made the Odeon, of which he was director, available to the rioting students, so that they could hold their political meetings there and have somewhere to sleep. They repaid him, finally, by breaking up his theatre, destroying his wardrobe, and spurning him as a weak and tolerant liberal. The government responded by sacking him.

Friday 10 May
Yesterday, while I was going round the South Bank, I ran into a workman who I have several times talked to in the past. He is a theatre fan. He told me that he thought the building would not be finished until 1976, the chief reason being the total lack of supervision or co-ordination.

Today the regional repertory directors went round the building and were impressed with it. It was the preliminary to another discussion about future collaboration. They were more practical than the Fringe, and much more concerned about how and what we were going to do. I think I have got them to believe—just—that they can regard the National Theatre as theirs to come and play in when they want[1].

Monday 13 May
The big event today was our press conference[2]. We held it on a boat. We embarked at Cadogan Pier in Chelsea and chugged off downstream to the South Bank.

---

[1] Several regional companies and Fringe groups did later appear at the NT, but the idea had to be abandoned early on because of lack of money.
[2] To announce eight new productions aimed at stocking up the Old Vic repertoire for the move to the South Bank. It was also announced that the latest information from the South Bank Theatre Board meant that the first public performance in the new building could be given in April 1975, or soon after.

A very good turn out of associates: Pinter, Schlesinger, Miller, Russell Brown, Kustow, Dexter. But no Larry. He had promised he would come, but I knew he wouldn't. His absence was commented on by many a journalist.

I was asked how I felt in the light of the failure of the first three plays of my regime. I said I wasn't exactly dancing in the streets, but I had expected opposition. I stood by *The Tempest* and *Next of Kin*, and *Eden End* was a special event. All the really awkward questions were of course in the private conversations after the conference itself.

We moored opposite the theatre and I described it. Most of the press got off at Tower Bridge and went back to Fleet Street. We chugged back to Chelsea.

John Schlesinger, fresh from the enthusiasms of Los Angeles, commented on the negative and downbeat attitude of the press. They weren't hostile — just indifferent.

To bed early, having reflected gloomily on the amount I have to do in the next month—what with Glyndebourne[1], continuing the editing of *Akenfield*, the NT's tour which will involve me dashing round the country, and a projected trip to Norway with Tim and Tazeena[2] to research for *Borkman*. I would really like a week sitting quietly at Wallingford.

Thursday 16 May

Associates' meeting. Jonathan Miller advanced the idea that we should, when the time comes, have the great popular entertainers in our new South Bank building now and again—Morecambe and Wise, Frankie Howerd, etc. It is a brilliant idea, providing they bring their audience with them, rather than making the intellectuals of London patronise what is left of the music hall. But the fascination was that Larry suddenly launched into a great speech about the way the microphone had killed the music hall. He said that any performer could overcome an audience with a microphone. The audience knew it and were cowed into submission. It was no contest. As far as the audience/performer relationship was concerned, all the gallantry was gone. The microphone was a gun that destroyed.

Wednesday 15 May

By car to Croydon for a symposium on regional touring. In the dark and cheerless cavern of the Ashcroft Theatre, theatre managers mumbled platitudes at each other, each seeing no further than his own problems and his own interests.

[1] To work on a second revival of *La Calisto*.
[2] Tim O'Brien and Tazeena Firth, his wife, the joint designers of *John Gabriel Borkman*.

96

I was asked to speak on the National Theatre's new touring policy. I don't know why it went well, but it did. I think possibly because I was so irritated by the proceedings. I spoke for about three-quarters of an hour and to my surprise quickly achieved that ease and fluency which occasionally makes public speaking such a seduction. I was holding the audience absolutely and knew it, speaking without a script, and getting my points across. After all the nit-picking and squabbling, somebody was speaking to the delegates about broad policies, and about hopes for the future, and ideals.

Tuesday 21 May
My Glyndebourne *Figaro* on television tonight. By the third act I was admitting to myself that it was the best television opera I'd seen. Then came the fourth act. This is supposed to be conducted in complete darkness —which is why the mistaken identity is credible. I begged them to shoot it in silhouette and they had agreed they would. But it turned out badly over-lit. I went to bed halfway through in a great rage. TV always over-lights. It cannot abide darkness (a strength of good movies) because it wants to work on the worst television set in the country.

Wednesday 22 May
Went to lunch at ATV with Lew Grade. His formal agreement with the National Theatre company to televise their plays is over now, but he wanted to continue discussions for the future. I was very happy to talk.

He gave his well-known Yiddish comedian performance for two hours and I laughed a lot. He speaks the same dialogue as his brother, Bernie Delfont, but it is even more self-deprecating. 'I'm not very good at scripts, I can't read a script, well you know I skim through a few pages, I get a feeling, a flavour. What's important is the package. What it's about. Who's doing it. Who's in it.' I should think he told thirty stories during the lunch. His memoirs should be entitled 'What are you doing to me?'

Friday 24 May
Christopher back from school for half-term. Jenny has stayed at school to work. Or at least that is what she says.

Preview of *Spring Awakening*. The disturbing quality is still very evident. Eight people walked out. It is not a question of the violence or the masturbation. The play questions fundamental values about children, parents, and their responsibilities to each other.

An excellent evening which went beautifully. I am very confident of Bill Bryden's direction.

Tuesday 28 May

Jonathan Miller began directing *Figaro*[1] rehearsals. I sneaked in and saw three American nuts playing Spanish eighteenth-century bagpipes. Jonathan, quite rightly, is wanting to break the Mozart sound.

Then a couple of hours with Bill Bryden. I asked him to join us on the South Bank as an associate. He was attracted to the idea[2]. He is particularly interested in running a young writers' group. This could be very good.

First night of *Spring Awakening*. A dreadful evening. The audience was stiff and hostile and not very held. The cast played magnificently, the best yet. But they did not get a response. The laughter was dimmed and the perception was not acute. God, how I hate first nights. My score must be now up in the two or three hundreds at least. They are a truly inhuman experience. There are so many people there for artificial reasons. Back home in considerable depression.

Wednesday 29 May

I could have written the *Spring Awakening* notices. They are patronising and lukewarm. Most of them speak about the dated impact of a shocker of yesteryear, which is very unfair. It is a remarkable play, remarkably done. But I fear for the box office.

Off to Norway late afternoon to research *Borkman*.

Thursday 30 May

Oslo: Jacky and I met Tim and Tazeena downstairs for breakfast. A Norwegian banquet of cheeses, herrings, porridges, hams. All that was fine, but the chatter of about two hundred Americans in a party made it sound like a bunch of transatlantic starlings gone mad.

We visited a large house on the outskirts of the town to see what a member of the new wealthy middle classes of 1860 or 1870 would build for himself. It had hardly changed since that date, inside or out. The owner is an anglophile, an aged Justice Shallow of about 6 ft 3 ins in enormous blue dungarees, an eccentric old bird who spoke happily of Gloucestershire and his visits there. He still rings the estate bell at midday every morning to signal the workers into lunch. There aren't any workers.

Then to Oslo's folk museum. Ibsen's study has been removed from his last apartment and recreated in the museum. It is spooky and unconvincing. But the mad, possessed portrait of Strindberg, which Ibsen had staring down at him each day, is there. Did Ibsen want to keep an eye on Strindberg, or did his paranoia need feeding by Strindberg keeping an eye on him? Clearly he needed a relationship with this new man.

---

[1] *Le Mariage de Figaro* by Beaumarchais, translated by John Wells.
[2] He became an Associate Director soon after.

We went round looking at nineteenth-century industrial developments. *Borkman* is about power, about the industrial revolution. He justifies his mania by the good it will do mankind. But the play casts a shadow forward into the future, when releasing the iron ore from the rocks causes pollution and misery.

We saw the Viking ships in their chapel-like museum. They are nothing to do with Ibsen certainly, but basic to Norway. These huge objects are some of the most beautiful things I have ever seen. And how threatening they remain. Imagine being about your business in Pevensey Bay in, say, the year 850 and seeing, on a fine summer morning, these huge black prows gliding into the beach. It must have seemed the Devil had arrived.

Saturday 1 June

Oslo: To the new Ibsen Centre at Skien. Two dark-suited earnest-looking gentlemen regarded us carefully as we climbed up the steps. We wandered past and on into the auditorium. They followed tentatively in the distance and finally accosted us. One was Dr Ostvedt, the director of the Centre. Was I Peter Hall? I suppose the O'Briens and the Halls did not look right. We were all casual, humping cameras.

Ostvedt is an old time European scholar. Very formal. He took us up to the farm above Skien where Ibsen's father retired with the family when he was bankrupted. We stood in the attic, and we saw the outside window where Ibsen used to present puppet shows. This is authenticated and was quite a telling moment. But the whole thing was like Shakespeare's birthplace at Stratford. No life, but a monument, a desperate attempt to find out why genius should happen.

We said goodbye to Ostvedt and drove an hour and a half through the valleys of Telemark for a late lunch in the most beautiful farm house, the home of an actor at their National Theatre—Flinn Kvalem. He wasn't there, as he was playing in Bergen, but his wife, a high-powered Oslo doctor, was our host.

It transpired that the National Theatre of Oslo had sent for us a van loaded with delicious cold goodies and champagne the 2½-hour journey through the mountains from Oslo to this farmhouse. Would we do such a thing in England?

Monday 3 June

To the Bergen theatre, a very pleasant little 550-seat auditorium with a large stage. Amazing architecture outside, Norwegian art deco, a fortress with Viking flourishes. I asked the director what his ratio of subsidy to box office income was. '91%,' he replied. 'No', I said, 'I don't mean your box office take, but your ratio of subsidy to income.' '91%,' he said. I observed that it didn't really matter whether the public came or not. He agreed.

Mid-afternoon plane home direct from Bergen to London.

Tuesday 4 June
Early morning work wading through piles of papers with a feeling of panic. It takes hours to get through trivia, whereas the real decisions, such as what plays we should do next year, get forced to the bottom of the pile.

Saturday 8 June
Read Howard Brenton's *The Churchill Play* now on at Nottingham. It is quite magnificent. New writing is the only way one can hear the voice of the present. And with this play I heard it alright. It was the same excitement as I have had in the past with John Whiting, Beckett, Osborne, Pinter. A voice which makes you revalue your own attitudes. I read the play right through without stopping.

Also read *Plunder*, one of the early Aldwych farces by Ben Travers. Beautifully made. The narrative line is very firm. And it is about something eternal, the equation of money and sexuality, and the greed people have for both, because one provides the other. A very funny play. We must do it.

Monday 10 June
The Tempest in Bristol. I hate hotels, so I hate touring. And most of all I hate re-doing plays in different theatres. The same old technical problems to be solved all over again, plus a great deal of new ones which you'd never even thought of.

It was a good evening though. The audience were extremely perceptive and picked up every point. And they gave the cast a wonderful reception at the end. I should think there were some 1,700 people in the house.

Julie Covington and Michael Feast had asked me to go and have supper afterwards with all the kids at a bistro in a back street. So I did, taking, to their delight, John Gielgud along with me. He entertained the table with reminiscences of Mrs Patrick Campbell and Ellen Terry until about quarter to one. A jolly evening.

Tuesday 11 June
Eight-forty train back to London, and straight to Max Rayne's ginger group, formed to bustle the builders and contractors. Yet there still seems an air of unreality about—very akin to our national situation. We all know we're heading for disaster yet nobody does anything about it.

Lunch with Gerhard Klingenberg[1] who was over here to see the premiere last night of the new Stoppard play *Travesties*. From the press this morning, it is another fantastic success for Stoppard. I am torn between

---

[1] Director of the Vienna Burgtheater.

being furious that we didn't have the play—he gave it to the RSC because they have John Wood who is one of his favourite actors—and relief that the Aldwych at last has a substantial hit. The relief has it.

Klingenberg was an amazement. A changed man. When I last saw him, in Vienna, he was a humourless, tense, dry Prussian, with hair *en brosse*: an archetypal German leader, all five foot six of him. Now his hair has grown and falls all over his face in soft arty waves. He smiles a lot, is relaxed, tolerant and much more charming. What on earth has happened to him? Is he in love? He said it was because he had come to a new philosophy about life in the theatre: nothing mattered very much. And the weekends must be sacred. I didn't believe him.

Wednesday 12 June

Peter Stevens warned me that he'd heard on the grapevine how very delighted NATTKE[1] are with their negotiations for working the South Bank. For they have set out a work structure without anyone so far getting down to mentioning how much an hour's pay would cost. We can't force the issue at this point. And they are in no hurry because the nearer we get to the opening of the new building, the weaker our position: we will *have* to open the theatre, so they will be able to murder us. We have a very militant shop steward in Kon Fredericks[2]. All this is going to make an interesting future.

Saw understudies of *Eden End*. The theatre is ruthless. An actor walks on the stage and within 30 seconds you know whether you want to watch him or not.

Off for lunch with Peter Brook who is here for a few hours. We fell to with a will, talking of all our problems, and the hour and a half was, of course, too short. He is one of my few real friends. I think we always warm each other's spirits to some extent. I know I'm always the better for seeing him. We discussed the RSC and its mounting deficit. He is convinced that the financial and artistic strains on both organisations will mean that we must live side by side by next year. I think he is probably right.

He sprang at me from nowhere a new wonder: the myths of ancient India. He wants to form a group and dramatize these myths[3]. His blue eyes gleamed as he talked. This, or so he says at the moment, could be his work for the next five years.

One area of work we got on to excited me greatly. We both feel that in a sense the concept of the director is moving away from the autocratic interpreter, the conductor who presents his view of the work, to someone

[1] National Association of Theatrical, Television, and Kine Employees.
[2] An NT stage technician, and Chief Steward of the NT NATTKE branch.
[3] Peter Daubeny presented the Kathakali Dance Company in two ancient Hindu epics, *The Ramayana* and *The Mahabharata*, at the Aldwych in his 1972 World Theatre Season.

who is much more like the trainer of a football team. The director trains and develops the group, but the group of course has to do the play, or play the match.

To the airport, where I gloomily caught the plane for Berlin to give a lecture[1]. I was considerably unnerved as we approached Tempelhof to see a large black Rolls-Royce, flying the Union Jack, on the tarmac. I was popped into it and sped straight off to the ambassador's residence. No trouble with passports or with luggage.

It was all the full gracious living. I had travelled with next to no luggage—just a large briefcase with a clean shirt and my tooth brush and razor hurled into a Harrods plastic bag. Even so, the housekeeper had 'unpacked' for me.

Soon I was in another Rolls on my way to dine with the army. The officer commanding lives in a huge and beautiful house by a lake. Gardens and interiors are impeccably kept and there are servants everywhere. His house is guarded by Germans.

All was very jolly and boozy. The wives all gossiped away, as doubtless they do every day of their lives, about postings and servants. The young men were what fascinated me. They had carefully calculated hair, of Army shortness but of slightly artistic longness. They were dressed in sharply cut suits with shirts with large stripes. Their accents were of upper crust stage Englishmen of the nineties. One confessed to a passion for amateur theatricals. But his conversation was mainly about gels, fishing in Scotland, and horse racing. The last forty years might never have existed. He was pure P G Wodehouse.

A fascinating evening. Here is the end of the British Raj. They now represent, as they must know in their heart of hearts, a diminished and unsuccessful country. The Germans are paying to keep them in the past. Six thousand troops are in Berlin in case the Russians' fingers get too itchy. And so this tiny group of people are kept in a manner to which only those in years gone by were accustomed.

Thursday 13 June

Berlin: Visited the new National Gallery. This has been built since I was last here. I think it is probably the most beautiful modern building I have seen. The Berliners call it the Coca-Cola factory. Why do we so often insult the new?

A quick dash at three o'clock to meet Peter Stein at his theatre[2] on the outskirts of Berlin. He is young, handsome, and crafty. He said his company would love to come to London to the National[3] but that of course he would

[1] The annual Queen's Lecture, a series endowed to commemorate the royal visit to Berlin in May 1965.
[2] The Schaubühne am Halleschen Ufer.
[3] They did—to the Lyttelton in Gorki's *Summerfolk* in March 1977.

have to put it to all the actors to vote on. Two minutes later he was making extremely definite demands in his own right. 'I shall need this. . . I shall need that. . . .' An autocratic democrat.

He spoke of Peter Daubeny who had attended the premiere of Stein's production of *Der Prinz von Homburg*[1] and had said at the end that he would take it to London if certain adjustments were made and twenty minutes cut. This Stein refused to do so Daubeny dropped the idea. I was not surprised to hear that he had been so quickly on to the man who is clearly the most important new talent in the German theatre.

Drove back to the Residence all the way down the Kurfürstendamm. Hot and crowded. Peculiarly German tarts, fat like suet puddings, with mini-skirts at their waists. Huge bottoms on display.

At seven o'clock to the Kongresshalle, which the Berliners call the Flying Oyster, to give my lecture. I think it went well. Certainly the applause at the end was prolonged. I can't say I much enjoyed doing it. I was standing at the side of the stage in a very bright spotlight, and the combination of amplification and reading from a text made me uneasy. I much prefer just to speak.

Friday 14 June
Berlin: The car collected me at quarter to ten, and I was driven straight to the aeroplane which took off on time, a miracle. I was, in the parlance of the Embassy, 'tarmac cleared'—which means a direct drive to the aircraft. I was at Wallingford by 1.30 and there swam, slept, and relaxed in the sun in the garden. A beautiful June day. Piles of work to do, but it appears that none of it is very worrying. Many scripts to read.

Saturday 15 June
At home again all the news is bad. I believe we are in for the biggest slump since the thirties. Fresh on my gloomy thoughts came Peter Shaffer[2], arriving for lunch and staying until half past eight. He was full of a new play. I know no one less restful than Peter. He talks compulsively all the time. But I enjoy it. Jacky said it was comical to see the two of us plop into the swimming pool and paddle up and down still talking nineteen to the dozen about the theatre. We could, she said, as well have been anywhere. Swimming was quite incidental to the main task in hand, which was talking.

Monday 17 June
My first meeting with Howard Brenton. A huge man, shy, a little fat, delivering occasional knockout remarks like a gentle pugilist suddenly lashing out. He is very like his plays, a sure sign of a fine artist. He is the first of the new, young ones to be utterly enthusiastic about the new building and

---

[1] By Heinrich von Kleist.   [2] The dramatist.

the possibilities of reaching a big audience at the new National. He will write a play for us and he wants David Hare to direct it.

Wednesday 19 June

Off to the Television Centre to record a programme called *Andre Previn Meets*. . . . He is apparently also meeting, or has met, Edward Heath, Morecambe and Wise, Ken Russell, and some young musicians who have just won international competitions. I thought I was likely to be the squarest of his guests, and so I proved.

There had been a message to go dressed casually. Apparently last week Previn, out of deference to Heath, appeared in a suit and tie, only to find that Heath rolled up in his Hello Sailor uniform of sleeveless shirt riding high on the belly.

I chose a black polo neck and my black-and-white dog tooth coat. Should have known better. I thought television cameras didn't strobe any more. My coat gave the cameras a nervous breakdown. So I had to decide whether to appear pot-bellied in a black sweater, or wearing one of the BBC's beastly standby coats. I chose to be pot-bellied.

A few words with Andre beforehand. We talked of our first meeting in Paris, when Leslie was making *Gigi* in 1957. A lifetime ago.

I always feel miserable after TV chat programmes. There's something so phoney and exposed about the readiness to talk. And there's the let-down of remembering what one has said, what one shouldn't have said, and what one would like to have said. This time, when we had finished the interview, Andre and I realised that we'd talked about music all the time and there had been no mention of the National Theatre. He hadn't brought it up and neither had I. So we recorded another piece to fill the gap.

Monday 24 June

Phone call to say there is a plan to film *Waiting for Godot* this August/September—principally because Dustin Hoffman wants to play Estragon. Will I direct it, and will I persuade Samuel Beckett to sell the rights? Well, I'll try. . . . I would love to do it.

In the evening I watched Panorama anatomising the career of Nixon. Terrifying.

Wednesday 26 June

Torrential rain today and everybody at the huts[1] near riot. Rain pouring through the roofs. Buckets catching the drips. We must make the place more habitable for the months that remain before we move to the South Bank.

---

[1] The NT's temporary offices—in Aquinas Street—during the company's years at the Old Vic.

Phone call from Sam Beckett during the day. I asked him about the film of *Godot*. He said, and I sympathise with his thinking, that if there was a lovely stage production of the play with fine actors that he had seen, he would be very happy for it to be filmed. But he didn't see it as a film in itself. Fair enough.

Sam had never heard of Dustin Hoffman. I said that perhaps he'd seen him in *The Graduate* or *Midnight Cowboy*. 'No,' said Sam, 'I don't really go to the cinema.'

Saturday 29 June

To London for the last performance of *The Tempest*. I saw the final twenty minutes. Fantastic reception. Gielgud obviously very moved. He said afterwards that for forty years he had been playing at the Old Vic, and this was probably his last performance there.

Monday 1 July

Sir Edward McAlpine held a lunch at the Dorchester for all the National Theatre dignitaries. A great deal of jovial establishment chat. I must have heard people offering to 'have a word with' someone at least eight times as a solution to some problem or other. But the atmosphere was good, because news on the South Bank is now promising. McAlpine's speak of the commissioning period for the building beginning in the third week of September. The opening of the theatre in April seems a reality at last.

Tonight was the first real test of *Akenfield*. Present: John Schlesinger, Harold Pinter, Michael Blakemore, John and Liz Bury, and Michael Kustow. Watching anxiously: Ronnie Blythe, Rex Pyke and myself. I have not been so appallingly nervous for years. What did they think? Well, they had all, they said, been very moved, and Schlesinger and Pinter particularly were most constructive and flattering. I was, in fact thrilled by the evening: by the response of my close friends, and by the possibility that I have of sharpening up the film a stage further.

Tonight's anxiety is directly related to one fact: *Akenfield* is far and away the most autobiographical piece of work I have ever done. It makes me feel very raw.

Tuesday 2 July

John Schlesinger rang and praised *Akenfield* at long length and acutely. I gleaned some very good advice from him. He begged me, even if a big distributor thought they could handle it, not to let them. He said it was a special film that must be nursed carefully by the Academy or the Curzon or some specialist cinema, and entered for film festivals. An ordinary distributor would show it in the usual cinemas and if it was not an immediate and spectacular success (which John doesn't believe it will be, and nor do I), would withdraw it and it would never be seen again. He is of course absolutely right. Rex and I must be careful not to be greedy. We have such a wonderful justification for greed, because we feel we must earn the maximum amount of money for the unit, since all the technicians share in any profits.

Albert Finney came to the Barbican flat in the morning. An excellent meeting. He said he now felt ready to take on the big parts. He wants to try to examine a rougher, more instinctive form of classical acting. He would like to do *Tamburlaine* and *Hamlet*. It is five years too late for Hamlet but he wants to try. I think he must. Tamburlaine is perfect for him, and Hamlet must assuredly be interesting.

Wednesday 3 July

Vogue taking pictures of the family and the Barbican flat. They did a fine, quick job on the roof garden, wheeling in white trellis work, and hundreds of plants, from a firm called Roots and Shoots. All this is dressed up as the real home of the Halls. As *Vogue* are peddling fantasies, I don't suppose it matters if they are true or not. I had an insane afternoon seeing people in my room and popping into others to be photographed. I saw Arthur Lowe who wanted to talk about his future, saying that he didn't want just to do Stephano in *The Tempest*. I said, and meant, what about *Plunder*? or *Le Bourgeois Gentilhomme*[1]? or Falstaff?

Just made it, exhausted, to the Vic to see a preview of *Figaro*. A dreadful evening. Granted it was the first time the actors had met an audience. But since I saw rehearsals, the comic business has grown and the seriousness been entirely lost. The whole play comes over as a charade with comic bagpipe music. I talked to Jonathan[2], who seemed very worried. I urged him to go back to his beginnings—his original conception—to make the play clear and hard. Trust the play, not the jokiness. And cut down on bagpipes. . . .

Thursday 4 July

This morning we took the press round the new building for the first time, to show progress. There were a few questions about Why Concrete? But generally speaking I felt it was a good thing for them to see how things were going. Denys Lasdun was brilliant with them. I stressed they were seeing an unfinished building, undecorated and not yet humanised.

Sunday 7 July

Lovely weather. Swimming and sunshine. Jenny and Christopher came back from school with a friend and enough luggage to set up house. I watched

---

[1] By Molière.   [2] Miller.

West Germany win the World Cup against Holland on television. It is said that a thousand million people were in the TV audience. Mass theatre of our times. Germany should not have won, they were the inferior team.

Monday 8 July
Left Wallingford for Reading very early to catch the 7.34 to Paddington. An amiable ticket collector told me it was cancelled—he didn't know why. He was rather like a countryman musing that the swallows hadn't appeared this summer for some inexplicable reason. So I caught the 7.25 instead, jumped in a taxi, and found myself to my surprise sitting in the office among the cleaners at 8.15. I had a quiet hour and a half dictating.

The ILEA have had a report that *Spring Awakening* is not suitable for children. I believe it is a play children *should* see.

To an NT Board meeting in the afternoon. Much droning on from a few about *Spring Awakening*, its filthiness, its unsuitability both for their elderly mothers and their young daughters. Would it not be more artistic to have something suggested, and done more briefly, than a large man waving a large penis and then literal and lengthy masturbation?

I said that the actors were not really masturbating, and if it were done more discreetly it would inevitably be more titillating. The scene *should* be horrible. . . .

It was then suggested it should be toned down for the regions for they, after all, were not ready to accept the depravities of London. I said I wasn't prepared to stand up in public and say we were censoring our work for the provinces.

John Mortimer said he welcomed the masturbating scene as it livened up the proceedings in what he regarded as a boring, old and tendentious play. There was hearty laughter at this sally.

Rayne handled it all very well, letting the anxieties have their head but pointing out firmly that this was an artistic matter on which they should comment but not insist.

Tuesday 9 July
First night of *Figaro* at the Old Vic. Jonathan has cut a lot of nonsense, and tightened and hardened things considerably. There is now a joy in the actors which does communicate to the audience. But the serious dialectic of the piece is not there. If it were, the play would be funnier. Apart from a scene where Figaro shaves the Count and one feels the imminent presence of steel at the aristo's neck, there is virtually no conflict. Above all I am bewildered by Jonathan's direction. He's an enigma, whose work I like and dislike in equal measure. That, I suppose, is talent.

The great shout of pleasure that greeted the end of the play proves that we have got away with it. But getting away with it is not much satisfaction.

Wednesday 10 July
The notices for *Figaro* are a good old mixture, but on the whole it seems we have got away with it with the critics too.

Comical interview with Tina Packer, who used to be a young actress at Stratford and is now running a classical theatre group in America. She had run the company as a democracy, three or four of them had intrigued against her, and in the end she had had to sack one of them.

I told her that, in my view, in twenty people you will always find two or three outright shits. And a group wants to be led. If it is not led, somebody replaces the leader. She said this was right-wing and Enoch Powell-like. I said yes, I supposed it was, but actors didn't go to work with groups, they went to work with the people who led those groups—Joan Littlewood, Ariane Mnouchkine, Peter Brook. They wanted leaders. And if she was running a group, she was a leader. She couldn't start something and then not take responsibility for it. Leaders must be checked, and abused, but they are certainly necessary.

Thursday 11 July
Guest night for *Figaro*. I was bowing and smiling to the Arts Council, to Jennie Lee, to Lord Goodman etc, etc.

I was able to tell my Board members that teachers were taking school parties to *Spring Awakening* at Oxford. . . .

Friday 12 July
Jacky and I to Liverpool, and by 2.40 we were at the University and I was being robed in those ridiculous garments ready for the honorary degree ceremony. I was first on of those being lauded, and stood for ten minutes while the laudation was spoken. What do you do on these occasions? Look modest? Look proudly arrogant? Pretend not to hear? Think of something else? It is an impossible situation. I dream of a sequence in a film where the ceremony is turned on its head. The graduate stands there while all his failures, vices and betrayals are read out, and people nod approvingly.

Everybody at the ceremony was very courteous, very open, and it was beautifully arranged. But what the hell did I do it for? The whole thing is an unpardonable vanity. I would like a doctor's degree from Cambridge and that is about it.

Sunday 14 July
I am enraged this morning by Harold Hobson's notice of *Figaro*. There are very few critics who when given an egg of talent in their hands can resist crushing it. They have the power; why shouldn't they use it? His review is not only mean to Jonathan and to the NT company, it is mean to Denys Lasdun about the building, which Hobson hasn't visited yet. I resolved

today to have a fight with him. Tomorrow when the heat has died I will write
him a rude letter.

Monday 15 July
Robert Cushman interviewed me for *Plays and Players* for some two hours.
He asked if I thought the critics were giving me a rough deal at the National.
I said I thought they were, but it had been the same at the start of the RSC.
He expressed surprise. How short people's memories are. The first two
years of the RSC were, by and large, hell, because of the critical abuse.

Tuesday 16 July
To school early to see Henry Pluckrose[1]. Very good reports on Edward
and Lucy. Henry said both the children would have to go into the private
sector to realise their full potential, and that ten years ago this would not
have been the case in London. But it was now, with the breakdown of the
state educational system.

Eric Johns, ex-editor of *The Stage*, interviewed me for a theatre annual.
He observed it was nice to know that youth was at the helm of this great new
enterprise. I reminded him that it was twenty-one years since he had first
interviewed me for *The Stage*.

John Dexter came back to the Barbican for drinks and a snack. He wanted
to say it was not the job that had been offered him in New York at the Met
that was making him leave us. He would have left anyway; he was so uneasy
about my new policy for the NT and the whole of my attitude to the theatre.
In the same breath he told me he was wholeheartedly behind me and my
attempt to make a new policy. But he then added that the company were
deeply unhappy, lost, unled, and there was a degree of disloyalty up and
down the corridors which he had never met in the theatre in his life.

I smiled blandly through it all and told him I was going to stay at the
National and that I had a lot of stamina. I respect his talent but not his
sighing for the good old days with Larry. He used to bitch in exactly the same
way then. An acutely depressing evening.

Wednesday 17 July
Woke early feeling low. I'm often astonished how some people whose whole
life is devoted to an art form which in basic terms is meant to encourage
human beings to behave better to each other and be more humane, can
personally on occasion be such shits: public moralists and private shits.

An emergency meeting with McAlpine's et al because the South Bank is
slipping behind again. When Max Rayne gave me the nod, I made my speech
about our continuing, big and expensive build-up at the Old Vic of produc-

---

[1] Headmaster of the Prior Weston Primary School in the City of London.

tions for the new theatre, and because of that our imminent bankruptcy unless we played there with these productions on time. I pointed out again how delay would mean a scandal, and said again I had every intention that the builders, the contractors etc etc, should be involved in the scandal with me. Everybody smiled, but it made an effect.

Lunch with Paul Scofield. As all great actors must be, he is deeply egocentric, and deeply instinctive. He does what he needs to do, whatever the consequences—and he should. In this sense he is the most bewildering of men because he is so modest, so genial, so utterly sensible and human, no one can believe that at the last moment he can back out if he's changed his mind. I still remember the nightmare of 1959/60. He had agreed to play Proteus, Malvolio, Shylock, and Thersites at Stratford, and only two months before we were due to start rehearsals, decided not to do it. The hectic rearrangement of the entire repertoire made necessary by this last-minute change is something I shall not forget.

Then in 1968 came our major quarrel over my Stratford production of *Macbeth*. I suppose it was my fault in some measure. I was a very tired man. And when I got shingles I should have given up the production instead of being noble and heroic. Anyway, it was a disaster. . . .

At lunch, though, Paul said Peter Brook and myself had given him his happiest and most creative times in the theatre. He wants at the new NT to direct Goldsmith's *She Stoops to Conquer*, and play in *The Guardsman*[1], in *From Morn to Midnight*[2], and *Othello*. All these were culled from various suggestions I made to him some weeks ago. Will he do them?

Thursday 18 July
Talked to the associates about an administrative reshuffle. But I made a great tactical error. I slipped in that after a year I might appoint a deputy director. There was immediate suspicion. Why did we need another top executive? Larry said that directors had come to work with me, not with a deputy. He said the company were unhappy, that they never saw me, that they didn't know what they were doing. He went on to point out that I was the boss, I must be seen to be the boss, and I must do some bossing. He thought I should forthwith give up my plans of directing for the NT *Happy Days*, *John Gabriel Borkman*, and *Tamburlaine* and concentrate for the next year on being the leader. By condensing all his comments, I exaggerate the intensity of them. But Larry, like Richard III, was indeed himself again. As in many situations of this kind, there was sufficient truth in his strictures for some of them to stick. But it is not the whole truth. I smiled through a great deal of it. And most of the rest of the gang rallied to my aid.

[1] By Ferenc Molnar.   [2] *Von Morgens bis Mitternachts* by Georg Kaiser.

Off for a drink with Reg Prentice[1]. Hugh Jenkins was the beaming host. Most of the subsidised emperors were there: Rayne, Claus Moser[2], John Tooley[3], Harewood[4], Kenneth Robinson[5], etc, etc. Nobody from the RSC—Trevor couldn't come. We all stood around singing lustily and loudly, like indignant cuckoos, for more money for our own organisations. Reg Prentice had one thing absolutely clear in his head. There was no more money for anything.

Friday 19 July
Jacky and I to Bernard Kimble[6]. We were faced by a disastrous situation. All my personal accounts are overdrawn. But even more troublesome is the fact that Kimble told me two years ago that I could manage financially at the National Theatre providing I also earned £5,000 a year from outside work. He is now telling me I must earn between £10,000 and £12,000 a year more.

Saturday 20 July
Read the Sophia Loren/Roger Moore film Dimitri de Grunwald is producing, and which he has asked me to direct. Called *Heaven Save Us From Our Friends*, it is a quite funny slick comedy, based on an old play by Moss Hart. It would be a job of work with no artistic pretentions, and a great deal of money. I moodily considered other money-making possibilities. There's a German film to act in if they meet my terms. There's my filmscript *The Last of Summer* which is still not off though certainly not on. There is *Conduct Unbecoming*[7] as a possible film. And maybe there are some TV commercials I can do. I ought to be able to get myself out of financial trouble. But what I really want to do is have a rest.

Tuesday 23 July
Lunch with Irene Handl to try to draw her about the little campaign she has been waging on Peter Nichols and Jonathan Miller to build her part in *The Freeway*[8].She of course denied this, said she was just eager to play a well-rounded character. But I saw in her eye the unmistakable glint of the tenacious star. Well, she is a star, but we can't have her unbalancing the play.

She's fascinating. Seventy-four and utterly eccentric in her reactions. She told me she hadn't come into the business until she was forty when, incredibly, she went to drama school having led up to that point an ordinary

---

[1] Secretary of State for Education and Science 1974–75.
[2] Chairman of the Board of Directors of the Royal Opera House, Covent Garden from 1974.
[3] General Administrator of the Royal Opera House, Covent Garden from 1970.
[4] George (Lord) Harewood. Managing Director of the English National Opera from 1972.
[5] Chairman of the English National Opera 1972–77. Chairman of the Arts Council 1977–82.
[6] Hall's accountant.   [7] The play by Barry England.
[8] A play by Peter Nichols, soon to be staged by the NT, directed by Jonathan Miller.

life as a housewife. She wrote her first novel, *The Sioux*, at sixty-five. She said that most of all in life she liked travelling. She would like to have been a cook with some expedition that went to the wilder parts of the world, looking for flowers and rare plants.

Peter Stevens was at the meeting of the NT's NATTKE members yesterday and said the atmosphere was terrible. The heavies among the stage hands were jeering, blinding, making catcalls and continually saying they were about to walk out if they were asked to work on Sundays and that's all there was to it. Kon Fredericks is quiet and watchful. They are his muscle.

To see the Louis Malle film *Lacombe Lucien*. I must confess to disappointment. Few films this year have had better notices: the word masterpiece was freely bandied about. It did not feel like that in the cinema. There was hardly anyone there. Curious that the public is almost never wrong.

What doesn't work is the casting of Lucien himself. The actor is an amateur, which is alright. But he has no sex appeal, which is not. I fear that the watchability of a film is entirely related to the sex appeal of its main characters. It always has been so and always will be so. I believe this to be the main reason why the public was not there tonight.

I find myself very happy at the moment, in spite of all the worries.

Wednesday 24 July
Read (at last) a 1948 play by John Whiting called *No More A-Roving*. Although Whiting was a very close friend and I worked with him for twelve years before his tragic death, I had no idea this play existed. Apparently he wrote it when he was a young actor at York rep. He sent it to Northampton to be performed and they turned it down. In the face of this rejection, he put it in a bottom drawer where it remained.

It is now a period piece. Two men and a woman who were involved with each other in 1939 meet ten years later. The complexity foreshadows Pinter; also the fascination with the minutiae of memory. It was a strange experience reading it: hearing again the voice of a man I loved very deeply. If only he had met with success at that time. His later serious plays have an aura of pretension—almost as if he were indulging himself in minority drama. Here he is showing a popular voice which could have become something forceful.

Thursday 25 July
Tonight was the big beanfeast given by the new chairman of the GLC[1]. I went in best bib and tucker. As the taxi approached County Hall I saw an enormous queue of long-dressed and dinner-jacketed people stretching the whole front of the building. Each one of them was going up to shake the

[1] David Pitt. Chairman of the GLC 1974–75. Created Baron 1975.

112

ove: Lords Cottesloe and
vier at the NT's 'Topping Out'
emony, 2 May 1973

posite top: With Denys Lasdun
he Greek theatre in Epidarus.
design is reflected in the shape
the Olivier auditorium.
ndon Weekend Television for
uarius

posite bottom: The huts in
uinas Street, used as offices by
NT during its time at the Old
. After the move to the South
nk they were pulled down.
n Haynes

ght: Peggy Ashcroft as Lilian
ylis and Susan Fleetwood as
bil Thorndike in Val May's
ibute to the Lady when it was
ven as the NT's last performance
the Old Vic, 28 February 1976.
he show was also given at the
c previously, on 6 May 1974.)
obby Clark

ove: Peter Hall's home at
llingford. There were trout in
lake

posite top: With Trevor Nunn
1968 when he succeeded Hall as
ector of the RSC.
uglas Jeffrey

posite bottom: Peter Brook —
other close friend and colleague
Hall's at the RSC — with his
Simon (left) and Hall's
nger son Edward

ght: Christopher, Hall's elder
, aged 14

Below: Christopher's sister, Jennifer –
aged 3 – with her mother, Leslie Caron.
Raoul Privé

Right: Jennifer as a teenager

Bottom: Jennifer as Helena in *A
Midsummer Night's Dream*, at the NT in
1982/3. *Michael Mayhew*

w: Edward with his mother, Jacky, in

Below: Lucy, Edward's sister, aged 3
Bottom: With Edward and Monk, the dog the children gave their father as a birthday present. *Keystone*

Above left: Edward, aged 11
Above right: Lucy, aged 9
Left: Lucy, aged 10

host's hand. It would have meant a twenty-minute shuffle along the pavement. On impulse I told the taxi driver to take me back to the Barbican: home to bed. I don't expect my absence was noticed.

Friday 26 July
Here is a terrible problem: the Sophia Loren/Roger Moore film of Dimitri's is on. Dimitri makes me a definite offer to direct it—£75,000 to be paid in three yearly lumps. Some of the filming is in Paris—but anyone can be brought there that I need to see, at Dimitri's expense. Can I do it? Should I do it? I said I would think. My own financial position is so serious that I certainly ought to. What concerns me far more is my workload.

Saturday 27 July
News came yesterday that Peter Brook would be arriving from Paris tonight for the weekend. He would be joining Natasha[1] in a visit to their little boy, Simon, who is staying with Edward at Wallingford. Simon is charming, a near-copy of his father. He and Edward are firm friends and chatter all day and most of the night. They are both intelligent, and highly physical: riding, swimming, continually dashing about.

Jacky overheard them talking as they lay in bed. Simon asked Edward which of his parents he liked best. Edward said he liked his father best because he worked hard, earned the money, provided the house, the food and everything. Simon said that those things didn't matter, he liked his mother best because she was softer, smelt better, and didn't shout, which his father did. They talked about who they were in love with. Edward said he was in love with a girl in London, but he had only seen her once. 'You have to be in love with someone,' he observed.

Spoke to Harold Pinter, who is on holiday in the country. He said: 'I think I might be pregnant.' This is great news. A play is on the way.

Brook arrived about half past eight and we dined and talked until midnight. He is in great form. He looks set for years of particular and well-financed work in Paris. I certainly hope so.

Monday 29 July
To Glyndebourne. Much talk with Moran Caplat[2]. We spoke of *Don Giovanni* or *Così fan tutte* in 1976 and 1977, and *The Magic Flute* in 1978. A happy journey of Mozartian work to look forward to.

Tuesday 30 July
To the House of Lords. A slow and ancient lunch with Lord Cottesloe and Kenneth Rae. The tempo was gentle under the Pugin decor. I am always

[1] Parry, Brook's wife.
[2] General Administrator of Glyndebourne Festival Opera 1949–81.

amazed by the ostentation of the interior of the Palace of Westminster, though it has a period charm now.

During the lunch, John Cottesloe confessed he was 75 which gave him two years over Kenneth Rae. There was a great deal of Justice Shallow-type talk.

The wine was good, and the service by sensible-looking Nannies was liberally laced with 'My Lords'. But the food was bad: dreadful canteen standard. How are the mighty fallen! The Peers of the Realm eat cold tinned consommé and Birds Eye frozen peas.

We all went after lunch to talk to Sir Martin Charteris, the Queen's secretary, about the opening of the National Theatre. At Buckingham Palace we walked through a world of early-Victorian taste, with something of the elegance of the Regency desperately hanging on. Charteris greeted Rae as a long-lost friend. I think there were shared connections with Eton or something. He expressed great relief at my ideas for an opening celebration at the National Theatre, rather than a play. With a good deal of table-banging and affectionate mirth it was established that the Queen didn't much like plays.

Thursday 1 August

Meeting with Kimble which reduced me to standard despair. He can tell me nothing about my involved life except that I am spending too much money and must cut down. Either that or earn some more. I need to earn about £7,000 fast to keep my huge family afloat. I am responsible for eight people if I include, as I must, my parents and aunt.

Friday 2 August

Meeting at which the NT office and front-of-house staff were urged to join NATTKE. This went down with a good deal of bewilderment and I think opposition. The point we were trying to make is that if the majority of our people are non-union members their lives will be run by the small groups of union people, mostly stage staff, who band together for strength.

Tuesday 6 August

The editing of *Akenfield* is finished. A feeling of unutterable relief. Of course, there are still things that could be done—alterations that could be made, cuts that could be improved. But I could go on for ever, and end up by frittering it away. Now it is over. It is five years since the summer day I began reading the book in the train from Goring to Paddington. And cried at the voices of the old men. I heard my grandfather.

Wednesday 7 August
Lunch with Harold[1]. He was illuminated, a man possessed. He said he was very excited about his new play. All he would tell me about it was that it had four men in it and, to quote him, 'somewhere or other there's a girl knocking about'. He said that for the first time for years he was overwriting, letting it all come out, and being less critical of his writing as he worked. He felt freer. He will complete the first draft this summer but does not expect the play to be finished until Christmas. Normally he finishes a play in weeks.

Associates' dinner. Most of the evening was spent in discussing our links with authors. I proposed that with certain eminent dramatists, Pinter, Osborne, Bond, we must commit ourselves to a relationship where we guarantee to do anything they write. John Russell Brown advanced the theory that writers often declined and never hit their former power again. I can't believe that talent ever diminishes for good.

Saturday 10 August
The new Osborne play that I've got, *Watch It Come Down*, is a wound of a play, uncomfortable to read. A group of intellectuals and artists are living in a converted railway station. They are destroying each other by every weapon to hand. There are signs though that Osborne is moving towards a new, calmer, more lucid form of writing. Perhaps a new strength is rising in addition to the invective. I like this play, but in a sense I wish I didn't. It is the most pessimistic and awful experience. Yet it is centrally a play for today—a play about England at this moment. I hope he will let us do it and I hope my colleagues will see its merits.

This evening a dinner at the Ritz with Dimitri, Carlo Ponti, Roger Moore and his wife, and Dennis Selinger, Moore's agent. Sophia Loren did not come—filming late: maddening. I don't know why I am continuing this charade. God knows I shouldn't direct the film. There are enough crises marching inexorably towards me. But money is needed, and every day the state of the economy gets worse and the prognosis for the future more bleak. Where will we purveyors of entertainment be in a declining world? Back on the sidewalks, busking. . . . The Ritz was empty, save for our little party. In the gilded room, with its *fin de siècle* splendour, the waiters outnumbered the guests.

Sunday 11 August
Jacky had arranged a vast number of visitors at Wallingford. So at least we were glad to see the sun shining. How could we have coped if it was raining? Trevor and Janet[2] arrived late. He is extremely pleased by the fantastic

---

[1] Pinter.   [2] Suzman.

success of his RSC production of *Antony and Cleopatra* on television. He says people in the RSC offices now say good morning to him in an entirely different way. I wonder if he's right. I think they say good morning in exactly the same way—it's just that he reads it differently.

Monday 12 August

To London on the train. I very much wanted to be in the office early. British Railways helped by cancelling the 7.34. There was, the announcer blandly said, a staff difficulty. Heads would have rolled for this when my father was a station master, but not any more. How reactionary one becomes....

A dreadful hour with Kimble. There is no hope for my future peace of mind unless I can cut down the cost of my family overheads. Something will have to go. But I cannot think what. I cannot sell Wallingford easily now that the bottom has dropped out of the house market. And worst of all, having just settled my parents there, I can hardly take to my heels and run.

That is my impulse at this moment: to take to my heels and run—from every responsibility and every family tie. Is this the fine gesture of the revolutionary saving his creative self? Or is it (and I think it is) the ostrich wanting to place his head in the sand? The truth is that work in the subsidised theatre can never earn me the kind of money I need to keep everyone in comfort. I knew this when I went to the National.

Thursday 15 August

The preliminary budget for our new South Bank building shows an expenditure of some £5 million a year. The cost of heat, light, insurance and skeleton maintenance staff alone is £1 million a year. Clearly I am cast as the pilot of the first theatrical Concorde. But then I brighten and reflect that I admire Concorde. It's one of the few beautiful things that our ugly century has produced.

I was appalled by this news, but succeeded in pretending not to be. I said that we must continue to hope that we can earn half our keep and be given half our keep. We might persuade £2 million subsidy, but not a penny more, so somehow the £5 million figure has to come down to £4 million.

To see *Pygmalion* with Tom Stoppard and his wife Miriam. It is well done, beautifully set, beautifully directed by Dexter. But I realised once again that Shaw's plays are carpentered to spell out their themes with a care which amounts almost to contempt for the audience. The play-making is so evident. But worst of all is the sexlessness of the proceedings. This is romance with no balls, a love story with no consummation, sentimentality without passion, and love without pain. It is really rather a dreadful play. Would I feel the same from a production of *Man and Superman*? I don't think so.

Friday 16 August
All day with Peggy Ashcroft reading through *Happy Days*[1]. Magnificent play. It excited me to hear her read it. Hard to do well but quite evident what has to be done. A very funny, touching piece: I think one of the masterpieces of the last twenty years. My spirits rose and I longed to begin on it.

Saturday 17 August
I had the doctor late last night. He found me over-tired, over-stressed, and not in good shape. He advised me to rest, which I did with the help of a large sleeping pill. Sat briefly in the sun this afternoon and then went back to bed. The walls appear to be moving in on me: a compound of dilemmas, professional, financial—and personal.

Tuesday 20 August
Bingo tonight at the Royal Court. An excellent evening, intellectual and mandarin and very elliptical. I feel that a touch of real success might make Bond the popular prophet that he sets out to be. His writing is fine, and the creation of Shakespeare at the end of his life one that stamps itself on the mind. Each age writes about Shakespeare in its own image. No surprise therefore that this shows him as a man who sold out to the bourgeoisie and no longer stood up for the progressive currents of his time. But there is a magnificent pessimistic awareness in him, a scepticism which Gielgud catches beautifully.

The scene in which Ben Jonson[2] visits Shakespeare at Stratford and has a boozy argument is one of the high spots of my theatregoing for years.

Today I was handed one sheet of paper outlining a television commercial for an insurance company's pension fund which I could do. £1,000 for two days' directing work. Ridiculous. . . .

Wednesday 21 August
Finally said no very firmly to Dimitri about directing his film. He accepted but wanted some help on the script. I had to agree. He said it would break the whole deal at this point if I walked off altogether.

Thursday 29 August
A rushed and dreadful day before I go to Hamburg tonight to do my bit of film-acting for money: to the barbers in the morning; to the finance and general purposes committee[3] in the afternoon; hurried packing, and a dash on a stuffy evening to the airport.

---

[1] By Beckett and soon to be staged by the NT, directed by Hall.
[2] Played by Arthur Lowe.   [3] An important sub-committee of the NT Board.

Friday 30 August
Hamburg: Barry Foster and I were taken to a nearby rosefield where my biggest scene took place—in long shot. On about the seventh take I dried stone dead, but continued to chat to Barry. 'I've dried stone dead,' I said. 'Never mind,' he said, 'continue talking. Say anything and wave your arms about a bit to make gestures. Give me my cue when you feel like it.' I did. We were told it was splendid.

Saturday 31 August
First plane back this morning. I was driven to Reading where we met the film unit for the insurance commercial, ready and prepared. There was some worry about the cast we had selected who were from a Bingo hall session. But the clients—Legal and General—thought the casting was wonderful. Half a dozen people wandered around: directors of the advertising agency, the writer of the script, the director of advertising for Legal and General. They were all dressed in studiedly casual clothes.

I enjoyed myself. The people were warm and responsive. The crew was excellent—indeed the best camera operator I have ever encountered. I felt exhilarated to be firing off film again.

Monday 2 September
Second day of the commercial in Reading. I finished shooting by 6.30. Everybody pleased. And I had enjoyed it. The 9.30 plane back to Hamburg in high spirits.

Thursday 5 September
Hamburg: Peter Stevens rang tonight, depressed. He believes our opening on the South Bank will now be June, and that our policy there is going to be vitiated because of insufficient subsidy. But on both counts I feel braced. Luxurious unreality has now given way to what is possible.

Wednesday 11 September
Back to London from Hamburg. Phone call from Pinter who told me he had bad news. I asked him what it was. I've finished my play, he said. I was delighted; I wasn't expecting it until Christmas. But he knows how difficult this may make our plans, for he will want it done quickly.

Good dinner with the associates. I told them we must look at a 40% cutback on our proposed South Bank budget. They took it well: were indeed braced by it, as I am.

Pinter arrived with a new short haircut. 'Hello, Harold,' said Bill Bryden, 'You've had your hair cut.' Then Michael Kustow arrived and said, 'Hello, Harold, you've had your hair cut.' Then Michael Blakemore arrived. Harold looked at him. 'Hello, Michael,' he said, 'I've had my hair cut.'

Friday 13 September
Settled down to read Harold's new play. It is called *No Man's Land*. I was amazed by it. It is not at all what I was expecting. There is an icy preoccupation with time; and the long sustained speeches have a poetic validity which would have seemed incredible in the days of the brisk, hostile repartee of *The Birthday Party*. I must read it again. It is extremely funny and also extremely bleak. A play about the nature of the artist: the real artist harassed by the phoney artist.

Saturday 14 September
Timothy and Tazeena O'Brien arrived to talk about their designs for *Borkman*. Tim had a few colour patterns and shapes to put up on the model of the Olivier in the new building. Because this is such an entirely new kind of auditorium, with a different focus and a different rhythm, I find it enormously stimulating. For so many years all my stage work has been based on the principle that less is more, and that colour is distracting and must be used with discipline. Yet sometimes less is less. We are out on the road of excess with *Borkman* and hope that it will lead to wisdom and balance.
 Read Pinter's play again. I begin to see how I will direct it.

Sunday 15 September
To Hamburg. Lonely in the vast hotel. The film continues to lurch on its way. Everything is chaotic. Ten or eleven more days of this in front of me....

Monday 16 September
Hamburg: Spent the afternoon working on *Don Giovanni*[1] as I wasn't wanted for filming. Wonderful to get to grips with this masterpiece: the penance of sex and its easiness in a feudal society; the Don with two faces— alarmed and restless in private, always eager for new stimulation, suave and attractive in public. He must be the vulnerable charmer. Without conquest he feels unconfident.
 Is Donna Anna lying about the night Don Giovanni is in her bedroom? The whole opera is about duplicity, masks, the risks people take when driven by instinct. It is concerned with disguise, physical and moral. Mozart's theatre is a theatre of madness, of impulse, of mistaken identities, confusing doubles, masters and servants swapping roles, the world about to stand on its head through joy and through passion: dark black shadows, hectic, dangerous games of hide and seek. And Don Giovanni in a sense waves his penis at God to see if God exists. Will He strike him down for his

[1] Hall's next opera at Glyndebourne, staged there in 1977.

immorality? For most of the opera, God is uncaring, indifferent. Taking no notice.

Wednesday 18 September
Hamburg: Telegram from Harold to ring him at once because he was finding it difficult to get through. I did this lunchtime. It was the classic conversation that I have had with him about every new play of his:
'Can it be done immediately?', says Harold.
'Well, I'm not sure, but I'll try.'
'But, I can't wait long, and I have this offer to do it in the West End; could you direct it commercially?'
'No, Harold, of course I couldn't direct it commercially'.
'I didn't think you could; who do you think should direct it if you can't—though of course I want you to direct it?'
'I don't know, Harold; we must sit down and discuss the matter very carefully.'
'I can't think of anybody,' says Harold, 'and what about Gielgud? Will he be free?'
'Well, he's with us.'
'Ah,' says Harold, 'then he couldn't do it in the West End?'
'No,' I say.
And so on and so on. I ended by telling him we would decide next week when we knew the positive opening dates of the new theatre.

Thursday 26 September
Hamburg: My last day of this session of film-acting. My anxiety about whether we would finish the shooting or not in time for me to catch the plane back to London hung like a pall over the whole day. I just caught it and arrived home tense and tired.

Friday 27 September
The classic day of a theatre director returning. All the news was bad. Among other things, we would appear to be lucky if the new theatre is fully operational by next September.

Saturday 28 September
Early call from John Gielgud. He had read the new Pinter play late last night and again early this morning. He was very enthusiastic and asked when we could do it.

Monday 30 September
At Denys Lasdun's this morning for an unbelievable meeting. Contractor after contractor reported either bad news or no news at all, broken dates or

no possibility of knowing when the job will be finished. The hand-over to us cannot now begin until May, and therefore an opening before autumn is unthinkable[1]. I banged the table and spoke of my commitments to artists etc[2], and that this is exactly the situation I predicted last winter. The water is now getting really rough.

Thursday 3 October
Associates' meeting. Larry's first appearance for many months. He looked awful—tired and worried. Blakemore and Miller began to be critical of the administration, but were not specific. Larry attacked the casting of our plays, said it wasn't the choice of plays, but casting. I told them the whole disastrous news of the postponement. We must tell the company and staff as soon as possible.

A tough day. Blows raining from every side. Just before I finished the evening, news came that Oscar Lewenstein is getting up a letter to *The Times* warning of the threat of the National to the theatre in general. He is asking all theatre directors and managers to sign it. How helpful progressives can be.

Friday 4 October
Company and staff meeting at midday. I gave the facts about the delay as honestly and fully as I could. Great gloom, great anguish, and of course immediate anxiety about people's contracts being terminated. I said these would not be terminated, but they would not be renewed when they expired. Slight ground swell, making me feel people think I was silly to believe in any completion date. Yet it was guaranteed, and we were requested to be ready. I shouldn't have believed in the completion date.

News that Equity has been raging this afternoon because they had not been consulted before the meeting this morning. They were issuing a press statement saying they were resisting redundancies. We must have a meeting on Monday with them to talk this crisis through.

Monday 7 October
Have managed to see an advance copy of the Lewenstein letter. I tried writing a pained card. But then thought the best thing would be to try and ring him tomorrow.

---

[1] Allowing four months for the mechanical and electrical installations.
[2] The build-up of the company and repertoire at the Old Vic had meant making commitments to a great many actors, among them Peggy Ashcroft, Diana Rigg, Albert Finney, John Gielgud, Ralph Richardson, and Paul Scofield—all of whose plans were now changed.

121

Meeting with Equity. One of them, puffed up, I hope, with a brief authority, objected in the most violent terms to the fact that I talked to the company without informing the union. I let him have it, saying that if he wanted a fight, I would be very pleased to have one. I said I thought Equity had come to discuss what we could do that was productive in this mess which was none of our making. And if he wanted to use it as an opportunity for union/management strife, I was perfectly prepared to take him on. He said he still wished to register his objections. I said I refused to accept them. So he withdrew them.

We managed to talk them into understanding the horrendous position the delay has produced. And we assured them that everybody's contracts would be honoured.

Special meeting to consider our budgets and our deficits. All the budgets we've produced are now out of date. But they all point to the fact that the South Bank building could very easily become a white elephant. Even without the cost of staging the plays, to run it leaves small change out of a million pounds. The Arts Council officials looked worried and reeled around. But they were a support.

Long talk with Peggy Ashcroft about changing plans and dates for the opening of *Happy Days* and *Borkman*. She is being utterly helpful and putting herself out. A friend as ever. Without her I could never have started the RSC. Now she is staunchly seeing me through one of the worst crises of my life.

Tuesday 8 October

Spent the morning trying to get Oscar Lewenstein on the phone to have a chat with him about his odious letter. He was refusing calls. I tried about six times and from the flurry and giggling it was perfectly evident he was there. So I wrote him a letter. Peter Stevens, though, got him this afternoon because Oscar thought he was ringing about something else. Peter pointed out some factual mistakes in the letter and Oscar refused to accept them.

Wednesday 9 October

Associates' meeting. No Larry. No Blakemore. No Miller. After dinner the talk became freer. The associates present expressed alarm as to whether Jonathan in his present disaffected state should be planning to do *The Importance of Being Earnest* and *Measure*. I spoke about my anxieties concerning my relationship with Jonathan. I knew that some plays would have to go from the scheduled repertoire[1] and I was worried that *The Importance* and *Measure* would have to be among them. It was obviously

---

[1] Each director's plans now had to be cut back because of the building delays.

insane to cancel *Borkman* with the cast we've got for it[1]. And wrong to cancel John Schlesinger's production[2] as he'd not yet done one for us.

Harold Pinter's birthday at midnight. We sang 'Happy Birthday'.

Thursday 10 October
Lunch with Howard Brenton. The postponements have affected his enthusiasm for the new building not at all. He is still writing away for us.

Went to vote, for today is the general election. I want Labour to win with a very small majority so that their dogmatic excesses are kept in check.

Friday 11 October
Labour is back with a majority of three. I am pleased.

Long conversation with Jonathan. I pointed out to him why, along with other plays, *The Importance* and *Measure* had to go: the saving was about £30,000. I said we should talk again in the spring about his plans and involvement next year. I don't want a confrontation at the moment.

Saturday 12 October
Wandered round the garden this morning and flew a model aeroplane with Edward. Visited my father, who looks pale and shaken after an operation, but rather better than I had expected. His spirits are high. Read *Happy Days* twice today. I begin rehearsing it on Monday.

Monday 14 October
Rehearsals began at 10.30. A cast of two, Peggy Ashcroft and Alan Webb[3], outnumbered by all the technicians and management.

Sam Beckett wandered in at 10.20. Trying to contact him during the weekend, I had rung up the Hyde Park Hotel, left a letter for him asking him to ring me, and sent a letter to his agent—all to no avail. Apparently he is staying at the Hyde Park Hotel under an assumed name. I asked him if he was staying at the Hyde Park Hotel under an assumed name. He said, 'of course not'.

Sam looks no different to twenty years ago: still the aesthetic, visionary face, the nervous energy. He walked round the room anxiously searching for his glasses while he held them in his hand. He is gentle, arrogant, not wanting to discuss but to assert. Yet never wanting to quarrel. The problem of the pacifist in a hostile world.

I asked him to talk to the cast. We discussed the set, the costumes. Then we began to go through the text. He had a few cuts and a few slight alterations. The primary one concerned the parasol that bursts into flames.

[1] Including Peggy Ashcroft as Ella, Wendy Hiller as Gunhild, and Ralph Richardson as Borkman.
[2] Of Shaw's *Heartbreak House*.   [3] Who played Willie.

This he said had never worked. The parasol is supposed to burn away because of the force of the unremitting sun. Sam has had trouble about that all over the world, with fire authorities and theatre technicians. He now asks that the parasol merely smokes and the material melts away like some kind of plastic under heat. He also, surprisingly, wants to cut an entire page of dialogue relating to the parasol. This disturbed Peggy because it is good and she has learnt it. And it also disturbed me because I think he's only cutting it out of a memory of all the difficulties of the past. I shall bide my time.

Beckett's theatre is as much about mime and physical precision as it is about words. Therefore I want him to tell us everything *by doing it*. There is no notation which can describe the precision of the physical business. We are lucky to have him here. During his fortnight with us we will gather, as it were, all the text from the page and all the physical action from him. Only then will I start to direct it. . . .

Exciting to be working with an absolute genius. The star-struck me came out again for a few moments. The first time in ages.

Tuesday 15 October
The letter from Oscar Lewenstein and thirteen other theatre directors is in *The Times* this morning as expected[1]. I am terribly hurt about it, although pretending not to be. I am not surprised at Oscar who is a classic public moralist. But some of the signatories upset me[2].

Afternoon of *Happy Days*. Sam continuing to talk us through it, giving meticulous physical and verbal instructions. The text sounds beautiful, balanced, rhythmic, incantatory, in Sam's gentle Anglo-Irish brogue. He is completely an Irish writer.

An evening meeting with the associates and the administrators to bring them up to date with the changes of plans caused by the postponment of the opening. Then a company meeting to do the same. I apologised, and hoped

[1] The letter warned that the NT might absorb so much government money that other theatres could be starved; and that it was attracting staff and technicians with salaries higher than other theatres could afford. Two days later Hall's strongly-worded reply was printed in *The Times*. He wrote that the NT would have little purpose if other theatres were weakened by it, and that the accusation about staff being wooed to the NT by higher pay was 'simply untrue'.

[2] The letter was also signed by: Lindsay Anderson (Associate Artistic Director of the Royal Court Theatre); Peter Cheeseman (Artistic Director of the Victoria Theatre, Stoke-on-Trent); Michael Croft (Director of the National Youth Theatre); Frank Dunlop (Director of the Young Vic); Michael Elliott (Joint Artistic Director of '69 Theatre Company, Manchester); Richard Eyre (Theatre Director of The Playhouse, Nottingham); Howard Gibbens (Director of The Bush Theatre); John Harrison (Director of Leeds Playhouse); Ewan Hooper (Director of Greenwich Theatre); Peter James (Artistic Director of The Crucible Theatre, Sheffield); Joan Littlewood (Artistic Director of the Theatre Royal, Stratford East); Charles Marowitz (Artistic Director of the Open Space Theatre); and Toby Robertson (Director of the Prospect Theatre Company).

124

that there would be a future for all of us. A melancholy occasion. And I was very nervous. This time nobody asked awkward questions. Too gloomy I suppose.

To the National Film Theatre, which is presenting a German cultural three weeks. Things were enlivened at the reception by a chance encounter. I was standing having a drink when out of the carpet there arose a surprised and embarrassed Oscar Lewenstein. He said to me, after a great deal of stuttering: 'I hope you were pleased with today's letter in *The Times* after all . . . it should provoke some healthy discussion.' I blew. I called him a shit and a creep, and pointed out that he'd refused to have factual errors corrected.

I felt better for a while, and then regretted it. I very rarely blow up. And it does no good whatsoever to engage in outright confrontations. Nobody ever wins. Oscar and I are now clearly implacable enemies and he will continue his campaign (he kept shouting between my words that they had been collecting lots of evidence) with all the justification in the world, for I have now insulted him. Still. . . there comes a point. And Oscar went too far today.

Thursday 17 October

I disturbed Peggy yesterday deliberately by raising the question of how Winnie *sounded*. We decided she was genteel, bird-like, but with a voice more incantatory, more legato, than Peggy's natural explosive emphases.

She came to rehearsal with the same thought that had come to me in the night: let her try to be slightly Anglo-Irish. It *is* Irish writing, and to hear Sam say the lines is to understand their texture. I had thought of Cecil Day Lewis's accent. So had Peg. He was a close friend of hers.

The consequence of trying a different voice destroyed all her inflexion patterns this morning and her memory was affected. But it's a step in the right direction.

Brief meeting with Michael Blakemore. He says he will do *Plunder* in the early summer and then stand by to do more productions for the South Bank when and if we ever get into it.

He spoke of Jonathan, saying he appeared to think he had left us for ever, or at least for the next year. I said that in my conversation with Jonathan I asked if he and I could look at our plans again in April. Blakemore is obviously on Miller's side, and seems to think I am trying to take all Jonathan's productions away from him—which I'm not. This division will undermine the health of our group unless I am very careful.

Ninth wedding anniversary tomorrow. I stand at several crossroads, in several areas of my life. That dangerous little man who leaps out of me asking why I am wasting my time with all this administrative nonsense, taking care of other directors, indulging actors, instead of getting on with my own creative work, has been much in evidence lately. But I remember my

125

Royal Opera House resignation[1]. I should never have gone there, and had to resign to save myself. I must try to get to the end of this National Theatre war with some semblance of victory. For war it will be.

Friday 18 October
A great deal of excitement in Fleet Street about the chaos caused to our plans by the building delay. And at the weekend Stephen Fay is writing a long piece in *The Sunday Times* and Richard Findlater is writing in *The Observer*. We now enter our first real crisis.

Sunday 20 October
The big Stephen Fay article is a well-informed, accurate, but depressing document of, I would guess, at least 3000 words. It is headed 'Unfunny things that happen on the way to the National Theatre.' The centre of it is that we are in trouble but at least we are getting over the crisis on our own terms and not becoming shrouded in the abuse of our enemies.

Thursday 24 October
Last night party for *Spring Awakening*. Sad farewells to many of the actors. The reality of the South Bank mess became even more glaringly alive: bitterly disappointed people.

I had my usual horrible experience at a large stand up party. I flitted from group to group with glazed eyes pretending to be relaxed and at ease. Those sort of functions still, after twenty years, unnerve me.

Friday 25 October
Conversation with Denys Lasdun telling me that a letter was on its way from McAlpine's warning me that criticisms about the delay on the building were emanating from the National Theatre and from me and that they would take appropriate legal action if this continued.

The main, front-page article in the *New Statesman* attacks the whole idea of the new National Theatre. I was able in the end to shrug it off. But it bit deep and went on distressing me all day. It must be answered.

Peg told me a joyful piece of gossip yesterday. The story is that I'm putting it about that the building is late to disguise the fact that the National Theatre company is in a great mess.

Monday 28 October
The first reading of *Borkman*. Ralph Richardson in fine fettle. Peggy reading with a deep instinctive understanding. The version I've done with Inga-Stina Ewbank sounded well and I was pleased with it. It has taken

---

[1] Hall was Director of Productions at Covent Garden 1970–71.

many hours' work, but worth it. This is a magnificent play which I know I am going to enjoy directing. And it is now in my blood.

I must stop worrying about all the attacks and all the pressures at the National. The vital thing now is to do a couple of good pieces of work so there's some demonstrable point in having a National Theatre. Otherwise we're properly in the shit.

The rush of the day continued. This afternoon worked on *Happy Days*. Immediately after rehearsal I went home, changed, and sped to the BBC Television Centre for an interview with Robin Day. I think it was alright. I was, underneath, extremely nervous. For Robin Day is a tough nut, and he was asking awkward questions and waving all the press clippings at me. I couldn't point the finger at the South Bank Board but made it absolutely clear that the mess we were in was not the National Theatre's fault.

Tuesday 29 October
The threatened McAlpine letter arrives—not from them but from their solicitors. I suppose their motive is to shut me up. If so it won't work. The building *is* late and there is going to be trouble.

On the other hand I don't want a Sydney Opera House-type public scandal going on and on and on. It will be damaging to us as much as to McAlpines.

Friday 1 November
Not a bad afternoon on *Happy Days*. Sam Beckett's last afternoon with us. We checked over most of the play in order to make sure we had his requirements clear. 'All true grace is economical,' he observed.

Peggy got through a great deal of the second act but the same problem kept emerging—unless she is allowed to feel it all very strongly, she will never know what she is hiding. But the slightest sign of feeling disturbs Sam, and he speaks of his need for monotony, paleness, weakness. This is where, unlike Harold, he is not finally a theatre worker, great director though he can be. He confuses the work process with the result. I suppose it's understandable. A writer of his meticulousness must achieve the phrase he wants very quickly as he sets it down on paper, otherwise he crosses it out. But an actor takes weeks of work to explore and then realise a few minutes of text.

Sunday 3 November
To Goodman's this evening for Jennie Lee's seventieth birthday. Found myself on the Jennie Lee-Harold Wilson table. Wilson looked extraordinarily well, not at all like a man who had just come through an election. The air was thick with self-congratulation: it was he and Jennie Lee who had

together brought the revolution in the arts, and the Open University. It's true.

Brief words with Hugh Jenkins who said that our budget ratio on the South Bank of £1 from the box office to £1.60[1] from the Exchequer was too much and I'd have to do something about it. My natural response is that he'll have to do something about getting us into the building, and paying for its fantastically high running costs. But I kept quiet for now.

Monday 4 November

Tinkered with the article for the *New Statesman* which I am writing[2] as a result of their attack. Got a rough shape on it.

Lunch with Clement Freud[3] to brief him for the forthcoming debate in the House of Commons—the second reading of the National Theatre bill, proposing more money to finish the building. He gives gloomy news for the future of the arts. He says we will of necessity march into the South Bank over the bodies of others. I don't like the sound of this at all.

He is allergic to cigarettes. When Yolande Bird[4] came in, cigarette between her lips, he retired in panic to the far corner of my office. His grandfather would be very interested in these symptoms.

Tuesday 5 November

Another MP, Gwyneth Dunwoody[5], came to see me for a briefing on the National Theatre debate. I gave her all the stuff. And there was a telephone message asking me to communicate with Renee Short[6]—also for the National Theatre debate. She poured sympathy over me, saying what a bad press the whole concept of the National Theatre was getting, and all my ideas for it. Hardly true, I pointed out: there were some stirrers and objectors with loud voices, but the publicity for the building had been good, and my ideas had been well received.

Wednesday 6 November

Down to Technicolor near London Airport. We ran two prints of *Akenfield* side by side—the first and the third. No question that the first is better. Our grader is a nice old boffin in a white coat who listens to me pontificating,

---

[1] In 1983 when these diaries went to press, the ratio was £1 from the box office to £1.20 from the Exchequer.
[2] The article, printed 8 November, said the new NT would be better value, artistically and financially, than the Old Vic. It would draw a far bigger and more varied audience, and provide many more opportunities for writers, actors and directors.
[3] Liberal spokesman on Education and the Arts 1974-77.
[4] A member of the NT staff, soon to be appointed Assistant Secretary to the NT Board.
[5] Labour MP for Crewe.
[6] Labour MP for Wolverhampton North-East and then Chairman of the Theatres' Advisory Council.

mutters that it needs a bit more red, and enters a hieroglyphic on his sheets. In the middle of the night someone unknown to the grader—or to me—will interpret this pinch of red his own way and the picture will come out more or less according to his guesses. All this is a very imprecise and impersonal way of working. Why do we take such care over the colour of costumes, the colour of makeup, if the print situation is so approximate?

Thursday 7 November

Many theatre people at the House of Commons tonight to hear the debate. I couldn't go but am told the Bill went through without too much holorum. George Strauss[1] brought up the old question of us overpaying and thereby attracting people from other theatres, but was apparently put down. Because of tonight everyone thinks the arts are not going to be cut to shreds after all. I hope they're right.

Dinner party at the Barbican for John Gielgud and Harold Pinter. They know each other but not well. They got on extremely promisingly. And by the end of the evening Gielgud's rate of conversation had halved itself. He normally talks all the time and very rapidly, out of nerves. Harold charmed him and was very specific about *No Man's Land*: who was who and what was what. We discussed at length the casting of Hirst. We all want Ralph if we can get him.

Jacky had gone out for the evening promising to return between 10.15 and 10.30 so that I could dash to the theatre to say farewell to the *Figaro* company. At 10.30, no Jacky. So Harold and John offered to babysit and I sped off.

When I got home again it was 12.30. John had left, but Harold was still sitting there benignly quaffing brandy and chatting to Jacky. He was saying he'd always wanted to spend his life teaching very small children. By 1.30 I had persuaded him downstairs into a taxi. Before then there had been many drinks for the road and cigarettes for the road. He was extremely warm to me, and assuring his wholehearted support of the National, and meaning it. I got him into the taxi and he sat with great dignity on the floor. He looked around him and observed, 'What's wrong with this fucking taxi?' I guided him gently up on to the seat, and he whirled off to Regent's Park.

So to bed, but I was awoken at six by Edward: Lucy was crying because she wanted to write a letter to Father Christmas. So do I. . . .

Friday 8 November

Albert Finney is banging the drum for the National Theatre in the *Evening Standard*, saying the actors must roll up their sleeves and get on with it. Very welcome talk.

---

[1] Labour MP for Lambeth, Vauxhall. Created Baron 1979. In 1968 he introduced the bill for the abolition of stage censorship.

Saturday 9 November
Afternoon with Tim and Tazeena O'Brien on the *Borkman* designs: a beginning, and a fair one. But it is tragic having thought of the play for so long in space, in the Olivier, to now be confined by the Old Vic's conventional box stage.

The O'Briens left in the early evening. I settled down to read Harold Pinter's play again. But should I direct it? I wonder whether it wouldn't be better to ask Harold to take it on himself, for my workload next year is ridiculous. No, I'll do it.

Wednesday 13 November
Clearly there is now no hope of the theatre opening until spring 1976 at the earliest—that is, a year later than we were promised in July at the Mc-Alpine's lunch. I begin to wonder whether I shall cling on to this job until the theatre starts. I begin to wonder if I want to.

Lunch with Cyril Bennett. He asked me to do *Aquarius* as editor and introducer: 22 episodes, one day's work a week, starting next October. I am attracted. It needs careful thought though.

Friday 15 November
Telephone conversation with Ralph who had been sent the Pinter script. He loves the play, says he cannot pass up the opportunity of such a fine part. He asked, what does it mean? Has Hirst committed some murder in the past? I was nonplussed by this remark. I said Harold was not a fellow of mysteries or enigmas. He was concerned with facts. So a murder, actual or psychological, has been done.

Saturday 16 November
Off to the airport to see Peter Brook's production of *Timon of Athens* in Paris at his theatre, Les Bouffes du Nord. It's a fine 1880 music-hall building with a high proscenium and ruined, cheap, rococo decorations, speaking of past pleasures, of old successful meetings between players and audiences. George Wakhevitch[1] has painted it here and there, brought up a little of the crumbling masonry, slapped a little faded red on the back of the circle walls. The theatre is in fact a ruin of great artifice.

There are no proper seats, only wooden planks laid out. The discomfort is extraordinary. In fact I hardly survived the last half hour. My knees were under my chin, my stomach folded in a shape to induce nausea, and the cheeks of my behind bruised.

---

[1] The stage designer.

The company is not good—twenty French actors who still orate in the classical style, and clutch each other hurriedly for dramatic effect. Peter deserves better than this. But just about everything else in the production is wonderful. There is a fairground atmosphere, a genuine informality. The cast sit round the acting space as part of the audience and then gradually get drawn into the play. The audience is in fact used constantly in a way which I have never seen brought off before. Practically all the text is spoken directly to them, with the actor appealing for endorsement. The play is about moral issues and the audience are asked to comment. It works partly because of the place, and because there is no division whatsoever between actor and audience, no barrier, no demarcation. But it works mainly because it has been done completely.

There is, though, something vaguely distasteful about seeing *le tout Paris* telling each other how *extraordinaire* the whole thing is as they sit hunched on planks, slumming it in the smartest clothes imaginable. Peter is such an innovator that he always gets mixed up with the trendies, even if he doesn't want to. But despite all the discomfort, and all the pretension, which chiefly comes from the audience, I would not have missed this for worlds.

Sunday 17 November
The morning with Peter Brook and lunch. There is a myth current in London that he has walked into a ruined old Parisian theatre and made magic, whereas we in Britain are spending millions on new theatres. The fact is that he has the most extraordinary deal with the French Ministry of Culture. They give a grant which completely covers all the running costs and the salaries and Peter merely sends whatever he earns at the box office back to them. He may play a great deal, or hardly at all, it depends on the needs of the group and the response of the audience. So do the seat prices. It really is a paradise for a theatre director. I am full of envy for Peter. He has never wanted to run a theatre. But this way he is getting his theatre without a heavy responsibility.

Tuesday 19 November
At noon to the Donmar rehearsal rooms to see the set of *Happy Days* for the first time. I am very pleased. It looks well and sits well. There was the usual actors' fussing—like dogs walking round and round a place where they are going to sleep.

Worked through Act I in the afternoon. Peg was very obstinate, resisting everything, arguing. She was like a horse who wanted to go, and I wouldn't let her. It is the usual tension with her in the last stages of rehearsal. She wants no detailed work, only to run. And yet if things are not working she finds it impossible to run.

Friday 22 November
Forty-four today. What happened to my thirties? It seems only yesterday that I was longing to be 35, fed up with being known as the young director. Well, I am not young any longer. I don't mind this, except there is so much I want to do.

Saturday 23 November
John Goodwin gave me a long and useful lecture about my increasing paranoia. He said I must expect to be attacked on all sides and that I must be as philosophical about it as I was in the sixties (I never was really) because the attacks would get worse. I was now, he said, at the height of my career, very successful apparently, very powerful: directing plays, films, operas, running a vast organisation, writing, appearing on television, making adaptations of Ibsen. . . . I was asking for it and would get it. I was no longer the young revolutionary being discovered, I was the Establishment that needed attacking. John said this would probably go on until my late fifties when I might hope to become a grand old man.

Good advice. But it doesn't alter the fact that I am as raw as burnt skin where some things are concerned.

Birthday lunch with the little children: paper hats and crackers[1].

Tuesday 26 November
Happy Days opened tonight at the Liverpool Playhouse[2]. To the theatre early for further work on the lighting. Then notes with Peggy and Alan[3] in the hotel. By the time I had got to the second act, Peggy's eyes were full of tears. She could take no more. This, I've always suspected, is a weapon she is inclined to use unconsciously in the last stages of rehearsal to get the director off her back, though her distress is real. We all spent an uneasy afternoon.

But she arrived at the theatre at 5 pm as bright as a button and full of apologies. We tidied up a few things and went into the first night at 7.30. Peggy rose magnificently to the occasion. All the anxieties and problems of the last week seemed to be forgotten. She acted with fluency and precision. I was really thrilled with the evening. The play received a very warm ovation.

Wednesday 27 November
The Liverpool notices for *Happy Days* this morning are excellent. Peg is in good heart. She held a levée in her bedroom and we went over the notes of

---

[1] A joint celebration for Hall's birthday and Edward's five days later.
[2] Following this week at Liverpool, *Happy Days*, because of the delayed opening of the South Bank building, went into cold storage until it joined the NT's repertoire at the Old Vic in March 1975.
[3] Webb.

last night. She assures me that I can now go off to clear my mind for *Borkman*. Alan is less willing.

Monday 2 December
John Heilpern to visit me at Wallingford. Two hours of hard conversation. He is writing an anti-theatre piece for *The Observer* saying theatre as a form cannot justify its place in society because nobody wants it any more—it is like the Church: something which everybody pays lip service to but is unnecessary, serving a declining audience.

Our argument was ferocious. It really came down to the fact that he was saying the theatre was a half empty glass and I was saying it was a half full glass.

I don't believe we need any more state-of-the-nation pieces about the theatre. The public is surely sick of them. We should get on and do some work.

Tuesday 3 December
The first rehearsal of *Borkman*. A stimulating though tiring day, riding all these mad horses: Wendy[1] bent into the shape of a victim ready to suffer; Peggy facing the world, eyes filled with tears, ready to break down; Alan looking angry and suspicious, chin jutting out, ready to be misanthropic; Ralph energetically swooping around like an old bull, tossing his head up and down in order to worry out the meaning. A lot of volts here and a great deal of talent. The play is wonderful, my first Ibsen. I think I can do it. . . .

It is a crucial production, the more so because of *Grand Manoeuvres*[2] which opens tonight. This is beautifully done, wonderfully directed, and technically very adroit, but the play is simply not up to the mark. My instinct told me not to do it. I was persuaded by Michael Blakemore. The lesson of the year is this: I am responsible, so I had better follow my own tastes and not compromise.

Wednesday 4 December
The critics are terrible about *Grand Manoeuvres*, and Michael Billington continues his what-on-earth-is-wrong-with-the-National-Theatre campaign. Muted atmosphere in the offices this morning.

A hard day on *Borkman*. Ralph is magnificent. He suddenly creates moments of pure genius. He is, like Edith Evans, all actor. It is an ability to plug in suddenly to reality. In rehearsal it is almost indecent to hear a line expressed so truly. It is not a line, it is life itself speaking.

---

[1] Hiller.   [2] By A. E. Ellis, directed by Michael Blakemore.

Dead tired at the end of the afternoon. Many nasty messages. There was news, though only a rumour, that Jonathan Miller was thinking of resigning. I've tried to keep him, but perhaps he should go. But I don't want him to resign at this particular moment and cause more public nonsense. We are in a very weak position after a bad season's work and, in particular, a series of bad choices of modern plays. We are also in the middle of a political controversy because we cost too much. And the new building is late.

Too much depends on *Borkman*. I don't like working under such pressure.

Thursday 5 December

Saw the costumes for *Borkman* this morning. Ralph arrived on his motorbike looking like an earless teddy bear in a large white crash helmet. He looked even more extraordinary when he left, for Peggy had left her cardigan behind. In order not to forget it, Ralph drove off wearing it.

He has a wonderful instinct about the opening scene. He feels he must be unnaturally, almost raffishly, happy and cheerful. One must see what a great, kingly, artistic, expansive man Borkman was at the height of his powers. Ralph does not want to look too black and pastor-like, but to contradict the images of gloom and neurosis with Borkman's ambitions, his joy in the world and progressive capitalism.

Michael Blakemore came in to close the day on a unique note. He said Jonathan had phoned him last night really on the boil and was now going to have a public resignation. I asked Michael what Jonathan was on the boil about. Michael dodged it by saying he didn't know. I don't know either.

Tuesday 10 December

Did a recording for the BBC on Michael Tippett. He is seventy at the beginning of January. Incredible. I was asked what was the most surprising and noticeable thing about Tippett when you met him. I said his youth.

Ran second act of *Borkman* this afternoon. Ralph is amazing. He more or less knows it. The first time through, he is fine: pretty precise. The second, he is becoming tired—so he doesn't say half the words at all but makes appropriate grunts, whistles and shouts which give the same kind of sound and rhythm and inflection pattern—very off-putting for the other actors. He seemed slightly surprised that they can't act with him when he's blowing like an old whale. He is an undoubted genius though.

Supper with Harold. He gave me a long lecture about leading a more sensible life—having time off, time to read, or time to do nothing, or time to see my friends. . . .

Wednesday 11 December
Meeting with Jonathan Miller. I asked him why he had been behaving in a Coriolanus-like way, booking himself up outside the NT, as I've now discovered he has been, so that there was no possibility of employing him for the next year or so; yet going round saying he was resigning as he was fed up with not being used. There was a complete breast-beating scene. He said he always loud-mouthed against authority, was always against the father figure, was verbally promiscuous. He said in justification that I had never been mocked at fortnightly intervals in *Private Eye*, had never had two years of abuse from running *Monitor*[1]. I asked him again why he went about saying the National wasn't using him. He apologised, asked to stay. I don't believe he will.

Thursday 12 December
Jonathan and I travelled back to the Barbican together for the associates' dinner. Harold looked quizzical when we arrived. He was wondering, in the light of a conversation he had with me last night, whether or not Jonathan would be appearing.

A good meeting. We discussed the dreadful Coliseum news. All the stage staff who were sacked for stopping Henze's *The Bassarids* have been reinstated and the committee of enquiry has criticised the top management heavily and said not one word against the union or the Coliseum workers. Yet we hear the Coliseum is full of trouble, that the militants are very active there, and that Covent Garden is to be the next for their attentions. Then the National—if possible—once it is in the new building. We must just wait for the confrontation which will undoubtedly come. And play scrupulously by the rules of the game.

A great deal of talk about the lack of candour in our associates' meetings. I said we were too deferential about our opinions and about our estimation of each others' talents. And we agreed that we must in future be much more ruthless in our criticism of repertoire proposals. Our main job was the repertoire. Everything else was incidental. There was more honesty about tonight than for months. We broke up in high spirits.

Friday 13 December
Meeting with Harold and John Bury about the set for *No Man's Land*. A house in Hampstead. Last century. Very rich. A clubland atmosphere. A great deal of money. Male. Brown. John showed us a sketch model which was a talking point. The problem is where to put the drinks cabinet: an altar

[1] A celebrated BBC arts programme that ran from 1958–65. Jonathan Miller fronted it 1964–65 and then produced occasional programmes for *Sunday Night*, which succeeded *Monitor*, in 1965–66.

to drink in the centre of the room, dominating without inhibiting the physical life of the play.

A stumble-through of *Borkman*. Quite encouraging. Ralph is wonderfully grandiloquent and noisy. Some of the speeches today he quite simply hummed and hawed. But I felt that though most of the cast didn't know what they were doing, I did. It cleared my head wonderfully.

The actors, having agreed that we must play it lightly, coolly, comically—making the tempo colloquial and repetitive, *never* significant—then played with the authentic cliché note of Ibsen doom, every line significant. But we will get there.

Sunday 15 December

An idea came to me during the day. Suppose the house in *No Man's Land* was not nineteenth-century but twentieth-century: rich Lutyens. We could then make all the back wall an alcove window and so give more dominance to the drinks altar—an altar to drink, set against 1920s leaded windows. I rang John Bury to tell him. He was excited.

Wednesday 18 December

Before the rehearsal of *Borkman* this morning Ralph said he'd had a sleepless night of alarm because he suddenly thought that the Pinter play was entirely about queers. I had said to him yesterday that I was going to cast Michael Feast in the play and that he would be wonderful because he has this androgynous quality. Ralph decided that perhaps he'd agreed to be in a play about four queers. I assured him this was not so. According to Pinter, the only homosexual is the character to be played by Terence Rigby—Briggs.

Dinner this evening with Trevor Nunn and David Brierley, Peter Stevens and Michael Birkett[1]. We talked about the problems facing the RSC and the National. Trevor and I, by one in the morning, had argued ourselves into a position where we didn't want to run large theatre organisations at all, didn't believe in them any more, and yearned for a small group of actors in a small situation. Big, we agreed, had no beauties about it whatsoever.

Tuesday 24 December

Usual fever of parcels, creeping about leaving stockings at the end of beds. Lucy and Edward have written very long letters to Father Christmas. Lucy the other day: 'Am I weally me? Or am I only dweaming?' I listened to the service from King's College, Cambridge, while swearing at having to fix the fiddly doll's house lights.

---

[1] Soon to become Deputy Director of the NT (1975–77).

Wednesday 25 December
Christmas Day. Euphoria with the children in the morning. Lucy's dolls'
house a triumph, also Jenny with her cape, Christopher with his gun,
12-bore, and Edward with his diving watch ('You can take it practically
anywhere')—all very successful. Sporadic games. We make music, which is
pleasant. And we watch television, which should be banned: *Laurel and
Hardy Go West* this morning; *The Bridge on the River Kwai* in the evening;
and as a late night bonus an anthology of Morecambe and Wise, as funny as
Laurel and Hardy, and quite as classical.

Friday 27 December
Jenny and Christopher left this morning for Chicago to join their mother,
then on to Mexico for a holiday. Jacky, Edward and Lucy went to Jacky's
sister's farm. I was left alone to work and think. I read several scripts,
walked and thought, and watched *Singin' in the Rain* on television.

Tuesday 31 December
New Year's Eve. I heard it strike twelve and then went to sleep. Let us hope
that next year will be better than last.

1975

Wednesday 1 January
To the Aldwych to see John Barton's production of Marlowe's *Dr Faustus*—a great broken-backed play that John has attempted to cure by using as narrative hunks of the original source book of the Faust legend. The curious things about the play are the common farce scenes that, according to critics, mar its centre. But I have always felt these should be done fully and as the reverse side of the coin. If the serious part of the play is the positive, then the farce scenes should be the negative. They are a fantasy. Surely Marlowe is getting at a basic truth here. A man who holds supreme power, or even imagines himself to be all-powerful, indulges in complex and—to saner mortals—comic fantasies, in which he appropriates all the wealth of the world or fucks all the women. I would like to see *Faustus* with the comic episodes done with mad surrealistic strength—a Ken Campbell show.

Thursday 2 January
I made the mistake of looking through *Plays and Players* this evening. Their bumper New Year edition contains summings up and awards from each critic. Every one of them knocks the year at the National and me in particular. Quite right I know. Nothing has worked as one had hoped. Michael Billington comments that *The Tempest* was not only the worst production of the play he had ever seen, but one of the four worst Shakespeare productions he'd seen anywhere, ever. A little extreme I feel.

Friday 3 January
Early morning meeting with John Bury and Harold Pinter about the *No Man's Land* set. I still wonder if it needs a little more edge. The model is recognizably an interior in a well-heeled London house. But at the moment it could easily be an environment for a naturalistic play of the thirties. It has to go beyond reality to a certain degree of surreality.

Borkman rehearsal. The first five minutes were spent with Peg maintaining the impossibility of doing one particular beat I had asked for. The words were wrong. Then, no, the words weren't wrong, the motives were wrong. Finally she said she would never be able to do it that way. And then proceeded to do it.

Sunday 4 January

Saw the *Borkman* sets on stage. The Norwegian stove, which we thought should dominate the room, is a bastard. It looks like a huge green phallus made for a surrealistic shop window. It is very scenic and unconvincing. It will have to go. The mountain top is, I think, going to work. But somehow the whole production gives me the feeling it was designed for the Aldwych. We haven't mastered the Vic.

Tuesday 7 January

This morning Wendy Hiller, who has been away ill, said she would try and come back to *Borkman* rehearsals on Thursday against doctor's orders. She sounded dreadful, wheezing and coughing and voiceless. Alan Webb is away ill too, so of course a postponement is lurking about in my head. But can I afford a postponement when the National Theatre's fortunes and my own are so low? The profession would scream at us for indulging ourselves.

I think it would be okay to open without Wendy, *or* without Alan, but not without both. I am particularly worried about the Alan situation. Ralph is an instinctive tennis player. If he finds himself playing a scene with an actor who doesn't interest him, he chunters through as quickly as possible. Alan forces him to play good tennis.

There was a ridiculous moment today at rehearsal when Peggy and Ralph sat side by side on the sofa. Peggy said it was much too high for her to work on, Ralph said it was just right. I soothed things over by saying we should practise with some lumps of foam rubber and get a compromise height. Ralph, as he left, his motorbike helmet securely on his head, winked and whispered to me: 'Don't touch that bloody sofa.'

To the Barbican very tired. I tried to have a sauna, but the phone kept ringing. One of the calls was from Peggy. She asked me if she was being difficult and I told her she was. She said she was fussed and tired. But her marvellous spirit to surmount crises began to appear when she realised Alan was possibly very ill, and the full ramifications of the Wendy situation. Peggy is one of the greatest human beings I know.

Thursday 9 January

Wendy returned this morning wheezing and swaying, able to talk or move, but not both at the same time. We meandered through Act I. I was quite pleased by her simplicity. When she's weak, she elaborates much less.

Saturday 11 January

Tested some boots in the lunch hour with contact mikes in the heels so that we can amplify Borkman's pacing round his room. Crazy, but it worked. Lunch with Ralph and Peggy, and they began reminiscing: how they met at Birmingham when she was eighteen, and he was twenty-four and a great hero of hers; how they were both together in the Robeson *Othello* in the late twenties with lighting so dim that Ralph secretly strapped a torch to his spear so he was visible for a soliloquy.

Rehearsed Act II of *Borkman* this afternoon and, two old lions that they are, suddenly they created magic. I provoked Peggy just before we began work by saying to her I thought she'd forgotten Ella was a spinster, a virgin. This worked the trick. An entirely new woman emerged, and Ralph responded to it.

Monday 13 January
I was behind my desk at six this morning—streaked through a great number of papers.

Run-through of Act I of *Borkman*. Horrid and interminable. Ralph thinks we should cut. So do I. But cut what? There are a lot of weeds in the text—odd turns of phrase which deflect from the main line. But they are there for a purpose: to show the obsessive side of the characters. This is the texture of Ibsen. And unless it can be played lightly and quickly, the repetitions are very boring. Ours are boring.

Tuesday 14 January
A drinks party at LWT for the TV critics who had just seen *Akenfield*. The *News of the World* was anxious to know how much I got paid for the film, and seemed shattered when I said it was £800 for what must represent a full year's work spread over five years. I bet they don't print it[1].

Wednesday 15 January
Harold told Peggy he was coming to the run-through of *Borkman* this afternoon, so Peggy, who adores him, got in an emotional state and said she couldn't possibly act if Harold were there. I began to lose my temper, saying I needed help too. She got more emotional. I just managed to control myself and cool the whole situation. I don't want her in an uncreative state this afternoon. So I stopped Harold from coming and got on with it.

Tuesday 21 January
Borkman's first preview tonight. Wendy played better, but Ralph became pedestrian and forgetful, so Peggy forced her lines out like exhortations. This, added to the inevitable withdrawal that always occurs when a play first meets an audience, made for a fairly disastrous evening. There were many laughs. Most of them good. But some of them so took the actors by surprise they thought they were being laughed *at*.

[1] They didn't.

I talked to the Old Lion after over a huge glass. He was very morose. He said he couldn't get a grip on the part, couldn't get the flow. But all this with great dignity and no pathos. He has great courage and never asks for sympathy. I admire him very much.

Wednesday 22 January

A bad night: fitful sleep; panic about the state of *Borkman*. I have a deep feeling it has gone wrong, and is not at all what I meant it to be. I have the excuse, of course, of illness in the cast. But shouldn't I have surmounted this somehow? Shouldn't I have shaped the play so that it had a clear intention and a clear line?

The preview this evening was better: more assured, more confident. Ralph played the second part magnificently. I talked to him afterwards at long length. He said that last night when he went home he said to Mu[1] he was afraid 'this was going to be a naughty one', but after tonight he didn't feel that any more. He knew he could play the part, knew it was his part, though whether or not he'd get there by the first night on Tuesday was, he said, debatable.

Sunday 26 January

A big day: *Akenfield* on television and opening simultaneously at a cinema, the Paris Pullman: a unique experiment.

Saw the *Aquarius* programme on all this early in the evening. Then off to the Paris Pullman to introduce the film. Then a dash down the road for our party and food and to watch it on television, where Cyril Bennett says it will be seen by between 5 and 7 million people if we are lucky. He was very jumpy, like someone at a first night. Everyone in the room had seen the film at least two or three times, so conversation, though muted, was general, and eating and drinking went on as usual. Cyril would have none of this. He sat on the carpet tensed and edgy, watching the screen as if the projector was going to break down or the actors forget their lines. He was terribly moved at the end and congratulated all of us at the way it had come over...

After that, I went back to the Paris Pullman and answered some intelligent questions from the audience.

Monday 27 January

The taxi driver congratulated me on *Akenfield* on my way to the theatre, and Princess Margaret phoned to say she'd liked it but didn't understand why one or two critics had complained it was difficult to understand the dialect. She hadn't found it difficult at all, 'Though of course,' she said, 'one did grow up there, in Norfolk at any rate.' The general reception seems to be

---

[1] Nickname of Meriel Forbes, Lady Richardson, wife of Sir Ralph.

good. Cyril is jumpy about how many people actually watched. We won't know for a few days.

This evening's preview of *Borkman* I shall not forget. Ralph played like a man possessed. The clear paranoia of the character was evident, and his power; all Ralph's avuncular softness was gone. The appearance helped. He had sharpened his nose, given himself a moustache, and two great sweeps of hair. He looks like a mad Toscanini.

I went to see him afterwards to say I was delighted. He said he had expected me to tell him to take all the new face off. I asked him if he would have done so. 'Oh yes', said Ralph, morosely.

I thanked him for being so courageous, being so ready to take such risks the day before the first night. He said that however hard one rehearsed, and however precise the work, acting on any first night was going out on a tightrope. One was quite inclined to fall off. So one might just as well do a pirouette into the bargain.

Tuesday 28 January
Borkman first night. I am very jumpy. I couldn't bear the prospect of sitting and stood nervously at the back. I had a very equivocal feeling at the end. The reception was warm but not madly enthusiastic. Have we pulled it off? Tonight I don't know, nor do the actors.

We went back to the Barbican flat for a small dinner party. Harold Pinter met Ralph Richardson for the first time. 'I am holding a poet in my hand,' said Ralph as he took Harold's proffered greeting. 'I am holding a great actor in mine,' replied Pinter. This little scene was enacted with sufficient humour for it to be delightful. Ralph was impressed by my flat. 'Very good digs,' he said.

Wednesday 29 January
Up early and read the papers. I couldn't believe it. Billington's notice in *The Guardian* was a complete appreciation of what I was trying to do in Ibsen, and very enthusiastic. Wardle in *The Times* was also very enthusiastic. I cried with relief. I don't think I could have stood another failure at the Vic and another series of articles asking what is wrong with the National. I have achieved too little there as yet to ride out failure. I am very very relieved; not elated, relieved.

Thursday 30 January
Cyril Bennett is over the moon. So am I. *Akenfield* had a television audience of 14½–15 million people throughout the country.

Associates' meeting. General feeling that if the Lyttelton is finished before the Olivier and the Cottesloe, we should start playing in it, *not* wait to have a grand opening when all three are completed. Let's get our foot in the door.

Discussion about me doing *Aquarius*. Doubts from Blakemore and Birkett. Michael Kustow reported that Jonathan, who could not come, was very much against it; he was asking how thin I thought I could spread myself.

Tuesday 4 February
Edward Heath has been chucked out decisively by the Conservatives. Tonight he has resigned, and William Whitelaw is now standing. I believe that if Mrs Thatcher is elected leader we are in for ten or fifteen years of solid Labour rule.

Wednesday 5 February
Long talk with John Schlesinger. He pitched into me about *Aquarius*. He thinks I shouldn't do it, that if I have any spare capacity, I should sit and think. He says that nobody can run a television arts programme, even as a presenter only, without getting heavily involved. So the opposition is about equal strength now as against those who think I should do it. I must confess to being very worried. We are on the brink of agreeing the contract.

Why do I want to do it? The money certainly—it will relieve the financial pressure. But also, I think, the desire to make small films.

Thursday 6 February
Session with John Bury about the set for *No Man's Land*. Our image now is an arch—protective, delicate, enclosing: a bland oval shape. But the colour of the model is still wrong: hot brown. I want it cool and elegant; green silks, parchment whites, bamboo greens: a Japanese feeling. John is a long way from that, and I'm not sure he endorses it. Harold came and was pleased with the shape, which was something.

Associates' lunch. We discussed the ridiculous position we are in. Insufficient money to stay at the Vic with an expanded organisation, yet if we reduce that organisation, we shall not be capable of opening on the South Bank when the time comes.

Friday 7 February
Lunch with Humphrey Burton[1]. Very useful on *Aquarius*. He said up to now it had been an experiencing rather than a critical programme. He thought I should go about it in a quite different way. I remain in a state about going about it in any way.

Dreadful meeting at the Arts Council. They say there is no more money. I put forward our idea of opening the Lyttelton as soon as it was ready. Patrick Gibson said there had to be an Arts Council enquiry into our future plans—staffing and financing—in order to head off criticism.

[1] Head of Music and Arts, BBC television 1975–82.

This little bomb was dropped at 5.15 just as I was about to leave. So I stayed on and missed every train to Bedales where I was due to lecture in the evening. Sue[1] acted as a real friend and heroine and drove me. I arrived at the school at ten to eight, and began my lecture at eight, very tense, very tired. A vast surge of adrenalin carried me through without notes. Jenny and Christopher were pleased and relieved, Jenny particularly. But for them being at the school I would have cancelled the lecture at the last moment.

Back to Wallingford at about a quarter to twelve, too dizzy and too depressed to sleep.

Saturday 8 February
Busy morning preparing for Edward's birthday party and pretending I was not stunned with tiredness. Jenny and Christopher mercifully helped. Christopher nobly refereed the small boys' football match. He sent off one team member for a few minutes for saying 'fuck'. Edward's dream of leading his team to victory became a nightmare. His team lost, and he was subject to every injury. Christopher played a dreadful joke. He built a pile of smarties in the grass, made a circle of the children round it, and whispered a secret animal's name to each of them. He told them he would call out each animal and give it three seconds to see how many smarties it could pick up; the one with the most would be the winner. He then solemnly said 'bear', and as soon as it was pronounced twenty children hurled themselves on a small pile of smarties. Poor Edward was at the bottom of a great mass of seething, fighting children. He was very indignant. Quite right.

Sunday 9 February
The Pinter play all clicked today. A feeling that I really know what it is about—opposites. Genius against lack of talent, success against failure, drink against sobriety, elegance against uncouthness, smoothness against roughness, politeness against violence. Now it is inside me I find it a wonderful play

Monday 10 February
First rehearsal of the Pinter. Very little said; just a reading. It came off the page beautifully. Everybody beautifully cast. Michael Feast[2]; Richardson, understanding it in his guts; Gielgud, doing a few virtuoso trills to find his way around it; Terence Rigby dour, thoughtful, and magnificently confident in the way he took the Bolsover Street speech.

Tuesday 11 February
An extraordinary day on the Pinter. The positions were right because the furniture was right. The furniture was right because I now know what the

[1] Higginson.　　[2] As Foster.

play's physical needs are. It went down very easily. Pinter wasn't there; we'll show it him tomorrow. The play is hard, complex chamber music, but I've got it.... A very satisfying feeling.

Dinner at Max Rayne's in Hampstead. First time to the millionaire's home, built by himself: beautiful architecture, high well-proportioned modern rooms, a huge garden outside with Elizabeth Frink horses and Henry Moore torsos dotting the lawns. At every turn in the house, fantastic paintings: a beautiful Braque; Vlaminck; Pissarro; Picasso; Matisse. Amazing wealth displayed with great taste.

Everyone agog at the news that Margaret Thatcher has been elected Tory leader with a huge majority. Surely no working man or woman north of the Wash is ever going to vote for her? I fear a lurch to the right by the Tories and a corresponding lurch to the left by Labour.

To Buckingham Palace for the Queen's reception for the media, at least I suppose that's what we were. Newspaper editors; television controllers; journalists and commentators; Heath looking like a tanned waxwork; Wilson; Macmillan a revered side show, an undoubted star; a few actors (Guinness, Ustinov, Finney); and all the chaps like me—John Tooley, George Christie, Trevor Nunn. And Morecambe and Wise.

It was two and a half hours of tramping round the great reception rooms, eating bits of Lyons pâté, drinking over-sweet warm white wine, everyone looking at everyone else, and that atmosphere of jocular ruthlessness which characterises the Establishment on its nights out. Wonderful paintings, of course, and I was shown the bullet that killed Nelson.

As we were presented, the Queen asked me when the National Theatre would open. I said I didn't know. The Duke asked me when the National Theatre would open. I said I didn't know. The Queen Mother asked me when the National Theatre would open. I said I didn't know. The Prince of Wales asked me when the National Theatre would open. I said I didn't know. At least they all knew I was running the National Theatre.

Home by 2 am with very aching feet. Who'd be a courtier?

Thursday 13 February
To the Dorchester for the McAlpine lunch. Alistair McAlpine looked at me rather as if I was a bomb that might go off. I was extremely charming to him.

Friday 14 February
Saw a run-through of *Heartbreak House*. Very promising. Fine cast, fine play. The performances are original; the play is well revealed.

It's the only Shaw play I really enjoy. I think I persuaded John[1] to do

---

[1] John Schlesinger. This was his first production for the NT, and about to open at the Old Vic.

some more cuts. I hope I also persuaded him that the madness and emotion should be greater in the second act—particularly after the burglary. Once something odd has happened, people's adrenalin remains high. They want to talk, to drink, to dispute. One thing is certain from this afternoon, Kate Nelligan[1] is a star. Absolutely no doubt about it.

Saturday 15 February
Absolutely exhausted. Stayed in bed most of the day stunned and miserable. I can't remember when I last felt so inadequate.

Monday 17 February
Spent most of the day getting my nose into *Tamburlaine*, my next production.

Took Edward to Oxford to look for some model electric cars. He gave me a long appreciative lecture about my abilities and how hard I worked. He also revealed how much he wished he could see me more often, which made me feel very guilty.

Tuesday 18 February
Hard work on *Tamburlaine*. I begin to understand it. I want to try it as a popular cartoon form of theatre, the actors discussing moral dilemmas *directly* with the audience. Each scene could have a strong emblem: a shepherd turning into a warrior; a scarlet banquet; three crowns carried onto the battlefield. All this to look like a stained glass window or a picture book cartoon, and expressed in strong emotional rhetoric. More Italian than British. Get away from the wit, the cool and the intellect, to something more passionate and exposed. More balls.

The text cutting process is working quite well. I must be careful, though. It is easy enough to reduce, but what you're left with can become monotonous, strident and naive.

Spoke to Larry on the phone. His voice was an octave higher and he sounded very odd, very abstracted. He said he was worried about me doing *Aquarius*. I did my usual patter about only presenting it. He did not seem reassured. He sounded vague and another person. It was a disturbing phone call.

Saturday 22 February
To Wallingford early this morning. Very tired again. How am I to protect myself from myself? I need to work at what is inside my head rather than distracting myself all the time. Otherwise I shall never do anything decent in the theatre.

[1] Who played Ellie Dunn.

Monday 24 February
Letter awaiting me at the office that Jonathan has resigned. I am in a way
very relieved. I shouldn't be surprised though if it will not provoke resignations from Blakemore and, if he can think of a way, Larry.

Tuesday 25 February
A depressing meeting on *Akenfield*. We have eleven cinema bookings in the
regions but no money to finance publicity. And the film is coming off from
the Paris Pullman on 15 March where the business has dropped completely.
Is it because everyone saw it on television?

Peg revealed she had seen Larry at Brighton on Sunday. The most
appalling thing is that a virus has attacked the muscles of his throat. For
some time they had to feed him intravenously, as the muscles for swallowing
were affected. Dreadful that a man who has spent all his life getting the last
note out of his voice should now find that his vocal cords are affected.
Hence the high voice I heard on the phone last week that worried me.

Wednesday 26 February
Excellent notices for *Heartbreak House*. They've seen what John was getting
at. I admire the production because it has revealed the heart of what is
probably Shaw's only truly emotional play. The set suffers from a decorated
restlessness, and lacks a feeling of the heart of Sussex, the green English
countryside, seductive and condemned to death. But that's a minor point in
an excellent achievement. Wild generalisations are being made: the
National is itself again, it's better than anything else. What has actually
happened is that we have had two hits after a succession of flops.

I have been asked, will I make two commercials to aid recruitment for the
Navy? I am, they know after *Akenfield*, so good with improvising with real
people. Would I do it with real seamen? Well, I might....

Thursday 27 February
Peter Stevens picked me up and we went over to the Minister. We had to
pick our way into the building through Fringe demonstrations. They are
lobbying for another million pounds so that they can pay their actors the
Equity minimum.

Fairly good meeting. The civil servants made a few ritualistic remarks
about the high cost of running the building. How could this be, they said?
Why wasn't it known? I said it must have been known because the DES is
funding the South Bank Board who, unlike the NT Board, are responsible
for actually building and designing the new theatre. I had the feeling they
were appalled by the money but fairly clear they had to do something to get
us in.

150

Sunday 2 March
Long talk with Michael Blakemore. I tried to draw him on Jonathan. He wouldn't be. He said he thought the trouble went back to when I didn't give Jonathan another production on top of *The Freeway*[1]. I said the trouble went further back, to when the associates expressed doubts about his wish to do an all-male *Importance of Being Earnest*.

Wednesday 5 March
Akenfield has done badly in the cinemas it has been to in the regions. Clearly there is no filmgoing public for it. The television experiment[2] hasn't worked.

To the NFT to see John Schlesinger's *Day of the Locust*. I find it difficult to write about this experience. The words 'like' or 'enjoy' do not apply. Schlesinger is now a complete master as a film director. There is a feeling for the medium in this work which I think is unrivalled. He has a perceptive and merciless eye, and he also has a definite personality: sceptical, ironic, and harsh. The picture is compulsive and it hypnotises you with its horror. I resisted it strongly but failed and was finally very, very upset. I wanted to rush out and make love and celebrate life.

Thursday 6 March
Emergency meeting at the Arts Council. Rayne has rightly responded strongly against the proposal, mentioned by Patrick Gibson a month ago, of an Arts Council enquiry into the likely costs of the National Theatre when it's on the South Bank. We sat there for two hours arguing. I said, let the enquiry, if it must happen, test and prove our figures on my policy. If the government won't give the money for this then let them be asked what money they will give. In the light of that figure we will formulate a new policy, if we can. I was very angry. So was Max. The danger is that those enquiring are almost certain to favour a small repertoire, inadequately staffed—and this would not allow the building to flourish. It would then look unproductive and thus absurdly expensive.

Gibson was on our side. Hugh Willatt was full of regrets but informed us that the Arts Council insisted on the enquiry. Angus Stirling[3] said we're not going to get the money we need to run on the South Bank unless there *is* an enquiry.

Why should we be enquired into, and possibly abused in public, for

---

[1] It had opened at the Old Vic in October 1974 to a poor press.
[2] The experiment of televising *Akenfield* country-wide before the film was released in the regions (and at the same time as its cinema showing in London). Normally, a film is televised well after its release to the cinemas.
[3] Deputy Secretary-General of the Arts Council 1971–79.

something we've not yet had a chance of doing? Shall I resign? No. I think I will dig my heels in and just be as dogged as possible and do what I want to do with the National in the meantime.

Monday 10 March
I reflected tonight on our plight at the National Theatre. Who wants the National Theatre at this point? The government don't because they have insufficient money for all the claims upon them. The Arts Council don't because they have not included us for extra amounts in their budgets. The media don't want us because it is very good news in this time of austerity and increasing puritanism that a £14 million temple of fun is a mistake and an aberration. The profession don't want us because they are fearful. So who does want us? Just us, I am afraid, and so it will continue until we actually get into the building and prove what it's for.

Tuesday 11 March
Worked early this morning. I must say I'm finding the psychological strain of rehearsing *No Man's Land* during the day and dress rehearsing *Happy Days* in the evening fairly unbearable.

Thursday 13 March
First night of *Happy Days*. Peg did well. The second act was marvellous. Pleasant supper afterwards: Michael Birkett and Maximilian Schell toasting Peggy. We spoke a good deal about the Horváth play *Tales from the Vienna Woods*[1] which Max is to direct for us.

Friday 14 March
Harold came to a run-through of *No Man's Land*. It wasn't bad. Gielgud in his wig for the first time: an extraordinary lank grey and sandy number, that makes him look—rightly—like a sad and dreadful creep.

Brief chat with Harold about the run-through. Then he got on to what really concerned him. He was wildly and happily in love, he said. He also said he had always resolved to be utterly frank with Vivien[2] but hadn't told her yet because she had been ill. I didn't ask who the lady was, or what Harold thought would happen when he did tell Vivien. I should think the explosion will be heard the other side of Regent's Park. But he certainly was jubilantly happy, and not terribly interested in his play, which I found endearing.

---

[1] *Geschichten aus dem Wienerwald* by Ödön von Horváth, translated by Christopher Hampton.

[2] The actress Vivien Merchant, Pinter's wife, who died in 1982.

Saturday 15 March
Phone call from America this morning: *Akenfield* has been very well received there, wonderful notices. But no distributor wants to take it on. They admire it, but it's not commercial.

Dreadful dream. My mother and father and I were looking at coffins, and selecting my father's for he had agreed to die that afternoon. Mother was in a frightful temper because the visit to the coffin-makers was so inconvenient she found it extremely inconvenient of father to decide to die on this particular afternoon. Father was, as ever, cheerful about the whole proceeding and accepting it with a good grace.

Considerable feeling of distress today as if I have been through some long physical disaster. I begin to think what is the point of working at this pressure and putting up with all the shit about the National Theatre. I have only 2½ more years of my contract to run so I shall be getting the new building open for somebody else to use. Is it worth it?

Sunday 16 March
The *Happy Days* notices are good, though there is a piece in the *Sunday Telegraph* about the rocketing costs of the National Theatre.

Long talk with David Brierley on the telephone. He believes the RSC may not have the funds to go on at the Aldwych after the autumn. One thing is certain: we musn't expand into the new building if at the same moment the RSC is shutting up shop at the Aldwych.

An interesting story told about Harold Wilson. Some eighteen months ago he came to see *Front Page* at the Vic. Mary Wilson was delighted because she loves the theatre; he doesn't. The only thing he said afterwards was that the poster up in the set urging the American people to vote for Coolidge was inaccurate: the election was not in the year of the play.

Thursday 20 March
We were talking about Jonathan at the associates' lunch. Michael Blakemore told an extraordinary story I had heard before, but not in detail. Jonathan gave an interview about Larry for Logan Gourlay's book,[1] and spoke freely as is his wont. He was sent the typescript of what he had said; also, later, a galley proof; and never commented on either. But when the book was in page-proof, and about to go press, a number of people read it, and it reached Joan Plowright who rang up Jonathan in great distress asking him if he realised what he had done. He was then appalled, and ended up by paying £700 of his own money to remove his entire interview from the book.

[1] *Olivier* edited by Logan Gourlay.

Saturday 22 March

I read *The Double Dealer* today. I don't understand the myth that it is difficult to bring off. It seems to be more clearly plotted, more vigorous, than anything else in Congreve and certainly more worthwhile than *The Way of the World*.

An hour on the phone with Harold this morning about *No Man's Land*. I have never done a play with him and seen so little of him. Love.

Monday 23 March

Last Tuesday Harold went to see Peggy and told her he was in love with Antonia Fraser. He also said he would have to tell Vivien, and that he was anxious above everything else that his marriage should not break up. Today Harold phoned Peg to say he'd told Vivien, who had, he said, taken it surprisingly well. I believe that by doing this he may be able to save his marriage. But I feel uneasy about his state. And also very uneasy about Vivien. Apparently the Antonia Fraser romance began some six weeks ago. Since when, it has raged passionately.

Monday 24 March

A vast article by Jack Lambert in *The Sunday Times*, headed 'Requiem for British Theatre', is causing some comment around the place today. It's over-stated—predicting 'the imminent collapse of our flourishing post-war artistic renaissance'—but rings a depressingly true note.

Peter Brook rang during the evening. He was very complimentary about *Akenfield*, though he rapidly moved into areas of philosophical thought about it which I didn't quite understand. He found the film a revolutionary attempt to go on to new ground, a mosaic, but with deliberately little dramatic tension.

We spoke of the new RSC *Macbeth*. Both of us were disappointed by it. Peter said there is a new kind of Shakespearean cliché which is not naturalism, method, or old style rant-and-boom. Each actor brings the part to himself and to his own problems, his own character, and devil take Shakespeare or Shakespeare's demands. So Brook feels that Nicol Williamson is not playing Macbeth, he's examining certain tendencies within himself.

Tuesday 25 March

Finance and general purposes committee this afternoon. Dick Linklater[1], there for the Arts Council, wondered 'Was it time to resurrect the idea of the RSC sharing the building?' And at a dinner party tonight with Jeremy Hutchinson[2], Peg's ex-husband and an old friend from years past, I men-

[1] Drama Director of the Arts Council 1970–77.
[2] Lord Hutchinson, the barrister.

tioned to Patrick Gibson that Linklater had raised this. Gibson looked startled, and said Linklater was speaking as an individual only, but what did I think? I said I thought that if a sharing of the building for the next three years saved £600,000 or £700,000 and could be effected without detriment to either organisation, we should be hard put to it not to do it.

Gibson looked thoughtful. He told me he'd had dinner at No 10 a few days ago and asked the PM if he knew the National Theatre was nearing completion, but as yet there was no money to run it. At which Wilson, startled apparently, said he had no idea things were in such a state. Gibson begged him to look into it.

Wednesday 26 March
Meeting at LWT about the failure of *Akenfield* in the cinemas. Cyril[1] in the chair. LWT is to take over the whole thing, and distribute it worldwide for television and cinema. In the meantime, the complicated debts position is to be worked out. Cyril was marvellous. There is real hope now of salvaging a mess and making possible earnings in the future for the people who made the picture.

Thursday 27 March
Train to Nottingham to see Trevor Griffiths's *Comedians*[2]: magnificent. I have liked Trevor's previous plays—*Occupations* and *The Party*—but they were cerebral, political, challenging the audience intellectually. This play fucks them; it achieves a full human congress with them. It is terrific.

The idea is original: a class to turn working lads into comics given by an old wise comedian who knows about truth and falsehood. There's only one problem with the play. In the third act, it is revealed what has made the comedian what he is; why he has not pursued his career, why he is so careful. It appears that he'd visited Buchenwald after the war. Now I don't think this will do. It is, to quote a memorable phrase about the Dirk Bogarde film *The Night Porter*, 'bumming a free ride on the gas chambers'.

A packed house and a really excellent production by Richard Eyre. Something occurred tonight between audience and actors.

Tuesday 1 April
Quite a good morning on *No Man's Land*. Norman Claridge, Ralph's understudy, stood in for him because he's got a fever. Norman did the big fall with over-exuberance, broke his glasses, broke his deaf aid, and drew blood on his head: good work though. Gielgud on form.

[1] Bennett.
[2] Presented by Nottingham Playhouse. The production was later brought to the Old Vic by the NT, and then moved to the West End.

Lunch with Peter Stevens to talk about the Arts Council enquiry. Things are better. They have commissioned an independent firm of city accountants, Peat Marwick, to look at the problems of the South Bank, our establishment there on my policy, and the costing for it. I am relieved. Done in this way I suppose the enquiry could be helpful.

To LWT to meet the *Aquarius* team. We discussed various ideas[1]: a film about John Makepeace and his hand-crafted furniture workshops; a possible trip to Paris to talk to Brook; and a visit to the theatre at Epidaurus, to some extent the inspiration for the Olivier, with Denys Lasdun. I left the meeting feeling vaguely elated, but also uneasy. There is going to be a lot of commitment.

Wednesday 2 April

To Hornchurch to open the new theatre there. A loquacious driver: 'Haven't they knocked down the Old Vic yet now you're going to your new place? It'll be scheduled for demolition surely?'

Reception at the town hall. In a biting April wind, I said a few words outside the theatre and the steel plaque which recorded I had opened it was unveiled. Then onto the stage. The mayor, a lady, introduced me informally and speedily. I made a short speech, got a big laugh at the beginning and was alright. The chairman of the trust thanked everybody, especially me, continually reminding his audience what a frightfully busy man I was and what an utterly modest man I was. I suspect it's the modesty that hides conceit. . . .

The opening performance was *Joseph and his Amazing Technicolour Dreamcoat*: camp, good melodies, slightly naughty for the Mums, slightly rock for the youngs. Tumultuous applause at the end. The evening was a success. I fled as quickly as possible, and managed to get back to London quite early. But I am glad I did it. It is another excellent new theatre.

Thursday 3 April

Associates' lunch. Harold threw open to the meeting his use of the word 'unscrupulous' in a speech of Spooner's in *No Man's Land*: '. . . The present is truly unscrupulous. I am a poet. I am interested in where I am eternally present and active.'

Harold says he chose the word unscrupulous because it shows the ruthlessness of the present, and its ability to lead as it were a life of its own. His sense is simply 'the present will not be changed' and I wish he would say that instead of 'the present is truly unscrupulous'. The associates threw words at Harold as if we were all mad crossword addicts. He went off to think.

[1] Hall had finally decided to front *Aquarius* for the series starting that autumn.

Desperate news late this afternoon. Mary Ure opened in a play in London last night and this morning was discovered dead in her bed. The rumour is that she had been drinking and took sleeping pills. She choked to death. Poor Bob Shaw[1]. And the eight children.

Friday 4 April

I ran across a wonderful quotation from a book by Mervyn Peake called *How to Draw*. It is sound advice for anyone working in the arts: 'It is for you to leave the spectator no option but to see what you liked; the curves or the jaggednesses; the outline shape or the shadowy patterns. . . whatever it may have been, the drawing must be about that—your choice; give him none.'

Round the South Bank early this morning. The Olivier continues to excite and the Lyttelton is nearly finished. The furniture, the carpets, the lights, the heating are all ready in the offices. Great feeling of lassitude about the place, though.

An hour and a half with the two inquisitors from Peat Marwick. Both intelligent, both, I felt, on our side and outraged that a building of this size should be put up by the government with no provision for its running costs. I talked too much, covered the main points, and probably tried to impress overmuch.

Monday 7 April

Rehearsing *No Man's Land* on the set for the first time, using the stage of the Royalty Theatre. The heating is off. The auditorium is freezing. Slight shock at first seeing the set: no proper lighting, no proper props, and therefore a slight lack of specific character. The shape is good though. I worked through all the problems with doors, drinks, glasses, etc. The Old Lions were in fine form.

Run-through this afternoon. Ralph was wonderful: absolutely creative, and making Hirst (one of the most difficult parts Pinter has ever written) crystal clear. John was hesitant and humble. At the moment he is inclined to play what the audience should conclude about the character rather than the character himself. Spooner is the proudest and most arrogant man you can imagine. If he ever plays humbly all the conflict has gone.

Tuesday 8 April

Breakfast with Harold Pinter. Much discussion about the play. After interminable conversation we came up with the line 'The present will not be distorted' instead of 'The present is truly unscrupulous'. The meaning is at least clear. And that is what we need at that point where the writing is very dense and the speaker of the line very show-off.

[1] The actor and writer Robert Shaw, then Mary Ure's husband.

A fair morning's rehearsal. I am a little worried about John. He's over-experimenting: playing it humble, playing it conceited, playing it creepy, playing it arrogant. It is a search for the simple key. Whereas the truth is that Spooner is many things and changes his posture from second to second. So there isn't a simple key.

Run-through this afternoon in costume: Gielgud's appearance is a triumph; Ralph's too. I talked to Harold afterwards and said I found the pauses less potent in this play than in his others. If over-stretched they made the whole thing very portentous. He said this was because *The Homecoming* and *Old Times* were primarily about sex and the pauses therefore reverberated with half meanings and suggested meanings. The pauses in *No Man's Land* are much more clearly a matter of threat and of tension, as in *The Caretaker*.

Wednesday 9 April
Good afternoon with John. I asked him to play Spooner as somebody hard, tough, and arrogant, the contrary of the visual image he presents. He doesn't need to play a failure, a creep; his appearance shows he is.

Thursday 10 April
An excellent day's rehearsal. There was of course no Ralph. He was busy yesterday and today playing *Borkman*. But I worked very hard with Gielgud, and with Micky Feast and Terry Rigby. Today John really broke through and became an arrogant and unpleasant man. I hope the unpleasantness will stay. He must not soften with the audience. Feast is taking off into a cold and remarkable performance.

Monday 14 April
More dreadful news following Mary Ure's death. Buzz Goodbody[1] has committed suicide. I hardly knew her. She was just after my time at the RSC. But she was so young and clearly very talented. There seems to be a spirit of destructiveness in the air at the moment.

John Gielgud's seventy-first birthday, so before our *No Man's Land* dress rehearsal there was champagne for the cast. At the rehearsal John was magnificent. He has it. I hope to Christ he keeps it.

Wednesday 16 April
First preview of *No Man's Land*. We had an initial twenty minutes of pure gold. The laughs came in the right place, the story was clear, Gielgud was in command. Then suddenly a section lost its edge and the narrative tension slackened. By the time Micky and Terry came on the play was dead and it

---

[1] The director.

remained dead for the rest of the evening. Pinter's plays are like very delicately balanced piles of building blocks. If one falls out, the whole bloody thing collapses.

Ralph very funny in his dressing room after. He said he didn't like his acting tonight. He knew where the ducks were but he'd fired at them either too late or too early. He'd taken off the occasional tail feather, but brought none down. John was also self-critical but aware he was getting nearer the shape of the part.

Thursday 17 April
Spent the morning in bed reading Michael Kustow's book *Tank*. Heavily influenced by Mailer, he writes a fact/fiction account of his life and particularly his years at the ICA. The key is a quote from Karl Kraus in the front: 'K has made a portrait of me; it could be that those who know me will not recognise me; but surely those who don't know me will recognise me.' Well, I don't completely recognise Mike.

I admire his amazing candour, which is American/Jewish/European, certainly not English. He tells all: his background, his sexual hangups, his thwarted ambitions. But he is not indulgent, not sentimental. And if anyone wants to discover what it felt like to live in London in the late sixties and be involved in the artistic hurly-burly, this book is a very good guide.

Interesting, though, is the number of voices in the book. Whenever Mike comes to an important subject, he flexes his metaphorical muscles and overwrites like hell. But sometimes the voice is even, simple, ironic, and shrewd. That is the man I like. And that is the writer. But then, the faults are what make the book moving.

At rehearsal this afternoon John asked Harold what the Briggs/Spooner scene was for at the beginning of Act II. What did it give the audience? What did it convey? Harold paused. 'I'm afraid I cannot answer questions like that, John. My work is just what it is. I am sorry.'

Saturday 19 April
Rumours are rife at the National that a big union confrontation is bound to come before long. Our NATTKE agreement has to be renegotiated for the South Bank, and Kon Fredericks is already teeing up his men.

Wednesday 23 April
The day of the Pinter first night. Spent some of it hanging pictures, moving furniture, and sorting out the flat: there is a party tonight.

In the theatre, Harold asked me before the play began to stick close to him. The *Daily Mail* has been ringing him and Antonia Fraser all day. If a reporter came up to him he would hit him, he said. 'You must remember my Portuguese blood.'

The performance of *No Man's Land* was our best: sharp, confident and precise. At our party afterwards John said to Harold that playing Pinter was like playing Congreve or Wilde. It needed a consciousness of the audience, a manipulation of them which was precisely the same as for high classical comedy. He thought it would be like playing Chekhov—where you must ignore the audience—but it wasn't. He's damned right.

Harold was last to leave the party. He said Vivien was now back, but he was doubtful they would stay together. The only thing he was certain of was his relationship with Antonia.

Thursday 24 April

The press for *No Man's Land* is good but careful. And maddeningly patronising: 'Surely not one of his best plays'; 'the Pinter puzzle'; 'the Pinter enigma'. None of them actually gets to grips with what the play means; indeed two, Wardle and Billington, get it wrong. They both declare that Spooner and Hirst knew each other at Oxford. The point is they didn't; they pretend they did as a weapon. The audience never make this mistake. If they did they wouldn't laugh.

But we have another success. The Old Lions are pleased. John's performance is magnificent, but there are other actors who could do it, whereas I do not think any other actor could fill Hirst with such a sense of loneliness and creativity as Ralph does.

Saturday 26 April

A quiet morning. Then to Paris, trying to collect my thoughts on Brook, whom I'm to interview for *Aquarius*. He is the man I know best and least among my professional colleagues; the closest friend, the coldest and the warmest.

Saw his production of *The Ik* at his Les Bouffes du Nord theatre, performed by his group, many of whom have been with him to Persia and Africa. The Ik is a tribe who, under the pressure of starvation, distort all forms of social behaviour: truth, family feelings, affection, pride, honour —everything is reversed. But we see the play through the eyes of Turnbull, the anthropologist, and unfortunately he emerges as a conventional Englishman abroad figure, a bit of a fool, and therefore the play's themes are simplified.

Sidelights on the nature of the company's life: they have no stage management, no stage staff, no technicians; and every actor is responsible for his own props and for his own transport. There is no bureaucracy or set working hours, and of course no unions.

All last week the group were away in a hideous new town some miles away from Paris doing improvisations and shows in schools, homes for delinquents, hospitals, etc. Is this forcing of the actor back into the community a

160

help to refresh his craft? Or a hope to change the community? Peter will not answer. He always answers every question with another question.

Sunday 27 April
Paris: One of the longest pauses I have ever heard in a conversation occurred last night when Michael Kustow, here to research for *Aquarius*, asked Brook what kind of actor he was looking for for his group. We all sat rivetted, watching him work it out. Small hands moved round, cutting patterns in the air. He removed two pieces of hard rice from his mouth, and replaced them on the plate of African spices. He then hesitantly began to answer the question. He wanted actors whose main motivation was not being actors. Acting for them was a means to an end. Well, what was the end? Social? Political? Aesthetic? Challenged, he came down to a mystical endorsement of truth: within the theatre truth burns between performer and audience.

Doing the television interview, I tried to be relaxed and to encourage Peter to talk. This is never a problem, but I wanted to make him simple, immediate and funny. I didn't want him to be the guru. After a short time I think it worked. We filmed some two hours of material and he said some wonderful things. I asked, why did he work as he did? He blushed and said because he liked it. He directed because he would not be happy if he wasn't directing. It was instinctive.

Paris looked beautiful this evening, low sun magnifying the buildings. Always femininely elegant, it is now prosperous and clean. By contrast, London is collapsing. But I have never been happy in Paris—all Leslie's *haut bourgeois* relations. I also always feel somewhat frightened abroad, uneasy. It's partly not being sure of the language, partly because I have never got over my terror of going out into the streets or into a shop alone. I prefer to hide. France and the French have always brought out a great inferiority complex in me. They are so noisy, so confident, so superior. And they speak French.

Sunday press of the Pinter good. But I still find myself depressed by the critics' inability to recognise the masterly way his talent is developing. Is the play that difficult? I can't believe it. Should the production have been more overt? I can't believe that either. Perhaps they simply do not trust themselves to respond emotionally.

Back to London this evening.

Monday 28 April
Spoke to Harold. He was at that very moment packed and about to leave home: 'The point is, I am at this moment leaving my home. I am leaving my house.' It is a tough business for him. He told me that whatever happened he thought that he and Vivien were now through.

Tuesday 29 April

Spoke to Hugh Willatt this afternoon because Peter Stevens has discovered the Peat Marwick enquiry people are reporting to a special sub- committee at the Arts Council which contains not only the Council's administrators but also some part-time members of the Council who are known to be not particularly sympathetic to the National. Willatt assured me that those we objected to were only advising. It would be a Peat Marwick enquiry, *not* an Arts Council enquiry; Council members would not influence the findings.

Well, if the report does not go our way, we will point out that the enquiry was influenced by prejudiced outsiders. Quite a useful card I think.

Friday 2 May

Quick visit to the Hayward Gallery to see an exhibition of British photographs: beautiful and extraordinary images, but a sadness, simply because these are not records of man's imagination—which is somehow indomitable in art, because it defeats time—but records of living people who have long since passed away.

Amazing to see how few advances there have been in photography. There are nineteenth-century action photographs with waves hanging immobile before they break, and hidden camera shots trained on unsuspecting people in a Salford market.

Tuesday 6 May

To the ICA tonight to see *Fanshen*, a play by David Hare based on a book[1] about twenty years in a Chinese village after the war. It's beautifully and lucidly performed by some very good young actors under the direction of Bill Gaskill and Max Stafford-Clark. It is also cunningly constructed, though a little aesthetic. I felt as if my soul had been laundered by the end. It is a thoroughly political play: undogmatic, exposing its ironies, but somehow never quite exposing them enough. Marxism is criticised but not routed. And I found the finish, where the girl dreamed of the revolutionaries waiting to come down from the hills, unbearably sentimental. Brecht managed to make characters in didactic political plays come to life through human inconsistency. However hard he tried not to, he always wrote about human beings. David Hare has not written about human beings. An excellent evening though, that I wouldn't have missed for the world.

Wednesday 7 May

To the Arts Council for an emergency meeting about our subsidy on the South Bank. There was the usual Arts Council debate. 'We quite see you want an extra £900,000; but surely you can do something with £600,000. It's

[1] *Fanshen* by Willian Hinton.

a lot of money.' But I know if we go into the new building under-subsidised we shall not be able to do the work and we shall be criticised for being the most expensive inadequate theatre in the kingdom.

Conversation with Rayne and Peter Stevens after the meeting. Rayne tells of a growing relationship with Denis Healey[1]. There are plans in a few weeks to show Healey the building and then have a private lunch. I hope we can achieve this before the country founders on the rocks. . . .

Rayne feels we should try to quieten down the press, discourage comment, about our need for more money. He didn't actually charge me with whipping up the present campaign in the papers[2]; he didn't quite have the nerve. I sat and smiled. He would not be able to pressure Denis Healey if there hadn't been a press campaign.

Saturday 10 May
A melancholy feeling today. It has been said to me quite a few times that I have proved a working-class boy can make it, can live among fine objects, and in expensive surroundings; now I should stop this nonsense and get on with living. This goes home. I have to get back to reality. I am over-extended. I work hard to earn money in order to have environments which I never have time to enjoy. Standard lunacy.

Wednesday 14 May
Early conversation with Albert[3] on the phone. He's saying yes to *Hamlet* as well as *Tamburlaine*, me directing. I can't say I have an overwhelming passion to do *Hamlet* again as a director, but I would like to see Albie play the part.

News that Ted Willis[4] is raising, in an arts debate in the Lords this afternoon, the question of me dividing my time between the National Theatre and *Aquarius*. I wonder what I have ever done to Ted Willis? It's all absolute nonsense. When Larry spent 48 days of one year narrating the Second World War television series[5] there were no questions in Parliament.

Thursday 15 May
The Guardian and *The Times* report Willis in the Lords, no other papers. The only trouble is that from now on the press will refer to my appearances

---

[1] Chancellor of the Exchequer 1974–79.
[2] Many major articles were appearing in the national press at this time, expressing concern at the NT's lack of sufficient government funding which, together with the unfinished state of the building, could delay still further the opening on the South Bank.
[3] Finney.   [4] The playwright. Created Baron 1963.
[5] *The World At War*, a Thames Television series shown in 1973.

in *Aquarius* as 'controversial'. It only needs one mixer to fix the label on any situation.

Went to half of *Love's Labour's Lost* tonight at the Aldwych—the second half because I wasn't able to leave the office in time for the first. To my surprise John Barton was there, seeing it again, and waving my ticket.

The production got universally favourable notices: Shakespeare as it should be done. In fact, it was Shakespeare as it was done twenty years ago. And one would think that by now the RSC could actually get the text right; I mean, say the right words. John Barton and I stiffened in horror. We sat there together, two bearded, tense figures of disapproval in an audience rocking with laughter. I do think it a beautiful play though.

Saturday 17 May
Left London for Athens this afternoon to do an *Aquarius* programme: Denys Lasdun at the theatre of Epidaurus which partly inspired the National's Olivier auditorium. I dumped my luggage at the hotel, was not allowed time to find my room, but was whisked straight off for drinks with Doxiardes, the Greek architect, at his apartment high up above the roofs of Athens. And there straight out from his terrace, at the same level, was the Acropolis—the first time I'd seen it: a wonderful experience.

Sunday 18 May
Athens: Wonderful morning at the Acropolis with Denys. I can't think of a better companion—a great architect describing great architecture. He pointed out all the various geometric anomalies. It is supposed to be the purest classical building in existence, yet the geometry is all the time humanised, bent as it were into impure life. The pillars are not entirely vertical: they lean in a little. The sides are not exactly straight: they curve.

I don't normally like ruins. But there is enough left of the Acropolis to feel what it was like. And one can study all the marvellous detail, the extraordinary, weathered marble. Perhaps it is age and time which make it so wonderful. Would I have liked it all new when it was shining in bright colours? Perhaps not. But now, worn into the landscape and trodden by centuries of feet, there is something inescapably moving about it. I thought of Byron coming here. And of Virgina Woolf. And of a host of others.

The place was packed. The thing I shall remember longest is the patterns the brightly coloured people made among the white marble. The natural patterns made by crowds always move me very much. If I'd picked up a loud hailer and asked them to stand in various places in order to film them everything would have been lost. Each group was composed naturally out of the preoccupations of its members. And each group's preoccupations were different.

Drive to Patre to see a concert by Theodorakis. I sat in the back of the car with Denys and Sue[1], and we talked and talked, mainly about the National Theatre. Sue spoke of what a strain it had been for twelve years of their life: the designing, all the fights for the money, and all the fights ever since. The children had grown up to hate the building, and would ask on weekends in the country, 'Please can we not talk about the National Theatre this weekend?'

Monday 19 May
My first introduction to the great theatre at Epidaurus. I was overwhelmed by it. The whole day was unforgettable. It's exactly as if someone had said to me, 'The Globe has after all been preserved on the South Bank, come over and have a look at it, then you might understand something about staging Shakespeare.' For here is a Greek theatre, and a masterpiece of architecture as well. Yesterday the Roman theatre by the Acropolis had left me cold: a brutal confrontation, the audience looking at the performers as their victims. But here, in a Greek theatre, everything grows out of the landscape. The first impression is one of intimacy, yet it holds 15,000 people. The second is one of perfect, simple geometry, yet every geometric calculation is slightly altered in the interest of grace and of humanity. Most extraordinary of all is the way the auditorium grows out of the hillside and, as you sit in it, seems to continue into the landscape, making a whole world of which the spectator feels a part. Why did they site it here? Because for the Greeks the landscape was alive, and full of gods who had a positive relationship with man. It is interesting to make a comparison with the Romans. They were engineers; like us they could move mountains. A Roman road cuts straight through the landscape, indifferent to its form. A Greek road is sensitive to the landscape, sensitive to its gods. So are their theatres.

We filmed all day. I uneasily shot my first trailer and, glazedly looking at the camera, said that *Aquarius* this week is in Epidaurus. What a joke. . . .

What curious work, though, today's Greeks do in this holy place — holy because it is the beginning of drama. I saw photos of their performances: artificially lit, yet here is the perfect theatre for daylight, with the hillside pouring into the auditorium. I long to do a play here: with nothing, and with daylight. But, say the Greeks, it is too hot. Well, too hot in July and August, when they have the festival, but originally Greek theatres were built to operate in the spring, in March and April. In ancient times, too, an enormous number of people lived near Epidaurus—enough to fill the whole auditorium. Now they motor from Athens—a $2\frac{1}{2}$ hour drive and only possible at weekends—to see scenic theatre in artificial light where the dramatic act should be part of nature.

[1] Lasdun's wife.

But how wonderful it will be to do Greek plays in the Olivier. I think I know how. I found the day unbearably exciting[1].

Wednesday 21 May

Back on the lunchtime plane. Associates' dinner tonight. The talk was mainly about us and the RSC, for we are being asked by the Arts Council to cost the total savings to the two organisations if the RSC used the Lyttelton instead of the Aldwych. But David Brierley has told Peter Stevens that they will not accept Shakespeare only there, and that they are expecting the Lyttelton for twelve months of the year. All this makes me uneasy. I feel we have missed a trick. Is this what the RSC really want, or what the Arts Council really want? In no circumstance should we allow the RSC to have the Lyttelton all the time. We would have one theatre, and they—with Stratford—would have two.

Thursday 22 May

The Peat Marwick report arrived this afternoon. It gives us a clean bill of health. A great relief.

Rang Dick Linklater and warned him the National was not prepared to help save the RSC by giving them the Lyttelton for twelve months of the year. I said we would become a one-theatre operation in order to preserve our rivals as a two-theatre operation. He agreed that each of us should have 50% use of the Lyttelton and 50% use of the Cottesloe. I rang Trevor and persuaded him to come and have supper.

Dinner with Trevor. He said, and I understand, that his first duty must be to preserve the Aldwych. His second duty, if that fails, is to go for a creative relationship with the National Theatre. I said what worried me was that as he and I had not made up our minds about our strategy there was a considerable danger that both companies would drift around in a grey area and the Arts Council would push us into untenable artistic decisions by default.

Friday 23 May

Took Trevor round the South Bank. He said to me that if he and I were walking round the building this morning unconnected with it, surely we would say to ourselves: there is no organisation that can possibly take it on at the moment without being crucified by it. I tend to agree with him. The building seems to demand martyrs. And I am going to be very careful not to be one. I asked him if he thought the real future lay in some sort of

---

[1] Hall's NT production of Aeschylus's trilogy *The Oresteia* opened in the Olivier Theatre in November 1981, and in June 1982 was performed at Epidaurus. Hall wanted to do the play in daylight, with a 6 am start, but the Festival organisers persuaded him not to.

association between us. He said he thought it probably did; only by that could we get the strength to use the building to its full advantage. However our priorities remain the same. In this muddled time, let us first go for independence.

Sunday 25 May
Skimmed through *In Search of Christopher Marlowe* by Wraight and Stern, which has been on my shelves for years. The book glosses over one very important area: the question of whether or not Marlowe was homosexual. I am convinced that he was. The plays glitter with the sensual excitement of the young homosexual. I think there are few things more creative that the young homosexual sensibility—more perceptive, and more tender. Unfortunately in the case of most artists, certainly most actors, age and maturity bring no widening of experience; simply a great nostalgia for youth. So to generalise dangerously, for there are several famous exceptions, homosexual artists tend not to develop as they grow older.

The book was very useful though for my thinking on *Tamburlaine*. The inscription on the presumed portrait of the young Marlowe, discovered in the fifties, reads, 'Quod me nutrit me detruit'— 'that which nourishes me destroys me.' An excellent motto for *Tamburlaine*; and for Marlowe.

Monday 26 May
Bad news this morning. Alan Webb has tuberculosis—a small spot on one lung. He has to come out of the repertoire immediately and rest for two to three months. I rang him. In a way he seemed relieved. He now knows what all his illnesses have been for the last months.

Thursday 29 May
Rayne rang with appalling news. Willatt had phoned him and told him the grant to the National Theatre next year, its first on the South Bank, was to be £1 million. Max in extreme gloom, saying there was no point in going on and he might have to resign. I was stunned. I couldn't imagine what they thought we could do with £1 million—£100,000 more than at the Vic. How could we do anything in the new building with this figure? I rang Tony Field[1]. He was very surprised at my disappointment saying in all his years at the Arts Council he never remembered a tougher battle by the officials to get something through. It emerged the Arts Council was offering us £1 million *more* for the South Bank. . . .

With an Arts Council grant of £1.9 million and what we shall get from the

---

[1] Anthony Field, Finance Director of the Arts Council from 1970.

Peter Hall's Diaries

GLC, possibly £300,000 but unlikely to be more[1], we shall have a total subsidy of £2.2 million in our opening year. That is about £700,000 short of what we estimate we will need. But we shall have to accept, do what we can, and use the huge expense of running the building alone as a way to get more money later. Only 20% of the expenditure on the South Bank is to do with art or anything I can influence; 80% goes on inescapable charges.

Apparently the Arts Council is not able to offer the RSC anything like what they require in 1976/77, and so feel that if the two of us can help our financial problems by a certain amount of sharing of resources, it was up to us to work it out and decide what the sharing should be.

Friday 30 May
Boring hour and a half with John Elsom[2] who is completing the National Theatre book started by Nick Tomalin. Elsom droned on, mainly about himself, his own education, his own obsessions. I shall have to see him again though. I don't think he got anything new out of me, but he wasn't trying to.

The RSC is about to launch its campaign to save the Aldwych. Trevor is apparently writing a big piece in *The Sunday Times* next Sunday.

Saturday 31 May
Read Howard Brenton's new play *Weapons of Happiness* this afternoon, commissioned by us for the opening of the new building[3]. The end is not quite right, but it is very fine. He is a magnificent writer.

Watched on BBC2 a dreadful long compilation of film material on the war in Vietnam. The waste, the waste. Hundreds of thousands are dead for nothing; a five-year-old boy was shown in hospital crying, emasculated by a piece of shrapnel. The whole hideous story is intercut with the hypocritical optimism of the American statesmen from Kennedy onwards—a revolting experience. What could they do there? You cannot wage partial war. You can either win or get out. Vietnam is the great humiliation of the Americans and it deserves to be.

Monday 2 June
To Nottingham. A wearing hour and a half talking about the National Theatre to a mixed audience of school children, adult drama devotees, etc. An eighteen-year-old professional sceptic asked me by what right I exerted such power over the theatre. How often did I check myself? I said every

[1] In the event, the GLC 1976/77 grant was £350,000.
[2] At the time, drama critic of *The Listener*.
[3] A series of plays by leading dramatists was written for the opening of the NT. As well as *Weapons of Happiness*, these were: *Bedroom Farce* by Alan Ayckbourn, *State of Revolution* by Robert Bolt, *Watch It Come Down* by John Osborne, Pinter's *No Man's Land*, and *Strawberry Fields* by Stephen Poliakoff.

168

day. And meant it. It is the standard orthodoxy of the moment to believe that no one must be in charge. Well, it always has been the orthodoxy amongst the young. But now we all give credence to it.

Watched Tony Benn and Roy Jenkins on *Panorama*. Benn now has a crisp haircut and suits and ties to reassure the working class; he's Tony Benn too, not the Right Honourable Anthony Wedgewood Benn, and he is cold as ice and very, very dangerous. I warmed to Roy Jenkins who was emotionally vulnerable and sometimes incoherent with amazement at the dogmatic tenacity of Benn. God help us if the referendum goes against Europe.

Tuesday 3 June
To Weymouth for the Navy recruiting commercials I'm doing. One is set in a pub, so the three servicemen we choose for this must look over 21 otherwise we are corrupting the youth of Great Britain. But it emerges the Navy don't have many people over 21; it is very much a young man's service. My abiding impression though was how extraordinarily unworried and unflustered they all look. Whether we were dealing with the Commander or a seventeen-year-old apprentice, every Naval face is well-fed, well-rested, unalarmed and unanguished, quite different from the faces in civilian life.

Lunch among the nobs, with the man in charge, our host. I was asked why I was doing commercials. I told them it was for money, and for practice in using a camera. There's nothing like the truth.

David Brierley phoned to say the RSC now had their subsidy indication from the Arts Council. They will get £1.1 million next year. But there is no promise of anything to bail them out this year. So they are in exactly the same position as we; rather better in a way for their grant represents a doubling, and the cost of their buildings is nothing like the cost of the South Bank. But the interesting thing is that the grant is given subject to them maintaining a full-time presence in a London theatre. So the bogey of merging can now be sent away.

Thursday 5 June
Another horrible day. I started with Bernard Kimble. There seems to be no solution to my own financial problems except to sell Wallingford, to move my parents, or to live in some sort of different way in London. Three places to run, which is virtually what I am committed to, is beyond anyone but a millionaire. The most sensible course would be to leave the NT.

Friday 6 June
Marvellous June day. To Salisbury with Jacky and the children to lay the foundation stone of the new Playhouse there. Quite a lot of it is already built. They are six months ahead of schedule.... The theatre is a repeat

design of the Colchester theatre, an excellent house, and will only cost £600,000.

I did the usual ritualistic television interviews. The chairman made a speech. I made a speech. I put the foundation stone in place, gratified I must confess by my billing. The trumpeters played out of tune, the church padre gave a blessing, and then the TV crew asked me if I could lay the foundation stone again as they had a technical hitch. Reality these days is only on film. 'Do it once again for the camera.'

We went to the Cathedral. It is years since I have been inside it. I think of all Gothic cathedrals it moves me most. It is all of a piece; there are no strange additions from different years, different periods. It is pure, cool, well-proportioned English Gothic, very contained.

The common market referendum results are a two to one victory for staying in. I feel elated as I haven't done since 1945 when Labour was voted back. I think our hope for the future is that England remains a moderate country. But moderates are easily taken advantage of by extremists. Enoch Powell is nuts, but it is evident that he is nuts. Tony Benn is nuts, but appears dangerously sane.

Saturday 7 June
A cloudless day, hot, still and beautiful. I stayed outside all the time and swam, read, thought. Alan Ayckbourn's new play, *Bedroom Farce*, is wonderful, a bit of a masterpiece. Not only does reading it make me shout with laughter, it has a serious and true heart, like all good comedy. The play shows many facets of married life, and, among all the jokes, is very sad. I would love to direct it.

Monday 9 June
Fascinating interview in *Theatre Quarterly* with Howard Brenton: 'I want to get into bigger theatres, because they are, in a sense, more public. Until that happens you can't have any worth as a playwright. . . . It's like getting hold of a Bechstein, hitting a really superb instrument, when before you've been shouting about with a penny whistle or a mouth organ. You realise how powerful the new instrument is, and varied, and how much fun.

'I think the Fringe has failed. Its failure was that of the whole dream of an alternative culture, the notion that within society as it exists you can grow another way of life which, like a beneficient and desirable cancer, will in the end spread through the Western world and change it. What happens is the alternative society gets hermetically sealed and surrounded. A ghetto-like mentality develops which is surrounded and in the end strangled to death. . . . I think in that sense the Fringe was a historical thing. Where it went wrong was when the Fringe audiences became spuriously sophisticated. That was when it was time to get out—it was becoming arty.'

Thursday 12 June

The Sandersons photograph[1] was taken this afternoon, fairly painlessly. The shot did not look too nauseating; pleasant atmosphere. The Sandersons representative came in and changed the camera angle because he said there was an awful lot of Peter Hall but not enough of Sandersons' wallpaper. Money!

Saturday 14 June

Drove to Stratford with Edward to see the *Hamlet* which Buzz Goodbody directed at The Other Place—the old studio-cum-rehearsal room. A good evening. It was particularly pleasant to spend some time alone with Edward. The amazing thing about this *Hamlet*, one of the best I have ever seen, is its complete certainty and clarity. Clearly Buzz was coming into her own. Her suicide is a tragedy.

Ben Kingsley's performance is shrewd, ironic, perceptive, paranoid. He's not romantic in any sense. Because this was Shakespeare in a room, it could be quick, intimate, and flexible. And how good it made all the actors seem!

Edward endured magnificently. He followed every word and understood very well. I asked him if he found the language difficult. 'Not at all,' he replied, 'They used to talk like that, full of thees and thous.' When we came out he said, 'It's just a rotten old hut not a real theatre, all dirty and grotty. Yet it has better actors than you would find in London where they've got all those beautiful theatres.'

Monday 16 June

First rehearsal of the one-man monologue *Judgement*, by Barry Collins[2]. It is very fine: but harrowing even to sit and read. I think it could last up to three hours, and Colin Blakely will have difficulty getting the controlled rhetoric. The violence and misery inside the man is conditioned by the form of the words. It is beautifully balanced prose. I told Colin he should read a couple of sermons of John Donne to look for apposition and balance in the phrases. God knows if he'll be able to learn the play or if an audience will sit through it.

Incidentally, Barry told us the Royal Court had been running an anti-National Theatre campaign backstage last summer and had put all our bad notices on its notice board.

---

[1] Hall had agreed to be one of several celebrities who took part in an advertising campaign for Sanderson's wallpaper. The slogan was "Very Peter Hall, Very Sandersons," or "Very Kingsley Amis, Very Sandersons," and so on.

[2] Based on an incident in the Second World War when seven Russian officers were imprisoned and left locked up, forgotten. Two survived by eating the others. *Judgement* is an attempt by the survivor who remained sane to justify what he did.

Peter Hall's Diaries

Tuesday 17 June
Last night of *Borkman*. Ralph was magnificent, one of the greatest perform-ances I have seen. Peggy marvellous too. I was actually proud of my own work tonight. It doesn't happen very often. Miserable party afterwards: standing around in dressing rooms saying farewell and promising we shall all be together on the South Bank. I hope we will.

Saturday 21 June
Glyndebourne: A beautiful performance of Stravinsky's *The Rake's Prog-ress*. The evening was dominated by the designs of David Hockney. They were very beautiful and striking, and because there is a camp, parodistic element in his work, they were not overdone. I wouldn't like to see him let loose on a less eclectic opera.

Wonderful moment at the curtain: Haitink[1] looking like an attractive potato, a Van Gogh peasant's face, the tails ill-fitting his peasant's body, flanked on either side by a couple of exotics—John Cox[2] in frills, and Hockney in huge bow tie and white shoes, dyed blond hair, etc.

Tuesday 24 June
Jacky and I took Christopher to Sondheim's *A Little Night Music*. It is beautifully directed by Harold Prince. But I always have the same experi-ence with musicals. I feel full of anticipation and glee before going to them. Here, I think, will be an evening of delight, that makes no demands on me and is a celebration. And within five minutes, I am wondering what the hell I am doing in the theatre. Musicals do so patronise the audience.

This one is an example. The Bergman film *Smiles of a Summer's Night* is reduced to a corpse of elegance, wit and outrageousness. It's stylish enough to delight the middle class, and naughty enough (there are many jokes about underwear) to deliver the odd sexual frisson.

Jean Simmons is wonderful, a star performer. She alone is worth the admission money; nothing else. Sondheim's lyrics are witty, camp and brilliant, but his music is abysmal: turgid and perpetual $\frac{3}{4}$ and frantic $\frac{6}{8}$, then sudden daring chromaticisms to show the musical theatre has caught up with Richard Strauss.

Thursday 26 June
Long, hot planning meeting. Douglas Gosling[3] and Peter[4] told me that our deficit for this year, which we knew was £250,000, was now running at

---

[1] Bernard Haitink, Musical Director Glyndebourne from 1978.
[2] Director of Production at Glyndebourne 1971–81.
[3] NT Finance Administrator from 1974, and Secretary to the NT Board from 1975. Is an NT Associate.
[4] Stevens.

£350,000. This is almost entirely the cost of building up and maintaining a repertoire at the Old Vic big enough for the South Bank.

It's strange actually, my change in attitude towards the National. A year ago I wished I hadn't taken the job. Now, with even more reason for regretting it, I feel very stubborn. I'm going to sit it out until that bloody building is alive.

Saturday 28 June
Papers full this morning of Mrs Thatcher giving the V sign the wrong—ie the rude—way round. It's somehow typical of her. She may be bright, but she doesn't live in the world of the majority.

Got up at lunchtime and sat in the garden in the afternoon reading Tony Harrison's volume of translations of Palladas, the fourth-century AD Greek misanthrope. One couplet summed up my feelings at the moment about the National Theatre:

'I was promised a horse but what I got instead
Was a tail, with a horse hung from it almost dead.'

Sunday 29 June
Depressing news in the newspapers. The country drifts towards economic collapse, the pound plummets, the unions continue to make selfish noises, and Wilson survives by refusing to take positive action.

To Stratford this evening for a gala to raise money. It was an amazing trip down memory lane: Tony Quayle doing a piece of Falstaff, reviving memories of 25 years ago; Peggy doing beautifully a piece from the *Wars of the Roses* and upsetting me dreadfully; and Michael Redgrave, weak with Parkinson's disease, doing Lear's awakening to Cordelia. Redgrave has always been a favourite of mine. Tonight he was simple, direct, and very moving. I cried. At the end, four Stratford directors since the war walked on—Tony Quayle, Glen Byam Shaw, me, and Trevor, in that order. There is a degree of continuity at Stratford, of handing over before changing, which is unlike any other theatre in the kingdom. It's sixteen years since I began at Stratford. But I hate going back to school. I'm not an 'old boy'.

Tuesday 1 July
Worked on *Hamlet* in the sun. Albert[1] with me all day. He is in excellent, form, though the *Daily Mail* reports today that his wife seems to be leaving him. He said he was thinking of going back to the simple life, one room and

---

[1] Finney.

living out of a suitcase. But it would be better, he remarked, if the one room was at the Dorchester or the Savoy with perpetual service!

Watched a documentary on dogs—their potential as disease spreaders, with worms that attack the eyes of children, and because the English allow their dogs to do anything, anywhere. Sixty tons of dog shit are deposited on London each day. I suddenly didn't like dogs any more.

Saturday 5 July

To Stratford to see the two *Henry IV*s and *Henry V* in sequence. Seated and ready by 10.30 am. I think *Henry IV Part II* remains my favourite play, although the most difficult structurally. The revelation was Alan Howard. The future beckons him to Leontes, Macbeth and Othello without any question whatsoever.

A quotation: 'Who is this chap? He drinks, he is dirty, and I know there are women in the background.' Field Marshal Lord Montgomery on Augustus John.

Sunday 6 July

News in the week's post that Bedales' school fees are going up to nearly £1,500 per annum. That's nearly three times what they were when Jenny and Christopher started there. Bedales won't survive as an interesting school if only the rich can send their children.

Wednesday 9 July

Lunch with Roy Shaw, the new secretary-general of the Arts Council[1]. He is humorous, definite, a believer in standards, a great friend of Richard Hoggart[2], and not dissimilar in attitudes and penetration. We managed to sort out much common ground about the National Theatre.

Friday 11 July

To Alan Ayckbourn's theatre at Scarborough to see *Bedroom Farce*, well directed by Ayckbourn himself. Supper with him afterwards. He told me that the play had been announced and publicised as the centre of the new Scarborough season even before it was written. It was due to rehearse on a Monday; he started writing it on the previous Wednesday, wrote all day Wednesday and most of the night, all day Thursday and most of the night, all day Friday and most of the night; on Saturday he typed it out, and on Sunday armed with some duplicated copies he drove up to Scarborough. He gave it to the cast on Monday morning, and after the reading collapsed in bed for

---

[1] Succeeding Hugh Willatt.
[2] The author and social historian. Chairman of the Drama Panel of the Arts Council 1977–80.

174

two days. He said this was the kind of pressure he needed, and usually induced, to write a play.

Saturday 12 July
End of Scarborough visit. It's been very worthwhile, getting to know Ayckbourn better, and understanding his shy cautious approach to the theatre, and his great understanding and respect of craft. He is a Rep animal, in many ways like Pinter, both of them produced by many years of hard slog in the regional theatres. They both know audiences.

What I saw of Scarborough this morning I very much enjoyed. Beautiful Regency buildings: a Brighton in the North, except it has the advantage of tall tree-covered cliffs. Another world though: tired, North Country faces off on their annual holiday; husbands and wives suddenly thrown together who sit silent on the beach, silent in cafes, with nothing to say.

Monday 14 July
Dress rehearsal of *No Man's Land* at Wyndham's Theatre, where it has moved from the Old Vic for a West End run. I am optimistic about the future of the play in this house. Giraudoux has a wonderful passage in *Ondine*[1] about theatre buildings embracing or rejecting certain plays. It is nothing to do with their intrinsic quality; it is just a marriage of play and place. Wyndham's likes *No Man's Land*.

Friday 18 July
Arts Council this afternoon. Another frustrating meeting. Pressure would be brought on the GLC to give us more, pressure would be brought on the Minister to see if we could get the money that the build-up has cost, pressure would be brought on the world at large. . . . A letter, they said, must go to the Minister at once. They looked at their watches. It was half past three on a Friday. Well we can't do it now, they concluded, and Gibson wasn't there on Monday so couldn't sign it then, and anyway they'd need Tuesday in order to draft it properly. Perhaps Gibson could sign it on Wednesday, which meant the Minister would get it Thursday or Friday? I am glad it is a matter of urgency. . . .

Back to the office in a rage. Obviously nothing will happen until September or even October. In the meantime we wait and, as a consequence, run up a huge deficit at the Old Vic.

Monday 21 July
When I come to look back on these diary entries I must remember that this July and August, this summer of inactivity, was the crucial time for the new

[1] Hall directed *Ondine* for the RSC at the Aldwych in 1961, with Leslie Caron in the name part.

175

National Theatre building. We haven't enough money to run it properly in its first South Bank year. But we have enough to make a start. Yet there could still be a possibility that the building will not be open for two or three years, that it will be allowed merely to drain away £½ to £¾ million a year, which is what it will cost just to keep it standing empty. It was planned when energy was cheap and when Larry, the Czar of the stage, was determined to design a theatre grander and more beautifully equipped than any in history. This he has done, but it's a legacy which may prove painful in this new age of dear energy and high labour costs. Standards may go, great schemes like the National Theatre may falter, but a little voice inside me still whispers amusedly: all I need to make a play is half-a-dozen people and a space. I don't need the South Bank; perhaps it is already a dodo?

Wednesday 23 July
To *Hedda Gabler* at the Aldwych in the evening. I was riveted by Glenda Jackson. She seems now to have found a way of making her private complexity public without being insistent or self-indulgent. A great actress in the making. But her performance, though keenly enjoyable, was rather wrong-headed. Hedda should hurl herself at man after man like a moth eagerly going towards a new lamp; she should initially be vital, full of joy. Glenda's Hedda was glum from the word go, bent on a course of self-destruction. I was struck by the fact that this was the last great pre-Freud play. After Freud, nobody could have written so un-selfconsciously those scenes between Brack and Hedda about the leading cock in the farmyard, and the importance of a firm, straight pistol when firing. . . .

Sunday 27 July
I read *Moll Flanders* in the vain hope that I could adapt it—or get somebody else to adapt it—for the Olivier stage. But I couldn't solve the problem. How do you narrate an epic story, full of contradictions, in the first person, with the voice of a seventy-year-old woman, while you watch her young self going through all the contortions of an amoral life?

Defoe is really the inventor of the pornographic style. Not that *Moll Flanders* is overtly pornographic. But it is titillating. Under the guise of a moral story, a moral lesson which all must note and learn from, he tells of Moll's countless husbands and of a life of crime. It's the beginning of the *News of the World* technique: 'Prostitution must be stopped . . . read all about it.'

Broody on *Hamlet*. There is enormous pressure on me from my colleagues not to do it as I want to, full-length. We simply can't afford it, they say. Overtime, and the impossibility of matinees, with the consequent loss of revenue, would put another £50,000 on the budget. So what am I to do? I took on *Hamlet* as a gesture of trust to Albert. I didn't much want to direct it.

But I now have a line, an excitement, something to get the adrenalin going. I don't want to *interpret* the play by cutting it.

Tuesday 29 July
More thoughts about my *Hamlet* production. It seems to me that we have come some distance in the last twenty-five years in understanding the rhythm of a Shakespeare play, how it operates, how one segment reacts on another. We have also come some way in understanding how to speak the verse. But we still cut the text like barbarians. Do we know *what* we cut? And don't we normally cut either to fit some preconceived theory for the production, or because we simply can't make the passage work? I think my future direction in Shakespeare must be to reveal the total object as well as possible. I feel in my blood now that I know how. The cost implications of full length will have to be got over somehow.

We may be waiting to move and uncertain, but I should think last week must be a record for the National Theatre: £13,000 taken at Wyndham's for *No Man's Land*; and £4,000—representing 82%—for *Happy Days* at Nottingham—£30,000 total income[1].

Came to London from Wallingford this evening for the last night of *Heartbreak House*. Very good. Larry, whom I'm to meet on Friday, was in the audience, the first time I have actually seen him since the autumn. He looks well, but much much older than he did last September. The suit hangs limply. I was heartbroken. For whatever his powers of recuperation —and they are amazing—he will clearly never play a major role on the stage again.

Thursday 31 July
Kon Fredericks has been elected steward again. He actually polled fewer votes than the moderate candidate, but 20 cards were disallowed by another extremist member on a procedural basis—as being incorrectly filled in. The legality of the extreme left is what gets them on.

Friday 1 August
To Roebuck House to see Larry. He is alert, humorous, with a mind dancing from subject to subject much as in the old days. But the scale of him seems to have been pressed, reduced; the strong physical presence seems to have gone—though with Larry you can happily never tell. He has surmounted cancer, surmounted phlebitis, and this recent muscular virus should have been the death of him, but he has surmounted that too.

---

[1] In 1983, the year these diaries went to press, the income for a capacity week on the South Bank, plus a week at 82% at Nottingham, would total about £137,000.

He told me that every muscle in his body was affected. He couldn't keep his eyelids open. He couldn't swallow, so he had to be fed intravenously. Only one muscle continued to operate properly—the muscle in his right thumb. This he used gently to press the bell for the nurse.

He has had to learn to walk again, to write again, and—most importantly—to train his voice again. It is still high, still a parody of its former self, but it is improving. And he is back to the gym, forcing himself to become right.

He said he didn't like going into town very much as crossing the road was now difficult. He could move at an even pace but if he needed to take two quick steps to avoid a car his knees might give way.

I found him friendly, cordial, helpful. He said he had to cease being an NT associate director this autumn, that anyway was when his contract was up, and the Board had been good enough to him already. I said he must nevertheless somehow take part in the opening of his theatre. He answered that he knew there would be disappointment if he didn't act in the new theatre, but he would sooner this, than have people disappointed if he did. I urged him to accept the presidency of the National. He said he would think about it.

Saturday 2 August

To a hot, depressing preview of our next production, *Engaged*[1]. After it was over, Michael Blakemore came up to the dress circle and discovered Birkett, Peter Stevens and myself still sitting there like three melancholy crows. Blakemore looked angry and asked me what I thought of the preview. I wriggled and said I would prefer to talk to him privately tomorrow, but he forced me to be blunt. So I told him that in my view the women were all wrong, that everyone was playing the play as if they themselves found it funny, rather than bravely and truly, and that the pastiche coda at the end, when suddenly all the cast burst into song, was a disaster. He asked why I thought it was a disaster. I said it was vulgar. Gilbert *is* vulgar, said Blakemore. I said Gilbert didn't write this particular vulgarity, that Blakemore was in fact putting his vulgarity on top of Gilbert's.

He said he was prepared to talk to me about all this providing it was understood that what was actually done was his decision. I said it was his decision entirely, for I would only get heavy with a production if the director had lost his way or if there was sheer professional incompetence going on, and neither was the case here.

Wednesday 6 August

News that Peter Daubeny died in the night. I am shattered, although I have been aware for months that this was coming. I suppose I have known him for

[1] By W.S.Gilbert. Directed by Michael Blakemore.

23 years, ever since, fresh down from Cambridge, I knocked on his door to ask him to finance a production I wanted to do of Lorca's *Blood Wedding*[1]. He didn't.

Peter was the most maddening, egotistical, paranoid person I have ever met. He was also very dear, very tender, a generous friend, and a fantastic enthusiast for the theatre. People loved to hate him, so they loved him too. And how he, chronically sick and loathing air travel, can have continued to get together the World Theatre Season every year, I have never been able to fathom. What courage!

And what was his motive? Not money—he and Molly, his wonderfully devoted wife, had money. I suppose it was for success, just a plain old-fashioned motive like success. Daubeny the Great. Well, he was.

First night of *Engaged*. As horrible as I thought it would be. People laughed and were welcoming for the first five minutes. Then it died.

Thursday 7 August
The notices for *Engaged* are not good but they are nothing like as bad as I feared, or as we deserve. I thought a full knife-job would be done. The BBC, though, has withdrawn from televising the production.

We will have to take it off after its scheduled 31 performances. Blakemore cagily agrees. It can't be continued for the South Bank; there is no pressure at the box office. We have therefore to replan our repertoire, and I spent much time in a series of tortuous meetings trying to rearrange everything.

Friday 8 August
Back to Wallingford this afternoon for my two weeks' holiday. I am laden with things to do, and may even do some of them. The first thing though is to lose weight. And to rest.

Saturday 9 August
Spent the day reading John Russell's book, *Francis Bacon*. Superbly clear, one of the few interesting bits of writing about painting I have read in years. It is not pretentious, and it helps you look at the pictures. I am sure Bacon is *the* painter of our tortured mid-century. There is in his work a recognition that the human body has now become somehow even more frail, even more subject to pain, abuse and torture; and he, the painter, playing God unopposed by his victim, is pushing this vulnerable flesh into even more exposed shapes.

Monday 11 August
I have lost six pounds in two days.

[1] Hall eventually directed it at the London Arts Theatre in 1954.

Wednesday 13 August
Unofficial news this afternoon from Peter Stevens. He hears the South Bank Board is going to receive the get-in money[1]; that it was indeed allocated before Parliament was dissolved last week.

Thursday 14 August
Peter Stevens's news of yesterday is confirmed. The get-in money is coming. I rang Max Rayne in France and managed to persuade him to allow some of our office staff to move to the South Bank on 1 September.

Sunday 17 August
Harold Pinter to Wallingford today, bringing with him his son Daniel who is to stay with us, seeing Jenny and Christopher, for a week or so. Harold was tense but pretending to be relaxed, anxious but pretending to be happy. Tonight Antonia joins him in his new rented home. Photographers and reporters are all round it. He has, he says, filled the house with flowers.

He left in the evening to go to the airport to pick up Antonia. Daniel wanders about solitary, silent, introverted, just as he was when he was a little tiny boy. But he is now bookish, a bit playing the poet. He's given to making cryptic remarks or suddenly asking difficult questions. He asked me if a quotation was from St Augustine or from St Thomas Aquinas—this out of nowhere. He found the gazebo and installed himself with his books.

Thursday 21 August
My holiday is nearly at an end. Part of me is glad of it, but another part is alarmed at what I haven't done. For I haven't read enough or thought enough. I've finished the *Hamlet* text, comparing Quartos and Folio; and I've managed to fillet it, with John Russell Brown's assistance, of practically all its punctuation except what is essential to sense.

Shakespeare's text is always absurdly over punctuated: generations of scholars have tried to turn him into a good grammarian. Even the original printed texts are not much help—the first printers popped in some extra punctuation. When punctuation is just related to the flow of the spoken word, the actor is liberated.

Sunday 24 August
Judgement all day at Aquinas Street. I believe it's going to be magnificent. But it's curious to rehearse a play that is a monologue of nearly three hours. You can't take it to pieces section by section and work on each in detail, because one section produces another in the emotional life of an actor. In an

---

[1] Funds to cover the cost of moving the NT organisation from the Old Vic to the South Bank.

ordinary play there are other actors who can feed the appropriate emotional level, but Colin[1] can't really feed himself without going through the entire play. So he does this at each rehearsal. We then talk and adjust and perhaps do a few lines, but not in any depth. We *talk* in depth rather than work in depth.

Thursday 28 August

Planning meeting this afternoon. All about the start of our move to the South Bank. Excitement in the air. We are off. . . .

I felt ill tonight, dizzy, and slightly nauseated. I must suceed in having an hour or two's break within the day. Rushing from one thing to the other is no good. Difficult to sleep when the room is revolving. The sleep revolves too. . . .

Monday 1 September

Afternoon at LWT on *Aquarius*. Chat with Derek[2] about the composition of the first programmes, and then to see some of them run.

The Epidaurus film we did is fair. It is beautifully shot, and Denys is very interesting when he's describing the geometry of the amphitheatre. But it all goes on too long, is too soft, and too repetitive. And I say 'yes' too many times so as to encourage Denys. . . . It is reverential and must be cut.

Then to Long Acre to see the rough of Russell Harty's film for *Aquarius*, *Willie and Our Gracie*, about two music-makers living on Capri, William Walton and Gracie Fields. It is a first-class piece of work, brilliant, humorous and very informative to fans of either or both. But there was one aspect that worried me. Old people are always dead give-aways—like children. Either they don't care, they can't be bothered, or they've forgotten to dissimulate, so their egos get more vividly exposed. Russell asked me what I thought, and I told him I found the film unnecessarily cruel. He bridled and said it was commercial, and another director who works with *Aquarius* said that in a commercial world this was what mattered. I got a little terse. I think being commercial has nothing to do with being cruel, and said so. If people are awful, they must indeed be shown to be awful; but it's a question of degree. I stayed arguing until late evening and, I think, upset Russell a fair amount. I believe he will modify the film though.

Tuesday 2 September

Went to St Michael's Church, Chester Square, for Peter Daubeny's memorial service. Molly looked elegant and strained, but courageous. There was the usual singing and liturgical chanting. Then Ralph[3] rose at the lectern with the poems he was to read and began 'Molly said. . .' and from that

---

[1] Blakely.   [2] Derek Bailey, producer and editor of *Aquarius*.   [3] Richardson.

moment a mood of intimacy, of sharing among friends, was established which carried us all through. I suppose I spoke for six or seven minutes. I risked being extempore and it worked; the danger always helps, like an acrobat without a safety net. I spoke about Peter's professional life; Richard Attenborough about him personally. At the end, a lot of nodding, smiling and kissing outside the church. Bill Darlington[1] had come to the service though nearly blind and deaf, bearing his 84 years with enormous cheerfulness.

To Molly's for lunch. Ralph said he liked my speech: 'I was just beginning to think, I wonder if this is the end, when it was ... Congratulations.'

Many friends: Trevor, Janet, the Donald Sindens, and so on and so on. Nicholas Daubeny was in his black velvet for mourning, but wore his father's brown army boots, now 35 years old, as a token of respect. He is terribly nice, and as eccentric as his father was.

Wednesday 3 September
A picnic lunch in the new building with our advance guard there: Richard, Peggy, Sue, Rochelle, and Mary[2]. The move to occupy at least the offices has begun with them. Spirits are high, although whether they will remain so if we don't all join them soon is open to question. A greetings telegram arrived from Lord Cottesloe welcoming us to the South Bank.

To the tailors to be measured for two suits for *Aquarius*, one black and one dark green. LWT is to pay £150 each for them. Christ.

Friday 5 September
Very good notices for *Judgement*[3] in the *Financial Times*, the *Telegraph*, *The Guardian*, and a rather flip one in *The Times*, not really bad, but irritating.

Saturday 6 September
Went to the Georgian Theatre exhibition at the Hayward. Interesting how an actor exactly mirrors the sensibility and the art of his age. The progress from Garrick's dry precision through Kemble's romantic classicism to Kean's romantic passion exactly mirrors what was occurring in literature. Who is the actor that represents our age? But our age is a mass of contradictory fragments.

[1] W.A.Darlington, drama critic of the *Daily Telegraph* 1920–69, and author. Died 1979.
[2] Richard York, the NT's South Bank Liaison Officer; Peggy Kessel, Assistant to the Technical Administrator; Sue Higginson, Rochelle Levene, and Mary Parsons were all members of Peter Hall's office.
[3] The play was presented as part of an NT experimental season at the ICA.

Sunday 7 September
Memory Lane day. Down to King's Lynn for Uncle Cecil and Auntie Elsie's ruby wedding anniversary. It must be twenty-five years since I was in King's Lynn—playing the First Outlaw in the Marlowe Society's production of *The Two Gentlemen of Verona*, directed by John Barton.

Cousin Tony gave today's party for his father: affluent middle-class house set in a secluded lane.

Jacky drove over from Wallingford bringing Grandma, Grandpa, Jenny, Christopher, Edward, and Lucy. Everyone wandered round the garden and in and out of the house eating too much and drinking too much. Terrible speeches, but very moving. Uncle Cecil said to me, 'There's a little touch of *Akenfield* here.' I chatted to everybody I could, trying to think of something to say. I was treated like visiting royalty, which didn't help.

Monday 8 September
Thought about *Judgement*. All in all I am pleased with its reception. A very dangerous thing has succeeded. The notices in *The Sunday Times* and *Sunday Telegraph* are excellent, and I think now we must move on to more performances[1]. Harold Pinter was the most interesting critic—he found all the attempts by the character to philosophise, to actually analyse a moral position, poor philosophy and, because of their great length, poor drama. He found the play much better when it stuck to the facts.

Wednesday 10 September
To a South Bank Board meeting. The usual gloomy recital of stage equipment for the new theatre still nowhere near ready. I got very annoyed and went far too far. I thumped the table and said that if we were now to wait for all the electronic marvels to be finished we might be waiting another two years before we moved on to the South Bank. They were not the essential thing about a theatre. What we wanted was to get in and act.

Off to St Paul's school in Hammersmith with Edward for the new boys' and parents' special afternoon, held the day before term begins. Well conducted, very ordered, touching too: crowds of little boys, constantly on the stir like branches in the wind, all dressed in new Harrods suits, slightly larger than they should be wearing. The expedition was a good idea because all the boys were taken off to meet their teachers and to look at their classrooms. The agony of tomorrow was over today.

---

[1] *Judgement* was later performed at the Young Vic studio, the Old Vic, and the Royal Court. In August 1977 it was revived with Ben Kingsley, directed by John Russell Brown, playing in the Cottesloe repertoire.

183

Thursday 11 September

Driven through beautiful autumn sunshine to John Makepeace's hand-crafted furniture workshops near Banbury. A happy day filming there for *Aquarius*, away from the pressures and anxieties of the NT. Interviewed the young people who work at Makepeace's. The image of the craftsman as an old man, gnarled hands, old skills, time no object, is a dying one. Makepeace employs very young men because he says they're the only ones who have the dedication and the concentration to meet the standard of work he demands.

To a Banbury hotel for the night. Derek Bailey down, and in a back room we recorded part of the commentary for the Epidarus film. I was tired and fell over words; also I sounded too pompous. I have to find a means of talking to the camera without projecting in an actorish way. It should be conversational, but not sloppy. Difficult.

Derek is uneasy. Our first transmission in the series is on Tuesday. He is also bracing himself for attacks on me. He asked me anxiously if there were going to be any more colour supplement 'Very Peter Hall, Very Sandersons' ads between now and Tuesday[1]. I said I'd no idea. He said if there were, we were dead. . . .

Friday 12 September

All has gone well with Edward at St Paul's, except he was very tearful this morning because yesterday at Assembly, when they called out the hymn, he looked at the page number and not at the hymn number, and therefore couldn't sing. He said everyone was staring at him and he felt embarrassed. Even worse, they all began to pray and he doesn't know the Lord's Prayer. He was very upset. He told Jacky, 'Mama, I want to pray.'

Monday 15 September

First reading of *The Playboy of the Western World*[2]. The Irish acting contingent was sitting round—Liam Redmond, J.G.Devlin, Harry Webster, P.G.Stephens. They've all been in the play many times. Poor, English Sue Fleetwood, having to be a County Mayo girl in that company. . . . But she read magnificently. The young Scot, Bill Bryden, began his opening remarks by observing that although he had often seen the play, it had never really come off. The Irish contingent looked amazed. . . .

Interesting point: if the actors drive through to the end of a sentence, instead of lingering on the incidental beauties of the phraseology, or pausing on commas, the text remains clear and hard and genuinely poetic. Otherwise it's over-lyrical and a wandering-scholar's idea of peasants.

---

[1] The press had already had much fun with this advertisement.
[2] By J.M.Synge. Directed by Bill Bryden.

Tuesday 16 September
Preparations this morning for my first *Aquarius* broadcast: hair cut, beard trimmed, and trying on one of the £150 suits. It's dreadful. I don't like the material, I don't like the cut, and it doesn't fit. But it will have to be worn today. Worked on the programme all afternoon. Then to the transmission. I think it was alright. At least I didn't hold them up, fluff, or make a mistake. But I must find a way to be myself with the camera. I can do it with an audience; I can do it directing; I can do it talking to somebody else. But with the camera. . . ?

Friday 19 September
Cambridge: Found myself sitting next to Mary Whitehouse at breakfast in King's College before attending the Royal Television Society conference[1]. She appears to me to be utterly showbiz struck. She said action must be taken against the BBC for an orgy film they have recently made for one of their Open University programmes. She thinks that either the chairman of the BBC or its governors should go to prison. And if they don't, she says she's going to refuse to pay her television licence, and be sent to prison herself. Her eyes shone like Joan of Arc. 'It's time I made a stand,' she cried. 'And a few months in prison would be very good for me.'

Moved into my office on the South Bank. I was very excited. Everything looks wonderful. The river glows outside the window. It is beautiful.

Monday 22 September
To the South Bank to work in my new office for the first time, and to begin *Hamlet* rehearsals. We had champagne out on the terrace to welcome the actors[2]. Albert wandered up twenty minutes late. He looks wonderful with his beard: a powerful, passionate, sexy Hamlet, glowering with resentment. I looked at him and felt cheered. A rough and ready, stumbling reading, with people falling over words or misplacing emphases, but it was good. It had vitality, and it showed conclusively that if you play on the line and keep going, think forward, the full-length play is neither too long nor too complex. I was amazed to find it read at just about three hours. Very encouraging. My spirits rise at the thought of doing Shakespeare again.

Tuesday 23 September
Went through second scene of *Hamlet*. The particular rehearsal room in the new theatre that we are using is quiet, has good daylight, height, and is properly warmed. After twenty-one years of rehearsing in cupboards, leaky

---

[1] Hall chaired the Entertainments Committee.
[2] The South Bank Theatre Board had made available to the NT company not only the offices in the new building, but also the rehearsal rooms and workshops.

halls, and bars smelling of last night's drink and tobacco, at last I am in a place with good conditions. I count this one of the greatest merits of our South Bank building. The work can be created in a proper place.

Thursday 25 September
Meeting at the Arts Council. Gibson told us that more money had been obtained from the Treasury for the National Theatre for running next year. We are guaranteed Arts Council support to £2.5 million[1]. So we've won... I can hardly believe it.... We're on. Max took me back to the South Bank flushed with victory and did a quick CO's inspection of the new building, complaining about the finishes, the white paint, the dirty fingermarks, and left in a cloud of cigarette smoke.

Friday 26 September
Good morning on *Hamlet*. Read and discussed right through to the end of the Players' scene. The cast is settling. So am I.

Celebration lunch: the Aquinas Street huts, the NT's battered old tin-roofed offices for the twelve years the company were at the Old Vic, are officially closing this evening. I didn't go—half didn't want to, half too tired. On Monday, all the staff will be in the new building.

Saturday 27 September
I've been dipping into Lord Reith's diaries. A record of egomania and paranoia. He hated everybody. He used his diary as a means of letting off steam. I wonder if I'm doing the same....

Monday 29 September
Big press conference to announce the opening of the NT in March, not in its entirety but theatre by theatre as each becomes ready, the Lyttelton first. Our 'foot in the door' policy, so that we can make a start despite delays. I suppose a couple of hundred journalists were there. The atmosphere was not alive but lethargic and bored, a bit puddeny. I felt fairly low key for the rest of the afternoon.

David Astor[2] came over to see the theatre. He was as engaging and nervous as ever. He said he never thought we would get in; thought in fact the scheme was finished and I had lost. That had never occured to me. All I've ever wondered was whether I would be able to sit out the waiting time.

Tuesday 30 September
Speedy lunch while my hair and beard were trimmed. Then over to *Aquarius*. I think I was more relaxed, but I always feel false talking from a

[1] See diary entry 29 May 1975 for the first indication of the Arts Council 1976/77 grant.
[2] Editor of *The Observer* 1948–75

script—or indeed talking with amplification. Still, we'd done a whole programme by 6 pm, with lots of tricky stuff on a Scottish Opera story written by Stephen Fay. Stephen was there and watched me recording. He had the air of sympathy one has towards actors who are giving a bad performance.... Gentle but embarrassed. Bodes ill. But at least I felt on top of it. An awful thing though is happening: the more expert, the more 'professional' I become, the more I hate doing it. *Aquarius* is all wrong for me. I am clear now how I *should* do it: absolutely ad lib, in my working clothes. At the moment I feel like a Harrod's window display: best suit, abstract background, fancy lighting, and a silly modern chair. What the bloody hell am I doing talking to people in such an environment? I am somebody who *works* in the arts, and the programme should reflect this. It's no good at the moment. I was wrong to do *Aquarius* at all. Too late now.

Saturday 4 October
Hamlet rehearsal this morning. Did all the ghost scenes. At lunch time a quick dash to the new Henry Wood rehearsal hall in Southwark: a beautiful eighteenth-century church which has been done up for orchestras to rehearse in. I went to have a few words with André Previn about Rubinstein, whom I'm to interview this afternoon for *Aquarius*. André told me that when he and the LSO recorded the Saint-Saëns piano concerto with Rubinstein, the old man insisted on doing the last movement nineteen times without stopping. He exhausted the orchestra. Also he still fancies the ladies. He took André's wife, Mia Farrow, into dinner and, so she told André, pinched her bottom....

Then to the Savoy to see Rubinstein for a happy hour and a half chatting to the maestro. He's 89 in January. He smoked his cigar vigorously and talked of this and that. He doesn't believe in talking about music, only playing it or listening to it. I sympathise.

Sunday 5 October
There's too much Hall in the papers today. A big piece about the new building in *The Observer* which gently sends me up for being a Sandersons-type showman. A story about Larry not appearing on the South Bank is in *The Sunday Times*. There's also some good, malicious comment here and there about *Aquarius*; *Time Out* absolutely takes me apart for doing it at all. The effect of this is actually not to increase my paranoia. I always find if there's a lot of criticism I can cope much better; it's the odd, sneaky little bit that upsets me.

Monday 6 October
To Covent Garden for nearly six hours of *Siegfried*. They were all there: Prince Charles, who was taken secretly in the dark from his box to the front

row so he could see the dragon properly; Edward Heath; Gibson; Claus Moser; and Georg Solti whom I haven't seen for about two years. He and I had a good talk in the first interval. He bewailed the collapse of all the democratic and liberal values of England; how we were letting 400 years of achievement slither down the drain through ineptitide and apathy. I agree. He asked me why I wasn't more militant about it.

Tuesday 7 October
Important findings at rehearsal. Hamlet is not so concerned that Rosencrantz and Guildernstern are spies; nor is he concerned in the Ophelia nunnery scene that he is being overheard. The scenes are not about these discoveries; he knows them in a flash. He's concerned about the honesty of the characters in their replies when he charges them with duplicity, and both the scenes show him trying to demonstrate his own philosophy, anxiously, vigorously. They are a pattern of misunderstandings.

And when Albert walked on to the stage and launched into the current problem of Hamlet—was he to be or not to be?—it was electric and urgent, not introspective. I'm sure that's right.

Thursday 9 October
To No 10 tonight for a dinner the PM was giving to honour Karamanlis, the Prime Minister of Greece. I was there as a representative of the arts and crafts. Wilson reminded us that democracy was a Greek word. Karamanlis was incomprehensible, speaking in a thick Greek accent, though key words such as 'EEC', 'Great Britain,' 'Cultural Understanding', swam up through the fog. After the dinner we stood around chatting on—so one of the PM's private secretaries informed us—one of the most valuable Persian carpets in the world, a masterpiece woven about 1520. Ash and wine were falling on it.

Talked for a while with Wilson. He told a story about how he lent Makarios a shirt when Makarios left Cyprus with nothing except what he stood up in. Wilson still hasn't had the shirt back.

Roland Penrose[1] was in a high state of rage that there isn't one single piece of modern art or modern decoration in the whole of the public areas of No 10, just eighteenth-century portraits, discreet representations of William Pitt the Younger looking romantic, and even discreeter photographs of this century's incumbents on the staircase. Penrose said they could at least have had *some* modern art—the odd Moore statuette, or the odd modern painting. He's right. But then the place is not designed to express any single person's taste. It looks like what it is: a temporary abode; furnished accommodation.

[1] The art historian and critic. Founder of the ICA 1947. Knighted 1966.

Friday 10 October

I was settling down in my office to a session with John Goodwin about the design committee, which was meeting this afternoon, when Larry walked in, looking old and uneasy. He'd asked Denys Lasdun to show him round the new building, so Denys was in attendance. It must have taken great courage on Larry's part to come and see everybody after a year, his appearance so different, feeling so frail, and being the man outside this wonderful place that he has created.

Saturday 11 October

Cold bad, sinus roaring, usual antibiotics, and consequent depression. We rehearsed the *Hamlet* graveyard scene this morning with a real skull. The actuality of the scene was immediately apparent; actors, stage management, everybody aware of a dead man's skull among us.

Jenny, up from Bedales, met me at the theatre. I showed her round. She said it was beautiful and that I was very lucky. I suppose I am.

Sunday 12 October

Clive James is very funny in *The Observer* about the Peter Hall publicity machine: says I need to be taken down a peg or two regularly. He apparently hasn't noticed that I am. I can forgive him his piece though because he's also funny, and rude, about Ken Tynan and George Melly.

Monday 13 October

Spent all morning rehearsing the first scene of *Hamlet*—four hours—and it was a wonderful experience. It's really why I do this job. Not for performances—not for plays—not for money—but for the satisfaction of having a really good rehearsal where the excitement of discovery spreads from actor to actor.

Max Rayne tells me that Harold Lever[1] warned him last night that there was terrific hostility in the government to the National Theatre and its money needs. Great! Then why did successive governments build it?

To *No Man's Land* at Wyndhams to see Tom Marshall play for Michael Feast who has laryngitis. The great excitement of the evening for me was to see Ralph—he gets better and better. His acting now has such truth, such high definition, and he is carrying out Pinter's wishes to the last letter. It's one of the greatest performances I have ever seen. Gielgud has become a little cosy. He wants a touch more acid. I will tell him. I suppose his essential niceness is always fighting through.

---

[1] Chancellor of the Duchy of Lancaster 1974–79. Created Baron 1979.

At the end Ralph chatted about *Hamlet*, telling me it was like the most amazing train and all Albert had to do was to get on it and rush along through cuttings, through stations, through tunnels until finally he reached his destination. He must not get off at any of the stations on the way.

Ralph made a wonderful speech about how acting, however beautiful a craft it is for oneself, has finally to be for *them*, the audience.

Tuesday 14 October

To Harley Granville Barker's *The Marrying of Ann Leete* at the Aldwych. I was struck by the likeness of this play and this dramatist to John Whiting. Why have none of our critics seen it? There's the same love of ambiguity, of elliptical expression; the same sense of humour, the same mandarin attitude; the same arrogant, almost wilful rejection of the audience. Neither Whiting nor Granville Barker care if they are understood. They feel a cut above the audience. But they are both wonderful.

Wednesday 15 October

An eighteen-hour day which started at 6 am with office work.

Saw a run-through of *Playboy of the Western World* which we open soon. It's very expert, very well placed, very well paced. It's curious though, that Bill[1] has done exactly what he said he wouldn't. All the cast, with the exception of Sue Fleetwood, Stephen Rea who is magnificent, and the meticulous Jim Norton, are sentimental and fey, and give a warm demonstration of what marvellous cute characters they are playing. The stage is full of the Little People. Bill said to me when he proposed the play that it must be hard, precise, totally unsentimental. He still means it to be. But there it is, as Irish as the Irish Tourist Board. I said this to him after the run, and he took the point. But what a magnificent play!

Associates' meeting which began at 6 pm and ended at midnight. Gillian[2] accused us of not seeing all the plays the NT puts on, or, if we do, of not going round to see the actors afterwards. This caused explosions. Pinter became very cross saying he could not be other than he was. Stevens said he never went round, but always saw the actors in the pub later. Blakemore said the only people he saw were the ones whose performances he had liked. I proposed they should all go round anyway. But they wouldn't. I then proposed they should go round if they liked it. That won some approval. The only thing everybody agreed on was that *I* had to go round....

We didn't sit down to dinner until late, and as the wine flowed freely so tempers got shorter and sentences longer.

---

[1] Bryden.   [2] Diamond.

190

Thursday 16 October
Not a bad day's *Hamlet* rehearsal, though I have a sense I am hanging on by my finger nails. Albert was very funny. He said he felt we'd just reached base camp and were now ready for the ascent. But as he looked round him with some satisfaction his face began to change expression. Did we really need all those pack animals, all that food, all those medical supplies, oxygen; what was oxygen doing? Where were we going anyway? At this point he looked up and did a huge double take—We're Not Going Up There!

Saturday 18 October
The Times is having a good go at me this morning for *Aquarius*: the wrongness of the appointment and so on. I think and hope I have now reached a peace in myself about the press. It's very obvious the battering is going to continue, whether I do *Aquarius* or not; whether I am over-exposed or not. I've been around too long, and have too much on my side, they think. So I must try and accept the knocks now and not be bruised. I shall not record any more of my paranoid reactions to press comment unless it is particularly interesting or awful[1].

Thursday 23 October
Hamlet rehearsal. Discovered the structure of the King's so-called prayer scene: I say so-called because he doesn't in fact pray. Claudius is in a sense the most honest person in the play—the man who sees most clearly his own faults and his own problems. The prayer scene is an open and candid discussion with the audience of his dilemma. It moves from the personal to the public—he asks the audience for their views, points out they too are guilty, and then goes back to the personal agony again. Hamlet's soliloquy in this scene, 'Now might I do it, pat,' is time suspended, a close-up with voice-over that lasts a few seconds. The speech rushes out while the sword is poised.

Friday 24 October
Bitty *Hamlet* work this morning. We were visited by the Minister accompanied by a bevy of civil servants and, most significantly, by Joel Barnett, the First Secretary of the Treasury. They were obviously very impressed by the building. The actors made suitable conversation with them when we broke from rehearsal for a few minutes.

---

[1] Two fairly significant newspaper articles appeared immediately after this decision of Hall's (one he did not always keep to). On 26 October, Philip Oakes reported in *The Sunday Times* that a newly-formed theatre company was out "to win the National's potential audience" and consisted of people, Joan Plowright among them, whose "love for Hall is several degrees below the norm". On 2 November, Michael Davie in *The Observer*, estimating Hall's total earnings, criticized him for doing *Aquarius* and the Sanderson's advertisement when the National was about to open.

Monday 27 October

Mentioned to Max Rayne that I would really have to get my contract extended. Otherwise I was going to work my guts out for the 18 months over the opening, which are bound to be rough and often unsuccessful, and then not have the opportunity to develop on that. I am a bit like a government carrying out a difficult legislation programme with no mandate. All the fault, of course, of the delays.

Wednesday 29 October

First night of *The Playboy*. Though the last act was magnificent, the performance was not fluent. Something to be proud of all the same, I think.

Thursday 30 October

Apart from one ridiculous statement that if we're going to make a gesture to the Irish drama, why don't we do a relevant play like *The Plough and the Stars*, *The Playboy* notices were excellent, some of them raves, and rather better than we deserve from last night's performances, though not I think better than the potential of the production.

Hamlet rehearsal this morning. I turned the closet scene on its head, cutting the bed. A closet is a withdrawing room, a place for disrobing, not the bedroom. It's a stage tradition, or at least twentieth-century tradition, to have a bed, and I had one at Stratford in '65. But a bed is really not what the scene is about. It's difficult to play around it, and you rapidly get to Freudian images—but only Freudian images. So instead I put two chairs on the stage and had Hamlet and his mother confronting each other. The scene was immediately more alive.

Friday 31 October

A very good investigation of the Ophelia mad scene. Sue Fleetwood in excellent state; instinctively she does wonderful things. She uses the circle of the stage as a garden from which she picks imaginary flowers to give to the characters she finds standing about her. Much better than those dry bits of poppy flowers which are normally thrust into the embarrassed hand of Claudius[1] and Gertrude[2].

Gravediggers this afternoon: Jimmy Devlin and Stephen Rea. The prose sounds wonderful in the Northern Irish accent, and they are funny by being utterly real. I did my Elizabethan accent, learned at Cambridge, to them. Amazing how close it is to Belfast; it's because of the Settlement of English and Scottish Protestants in Northern Ireland in the seventeenth century, after which the area became a backwater and the accent stayed largely unchanged.

---

[1] Played by Denis Quilley.　　[2] Played by Angela Lansbury.

Tuesday 4 November
Aquarius this afternoon. A drink with John Freeman[1] afterwards. He was very cordial, and advised me to hold firm despite the criticism I was getting. He'd had it in the past. He said if the people one was working for could justifiably accuse one of not doing the job properly because of other commitments, then there was an argument. If not, not. He also said he would be prepared to make a case for me at any time—why it was better for the director of the National Theatre to do *Aquarius* than not.

I had need of his support. In the break, Sue brought me stuff from the office, with news of the meeting Peter Stevens had had that afternoon with the Arts Council. He reported there was a witch hunt on me—about my salary—about my outside work—about *Aquarius*. . . .

Thursday 6 November
Interview with Judith Cook for the book she is writing, to be called *The National Theatre*. She handed me out a lot of pity for the way I was being attacked by the press. I smiled blandly and said I didn't mind. Liar.

Watched *The Browning Version* film[2] on television tonight. Old memories stirred. I directed this play with John Barton at Cambridge in the summer of 1952, before I took off and directed everything in sight in my last year. The film is still excellent, particularly Redgrave's performance. Schoolmasters don't change.

Friday 7 November
A big, powerful piece by Janet Watts in *The Guardian* this morning about the crisis in the theatre, the theatre in general: powerful because it's well-argued and unprejudiced. It does raise the old question though: how the hell are we going to open—our greedy great mouth stuffed with millions of pounds—when other theatres are going to the wall? Jonathan Miller made all this very clear in some statements that were quoted in the article.

Ran Part 1 of *Hamlet*. Promising, but I feel I am losing my grip. Is it my usual deep-seated desire towards the end of rehearsal time to have a crisis, to have things go wrong so that I can heroically make them right at the last minute? These *Hamlet* rehearsals have been so organised, so organic, so creative, that I don't want a great big panic at the end.

Wednesday 12 November
A talk with Max Rayne who raised the question of the extension of my contract. He said the Board wished it to happen, but it was a pity it was coming up when there was all this press controversy; for one thing, the Minister had asked that any extension should be exclusive, not permitting me any outside work. I said if that was the case, I wouldn't be extending it.

[1] Chairman of LWT from 1971.　　[2] From the play by Terence Rattigan.

Peter Hall's Diaries

Thursday 13 November
Victor Mishcon dinner tonight. O'Brien, Leach, Mischon, Rayne all agreed that my contract be extended from next June for a period of five years on roughly the same terms, and that it would not be exclusive. So there's another turnabout.

Monday 17 November
This morning Daniel Thorndike asked Michael Melia 'Who's there?' and Michael Melia asked the voice to unfold itself. We were rehearsing *Hamlet*, the beginning, in the Lyttelton auditorium, and they were the first actors to speak on a stage of the National Theatre.

A thrilling day. Sets and costumes patchy, half-finished, but everything working. The theatre looks well, the actors dominate it easily, and—most important—the acoustics seem to be perfect. I tried experimental lighting cues with David Hersey[1]. What we did would have taken about six hours with conventional equipment. Yet now, on the new computerised board, we were able in two hours to dash through various ideas.

Tuesday 18 November
A reasonably smooth morning's rehearsal. The same old problems with the gravediggers as I remember in 1965[2]. Where can you keep the spade? Where can you put the coffin? How does Laertes get in and out? How do the gravediggers get in and out? I almost feel like writing a slim paperback entitled *How to Cope with the Grave in Hamlet, To Assist Aspiring Directors and Designers*.

I am excited by the state of the play, but depressed by how much there is to do. I have to work hard now and with enormous concentration, and a sure touch. The trouble is that when you say that to yourself, you never work with any touch at all.

Friday 21 November
John Barton looked briefly in at *Hamlet* rehearsals on a visit from the Aldwych; greetings, handshakes, smiles. He looked awful: tired out; I was appalled. Then another ghost walked in: Birkett was conducting Peter Stein round. Here is the young Stein, an undoubted genius, but already looking absolutely clapped out. This is what the theatre does to you.

Saturday 22 November
Forty-five to I've been doing the job for twenty-three years. I suppose I could do it strenuously for another twenty if I'm lucky. A mortal thought to get things in perspective.

---

[1] The lighting designer.
[2] When Hall directed *Hamlet*, with David Warner in the name part, at Stratford-upon-Avon.

194

Wednesday 26 November
Tense atmosphere at *Hamlet* rehearsal this morning. Poor Angela Lansbury has to leave tomorrow for three days in Los Angeles as her mother has died in Hollywood. Our rhythm of work disturbed. I tidied up a few things, and then we went into the run-through. It was not bad, slightly jumpy, slightly crude, things which had long been secure going awry, Angela obviously working under great strain. She came on for the Ophelia's death news and started the 'One woe doth tread upon another's heels so fast they follow. . .' speech with the most amazing emotional complexity. Then she stopped; nearly went on; tried to control herself; tried to go on. The silence lasted for ever. Denis Quilley collected her into his arms. Her grief was too much. An extraordinary moment. Everyone in the cast felt the reality of death—and the second half of *Hamlet* particularly is about death.

I have a feeling there is something wonderful in this production if only I can bring it home.

Thursday 27 November
A long session with Roy Shaw who came for a drink. He went through all the much aired complaints against me: *Aquarius*; earning too much money; Sanderson's newspaper ads; percentages from *No Man's Land* in the West End, etc. He said he was entirely on my side about all these things—he just thought there had been mistakes in timing. I told him that the percentage question was general theatre custom—that whenever commercial entrepreneurs make money out of exploiting work from the subsidised sector, the creative people concerned with the work are paid their market rate. But I really got sick of defending myself as if I were some kind of criminal.

Friday 28 November
Edward back from school and unwrapping his birthday presents. He told me he'd done a handwriting test in which he'd had to write down five famous people. His five were Shakespeare, Tchaikovsky (which he couldn't spell), Rolf Harris, Peter Hall, and Sir Francis Drake. I bridled, saying I wasn't quite in that class. He said I was better than Rolf Harris.

Saturday 29 November
Last *Hamlet* rehearsal in the South Bank rehearsal room. We now go to the Old Vic where the production will open and play until the new building is ready.

Monday 1 December
Hamlet technical rehearsal, endless exits, entrances, light-cues, etc. Like all technicals, a test of endurance, patience, and tenacity; and something I think I've been getting worse and worse at as I get older. I become more

petulant and more perfectionist: an unfortunate combination. This one lasted from 11.30 am until 11.30 pm. It went surely, but by the end we were at least three hours behind. It's worth bearing in mind that any technical rehearsal needs about four times the length of the play to get it into first shape. It then needs going through again so that everybody can try to remember what they have learnt.

Tuesday 2 December
The technical continued all day again today. What other profession demands that you go beyond the limits of your physical endurance, and yet keep your judgement? Fighting a battle, I suppose. Full responsibility and judgement are supposed to need rest and time off. You don't have it in the theatre.

Dress rehearsal tonight. Considering the tiredness of everybody, it was fair. The usual actors' sense of being freed of the boredom of technical problems: at last the play is returned to them. So at this stage they often act with a greater freedom and a greater sense of risk than at any other time. To some measure that happened tonight. There's excitement in the air—as if we might be doing something really important. I took pages of notes though. . . .

Wednesday 3 December
After our notes following the second dress rehearsal tonight, Albert told me quietly that he had had bad news. His father had died at ten to seven—just when he was playing the scene with the King his father. He was very upset, but extremely brave. He was very close to his father. He reminded me of a story he told me last summer. Sometime back he suddenly realised that he'd never told his father what he meant to him—how fond he was of him, how he respected him. His father was in a nursing home, ill, so Albert sat down and wrote him an eight-page letter trying to put into words his feelings. There was no answer. After a time he rang up and asked if he'd received the letter. 'Oh yes,' said his father, 'there's a reply in the post for you.' It read 'Dear Albert, thank you very much for your letter. Love Dad'. . . .

Thursday 4 December
Everything is now becoming *Hamlet*: the outside world is receding.

First preview. An undoubted success with the audience; a marathon for the actors. The first act was pretty wonderful, though Albert had difficulty in the early part to curb his emotion about Hamlet's father's death. I felt terrified for him. He said afterwards that he knew if he let his emotion run away with him, he would lose control. He therefore had to check it forcibly. And in a way that part of the performance was drier than it should have been.

196

The second act went less well than the first. What is the solution to the second part of *Hamlet*? It's puzzled me all my life. The soliloquies cease, and the audience start looking at something that is no longer the public discussion of morals and ethics that the first part was. Hamlet returns from England and muses philosophically to his friend in a graveyard—and at great length. There is the 'comic relief' of the gravediggers and Osric. And there are the accidental slaughters. But where is the tragedy? This play is the first statement in Christian literature of the unbeliever—the man who believes in nothing. Whatever the divinity is that Hamlet believes in at the end, it is ruthless, casual and unthinking. And his dying statements are hardly reassuring. He doesn't live to hear the news from England. What is the news? His wilful action in sending his two friends to their death? And who is his successor? Fortinbras, a military man who for a fantasy or trick of fame goes campaigning? For honour? What is honour?

I am very puzzled. The second act is not right. It doesn't make the statement that is worthy of Albert's questing anarchic personality. I hope the answer will come.

Friday 5 December
Second *Hamlet* preview. Albert said to me afterwards that there were pieces of the play when he really felt the stage belonged to him—a sense of ease, of freedom, of oneness with the audience. I felt it too as a spectator. But my mind had begun to churn during the second part—the way it withdraws. Partly, of course it's because the soliloquies cease. But it occurred to me tonight to ask the question, do they? I am sure Hamlet should *continue* his dialogue with the audience—particularly in the graveyard scene. By the end of the performance my head was buzzing. I thought I had it. If Hamlet addresses a good deal of his graveyard humour to the audience—so that the lawyer, the politician, and my lady painted an inch thick are out there, in the audience, then the contact continues and the play goes on building. I said some of this to the cast—and then a lot more to Albert. Albert, Elijah Moshinsky[1] and I were pounding round the Vic stage until well after midnight shouting with discovery and excitement. I went home, my head alight.

Saturday 6 December
It always alarms me that the mind will not have ideas to order. So what sort of state does one have to be in for the mind to work? I didn't sleep a wink last night. I went through and through the second part text, with a mounting feeling of excitement that I had solved it.

---

[1] Hall's assistant on the production.

Today was the hardest day's work so far. I began rehearsing at 11 am and worked straight through until 5 pm, not stopping for lunch, and then continuing to give notes until the third preview began.

A fascinating evening. The first act suffered a little. Albert was tired—not so much I think from the day's work, but emotionally tired from the events of the week. But the second half took off and proved my point. It's insistent and overdone, but the fact that Hamlet talks to the audience in the graveyard scene justifies the length of the death passages—and then, having mocked us and himself for our ambitions and our aspirations, because we will come to nothing but skulls in the end, death comes fully into his own life again with the entry of the coffin of Ophelia.

The actors are in a marvellous state at the moment—like a trained orchestra who can play the piece and will move it in any direction the conductor wants. Albert particularly is flexible and eager to live dangerously.

Sunday 7 December

Spoke to Albert and urged him to go the whole way in the first part in rawness and pain; also in Hamlet's search for the ideal—whether it be a play, a method of acting, or a woman. Only a great idealist can attain the level of cynicism which Hamlet reaches by the end of the play.

Monday 8 December

Tonight was the first alarming preview that there's been—alarming because I confronted for the first time the possibility of failure. And I mean it—for the very first time. Up to now I have always been supremely confident about this work. I was aware it would not get universally liked. What *Hamlet* ever does? But I thought it was going to be a break-through. After tonight I am not so sure. What happened?

Well there was a frantic air on stage: of people trying too hard, forcing their emotions. Perhaps they're too tired. Perhaps I'm giving them too many notes. Or perhaps they all feel they're in something extraordinary, so each night must get better than the last. Everything was strained, everything was pushed, and I began to dislike the second act. Its intention is absolutely right, but its execution is mannered.

Signs of revolt when we all met after the curtain call. 'Are we not to get any time off?' asked Roland Culver[1]. Groans and restlessness at the prospect of more work tomorrow. The elastic is beginning to fray thin. But not with Albert. He seems as resolute as ever. But tonight I was frightened. I must try to be less nit-picking tomorrow.

Troubled dreams. Once more I was thinking how much depends on this production: a foolish thought.

[1] Polonius.

Tuesday 9 December

A long team talk this morning. We discussed why the performance last night was so over-eager, tense and tight. It seems that the actors were disturbed by the slippery floor which had been polished just before the preview—it is impossible to act unless the feet are firm.

There was a good deal of grumbling, a good deal of concern about changes, notes, overwork—all justified. I don't know what the talk achieved except that a few skeletons were brought out of the cupboard and rattled.

A much better preview this evening which cheered me enormously—and the cast. Many things went wrong though. The cock didn't crow, the ghost didn't come up in his trap in the closet, and a gun went off by accident during Hamlet's dying speech. Worst of all, Roland Culver had a monumental dry that went on and on and on. But I believe we've done the play right.

Wednesday 10 December

Opening night tonight. I feel reasonably calm. This is the closest I have reached to the heart of a Shakespeare play in my own estimation; it is the production which over the last fifteen years has the least gap between my hopes and the facts on the stage. It is also pure and clear. On my instinct I have discovered a great deal about Shakespeare which I have always known in my head: the way scene must follow scene; the way lines are written for coming on and going off; the way every scene has a thematic line five or six lines in, to catch the audience's attention so that they know what the scene is about. And the production is the closest I've ever got to a unified style of verse speaking which is right. I feel now I know how the verse should be treated. In Stratford days what I did was intellectual. Now I have found a way of doing it which is based on feeling and passion. It has been a very satisfying experience. I can see marked clearly the path ahead to *Tamburlaine*[1].

Warm up of the cast this afternoon. I gave them one note: if you don't feel it, don't 'act' it. Then into the first night.

The audience were very attentive and the actors did well. All in all it was our best performance. The last scene has never gone better and I felt an actual tragic purgation in the house. The reception was really thunderous. I've heard it as much for Callas, but that's about all. Everybody very elated. I believe we're going to have a contentious press, but on tonight's evidence we have achieved something big.

Man leaving performance (snorting): '*Hamlet* is not as contemporary as that. . . .'

---

[1] The production scheduled to open the Olivier auditorium on the South Bank.

Thursday 11 December
Some of the critics are wonderful, some are dreadful. Why are they, the bad ones, so angry? I suppose because this is a different kind of Shakespeare, undecorated, and in some sense uncomfortable.

Albert is still elated; not put down at all by the abuse, which is vociferous here and there. I tried to keep myself up all day, but the reaction is dreadful. Round to see the cast. They're a bit bewildered, but there is a sense of strength and courage back-stage.

Finance and general purposes committee meeting this afternoon. Nothing much of interest. At the end I was handed a slip of paper with the London theatre critics' awards on it. The NT has collected 6 out of 10. Not bad.

To a late dinner at the Savoy with Max, Goodman, Drogheda[1], and the Healeys. Denis Healey is almost the only practising politician I have ever talked to whose interests extend beyond the political kitchen. He and his wife enjoyed *Hamlet* tonight very much. He said that when he read some of the press this morning he almost cancelled his tickets, for he had a hard day ahead in the Cabinet arguing with colleagues about cutting each of the Minister's budgets. To sit through a four-hour controversial *Hamlet* after that would be too much. . . . But on the contrary he felt elated.

Friday 19 December
Dinner at the Dorchester with Albert. An excellent evening. He was most complimentary about the *Hamlet* work and about the experience of working with me—wants to go on, is determined to tackle more big roles, and determined to stay with the NT, with the occasional film away.

Interesting point. He told me he'd had great difficulty in playing the last part of *Hamlet* because of his long time off stage. He would come off after 'How all occasions', have a Guinness, relax, and even have a little sleep. But when he at last came back to do the graveyard scene he couldn't get himself going again. He said that now he was adopting a different technique. On coming off he jumped into the shower and while soaping himself vigorously thought of the fight with the pirates and all the activity that was crowding in on the life of Hamlet. He then didn't relax but came on again as keyed up as possible. He said he loved playing the part so much he resented this long gap when he was off stage.

Monday 22 December
Up from Wallingford on the train. Came to the flat first to check the mail, and was very happy to find that Christopher has been awarded an Exhibition at St Catharine's. This will do more for his confidence than anything.

News this morning that the Queen doesn't want to open the building until

---

[1] Chairman of *The Financial Times* 1971–75 and of the Royal Opera House 1958–74.

it's all finished, and therefore suggests October, after Balmoral. I can't say I'm sorry about this. It might, I suppose, give contractors and people an excuse for going slower, but then in the past the imminence of a royal visit never did anything to speed them up. I think it's good news. It means the whole place will be well and truly opened and buzzing before we get down to the official formalities.

Tuesday 30 December
To London for *Aquarius*. We recorded the programme—a good talk with Clement Crisp[1] on Nijinsky and Isadora Duncan. In the break, enter Sir Fred Ashton and Lynn Seymour, Lynn to dance the little Brahms waltz inspired by Isadora which Ashton has choreographed for her. It's a pity I didn't talk to him about Isadora on the programme. He saw her at sixteen, and told me she was really a kind of intellectual strip teaser, taking off gauze veils one by one and draping them over the piano; huge thighs, he mused. But he'd obviously been very impressed by her artistry. She was, he said, the first Earth Mother.

Wednesday 31 December
Quiet day in Wallingford re-reading *Tamburlaine*. Didn't move from the text. I begin to get into it.

    Christopher and Jenny have gone to Scotland to stay with friends. Peter and Natasha Brook's son Simon is rampaging here with Edward. I am deep in Marlowe.

---

[1] Ballet critic of *The Financial Times* from 1960, and author.

1976

Friday 2 January
A good day reading and thinking about *Tamburlaine*. What a magnificent work: powerful, comic, and penetrating. But I bet the critics will not see past Marlowe's reputation. They will talk—as they nearly always do—of his mighty line, of barbaric show, and of superman heroes; no recognition of character, conflict or, most importantly, theme.

Thursday 8 January
To *Plunder* first preview. It's messy, and a good deal of it simply doesn't work. I think Michael Blakemore, because he knows he camped up *Engaged*, is so keen to make this real, he's forgotten it also has to be presented as farce. When I spoke to him he listened with a half smile and then promised to think about it. But he's as open as a clam. I do find it difficult to work with him.

Monday 12 January
Lunch with Peg[1]. Eventually she got round to talking about *Hamlet*. She hated it. She thought that it was gabbled and imprecise; that there was no virtue in the full text; and she didn't like the speaking direct to the audience. In short, she didn't get it at all. She was very upset by this and so was I. It's not usual for her to misunderstand what I'm up to.

A tussle with my conscience and then a decision not to go to tonight's preview of *Plunder*. Word reached us today that Ben[2] didn't really like it. But Michael Blakemore is insisting all is going well. There seems nothing I can do. I see no point in making efforts to work with somebody who has no desire to work with me. Michael gets stuck in a dogmatic theory about the way to do a play and doesn't seem to realise it could be wrong—or needs development.

Tuesday 13 January
Lunch with John Bury, flushed with his Prague triumph[3]. Much talk about how we want *Tamburlaine* to look. Well, I say 'much' talk. Because we know

---

[1] Peggy Ashcroft.   [2] Travers, author of *Plunder*.
[3] He was the co-winner of the Gold Medal for Scene Design at the Prague Quadrenniale, 1976.

each other so well, I just showed him my scribbles. John whacked his thigh, said he would make roughs, and announced, 'Yes, that'll be alright.' Sometimes he takes the lead; sometimes I do.

To a Max Rayne ginger group meeting. A dozen or so defensive contractors there. It's now clear that what I predicted long ago will happen. We shall be in the new theatre but there will be no stage flying equipment and no stage machinery ready; consequently our costs will be a great deal more than planned because of the extra stage hands needed. Even so, we must start, we must begin. Truth is, the consultants have had little discipline imposed on them by the South Bank Board to stop them dreaming the most extravagant dreams. I did a little table thumping and then crept off to do *Aquarius*.

Wednesday 14 January
To an NT Board meeting. Peter Stevens and I said we would prefer not to do a detailed South Bank budget at this stage because there were so many things outside our control; why waste time now on detailed financial speculation? Dick Linklater got sniffy. He said that if we exceeded our grant we might be closed down. My nightmare is that we stage two or three flops on the trot in the summer (it happens to many theatres), there is a storm of abuse, and we are at the same time £250,000 to £300,000 in the red.

Plunder first night. Audience suspicious and cast a bit tense. Not a very good evening.

Thursday 15 January
Up early this morning and opened the newspapers with trepidation. Fortunately they're kind. There is obviously a great cordiality towards Ben Travers and a recognition, which is absolutely justified, that *Plunder* is a fine play with fine dialogue. I am very glad, though also angry, because most of the actors are first-rate, capable of doing an original and creative job, and what we have delivered is a conventional and 'expected' production.

Friday 16 January
First reading of *Watch It Come Down* this morning; Osborne, looking curiously pink and strained, present. Bill Bryden[1] made an incoherent speech, but it was engaging: his enthusiasm for the play bounded through like a great big puppy.

As the actors read, they became quieter and quieter: private mumblings. I had to follow with the text. But it's a wonderful cast[2], and I think a powerful play. The first act has vigorous sardonic humour, and the second is one of the bleakest most terrifying I have heard outside Strindberg.

---

[1] Its director.
[2] Jill Bennett, Rowena Cooper, Susan Fleetwood, Angela Galbraith, Michael Feast, Frank Finlay, Michael Gough, and Peter Needham.

Sunday 18 January
Alone today in the Barbican flat until 5 pm when Jacky and the two children arrived. Rather wonderful to be alone and have the privacy of my own thoughts. Those thoughts today are about *Tamburlaine*.

Some phoning around lunchtime: three quarters of an hour talking with Blakemore. He made a protestation of faithfulness to me—although saying that there was much in the organisation that he disagreed with. Ah. . . .

To bed early for more work on *Tamburlaine*. One of the *real* tyrant's (not Marlowe's) choicer atrocities: he knocked down the wall of some city he was overcoming and built it up again with two thousand living prisoners piled on top of each other and cemented together; they were then left to die; and the wall presumably to crumble. Fortunately it's not in the play.

Monday 19 January
Today's event was a very preliminary reading of *Tamburlaine* by some of the cast. Well, it works, and is a magnificent part for Finney: tough, vital, funny and with a great tragic dimension at the end. He will be remarkable, I think. Some quite impressive talents revealed, but I was alarmed at the amount of weight demanded by the two plays that make up the whole work. These are men of power, leaders, so it needs not one Denis Quilley, but four or five. The first play is not very hard: it has a wonderful Boys' Own Paper story energy, and a good deal of humour and incident. The second is much more difficult: the disintegration and moral corruption of Tamburlaine. With the light cutting I've done, each of the two plays will last two hours: four hours playing time in all.

Thursday 22 January
John Goodwin came to see me angry and wanting to resign. The thunder cloud of temperament has burst. He said the press office are unhappy; we make too many demands at a hectic time for them; those in my office are too brisk, too unfeeling. I stayed late sorting it out: passions high, much tears, general shouting. To quote Edward Albee: 'There are so many martyrdoms here.' But underneath it all, I have a sense of unease. People I love are being hurt and overtaxed. We are working too hard to get this damned place sorted out.

Went to a dinner at Rules given by Gielgud and Richardson to Harold, Antonia, Jacky and me, to celebrate the end of *No Man's Land*. A Ralph story: 'You know cocky I've tried to *sell* Hirst to the audience. But somehow I can't make it. I try, I work at it every night, and sometimes I think I am quite near it now. But when people come backstage afterwards they look at me and say, "Ah, those falls. . . ." or else, "Ah, those blue socks. . . ." but they never say, "Ah, Hirst."'

A moving story, because Ralph has had nothing like the credit he deserves for a great performance.

Sunday 25 January

Quiet day in Wallingford. Very very cold. I played hopscotch with Lucy this afternoon, but the air bit too much to go for a long walk. Played music, thought, and read papers. Back to London this evening. I am now even nervous about time off. I dare not relax.

Tuesday 27 January

Did a brief *Aquarius* this afternoon on Euan Uglow. Wonderful paintings. One in particular, called *Summer Painting*, was hard, precise, with an amazing sense of structure. I had my usual reaction, I wanted to own it, to live with it. Easy if one had £3,000 to spare. I don't.

Back to the theatre. A sense of unease. The opening is coming very near. One of the accounts department staff has written an abusive letter to Peter Stevens about the management, and left. Everybody is under strain. Is it my paranoia, or has the fun gone out of the thing? Somehow it has to be got back.

Wednesday 28 January

Up late for me, 8 am. A sluggish start to the day therefore. I worked at home all morning, grinding away on correspondence and worrying about our general tactics. I very much doubt whether the Lyttelton will be ready for the opening season in March, which is now booking; or the Olivier ready in the summer; or that we shall have enough money to run the Cottesloe.

Denys Lasdun arrived in a great state because he said the curved shape we have given to the Lyttelton stage front ruined the straight lines and angles of his architecture. I explained that the reason was because the stage had to accommodate the productions transferring from the Old Vic without changes being made to them. I soothed him, and said John Bury and I would look into it, but that far more bothering was the problem of getting the theatre finished at all, whatever the front of the stage. This went home with Lasdun and he looked more and more worried. But what can be done? We're on a course now that we have to go through. The people who will suffer are not the consultants, not the contractors, not the architects, not the builders, but the actors and the administration of the theatre. I sometimes feel I am all set up to be a great sacrificial victim: the white temple's first blood. That is not the way I am going to behave. I must believe in my own capacity to succeed. I'm not sure I do any more.

Peter Stevens champing round the office this evening concerned about the budget. We still can't get it down low enough, and he is fearful the Cottesloe will be axed.

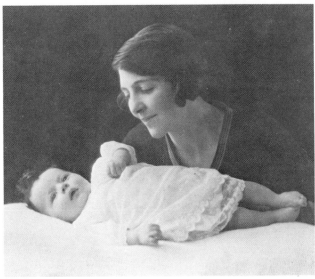

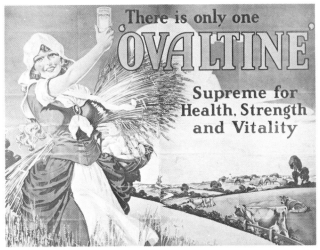

ove: Hall's father, Reginald, a
ntry stationmaster. Hall was
e-struck from an early age,
ly because of the cheap train
s to London that his father, as
ilwayman, was able to provide

right: Peter Hall as a baby
was born in Bury St. Edmunds
930) with his mother, Grace

dle right: 'My five-year-old
a of God was the Ovaltine
ter of a peasant earth-mother'

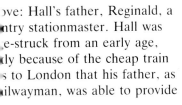

ht: F. R. Leavis, 'more
uence on the contemporary
atre than any other critic'.
Angeloglu, Camera Press

'Here comes Steve McQueen — flitted across the screen for ten seconds in *Akenfield*.'
Express Newspapers

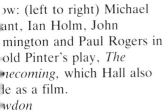

osite top: Young Tom Rouse,
ed by Garrow Shand, in a
er ploughing scene from
nfield

it: Ronald Blythe (far left) as
parson, during the filming of
nfield, which was improvised
local people. Blythe is author
he book

ow: (left to right) Michael
ant, Ian Holm, John
mington and Paul Rogers in
old Pinter's play, *The
necoming*, which Hall also
le as a film.
wdon

Above: With Paul Scofield rehearsing
Amadeus.
Nobby Clark

Left: Celebrating John Gielgud's 71st
birthday, 14 April 1975, during rehearsals
of *No Man's Land*.
Anthony Crickmay

osite: The Queen and Prince
p at the royal opening of the
onal Theatre, 25 October
. 'The special fanfare version
od Save the Queen sounded
ible with many mistakes by
Household Cavalry
peters.' *Nobby Clark*

t: Jennie Lee.
era Press

ow: The highest-priced stamp
e European Architectural
itage Year set, April 1975.
Post Office

osite: Members of the NT
rd at the time of the opening,
gh also included, marked with
risks, are non-members who
nd meetings. Behind Lord
ne, chairman, are − left to
t − Michael Birkett* (then NT
uty director), Denis Andrews*
ts Council assessor), David
es* (representing the DES),
er Hall*, Sir Ronald Leach
E, Maurice Stonefrost (at
k), Harold Sebag-Montefiore,
vey Hinds, Yolande Bird*
istant secretary to the Board),
Horace Cutler, Lord Mishcon,
glas Gosling* (secretary to the
rd), Lord O'Brien PC, GBE,
mond Carr, Alfred Francis,
ence Spencer. Members not in
picture are Illtyd Harrington
John Mortimer.
is J. Arthur

ht: Lord Goodman.
nera Press

Top: The National Theatre
Company at the opening of the
Olivier. *Nobby Clark*
Above: Ralph Richardson
inaugurating the NT, 16 March
1976. 'In peaked cap and exuding
geniality, he lit the blue touch
paper and the rocket zipped up
over the Thames'
Right: Julie Covington as Dorothy
in *Jumpers*. Stoppard's play,
directed by Peter Wood, was first
seen with Diana Rigg in that part
during the Olivier regime at the
Old Vic, and was revived at the
NT under Hall. *John Timbers*

Thursday 29 January

Cyril Bennett says he wants another 26 *Aquarius* episodes from me next year. I must do it, for news came today that it's going to cost £1,500 a year to send Christopher to Cambridge, which I suppose means earning between another £7,000 or £8,000 a year to have that clear after tax. So there's no choice about whether or not I do *Aquarius*, desperate though I am to cut down on my work.

Took a little tour of the Lyttelton and Olivier theatres alone tonight. Tried to imagine how *Tamburlaine* would be in the Olivier. The Lyttelton is at last full of the contractors' people—some two years late, they are working round the clock.

Friday 30 January

An hour with Professor Bernard Crick who is writing articles on the RSC and the National for the *Times Higher Educational Supplement*. I've seen the one on the RSC: not bad. I can't imagine what he can write about the National because there isn't a National at the moment. There's the National as it was under Larry, and the National as it might be under me in a couple of years' time. At the moment we are, and have been, only responding to crises.

Trevor's sense of Puritan duty made for a very bloody evening at Michael Birkett's house where he, David Jones, John Barton, and David Brierley from the RSC, and Michael Birkett, John Russell Brown, Peter Stevens and myself from the NT, all had dinner. Our object was to lay down some rules of behaviour between the two organisations. I first of all made a suggestion to Trevor: that each year the Olivier should have one Shakespeare play in its repertoire, which on the whole would be planned twelve months ahead. But, I said, there was a difficulty about this which ought to be sorted out. As Stratford always planned its repertoire about four months ahead, it would be easily possible for Stratford to pre-empt the NT by getting the same play on just before us, thus bringing all the problems of clashes, waste of public resources, etc. Trevor, though, absolutely refused to work out anything. He said that in effect the 37 plays of Shakespeare belonged to the RSC and they had to do them as they needed to do them. He reminded me that that was what I had said to Larry in the sixties.

He was the same about artists. What he proposed was that if either of us wanted an artist who was with the other, we should ring up, and if the answer was, please don't approach this actor at the moment, he or she is central to our work, the other would hold off; the actor would never be told. I think this is wrong. I cannot see how we can carve up actors' lives between us, without reference to them. We can't have secret deals.

So our meeting got us nowhere.

Sunday 1 February

Our prop men want a 50% increase because they're moving from the Old Vic to the South Bank: they're doing the same job but it's in a different environment. We've said no. So our friendly NATTKE steward, Kon Fredericks, has got our whole stage staff to agree that while they will continue to work they will not, during this fit-up period in the new theatre, touch any of the new machinery until the management make a more realistic offer. They know that now we're nearly open we're vulnerable.

Carpets going down in the front of house. I like the look of them. The public areas will really be dazzling.

I've finished recently a book, *Your Isadora* by Francis Steegmuller. It's a record of Isadora's affair with Gordon Craig. The love letters are wonderful. She was an open, vulnerable creature. Craig was a careful, egocentric shit: too proud to fail, either in his profession or in his personal life. He never risked commitment of any kind. At one time he had the whole European theatre at his feet and could have worked anywhere with anyone: with Reinhardt (refused), with Stanislavsky (one production, the *Hamlet*, five years to make and rehearse), and there were many many other offers. I believe he turned them down out of fear. Even genius is no good without courage. He was a great artist and an awful human being.

Monday 2 February

Larry arrived at midday in a very strange mood: something manic and disturbed. He said he couldn't appear in the special show we are giving on 28 February, our last night at the Old Vic. I said I didn't know how we were going to announce his non-appearance. There would either be a press campaign speculating on his serious illness again, or a campaign speculating on his refusal to work with me. Anyway, we agreed we should make public that he was indisposed and not able to be in the show a reasonable time before the performance, and that Albert should take his place.

Why won't he take part? I don't know. Is it that he doesn't want to be seen helping?

Evening associates' meeting. Many topics discussed. I got rid of everybody by 10 pm and slept until 4 am when I woke up in absolute clarity and began work.

Wednesday 4 February

Tonight was the acoustics test. The Lyttelton was packed: 700 contractors, engineers and their wives and children, plus a couple of hundred from the theatre. Great excitement. I shall never forget seeing the foyers full of people for the first time. But the best moment to me was when, at the beginning of the test, Albert and Gawn Grainger walked on to the stage and talked to each other deliberately making no sound: a nice start and a big laugh. At intervals gentlemen came on and fired revolvers and let off maroons, and others rushed about the auditorium measuring the results. There was singing, and I played the piano for the accounts department in three songs. The gentleman I was accompanying in an Irish ballad cut two pages in the middle and I had to do a quick rescue. Denis Quilley, clutching his stetson, sang tough guy Howard Keel songs from the past.

The lights failed at quarter past ten but Albert continued to tell jokes in the dark. The theatre works. Hearts were high by the end of tonight.

Friday 6 February
After a meeting today I asked Rayne what was happening about my contract. I had heard nothing, though some time ago it had been made clear that the Board were extending it for another five years. If it wasn't coming through, I wanted to know. I said the precise position would affect my feelings about my work for the next two years. He assured me it was all a mere formality. Well, let's see the formality finished. I think I'm boiling up for a big blow-up with him. Still it's the end of the week, and we all feel under siege. Everybody is overworked, overtaxed, and very anxious. Perhaps we're all over-reacting.

Sunday 8 February
Finished the Dimbleby book[1]. There's a most moving section. He's aware the young turks of the BBC are against him, that they want him out. And yet he is continuing to work hard, while keeping it quiet that he has cancer and is in continual treatment. At that moment T C Worsley in the *Financial Times* wrote a big attack saying what was wrong with the BBC was Dimbleby, his time was over and he must go, which Fleet Street joyfully took up. So he had to surmount all that too. He showed enormous courage in his last six years.

Monday 9 February
Saw Larry Malkin of *Time* magazine. He'd briefed himself with Ken Tynan and Jonathan Miller. He said that *Time* always spoke to the enemies. I had the same replay of Tynan's views that Michael Billington produced when he interviewed me last week: the National Theatre was now too important to be run by one man; it must have at its head a bureaucrat, a technocrat, a scholar of the theatre, not a director or actor.

I expect my talk with Malkin will add up to two lines in the European edition. *Time* takes over your life and then often prints nothing.

To Tony Crickmay to have my picture taken by him. I was as uncomfort-

---

[1] *Richard Dimbleby* by Jonathan Dimbleby, his son.

able as usual. I don't mind television, I don't mind trying to act in a film, but to stand around and hope the camera will capture me I find acutely embarrassing. Crickmay made it as easy as it can ever be.

Wednesday 11 February
Willie Wright[1], the man from the DES, came up to Max and myself after today's South Bank Board meeting and said the official position had to be that the South Bank Board could take no responsibility for the extra costs we were incurring by ordering temporary equipment to replace the equipment that was not working, but that we should get on with the opening and keep a very careful log of all money; it can be argued who pays later. That of course is what we have got to do. But if everything goes wrong and we have enormous deficits, I am quite sure that all this expenditure will be used against us. The English Establishment only bends the rules for success.

Thursday 12 February
Today, a radio interview and an interview with two American journalists. Steady stuff. I've now done so many of these, I feel if I'm kicked I can start speaking the National Theatre pitch like an automaton.

Sunday 15 February
I ran Max Rayne this morning and had an appalling ding-dong with him for an hour. He went on about our treatment of the protocol committee and the catering committee; he assassinated Birkett, annihilated Goodwin, and passed a few nasty remarks about Peter Stevens, and myself, all the time talking nineteen to the dozen. Some very hard things were said. I asked him if he was running the theatre or I; he could hire me or fire me, but until he fired me, I was doing the job. I told him we were all in great discomfort and irritation and feeling very insecure. Max finished by soothing me down and flattering my ego. I was, he said, a wonderful administrator and artist. He had destroyed me on both counts earlier.

Had a blessed, quiet evening at Wallingford on my own. The family went back to London at the usual time. I stayed; to think of *Tamburlaine*—which still eludes me.

Wednesday 18 February
A catastrophic dress rehearsal of *Plunder* last night in the Lyttelton[2]. The thirty-second scene change took forty minutes. None of the communication

---

[1] C.W.Wright, Deputy Secretary of the DES 1971–76.
[2] All the productions then playing at the Old Vic were also being rehearsed on the Lyttelton stage for their opening there in March.

212

systems is working—no cue lights, none of the flying. You can't time a curtain in or out. The whole situation is horrifying. Shall we make the opening?

Brief session with yet another writer from *Time* magazine—this time their man from New York. People who work on *Time* do take themselves frightfully seriously (as I suspect we in the theatre do too). It's that circulation all over the world I suppose. They also spend so long sharing with you the problems of getting their stories passed by their editors, chief assistant editors, chief executive editors, and so on up to God, that they very rarely have the time to ask you anything about yourself.

To the first preview of *Watch It Come Down* at the Old Vic. I never remember an audience more nervous. They were terrified about what was going to happen next. The play is very strong, I think very good, and Bill has directed it wonderfully. But I guess it will be received with detestation by many people. Osborne has an amazing ability to draw into himself all the sicknesses of the moment and make plays which express whatever our current mood is with great complexity. He did it with *Look Back in Anger*; he did it with *The Entertainer*; and now I think he's done it with *Watch It Come Down*—though where he can go next, after the extreme self-laceration that this play reveals, is a question.

Friday 20 February
Hamlet dress rehearsal in the Lyttelton tonight: 7 pm to nearly midnight. Who would have thought a problem in the new theatre would be that the front-of-house doors didn't fit, and that the automatic closing devices made them squeak. And as the backstage areas are like an echo chamber, every door squeak is audible for miles. It drove me mad. We asked for the doors to be fixed last November. Nothing has been done.

News came from the Vic about the reception of *Watch It Come Down* at tonight's preview. There was a bit of a riot: boos and cheers, and cries of rubbish and bravo. That's the stuff. . . .

Tuesday 24 February
A ghastly afternoon's rehearsal of *Borkman* in the Lyttelton. The noise of banging and hammering all over the building made it impossible to concentrate. Added to which there was a large electric drill going like a nightmare at the dentist. So the actors were completely inaudible at times. Nothing to be done. The workmen just say 'If you want the theatre open. . . .'

Wednesday 25 February
The Osborne notices are disappointing: they are neither hostile enough nor enthusiastic enough. Irving Wardle in *The Times* and Michael Billington in *The Guardian* reserve their position. There's only one real stinker, in the

Daily Mail, which rejoices in the headline, 'Oh no John.' The new territory that Osborne is trying to chart is not commented on.

The disabled are hopping mad. They've issued a press release saying their needs have not been adequately met at the new National Theatre[1]. This is causing great happiness in Fleet Street. Here we go. . . .

Thursday 26 February

We decided today to go manual with the Lyttelton backstage equipment and bypass the electronic system. This means that over the next months we shall have to install a manual flying system ourselves, line by line. I had a drink with some of the stage crew in the bar. The cry 'We've gone manual' was one of jubilation. Power and performance were back where they needed to be, in the hands of the operators, the human touch. All we need is a space, an audience, and some lights. That is all we're going to get in the Lyttelton.

Friday 27 February

Great sense that everything is about to happen. The opening is near.

Saturday 28 February

This evening was the National company's last night at the Old Vic. We presented the special entertainment to honour Lilian Baylis, *Tribute to the Lady*. There was a warm feeling in the house, not too much sentiment or too much nostalgia, and I think we surmounted the absence of Larry fairly well. Albert did magnificently in his stead: he was charming, dignified, and put the audience and the cast at their ease. Ralph told stories about the addiction of Harcourt Williams[2] to Bemax, and got as many laughs on the word Bemax as the best stand-up comic. John Gielgud began Hamlet's 'Oh what a rogue' speech at such a high pitch that I feared he would go into orbit; he did. Peggy was superb; I think her performance of Lilian Baylis is one of her greatest achievements; it seemed like a reincarnation.

Denis Healey and Roy Jenkins were there as well as what seemed like most of the profession. A crushing party afterwards where everybody roamed all over the building. We left at half past one and it was still in full swing. It should have been Larry's evening, but he had refused to accept it, so it was the company's and it worked. Larry was given due homage and so was the Vic, and the audience loved it.

I had a word with Sybil[3] in the audience before the performance. She's now nearly 93 and looks amazingly delicate and white. I kissed the cold skin and said, 'Hello, Sybil, I am very glad that you are here.' She smiled with a

---

[1] In 1981, the Year of the Disabled, the British Tourist Authority officially acknowledged 'the outstanding contribution made by the NT in providing facilities for disabled visitors'. [2] Director of the Old Vic 1929–33.   [3] Thorndike.

great deal of the old radiance and said, 'Dear Peter, I am very glad that *you* are here—at the National. . . .'

Radio, TV and many journalists asked me to comment. Had I no regrets? Wasn't it rather a sad occasion? I kept on saying I had no regrets whatever. I was delighted to be leaving the Vic. I had fought for this for three years. This was the moment I had been waiting for. We were moving.

All that was true. I didn't join the National to run the Vic. It's a fine old theatre, but it's not what I came here for.

Sunday 29 February
A quiet day in London. The Sunday notices for the Osborne play are much better than I had feared after seeing the tepid dailies. The overall impression is of quite a success.

Went for a walk round the city with Christopher and dropped in on the Whitechapel Gallery to see a strange exhibition of inflatable figures lying corpse-like in ultra-violet light, and a man etched out in tiny gas jets, all in the dark.

An evening of television and nothing. An ominous sense that all hell is about to be let loose next week.

Friday 5 March
Ran into Harry Pugh[1], who made an amazing speech to me. It was terrible, he said, that we'd had to endure such difficulties in this run-up to the Lyttelton opening. The contractors and the consultants were all agreed that we must not suffer in the same way in the run-up to the opening of the Olivier. Therefore, he said, they want to test and finish all the equipment there before letting us in. I said this was unacceptable, as I didn't believe that if we gave them more time things would be any more finished.

I know there's a report going to the South Bank Board in which they are going to try and bring this one off. But I am not going to let them.

Saturday 6 March
I talked to Richard Pilbrow and my worst suspicions were confirmed. They are extremely late completing the Olivier. For instance, they haven't yet even started putting in the switchboard, and instead of thirty people working on the stage wiring there are—wait for it—four. So, said Richard, it would be much better if they absolutely finished the Olivier before handing it over to us, but of course later than we had planned. I told him if this came up next Wednesday at the South Bank Board meeting, I would oppose it resolutely and there would be a confrontation. He looked rattled.

---

[1] An Associate of Denys Lasdun and Partners.

The Olivier obviously *won't* be ready on time. I need this like a hole in the head while we are struggling with moving the Old Vic productions into the Lyttelton for its grand opening next week. And the Cottesloe apparently is now delayed too. It's a disgrace and ought to be seen as such in public. If I am not very careful though the disgrace will be laid at the door of the National Theatre. It's the fault of the South Bank Board and their contractors.

There is clearly a big feud going on between McAlpine's and the architects. No one is handling the situation at all properly. We have asked repeatedly for a gang of a dozen men who can go round de-snagging — making lavatories work, correcting doors etc etc. McAlpine's have ignored this. Everything is a special job which has to be indented for and go through the office. And costs a fortune. I spent most of the day with my mind seething, wondering what to do.

Dress rehearsal of *Happy Days* in the Lyttelton. We had an invited audience of 150. The back of the stalls was like an oven, the front freezing cold; and the play was hardly audible for the din of the air conditioning—it's like some vast ocean liner at sea. Peggy in fine form though.

I wandered about under the stage after the performance trying to trace the noises. There appears to be a big roaring furnace right below the front row of the stalls, and the sound is coming up into the auditorium.

Didn't sleep. I have the feeling we are going into a very bad time.

Sunday 7 March
Dreadful night. Head too active. Too tired to move, go out, do anything. Didn't go to Wallingford. Didn't stir from the flat. Spent the morning on the telephone, while lying in bed. I was almost scared to relax. We must play our planned Olivier repertoire somewhere or other, no matter what—perhaps in a tent near the site—or the company we have built up will disintegrate. If we postpone the Olivier opening now, and send actors away, I don't believe we shall ever properly recover, either in the profession, or with the public.

No Sunday papers in London today: a strike by the distributors. They have them at Wallingford but apparently there's nothing, thank God, about the National. I'm sure there's going to be a big press attack from somebody within the next ten days—either against the National or against me. The target is too big; the noise we've been making too loud. Someone will come out of the woodwork. Perhaps Jonathan Miller?

Mooned about all day feeling like a cabbage. Splitting headache. A sauna bath did little to make things better. Just too bloody tired.

Monday 8 March
To the theatre. All activity. Sense of preparation. Today we start a week of opening to the critics all the five productions we've transferred to the

Lyttelton from the Old Vic. So this is the critics' first ever experience of the new building as a working playhouse.

Talked with Jack Kroll of *Newsweek* at midday. Then down to the auditorium to listen to the air conditioning—appalling noise. The input makes a low hum, a distant growling with the occasional throb. And the extractors hiss. The weary smiles of the experts in the auditorium show that they know what I fear: that the bloody thing will never be silent. It's the curse of the modern age, this acceptance of machine noises. We arranged for it to be shut off—all of it—during the actual playing of today's matinée of *Happy Days*.

At 1.30 pm, in the freezing cold, flurries of snow around me, I talked straight to camera for a Central Office of Information film about the building. Five minutes they said. It took more like 25. Taxis, noise, people staring. . . .

Full of adrenalin I rushed back into the foyers. The place was filling up, the bars open, the bookshop selling books, all the familiar first night faces looking a little startled in the afternoon light—but pleased I think. There was a great sense of excitement in the air, and I must say the building looks magnificent.

I've never seen so many wheelchairs. It looked like a convention of wheelchairs. I suppose the publicity stirred up by the disabled, protesting that our arrangements are inadequate, has encouraged them to try us out.

No bells yet working to summon the audience. So the house manager had to walk through the foyers with an old electric bell and battery strapped onto a piece of plywood, holding it up in the air and ringing it. How English. . . .

As I dashed in I was caught by a radio reporter. I gave a brilliant interview, and then he discovered he hadn't turned his tape recorder on. Generally, there was much bobbing and bowing to the media.

Peggy gave a superb performance of *Happy Days*. The house was full, intelligent, and responded well. Larry was there, looking, I thought, genial.

In the evening we did *Plunder*—a fair performance. The interval was too long, and the scene changes as well, but the revolve had broken down and we were turning it by hand. Also the audience suspected imminent bombs —very helpful to a farce—because a GLC man in peaked cap and uniform marched to the centre of the proscenium and faced the audience at each scene change, rocking up and down on his heels like a conceited schoolmaster. This was because the GLC has decreed that he keep close watch on the fire curtain—which rises from the floor—in case someone is impaled on it.

Some sense of achievement today: two plays launched; two audiences satisfied. I am very pleased.

Tuesday 9 March

Lunch with Richard Findlater for an *Observer* piece, 'Whither the National Theatre? The penalties of success'. I said let's have some success before we start talking about penalties. He revealed that *The Observer*'s official policy was now fairly hostile to the National: anything big needs hitting.

Pandemonium this afternoon trying to tidy up *Hamlet* for tonight's performance. One of those Marx Brothers two hours; but we got it done. Desperately tired tonight, and unable to watch the play right through; I popped in and out. I had asked the cast not to push too much, not to shout. It is an intimate theatre and they should use clarity and truth, not inflation. But somehow the rough edges showed. The play didn't work; and the reception was rather disappointing.

The actors were all very down at the end: a feeling that they'd given a fair performance, but somehow just missed it. I have a sense of morbid disappointment. This *Hamlet* will never be seen as I meant it. No, that's stupid! I think we're all suffering from reaction to yesterday. It feels like Friday now, and it's only Tuesday.

Last night when I walked into the auditorium to see *Plunder* I noticed to my horror a lot of little wooden stands with hygrometers merrily whirring away on them. They were testing the temperature and the humidity. Seats had been closed off and a lot of the audience were looking wonderingly at these white machines. I said they must go. I had the usual answer of course—if they're not there the heating will never work. I repeated that tonight, at least, they must go. So they went.

I had a big attack this evening of What's-It-All-For. We're winning, I suppose. But I know there's going to be an avalanche of abuse at the end of the week.

Wednesday 10 March

Gathering of the South Bank Board to discuss that since the last meeting, a month ago, the delivery of the Olivier to us for rehearsals etc has moved from the beginning of April to the end of June, the only explanation being 'electrical difficulties', and the quite spurious argument that the technical consultants don't want the National Theatre staff to go through hell again—they want to finish before we go in.

Lord Cottesloe rather touchingly, in his most Polonius-like way, read out a little prepared speech written in meticulous Etonian handwriting on his own House of Lords notepaper, recording that we must all stand together. He was just about to call the consultants in, when I asked if I could have a few moments off the record. I said we were not prepared to accept that the consultants must finish the work first. It was only a way of them giving themselves more time. We had every intention of getting into the Olivier as soon as possible—not though to the extent of ruining the plays. If that were to be so we would stage our planned repertoire in another theatre. But perform we would. . . .

The consultants then came in and had their say but it didn't actually mean very much because I had provided a background. The delays and extra labour so far on the South Bank have cost us about £125,000. God knows what the final figure will be[1].

A dreadful dress rehearsal of *Borkman* which opens in the Lyttelton tomorrow. Scene changes long. Lighting cues wrong. Peg quite good. Ralph saying amazing things. Wendy distant and hiding. The revolve broke down so Ralph was wandering up the mountain for what seemed hours. He was shy and ashamed at the end, like he always is after a performance, even when he's given a fine one. He is never satisfied with his own work.

John Goodwin is preparing me for the bruises at the end of the week[2]. The *Standard* is running a big story about how on earth are we going to fill the 2,500 seats each day. *The Observer* is considering what our effect will be on the rest of the theatre—bad doubtless. And so on and so on.

Watch It tonight. Four productions in, one more to go.

Thursday 11 March
Borkman this evening was, I'm afraid, lousy. Peggy played the second act very well, and things cheered up a little, but she was in tears after it had ended. Ralph was in tears too, or at least one tear was trickling down his cheek. He said, 'Old fellow, I so much wanted to be good for you tonight, and I know I wasn't. . . .' What could I say?

I sat with him for a time in the dressing room while big beakers of gin revived him. Donald Sinden called full of glee and exuberance. He had, he said, loved it. He looked at the dressing room, heard the air conditioning, and remarked it was just like a ship. 'Oh yes it is,' said Ralph. 'But being in the theatre *is* rather like being in a ship. We go on a perilous voyage knowing we may capsize at any moment. We have to look out for rocks—and mermaids.'

Natasha Parry called too. She told Ralph she was coming again, bringing Peter[3]. Ralph was very cordial to her but said to me afterwards, 'Who was that? Peter who? Hello, I thought, we're on thin ice here, I don't know any Peters, except this Peter. . . .'

[1] The end figure was £377,407. This was paid off over the years, largely by the NT itself, partly by the South Bank Theatre Board, and finally by the Arts Council, whose special grant of £173,597 in 1983 cleared the deficit.
[2] The critics were holding back their reviews until they had seen all first five productions in the new building.
[3] Brook, her husband.

Friday 12 March
The critics response to the new building, the Lyttelton, and this week's productions is given masses of space today. It's enthusiastic. Everyone has a little go about something or other, but the overall impression is success: a bit of a triumph. Our big gamble of bringing the new theatre to life now and not waiting for it to be completed has paid off.

Monday 15 March
McAlpine's lunch in the Pavilion Room of the Dorchester: McAlpine father and son; Goodman; Lockwood; Rayne; Cottesloe—the cultural establishment. A good deal of congratulation about having got the building going at last. Cottesloe repeated his joke of last week—'Well, we're not out of the wood yet, but at least we're in it!' I was there to sour the proceedings by pointing out that if the contractors didn't hand the Olivier over to us by July we were likely to be playing our Olivier repertoire in a tent on the back car park. Some consternation, but the point went home.

The gala £10 performance of *Plunder*: all the nobs of the land, champagne, salmon in the restaurant, Rayne hither and thither. The building is certainly a success; one could feel it again tonight: great warm pleasure in everybody. Even better, the nobs had obviously expected a high-minded cultural evening, and what they got was a simple play with lots of laughs. They were delighted and I think the play has never gone better. Max begged me to make a speech; so I did; short.

By the end it was too late to go to a restaurant. So the children and I bought fish and chips in the Waterloo Road and took them home to eat.

Tuesday 16 March
Session with Douglas Gosling on our budget, which is already in ruins. Our plans are destroyed by the delays, and our costs are escalating wildly. Bar profits are up though. . . .

The big surprise news of the day is that Harold Wilson has resigned. Fleet Street was caught napping. They are furious they didn't know. He says he just wants to retire. This is so simple it might be true. Yet I can't believe a man so dependent on power for his very breath would give it up this easily.

There was a queue outside the box office at 5 am this morning. It opened at half past eight and by quarter to nine all the seats were gone.

I was on parade to meet Princess Margaret at 7 pm, escorted her into the auditorium, and as the national anthem finished I ran for the roof where Ralph and half the press of London were waiting for him to inaugurate his rocket. Called Ralph's Rocket, this will be fired every night when the curtain goes up[1]. Ralph in peaked cap and exuding geniality lit the blue touch

---

[1] Later the rocket was fired only before every first night.

paper and the rocket zipped up over the Thames. Everybody cheered. I then took him down to the director's box, where he watched a little piece of *Hamlet*, nodding and tutting. I don't think he liked it. But he went off into the night, happy and gracious. 'I love fireworks,' he said, 'they are so unnecessary.'

Wednesday 17 March
Associates' dinner. I thanked everybody for their efforts in opening the Lyttelton. John Bury on behalf of everybody thanked me, very generously. A celebratory mood.

Throughout all this Blakemore looked tense and drawn. He had asked earlier to be put on the agenda to talk. He needed, he had said, 25 minutes of our attention. He wished to read a paper to us. He wanted no interruptions. And he wanted peace. He didn't want people bringing in food, sandwiches, drinks etc. Before he actually read his paper he said he had discussed it with nobody, and that it had been typed outside the organisation. He handed out nine copies, enough for everybody. Then, his eyes staring, his voice high-pitched, he read an attack on me.

His main point was that the associates had no power. They were a rubber stamp, and were not consulted. But what angered me were the techniques Blakemore used. He said the actors getting high salaries had Laurie Evans as an agent, and Laurie Evans was my agent. He talked of me getting four per cent of NT productions I'd directed when they transferred to the West End, though he must know that it is the practice of all subsidised theatres to allow their people to earn proper commercial rates if outside commercial interests are making money out of their work. He declared I was indeed the person best fitted to run the National Theatre, and was doing brilliantly, but I needed to be saved from myself. It was being said that I was feathering my nest, although of course he didn't mean to imply that I was.

I had the greatest difficulty in controlling myself. The embarrassment round the table was acute. We argued the matter out until half past midnight. I refuted Blakemore's facts, pointing out that everything he mentioned had been brought to the associates, and all the financial details had been passed by the Board. He tried further allegations: there was revolution breeding in the company; attacks were being prepared from outside; the technical staff were unregarded and unappreciated—and felt it. Harold Pinter asked him to be specific. 'I cannot name names,' he said.

I took all his points in turn and dealt with them. His chief one remained though—did the associates have less power than they wanted? Blakemore was for having them designated as an advisory body. I said I didn't want advice; advice was easy. I wanted responsibility, commitment.

In the end, he asked the associates to take his paper away with them and study it. But they all individually returned it to him. Their gesture refused it.

I was very shaken, and very upset. I don't at all object to discussing the powers of the associates. But what else were we dealing with? What was his motive? He can't seriously have wanted to turn the associates into an advisory body. I suppose he dropped his bombshells either to create a situation in which I resigned, or in which he could resign with a good clean puritan conscience. I just don't know. Was he expecting support from the associates? He didn't get it.

I must remind myself that nothing in the theatre is as bad as it seems. Things move; problems resolve. I must be careful of my own paranoia. A situation like this could make it run rampant. That is the chief danger.

Thursday 18 March

Finance and general purposes committee. Mishcon thinks that as the National Theatre we should play the national anthem before every performance. I told him it was now practice to play it at the beginning and end of seasons, or in the presence of royalty, and that was the custom at all other theatres. Yes, he said, but they were not the National Theatre. God help us if we are once more going to spend, in the immortal words of an alderman at Stratford-upon-Avon in my time there, a couple of minutes at each performance 'remembering the privilege of being British'. I can still see Michel Saint-Denis's wide-eyed disbelief at this remark when the national anthem was an issue at Stratford in the early sixties. It is not a good tune to raise a curtain; and was only introduced in the 1914–18 war to encourage patriotism.

Friday 19 March

Woke up still thinking about the Blakemore business. Like a fool I gave my copy of his paper back to him. I should have kept it. I am sure it is defamatory and would be useful to have in my hands. So I rang for it. But he refused; said he wanted to correct it because there were certain errors of facts and perhaps mistakes of emphasis. There certainly were....

Off to see Georg Solti in North London in his new house: a soundproofed room, wood lined, with wonderful hi-fi equipment and a glistening piano—a womb of music. He'd been on some mad lunch with Michael Birkett and others: drinks at the House of Lords, then *hors d'oeuvres* at Pomegranates, the main course at some other restaurant, and so on. He said he didn't like drinking in the middle of the day....

Blakemore came to see me in the evening. I was very blunt. He said he was being very frank too. He told me he had committed errors of fact and of implication, and he apologised, but his main point remained: the associates had insufficient power.

He said he admired me but couldn't stand my greediness—for work,

222

for money, for success, for power, for position. And he couldn't stand the fact that I was so energetic. He agreed, though, to retract at our meeting tomorrow evening the defamatory implications of the paper so that we could discuss what was important—the situation of the associates.

Saturday 20 March
Special meeting of the associates. Everything kept deliberately low-key. No one disagreed that all matters of policy should come to them, that they could ask questions and seek information on anything they wished, but that I reserved the right, having taken the consensus view, to overrule them.

The Board employs me, but I choose the associates. I want them as a body to argue with, a group that can check and criticise me. Ultimately, having listened to them, the decision has to be mine. But to overrule them would be a very foolish thing for me to do.

It was decided, therefore, to leave things as they are and to try to make everything work in the way designated. The storm has subsided.

Watch It Come Down played to a capacity house tonight—the Establishment out in force, hating the play. But we've had the world and his wife at the theatre all this week, and it's a real success. I suppose everything is put into proportion once the building is alive. Now it will have a daily rhythm working as a theatre, and we shall know what we're there for. Blakemore picked his time badly.

Sunday 21 March to Friday 26 March
In all the welter of publicity about the opening there's one paragraph in the article in *Time* that I want to record: 'By the time he finished Cambridge, Hall had already directed several plays and, perhaps more significant, studied English under F R Leavis. Even though Leavis hated theatre, he made a lasting impact on Hall with his scrupulous examination of a text, particularly for its ironies and ambiguities and the sense that a work of art must be placed in a social context. Hall more or less applied that lesson in his celebrated *Wars of the Roses* productions, where the protagonists were not seen as gallant warrior kings but as bloody power buccaneers. Hall clearly believes that to immerse an audience unforgettably in a play, the cast and director must locate and pinpoint the vital element that T S Eliot once called "the present moment of the past".'

That's a marvellous phrase of Eliot's. Where does it occur?

I have been thinking about *The Oresteia*. If we are going to do it we must do all three plays in one brave gesture. So I've asked Tony Harrison to give me his version of the first, *Agamemnon*, by the autumn, then to get on with the other two plays, and in 1977 we will stage the whole trilogy.

I'm told the *Evening Standard* is sniffiing about preparing an anti National Theatre story to be written by Gaia Servadio, probing at my salary, my involvement in film companies, whether I have a chauffeur-driven car, whether the Barbican flat is paid for by the NT, etc. Someone is putting them up to all this.

Have read this week a biography of Edmund Kean by Raymond Fitz-simmons[1]: an interesting economical story of a great actor, the Byron of the stage, dead at 45, a monster of egoism and paranoia. His life was spent struggling to maintain the supremacy he was given at Drury Lane in his twenties—a struggle aided by hot brandy and two or three whores each interval in the dressing room. Some interesting things:

During the great Cox scandal—the case brought against Kean because he was having an affair with an Alderman Cox's wife—Hazlitt wrote: 'Let a great man fall into misfortune, and then you discover the real disposi-tions of the reading, seeing, believing, loving public towards their pre-tended idol. See how they set upon him the moment he is down, how they watch for the smallest slip, the first pretext to pick a quarrel with him, how slow they are to acknowledge worth, how they never forgive an error, how they trample upon and tear "to tatters, to very rags", the common frailties, how they overlook and malign the transcendent excel-lent which they can neither reach nor find a substitute for.... Who that had felt Kean's immeasurable superiority in *Othello*, was not glad to see him brought to the ordinary level...? Such is the natural feeling. And then comes the philosophical critic, and tells you with a face of lead and brass that "no more indulgence is to be shown to the indiscretions of a man of genius than to any other!" What! you make him drunk and mad with applause then blame him for not being sober, you lift him to a pinnacle, and then say he is not to be giddy. You own he is to be a creature of impulse, and yet you would regulate him like a machine, you expect him to be all fire and air, to wing the empyrean, and to take you with him, and yet you would have him a muck worm crawling in the earth!'

There is also in the book a nightmare description of Kean's attempt to play Henry V in 1830 when, though he was only just into his forties, his memory had deserted him. He couldn't learn the part. His spirits had never completely recovered from the outcry that followed the Cox scan-dal and the thought of another persecution sickened him. In a personal letter to his friend W H Halpin, editor of the *Star*, he wrote: 'Fight for me, I have no resources in myself; mind is gone, and body is hopeless. God knows my heart. I would do, but cannot. Memory, the first of goddesses, has forsaken me, and I am left without a hope but from those

---

[1] *Edmund Kean, Fire From Heaven.*

old resources that the public and myself are tired of. Damn God, damn ambition. The soul leaps, the body falls.'

I find that a very moving statement of any great actor's decline. Loss of memory is the thing that haunts them all. It's strange too that the late eighteenth and early nineteenth century had this ability with words. Kean behaved like a scoundrel, leched like a madman, was a liar, a drunkard and a megalomaniac of impossible proportions. And he, in common with nearly all his contemporaries, wrote like a god. As with writing, so with furniture, with houses. Between 1750 and 1830 English taste was secure.

Monday 29 March
Tamburlaine work this morning with John Bury. Haunted all the time by the problem of scale in the Olivier. We really don't know what the size of things should be in that auditorium.

Great worries about the *Evening Standard* and Gaia Servadio. I have arranged to meet her on Thursday evening.

Tuesday 30 March
Christopher's birthday; he's nineteen. . . .

Lunch with Cyril Bennett. He confirmed that he would like me to do another series for *Aquarius* and hoped I could.

Wednesday 31 March
To Arnold Goodman at 10.30. I told him the whole sordid Blakemore story and that the *Evening Standard* was preparing a big attack. He was sitting magisterially taking his breakfast and asked me to join him, so I had grapefruit and a coffee.

His main counsel was to let what is going to happen happen. He said everybody knew there were lots of scurrilous dogs barking round my ankles—as there were round the ankles of anybody who was envied. Most of the curs wanted my job; ignore them. He was, though, disturbed enough to urge me to share it all with Max Rayne. So it was arranged that early this afternoon I should join them both at Goodman's office.

There I told my story and got everything out—Blakemore's attack, Tynan stirring the press, the Miller disaffection, my particular anxiety about all this because my contract is soon to be renewed. Max expressed surprise at Blakemore. Arnold said the only point of having chairmen, chaps like Max, in the background of artistic enterprises was to help fellows like me when they were attacked. Max declared at one point that he'd always thought it was a mistake for me to do *Aquarius*. Arnold thought this was preposterous —*Aquarius* had helped me and it had helped the National: made me better known, and earned me a few bob. I told them I was going to see Gaia

Servadio tomorrow, and they agreed this was probably a good thing, and then just to take the consequences, whatever they might be.

As I was leaving the theatre in the late evening Blakemore popped his head into my office and said nervously that he'd heard I was seeing his friend Gaia Servadio. He wanted to assure me he hadn't shown her his paper. She'd pumped him, and he'd told her as little as possible. I said that if he assured me of that, of course I had to believe him.

Thursday 1 April
Saw Gaia Servadio. She has a vague Italian charm, and was very misinformed about me. She told me I had a film company with a registered office, the address of which was my home in Wallingford. She said I made commercials regularly and she'd heard that I cancelled a *Hamlet* rehearsal in order to go and make a commercial for Liberty's one afternoon. This, in fact, was the Makepeace *Aquarius* film, though I didn't actually go when they shot a Makepeace table at Liberty's. She asked me about the furniture in the office, my salary, why I did so much etc etc. It was all the old rubbish. I tried to be as cool as possible but I don't think I was very successful.

Friday 2 April
To Vienna in the mid-afternoon for the Jubilee celebrations of the Burgtheater. Usual crowded aeroplane. I hate air travel, I hate travelling, I hate new places. I'd much sooner be at home.

Saturday 3 April
Vienna: I talked at length to Klingenberg, Intendant of the Burgtheater. These Jubilee celebrations are virtually the end of his contract; he leaves in three months, has a year off, and then begins at the theatre in Zurich in the autumn of 1977. I can't imagine that to move from Vienna to Zurich is much of a step up. Yet Klingenberg seems extremely happy.

It's extraordinary the way they go on in the German theatre. Intendants have only five-year contracts, and move from theatre to theatre, I suppose simply to increase their salaries. The consequence of this perpetual musical chairs is that they do three years' work in which they actually make some mark, and then the last two are fairly useless because everybody knows they are going.

Sunday 4 April
Vienna: To the theatre in the morning. I am put in the row of visiting Intendants: Everding from Hamburg, Buchwitz from Zurich, etc etc. They all look like fierce career politicians. The curtain rose at 11 am sharp on a packed auditorium. The veterans of the Burgtheater are in the front rows. The amazing thing about this theatre is that after five years

you can't get fired, so they have a wonderful collection of old actors who will eventually retire on a pension very nearly the same as their finishing salary.

Ewald Balsar and Paul Hoffman started the proceedings with a poem by Goethe and the proclamation by Joseph II founding the Burgtheater two hundred years ago. Guests from overseas paid their tributes. Klingenberg spoke; the Minister of Culture spoke; the Chancellor spoke. I have never heard so many people say so much about the theatre making a healthy, socially democratic society, and about the poet being the critic of mankind and the actor his mouthpiece. But how can reverence be avoided on these occasions, even though reverence has nothing to do with the theatre and nothing to do with entertainment?

Back in London by 6.30 pm and to the Barbican very worried still about Gaia Servadio and the *Evening Standard*. John Goodwin rang. He thinks I should see Charles Wintour[1], offer to tell him the background, and point out that I am going to sue if the *Standard* defames me. But I don't know. So I do nothing. Which I shall doubtless regret.

Monday 5 April
National Theatre Board this afternoon, a fairly smooth and equable meeting. My contract got nodded through with acclamation. So I am now at the National for another four and a half years. I am glad.

Wednesday 7 April
Breakfast with Terry Hands[2]. He said that with his production of *Twelfth Night* at the Comédie Française, his Stratford *Henry* plays visiting Paris, and his *Otello* at the Paris Opera in the summer, he thought he had Paris pretty well locked up; now he was moving on to Vienna and Salzburg; his only real competition in Europe was Strehler. Are we, I said, all in a race? There is plenty of work, and room for plenty of people. I talked to him about doing something on the South Bank and he's keen.

Lunch with John Osborne, who said he would write a play for us about the Third Reich.

Gave a talk on Beckett in the Lyttelton to an audience of about 500. Peg rather threw me by interrupting from the wings (unseen) when I was speaking about *Happy Days* saying, 'It's not sand, it's earth.' She gets very het up when I say that Winnie is buried in sand. 'It's earth,' she trumpets.

---

[1] Editor of the *Evening Standard* 1959–76 and 1978–80. Simon Jenkins was editor in the years between.
[2] An Associate Director of the RSC 1967–77. Joint Artistic Director of the RSC, with Trevor Nunn, since 1978.

Thursday 8 April

To No 10 for dinner. Callaghan is a much more relaxed, genial and reassuring host than Wilson, who is inclined to look embarrassed and slightly shifty, as if he were thinking about something else. The main object of the dinner was to promote British theatre in Iran, and the Empress was the guest of honour. Apparently we hope for fat export orders on stage equipment. . . .

Saturday 10 April

To Wallingford. Moody day: I am dead tired and feel threatened, and the therapy that would really make me happy, work on *Tamburlaine*, I can't get right because I haven't had time. I am at the National now, if I last, until I am fifty. Then what? No more theatre surely. Too old for films. Politics? Stupid I know to be thinking about what I could be doing at fifty when I am not doing adequately what I should at forty-five. When you feel threatened, the future is threatening too.

Monday 12 April

Lunch meeting to discover how things are progressing with the Olivier. A dreadful atmosphere: weary, smug, hopeless. The news is, of course, worse than we could have expected. In the last month, they have lost a month. What can I do? Play *Tamburlaine* somewhere else? I am very foxed. I must think.

Peter Softley[1] said two amazing things when I was complaining about air conditioning noises. I was hearing the air conditioning, he said, because the theatre was so quiet and had such good acoustics. He also said the actors were hot not because it was hot but because this perfectly designed theatre had no draughts. The perils of perfection! The air conditioning *is* noisy. And it *is* hot.

As I reeled out of the meeting, late and confused, Sue handed me the *Evening Standard*. The article is in, headlined 'Is Peter Hall Now Stretching Too Far?', and so like Blakemore's paper that for him to disclaim any connection seems absurd. It's inaccurate and, I would say, defamatory. And it dresses itself up by the technique of saying that nevertheless I am the best man to do the job, the most talented, the most energetic. I feel winded and alarmed, but at least it's now printed. Quickly down to the theatre to rehearse: the therapy of work. As far as the general public is concerned the article doesn't matter; it's tomorrow's fish and chip wrappings; and showbiz people are expected to be energetic and earn a lot of money. But it's bad within our own organisation, and within the cultural establishment.

[1] A Partner in the firm of Denys Lasdun and Partners.

First night of *No Man's Land* at the Lyttelton: audience very held, and cheered.

Wednesday 14 April
South Bank Board meeting. I asked if we could just be given some firm date—any date—for the Olivier. Silence. Was it, I said, wrong to ask to open on 15 July? Silence. Was I right to ask to open on 15 July? Silence. We agreed to meet again at the end of the month. And I have concluded to myself that we shall not be opening *Tamburlaine* on 15 July.

Bill Bryden tells me that Blakemore has rung from Biarritz, where he is on holiday, asking if there's any news arising from the *Evening Standard*.

Sunday 18 April
Big storm in the papers about the amount conductors are being paid: Solti, for example, gets £3,000 a concert. So what's the problem? They are unique men, very rare. It's another instance of our society believing that no one should be better than anybody else; not even better, just different.

Walked in the countryside a couple of times: bright, tender colours, that yellow-green which lasts in the spring for just a couple of months —stimulating and melancholic. Read *Bedroom Farce* and adored it again; that I shall enjoy directing. And read *Tamburlaine* and worried and didn't sleep.

Monday 19 April
Perfect hot morning: sat outside and finished reading *Present Laughter*. What a wonderful play it would be if—as Coward must have wanted—all those love affairs were about homosexuals.

Tuesday 20 April
Began rehearsals of *Tamburlaine*. Not really in command: nervous and a bit incoherent. We chatted and discussed this and that and then began reading the play.

Went home and to bed early. Watched a piece of Garbo's *Camille* on television. Apart from her, it is unutterably vulgar and bad. The studio sheep run round the idyllic country estate where apples and pears are on the studio trees at the same time as the tulips are blooming—and if the sheep really were there, all those carefully tended trees would be eaten away to nothing. Fantastic unreality.

Wednesday 21 April
Second day of reading *Tamburlaine* with the cast. Finished mid-morning, then I put part of it on its feet: just a couple of scenes. A relief to see it

stumbling into some kind of life. But I am terrified. I haven't got its measure. I don't know what I'm doing. I think the approach is right, but I am not working freely, spontaneously, confidently. I am haunted by 1963 when I cracked up.

Thursday 22 April

Felt a little better this morning about *Tamburlaine* but still have no sense of freedom. What am I doing? I am in a rat race that I don't much want to win; you can't win anyway. I am worried about rehearsing a production of a play I'm not prepared for, with no opening date, in a theatre that isn't finished. I am living a life without relaxation—just work, work, work.

The London reviews following the release of *The Homecoming* film here are coming in. Some very good, but the heavies are still wanting to deny my possibility as a film director. I am not much upset by this. *The Homecoming* film is a long time ago—and it exists.

Friday 23 April

Another long morning grappling with *Tamburlaine*. To be open when you work, to discover, you have to be quite relaxed. I'm not. I can't quite feel what the actors think. Are they approaching it as a far away object, tentatively, but with some interest? Or do they feel that the director doesn't know what he's doing—the ultimate nightmare of any director?

Saturday 24 April

To the Royal Court to see Sam Beckett's Schillertheater production in German of *Waiting for Godot*. This is a masterpiece. Absolute precision, clarity, hardness. No sentimentality, no indulgence, no pretension. The ghost of Buster Keaton hovers over Estragon and Vladimir. Vladimir very very tall. Estragon small, comic, and heartbreaking: a very great performance this. The production is also quite, quite beautiful. It revived my shaken faith in the theatre. I think one of the things, among many, that is wrong with me at the moment is that I am not seeing enough theatre to keep my juices running. Enough good theatre that is; well, any theatre at all.

Sunday 25 April

The Sandersons ad is in *The Observer* again. Hateful. It was a mistake.

Sunday 2 May

I have had some peaceful time this last week, sitting in the Wallingford sun.

Peter Stevens rang to tell me what had happened at a recent meeting with the contractors. Harry Pugh continued to hope for an opening in July, but everybody else said it was more or less impossible. So now we are to consider being able to use the Olivier for limited rehearsals only during the summer and a possible opening of *Tamburlaine* in September or October.

Monday 3 May

Quite a good morning on *Tamburlaine*. Told the company that there were problems over the Olivier, that we might not open for months. I felt I had to. Rehearsing a play with no opening date is like protracted necking with no possibility of an orgasm.

To the Festival Hall for its twenty-fifth birthday: Queen Mother waving, trumpeters trumpeting. But it takes the British to celebrate the birthday of a great concert hall by not giving a concert. The programme was unbelievable. First a pretentious work-music-and-picture show, then an appalling film. I guess there must have been a committee to consider what to do, and someone had said it was too simple to give a good concert, 'We must use our imaginations.' Very few people should be allowed to use their imaginations. Mostly what is wanted is the obvious, *but very well done.* . . .

Thursday 6 May

To the DES for a meeting with Jack Donaldson[1]. Rayne present, also Pat Gibson and the usual bevy of note-taking, worried-looking civil servants. Hot day. Donaldson in shirt sleeves, welcoming and cordial, with jokes about being a new boy, needing to understand.

Well, we tried to make him understand, specifically our projected deficit. Where is it going to come from? Do we go out of business, we enquired? The deficit is produced by the building being late. We've had to spend money on our own equipment. And we have now lost huge box-office income because the Olivier is late. Donaldson and the civil servants said they understood the problem although they had as yet no solution.

So what did I feel at the end of the meeting? At least we'd made our case. Gibson was standing firmly behind us. And everybody realises that the theatre has to go on, and that extra money has to be found.

Driving me back to the National in his ancient Bentley, Cottesloe observed he was perfectly prepared to have his head delivered on a silver salver if it would help the situation.

Friday 7 May

Talked to Albert at lunchtime. He says he can stay until 15 January. That's an enormous help. I can begin re-scheduling the Olivier. At a company meeting, I told them that the opening would now be late autumn. There was

---

[1] Lord Donaldson, who had just replaced Hugh Jenkins as Arts Minister, and held the post until the end of the Labour Government in 1979.

an atmosphere of scepticism. They probably don't believe any date any longer. I wouldn't.

Monday 10 May

Blithe Spirit this morning, first reading. Cast looked very good in a biscuit-coloured nineteen-thirties set. How wonderful to have the set there on the first day of rehearsal. Harold[1] addressed them: 'Noël Coward calls this play an improbable farce. Well, I just wish to make one thing clear—I do not regard it as improbable and I do not regard it as a farce.'

Tuesday 11 May

Back to *Tamburlaine* this morning with some delight. I am now burrowing away to find the point of each scene. The exciting thing is that it's there. There are definite emblematic beats of emotion, section by section, which you can analyse. They dictate where the actors are standing, and they dictate the overall intention of the play. The actors must move from one mood to another like a film cut. Put the clear images together, emotional and visual, and you have a play with contradictions which perpetually disturb and stimulate the audience. That is Marlowe.

Sam Beckett over this afternoon to see the new building. He was thrilled with it, particularly the Olivier. His face is even more extraordinary: dark *Endgame* spectacles, the eyes pale and watering, the appearance sometimes hawk-like, sometimes child-like, but definitely a bird—a bird in his movements, his shyness, and because of occasionally a certain predatory hauteur. But he was warm, charming, smiling and affectionate. No distrust, no uneasiness: very free. He wants us to do *Godot* at the Olivier. I begged him to do the production himself. He says he can't face it again. He is seventy and any energy he has must be used on writing. He told me I could have his production notes; he had written them out long before he rehearsed the play. It had taken him months. I said it was an amazing thing for a director to write everything out beforehand, and to my mind a bit worrying. He agreed, but said he wasn't a director; he was a writer. In rehearsal, he gave the actors his images with great precision, but had to write them down first. That was how his imagination worked. It was neither better nor worse than any other way.

He said that in the actual performance there was only one alteration to what he had set out in advance in his production notes. It comes when Estragon has to move across the stage on the diagonal from the tree to the stone. In the notes, Sam says Estragon stops halfway for a beat and then goes on. In the actual production he did not stop. . . .

---

[1] Pinter, the play's director.

I enjoyed my meeting with Le Grand Sam. I told him as he was going off in his taxi not to pay for it as I had ordered it on my own account. He smiled in mock horror, putting his hand over his lips and bending up his great gaunt frame into an expression of mock amazement, like a child on a wicked trip. Not at all the bleakest playwright in the world.

Back in the office we struggled with re-scheduling the Olivier and repairing the collapse of our plans. In the middle Sue brought me a letter from Michael Blakemore. He's offered his resignation. I can't say I'm surprised.

Wednesday 12 May

South Bank Board meeting. Cottesloe instructed the consultants and the contractors to allow us into the Olivier on 6 July for uninterrupted access for rehearsal, whatever the consequences might be.

Bill Bryden let slip at tonight's associates' dinner that Blakemore had confessed to him and Pinter that he had seen the Gaia Servadio article in typescript. Blakemore hadn't inspired it, we were to understand; he'd just read it.

Thursday 13 May

Tamburlaine rehearsal this morning. Not easy but stimulating. A feeling all the time of being near something extraordinary. I am starting to enjoy it.

This afternoon we interviewed possibles for running the theatre catering. A fair selection. One Swiss, thirty, with bright blue eyes and a cutting manner seems the best. His metaphors were all predatory. He spoke of his desire to get his teeth into something, flashing brilliant white teeth. Later he wanted to get his claws into something. We decided to have him.

Friday 14 May

Working on *Tamburlaine* in the Olivier with John Bury and John Heilpern[1]. I yearn for invisible entrances, some way of making actors materialise on to the world. The Barbican is going to be much better than the Olivier from this point of view. But then it should be. John Bury and I saw to that[2].

Afternoon spent working out numbers with charts. How many soldiers, how many body bearers, how many litter bearers. The side of directing that bores me. It took hours.

Sunday 16 May

John Gielgud phoned, responding to a letter from me. We talked of possible parts. He said Larry came round after the performance of *No Man's Land* on

[1] Hall's assistant on the production.
[2] The design of the RSC's Barbican Theatre was the result of a close collaboration between Hall and Bury with Peter Chamberlin, the architect.

Friday and told him and Ralph that he couldn't hear either of them, and went to sleep. He threatened to return on Monday night—the play's last performance—when he hoped he'd be able to hear it. Ralph is very upset: why is Larry so harsh? John, who is furious, is more down to earth; he says he suspects Larry is going deaf.

Tuesday 18 May
Dinner at Denys Lasdun's. Good food and good company but too many people. Denys at one point became very touchy about his building. I said he mustn't be paranoid—that was just like me. He said I was the last person in the world he would think of as paranoid: I was an extrovert, taking it all in my stride. I suppose that's a tribute to my mask.

Wednesday 19 May
Tamburlaine rehearsal in the morning. Its strength as an intricate structure comes home to me; and it uses the Morality Play technique of demonstration in order to be totally immoral: an immoral Morality Play.

Peter Shaffer for lunch. He spoke jokingly of all my enemies. He said he'd had dinner with Larry in New York who had gone on for an hour and a half about the way the new NT management had treated him, the way the Board had treated him, the things he could tell, etc etc.

I showed Peter the Olivier Theatre and he was excited. He promised his next play to us. . . . I wonder. . . .

Last night of *Borkman*. Sad to see it go. Drinks at the end. Ralph said he'd never really got the part; that he was sorry; that it was irritating. In fact, he's achieved it magnificently. He's always discontented with his own work. Peg looked weary, said she was glad to have helped open the theatre, but had had enough of *Borkman*.

I don't think the production is as good as when it started. Its peak was at the end of the run at the Vic when Ralph really had got somewhere. He did an amazing heart attack last night though, quietly hooting like some vast owl as the last pain struck him.

Thursday 20 May
To Simpsons for Peggy's birthday tea party celebrating fifty years on the stage. Trevor and the RSC there; also Tony Quayle; a lot of us circulating in the Edwardian decor.

John Osborne has returned from the States and found my letter about the decline in *Watch It Come Down* business, for an angry postcard arrived today saying he is dropping writing and taking up weaving. I phoned him and placated him. We can't take the play off if he objects, not at least until it does worse business than now and for much longer.

Friday 21 May
Meeting with John Osborne: Bill Bryden there; and Peter Stevens with the box office statistics. Osborne was implacable, but very charming with it. He thinks a subsidised theatre ought to have one box office failure in its repertoire and that we mustn't behave like a commercial manager. To a point I agree with him. We will have to work out a philosophy towards dramatists. They'll have to know how many performances they're guaranteed and how their plays will be treated in the event of failure or success. Stevens pointed out that if we played to bad business for too long it would prejudice my position with the Board about doing new plays. An exact balance has to be struck.

Saturday 22 May
Slept fitfully and stayed in bed until noon, dozing uncomfortably and waking with worry. I tried again to work out a new repertoire for the Olivier, but my heart wasn't in it. I walked round and round the garden thinking. I have *Tamburlaine* in my hands, but can I do it? I have a theatre in my hands, but can I run it? I am in such a state that I begin to wonder whether I am ill.

Sunday 23 May
Dress rehearsal of *Hamlet* because it's been out of the repertoire for a month and returns to the Lyttelton tomorrow. Albert was streaking up and down demonstrating his strength and dexterity, like a child back in the water at the beginning of the swimming season. He was just too bloody fast to investigate the text. I told him this after the performance and begged him to spread himself tomorrow night, and to make the first act last another five minutes if necessary.

Monday 24 May
Hamlet: Barbara[1] let her emotions rip, and Albert slowed up and investigated. The first act was seven minutes longer. Good. I went to see Albert in the interval. He sat there covered in sweat crying his eyes out. He cried and cried and cried. I asked him if he would like me to go. No, he said, he felt tonight he'd unblocked something in himself. I agreed. What we'd had before was energy, ferocity, and agility. What we had tonight was a man exposing his own heart in return for the audience's gift of those few hours of their lives.

Tuesday 25 May
I forgot to report on a representative of the DES who yesterday enlivened a very boring South Bank Board meeting. He's an eccentric: old tweeds,

---

[1] Jefford, who had just taken over from Angela Lansbury as Gertrude.

baggy trousers, straying tie; the image of a nineteen-forties left-wing schoolmaster. He whistled occasionally, and at one point was singing quietly to himself. Victor Mishcon made one of his more elaborate speeches saying the design committee was now going to consider its attitude towards busts. At this point the DES representative broke into hysterical laughter. Victor fixed him with his hard stare, practised by years of being a successful solicitor, and said that he didn't make that remark in order to allow attending officers to snigger. He said it with great charm....

Thursday 27 May

Reading of Howard Brenton's *Weapons of Happiness* this morning. David Hare[1] tight, restrained; Brenton generous and pleased. I look forward to it.

A dash to St Paul's for the first form music concert—Master Edward Hall playing his cello a little hurriedly but with some confidence.

Back to the theatre for a planning meeting, all fairly routine, then with Jacky to Chelsea Square for dinner with the Osbornes, just the four of us. The evening passed very pleasantly, oiled by liberal quantities of alcohol. John and Jill[2] conduct a constant banter of war, mocking each other, usually sexually, much like the two characters in *Watch It Come Down* — except tonight we were in comedy and not in tragedy.

Peter Stevens is wrestling with Brenton and Hare over the number of performances we can give *Weapons of Happiness*. I think 30-35 guaranteed performances is fine with us having the right to take the play off if it falls below 65% seating capacity.

Saturday 29 May

To Bradfield College to see the boys there in *The Agamemnon*. Their Greek theatre is made out of a chalk pit. The evening was very illuminating—and showed up a lot of problems. The Chorus didn't work, partly because the music was *conclusive*. Aeschylus is entirely ambiguous and contradictory all the time. To sing resolved cadences with great affirmative climaxes is absolutely foreign to him, and fragments the drama into little scraps. A lesson could be learned from Monteverdi here—always starting the next phrase on the resolving chord of the previous one.

I thought all the boys at Bradfield learnt Greek—which was one reason why they did Greek plays. Not a bit of it. Only one member of the cast was a Greek scholar; five of them had done Greek O level. But the

---

[1] The director.
[2] Bennett. At the time, John Osborne's wife, and playing a lead part in *Watch It Come Down*.

majority, including Clytemnestra, had learned the text by heart in the language lab and then recited it. They knew what it meant, but they didn't know Greek. So here we were watching a play in a language which neither the actors nor the audience understood. Yet the emotion communicated.

I was struck by the nineteenth-century tradition of the classics where Aeschylus, Euripides, and Sophocles are thought of as good public school types and members of the Church of England. Next to me sat a bishop, gravely following his Greek text, while the story of cannibalism, murder, and corruption was enacted before us. To the Renaissance the classics were subversive—almost revolutionary. But to the English public school they were pillars of conformity.

Tony Harrison and Harrison Birtwistle[1] were also there learning lessons. When we come to do *The Oresteia* we must condense—they didn't, not enough; have masks—they didn't; and the Chorus must *use* their bodies—they didn't.

Tuesday 1 June

Watched the Raoul Walsh film *The Roaring Twenties* on television; James Cagney playing the lead, Humphrey Bogart still a supporting actor. In this film, made in 1940, Bogart gives the only few seconds of untrue acting that I have ever seen from him. When he's threatened by a gun and knows he is about to be shot, he panics. His face quivers, his hands flap about. It's very melodramatic and is a shocking blasphemy from such a great actor. I realised tonight what James Cagney's appeal is: he has bedroom eyes.

Wednesday 2 June

I committed one of my madder acts today, addressing the annual conference of the Women's Institute: 6,000 women in the Albert Hall—hatted, flower-patterned, true blue. When I went on to the platform, the noise of chattering was indescribable. I spoke for about 25 minutes. Of course the speech was amplified. You hear your voice coming back to you from those vast caverns, so you hear what you said and you then think it was a very silly remark to have made. Anyway the speech went well and I hope did some good for the National Theatre.

Meeting with John Schlesinger. He wants to direct *Julius Caesar* with the younger actors—to hell with the stars. He thinks we've got a fine company of new young talent and that it should be used. I absolutely agree. But I stressed one thing: the risk is enormous, and if it doesn't work, I don't want him turning his back on the theatre and the NT.

---

[1] The composer. Head of Music at the National Theatre from 1975. Is an NT associate.

Went to see *One Flew Over the Cuckoo's Nest*: a superbly made film, and Jack Nicholson amazing, but it's of dubious morality. The mad people are the goodies, so they are charming and not too mad, and our chief way in is through Jack Nicholson, who is not mad at all. The doctors and nurses are baddies and they *are* mad. It's fascinating that the biggest success of 1975/6 should be a film which is as obsessed with madness as the Elizabethans. It's certainly typical of violent, sick, disturbed America. I admired it but was not convinced by it. There is a full demonstration of electric shock treatment. I always hate to see this; it took me back to 1963 when I was threatened with it. It is the dark ages of brain medicine. Terrifying. I didn't have it.

Thursday 3 June

Lunch with William Douglas-Home. He told me a wonderful Ralph Richardson story. Said Ralph to him: 'Tonight while Mu was sitting at the dressing table taking off her make-up, my parrot flew across the bedroom and bit her. Now the vet is coming round with a gun to shoot it.' WDH: 'Why don't you keep it in a cage?' RR: 'What a good idea. . . .'

To the Albert Hall for a concert of American music with the New York Philharmonic conducted by Lennie Bernstein. In a piece of Charles Ives, Bernstein did the hammiest thing I have ever seen a conductor do. The strings play pianissimo on a long sustained note throughout it and it ends with an infinity of high, held sound. Having reached that, Bernstein crept away from the platform leaving the orchestra to finish the mystery on its own. It brought the house down.

Lennie also played *Rhapsody in Blue*, he in a double spotlight but the lights lowered on the orchestra: many wrong notes, and a great deal of New York chutzpah. He is a superb showman. . . .

Then to the Savoy for a Cyril Bennett supper with Lennie as guest of honour. I had a good-humoured argument with him about Gilbert and Sullivan. He adores it; thinks it's wonderfully witty, wonderful music, and central to England. I think it is sexless and camp. He begged me to look at *The Mikado* again because he would love to do it with someone who hated it so much. . . .

Tuesday 8 June

To David and Pamela Harlech's[1]. Dined out in the garden. Very *Vogue*. Not really my scene at all. Much talk from Pamela about the Tynans, their bitterness against me, and their imminent move to California. She thinks he will become the crowned critic of California; an expatriate genius like Isherwood. I hope she's right.

[1] Lord Harlech, President of the British Board of Film Censors from 1965, and Lady Harlech.

Sunday 13 June
Perfect summer day. To Glyndebourne with Christopher to see Verdi's *Falstaff*. The production by Jean-Pierre Ponelle was excellent, real strength and force, and the work is wonderful.

Good to be in Glyndebourne again; good to see the gardens and the beautiful summer sun and all the many friends I have down there. The usual consumption of quantities of chilled white wine. To bed about midnight after gossiping with the Christies. Mary Christie told me that yesterday they'd had Gaia Servadio and her husband in their party and the lady had gone on and on about me throughout dinner. The burden of her song was that it was disgraceful that I should be using my National Theatre position to bring my 1977 production of *Don Giovanni* to the Lyttelton next year[1]; disgraceful that I was doing *Aquarius*; and no one in the profession would now work with me. Mary said she was amazed.

Thursday 17 June
Lunch with John Barber[2], my invitation. All the familiar questions came up. Are you playing safe? The West End is very against you because you are doing commercial plays. How do you feel because so many of the profession won't work here and dislike you personally? I asked him who, for instance. Jonathan Miller, he surprisingly said. I quoted a Turkish proverb Lasdun told me: 'The dogs bark but the caravan passes by.'

He recalled in glowing terms the Wolfit/Guthrie *Tamburlaine* of the nineteen-fifties: the enormous battles and the huge map of the world that Tamburlaine rolled out on the stage and walked over at the end. I nearly told him that we were having a very small map, but managed to bite my tongue back.

Friday 18 June
Two hour session with John Heilpern sorting out where we are with *Tamburlaine*. During this we got on to *Hamlet* and whether or not my production lacked a point of view. I said it did, if having one led to a simple thesis. It is perhaps too complex in that it tries to make clear each component part of the play. What the critics have grown used to in this country, and I am as responsible as anybody, is a simplistic theory grafted on each production. It makes it far easier to understand the play and far easier to criticise it.

---

[1] As part of a Don Juan season, which was planned to include, as well as the opera, Molière's play, Horváth's *Don Juan Comes Back From The War*, and the full-length version of Shaw's *Man and Superman*. Later the idea of a cohesive season was abandoned because of the NT strike that summer, but the opera was still staged in 1977, the Horváth in 1978, and *Man and Superman* and the Molière in 1981.
[2] Drama critic and theatre columnist of the *Daily Telegraph* from 1968.

Big inquest this afternoon with the full *Tamburlaine* company. I tried to explain what we'd found in the last weeks. The actors must *represent* a character rather than being it. They should present the narrative and the emotion to the audience, and ask for a judgement from them, support or denial. This doesn't mean they shouldn't feel; they must. But they need a Brechtian sense of narrative, plus emotion. They are all also, in a sense, opera singers. They have specific little solos which have to be fully taken. The play is an intricate mosaic of extreme emotions and there is no bridge from one emotion to another; no Stanislavsky comfort. It is the break from one mood to another which gives the play its vitality.

We have seven weeks rehearsal before the first dress rehearsal, and a great deal of work to do.

An excellent preview of *Blithe Spirit* tonight. Coward is truly a remarkable craftsman; the play builds and builds in the most sure-footed way. You think he's going to overbalance, but he doesn't. Harold has directed the production extremely well. The characters are wonderfully etched and the lines are beautifully tuned. Richard Johnson[1] is absolutely magnificent.

Sunday 20 June

Something further to note about *Tamburlaine*. I have never worked on an Elizabethan text with a more precise structure, in its scenes, its writing, and its people. I now believe that no scholar has properly understood what is going on. It is very calculated. Not primitive.

Monday 21 June

Today we rehearsed the storming of Damascus, the slaughter of the virgins, Bajazeth beating his head out on the cage, his wife Zabena doing likewise, Zenocrate lamenting, Tamburlaine letting off her father, the Soldan of Egypt, then making her Empress. All that in ten minutes. I plodded through it, for I am not well and don't know what's the matter. I can't sleep or rest properly and I have this growing anxiety inside myself: paranoia is rampant.

It was not helped by a lunch I had with Roy Shaw. He said there is growing opposition among MPs to our extravagance—particularly from Renee Short—also hostility among the regional theatres and officers of the Arts Council. And last week he had lunch with five leading West End managers, during which Donald Albery[2] spent the entire time saying we were a scandal and that there should be an enquiry. Terrific. . . .

It is amazing the frenzied efforts the opposition are now making to stop this building fully coming to life. I suppose their hysteria is a measure of their

---

[1] As Charles.

[2] The theatre producer, and Chairman of the Theatres' National Committee 1974–78. Knighted 1977.

fear.... A compliment. Lots of people are coming and lots of actors are being employed.

Thursday 24 June
First night of *Blithe Spirit*. The air conditioning has broken down and the heat was tremendous. There was about 50% less laughter than at any of the previews, so all the actors forced. Drinks and sandwiches with the cast afterwards. Graham Payn was there, who lived with Noel Coward through-out his last years. He said Coward would have loved the evening because at last the play was centred on the marriage between Charles and Ruth; Elvira and the medium, Madame Arcati[1], were incidentals. He's damned right. That is what is brilliant about Harold's production. But I fear it's been seen tonight at less than its best.

Friday 25 June
Blithe Spirit notices are not very good and not very bad; genuinely mixed. I'm sad.

Wednesday 30 June
Long meeting with Christopher Morahan. He would like to come to us in February as an associate director with an option at the end of six months that we could either seal the bargain or decline it, and so could he. He is a master craftsman and he knows the whole repertoire. I think he would provide a centre of sanity and knowledge. I loved working with him at the RSC[2] and would, I'm sure, again.

Tuesday 6 July
Moved *Tamburlaine* from the rehearsal room to the Olivier to rehearse on the stage there for the first time, though it's still of course far from finished. The actors are like delighted fish in new water. A good day.

Wednesday 7 July
Saw the dress rehearsal of *Weapons of Happiness*. It looked visually exciting and was full of meaning. Brenton is an extraordinary dramatist. He writes two lines of seemingly naturalistic speech, then in the third line a bomb goes off which illuminates the whole past of the character and the conflict in which he lives. I think Hare has directed wonderfully. I cannot

---

[1] Ruth, Elvira and Madame Arcati were played respectively by Rowena Cooper, Maria Aitken, and Elizabeth Spriggs.
[2] Morahan directed Jules Feiffer's *Little Murders* at the Aldwych in 1967. It was his first stage production, though he had been a television director from 1957, and Head of Drama for BBC TV 1973–76.

see the play being the theatre-filler of all time, but I think we shall be proud of it.

An interesting thing about *Weapons*. The stage crew don't really like it. Quite a number of them are political, but they don't like political plays. Some also don't like plays with 'fuck' and 'shit' in the text, though these words they use without cease when they are working.

Friday 9 July

Early to a Long Acre studio to see the rough-cut of LWT's National Theatre film, which they are transmitting soon to mark our opening. That part of it which covers recent history gives a fair impression of the agonies of the last years, though I think there's a bit too much emphasis on knights and dames and Rolls Royces arriving for galas. I am shown at various stages of anxiety, and Jennie Lee is overheard saying I am an empire builder. But there's nothing much wrong with the film, except that it's a bit dull and worthy at the moment.

Tidying up the first play of *Tamburlaine* this morning, and this afternoon the first run through of it. Albert is in terrific form: one feels all those years of his youth in Manchester studying stand-up comics. One thing I know very strongly about *Tamburlaine* now. It reeks of the theatre as the circus reeks of sawdust and horse shit. It's not an intellectual's fantasy. It is highly organised and craftily constructed, and every actor is given his aria.

Larry has responded to my letter asking him to speak the prologue to *Tamburlaine* for the opening of the Olivier. He obviously is not going to do it, but doesn't know how to say no.

Saturday 10 July

The Royal Air Force drama group were here today holding their open day in the theatre. So I went to talk to them. I'm always amazed to meet people with hobbies. I can't conceive spending one's life in the RAF and having a passion for drama, and as a result putting one's main efforts into an amateur activity. My work is my hobby, and I am thankful for it.

Tuesday 13 July

A very bizarre meeting with Rayne, Mishcon, Michael Birkett, and Larry. Larry was at his most Richard III: smiling, charming, constantly saying how generous all of us had been, but obstinately refusing to agree to anything that we wanted him to do. He said it had been the sweetest idea to ask him to do the prologue for *Tamburlaine* at the opening of the Olivier but it would look very greedy for him to step in then. I said it was his theatre, it bore his name, and the company would be delighted. So he said he didn't much like the prologue anyway. Shakespeare did that sort of thing better. . . .

We then moved on to the royal opening, now fixed for 25 October. Larry thinks there should be a ball in the Olivier with an orchestra on the stage. But if we were intent on opening with a play then all he was prepared to suggest were revivals of single acts from productions from his regime (which we do not have in our repertoire and the scenery doesn't exist). He left to catch a train to Manchester, and we all ruefully surveyed an impossible situation.

Wednesday 14 July
First night of *Weapons*: a wonderful performance and I was very, very proud. The audience was full of young people clad in deliberately tattered jeans. They were amazed, said Gillian Diamond, that we were doing such a play—it upset their settled response to us. Party afterwards. Happiness all round.

Thursday 15 July
Disappointed in the *Weapons* notices this morning. Michael Billington is full of praise, but has qualifications; we need a few absolute cheers. Irving Wardle is grudging, and unfairly adds that we shall be able to flourish the production as 'evidence of radicalism'. Thanks. Michael Coveney[1], though, is wildly enthusiastic.

Saturday 17 July
Crowds of people milling around the theatre this lunchtime: a kite-flying festival by the river, a Dixieland band playing on the terraces, hordes of children watching a puppet show near the main entrance, a full house for the *Hamlet* matinée. Wine is flowing freely in the bars. It's the way this building has to be—a place for a party.

Round to Ralph's to discuss his future plans. He had promised a sandwich and a glass of wine, but this turned into a bottle of chilled Chablis each and a lobster. We talked about Larry and his ambivalent attitude to the National and to me. But Ralph said gently that, as soon as he saw him, the charisma, the size of the man, took over, and he loved him again. I know what he means.

Monday 19 July
Yvonne Mitchell, Harold Hobson and Richard Mills[2] have all agreed to join our Board. This should really help matters.

---

[1] In the *Financial Times*.
[2] Chairman and Chief Executive of Bernard Delfont Ltd.

Tuesday 20 July
All day running *Tamburlaine*: first play this morning, second play this afternoon. It was the first time we've done them together, and I am sure now how to present them. They must be given in the same evening, as two parts of a whole, with a 35-minute interval between each, not longer.

Friday 23 July
Healey has made enormous cuts in public expenditure, and it is pretty certain the arts will be included.

Sunday 25 July
Buffet supper on the terraces of John Gielgud's home in the country. It is now finished and very beautiful, but a little like living in the William and Mary wing of the Victoria and Albert Museum: decorated out of its life and rather impersonal; exquisite taste though. A happy paradox: there is John standing in the middle of his palace, the wonderful salmon and chilled white wine spread out in the background, and saying mournfully that he's broke and can't even write a cheque. He looks as if he should be wearing a full-bottomed wig.

Monday 26 July
Board meeting this afternoon. Nothing of note, except we again registered with them the size of our deficit. We are spending not earning. Because of the delays on the Olivier and Cottesloe theatres, we haven't been able to earn our full box office income.

Tuesday 27 July
Tony Harrison came bearing gifts this morning—his first rough draft of *Agamemnon*, in silver cover with the title in stylish type prepared by his daughter. He is obviously excited by what he has done, but I had to warn him that I couldn't give it proper consideration for a while. He's now off to New York, translating *The Bartered Bride* for the Met, which John Dexter is directing.

A dash through the sunlit streets just after lunch to meet with Goodman and Cottesloe in the visitors' lobby at the Lords: another world: Victorian Gothic, thick carpets, and slow speaking lordships. I'm going to need all the support from the Establishment I can get come next autumn when the size of our deficit is revealed, and there is an uproar. But I felt that this afternoon's meeting gave me the full backing of Goodman and Cottesloe.

Looked again at a rough-cut of LWT's National Theatre film. Larry's contribution is wonderful; he is the star. He delicately hints that the Board had not liked any of his ideas for a successor. Then, while paying tribute to me, he says they must have had me in mind all the time, but I was not a rival, rather a friendly enemy, someone who'd been on the other side of the river. So he shows how hurt he was, and how wrong the Board was, and yet he's nice about me. It's an absolutely masterly performance.

Wednesday 28 July
Did a long interview with Derek Bailey this morning for the National Theatre film. He threw me a few nasty balls: did I delegate enough? didn't I only have yes-men, whereas Larry had had people who disagreed with him creatively etc? I did my stuff.

Thursday 29 July
Today was one of the worst and longest since I joined the National Theatre. Early this morning I got a note from Peter Stevens about a meeting last night with the contractors. They're suddenly expressing surprise that we need a lift in the stage for *Tamburlaine*. To get the lift, they now say, we need special permission from the architects, and from the local authorities. I believe they are bluffing. I think they don't want us there. They want us to leave the stage entirely to them to finish the job, which in that case would be in many years' time.

So I went into action, rang Cottesloe and said the contractors and consultants didn't seem to be appreciating his directive that the opening of *Tamburlaine* must come first. I then tried to sort out the realities of the crisis. Of course everyone is on holiday, so I left nasty messages at all their offices. The meetings and screamings went on all day and in between I kept on dashing into the theatre to try to rehearse. There a pale and amazed John Heilpern was valiantly keeping things going with the help of Albert. At one stage we all rushed out on to the terraces, John Bury leading, to find a space for an outdoor rehearsal, because I'm sure we've now reached the point where we've somehow got to do the play in public terms, and this could be with a non-captive audience of the people passing by. There's a fine site where the main stairway leads up from the esplanade.

Most of the afternoon was spent arguing about priorities. The contractors and consultants are now a further three weeks behind. I don't know how we're going to keep the production together if this means another postponement of the opening.

I returned to the Barbican exhausted and extremely depressed, and read Tony Harrison's *Agamemnon* to cheer myself up. He's on to something wonderful. It's the most vital and immediate Greek translation I have ever read. The adrenalin started to rise again. Somehow I must just persevere.

Saturday 31 July
Saw the National Theatre LWT film again. It's turning into something good now. I asked Derek Bailey if he would cut a few of the more pretentious lines

I said to the *Hamlet* cast at the rehearsal he had filmed. He made ritualistic objections, but he will. I also advised him to cut down the shots of machinery whizzing round the stage and Richard Pilbrow talking about his modern technology, when in fact we can't fly an ordinary flat, and the machinery does not work.

Monday 2 August

I've often sat in theatres at bad dress rehearsals and prayed that the building would be burnt down that night. I thought my dream had come true this morning, and the South Bank problems had been removed, for as I arrived, fire engines were at the doors. But the fire was soon dealt with, alas. It had been caused by some clown of a welder allowing sparks to go through a hole in the wall into our store of fabrics.

Again ran the whole of *Tamburlaine*. It was dull and dead. I simply cannot get the cast to understand that this is public, not private utterance. Tonight I am very alarmed. I feel that once more I have lost my way. It is unquestionably the hardest thing I have ever done. Can I convince the actors to endorse the style?

Tuesday 3 August

On to the outside terraces where we did about an hour of *Tamburlaine*. Revelation. Denis Quilley[1] immediately started talking to bystanders, and his performance became free, open, and necessary. Peter Needham up on the concrete battlements as the Governor of Damascus suddenly became full of power, full of emotion. It's a curious thing to me that there have been many attempts to recreate the Elizabethan stage, but has anybody understood that the basic thing about Elizabethan theatre is that it was played in daylight? The actor saw the eyes of the audience.

Another interesting thing about *Tamburlaine*: it has to be high, astounding, and unsubtle because it was designed to interest and excite theatrically a noisy and unsophisticated audience. It's a bit like the great epics of early silent movies. It works in broad ways. By Shakespeare's time the audience had become more sophisticated, and it was not necessary to be so crude to hold their attention.

I must have dinner with Albert. He's tense and worried because of the size of the task. But I suspect he's also a little fed up with me. He hasn't been getting from me what he needs because of all my worries.

Wednesday 4 August

We ran part one of *Tamburlaine* in the rehearsal room this afternoon, armed with our experience outside on the terrace. It was very exciting, very open, very public. Now the company understand what I am driving at. I remember

[1] Who played the parts of Bajazeth, and Bajazeth's son, Callapine.

some eight weeks ago a basic discovery of the production—that in this play an actor cannot speak thirty lines of blank verse to another actor's eyeballs. It must be shared with the audience—told like a story teller. At last the cast are doing this, but because they feel it rather than because I tell them to.

Thursday 5 August
Long and amiable dinner tonight with Albert. I think it did a lot to heal the tensions I have felt between him and me over the last few weeks. He spoke of the opposition to me in the press and elsewhere, and said it was not possible to stop people saying what they thought of you in public if you were publicly known. You had to be like a willow: bend with it and then return to your original position. I think that's easier to do if you're an individual than if you're part of an organisation. But I knew he was reassuring me and I was grateful.

Sunday 8 August
Depressing acoustics tests tonight in the Olivier. The sound was not too bad in the centre of the auditorium but at the sides it was dreadful, and the noise of the air-conditioning is very intrusive... of course.

Monday 9 August
Tamburlaine, part one, outside this afternoon: a full run with props and odd bits of rehearsal costumes, the musicians either side. It was really encouraging, popular, broad, and clear in its narrative. The audience passing by loved it. So did the actors.

Tuesday 10 August
Walked round the Olivier stage with Simon Relph[1] and looked at the growing *Tamburlaine* setting. I was alarmed by the lack of progress, and made a whole series of critical comments while Simon kept making reassuring noises. I suppose everyone is so doubtful of the play opening on time that they have not pulled out their last efforts.

Wednesday 11 August
Our stage staff have refused to work in the Olivier while being on call for the Lyttelton. So this-afternoon we had to take the issue to ACAS[2]. News came tonight that they had ruled in our favour and instructed the men to return to work in the Olivier for fourteen days while we sorted out a new agreement.

[1] The NT's Technical Administrator 1974–78.
[2] Advisory, Conciliation and Arbitration Service.

Thursday 12 August

Sneaked off to the Academy cinema to see, I suppose for the fifth or sixth time, Buster Keaton in *The General*—a great refreshment. Keaton is masterly, so moving in the stony immobility of his face. I remembered that face tonight as I saw it when I met him in Hollywood in the late fifties — raddled with drink and with suffering.

Friday 13 August

A date which lived up to its reputation. We were due for our first technical rehearsal of *Tamburlaine* tonight, but Simon came to see me to say the stage staff had refused the ACAS ruling and voted against working in the Olivier while they were on call for the Lyttelton. In the Olivier, nobody but the stage management and production team was there. Kon Fredericks was lurking about under the stage to make sure we didn't rehearse even a cue.

I am heart-broken, but we must stand up to the wreckers among them now, or the theatre will not be a place in which to work for the future. If *Tamburlaine* has to go to the wall, it must.

Jacky and the children returned from two weeks in Corfu tonight; a fact which was celebrated on this perfect day of bitter disappointments by an almighty row about why I hadn't gone to meet her.

Saturday 14 August

Tamburlaine, part two, on the terraces outside. The first half-hour was dire, like thumpy early Shakespeare history writing. There was no element of irony, and therefore the comedy was lost. But after this bad start, things picked up, and by the time of the play's descent into utter blackness, it was holding very well. The response of those watching was tremendous and most people sat rapt on the hard benches or stood in the crowd for the two and a quarter hours.

Confirmed to the company that because of industrial action we were entering a period of strife and must be prepared for anything.

Sunday 15 August

A hot, hot day. Mainly thought and thought about the stage staff dispute. Three telephone calls with Simon and even more with John Goodwin. He said we were not experienced in union negotiations, were all green at such things, and must be sure of our ground before we risk a long strike, serious loss of audience, and damage within the organisation. Well, I know we are going to be damaged in the short term, but we shall be damaged in the long term if we allow the stage staff to have their way. So we're over the top tomorrow.

248

Monday 16 August

The big day. Good news to start with: Jenny's A level results are A for English, A for French, and C for Art.

Suspension notes were issued at 9.30 am to all those refusing to work in the Olivier. By just after 2 pm the stage staff, electrics and stage props had left the building on unofficial strike. The union then disowned them and suspended their membership; we stopped paying them.

Great complications; many meetings; press statements. Phone call to Max who was abroad. He overwhelmed me with sympathy, and said it appeared to him I was handling the situation properly as far as he could tell from that distance, but would I talk to Arnold Goodman, Victor Mishcon, and Hugh Jenkins in that order? He reaches for people like someone seeking a handrail when they get out of the bath.

In the evening picketing had started outside, with Kon Fredericks and his merry men handing out a quite inaccurate leaflet. I think there is great suspicion of the management and that Kon is winning sympathy. Ed Berman and his group played jolly street theatre on our river terraces while the audience for the Lyttelton were given their money back. A grotesque situation.

The union assured us they were not going to back down. 'We are going to discipline our men,' said Paddy McGrath, the acting general secretary of NATTKE. He added that if by Thursday the men had not gone back, NATTKE would propose that we re-engage a different lot. I don't believe it.

With *Tamburlaine* on the boil, and the whole of the future of back-stage work in the new building at stake, I have to play a waiting game until I see what's going to happen.

Paddy McGrath tonight apparently behaved exactly like the union representative in *Weapons of Happiness* trying to persuade the strikers to be disciplined, and he met with the same response: the strikers threw potato crisps at him.

Tuesday 17 August

A very unpleasant atmosphere around the building. No one is working, simply discussing the dispute. There's a lot of talk about threats of violence and intimidation, and there is a rumour that all our good electrics staff who should have reported for the *Tamburlaine* technical rehearsal last Friday night, and would have reported, were informed that there'd be some broken limbs if they became scabs.

Long session with John Wilson, NATTKE's general secretary, Simon Relph, Peter Stevens and Victor Mishcon. We stood firm in our support of the conciliation board's decision. Wilson gave an impressive performance. His expressed determination to clean up the union and make labour relations at the National decent and honourable are our only hope for the future.

Wednesday 18 August
The atmosphere today has been interesting and terrifying. I can only compare it with a corrida, a bullfight at full pitch. There was a feeling of destruction, of blood. I am not exaggerating. During the day the pickets increased and the feeling of imminent violence increased with them. I have never been at a death, although I have been at a birth. There was the same feeling of archetypal change in the air.

We made an offer in the morning for the men to return to work under the terms set out by ACAS, for the suspensions to be lifted, and no disciplinary action taken. This was refused and refused hotly. By just after lunch Wilson was saying he was going to withdraw the cards of those outside, and allow us to engage new men. He went back to his office to work things out. But when he returned to the theatre, he brought with him one of the NATTKE representatives who had sat on the ACAS conciliation board. This man, sweating, twitching and nervous, began a halting speech saying he wasn't sure the board's finding was properly drafted. Then Wilson produced a piece of paper with five points on it which he said were what the moderates outside had got the extremists to agree to. The points covered a return to work, a waiving of the suspension, a continuing of negotiations, and the men working in the two theatres but with the stage team divided into two flexible units, one in the Olivier, the other in the Lyttelton.

Our first reaction was to refuse it. Our feelings were strengthened by a visit from our best middle management. They would have to leave, they said, if the men were taken back. They all made the same plea. They care about this theatre, they want it to be a place that works at high standards. But standards are slipping badly because of the attitudes of those in the stage staff who are producing an evil atmosphere.

Mishcon, Stevens, Relph and I went on debating. Stevens and Relph were for sacking the men tomorrow morning. I kept reflecting that direct confrontation was usually disastrous unless the timing was absolutely right.

During the course of the evening, the picketing increased. People were not molested but they were shouted and jeered at. Kon kept trying to get every other NATTKE member out. If this theatre becomes an industrial battleground and is closed pending an inquiry, it will be international news, and a vivid example of the government's inability to act effectively even with comparatively simple industrial relations. Kon appears to me to be having his finest revolutionary hour. The former actor cuts a romantic figure on the barricades.

Around 11 pm Wilson came to see us again and said that if we wouldn't agree to the five points, he would take us all to ACAS in the morning and was perfectly sure they would rule that the management was being intractable. This was the moment I had foreseen. We were being put in a position where we were refusing a compromise solution which would get everything back to work while a new agreement was worked out; and where Wilson's interests and ours would no longer be the same, and we would be beaten into the ground. Also, a refusal of the five points would, I was sure, unleash unholy violence all through the theatre.

So I decided we must accept and trust Wilson to tidy things up next week. But Peter Stevens and Simon Relph did not support me. They regarded the decision as craven, and wrong. But I was clear that out of the two black possibilities confrontation would achieve nothing, and compromise might get us into play again. Mishcon entirely supported us on behalf of the Board.

So Wilson left the building at 11.30 pm and told the waiting pickets that the points had been agreed. Kon had gone home, but Ralph Lawrence, the brawn and muscle man, was still there. He said 'Thank you very much, Mr Wilson' and they all pissed off home.

All hell then broke loose round me. Peter Stevens and Simon Relph offered their resignations and there were reports of all middle management resigning too. Peter told me I had damaged the organisation irreparably and didn't realise what I had done. I limped home dispirited, faced with the loss of some of my best people, but still convinced that the course I've taken is the better one. I am also convinced that I don't want to work at this theatre unless the bully boys eventually go.

Thursday 19 August
Aftermath day. I slept for about two hours, woke at four, and went on turning the thing over in my mind. I felt sure I'd made the right decision last night.

In the theatre, Simon asked me what his position was. How could he go on negotiating the new agreement? How could he stay? I said I had no objection at all to him saying to the men as they returned that if he'd had his way they would have been out and we would have continued the strike by sacking them, but that I had overruled him in the interests of trying to get the theatre working by rule of law, and he had accepted that ruling.

Simon cheered up a little over this, but was still anxious to know whether I wanted him to go on with the negotiation. By God I do.

I met with the middle management and tried to explain my decision. At first I didn't think it did much good. But during the morning I think most of them began to understand.

Meanwhile chaos reigned downstairs. Kon and his men were still manning the barricades, saying that nothing was official, they'd seen nothing in writing, and picketing must continue: all very romantic and stirring stuff. So when Wilson arrived he had to get this stopped before he addressed all the NATTKE employees and conducted a vote on whether the men should come back or not on the management's acceptance of the union's proposals. There was a majority in favour of the men returning, and Wilson came up to my office and asked for a memorandum setting out the five proposals, which we and he would sign. Rochelle[1] refused to type it and tore it up. Sue stormed out. Simon, who was the right person to sign it on behalf of the management, said he didn't want to. I didn't want to either simply because I didn't want to undercut Simon's position. At last Peter Stevens signed it.

I asked Wilson if he would talk to middle management because his union had a bad name in the building and I thought it would be well for him to understand the strength of feeling. I don't think many emperors of the trade union movement would put themselves up before a non-union management meeting, some forty or fifty strong, and be mauled for two hours, but that is what he did. I gather his performance was impressive, but I heard it also called tricky and evasive. Anyway there is a feeling of uneasy peace. Also a feeling that we've got to take more responsibility to stop wild men doing what they want. There could be a bigger membership of NATTKE out of this, which would be good. The majority of our staff are not members. If they all joined, things would be healthier because a small group of extremists could not overrule them.

At the end of the day the flood gates burst. I felt so sick of everything and everybody. Reaction I suppose. If only I could care less about this building and what it means to so many people. It's only a job after all.

One thing's certain. I am learning about industrial relations.

Friday 20 August
Some feeling this morning among everyone of returning to normal: battered and bruised but back in play again[2]. Simon's been negotiating all day on the new agreement with Wilson who is anxious to get it signed and can as little afford for things to go wrong as I can. His head is on the block with mine. NATTKE must be able to show the National Theatre to its members everywhere as the best theatre in the country.

The first technical rehearsal tonight of *Tamburlaine*. We're doing what should have happened last Friday—a week lost. An amazing demonstration of 'We're all professional fellows who deliver the cues as you want

---

[1] Levene, secretary to Peter Stevens.
[2] During the strike a total of four performances were lost.

them and let's be helpful' from the stage staff. There is a rancid smell in the air though, and all our smiles are fixed.

Saturday 21 August
More *Tamburlaine* technical rehearsals. We start our full dress rehearsals soon. But I very much fear the men backstage may be out again next week over negotiations for the new agreement. No, I don't fear. In a way I hope they will.

Back to the Barbican flat to see the National Theatre film transmitted on television. Quite a lot about it in the press today. *The Times* prints in its entirety Larry's remarks about his astonishment at me being his successor. I didn't like the film too much. Rather 'in' I thought, and too concerned with gossip and not enough with fact.

Tuesday 24 August
The NT Board at the meeting today endorsed all our actions over the strike, so did Tony Field for the Arts Council. The DES and GLC representatives asked for a few clarifications on odd points, but all went well.

Second dress rehearsal of part one of *Tamburlaine*. I am enormously encouraged. The visual size of it and sound of it are coming together to make a great cosmic Punch and Judy show. It goes back to what I originally felt about the extravagance, the caricature, the shocking elements of the play. I felt it but didn't know how to achieve it. I think we're really on the way now.

Max was in the theatre tonight among the staff being friendly. He's obviously worried about the pressure we're all under.

Wednesday 25 August
Tamburlaine, part two, technical rehearsal today. More difficult, more complex, than part one.

By this evening it looked as though Wilson is going to deliver the new NATTKE agreement tomorrow.

Thursday 26 August
At about 5 pm I went up to the conference room and signed the new NATTKE agreement with Wilson. Among our 17 shop stewards, there was one anti, one abstention (Kon), and the rest were finally for it. And the agreement, apart from a conciliation clause, is exactly the same as one that was thrown out seven weeks ago.

The men were asked if they would give us a dress rehearsal of *Tamburlaine* although the new agreement doesn't come into force until Monday. They refused. The company were furious. If anything was needed to show the disruption between company and back-stage staff, this was it. It is going to take many months to heal.

Sunday 29 August
All day cutting *Tamburlaine*. A great struggle. I managed to lose 25 minutes, but only by chipping within speeches, which the actors will find hell.

Monday 30 Agusut
I managed some objectivity about *Tamburlaine* at the run-through rehearsal tonight. Before, it seemed I was in the play, suffering and sweating at each moment, and cursing as each thing went wrong. Tonight I was able to be dispassionate, and made judgements. The fantastic makeups have to go, the costumes have to be stripped down, the lighting has to be extremely simple. The production over the last week has become spangled like a Christmas tree. In a way we need to go back to the directness of the terrace perform-ances outside.

Harold was in to see the rehearsal. He was, he said, bowled over by it. This encouraged me greatly.

Wednesday 1 September
At a meeting this morning we decided that Monday 4 October, was the right opening date for the Olivier and *Tamburlaine*.

Thursday 2 September
I hear word that the bloody-minded lot in the stage crew may follow the letter of the new NATTKE agreement by working to rule next week. Yet the agreement says that overtime is recognised as essential for the operation of the theatre, and that the men will normally work it. They won't if they work to rule. They insisted on this clause because they didn't want a bigger staff on smaller pay.

Saturday 4 September
The first dress rehearsal of *Tamburlaine*. It was before an invited audience. Part one worked very well. It's rough, crude, but it does hold. Part two trailed away somewhat. My head is full of the play, bursting with the play.

Sunday 5 September
Day in Wallingford. Harold, Antonia and two Antonia sons arrived for lunch. He was expansive and relaxed, and Antonia was amiable. But there was a great deal of nervousness in the air, I suspect coming from our inability to feed such quantities of people and wait on them with no help at all. Jacky and I are not relaxed hosts, to put it mildly. Harold left at half past four by taxi to the airport, off to America. He played a wistful game of cricket on the lawn with the boys before going: farewell England, farewell summer.

Monday 6 September
Six stage staff men, against the spirit of the agreement, have refused overtime. They are also threatening to bring *Tamburlaine* dress rehearsals to a halt. Here we go again. Home very depressed. I begin to think there is a curse on *Tamburlaine* and the opening of the Olivier. So tired tonight I was steadily and consistently dizzy. Went to bed, but felt too ill to sleep: had that dreadful feeling of not daring to sleep. I suppose it's a deep-rooted fear. One feels one won't wake up.

Tuesday 7 September
Talked to Gawn Grainger about the stage staff situation. He said he thought his fellow actors would go mad and occupy the building if there was further disruption. I asked him to see if he could stop such a move. Militancy is what Kon wants.

Went round to LWT and in great fatigue watched Russell Harty's *Aquarius* film on Edna O'Brien. It's magnificent: as irritating and lovable as Edna herself; her vein of sentimentality is offset by that sharp eye and those acid little phrases. I enjoyed it very much.

Wednesday 8 September
A somewhat stormy meeting with Max Rayne, who went on about the book by John Elsom on the history of the National Theatre, soon to be published. Max had been sent proofs. Perhaps there was something in the criticisms it made of me, he said, because he was getting complaints against me from so many quarters. That at least is the gist of what he said, though hardly so crudely. He's very twitchy, very nervous; and I suspect he's worried that he may have backed a loser in me rather than a winner.

Lucy liked her new school today—the City of London Girls School. I was highly favoured by being asked to take her there early this morning, so with school uniform and looking like a small Renoir child she toddled off quite happily. She told me on the phone tonight the only problems were that she didn't know what the Lord's prayer was or what to do about hymns. I have brought up another pagan.

Thursday 9 September
Elijah Moshinsky wandered into the office today looking pale. He said he'd had a late night two-hour phone call from Jonathan Miller who said he was writing a big article for *The Observer* about the theatre at large, but specifically attacking the National, and wanted news about how *Tamburlaine* was going. Was it true it was costing £$\frac{1}{2}$ million? He told Elijah that he and Michael Blakemore and Ken Tynan were convinced that John Elsom's National Theatre book, after he—Elsom—had had talks with them, was going to be awful about me, and he wondered if I was getting rattled. Miller

said they were like guerillas that struck in the night. And they would go on striking.

Albert began to take off in the *Tamburlaine* dress rehearsal tonight and the play began to have its passion. It didn't help the actors that they wondered all evening whether and when the stage staff were going to leave. Most of them left at 9 pm, refusing to work overtime, but we got through and the cast were triumphant at the end.

Friday 10 September

It seems that Kon is now fed up with Ralph Lawrence, the leader of the men who have refused to do overtime, and is encouraging Simon to sack him. I bet he is. It would be a perfect case of victimisation and all the men could be led out again. We decided to give Ralph a final warning, and tell him that if there were any more breaches he would be sacked. He was brought in to me like the wicked boy before the beak. Simon let him have it; I let him have it. He admitted he had behaved badly and deserved sacking. He then burst into tears, and left vowing *Tamburlaine* would be perfect on Monday and the troubles would cease.

Saturday 11 September & Sunday 12 September

A day and a half of rest and *Tamburlaine* thinking. We have been saying for months that it's an immoral play in a morality play structure. But it is actually attempting to prove there is no God. Tamburlaine dares God (or Jove or Allah) to stop him, and God does nothing. I was very impressed on Thursday night by the feeling of absolute evil that was unleashed in the auditorium. What we need to add now is a man who is constantly challenging God to prove Himself, to prove He exists. That is the core of the play. It is the first atheist play, and in a way the first existential play. It is utterly bleak and cynical, and I don't believe we are delivering it as such. At the moment Albert's relationship with God is not that of a cynic who doesn't believe he exists. It's rather that of a man of great chutzpah who can use the idea of God as a sanction. But by doing this he indicates he believes in him. I think that is quite wrong. Every mention of God has, in some way, to be a challenge. Albert was very excited by this thought so perhaps it will pay dividends.

The other problem frankly is the shape of the second part. I've always been aware in my blood that there was something wrong with part two; not its emotion, but its architecture. I have resisted rearranging scenes because all these months of work have made me have the greatest respect for Marlowe. But this weekend I had to face the fact that either I have failed to grasp the structure, or the structure doesn't quite work. My old theatrical horse-sense tells me something has to be done.

Monday 13 September

It emerged during the day that the dispute with those of the stage staff who are working to rule was likely to be settled. I think they've begun at last to realise that they might as well have the overtime money themselves as let it go to the casual labour we were going to have to bring in.

Tuesday 14 September

Worked on *Aquarius* this afternoon: a very good film by Jeremy Marr on British reggae. Good music; good, strong, arrogant personalities. I didn't enjoy my contribution much, except that, after experiencing all this black culture from Brixton and Stoke Newington, I was able to say 'and next week, Miss Janet Baker.' Diversity. . . .

Wednesday 15 September

With some temerity this morning I began rearranging the order of scenes in the second part of *Tamburlaine*: a colossal job but it went well and I was able to achieve a runthrough of it by late afternoon. There is now a completely different rhythm.

Went to an NT Board dinner of the big four—Rayne, Mishcon, O'Brien, and Leach. I had a definite feeling all evening that there were things they wanted to say that they couldn't say. Victor made his well-known speech about how wonderful the RSC was, and how much cheaper than us, with a smaller company, smaller production costs etc. Max criticised us all for being so overworked, so tired, so wanting in holidays. I was demolished for being too energetic, for doing too much, for directing plays when I should be running the organisation. But it was all done most subtly and politely and without any unfairness.

Home tired but full of determination. I wish though I wasn't so worried about *Tamburlaine*.

Thursday 16 September

News that Larry is coming to the first *Tamburlaine* preview tonight. It's all over the papers today that he opened Michael Elliott's new Royal Exchange Theatre in Manchester. Yet he won't come to the Olivier at its opening on 4 October. 'No, no', he says, 'it's your evening—yours and the actors'. . . .

Finance and general purposes committee meeting. The Arts Council representative warned us that next year was going to be a question of survival, not expansion, which means that everything new, progressive or dangerous may have to be cut. Many of the Board don't mind too much. They think we can succeed by just doing *Blithe Spirit* for ever. Or *Hamlet*. . . .

Monday 20 September

A piece by John Higgins[1] in today's *Times* is excellent but makes me appear somewhat embattled. It talks of the guerillas mustering to attack the South Bank and gives an impression of Hall paranoia which I certainly didn't think I'd conveyed in my interview. Perhaps I did.

Finished reading the *Theatre Quarterly* on Gordon Craig's Moscow Art Theatre *Hamlet*: an extraordinary story of the relationship between him and Stanislavsky. It's interesting to see Stanislavsky's psychological realism, and Craig's new yearning for visual symbolism, both cracking their heads on Shakespeare's absolutely authoritative text. An object lesson in two different aesthetics both getting in the way of the play.

Rang Jill Bennett because I had heard she was very poorly. She said the crisis with John was continuing[2].

An uncomfortable morning with Max Hastings, who is to write two—two, mark you—big articles about me and the National in the *Evening Standard*. He asked all the usual questions. How much do I earn? Why do people resign? Why is everybody unhappy? Aren't the actors overpaid? etc etc etc. I was immediately driven to the 'No, I am not beating my wife' position. I think it was a mistake to see him.

Tuesday 21 September

I was thinking about Max Hastings: apparently charming; intellectual expression; engaging glasses; scholarly air; open manner—casual, neat, business-like. But the eyes are shark-like and they pounce. He knows nothing about the theatre. Indeed, I'd wager he's never seen a play at the National. Is he a professional axe man who's been asked to wield the axe? I am still feeling I shouldn't have seen him.

There are some awfully nice remarks tonight in the *Standard* about *Hamlet* without the prince—ie the Olivier theatre opening without Olivier, and Joan Plowright refusing to make any comment about what Larry thought of the new regime.

A refreshing afternoon over at LWT talking with Janet Baker, an old friend, who spoke frankly about what it was like being a singer. It'll make a good programme. But my goodness, she seems to be together, that woman. She knows what she wants, and she knows the sacrifices she has to make in order to get it. She also treats her talent not as a meal ticket, but as a serious responsibility that's got to be used to the full. She's a very remarkable person.

---

[1] Arts Editor of *The Times* from 1970.

[2] Jill Bennett and John Osborne had just separated after eight years of marriage; he later married the journalist Helen Dawson.

Jumpers opened tonight at the Lyttelton[1]. We all went as part of Jenny's birthday treat. Excellent evening. Julie Covington wonderful[2]. Michael Hordern[3] a trifle subdued, which I didn't mind.

Wednesday September 22
Max Hastings's first article is in the *Standard*. Really a replay of Gaia Servadio's piece. For some reason the *Standard* wanted to do it all again. Not as bad as I had feared but pretty upsetting.

Rehearsed the end of part two of *Tamburlaine* and tried blowing up John Gill, as the Governor of Babylon, using electrically-operated small explosive charges in his costume, as in films. Quite satisfactory, but still a bit comic. Another preview tonight. The actors really took the play and made it their own. Very good.

Thursday 23 September
The second Max Hastings article absolutely winds me. It is very personal, and very horrible. The source material seems to be Elsom's book. Did Hastings see it in advance of publication? I found it all much harder to take than I had expected. I hardly dared walk round the building for a little while. I don't know which I dread more, people's pity or their pleasure at seeing me kicked. I sense both.

Session with Maximilian Schell on *Tales from the Vienna Woods*[4]. He is impressed by the keenness and helpfulness of every department; how nobody works office hours as they do in the state theatres of Germany; how everybody cares. All these were welcome sounds.

Friday 24 September
Phone call from Goodman comforting me about the Max Hastings articles. He found them vindictive, and said he was writing a letter to the *Standard* which would go round on Monday. Very kind of him. Everyone is being extraordinarily nice to me, and I am pretending to look brave. Taxi drivers and the porters at the flat laugh and say they are always reading about me in the papers these days.

Saturday 25 September
Difficult day. The stage was ready late for our rehearsal. I was also aware of everybody looking at me to see how I was taking adversity. I don't think I was taking it very well. I was irritable and flustered. And I kept on having moments of absolute despair when my spirits would fall to the depths.

[1] A revival of Peter Wood's Old Vic production of Tom Stoppard's play.
[2] As Dorothy.   [3] As George.
[4] Horváth's play, which Schell was about to direct in the Olivier Theatre.

Monday 27 September

A tough Board meeting. Max questioned everything: expenditure, box office returns, repertoire in the future. We fought back strongly. At the end he referred to the *Evening Standard* articles and said he wished to record the support of the Board in their confidence in me.

I then rushed off to the preview, feeling not at all like it. But I was pleased. The end of the *Tamburlaine* tunnel is in sight, and I went to bed far more contented.

Wednesday 29 September

Peter Stevens spent all morning amassing factual errors in our proof copy of the Elsom book. Do the press attacks, the feeling in Fleet Street that they must have a go at me, stem from that? I am better in myself and almost through it, but it's been an enormous time-waster and has ill prepared me, the company, or the public and critics for the opening of the Olivier with *Tamburlaine*. This event is now set up to be a huge flop.

Thursday 30 September

Wonderful article in the *Standard* today by Tom Stoppard taking Max Hastings to pieces. Arnold's letter is also there, and Peter Stevens's calm refutation of the facts. But over everything hangs my anxiety about Albert, who has a heavy cold. What a gamble the theatre is. After six months of struggle we can suddenly be totally at the mercy of Albert's health.

Friday 1 October

On the phone to Albert, I discovered to my horror that he hadn't seen a doctor or taken antibiotics. He sounded ghastly. And I feel a fool. He always takes such scrupulous care of his health that I'd assumed he was treating himself properly. So I went round to see him: Brompton Square elegance, French chic, antique furniture and correct carpets; but all messed up by a multitude of cats and a pack of slobbering dogs. Albert sat in his study swathed in dressing gown and track suit, with a curious listless air and a very removed expression. He was not the Albert that I know. He had no fight and he appeared defeated. He's pretty ill.

It seems he didn't want to start antibiotics; they pulled him down and he didn't think he could then play the part; so he thought he must just lick the cold on his own. The trouble is he hasn't. It's now bronchitis. He's full of fever and he wheezes and puffs like an old traction engine. I said to him that I thought it was impossible for him to play tomorrow's preview. To my surprise he agreed listlessly. Rang the doctor, and then saw him. He said he would try to get Albert back for Sunday night's rehearsal.

Saturday 2 October

The doctor confirms today that Albert has serious bronchitis. He's having bronchial therapy which means being hung upside down while your chest is beaten and the gunge drops out.

Max Rayne in a state because of *The Guardian* leader[1]. I hadn't seen it. It is another familiar attack. This time with more strength because it's more reasoned.

Sunday 3 October

Off to Cambridge today to deliver Christopher for his first term there. Entire family and a great deal of luggage jammed in the Range Rover. Cambridge was grey, wet and autumn-like with lots of absurdly young-looking students arriving bewildered, carrying large trunks and paper bags, proud parents in the background. Christopher was deeply thrilled to take possession of his rooms. They are small and poky, and I'll wager extremely cold, but they are his kingdom.

The company met at 6 pm and we rehearsed both parts of *Tamburlaine*. It was marvellous: light, flexible, and thrilling in its ironies. Albert was there but looked ghastly and was perspiring the entire time. He got through though, and by the end was rejuvenated and determined to do the big opening tomorrow.

Monday 4 October

My father is 75 today. Christopher starts Cambridge today. And the Olivier opens today, at last—for at midday the doctor said Albert could make it. Met with the company for a team talk, and stressed to them that they must be arrogant and confident and play it cool; make the audience come to them. By 4 pm the hordes of familiar first night faces were beginning to muster. I was interviewed, and television news asked me to reply to the mounting wave of criticism. 'What mounting wave?' I asked.

The performance began early, at 5 pm, because of the play's length. I can't pretend I knew very much about how it went. Jacky and I lurked in the director's box, well away from everybody. But the house was attentive and the company displayed magnificent nerve. Albert sounded badly bronchial for the first three quarters of an hour, but gradually the tubes began to clear and his confidence grew as he realised he would be able to get through. At the end there was the sort of ovation that is usually reserved for opera and ballet, and it was not just for Albert, but for the whole company.

[1] Headed 'The Colossus of the South Bank', the leader commented that Hall's critics depicted him as an emperor of the theatre world, and it went on to recommend that two new artistic directors should join him to 'reduce Hall's power to proper proportions and allow other ideas freedom'.

Tuesday 5 October

Woke after a fitful night feeling as if I'd been steam-rollered. The notices are good, though. There are the usual clichés about Marlowe—his blood and thunder and mighty lines—and nobody sees the play as the great a-morality that it is. But Albert gets praise, so do the company, so do I. We have a big success, and it is all very much better than I feared.

During the afternoon news came of Max Hastings's latest carve-up. Somebody has given him an Arts Council working party's report on us which we refuted months ago and which was not accepted by the Arts Council itself. So it's all in yet another double-page spread in the *Standard*, the fourth running. Hastings leads off by saying it is only a matter of time before there is a full scale enquiry about the extravagances at the National. All the old hoary and mostly disproved accusations are there. I find it extraordinary that the *Standard* pursues this campaign. It can be of little interest except to a few hundred people in the theatre.

Home tonight feeling awful, and not wanting to continue with this life or with this job.

Wednesday 6 October

Most of today spent in session with Peter Stevens and Simon Relph. Stevens proposed that I get two associate directors to run the Cottesloe and Lyttelton respectively, not assuming full responsibility but to implement my policy. I told him he was living in a fool's paradise. In all my years at Stratford, I learned that the only way a John Barton, or a Trevor Nunn, or a Clifford Williams, or anyone, can actually run a theatre on your behalf, is for them to run it on their own behalf. They have to be given power, they have to have responsibility, and they have to keep to the budget.

A very interesting couple of hours with Stephen Fay. He's writing a National Theatre piece in *The Sunday Times*. He asked me to speak frankly. As I trust him, I did. I didn't tell him anything he didn't already know, I'm sure.

Friday 8 October

A very helpful piece in *The Guardian* this morning by Michael Billington blowing the whistle on the detractors and giving some indication as to why they are against us. I feel cheered.

Saw *Yahoo*, Alec Guinness's entertainment about Jonathan Swift at the Queen's Theatre. Guinness appears to have at the moment a bad attack of 'the lovelies'. He seems to me to want, above all, to be loved by the audience. A pity when he is such a superb technician, and has such an amazing sense of character. What we received tonight was a gentle half-smiling ironist about as far away from the ferocious misanthropic Swift as a duck-pond is from the Pacific Ocean. Guinness said the famous line, 'Today

I saw a woman flayed alive, and you would hardly believe how it improved her appearance for the better', with a rueful, gently mocking smile.

Saturday 9 October
Saw the *Tamburlaine* company, gave some notes, and then left for Wallingford absolutely flattened with tiredness. I always have withdrawal symptoms from a production as soon as it's opened. But this time, the feeling is acute.

Sunday 10 October
The *Sunday Telegraph* and *The Observer* on *Tamburlaine* are marvellous, and Levin (in *The Sunday Times*) is dreadful: hates Marlowe, hates the play, hates what I have done with it. He is so absolute that I can't even argue about it to myself.

Stephen Fay's *Sunday Times* piece—commenting that we are the centre of the biggest row in the theatre since 1848, when the National Theatre was proposed—is balanced and clear. He reports 'a veteran' as saying that we are the target of 'an incredibly spiteful and envious campaign' inside the profession—and Fay points the finger.

Monday 11 October
To the Connaught for Max Rayne's lunch for new Board members. Of these, neither Lady Plowden[1] nor Yvonne Mitchell could be there, but Hobson, Hugh Jenkins, Richard Mills and Rafe Clutton[2] were. I am much encouraged by this strong injection. In Richard Mills we have a clear headed commercial theatre man. In Rafe Clutton, a surveyor, we have an obviously fair-minded new member on the side of the angels. Hobson I think will support me in a crisis, certainly over plays. Hugh Jenkins is a firebrand but knows how the Ministry works.

Much talk about policy, costing, being commercial. Tony Field kept uttering dire warnings about the future, but when pressed thought we might next year get a little more money from the Arts Council. Meantime, the Board look glum. We are still badly in the red, all due to the delays.

Thursday 14 October
Saw a run-through of *Il campiello*[3] which I enjoyed in many respects. It is true, not vulgar, and with a great deal of infectious charm. But I am worried by the medley of accents—principally Scottish—that Bill Bryden had drawn from his cast. I think the production will work with audiences, but the critics will accuse us of doing a thin old play. It's nothing of the sort of course. It's

[1] Chairman of the Independent Broadcasting Authority 1975–80.
[2] Partner in Cluttons, Chartered Surveyors, London, from 1955.
[3] By Carlo Goldoni; English version by Susanna Graham-Jones and Bill Bryden. Directed by Bill Bryden in the Olivier.

cunningly contrived and beautifully observed. But somehow the language is wrong. I am uneasy.

Bill Allan from the press office had lunch today with John Elsom, at Elsom's request. Elsom gave himself out to be a fair man above intrigue and gossip. His position is that he doesn't trust anybody, neither the faction against me, nor me. He said his book had to deal with all the *Evening Standard* controversy because the articles were now part of history. I believe that the articles were based on the last chapters of his book in draft form, and these chapters must now be rewritten to take note of the *Standard* articles. It's the press feeding on itself.

Sunday 17 October

I hope to stay in Wallingford for the next few days, and shall not over that time, unless there are significant happenings, be adding to this diary of pressure. I must try and stop working while I am here. But I am worried about next year's repertoire, worried about the organisation, worried about my own development in the next couple of years (what plays shall I do?), worried above all about the mess of my personal life. I know what I want, but I have to have time to do it, and an uncontentious atmosphere in which I can think clearly and strongly. My life is now all work. That is no life. The last year is the worst I can remember. The theatre is open, but at what cost.

Wednesday 20 October

Up to London to see the preview of *Il campiello*. I thought again what a superb dramatist Goldoni is—so accurate, so economical. And the audience were adoring it. They recognised the human behaviour, which is what the comedy is about—not wit, but a recognition of an awfulness which you've met in your own family, or a tenderness which you've experienced in your own heart. Perhaps it will work after all. I don't know.

Thursday 21 October

I am told Larry has been coming in every morning between 8 am and 8.30 am and behind locked doors in the Olivier rehearsing his speech for the royal opening on Monday. I have to admire his professionalism.

Sunday 24 October

I have just finished reading *Clayhanger* by Arnold Bennett. I have never read Bennett before, perhaps because he was out of fashion in my youth. I really admire the precise observation and the relish with which he writes. There are some wonderful things. For example, he refers early on in the book to the 'interestingness of existence'. Another beauty: 'Edwin was one of those who learnt quickly, by the acceptance of facts. And he now learnt that profound lesson that an individual must be taken or left in entirety, and that you cannot change an object merely because you love it.'

Monday 25 October
To breakfast with Goodman. The spectacle of this latter-day Samuel Johnson tucking into his eggs and bacon while talking to his secretary on the telephone and dictating to her a congratulations and good wishes telegram on today's royal opening to be sent to me, who was eating breakfast opposite, will stay for a long time.

I went to talk about the Elsom book. Goodman advised that I should not take legal action now but wait for Cape to publish and then perhaps do something. He said he would talk to Max tomorrow and advise him on a correct approach. He thinks a letter should be sent which says that having checked out all the factual errors the Board feel they can no longer regard the book as an official history of the National Theatre.

Arnold is quite sure the malice and envy will pass in time. I hope he's right. It's a long road to journey.

Off for a haircut and beard trim, then back to the theatre for a rehearsal of the royal arrival: the BBC, Mishcon, Rayne, Michael Birkett, and various dignitaries all present. Our positions were governed by where the cameras were and where the lights were rather than by any natural feeling. TV news bulletins create life rather than record it.

It came on to rain heavily this afternoon, naturally. Before that, the outside of the theatre was looking very attractive: brass bands, funfairs, stalls with hot dogs etc. But by 7 pm, when we were all lined up at the entrance for the Queen, the rain was torrential.

A score or so of the Fringe demonstrated with banners and leaflets, chanting 'Whose National Theatre? Whose National Theatre?'[1] They were all packed into the cheering, applauding, singing crowds, some six thousand people watching the arrival of the royals and getting wet outside.

It seemed inside that most of the artistic and political world was there. Denis Healey looking cheerful in spite of the fact that the pound has fallen through the floor today; Norman St John Stevas telling me not to worry, it was because the building was a success that the worms were now coming out of the woodwork; Larry much in evidence but not particularly warm to me. I should think sixty or seventy people commiserated about the *Evening Standard*.

Campiello went very badly indeed and I was deeply ashamed. The presence of royalty nearly always ossifies the public in a theatre, but this

---

[1] A poster by Tom Phillips, issued for the opening, had the slogan 'The new National Theatre is Yours'.

particular play meant nothing to this posh audience. The actors were like men struggling through a nightmare. And the special fanfare version of God Save the Queen, which we'd commissioned from Howarth Davies, and which had sounded well when it was rehearsed, sounded horrible, with many many mistakes by the Household Cavalry trumpeters.

The one undoubted success of the entire opening ceremony was Larry who, before *Campiello* started, made an elegant, though over-written, speech. The audience gave him a standing ovation. So they should have done. But it was difficult for a play to follow that.

HM did her job magnificently. She didn't eat and she didn't drink. She chatted well everywhere, was extremely gracious to everybody, and worked with a will. The atmosphere was warm and friendly and it was a party. But the play was dreadful.

Why did we open with *Campiello*? Well, any play on this occasion was a risk, and we didn't have a choice, with all the changes of dates and schedules. I thought something light, short, and amusing might serve. It didn't. We have made our piece of history.

Tuesday 26 October
Campiello shown to the critics tonight. The cast were cheerful beforehand because they thought nothing could be worse than yesterday. But it wasn't much better. It has the feel of a flop.

Wednesday 27 October
The notices for *Il campiello* are appalling. Not one is good. Also, after an amazing string of successes I have an unpleasant feeling we could now be in for a run of badly-reviewed work. To come are Thomas Bernhard's *The Force of Habit*, the kind of middle-European play that pleases few drama critics; a revival, in the Olivier, of Albert's *Hamlet* which those who didn't like it before will be furious at seeing again; *Tales From The Vienna Woods*, an extremely tricky thing to sell; and then a young, rather under-weight cast in *Julius Caesar*. If *Caesar* were coming after a more solid repertoire it would be alright, but I think by the end of March we may very well have run out of credit with the critics. Can I do something to help matters? Not easily. This place has to plan too far ahead.

Thursday 28 October
Off to the Arts Council for a three-hour meeting. We got a lot of things out into the open. They kept on and on about extravagance, particularly 'my reputation for extravagance'. Their latest was that they had heard a story that we had filmed three actors at enormous expense for the role of Cassius in *Julius Caesar*, and then flown the film by special air freight to its director, John Schlesinger, in America because he couldn't be here to do the

auditions. In fact the film was on video tape, Michael Birkett did it himself, it cost £40, and we sent it in the special diplomatic bag Paramount runs between London and Los Angeles for free. So that story was disposed of. National Theatre extravagance stories are being collected. I was fairly tough about their attitude and invited them to be tough to us, which they were. So it wasn't a bad meeting.

Friday 29 October
Interviewed for an American TV chat show. They did a big build-up: 'And now we are very honoured to have on the programme the famous inter-national actor, I mean director, who founded the Royal Shakespeare Company and is now running this great modern theatre, the National Theatre. Ladies and gentlemen it is a pleasure to welcome on to the show, Mr Peter—I'm terribly sorry, I can't remember your name.' So we cut and started again. The interviewer never really recovered.

Full houses tonight in the Olivier and Lyttelton. The public has taken the building to its heart. The foyers absolutely packed with people. This is what it is all about. But my God, what a lot of work this place is going to eat up.

Sunday 31 October
Poor Edward depressed this afternoon, going back to school after half term, because he's been shifted down from the first stream to the third. He observed, 'My days of success are over.' I talked about getting back on to the horse as soon as you've been thrown. But he said he didn't seem able to go on as I did in the face of failure and abuse and misunderstanding. There's a true melancholic Pamment there[1]. His temperament will take him far— and he's a brilliant boy.

My own head will not stay still. Many problems. I don't think this theatre's going to submit. I have managed to force it open, but it's for those who come after me to do something with it. That's my fear anyway. There also speaks a true Pamment.

Monday 1 November
All day spent arguing about future plays. I felt better at the end of it than I have for weeks. We are grappling with the thing that matters most—what is on our stages. Suddenly we could become a theatre that does obscure and possibly bad European plays instead of the great central repertoire of the classics. With all the shit that has been flying for the last few months, at least it was not possible for us to be attacked because we had poor houses. Now I fear we could get them.

---

[1] Pamment was the maiden name of Hall's mother.

Yevgeny Yevtushenko read his own poems in the Lyttelton tonight before the play started, and behaved like an egomaniac clown. He used Denis Quilley and Brian Cox, who appeared with him, as his creatures. He rolled his eyes and over-inflected like the worst ham in the world. I have never seen a more dreadful display of selfishness. While they read he scratched, whispered, walked about, sipped water.

But a wonderful feeling in the foyers. Partly because he drew a full house in the early evening and also because we have packed business for the plays too. I always walk round the foyers to cheer myself up.

Tuesday 2 November
Most of the afternoon with Peter Wood. A little trip down memory lane. He's been a director for 22 years, I've been a director for 23 years, and we met at Cambridge. I gently led him into thinking whether he would like to be an associate. He said he would. I was pleased with that.

Wednesday 3 November
Scofield to lunch. All as easy as winking. He will do *Volpone*. He may do *Madras House*. And once he's played in the Olivier, he'll confirm whether he'll do *Othello*. We had a very good talk about *Volpone* which I certainly don't have much idea about yet, though we both thought Ben Kingsley would be wonderful as Mosca. We agreed that our meeting was like a homecoming.

Friday 5 November
On Concorde to Washington, by courtesy of the American producers of *No Man's Land*, to work on the production there before it opens in New York on Tuesday. A beautiful aeroplane, beautifully designed; lovely colours inside, rich browns, and real leather upholstery on the arm rests. It's quiet, but then I suppose it's quiet because it leaves its noise to others. It was half empty, and stewardesses urged more and more caviar upon me to save it being wasted. Excellent wines. The first time I have enjoyed an air trip in years.

On landing I was met and whisked to the theatre, arriving at 7.15 for curtain up at 7.30. Such timing always gives me acute pleasure: a sense of fitting everything in, of doing the impossible.

The theatre, the Eisenhower, is beastly and cavernous, although reckoned to be intimate. The usual American audience: they talked, they were late, they rattled their programmes and banged their seats. But the play 'went', though I don't think it would stand a chance without the two Lions, who seemed delighted to see me; really delighted. John gossiped away like mad, and invited me to supper tomorrow night. Ralph hugged me and said how wonderful it was to have come on Concorde.

Saturday 6 November
Washington: Had a good look at the Kennedy Center this morning. The outside, facing over the Potomac, is beautiful, with slender willow trees and gentle fountains against white marble. But this is a pompous place, full of pretension and *very* rich. Huge parties with guides are taken round while statistics pour forth: this was given by Sweden, this was given by France, this is the largest, the biggest, the something or other. . . . I can't imagine anyone sitting down on the carpet here as they do, thank heaven, on the South Bank.

Monday 8 November
Washington: Appalling news from London. Yesterday a good friend, Cyril Bennett, threw himself out of a window and is dead. I cannot believe it, though I know he's been going through hell personally and that things have not been good lately for the commercial television companies. I remember the time about three months ago when he rang me to come and have a talk about life. He said he felt I could help him somehow. But he cancelled, and over the last couple of months I have been thinking I should see him—just that uneasy sensation that you should be seeing somebody, yet you don't follow it through. I can't believe he's gone.

Tuesday 9 November
New York: Opening night of *No Man's Land*. There was terrific excitement in the house and the actors rose wonderfully to the occasion. I have rarely seen the two Lions roar better. Fantastic reception.

Wednesday 10 November
New York: Wonderful notices this morning for *No Man's Land*: a hit, a hit—but it feels curiously remote to me.

Thursday 11 November
New York: Spent the morning with Ralph and Mu. Ralph does not want to leave the National—or, happily, me. He made a speech saying he'd like to stay there for the rest of his life.
Tonight I took Mu to see Joe Papp's show known as *Coloured Girls*. . . . The full title is much longer. Seven girls tell the story. They sing, they dance, they explain the onset of maturity, the first affair, the marriage. What interested me was that all of them performed not to each other but directly to the audience. They were narrating, but experiencing at the same time. The house, half black, responded with audible comments, cries, cheers, laughs, shouts of approval, applause on every other line. This was an extraordinary experience, as near Elizabethan as anything I have ever seen. Culture shock:

to walk round the corner from this show (it only lasted an hour and a half) to the two knights elegantly rolling out their Pinter periods.

Saturday 13 November
Back in London last night. Can't say I feel my normal self. There's a mountain of correspondence in, of course, including a copy of a letter from Hugh Jenkins to Max Rayne saying that the Board should now have a play committee to prevent disasters like *Campiello*. Ça commence.... *Campiello* is a beautiful play by a master. What play committee would refuse it? No, if they follow that line of thought, they'll need an artistic direction committee to vet dress rehearsals and previews.

Talked to Derek Bailey. He's shattered by the Cyril Bennett tragedy. Derek was at LWT's three-day conference last week and said that at the end the feeling was buoyant and optimistic with a terrific vote of confidence in Cyril. The next day he killed himself. Why? Loneliness I suppose. The big ebullient wisecracking tycoon was desperately lonely.

Derek gave me a feeling there'd be no *Aquarius* for me next year. No surprise. I haven't been doing it well and it hasn't been good. Well, it's been passable; but that isn't enough. The commercial companies don't expect arts programmes to get ratings, but they do expect them to get attention—which means press—and *Aquarius* has been getting next to no attention. I suppose it serves me right for being greedy and thinking I can do something as difficult as that with one hand.

Sunday 14 November
Dreadful notices for *Force of Habit*. Levin observes that after *Tamburlaine*, *Campiello*, and *Force of Habit* there is nowhere for the National Theatre to go but up. That will teach me.

Wednesday 17 November
Tartuffe visiting the Lyttelton from the Théâtre National Populaire. I have in the past found Roger Planchon's directorial touch light, ironic, and rich, but this was heavy and full of philosophical implications. It looked to me like a production that had been worked on too much.

Reception at the French embassy. Bumped straight into Gaia Servadio whom I mocked and called a liar with the biggest smile. The room was divided between those who thought *Tartuffe* marvellous, and those who thought it awful. But something had occurred. Theatre had released indignation and argument again.

Home much too late. I hate gatherings of the Establishment, I suppose because I play their game, and hate myself afterwards for having played it.

Max Rayne tells me there has been an objection from the Palace about our special fanfare version of the National Anthem played at the royal opening. But then, the London Sinfonietta played it well and the Household Cavalry played their contribution extremely badly.

Monday 22 November
Forty-six today; fifty in sight. The good thing I suppose is that I have reached a point most people reach in their fifties rather than their forties, so I reckon I can sit out the swing of fashion against me. But I am doing too much. If I can get this theatre right and devolve it so that major directors are running segments of the company then I will have done something. But that requires a lot of thought and a lot of steady progress. The main thing I need is time, and time is what the Board may not give me.

Finance and general purposes committee: what a way to spend a birthday. We've reduced our deficit dramatically, and made over £100,000 by outside commercial exploitation of our work. After the meeting Max asked me in a whisper if I had yet heard from Downing Street. I asked him if the Prime Minister was coming to a performance. 'No, no,' said Max. I then realised what he meant, so said I hadn't, and didn't expect to as I was currently the most controversial figure in the English theatre.

Tuesday 23 November
Tonight the TNP gave us Marivaux's *La Dispute*. Patrice Chéreau is a master director, but I've never seen a play so warped out of its true guise. The production is creative and extraordinary, but it's full of French bullshit. Most irritating of all, it is lit very artily so that you cannot see anybody's face. There's also a cobbled-up prologue from the writings of Marivaux, and the whole thing is three hours without an interval.

Thursday 25 November
Rather a morbid talk with Peter Stevens. He sees January as the month we are run out of town. He fears we will not be able to effect the cutbacks we should make to our repertoire if we are to reduce our deficit still further, that *Tales from the Vienna Woods* will be a flop and a very expensive flop, and that following *Campiello* and *Force of Habit* it will finish us. I don't see it like that. I think with Schlesinger doing *Caesar*, Scofield joining, and Gaskill[1] and Morahan lining up, we are moving towards a more secure future. We must of course do a good job with *Vienna Woods*, for you're only as good as your last play, but I think we will survive, just.

---

[1] William Gaskill, who was to direct Granville Barker's *The Madras House* in the Olivier.

I actually feel much better about everything. It was therefore strange tonight that I had the most graphic dream that I had cut my own throat. I woke up thinking there was blood round my neck. It was sweat.

Monday 29 November
Good meeting with John Heilpern. He talked to me about his inclination to become a director. I talked to him about my wanting to examine a theatre in which the actor's awareness that he is acting, his awareness of presenting himself, forces the audience into an involvement. That is what is different to the realism of television and cinema, and why I believe the live theatre could expand. Above all, that is what the Olivier theatre is about, and the Olivier is why I am here. The openly public presentation of a true emotion is my objective, my aesthetic, and it goes for Chekhov in the Olivier as much as it does for Shakespeare.

Thursday 2 December
To Lincoln's Inn for the dinner given by Goodman for Robert Anderson, chairman of the Aspen Institute and of the Atlantic Richfield Company—the man who has saved *The Observer*. Our prestige and our traditions can only be supported now by American capital.

Everybody kept sympathising with me for the battering I was getting in the press and expressing hopes I would hang on; there was a distinct feeling in the air that I wouldn't.

No taxis and of course I didn't have the limousine cars of the rest of the guests. So I walked from Lincoln's Inn to the Barbican through the freezing night.

Friday 3 December
I woke up suddenly at 6 am with an absolute understanding of what should be done for the royal opening—the first part of *Tamburlaine*. It was a bit of a disappointment to come to and realise that the royal opening had happened in October.

Wednesday 8 December
Up at 5 am to do paperwork. I worked for eighteen hours in all today without stopping: mad.

Auditioned a singing dwarf for *Volpone* in my office—David Rappaport. He stood by my glass-topped desk and sang a song unaccompanied. The experience was very Jonsonian.

South Bank Board meeting. Max was extremely brisk and distant. Is the *putsch* beginning, I ask myself? I don't record this in paranoia. My whole situation now with the National is so farcical that I either do it on my terms, or depart.

272

Associates meeting tonight which went on until 11.15 pm. I sat there realising that you can't run three theatres by committee, but that I can't run three theatres by myself.

Sunday 12 December
The notices for Edward Albee's *Counting the Ways*[1] are appalling, particularly from Levin who takes the opportunity to give more bad notices to *Tamburlaine, Force of Habit*, and *Il campiello*. I know I am prejudiced, but *Tamburlaine* is in another class. I am hurt, upset, and frightened. Another nail in the coffin?

Monday 13 December
Up to London early this morning by train with two suitcases full of scripts and papers, and a cardboard model of *Volpone* in my teeth: not the right equipment for the rush hour. Planning all day. Broke off in the middle to talk to Lindsay Anderson. He told me the Royal Court is in terrible danger—Nicholas Wright and Robert Kidd[2] are leaving and somehow he's got to help. There was that awful pleasure in the air at the ill-fortune of others. Well, it could be coming to me over the National.

Wednesday 15 December
The NT Board gathered this evening to present a Laurence Whistler cut bowl to Larry. He said how tired I looked; begged me to tell him I was alright; hoped I was alright. . . . I had a feeling during the gathering that the sands were running out for me. Certainly there was less cordiality than usual from all the Board members.
    The Aldwych has another enormous success with *Wild Oats*[3]. I am glad for them. But I am sure if we'd done it (which we nearly did two years ago) we would have been criticised for disinterring a minor classic instead of doing Sheridan or Goldsmith. That is the way things are at the moment. I try to be a happy fall guy, but it's getting tiring.

Thursday 16 December
Tennessee Williams in for a drink: a tiny man in a wonderful beige coat and a large ten-gallon hat. He wanted me to read his new play again; he has rewritten it. He said, though it needs to be heard in his soft Southern accent: 'The lady who produced my new play on Broadway organised a seminar. As I went into the seminar I saw that the notice for closing the play was up on the stage door notice board. I thought this odd as I was doing the seminar to

---

[1] A short two-hander, directed by Bill Bryden, put into the Olivier repertoire in the evenings to allow matinees of the extra-long plays, *Hamlet* and *Tamburlaine*.
[2] Joint Artistic Directors of the Royal Court Theatre 1975–77.   [3] By John O'Keefe.

boost business. After the seminar I asked the lady producer why the notice was up. She said she had no more money. I told her this was a shock to me as I had a cardiac condition. I threw myself down on the floor. She screamed and called for a doctor. I rose from the floor roaring with laughter.'

Tennessee has always had the ability to say the most dramatic, sometimes sentimental, things with an enormous sense of self-mockery. Peals of laughter at himself are always underneath his talk. It's underneath the dialogue of his plays too. That's how they should be acted. The greatest guide to playing a dramatist is to listen to his tone of voice in ordinary life: Beckett, Pinter, Shaffer, Stoppard, Ayckbourn, Brenton—I could go on.

With Jenny to the first night of John Schlesinger's film *Marathon Man*. Jenny wanted to leave after the first twenty minutes, the sense of impending violence is so great. It is a wonderfully made film: never has John been more adroit. It's an indictment of 'them'—the secret police, the CIA, authority. Larry gives a very theatrical demon king performance as the wicked German, and so in a way makes the horror easier to take. The rest of the actors, particularly Dustin Hoffman, are so real it is unbearable.

I suppose you could say the film has an Elizabethan love of horror. But I think John has taken a conventional thriller plot and filled it with his own obsessions: the Jewish question, the minority question. And over it all hangs the nightmare sense that sooner or later you will be 'got'. It's horrifying.

Friday 17 December

A big NT Board meeting. The tactic the opposition adopted was to say that they had heard it said, though they themselves were not necessarily agreeing with it, that *Campiello* was an awful play, *Force of Habit* a dreadful play, and *Hamlet* should never be done un-cut. Victor said lightly it embarrassed him when a great lady, the predecessor of Hugh Jenkins (he meant of course Jennie Lee), asked him if these were the plays she had fought for in building the National Theatre. He then made the suggestion that there should be a committee of play experts, people who advised.

I let it all go on, trying to keep cool. Then I hit back for two hours. We have had three flops on the run, I said, but what about the eleven successes before them? And how can they, in the muddle and delays of this particular year, properly judge our policy or our repertoire?

John Mortimer was excellent and got us away from detail and on to clear principle. Should a Board read plays? No, it clearly shouldn't. Harold Hobson declared our repertoire this year was impeccable, but thought with reason that the production and casting of some of our work had not been up to scratch. Yvonne Mitchell was very strongly for what had been done, and against any undue influence by the Board on repertoire, so was Collins[1], so

---

[1] Philip Collins, Professor of English at the University of Leicester from 1964. Member of the Arts Council Drama Panel 1970–75.

was O'Brien. Thank God for a new and stronger Board, and also thank God
I am good with committees.

Saturday 18 December
News of our own Christmas cabaret for the staff last night to which I should
have gone, but didn't, for I am becoming more and more withdrawn.
Apparently its targets were somewhat obvious, but fun was had by all.
Simon Relph was to have appeared as Kon Fredericks, but it was pointed out
to him by some of the back stage lads that if their union official was mocked
there would be trouble.

Sunday 19 December
Finished James Forsyth's book *Tyrone Guthrie*, on that sad, mad Don
Quixote. It gives a good picture of his eccentricity—and of his curious
inability to stay anywhere. Whenever he was starting something, he was
already leaving—whether it was the Vic, or the Edinburgh Festival, or
Stratford, Ontario, or Minneapolis. From the book it seems it was a fear of
being hurt; he preserved his own skin. Forsyth records the closing of the Old
Vic School; the big row with Larry, Ralph, and John Burrell[1]. And
Guthrie's peculiar English flippancy, and distrust of sex, come through well:
he was a Gilbert and Sullivan creature, which is why I suppose he loved them
so much.
    There's probably never been anyone who could handle crowds or move-
ment or pageants on stage better; nor anybody of genius who kept human
feeling and reality so much at bay. He encouraged the audience not to be
challenged, not to feel. He distracted them all the time with marvellously
inventive stage business. He was a director whose technique I idolised, but
whose work—because of its aridity—I finally hated.

Monday 20 December
I may be kidding myself but I feel the worst is over as far as our stage work is
concerned. Stevens doesn't agree and is predicting Götterdammerung. I
believe if we can survive *Vienna Woods* we will last.
    On home fronts, I am approaching a big crisis. Things cannot go on as they
are. Only one pleasure in a perfectly ghastly day—Jenny's absolute delight
at her Cambridge news. She has won an Exhibition at Newnham. I am
excessively proud.
    Up most of the night, and rose at 4 am.

Wednesday 22 December
The Christmas madness is upon everybody. Work is coming to a halt. Drinks

[1] Joint Artistic Director of the Old Vic company with Olivier and Richardson 1944–49.

with Tony Harrison and Harry Birtwistle about *The Oresteia*. This is the most exciting project I think I have ever contemplated.

Then the *Aquarius* Christmas dinner at Luigi's: a rather ghoulish feast, and everyone drank too much. Derek made what sounded like a valedictory speech to *Aquarius*. Well he may be right. It is a unit that has lost heart. I fear that the programme is now not successful enough for them to have any pride. And they lack a leader—me.

Friday 24 December to Tuesday 28 December

Christmas: the usual expectation and the usual disappointment. The children delighted; the in-laws and my parents monosyllabic. Too much eating and drinking. A sense of occasion where nothing happens. So there is no occasion. I read a mass of plays, but the main task was *Volpone*. Ralph phoned on Christmas morning to say Happy Christmas. I was very touched.

I have been thinking further about the Tyrone Guthrie book. It's encouraging in a way that he went on working until his seventies—but only by rushing round the world and always keeping on the move. I am afraid I am more sedentary and dislike travelling. So when I finish at the National, which may be soon, what can I do? There is nothing for me in this country. But the book encouraged me in a way. While there is life there is hope of exercising one's talent, whatever sort of state it's in.

Friday 31 December

The end of this rather horrible year, seen out in bed reading Cole Lesley's gossipy but touching biography of Noel Coward[1]. I remember him as a very generous man, loving Pinter, and firing off telegrams of congratulations to whoever won his enthusiasm. Very interesting to see the movement of fashion in his life. After being the voice of the new generation in the twenties and a glittering success in the thirties, he moved during the forties, fifties and early sixties into being derided by the press as a minor talent. He had great courage. I found his cry of 'Rise above it' very moving. And I admired his capacity to put distance between himself and a flop very rapidly by travelling.

Then came *Hay Fever* at the National, being discovered as an old master, and a knighthood. It's a perfectly shaped creative life, ending in a blaze of glory and adulation. I can't help thinking though that during the difficult years, his talent did in some sense become disconnected from reality. Too much showbusiness camp, I suppose. You can't live off the theatre. It's imitation. There needs to be some life to imitate in your work.

---

[1] *The Life of Noel Coward*.

1977

Saturday 1 January
All day on *Volpone*. I am finding the play, and Jonson himself, extremely sympathetic at this moment because he deals with malice masquerading itself in moral virtue. When I look back at this last year, several people in my life seem characters from a Jonson play. But, my God, what a writer! I am specially struck by the virtuosity of his verse. The conversational tempo and variety is amazing. Purely as a versifier, he's more exciting in many ways than Shakespeare—more intellectual, more conscious, less instinctive, less naturally mellifluous; always stimulating.

Tuesday 11 January
To *Chorus Line* at Drury Lane this evening. It manipulates the audience brilliantly, and is of course most expertly done, with the most precisely timed lighting cues to music that I have ever seen in my life. But the show is a sham, it's kitsch at heart. The girl who desperately wants the job, and shouldn't get it, does of course get it, otherwise the show itself would not be commercial. Bullshit really, reeking of double Broadway standards.

Wednesday 12 January
Routine South Bank Board meeting. Max Rayne greeted me with the news that I looked washed out. I am sure I do. He was tanned from his two weeks in the West Indies for Christmas.

Saw a number of young writers including Stephen Poliakoff, Robert Holman, and Shane Connaughton: a mixture of amiableness and suspicion. We are an institution they need, but which they do not wish to join.

Thursday 13 January
Brian Mitchell of the stage staff said he'd take a bet with me that *Tales from the Vienna Woods*, which opens in a fortnight in the Olivier, would be a great success. I refused the bet.

Friday 14 January
Peter Shaffer to lunch. He was very cordial, very warm, promising a play and commiserating (of course) about the campaign that has been waged against me during the last year. He says the tide is turning and there is a good deal of disgust at the malice. I am getting tired of sympathy though.

Stuart Burge, who has agreed to run the Cottesloe, phoned me because Hugh Willatt and Jocelyn Herbert[1] have begged him to request me to release him so that he can go to the Royal Court immediately as its director. The argument is that unless I do, the Court may close forever. It's good old-fashioned blackmail and very upsetting, even though I know it's over-stated. Stuart is torn. He says it's his duty to go to the Court, although he recognises that emotionally he wants to come to us and is committed. I said I didn't think it was any good doing things in the theatre out of a sense of duty. What did he want to do? He offered to come for six months and then go on to the Court. But what use is that to me? I want commitment, not short-term help.

This is a hideous blow. I feel the pressure of too much work building up on me once more, and at least I thought the Cottesloe would now be taken care of. If Stuart has really changed his mind, then of course I must let him go. But as he's being pressured, I shall try a little pressure back.

Saturday 15 January

Well over a thousand people queued for the last performance of *Hamlet* tonight, and hundreds were turned away. Before it started I made the long tour round the company saying goodbye: to Denis Quilley, to Barbara Jefford, to Philip Locke[2], and to many another who has upheld me through these last desperate seventeen months. Albert was as cheerful as ever as he prepared to play *Hamlet* full-length for the seventy-second time. He asked me to keep the theatre in order until he got back.

Monday 17 January

First day of rehearsal on *Bedroom Farce*. I told myself the play was not a problem, that I knew it, and that anyway Alan Ayckbourn was shortly joining and directing it with me—so there was no need for my usual fears before beginning a production. The actors read it, very relaxed, and we began. I then had all my usual fears.

It is, though, quite wonderful: accurate in observation, precisely engineered, and beautiful in its execution. The actors responded with the joyous recognition of being involved with a marvellously human text.

Stuart Burge to lunch. He looked ghastly and was in a terrible state. He's been got at even more to save the Court. Meantime there are messages to me from Hugh Willatt to ring him about it, and telegrams from Michael Codron[3] begging me to release Burge. My stance is that Stuart must do what he wants to do. And I mean it. Today, he very definitely still wanted to come to the Cottesloe.

---

[1] The designer.   [2] Who played Horatio.   [3] The producer.

Tuesday 18 January
Stuart Burge came in to—as I thought—sign his contract with us, drafted exactly as he wished. But he has now decided he must go to the Court. So I have released him. And I am in a mess.

Wednesday 19 January
Spoke to Hugh Willatt at lunchtime, who thanked me for being public-spirited about Burge. Public-spirited be damned. I have had to bow to the inevitable and it's upset me very much.

Friday 21 January
Peter Stevens's cut-back programme looks very nearly possible. We're in sight of making an even bigger dent in our money problems—always assuming the grant is what we expect—and we've reduced the staff by some 60 people.

First preview of *Vienna Woods* tonight. Encouraging on the whole, and the reception at the end was tremendous. But the actors fell into sentimental patterns as they sensed the audience enjoying themselves, and the play then became a boring Victorian melodrama. It should be hard, cryptic, cynical, all the time. There is a great deal of work to do and it's shirt sleeves up and into action to work on the production with Max[1]. I'm going to sort out the technical stage problems for him so that he can be where he should be—with his actors.

Saturday 22 January
Work on *Vienna Woods* this morning, and all the company together for notes at lunchtime. At Max's invitation I spoke my thoughts to them. I had intended to keep to technical matters, but Max gave me a cue to go further and I did. I had discussed with him last night the dangers in the performance, so I said that the audience's pleasure at the story had trapped the actors into indulging their feelings, and the stage was awash with sentiment. Also, the music making, instead of being schmaltzy and to be taken critically, had become hearty English party singing, and sweet, well-loved waltzes.

This afternoon Max put the company through five hours of hair-splitting notes; and there was smouldering anger about the place, the result of many days of unrest.

The preview tonight was both better and worse. Better because it was harder and lacking in indulgent pathos, worse because the actors were tired and fed up. Yet no English director could have led the company with such certainty into the heart of Horváth as Max has done.

[1] Maximilian Schell.

Wednesday 26 January

The first night of *Vienna Woods*. The play went well, all in all the best it's been, though the edge was still a trifle blunted. The Austrian ambassador was there, plus a very amiable Arnold Goodman and an extremely frosty Jennie Lee, who I suspect thinks I should be removed from the National. Drinks with the cast afterwards. Max Schell made a speech and gave everyone a long-playing record that he'd made of rehearsals almost from day one.

Christopher Hampton[1] was depressed at the party after the performances because he had run into Bill Gaskill, who was very critical. So had I. But I deliberately didn't ask Bill what he thought because I guessed. I don't mind people not liking things, but they should keep their mouths shut on first nights, and I knew Bill wouldn't.

He told Chris the play showed facile pessimism, and was dated rubbish with no true social point of view. Will the press say this tomorrow? They could. Or they may like it because it's different, foreign. But I don't care too much because all in all it is now a good piece of work

Thursday 27 January

The notices for *Vienna Woods* are excellent. We are praised for what we are trying to do and Max comes out of it as a hero. A great lightening of the spirit detectable round the theatre at lunchtime. The morning after an opening, the reek of success is as immediately detectable as the reek of failure, with no word said. I remember Larry saying success smelt like Brighton. Is that why he lives there?

Monday 31 January

Quite a lot of problems came up during today's NT Board meeting. The enormous loss of box office income anticipated because of the delayed openings of the Olivier and Cottesloe has been reduced in this financial year to only about £200,000—entirely due to exceptional business. But because we've done well, we are going to be penalised. The £200,000 loss will be carried over to 1977/78. If it were a lot bigger we would have to be bailed out. Classic government finance.

Wednesday 2 February

Had lunch with Terry Hands. He rang asking if he could see me. There is no hope any more of his marriage to Ludmila Mikael[2] surviving. He wonders how to keep his little daughter so that she can be educated in England; she is only two. I told him we must find him good legal advice and he must stick to it. I am very aware of Terry's problems, having lived through them myself.

[1] The translator of *Tales from the Vienna Woods*.
[2] The French actress. She and Terry Hands subsequently divorced.

That is why he came to me. He told me his wife sat next to Leslie on an aeroplane quite by chance recently. They fell to talking about British directors and being married to them. Leslie said the main problem with British directors was that they worked too hard.

Sunday 6 February to Sunday 13 February

At the Imperial Hotel, Torquay, trying to rest, relax and stop worrying. Desperately lonely and I nearly went mad. On the other hand there's been a bit of peace.

The hotel was fairly empty, and luckily nobody spoke to me, save the odd porter or waiter who'd seen me on the box. But there was a lot of nudging among the half a dozen ladies wintering there in solitary luxury, all sitting at separate tables in their turbans, husbands I suppose having departed with the mandatory coronary.

I took a sauna every morning, swam in the pool, looked at the sea, walked a little each afternoon, mostly in the rain, and tried to sleep. I like seaside places out of season. The cheap souvenir shops are shut, the rotten cafés and amusement arcades out of action until the spring.

Jonson is becoming more and more of an obsession with me, and I did a great deal of work on *Volpone*. I feel as secure about it as I ever can about a new production; I have it inside me. Talked on the phone to Scofield, all a-bubble about playing it, which bodes well.

Have been reading Ronald Hingley's *A New Life of Chekhov* all week. Curious the portrait of the man that emerges: reluctant to commit himself to a woman and therefore very attractive to them. They came round him like bees and he discouraged them with a light mockery. Half of him is actually a-sensual, against food, against high living, against sex; something in him wants to remain totally untouched. The other half is a thorough-going sensualist.

I feel better after my rest. I have spent all week trying to quieten the terrors which rise in me when I face the thought of the next eight months. The work ahead is enormous and inescapable.

Monday 14 February

The GLC have given us no increase on their grant for next year, not even enough to allow for inflation. It is a mark of signal disapproval and our chairman doesn't avoid telling me so.

News of the series of dreadful meetings John Goodwin has had with John Elsom going over the proofs of his book. Elsom said that writing it nearly gave him a nervous breakdown. He also told Goodwin he believes a National Theatre should be 'slightly stuffy'. Goodwin finally challenged him by asking how, if his criticisms in the book were true, did I successfully run Stratford and create the RSC. 'Ah,' said Elsom, 'but he's changed.'

First rehearsal of *Volpone*. I chatted about it somewhat incoherently, then we began to read. Interestingly enough, the text immediately took wing. It reads aloud much more easily than it reads in the head. Scofield for lunch: warm, expansive, and eager to work on the play. I get very much the feeling it's our second honeymoon.

Tuesday 15 February
Bedroom Farce rehearsal this morning, or rather not. I went down and saw Alan and it is clear that after my week away he would like to get on with directing it by himself for a few more days, so I left it at that.

Aquarius: an exhausting two hours allowing Ken Campbell to talk at me, playing straight man to his comic. He is a total anarchist and impossible to pin down. He more or less said it was a crime to be serious.

Then a meeting with Derek Bailey about the future. I told him I couldn't contemplate doing *Aquarius* next season, even if wanted. He was obviously relieved by this and said he was thinking of producing it then without a presenter, a front man, because it would leave more money for the programmes themselves. But there's never been a weekly show of this kind, without a talking head. You need one because there is so much information to be given. The audience won't read it on the screen, and voice-over is boring. So Derek's undecided. I'm a bit sad I've finished with the programme, but very pleased to have one responsibility off my shoulders. I have enjoyed it sometimes. But I haven't been enough involved; I couldn't be. And I don't like half doing things.

Monday 21 February
Good news from the box office. *Vienna Woods* is now a complete sell out. And there are phenomenal advance bookings for everything, the best yet. The support of the public is growing, and the place is really taking off.

Tuesday 22 February
Good rehearsal this morning of *Bedroom Farce*. Then a very interesting afternoon working on *Volpone*: Ben Kingsley[1] is a great asset, and Dave Rappaport came bustling in to be a perfectly normal, joyous dwarf; he really brings an enormous quality to the play which it would otherwise lack; he is disturbing yet utterly charming and comic. I'm sure that's what Jonson is about. The villains in the play, the most condemnable people, have the most lyrical language, the most profound perception of beauty.

Thursday 24 February
No Man's Land, back in the Lyttelton repertoire since January[2], finished

---

[1] Who played Mosca.
[2] Following visits to Toronto, Washington, and New York.

tonight after a grand total of 378 performances. Harold benign. The cast presented him with a tiny cricket bat marked 378 not out—for no one believed this was the end of it.

Saturday 26 February
Volpone rehearsals morning and afternoon. First day with Gielgud there[1]. He came in like a fine-bred horse eager to career anywhere, even down the wrong road, but very creative, very brilliant, and very very funny. I'm a lucky fellow to have him. I think he will be wonderful.

Tuesday 1 March
Birmingham: *Bedroom Farce* opened a week's pre-South Bank run in the Alexandra Theatre tonight. Full dress rehearsal this afternoon to an invited audience, mostly young from colleges. They were like wild beasts let out of a cage. From the first line they roared with laughter. The actors had actually to tame them. An alarming experience, but a good one to have before the actual performance which we were into within a few hours. It was a great success, an excellent beginning for the production. Alan Ayckbourn says it's the best launch of a play of his he's ever had. I think we have something that, whatever the critical response, can fill the Lyttelton for many many months.

Thursday 3 March
Birmingham: Breakfast session with Ayckbourn going over all our various notes. I like him and we haven't had a cross word, but God he's nervous: masks everything behind a jumpy mockery. He begins to settle down with me though. I hope we can work together again. I believe we shall.

A long notes session with the cast. It was uphill work. They already have that rather pleased remoteness which actors achieve once they have been in front of an audience. The director, who used to be the centre of their working life, is now an adviser on the sidelines, rather like a football trainer shouting helplessly from touch while the chaps get on with playing the game.

Incidentally, I don't think I've ever known a more miserable, insecure, and paranoid group of actors than this *Bedroom Farce* lot. It's not that they're difficult; rather, they are all individually thinking they themselves are not particularly good. Maria Aitken[2] murmurs gloomily that she's heard this always happens with Ayckbourn. I think in fact that there's nothing sadder than playing uproarious comedy. There can be no emotional release. The satisfaction is manipulative rather than sharing a feeling. Albert Finney once told me he feels frustrated at the end of a farce, but elevated and high at the end of a tragedy. It's a particular problem with this

[1] Who played Sir Politic Wouldbe.   [2] Who played Susannah.

285

play. The laughs are enormous and continuous, yet if any actor actually plays a laugh, or encourages one by even a lift of the eyebrow, the whole structure collapses. The actor feels like a man addicted to drink who is left in charge of a pub, but mustn't touch a drop.

Friday 4 March

Birmingham: News came to me from time to time about today's opening —at last—of the Cottesloe Theatre, with Ken Campbell's extraordinary eight-hour show *Illuminatus*. Apparently it's packed, but there are many dazed critics who imagine it's a put-on. Well, in a way it is.

A stimulating dinner with Trevor. We spent some time lamenting our separation, still wishing we were working together. He said it was nonsensical of me at this productive stage of my life to be considering, as I was, giving my time to running a studio in the Cottesloe in which directors could be developed. He pointed out that he and Terry Hands and Robin Phillips and John Barton, etc, etc all came to the RSC in the sixties because of what I was doing there on the main stage, not because of studio work. He asked me if my dream was still the same: to run a small company of treasured actors in which I staged three quarters of the productions. I said it was. He said I should do it. The thing is *how*, in my current situation? The National is so large, its demands so huge. How can I have my cake and eat it? I must think, I must think.

Trevor told me quite a lot about his attempt eighteen months ago to form a cooperative of 23 actors and himself. He supposed there was a kind of dishonesty in it because they didn't believe, and perhaps it was right of them, that he was sharing his power equally with the group; and in the event only three actors agreed to sign on.

Sunday 5 March

Back from Birmingham this morning. After lunch, to the Cottesloe to see *Illuminatus*. It's mad, and deliberately kitsch, and it shows Ken Campbell's acute intelligence at work. Some wonderful things: Chris Langham's extremely impressive performance—energetic, naive, goofy, true, very funny; and Dave Rappaport's twenty-minute turn on his own in which he discusses how he's taken on the world and tried to screw it up in all sorts of minor and major ways, each springing from his various phobias. The sight of his final phobia—self-phobia—is amazing. He hurls himself round the stage trying to get away from his own diminutive body, his own tiny unwanted limbs.

A good feeling about the whole National tonight. Standing room only in the Olivier, Lyttelton, and Cottesloe. At last, at last, they are all *three* working.

Monday 7 March
Quite good notices today for *Illuminatus*, even from Milton Shulman[1]. I
ran into him yesterday at one of the intervals and he rounded on me. He said
it was outrageous the critics should be asked to sit through a play as long as
this. He was very stroppy and I got angry back. He then said the National
was now a year old, with all three auditoriums finally open, so he was
thinking of doing a piece and would I see him. I said I was afraid I wasn't
seeing any writers for the time being because I was fed up with misrepresen-
tation and prejudice. I should have added that I was particularly fed up with
the *Standard*.

To Cardiff for *Bedroom Farce*, which is there this week before opening in
the Lyttelton next Wednesday.

Tuesday 8 March
High-speed train back to Paddington, with British Rail breakfast. *Volpone*
rehearsal at 11 am. Ben Kingsley and Paul took two hours to get into the
play, and the work was slow. I notice Ben has the same habit of over-
emphasising individual words that Sue Fleetwood had when she also came to
us from the RSC. It's *explaining* the text rather than *being* it, and it's a habit
over there now.

Melancholy evening; big nettles to be grasped. I am very tortured about
whether I even want to go on with this National Theatre nonsense, and if I
do, who am I to get to help. For at the moment it is assuredly too much for
me.

Wednesday 9 March
Lunch with Terry Hands. He is attracted to the idea of joining us. He said he
must talk to Trevor. I said until he had made a decision, nothing should be
mentioned either to Trevor or to the associates at my end. He must have
made a firm commitment before we get into the inevitable hassle.

Meeting of the entire staff and company to talk about our financial
position and our programme for next year. I was very uncomfortable. The
trouble began because I had to mention the word redundancies. The
militants among the stage staff then started attacking and passing judgements on the amount of money spent on scenery. I might have countered by
pointing out the amount of money spent on stage staff, particularly with
their overtime, but I didn't.

When you have disruptive elements, it is a painful experience for many to
be at a full-scale get-together of this kind. The disrupters are only a minority
but they distress the majority, so the meeting, instead of being something
which makes the organisation cohere, is just depressing and fragmenting.

---

[1] Drama critic of the *Evening Standard* from 1953.

Then an associates meeting. Most of the evening was spent exploring new thoughts I have had. Ideally, I said, I would like two crack companies in the Olivier of fifteen or twenty actors each (serviced for minor parts from a central pool), one directed by perhaps a newcomer to the organisation, the other by me. I would also like someone to run the Lyttelton, and someone to run the Cottesloe.

We didn't get through any of our agenda but spent all the time discussing these things. Harold bowled me a googly at one point by saying I would hardly have gone so far in my thinking without having a secret candidate from outside to direct the other Olivier company. Who was it? I said I wasn't prepared to say yet.

Home very late with horrible sinus, eyes streaming. So this is the creative life. . . .

Thursday 10 March

Lunch with Scofield. I floated over his nose the notion of him joining a small crack ensemble in the Olivier committed to me, with me committed to them. He reacted very well and, significantly, he took me aside after the *Volpone* rehearsal this afternoon, and said he thought it a most exciting and marvellous idea. But then, as I have continually to remind myself, you can never be certain of Paul until he's actually there and doing it. He is, though, happy at the moment: happy with the play, and I think happy with me.

Some jollity this evening: Kon Fredericks is reported to have told *The Guardian* and the *Express* that the shop stewards are resolved that if there are any redundancies there would be a strike, unless I took a cut in salary and gave up the Barbican flat.

Friday 11 March

Christopher rang me from Cambridge very shaken. He had been to a lecture by Jonathan Miller on the theatre in society, and it was really an attack on me and the National. Jonathan said, among much else, that he'd left the National because he wanted to get away from the vodka-and-tonic expense account form of theatre, and back to the grass roots and reality. Christopher said the awful thing was that a crowded house of students swallowed all the bullshit.

Sunday 13 March

All day at Wallingford, mainly phoning. Long talk with Pinter who is for my new scheme of two small Olivier ensembles, and a director each for the Lyttelton and Cottesloe. Talked as well to Peggy Ramsay[1] who overwhelmed me with praise, said the tide had turned, and that the entire profession

---

[1] Managing Director of Margaret Ramsay Ltd, play agents.

was saying what a success I had made of the place. It's so rare for me to get an ego rub these days, I responded happily.

Stayed behind this evening while the family went back to London. Watched *The Ambassadors* in one of those glossy Sunday television productions well removed from any form of reality. I don't really *like* Henry James, I certainly don't like him dramatised, and worst of all is to have him dramatised on colour television. But there were compensations: Scofield was very subtle and ironic and handled the vast sentences beautifully; Lee Remick was excellent; and Delphine Seyrig very haunting and true. What came forcibly home to me was how like James Edward Albee is. *Delicate Balance* and *All Over* are the children of the late Jamesian novel.

Wednesday 16 March
First night of *Bedroom Farce*. I was a little disappointed, though things got better in the second act and the play got a warm reception. The actors came out of it well.

Thursday 17 March
We have an unqualified success with *Bedroom Farce* from the notices I've read this morning, though John Barber in the *Telegraph* concludes by saying it is nothing short of scandalous that the National Theatre should stage a play the commercial theatre would snap up. So what are we to do? Refuse a good play if we fear it might be commercial?

First preview of *Julius Caesar*. I don't think it's going to work. I believe we shall be slaughtered for the weaknesses in the young and inexperienced cast, for all the clarity of Schlesinger's direction. A great great pity, just when we've turned the corner. There's little I can do. John is thoroughly receptive and open to suggestion: he takes what he needs and rejects the rest, and that is all I ever ask. But I fear that neither he nor anybody else is going to make this one a success.

Friday 18 March
To see Max Rayne. We settled down to a lunch of asparagus, lobster, strawberries, and chilled white wine. He was out to soothe my ruffled feathers. He assured me we were now over the worst, and would finally somehow get the extra money we needed. Then he explained he had great confidence in us all. I said we didn't mind giving him any facts and figures, and accepting criticism, but we did get dispirited when the criticism was so total and he was so constantly asking the opinion of outside experts.

We ended with him declaring there was no one who could run the National Theatre but me; and with me thanking him for his unremitting fight on our behalf. . . .

Back late for my *Volpone* rehearsal, and of course cross that I had lost so much of it. Paradoxically, it was the best rehearsal I have yet done on the play. I found myself absolutely brimming with ideas, communicating easily with the actors, and the whole thing came to life very quickly. How can one explain these things? You do your prep, you sleep well, you think about it carefully, you are undistracted—and the rehearsal is like lead. You rush about like a flea in a fit, like I have today, and the work goes magnificently. It was worth being a director for those couple of hours.

Saturday 19 March

Associates' meeting. Much talk about the new scheme and who would be joining to run one of the two Olivier ensembles. I said I couldn't yet say who are in my mind as possibilities. They are of course Brook, whom I am trying to get in touch with; Bill Gaskill, who wants to keep himself free until July or August; and Hands who is now playing funny buggers with me and not answering phone calls. So I don't think I stand much chance of getting any of those. But I must try.

Chris Morahan very impressive at the meeting. I am quite sure he will take the Lyttelton.

Tuesday 22 March

Dined with Brook. He told me I should follow my instincts, form my own Olivier ensemble, and work away calmly and solidly on a body of work. He said it was up to me to hand on traditions, that in many ways I was a traditionalist. What I think he was also saying was that in a time of dogmatic revolution, tradition itself is a revolutionary force and must be safeguarded. It's an interesting role for me: a conservationist, a hander-on. But it is a role I feel comfortable in at the moment. Certainly the radical questioner that I suppose I was in the sixties is not what I am now. There are different radicals about.

The movie Brook is starting will take at least twelve months, and he's not really free for another two years to consider what he might do at the National. But he said we had to work together sometime again though he made, of course, no commitment.

Wednesday 23 March

The *Caesar* notices are dreadful. The audience were ahead of the play at the opening last night and that always spells death. I saw a great number of dispirited actors, all in shock.

Up to the Manchester Exchange Theatre to see Albert and Leo McKern in *Uncle Vanya*. It was wonderful to see the play again, and I think both actors were definitive. I felt that Leo's Vanya actually ran the estate, had work-soiled hands, and that Albert's Astrov was a country doctor wading through shit and mud in order to save peasants from cholera.

Thursday 24 March
There's a postcard in from Terry Hands saying his silence wasn't at all because he wanted to say no, but because he was trying to think of ways of saying yes.

Friday 25 March
Lunch with Chris Morahan. He said a definite yes to running the Lyttelton, so there is the first of the new team.

Most of this evening with Terry. He said he was going to resign from the RSC anyway and was intending to do it at the beginning of next week, giving a year's notice. He will then write me a letter saying yes or no. I think he may say yes. But I'm not certain. A good talk however, and he's obviously very tempted.

Jovial Chancellor Healey in the audience tonight, apparently unworried by his budget, and adoring *Bedroom Farce*. The house actually reeled out exhausted by laughter at the end of this evening: very gratifying.

Monday 28 March
Volpone rehearsal on stage this morning. A long session working at the Court scenes. I finally solved them physically—a wonderful pile-up of people centre stage. Something stirred in my memory and I remembered I had done the same sort of pile-up years ago in the last scene of Gogol's *Government Inspector* at the Aldwych. Am I copying myself? I don't think so, it's just that I'm the same chap.

Rather flat finance and general purposes committee meeting. A Board member asked, was it really right for us to do *The Crucifixion*[1] outside on the terraces on Saturday when there was a possibility of rowdiness and, dare he say it, blasphemy from 'undesirable and uncontrolled elements'. I was dumbfounded.

Tuesday 5 April
Lunch with Christopher Hampton. He told me to my surprise that he was at school with his fellow playwright David Hare. They were both at Lancing together. David apparently was head boy, which must be where his insistence on wearing pullovers with holes in comes from.

Tuesday 12 April
Run-through of *Volpone* this morning. It is much much too long, well over three hours without counting the intervals, and I don't know where to cut,

[1] A part of *The Passion* [see diary entry of 21 April 1977] which was performed outside in the open air to a huge crowd on Easter Saturday, April 9.

for the actors have now grown fond of the text they are playing and fond of their own technical dexterity with it. I've mistimed things. We should have been at this stage of rehearsal in the middle of last week, then I could have done something. Now I'm not sure whether we can. What an idiot.

Scofield, usually a slow cooker, not getting there until the very last minute, revealed himself as a magnificent Volpone who knew exactly where he was going. There was a radiance, a pleasure, about him which was remarkable.

Long meeting about Hayden Griffin's designs for *The Madras House*. They are very good, but of course expensive. You can't, in the Olivier, do a four-set naturalistic play, with real rooms, as this is, without spending a lot of money. There is a feeling we should cancel *Madras House* as a sign we're taking our economies seriously. But what would be the point? We have to stage such plays, and there is no such thing as a cheap production in the Olivier because of the scale of the place. All we would do if we cancelled it would be decimate the repertoire, offend Scofield[1] and Bill Gaskill[2], and show we shouldn't have planned it in the first place. So I said we must go ahead.

Wednesday 13 April

A better day on *Volpone*. The actors are all naturally and rightly resisting cuts. They've built acting patterns, understand the text and love it, and don't want great lumps of it ripped out. I fear I have left it too late. My other fear is that if I butcher the text too much, we shall reduce it to a silly caricature structure: all the wonderful complexity and irony and layer upon layer of contradiction will be gone. We shall not be doing Jonson but a farce.

Thursday 14 April

Run-through of *Volpone* this afternoon. We are over the hump. The way is clear. The vigour and clarity were a joy to watch.

Friday 15 April

Terry Hands on the telephone this morning said yes to joining us, and that he would be writing to me. So I feel pleased. But why do I also feel uneasy? Because I don't actually believe he is coming.

Wednesday 20 April

Dress rehearsal of *Volpone* with quite a lot of people watching—mainly company and friends of the company. High tension on the stage, high nerves, and a good deal of worry. But the play worked on the spectators. Scofield was in a great state in the interval because all the fur trappings on his

---

[1] Cast as Constantine Madras.   [2] Director of the production.

Volpone robe are moulting: hair in his mouth and throat made speaking almost impossible. Actors do love to seize on martyrdoms at this stage of work. It's understandable.

Thursday 21 April
Went into the Cottesloe and saw them rehearsing *The Passion*[1] there. Bill Bryden has achieved something extraordinary. I have the feeling the production could be a great success.

Then I wandered about giving stray *Volpone* notes to any actors I could find before the play's first preview tonight. John Gielgud wants to re-focus his performance and make it realer. So, while the stage was being prepared, scenery being humped around him, hammers knocking, and Kon Fredericks strolling here and there looking self-important and angry because actors were interrupting the technicians' time, Sir John rehearsed. In the middle of it all I mentioned something to do with over-playing. He blushed and said, 'Will I never learn? Still my old tricks after years and years and years: anything for a laugh, and because of that I don't get it.'

Packed and responsive house at the preview. Last night I was convinced some scenes would have to be cut. Now I am not so sure. I must be careful. And I must be clear-headed. If only I wasn't so fucking tired. I feel incapable of making sound judgements.

Saturday 23 April
Guest night of *Volpone* with the Prince of Wales there. He talked immediately and engagingly with everybody he met, and seems to have none of the Queen's shyness. I give him top marks for professionalism, and the evening, potentially a glacial event, went quite well.

Christopher up from Cambridge in a gloom about his examinations and convinced he's going to be thrown out.

Tuesday 26 April
Very nervous all day because of *Volpone* opening this evening. John Goodwin gave me comfort by pointing out how the launch of the new theatre had succeeded despite so much being against us: the swing against institutions, against large buildings and modern architecture, against nationalised art or industry of any kind, against expensive cultural enterprises at a time of recession.

I tried to watch *Volpone* but couldn't and was in my office most of the evening. It is unusual for me not to have the guts to sit out a first night. I gather the play went well, certainly the reception was good. Quick backstage

---

[1] A selection from the York Mystery Plays, in a version by Tony Harrison and the Company, directed by Bill Bryden.

congratulations: Paul relaxed; it seems he gave his greatest performance in the play so far.

Wednesday 27 April

The press for *Volpone* is good. Michael Billington finds my approach too academic, not social enough; and he writes that the monstrosity in the play is not venal enough. But I think he ought to listen to the prologue. Jonson's satire is healthy, not sick. It is lusty, full of juice, not the misanthropic mood of the middle plays of Shakespeare. I am mightily relieved this morning, though.

Off to Glyndebourne to start *Don Giovanni* rehearsals. I was standing in the opera house before ten: familiar smells; winter damp not yet banished by the hot summer audiences. It's four years since I did *Figaro*, and a bit like coming back to school. The same faces saying hello, all very welcoming.

By 11.15 rehearsals had begun. Benjamin Luxon[1] on the balcony, athletic as ever, was invited to jump off. He did. And damaged his foot and leg. He returned at 2.15 from hospital on crutches. A great start.

In the evening, driven back to the National by Sue. Tonight in all three theatres there were things I am proud of—*The Passion* in the Cottesloe, *Volpone* in the Olivier, and *Jumpers* in the Lyttelton. It was the last night of *Jumpers* and at the end the audience gave a standing ovation. I saw bits of *Volpone*, and nearly all *The Passion* which is really excellent: it has no pretension and there is an absolute honesty about the acting and the attitudes towards the roles. I am very thrilled Bill has done such a marvellous piece of work.

Friday 29 April

To Brighton to see Ralph in William Douglas-Home's *The Kingfisher*. Supper at the Royal Crescent Hotel with Ralph and Mu afterwards. Mu left when we'd finished to go to bed. Much talk. Ralph said he wanted some good strong glue to bind him and me together. He wanted to be with me just as early on in his career he'd been with Barry Jackson and later with Binkie Beaumont, and now he'd every intention of finishing his last years at the National. But what to play? As the drink flowed, much else came out. He'd seen Larry at Brighton last week who had said he'd never go on the stage again. But, said Ralph, in another couple of years he would return and knock them all flying: he was the greatest actor alive.

By 2.15 in the morning, Ralph, in his dressing gown and slippers, seeing me off, was acting out in the foyer of the Royal Crescent Hotel how he had stormed down into that very foyer years ago to complain about the bacon to the lady who ran the place, and walked straight into the funeral of her

---

[1] As Don Giovanni.

husband, with mayors, various dignitaries, and—according to Ralph—a police escort. As he looked at the weeping widow, the complaint about bacon froze on his lips.

Wednesday 4 May
To see Robert Bolt's *State of Revolution* in Birmingham, where it's playing a week before opening in the Lyttelton. It is brilliantly acted, captures well the turbulent lives of the Russian revolutionaries, and will certainly establish Christopher Morahan as a major director with the company. But I am worried. What I read was an anti-Marxist play. Yet in performance it seems to be too soft, too fair, too reasonable, too liberal in its understanding of the extremists' point of view. I understand that it needs to be objective, but it mustn't be cosy. All this was said after the performance to Chris and to Bob, who were receptive and very open. I am glad I went, for they needed to be challenged.

Thursday 5 May
On the train back to London I wondered what I got from this life, why I did it, and why I seem incapable of calming down. I ate a large breakfast to reassure myself.

Tuesday 10 May
The expected letter is in from Scofield. He won't, after all, commit to the group of actors I am hoping to gather for my crack Olivier ensemble. He doesn't want to commit himself so far ahead, only wants to stay until his contract finishes in December and then see what happens. Mr Caution strikes again. It's a repeat of the same situation I have had with him many times over the years: initial enthusiasm and terrific warmth; then withdrawal. But I believe he will do *Othello*.

I heard this afternoon that there was a letter from the Prime Minister at Wallingford. I rang my father and asked him to open it, thinking it was something to do with the NATO foreign ministers who are visiting the National this week. It was the recommendation for a knighthood. I don't want it, I really don't: I'm too young to be labelled a member of the Establishment. Yet there's no doubt it will help combat all the mischief-makers and the horrors.

Friday 13 May
At Glyndebourne. Sue down at lunchtime with an enormous number of fiddling things from the NT.

I've filled in the form accepting the knighthood, but not posted it. I still don't know what to do.

Wednesday 18 May
Spoke to Harold Pinter about this and that and mainly about the knighthood. He said his rule in life was to accept everything that was offered provided it was offered with a good grace. Finally, I suppose I will accept.

Wednesday 25 May
Guest night of *State of Revolution*. It's better but still too fair. I wish it was more passionate in its condemnations. If you're going to write a play taking Marx, Lenin and Stalin apart, then do it. You can't have it both ways.

I met an angry Jennie Lee at the end who said Bob Bolt had falsified history; what about the Cordon Sanitaire the West threw round Russia at the end of the war? I said I didn't think that was Bob's main concern. But she wouldn't have it. Her eyes glowed with romantic fire and she spoke of her communist father, and of her visits to Russia in the twenties and thirties with Nye[1].

Thursday 26 May
The first night of *State of Revolution*. I went up from Glyndebourne, and between my leaving there and arriving at the theatre, a crisis had blown up. A plumber, Ralph Cooper, had been fired last Tuesday after all the necessary warnings in writing about his inefficiency had been gone through. But he's a shop steward. So Kon Fredericks, our chief steward, and his merry men are threatening a strike. There was a partial strike this evening which could have ruined the first night, but it failed. Tomorrow I think we face industrial action.

Friday 27 May
Some of the notices of *State of Revolution* are very good, and some just mild. But the real revolution this morning was down at the theatre. The workshops, the stage staff, and some others came out on strike and began picketing. It is in a way a replay of last summer, but it's also very different. Then we had no agreement with NATTKE for working the new building. Now we have. If the plumber has been wrongfully dismissed, there are proper means of arbitration to decide whether or not he should be reinstated: what we're talking about now is rule of law. An even more important difference to last summer is that the majority of the staff have now joined NATTKE. There is therefore a very large body of moderates who are not likely to be taken in by extremist behaviour or by half-truths.

I was in the theatre for fifteen hours negotiating, discussing, and wondering. The day was a series of cliff-hangers. Could I return to Glyndebourne where it was my final *Don Giovanni* dress rehearsal? The hours

---

[1] Aneurin Bevan, her husband.

ticked by and in the end, of course, I didn't—the first time this has ever happened to me.

We fought to save tonight's performances of *State of Revolution*, but we couldn't. There aren't many people actually outside—about 80 or 100—but many more are reluctant to cross the picket lines. Here we go again....

Saturday 28 May

An offer came this afternoon from the strikers to return to work if Cooper was reinstated without an enquiry, and could at no time be dismissed in the future. They have to have their little jokes.

There is today the same atmosphere of blood and of violence that I remember from last summer. There is the same need to stay in the theatre in case something happens, something breaks. There is the same feeling that one must keep a cool head and a long view; the biggest danger in labour relations is over-reacting. But in this strike the majority of our organisation want to understand, want to heal, so I believe things may come right.

Audiences turned away again. It's bizarre that sacking one inefficient plumber can bring a vast building holding three theatres to a halt.

Sunday 29 May

Bernard Levin salutes Bolt's play as a masterpiece. The other Sunday critics are stuffy. I never remember a play getting such mixed reviews. Normally 'mixed' is a euphemism in the theatre for bad notices. But these are genuinely mixed: some brilliant; some terrible.

A piece on the strike by Stephen Fay in *The Sunday Times* is excellent straight reporting and will I think anger the strikers considerably[1].

Monday 30 May

At the theatre before 9 am. My taxi went through the pickets without trouble. I met the acting company (the Equity members) and explained the position. It passed well, with intelligent questions. When I'd finished the actors convened another meeting and invited Kon to address them. I heard many reports. The most interesting was Harold Pinter's. He said Fredericks was full of charisma, spoke with lightness and agility, and provoked misunderstanding by distributing veiled attacks in all directions; but the final effect was neurotic and emotional.

At midday I held a full meeting of everybody in the organisation.

---

[1] Headed 'Two Wash Basins Halt National Theatre' the piece reported that the strike stemmed from the failure of a plumber to fix two wash basins, but that 'the real reason ... is the management's determination to make a new agreement stick'. Kon Fredericks was quoted as saying, 'We won't abide by a majority decision.'

Michael Bryant[1] was chairman. Those on strike outside were invited in, but refused to come. I'd expected heckling and abuse, but the gods were with me. I spoke very feelingly, and knew I was getting through. I said compromise was impossible, and that both sides must submit to the rule of law. There was no interruption, total silence, and quite an ovation at the end.

After I and the others representing the management had left, the meeting asked the strikers to come in and put their case, which they refused to do. So all the actors, and a great mass of the non-striking NATTKE membership, well over two hundred people, went out to where the strikers were, on the riverside terraces in the sunshine, and argued with and harangued them. Talk about political democracy, here it was—working.

In the afternoon Kon spoke to a full NATTKE meeting, and soon afterwards there was a feeling that support was running away from us. Chris Morahan said that if people could change their loyalty to management so quickly there must be a considerable distrust. I think there is, partly because Kon has fostered it, but mainly because people are very volatile in a situation like this.

By 8 pm we seemed okay again, and by 9 pm in the Green Room there was a mood of euphoria. If NATTKE aren't able to do their job of controlling their members who refuse to recognise agreed disputes procedures, we'll form our own union, was the feeling. I think something has started that could save us, but I'm not sure. Kon is not one to give up easily.

I was talking without stop today for thirteen hours—on sandwiches.

Tuesday 31 May
In early. Pickets still active. The whole of the press thunderous: front page stuff. On the whole they are reporting accurately.

This morning began with high hopes that were quickly dashed. John Wilson, NATTKE's general secretary, met the full membership inside. He had them in his hand. I believe that if he'd said immediately that the men outside had acted illegally and he was going to suspend them and call for new elections, he would have had an overwhelming vote of support. But instead he apparently started with some severe criticisms of the membership, of Kon, and of others. Before the moderates knew where they were the whole thing was in uproar. Kon came in and challenged Wilson, and there was very nearly a vote of no confidence in the general secretary. Chaos.

After lunch Kon and the other stewards, striking and non-striking, came to see me. He called for the instant reinstatement of Cooper, and an

[1] The actor.

298

enquiry—wait for it—into the running of the National Theatre. He said if the enquiry found Cooper had been dismissed correctly they would all be very sad about it. But under no circumstances could Cooper be dismissed now. I felt very cool, so I was able deliberately to lose my temper and throw out Kon's proposition. Rather than accept that, I said, the theatre should remain closed; we must abide by the rules of the NATTKE agreement.

I then talked to a shaken Wilson and persuaded him to take me this afternoon to Len Murray at the TUC. So this afternoon we all sallied forth. I made it clear the union was in trouble, and I'm sure Murray knew it. But while we were there news came that the strikers were willing to go to arbitration—so back to the theatre which was besieged by newspaper men and television cameras. There at a NATTKE meeting it was agreed that the strikers return to work tomorrow morning, but that arbitration proceedings should be set up and Ralph Cooper be reinstated, pending the outcome of the arbitration.

Why has Kon caved in? There are many rumours in the air. It's said that he was losing support and, as well, that it was clear there were enough working people inside the building for public performances to start again.

Against all this has been my anxiety about *Don Giovanni* at Glyndebourne. Never before have I finished a production *without* finishing it. I often wonder whether all the obsessive things one strives for in the last few days of rehearsal are really worth it. Do they make that much difference? I know in my heart they do. I also know in my heart that I am capable of a definitive *Don Giovanni*. I fear that in these circumstances I may not quite have done it.

Wednesday 1 June

Notices for *Don Giovanni* this morning are all excellent. It seems to be very like the *Figaro* success in that what I've done is to some extent controversial. For example, William Mann in *The Times* criticises me for not allowing Don Giovanni to escape at the end of Act I, saying that this must happen. He should look at the text again. Don Giovanni does *not* escape.

The strikers came back today and there were performances tonight[1]. The box office has virtually stopped though. Front pages shout that you are closed, but when you're open again it's not much news. I put myself about, looking I hope calm and detached, which I am certainly not feeling.

---

[1] During the strike a total of 13 performances were lost—4 in the Olivier, 5 in the Lyttelton, 4 in the Cottesloe.

Sunday, Monday, Tuesday 5, 6, 7 June

The long holiday weekend for the Queen's Jubilee. I've lumped the three days together because for me they all passed in much the same mood. I swam, sat in the sun until it rained, and slept. Not a single phone call and no need to talk to anybody: a blessing.

I watched Larry's *Henry V* film on television for the umpteenth time. It's still beautifully shot; silly remark—it always will be. But I still dislike all the Elizabethan theatre scenes, so patronising and bad. Why do we have to assume that our theatrical ancestors were crass, vulgar, and untalented, particularly when they fostered and produced Shakespeare?

Wednesday 8 June

Back to work, full of nerves and false starts. Not very good business at the box office throughout the holiday period: the strike has taken its toll.

Max tells me he's received a letter from Larry saying he was fed up with being asked what was going on at the National when in fact he was not involved at all, and he wished to resign as a consultant director. This has long been inevitable.

Friday 10 June

It's sure now that I am in the honours list tomorrow: the press office have been rung up a lot during the day for pictures. The certainty upsets me frightfully. I almost rang the Prime Minister's office this afternoon to find out if I could tactfully withdraw. Then it seemed ridiculously havering, so I let things rest.

Saturday 11 June

Phone calls and telegrams all day for the knighthood. People very warm and generous. Ralph rang up and said 'I'd had you down as a duke after what you've been through, but this will do.' John Gielgud was made a CH on the same list and said to me that he'd done nothing really except survive to seventy-three.

Sunday 12 June

Down to Glyndebourne for *Don Giovanni*. I really enjoyed it and thought myself a lucky fellow: lucky because though I never felt I had quite achieved what I wanted, the singers have gone a long way towards filling it out.

During the long interval Moran Caplat gave a banquet of all my favourite foods—lobster and melon and wonderful white wine. To warm me to the idea of directing *Così* next year?

Tuesday 14 June
It looks as if the plays I shall be directing at the National over the coming twelve months are *Country Wife*, *Cherry Orchard*, *Macbeth*, and perhaps Otway's *Venice Preserv'd*, certainly one other production. So I am more than ever tortured now about whether I can do *Così* at Glyndebourne next summer. I think it has to go. And I am not too pleased about doing *Macbeth* again, but I do owe it to Albert.

Saw Mu Richardson who'd had the Oliviers to supper last night. She'd said beforehand, 'Now Ralph, let's have no mentions of the National Theatre, or of Peter's knighthood, or of CH's'. So Ralph tactfully did not mention these subjects. Neither did the Oliviers. I must say their congratulations have been deafeningly silent.

Wednesday 15 June
Albert in to see me mid-morning looking ten years younger, bursting with health from his holiday, and just off to America. I wish dealings with all actors were as pleasant as they are with Albert. He told me he didn't really like *Brand* which I'd proposed to him. It had no joy. He said he didn't mind climbing Everest, but if he did he wanted to look at the view from time to time; these Ibsen characters kept their noses resolutely fixed on their boots. I know what he means, though I stay passionate about the greatness of the play.

To David Edgar's *Destiny* at the Aldwych. It was the last performance and the place was packed: queues round the theatre of young people busy flogging Marxist newspapers to each other. Edgar has a fine command of structure, of conflict and of character. And he can write. I was never bored. But what does the play say? Merely that the right-wing is always to be watched; and that Hitler was a bad man. The far-left is treated with tenderness, with idealism, and they speak with quiet voices and wonderful sincerity. They are also cast with the best actors. If only Edgar had had the courage to be as critical of the extreme left as he is of the right.

Thursday 16 June
Late night supper with Terry Hands. He kept on urging me that he has to be number two in the National. What to do? I think Terry has to come in, but not as deputy director. I must think.

Friday 17 June
John Wilson rang this morning telling me that Kon Fredericks was trying — but as it turned out had failed—to get another strike going today. He had issued a very silly leaflet entitled 'A Sell Out[1]'.

[1] The leaflet claimed that Wilson had refused all the strike committee's suggestions as to the composition of the Arbitration Board and had finally 'sold out' the NT membership 'in collusion with the National Theatre management' by asking ACAS to appoint just the one arbitrator, 'in direct contravention of the terms on which we recommended a return to work'.

To a preview of *The Madras House*. It's caviar to the general, and I don't believe it will be a commercial success. I just hope we get marks for rediscovering a masterpiece. Bill Gaskill has directed it beautifully, and the design really shows what power the Olivier can have, even for intimate, naturalistic scenes. It's extraordinary to think that when Granville Barker wrote it he cannot have been familiar with Chekhov. And it's ten times richer than anything Shaw did at this period, for the characters are not simply the mouthpieces of the author. They are alive, and contradict each other. Though the play seems to ramble on in a spacious way, it is soon evident that every single action, every single character, is related to one problem—the role of woman. I'm very proud we've done it. And what a relief to see a production and have next to nothing to suggest to the director.

Saturday 18 June
Christopher suddenly back from Cambridge, so fed him, and dashed late to the Aldwych catching only the last part of the Donald Sinden *King Lear*, which finishes tonight. Again there was this slow, over-emphatic, line-breaking delivery of the text. The actors are so busy telling us the ambiguities and the resonances that there is little or no sense of form. You cannot play Shakespeare without a sense of line. RSC Shakespeare is getting slower and slower.

Trevor has staged it well, but it is Ruritanian: rifles and gunfire. Why, oh why?

Monday 20 June
A long and late dinner with Harry Birtwistle and Tony Harrison about *The Oresteia*. I thought Tony was going off the boil because of all the delays, but not a bit of it.

He spoke of how wonderfully he was treated by the Metropolitian Opera House when he went to New York to work on his translation of *The Bartered Bride*: an apartment, adequate expenses. I said that was the difference between Britain and America. But on reflection, I am not sure I'm right. Isn't it that we here are inclined to disregard writers, and think they should only get big rewards if they are a box office success? We are conditioned to think of them as earners of royalties, and that's that. What I would like to do is give Tony Harrison a regular salary. But how can I?

Wednesday 22 June
Spent all afternoon working on the management's arbitration submission over the sacking of Ralph Cooper, the plumber. I had that same sickening feeling that I had in my divorce case all those years ago. The law has little to do with truth or intention or human feeling or pain. It's to do with

manipulation and semantics; and the sanction is always a righteous cleverness. It's not *being* right, but playing it right.

The union's submission is amazing. It appears to say that the first two warnings to Cooper for inefficiency were correctly given but the third was not because an unofficial strike interrupted the proper procedural course! I suppose what the union want is for the arbitration to find Cooper was correctly dismissed, but there were procedural difficulties on the last warning, and therefore we should give Cooper another chance and allow his first two warnings to stand.

Thursday 23 June
Half the morning spent with Terry Coleman for a *Guardian* interview. I like and admire Coleman, but it was a depressing interview for me because all the old rubbish came up again. My salary. My four per cent on transfers to the West End of my own productions. *Aquarius.* Who pays for the Barbican flat? Am I a dictator? I think his line is that I've had a terrible beating and survived well, that the building is successful, and what's more I've been knighted. Ho ho. Even so I had to wade through the shit once more. And I'm afraid that when he began bringing out the old Miller/ Blakemore accusations I just blew and called them a couple of bastards and gave him a short sharp rundown on the circumstances in which they both resigned. Christ, I'm fed up with all this. From now on I must say to journalists in advance that there are some subjects I'm not prepared to talk about.

Feverish work on the management's arbitration submission. Meanwhile, our own industrial troubles are put into perspective by the horrible picket at Grunwick. The country gets more and more like Germany in the twenties. And there's clearly a jolly band of extremist brothers on picket outings at Grunwick to see that it does.

No notices in the morning papers today for *Madras House* due to the critics having deadline problems. The two evening papers were both good but both indicated that the production was too long and rather worthy. Oh God! This is one of the best bits of work I've seen for years. Is it going to be patronised?

Friday 24 June
Peter Stevens and Sue finished the management's arbitration submission and it winged its way to the arbitrator this afternoon. It reads well.

The Grunwick business grows worse and worse: people hurt and horrible brutality; extremism on both sides. I was rather horrified to see a red notice up on our stage door noticeboard asking people to support democratic trade unionism by joining the pickets at Grunwick.

This week I have felt the seeds of a strong desire to leave the National Theatre. I can't remember having had this so intensely before, though it's something I forget, like pain. But when it occurs it is absolutely valid and unanswerable.

Saturday 25 June
Read George Kaufman's *The Man Who Came to Dinner*, hoping it would be the answer for Christmas in the Olivier, directed by Peter Wood. But it isn't. It's a gaggy commercial piece with no real heart.

To the theatre this afternoon for the Flying Thespians[1], who are at the National for their open day. I spoke to them for an hour, mainly about Jonson. They seemed surprised that I felt a director should not start rehearsals with the moves blocked out and dictate them to the actors—that, instead, the physical life of the play should evolve. What if you haven't got time, they asked. Good point.

To Wallingford this evening. Things are not happy in my life at home.

Sunday 26 June
All told, *The Madras House* has been well received by the critics. It is a big success.

So much work and worry I don't know where to turn. I should actually stop for two weeks. But I can't find the time.

Wednesday 29 June
Kon had an unofficial meeting with our Equity deputies at lunchtime and told them about what he claims is the betrayal of Cooper and the workers.

It seems the deputies, despite their distrust of Kon, swallowed this whole and went back and told it to the actors without asking for the management or union point of view. As a result, poor Chris Morahan took a heavy beating from some of his company in *State of Revolution* and was visibly shaken by it, muttering that though a progressive himself he thought there were too many liberal *Guardian* readers in the theatre. I have realised during these last weeks the danger of the fair-minded liberal. He believes every man is as fair-minded as himself. He's therefore easily preyed upon and abused.

John Wilson keeps saying he has Fredericks on toast. Yet he must know that he can't move against him without the risk of bringing our theatre, and a lot of others, to a standstill. Perhaps he doesn't mind about that. Perhaps he feels, as I do, that blood has to be let. We cannot continue to work in this atmosphere and in this way. A thumping awful strike may be the only way we shall get out of it—a desperate thought because the theatre was full again

[1] The RAF Amateur Dramatic Society, of which Hall, who was in the RAF on National Service 1948–50, is President.

Top: Samuel Beckett.
Bobby Clark

Above: Alan Ayckbourn.
Anthony Crickmay

Top right: Edward Bond.
Chris Davies

Middle right: David Hare.
Jenifer Rima Beeston

Bottom right: Howard Brenton.
Laurence Burns

and below: Mark McManus as Christ
he Crucifixion on the NT river
ices, Easter Saturday, 9 April 1977.
Albion Band is on the platform near
river. The crowd was made up of
ers-by. *Nobby Clark*

Bottom: *Lark Rise* in the Cottesloe. The
audience were not only onlookers, but
active participants.
Michael Mayhew

Above: Rehearsing *Tamburlaine* on the terraces. Albert Finney is in the straw hat. The audience were passers-by.
Nobby Clark

Left: Albert Finney.
Zoë Dominic

Opposite top: Christopher Morahan with Barbara Flynn at rehearsals of *The Philanderer*.
Reg Wilson

Opposite bottom left: Warren Mitchell with Michael Rudman at rehearsals of *Death of a Salesman*.
Michael Mayhew

Opposite bottom right: Bill Bryden.
Michael Mayhew

Left: The *Hamlet* poster, which was printed in silver and black; and the *Tamburlaine* poster, printed in gold, scarlet and black. *Hamlet* officially ope[ned] the Lyttelton on 16 March 1976; *Tamburlaine* opened the Olivier on 4 October 1976. Both posters were desig[ned] by Richard Bird and Michael Mayhew

Below left: some typically enthusiastic press comment when the NT opened. Right: examples of comment when the euphoria turned sour, with the chaos of the strikes and with attacks on Peter Hall for alleged extravagance and for, in one instance, showing aspects of a South Bank Tamburlaine

Top: Kon Fredericks (left, with papers) listens to NATTKE members at a meeting about the strike, outside the NT.
BBC Hulton Picture Library

Above: An addition to the mural in Upper Ground, behind the NT.
Michael Mayhew

Left: Ralph Cooper on picket duty outside the NT.
BBC Hulton Picture Library

tonight, having climbed slowly back to its old succcess in these last painful weeks.

In bed by 10 pm ready for the arbitration tomorrow.

Thursday 30 June
To ACAS in Westminster for the arbitration. Tight security: everybody signed in. Kon was hanging about outside, pale and unshaven. A Kafka-esque building with the usual run-down tattiness of government offices and seemingly infinite. Only the smell of borsch and cooked greens is needed to complete the Kafka picture.

Soon after 10.30 am Z T Claro, the arbitrator, came in. The union said they couldn't defend Cooper because he had refused to appear at the arbitration or make a statement, either written or verbal. I was convinced that many liberals in our organisation would never accept the ACAS findings if they condemned a man in his absence—even if he chose that absence. So towards the end of the proceedings, which had nevertheless dragged on, I suggested the union should have more time to persuade Cooper that he had to be represented[1]. Claro and the ACAS heavies thought this a good idea. As a result any arbitration is postponed, and we meet again in a month or so.

Tuesday 5 July
First night of *Bow Down*[2] at the Cottesloe. I looked in but didn't stay as I have to come tomorrow night with Princess Margaret. She won't like it a bit.

I am full of antibiotics for my eye[3].

My personal life is about to undergo some revolution.

Wednesday 6 July
Lucy's school concert this morning: little embarrassed girls grinning shyly at the audience, reciting A A Milne, all spick and span in school uniform—a vanishing society. Dashed down to Wallingford this afternoon to see Auntie Gee who last night had a stroke[4]. The doctor said she was not a person who had in any way come to terms with the idea of death, and asked me if I had. I said I hadn't but I would like to. I know that when I die my remains will go into the cycle to make more life, that life in that sense is eternal. But the rage I can see in Auntie Gee, I fear I shall feel myself when my time comes. Life may be eternal, but what happens to me?

[1] Cooper's decision not to appear did not change between this hearing and the final hearing on 11 August 1977.
[2] A music theatre production by Harrison Birtwistle and Tony Harrison, put on with two other pieces.
[3] Hall's eyes, in particular his right eye, had been troubling him for months.
[4] The sister of Hall's mother; she later recovered.

Back to the Cottesloe for *Bow Down*—a fairly disastrous evening. Princess Margaret was very affronted by the whole thing, and afterwards said she didn't think she should have been invited. This surprised me, though *Bow Down* is certainly strong, cruel, and somewhat upsetting.

Friday 8 July

A holorum on the phone with Glyndebourne this morning. The three maskers in *Don Giovanni* have refused to sing the trio in their masks, and Bernard Haitink has supported them: questions of balance, intonation, etc etc. I was in an immediate rage—most of which I put on. Had a phone talk with Bernard at lunchtime who backed off a bit when he realised how strongly I felt. The point is lost if they take the masks off before they reveal themselves in the ballroom. He asked me if I could be at Glyndebourne at 5 pm to explain to them. I said I would, dashed down, and arrived late in a perfect lather. I went to the Green Room but the singers were not there. I found them just before they went on stage, shouted at them, and told them that if they wouldn't wear the masks I wanted a full rehearsal tomorrow to reconsider the scene. So they wore them. They then proved how silly they had been by singing the trio perfectly and with perfect intonation.

The usual Glyndebourne over-wining at a party in Moran's office after the performance, but a pleasant and successful evening. I sat up until 3 am talking to George and Mary Christie. They begged me to do *Così* next year no matter what.

Saturday 9 July

Glyndebourne: More talk about *Così*, this time with Moran. He said he wasn't going to accept my refusal: I *had* to do it. We went round and round the same problems, and ended up having decided nothing. I just have to sort out next year before he will take no for an answer. I am in a muddle. I do want to do it. And they meet me more than half way. What to do, what to do? Moran's main point was that Glyndebourne would be in a worse mess if I walked out on it now than if I walked out on it next year—next year would be a crisis, now would be a catastrophe. He is a clever old fox.

In the evening, a Christie family dinner of shepherd's pie with the children in the kitchen. Much nicer than salmon and strawberries and cream in the candlelit restaurant.

Thursday 14 July

My brain is boiling. I'm really not well. On the personal front things couldn't be worse. And my financial position is desperate. I also cannot see the way to run the Olivier next year: Gaskill or Hands (who has gone very quiet)? One company or two? The Gaskill problems were slightly sorted out by a long conversation with him tonight. We talked of plays, and he had a good substantial list. But it's clear to me that he hasn't the appetite for the number of productions we will need from him. I pushed him and he recoiled; I backed off and he came towards me.

Saturday 16 July, Sunday 17 July
An awful weekend in Wallingford: emotional scenes all round. Christopher, who has been a marvellous support for the last month, is off to Canada and America for four or five weeks on Tuesday and I think he should take the trip—but his travels, and Jenny's, have caused much tension.

I tried to do some work on *The Country Wife*, my next production, and skimmed through *L'Ecole des Filles*, the bawdy book which mentions it and which Pepys couldn't resist buying and then burnt for fear of contaminating his shelves. It is pornography and it tells how one young woman teaches another the delights and arts of love. I also skimmed through some of the Earl of Rochester's writings including the 'filthy' play attributed to him, *Sodom*. One beautiful line in it: 'On this soft anvil all mankind was made.'

The only peaceful moment during the weekend was a quiet swim in the rain tonight. But my eye is troubling me again, and there's no doubt the sight is declining.

Monday 18 July
Board meeting this afternoon. We looked at the melancholy future facing us, with a hugely mounting deficit. We have two big problems. The building is seriously under-subsidised—because it was impossible accurately to assess its annual cost before it was fully under way. And the stage machinery doesn't yet work properly—therefore much of it has to be hand-operated, which is expensive. All we can do is cut production costs, mainly by doing fewer plays. The Board said they wouldn't wish this, but we are contemplating closing the Cottesloe by the end of the year.

Tuesday 19 July
There is much to do, much to decide. But I have no feeling of real purpose when, as now, I am not rehearsing. I could never be happy if I didn't direct, didn't at times live in the rehearsal room.

Wednesday 20 July
It looks as if we are getting near a structure where Chris Morahan runs the Lyttelton, Bill Bryden the Cottesloe, and Terry Hands and myself the Olivier. The real problem is will we survive with sufficient funds to do it. We are virtually powerless to alter our financial position. The government pay policy is completely broken: union after union through the country is putting in extravagant claims—NATTKE want nearly 30%. We haven't got anything like it.

Off to Buckingham Palace for the Queen's Jubilee party. About 800 people there, the public rooms all open. At first I was horrified because I could see nobody I knew. But gradually I identified a few faces. I saw Julian Bream[1], whom I haven't met for years. He's converted an old chapel into a recording studio where EMI allow him to record anything he wants; he has it made, I would say. I also saw Janet Baker who looks absolutely blooming with health although she'd just finished giving a concert at Chichester and had driven up for the party. Singing is such a physical business it can actually produce health just as it demands it.

The Royal Family wandered through speaking to whoever took their fancy. Breakfast was served at 1 am. I came out of the press of people bearing three plates of sausages and scrambled eggs, a cigar between my teeth, and nearly knocked the Duke of Edinburgh over. He greeted me cheerfully, and a red-coated flunkey removed the cigar from my mouth so that I could speak.

The thing that gave me most joy was this. I was walking across the reception rooms when I heard a voice crying 'Cuckoo'. It was Princess Margaret. We paid our respects and chatted away. In the background the band of the Coldstream Guards were playing selections from Gilbert and Sullivan. The Princess invited me to choose the next piece of music. I said I would like something by Harry Birtwistle. She didn't find that funny and went into a long pout about her evening at Harry's *Bow Down*. I, with enormous smiles, told her what frightful trouble her dislike of the production had caused us because what she thought had so disturbed the chairman. I then moved further through the crush and met Max Rayne. He asked me if I'd seen *her*. 'Who?' I asked. 'The Princess,' he said. 'I'm keeping well away from *her*.'

Friday 22 July

Session with John Bury on his design for *The Country Wife*. He showed me his first rough model. I'm not sure if it works. Restoration plays are a new world for me.

Sunday 24 July

Spent most of the day doing paperwork and only got round to what matters, *The Country Wife*, in the evening. Studied again John Bury's first model. If the setting itself were an island of attractiveness, the dirt, sweat, and lust of the people on the stage would present a greater contrast. I begin to feel it. I think the people must be grotesque, and express the characteristics signalled by their names: Fidget, Squeamish, Horner, Pinchwife. They are all

---

[1] The guitarist and lutenist.

extreme; Jonsonian I suppose. So they're super-jealous, ultra-innocent, and always exuberantly hypocritical.

Wednesday 27 July

Yet another eye specialist this morning, the umpteenth I've seen, all of them with different diagnoses. This one concludes it's herpes from the shingles I had years back at Stratford, which keeps on reactivating itself, and that there's very little I can do except try an even more fat-free diet. The surface of the right eye is bubbling with little blisters, like a tarred road on a hot day. He says there is nothing wrong with the sight underneath the blisters. But they can't do anything about the blisters. I shall just have to live with it, I suppose.

I am getting tired of the office. It's lonely and I miss rehearsal; yes I do. Rehearsal produces overwork, but it's what I am chiefly here for. I feel frustrated and uneasy banging around in an office all day to little effect.

Friday 29 July

A happy lunch with Ralph. The restaurant was quiet and regal, while he commanded everything. He said 'I don't mind dying. I know I haven't much longer. I hope it won't be too painful, but I'm ready. I'd like to go on acting for a few more years though.' He talked of love and marriage: 'It's just luck really. No one can know. There can be physical attraction, and that is nice, but to be married to somebody takes a long while. You don't know till you've done it, and then it's too late.' He made me a long and flattering speech about not doing too much administration. I was a director, one of the most sensitive he'd ever worked with, and I must direct; I mustn't get my priorities wrong. In the same breath, though, he observed I should stay at the National for at least another five years. He also said that too many talented young men were being cushioned from learning their craft. They were almost proud, for instance, of being exclusively Royal Court dramatists. Their tiny audiences made them feel important. He said that if they were not cushioned by subsidy, they might learn to tell their stories a little more clearly. He has a point.

Well into the afternoon, and after nearly two bottles of wine, I walked him northwards towards his home off Regent's Park. We dropped in on the Scolar Press at the British Museum to get a facsimile of *The Country Wife*. He bought it and inscribed it for me with a flourish. There were no taxis, so I popped him up Tottenham Court Road and saw him striding off, cap level and stick flourishing.

Saturday 30 July

Message from the doctor who looked after me years ago in Stratford: it was the left eye that had the shingles. So Wednesday's diagnosis is nonsense. It's the wrong eye.

Saturday 13 August
From the first of August until today I have been chiefly in Wallingford. I resolved I would not keep this diary, but I must summarise a few things.

I read a good number of Restoration plays and began to get into the period. I also read Frances Donaldson's book, *Edward VIII*. It's a marvellous biography, ironic, factual, and it illustrates the awful processing and conditioning that can keep the royals from any kind of reality. Baldwin is the best on the abdication: 'The last days before the abdication were thrilling and terrible. He would *never* listen to reason about Mrs Simpson. From the very first he insisted that he would marry her. He had *no* spiritual conflict *at all*. There was no battle in his will. I tell you this and it is true. . . . There was simply no moral struggle. It appalled me.'

I spent most of my holiday planting and making the water garden, and wiring it with lights: silly manual labour, but it was something to do to stop my mind racing—I got my hands dirty.

I saw *Henry VI Parts 2 and 3* at Stratford. But the plays do not work uncut. They are a monument to the young Shakespeare's hubris in trying to write a national epic before he was ready. What an extraordinary thing to have done: three plays about the Wars of the Roses—I suppose to take on *The Oresteia* on its own terms. He couldn't do it though, not until the *Henry IV*s.

Monday 15 August
We have the findings of the Ralph Cooper arbitration[1]. It gives the union three out of ten and us eight—though whether the union will actually do anything about putting its house in order, or disciplining Kon Fredericks and the stewards, remains to be seen. Cooper stays, but on second warning, so he has to behave himself.[2]

Tuesday 16 August
My Glyndebourne *Don Giovanni* opening in the Lyttelton tonight for five performances[3]. The London Philharmonic are having great difficulty fitting into the orchestra pit. If we do opera again in the Lyttleton the pit will have to be wider which means dropping more of the stage. The sound is not as bad as I feared, but not as good as I hoped. You can hear the full spectrum—but the orchestra sounds as if it's in the next room. Haitink was rattled but very professional; so were the singers.

---

[1] In broad terms, the findings were that the management had 'reasonable grounds' for terminating Cooper's employment, but indicated that, as Cooper was a shop steward, a senior NATTKE official should have been present for 'discussion and consideration' before he was actually dismissed.

[2] Cooper was dismissed in February 1978 because of further incidents of unsatisfactory work, and later claimed wrongful dismissal before an industrial tribunal, but lost.

[3] See diary entry 13 June 1976.

Wednesday 17 August
A reasonably calm associates' meeting. We made the decision that there should be no visiting companies—regional or from abroad—in the next year. We can't afford them.

Saturday 20 August
Talked to Scofield. He said he still couldn't make up his mind about *Othello*. I popped *The Cherry Orchard* in front of him but got no response. I mentioned Peter Brook's idea that he do a joint National/RSC *Antony and Cleopatra*. Paul said Antony was a part he'd been avoiding all his life; he gave no indication of whether he intended to go on avoiding it.

Read until late, ferreting through a book on Restoration actresses, trying to get a feel of what the theatre was like then. It was a surprise to learn that Restoration playhouses were smaller than the Cottesloe and, as they played mainly in winter, extremely chilly. The audience sat dressed in all their finery, and their warmest clothes: cloaks, surcoats, gloves. Actresses always displayed their shoulders and a good deal of their breasts, and consequently were freezing cold. Important ones, such as Mrs Bracegirdle, had solo dressing rooms, and the ultimate luxury was to have a fireplace with a seacoal fire. They would then rush from the stage, get warm by the fire, and wrap up their rosy shoulders.

One of the main attractions of the Restoration theatre was of course the display of the actress as a new phenomenon. About 90 of the 350 Restoration plays contain women disguised as boys, many of whom at some point reveal that their masculinity is false by stripping open their jerkins, or having a man feel their bosoms.

Restoration theatre gives me the overwhelming impression of a sex-orientated, fashionable club: the Playboy Club of the day.

Wednesday 24 August
Simon Relph was speaking today of the elite education we'd all had. He'd been sent to a good school and arrived almost automatically at Cambridge without realising how lucky he was. So, he seemed to imply, had I. I was furious. I suppose it's inevitable now that people think I was born with a silver spoon in my mouth.

Thursday 25 August
Most of the afternoon with Harold Pinter. He was very expansive and happy and during the conversation I discovered why. To quote him, 'Something is afoot.' He means that a play is on the way. He wasn't specific, but he's writing again; being in no man's land is over. He's moved into Antonia's house and he has a little study there where he feels at peace. His books are up, and he can work. Hard graft is required he says, but I can expect a play.

Saturday 27 August

I think we're going to have a bad autumn at the theatre. I can't imagine the Arts Council will bail us out of our vast deficit without trouble. And although Peter Stevens is confident our offer in our new NATTKE agreement has been well understood and virtually accepted, my spies tell me otherwise. I am quite sure Kon Fredericks will want to join those defying the government's pay policy. And I think he fancies the front page.

It's interesting that the main body of workers at Leyland have today revolted against their shop stewards' call for a strike. Is this an encouraging sign of the times? I believe in the final good sense of the British people, but by Christ they have to be in trouble before they wake up. I feel the country isn't yet in trouble enough.

Wednesday 31 August

Our NATTKE offer this morning was refused, but it was agreed that if there was a £7.00 a week increase all round, which amounts to a rise of just over 10%, Kon would be prepared to recommend it[1]. So he's still Czar-ing it: Wilson has done nothing to discipline him or regulate his behaviour.

Thursday 1 September

Lunch with Tony Field to exchange some thoughts before a key Arts Council meeting next week. He said it was perfectly clear we were underfunded because of the enormous running costs of the building alone, before we've even staged the plays; and perfectly clear we were a success. He also saw why Max and I continued to affirm as our case for extra funding the special nature of the National Theatre. But he does not think that helps our cause much. Except for the amounts involved, our situation is no different to Sheffield or Birmingham or Nottingham—all new theatres where the huge costs of running the buildings had not been taken into account. He urged therefore that we should lobby for more money for the Arts Council as a whole, rather than for the National Theatre. I see the point, but doubt the wisdom. It helps him, but I'm not sure it would help us.

Tuesday 6 September

Worked at home. Then visited Arnold Goodman. We spoke of the National Theatre's money problems. His view is that the cost of the building, as distinct from the cost of its productions, will somehow have to be taken care of by direct government funding, otherwise our Arts Council grant will always look unbalanced in relation to others.

---

[1] The NT's new NATTKE agreement, for September 1977 to August 1978, backed by the union, was accepted two weeks later. It allowed for an increase of 10.14% overall.

Wednesday 7 September
Victor Mishcon, Ronald Leach, Peter Stevens, Rayne and myself to the Arts Council. Present there: the new chairman, Kenneth Robinson[1], Tony Field and Roy Shaw.

A good two hour meeting. They suggest that of our deficit, the greater proportion should be settled now as caused by the delays and deficiencies of the building. They are prepared to go and fight for that—providing we will take on the remainder and try to pay it off over the next two or three years. This was agreed. There was a great deal of talk about getting the building and its maintenance away from us and made directly the responsibility of government. It was fairly inconclusive. I think this problem will go on being passed from government department to government department for the next few years.

Leach was concerned that because we are not an on-going concern in our present financial state our auditors cannot give an unqualified pass to our accounts.

It was interesting that there was no talk of economies, or extravagance. There was comment about our great success, and that we could hardly be expected to earn more money ourselves.

Sunday 11 September
Wallingford: Terry Hands arrived on his way back to Stratford from Paris. He said he had to pause about my proposition as Trevor had now offered him joint direction of the RSC. I said he had given his word to me. He admitted this and asked for another week to think. I could do nothing. It's obvious he's going to stay with Trevor. So the whole of next year's plans are in disarray and I have to start again.

Wednesday 14 September
A production meeting on *The Country Wife*. I am now very pleased with the sets: elegant, gracious, and *real*.

Dress rehearsal of *Happy Days*, which is back, briefly, in the Lyttelton before going to Canada. It's amazing how the arrival of John Neville as Willie has changed Peggy's performance. He's very powerful and it's made Winnie more vulnerable, more dependent on her hateful husband. Yet he only says 42 words from a hole under the stage. What an extraordinary thing communication in the theatre is.

Dreadful associates' meeting. I was deeply depressed because I was reporting to my colleagues the utter failure—for I'm sure Terry won't come—of my two-company scheme in the Olivier, which I have been working on for five months.

[1] Succeeding Lord Gibson.

Peter Hall's Diaries

Monday 19 September
Late tonight Terry Hands came to see me. An unpleasant conversation. He tells me he is staying with the RSC and will become joint director of the company with Trevor immediately.

I tried not to get emotional.

Friday 23 September
Started *The Country Wife* at last: it's so good to be back in rehearsal again. I looked in at the dress rehearsal of a revival of *The Passion* and saw Albert wandering about in mayoral robes trying to learn his lines[1]. He said he didn't really think he could bring credibility to the role of a blind man if on stage he had to read his script. . . .

A chat with Scofield in his dressing room before *Volpone*. I discussed with him, and independently with Ben Kingsley, how the play is now working. They have, rightly, got much more ruthless. I think the sadistic thug in *Volpone*, the utterly selfish fascist, must in the end come out. We never in rehearsal got the scenes right that should show the cruel streak. They weren't cruel enough. At last both Paul and Ben have the predators' pleasure in total destruction: a mounting excitement as they fall upon the carcass. Paul said it worked absolutely in performance, though Michael Medwin[2] was a little startled that he had got so horrid to him and was wondering whether it was personal. . . .

Saturday 24 September
A very painful lunch and afternoon with Trevor. We went through the whole Terry Hands story. He says Terry didn't tell him he was totally committed to me until this last Tuesday. I feel completely betrayed by old friends. I suppose what hurt me most was that Trevor suggested nothing to help. He might have said that Terry could still do a production for us. But he didn't. I found the whole situation unutterably depressing. It's the end for me of nearly twenty years of trusting and loving association with the RSC, and I can see very little which is good in the future.

Monday 26 September
Off to the Warehouse for Trevor's *Macbeth* production. It is magnificent: refreshing, invigorating, utterly clear and original; also the only *Macbeth* I've seen which works. And my admiration for the subtlety of the acting[3] is unbounded. But by doing Shakespeare in a tiny room you do actually sidestep the main problem we moderns have with Shakespeare—rhetoric. We don't like rhetoric, we mistrust it: our actors can't create it, and our

---

[1] He played Annas.   [2] Who played Corvino.
[3] Ian McKellen and Judi Dench as the Macbeths.

314

audiences don't respond to it. So how on earth do you do a great deal of Shakespeare? It's the problem that will often confront us at the Olivier and at the Barbican. The subtlety I saw in this *Macbeth* would have delighted the eyes of Leavis, but it was only possible because of the scale. In a large theatre something different would have happened—not intellect, but passion; not irony but emotion. I am sure that historically the tendency in the seventies for the classical companies to work in tiny spaces will be seen as a cop-out. For all that, it was an evening which made me proud of my profession again, and full of admiration for Trevor. He is now a master. He has done the play three times before, and it has obsessed him for five years. This time he's really made it. He is now one of the four or five directors whose work I would cross mountains to see.

Tuesday 27 September
Strange news at lunchtime: Kon Fredericks has resigned as our chief steward. Why? The political zealot never gives up. Now he is just a member of the stage staff, without official position, he will have more freedom of movement. Will he use it?

Wednesday 28 September
All day on plans and planning, and spent hours tonight trying to sort out whether or not we should do *Macbeth* in the light of the RSC's current production, and whether or not we should do *The Cherry Orchard* because of Peter Gill directing it soon at Hammersmith. The problem is that both our productions were planned before the RSC decided to bring their *Macbeth* to London, and before Peter Gill decided to do *The Cherry Orchard*. We *have* to plan so far ahead in an organisation this size. What to do? I feel very insecure, and am changing everything. Which is ridiculous.

Thursday 29 September
Huge piece in the *Daily Mirror* saying the National Theatre is a waste of money and apparently only exists to allow me to embody my fantasies of power! Is it all starting again?

Sunday 2 October
Drove Jenny to Cambridge for her first term. The drive was peaceful and I enjoyed going to Cambridge again, particularly on this day of soft autumn sunshine. Many young new faces arriving, either frightened or aloof. Jenny is pleased with the look of Newnham. She was slightly nervous, slightly sad, but very excited. We walked round a bit together, chatting of this and that. She's very sympathetic and a friend. I do hope she'll be happy at Cambridge. I suppose its twentyseven or twentyeight years since I began there. Time is bewildering: it was another world, another society, but still the same place.

Peter Hall's Diaries

Monday 3 October
At lunchtime I heard that Peter Gill's *Cherry Orchard* production is to open in January, just a month before mine. Perhaps one shouldn't worry about that but simply get on with it. But I am in a bad state. I must calm down and get back my confidence. It's not there with rehearsals of *Country Wife*; it's not there publicly; or with the Board; or in my private life. It's all a bit of a balls-up at the moment.

Wednesday 5 October
Peter Wood phoned Sue today giving support to me, and saying I must be careful. He saw the signs all over again of the crack-up I had years ago rehearsing *The Wars of the Roses* at Stratford.

Saturday 8 October
Early morning examination in Harley Street: electro-cardiograms, running about, listening to arteries etc etc. The doctor gave me a bit of a wigging and concluded that my cholesterol is too high, that I put too much stress on myself, am too fat, possibly smoked too much, but that the machine is in good order, at the moment. So that's something.

Sunday 9 October
I used my few hours weekend break at Wallingford to get myself together. I read *The Chaste Maid of Cheapside*[1], *The Shoemaker's Holiday*[2], the Julian Mitchell version of *Henry IV*, *The Rape of the Sabine Women*[3], *The Silver Box* of Galsworthy and also his *Strife*. I wanted to clear my head about the repertoire and also calm myself by absolute disciplined work. It succeeded.

Monday 10 October
The train back to London this morning took one hour, the passengers standing pressed together in the corridor. That comic British thing happened of everyone pretending there was no one else standing right against them.

A boring, 6½ hour Board meeting. Everything quite amiable, but we are now at the crossroads: we must get more money in subsidy or the building is impossible to manage. I suppose we shall know in about three months.

Peter Stevens discovered that Camilla, his secretary, has been dosing not only herself with Valium, but secretly him too, in his coffee, in an attempt to make their working relationship better.... What a resourceful lady.

---

[1] By Thomas Middleton.   [2] By Thomas Dekker.
[3] A nineteenth-century Austrian play by Franz and Paul von Schönthan.

316

Saturday 15 October
Watched a television version of *Fidelio* by the Berlin Opera. Rather
sentimental, and it didn't use the greatest power of television—to soliloquise
straight at the camera. Instead there were fancy shots of singers singing
radiant generalisations to the heavens. Worse, as it was post-synched, they
were miming to their own play-back. This may enable us to have big close-
ups without seeing expensive dental engineering, but the sound and the
passion of singing has to be expressed muscularly. You have to *see* them
sing.

Sunday 16 October
By train to Peterborough with father to see Uncle Cecil[1] who is very ill. I
hadn't allowed for Sunday working, when the railways rebuild their tracks,
so we took a long and complicated route. But happily it kept my father
talking and reminiscing as station after station was passed where he had
served as a relief station master 25 or 30 years ago. I think he enjoyed
himself. But he did not enjoy—how could he?—seeing Uncle Cecil at the
hospital, who cried a bit, but very controlled and heroic. He then went on
joking and being the same old Uncle. It is clear we will not see him alive
again.

Tuesday 18 October
A quite good day on *Country Wife*. Albert[2] energised the rehearsal,
sparking all the time. I had one or two moments of sheer fatigue when my
mind was a complete blank, for I am not yet comfortable in this, to me, new
world of Restoration comedy; I am not moving freely, understanding and
creating. But there are glimmers.
    First night of Feydeau's *The Lady From Maxim's*, in the Lyttelton. I
skulked in the box at the back of the circle and wished it would take off,
which it honestly didn't. I kept running into tight-lipped critics who seemed a
little obsessed by John Osborne's piece knocking them in *The Sunday Times*
last weekend—though it was surely John just having fun? It always amuses
me how those who dish it out can seldom take it.

Wednesday 19 October
Lady From Maxim's notices. John Mortimer gets praise for his translation,
which is deserved, but the actors get patronised, and Chris[3] gets told his
production hasn't quite done it, which as yet is true. But I don't know
anybody else in this country who could have built it better. It will become
very considerable. At the moment though the audience is slightly ahead of it

[1] Brother of Hall's father.   [2] Who played Mr. Horner.   [3] Morahan.

instead of running to catch up. It is extraordinary how an audience as a whole is sharper than any single member of it.

Heavy day's *Country Wife* rehearsal. I only did half what I should have done, but I see more and more how performing in the Olivier must be of a public, outgoing nature. It's not a question of being untrue, but of not burying yourself in your fellow actors' eyes. I think this is important for Restoration texts anyway. Originally, after all, the actors acted on a platform space to an audience of gallants and wits on either side of them as well as in front. And they were playing those same gallants and wits, sometimes the very individuals. There is a sense of representing the audience. It's something to bear in mind for the public style of the play.

Thursday 20 October
In through the back-door early this morning to the Fabergé exhibition at the V and A, kindly arranged by Roy Strong[1]. If I had thought we were to saunter alone among the pieces I was mistaken. There was a full house of other privileged people.

The objects are not art, they are consummate craft: the toys of the royal families of Europe. They don't tell us anything about the flowers and animals they represent. I shan't, because of them, look with a changed vision—which is the measure of real art. But the pieces are exquisite, amusing, and unbelievable, the perfect symbol of a society about to disappear.

Monday 24 October
Bad morning rehearsing. I am not working well. The ideas aren't there. It's heavy. And I am not enjoying it. There's no instinct. Only thought. What on earth to do?

Tuesday 25 October
I am worried about Peter Stevens. The building is at last fully open, but he like many of us is not enjoying the continued pressure. I think he's a pioneer anyway, an instigator, not a fine tuner. I suspect he'd like to go.

Wednesday 26 October
A talk with Edward Bond which I believe I mishandled. I told him we couldn't do his new play *The Woman* in the Olivier until next autumn, but we could do it in the Cottesloe in the spring. He said he would have to consider his position, but the clear implication was he was withdrawing the play. What did I do wrong? Well, I did mention that we had to play to 80% in the Olivier, and as a consequence he gave me a short talk about the wickedness

---

[1] Dr. Roy Strong, Director of the Victoria and Albert Museum from 1974. Knighted 1982.

of the National Theatre having to be commercial. I asked him to tell that to the Board and the Arts Council.

Long conversation with his agent, Peggy Ramsay, when I got home because I was very worried that I had lost him. She says he is in a bad state anyway, and if I had asked her advice she would have told me to leave him for a week or two. He's in the middle of a big row with the RSC over the play they've commissioned and is anti everybody at the moment. It made me feel slightly better.

To the revival of *The Passion* in the Cottesloe, which was a memorable experience again, a wonderful event.

Sunday 30 October
Most of the day spent on *The Country Wife* focusing it, getting my mind clear, and cutting a little. It's damned elusive. I know what the result should be but I just can't get it. It is not my sort of play. I am not engaged.

Monday 31 October
I ran out of steam during this afternoon's *Country Wife* rehearsal, and think the company felt let down. I should never have done this play. It simply doesn't generate the right responses in me. I can't get through the language. . . .

Tuesday 1 November
Worked early, and then climbed into the Moss Bros suit ready for the Palace. The theatre wardrobe has discovered that the correct thing for investitures is black waistcoat and black hat, so that is how I appeared. Much the same drill as thirteen or fourteen years ago when I got the CBE. A grey-haired colonel of the Royal Household briefed us all in amiable military fashion. His eyebrows went up from his nose at about 30 degrees each side and were jet black strips, as if applied with Elastoplast. I was put with some of my fellows in the first waiting room, and my heart sank. I am going to have to talk to complete strangers for the entire morning, I thought. Happily Alexander Gibson[1], an old friend, arrived, and as he's a G and I'm an H we went through the process together, whispering like naughty boys. The Queen Mum officiated. It is remarkable that a lady of 76 or 77 can stand in the same spot for an hour and three quarters and, apparently without being prompted and without a crib, remember a little something significant to say to over a hundred people in the right order. The Guards band played the same music I had heard for the CBE. Selections from *Oklahoma* came up, and Gilbert and Sullivan, appropriately 'When everybody's somebody, then

[1] The conductor; Hall's first opera production, John Gardner's *The Moon and Sixpence* at Sadler's Wells in 1957, was with Gibson.

no one's anybody.' If they'd had some divertimenti by Mozart or Haydn or any of the eighteenth-century occasional musicians, the live muzack we heard would have been bearable. And I think we should have been given a drink. There was a sense of suffering like guardsmen on parade in honour of ceremony.

Wednesday 2 November
A fair day's work on *Country Wife*. I have almost no time left now before it opens and am in a nightmare grip of knowing that it's no good and that I am not the man to be doing it. One of the hardest things about a director's life is that you know when you've made a mistake, yet you have to see it through with a brave face. Lunch with Albert who is bursting with energy and very tactfully told me lots of things that were wrong with the production. He was right, right all the way....

Thursday 3 November
The *Evening News* rang up this morning to announce they had it on good authority from someone high up in the GLC that the National Theatre was half a million pounds in the red on its current account this year, would shortly not be able to sign cheques, and would be closing down unless more money were found. This is fairly near the truth. Perhaps a story now could be helpful because it would dramatise the present deadlock we are in.

Dinner at the Barbican flat with Peter Shaffer and his sister-in-law, the wife of his twin Tony. Peter has a delicate, feminine way of finding out what he wants to know—and also revealing what he's up to. I learnt that he was writing a new play, that we would get it, and that he wanted John Dexter to direct it but wasn't sure Dexter would come near the National.

Friday 4 November
Peter Wood came to *The Country Wife* run-through, and was helpful and encouraging in a guarded way. He would direct the play entirely differently to me, probably much better, and he didn't therefore talk about it as I was doing it but as he would. It was invaluable though, the gesture of a friend.

In the middle of the run-through Sue came in with the *Evening News*. Front page, entire[1]. As a result the whole Fleet-Street pack are baying. Stephen Fay has to be seen tonight. The *Mail* is doing a story tomorrow. Max

[1] The NT was 'thought to have lost nearly £500,000' since April. This was the core of the story, as expected. And it reported Hall as commenting that the building alone cost £1 million a year to run before anything was put on the stages. Angus Stirling, Deputy General Secretary of the Arts Council, was quoted as saying the NT was 'remarkably successful' despite 'intractable' financial problems, and that the Arts Council and GLC were in 'continuous discussion' with the theatre over resolving the difficulties.

Rayne is wondering whether there should be an emergency meeting of the Board.

I am glad the boil is burst, though I am getting bloody fed-up with being written about rather as if it is my fault that there were delays in completing the NT which led to loss of revenue; that men have to be paid vast overtime to do the work of stage machinery which isn't yet functioning properly; and that the building itself costs far more to run than any other theatre. . . .

I have no idea if we shall weather this storm or not, but it had to come.

Monday 7 November
The media storm continues to rage. An article by me in the *Daily Mail* looked well, and I think quite entertainingly answered an attack on Saturday in the *Mail* by its drama critic, Jack Tinker, who thinks we work extravagantly. There was a helpful piece in *The Guardian* by Nicholas de Jongh, and a sympathetic leader in the *Evening News*, saying 'the only answer is more money—much more—from the government'.

Wednesday 9 November
Extraordinarily jumpy and nervous South Bank Board meeting. Now the shit is hitting the fan, everybody is much more concerned about the minutes, the record, who is responsible, and who said what to whom.

Walter Ulrich[1] had a fairly strong disputation with Tony Field who said the Arts Council had provided all the information about the delay costs to the DES. But Ulrich was not satisfied. So Mishcon, full of urbanity and with sharp teeth, bit most graciously into him. Max Rayne was emotional. Do people not want a National Theatre? Why are we all suffering? All this rumbled on until I left for the dress rehearsal of *The Country Wife*.

Monday 14 November
A bad day's rehearsal. I was tetchy, tired, and anxious—anxious, truthfully, more about the future of the National than about *The Country Wife*, though I was also feeling that I had only a few hours of work left on the production to make a miracle. But effort never makes miracles. *The Country Wife*, as I have done it, is ordinary, unfocused and boring. I am ashamed of it. I have brought to the play all the inspiration I would bring to a routine game of draughts.

Tuesday 15 November
Peter Stevens reported to me today an unbelievable meeting yesterday at the DES. Ulrich, in the chair, declared it had been our decision to open the building before it was finished and they had never asked us to. Stevens

---

[1] Deputy Secretary of the Department of Education and Science from 1977.

vigorously contested this. He said the spirit was always one of collaboration. He also pointed out that throughout all our deliberations, an assessor from the DES had been present. But I foresee ugly times ahead. If anybody did this in commercial life no one would ever do business with them again. It's truly outrageous.

Wednesday 16 November

Sad news early evening. Uncle Cecil died this afternoon. I talked to father who sounded very frail and mortal. Poor man; his youngest brother goes before him.

The fireman's strike is growing uglier. The dons are demonstrating in Westminster. And I think we are about to close. No, that is nonsense. Goodman said this morning, just go on as properly as you can and if you absolutely have to, run up the deficit. He is right. Posterity would not thank us for closing the National Theatre so soon after it was opened.

Thursday 17 November

Morning with Bernard Kimble. I was more than a little depressed to find that after nearly twenty-five years of success as a director I was contemplating a life with no security, no savings, and no assets. Still, I have chosen the way I live, and I have never been sufficiently interested in my own finances. I would sooner work. And I spend money in order to work.

Monday 21 November

An interesting dinner with Kenneth Robinson. He asked me in so many words to be patient, to hang on. I replied my strategy was very much to do that. He said there was a terrible war going on between the Arts Council and the DES about which of them was obliged to rescue us in our current financial plight, and we were in the middle. He also said the politicians were nervous about us on a number of counts: budgetary control; should an artist run a big enterprise—wouldn't a top Civil Servant be better?; labour relations—we'd had so much publicity about the strikes; and dirty plays. This last was becoming, he said, a very live issue, particularly with the paedophilia in *Lavender Blue*[1].

I told him that controversial plays cause no trouble if the critics give good notices; once they question artistic merit, the vultures descend. I also mentioned that we were hard at work cutting back next year's budget. He seemed fairly reassured but still worried. Obviously we're a problem child.

---

[1] A new play by John Mackendrick, which had opened at the Cottesloe a week and a half earlier to a poor press.

Tuesday 22 November
My forty-seventh birthday, but a melancholy day: Uncle Cecil's funeral —
pork pies, sandwiches, and booze in Auntie's little house over the store.
Then a terrible service, with an out-of-tune organ, followed by the long ride
through the black, low fens to Peterborough for the cremation and the
discreet drawing of the purple curtains as the canned music fades. It was all
so very like *Akenfield* that I constantly felt embarrassed.

Wednesday 23 November
At Max Rayne's, considering our cuts for next year. The main worry—and
one I was happy to encourage—was that the proposed savings on the plays,
the productions, and the company were nearly £700,000, whereas the
savings on the servicing and the building were only £150,000. I scared
everyone so much with tales of contraction in box office revenue as a result
of the massive cut-back on the plays—which are what, after all, we exist
for—that it was agreed we should increase the plays budget somewhat and
make greater cuts elsewhere. This is sensible, though there will be squeals
and redundancies.

Thursday 24 November
I find it difficult at the moment to believe in my heart of hearts that our
administration is going to survive our present deficit problem. Either the
money will not be provided at all, or it will not be enough and given with such
heavy strictures on its use that our alternatives will be to resign or stay and be
castrated. I think there is a faction that wants the theatre closed so that the
contractors can finish, and there will then be the opportunity to form a new
management and start again.

It would not be easy for us to mobilise public support, for we seem to have
few friends in the media. Truly we are in very deep trouble, and I cannot
think what to do. It seems to me that all these years of effort are about to be
wasted.

Tuesday 29 November
First night of *The Country Wife*. A very good reception, but I fear the worst.

Thursday 1 December
On the whole, horrible notices. They speak of stridency and of nothingness.
Unfortunately I think they are right. I don't even feel resentful, just hurt.
My search for classicism is not working out.

Read *The Cherry Orchard* twice today. Felt nothing, only fear. Confidence has gone I'm afraid, so it's probably better that I get straight back into
rehearsing again.

Friday 2 December

First rehearsal of *The Cherry Orchard*. Susan Littler not there as she has a temperature, but everybody else was[1].

The most wonderful play ever I think. Its economy is extraordinary. I don't feel I yet quite have it in my heart. I am almost in danger of admiring it too much.

Lunch with Ralph. He begged me to find someone who could take some of the weight of running the National off me. He suggested Tony Quayle. It made me think. Quayle was the best theatre runner apart from George Devine I have met in my life. But I'm sure he wouldn't do it. He left Stratford to get away from all that.

Ralph complimented me on my nerve and healthy looks. Little does he know.

Caught an evening train to Cambridge to see Jenny and Christopher. Great warmth, great jubilation. They talked nineteen to the dozen about life, literature, theatre, films; it all came tumbling out of them. I hinted that big changes were coming in my personal life. They looked worried but were very sympathetic.

Saturday 3 December

Cambridge: Slept well in a guest room of St Catharine's. Breakfast in the appalling new hall: a jumble of late fifties clichés, mainly Danish and cheaply done. Jenny showed me round Newnham. I asked her if it was strange being in an all-female college after all those years at Bedales. She said it wasn't because there were plenty of men about and many lived with the girls in their rooms. . . .

Tonight, late, *The Cherry Orchard* clicked. I think Chekhov is a subversive—a cryptic, cynical, abrasive subverter of everything simple and dogmatic. But he's a humourist. He makes fun of the Left, he makes fun of the Right, and he makes fun of love. I am sure his own peculiar relationship with women and his apparent backing off from sex was not because he was undersexed or slightly homosexual; rather it was that sexual passion is a simple, abandoned, in a sense *dogmatic* emotion. And to Chekhov, I swear, it was ridiculous. Again and again in *The Cherry Orchard* every strong, clear, simple emotion is undercut by something ridiculous.

Sunday 4 December

Today's notices for *The Country Wife* are bad, like the dailies. It's a failure. Well, I knew it was.

---

[1] The cast included: Judi Bowker (Anya), Susan Fleetwood (Varya), Helen Ryan (Charlotta), Dorothy Tutin (Ranevskaya), Albert Finney (Lopakhin), Nicky Henson (Yepikhodov), Ben Kingsley (Trofimov), Ralph Richardson (Firs), Terence Rigby (Pishchik), Robert Stephens (Gayev), and Derek Thompson (Yasha).

Monday 5 December
John Bury showed a cardboard model of *The Cherry Orchard* set. I ripped a piece of it away. Ralph then fell on it and tore a section into little bits. Everybody offered their ideas. The stage management looked shocked, and the production department were horrified. Was this the way to work? Was this the way to treat a designer's model? The answer is of course, yes. We all then collaborated about the physical needs of the production and as a result found something which wouldn't otherwise have been seen. By the end of the day I think we had a solution.

Wednesday 7 December
Lunch with Albert. I felt I hadn't been in close enough contact with him during *The Country Wife*, certainly I hadn't helped him. I talked frankly about the pressures on me: that I was trying too hard because everything at the National must be a success. I said I thought he'd done the same: he was playing the leading actor of the company, taking the responsibilities of the whole theatre on his shoulders, and it had affected his voice, his freedom, his whorishness as an actor. So we decided to try to make our next bit of work freer, less puritanical.

Thursday 8 December
South Bank Board meeting: an emergency one called to discuss our application for funds to meet the huge delay costs. There'd obviously been a deal done in advance. Rayne and Mishcon were fighting much less than before; they had clearly been told to cool it and everything would be alright in the long run.

Associates' meeting tonight. Most of our time spent discussing finances and the general strategy. I was much strengthened by the support I received. We felt we should budget on the minimum work we needed to do to justify the building, stick by that, and if we are told to do less, then we still continue to operate at the right level. And if the Board as a consequence feel it necessary to sack us, that's that.

This was our first austerity associates' meeting—no food, no wine. Harold left early as a sign of protest, to have his dinner.

Friday 9 December
A lovely day on *The Cherry Orchard*. I shall never forget Ralph walking through the last bit of Firs; not acting it but commenting on it to himself and to us. 'Now I come through the door in my slippers. Good heavens, there's nobody here. Good Lord, they've all gone. So I go off to the window and look out. Can't see anything. So I go over to the sofa feeling very tired now, sit down, drop my stick, too tired to take it up. So I lie back, want to put my legs up, but can't, I'm too tired. Then I die. . . .'

Peter Hall's Diaries

Saturday 10 December
Eating up Chekhov now at a great rate—the stories and books. This is a complex and elusive man and the laugh is on all the critics who try to possess him. I am also quite sure that his reluctance to fight, to engage, to be simple, is why he was always so fly-away with Stanislavsky and the Moscow Art Theatre people. He didn't want a confrontation. If they got the play wrong, let them. What does the text say? That is all you have to guide you.

Tuesday 13 December
I didn't feel happy at rehearsal today: the same nightmare feeling of loss of confidence, loss of freedom, that I had during *The Country Wife*. Once again I was perplexed. What should I do? It's a question that can't be asked. A director must know the text backwards, and unless his invention is free, unthinking, as inspirational in a way as an actor's, there's no production. Today I was once more pedestrian and wooden. And appalled.

Tuesday 20 December
Went into the Cottesloe late to see the preview of *The Hunchback of Notre Dame*[1] and found Dave Rappaport leading the audience in community singing to the words of 'Bums and Tits, Bums and Tits, Having it Away. . . .' Christ, I thought, here is the National Theatre's family Christmas show. . . .

Wednesday 21 December
My main concern today was *Hunchback*. I am sure it is a fault in me, for Michael Bogdanov's production has vigour and vitality and is a romp. But it is simply not my kind of show. Mind you, the show was voted a great success by the young Halls at breakfast this morning when there was a spirited rendering of 'Bums and Tits'. The theatre is telling all people who bring small children that the show is a bit rude. We tried this tonight. No one objected, they just giggled and went into the auditorium.

Sunday 25 December
I finished *The Honourable Schoolboy*, John Le Carré's new book, early this morning. I've enjoyed it very much. I like his tone—humorous, deflationary, and yet capable of a baroque use of words and images. It sometimes leads him to excess, but then his whole idea of life as a series of conspiracies is an excess in itself.

Subdued Christmas, though the children a joy and excited. The usual rituals, over-eating and over-drinking. I felt very peculiar all day because this may be my last Christmas at Wallingford and a saying goodbye. Things are now finally breaking up. Why have I loved Wallingford so much? I suppose, in my vanity, it has been important to me because it proved to me

[1] A play by Ken Hill from Victor Hugo's novel, directed by Michael Bogdanov.

that I have arrived. It is a beautiful house, with the possessions I like, and country space. Every weekend, whatever else, I have been reassured by the emblem of Wallingford. I suspect it will be very good for me to live without it.

Wednesday 28 December
Rehearsed *The Cherry Orchard* Act 1 all day. Sue Fleetwood is actually making Varya funny. It's clearly what Chekhov wanted. The characters are all funny. They are totally egocentric, living their own fantasies. They avoid emotion by changing the subject. They hear what others' problems are, but don't listen; that would be dangerous. They therefore emerge as quite ruthless with each other. It is very Russian, unsentimental, and un-English.

Saturday 31 December
To a New Year's Eve party at Covent Garden. The first performance of *Die Fledermaus*, which was televised to millions all over the world. I was irritated at so much talent, time and money being spent on such a boring piece. Lord Donaldson assured me that the National was going to be alright in 1978, that somehow they would see us through. But what does he mean? And where is the money?

1978

Monday 3 January
The Cherry Orchard on stage today. Fairly worrying. I don't think it's in the right theatre. Chekhov I feel is too tender, too delicate, for the Olivier. I hope to Christ I am wrong.

Thursday 5 January
I think I understand the 'absurd' aspect of Chekhov in a way I have not seen analysed. His characters are so self-absorbed they are almost indifferent to other people's troubles. They blame others for being sad; they very rarely sympathise with them. From this total absorption in self comes Chekhov's comedy, for it means that every character says something surprising. It's a quite harsh atmosphere but loaded with emotion.

Saturday 7 January
To Hammersmith to see a preview of *The Cherry Orchard*. I admired it. It has clarity, simplicity and elegance, is more Scandinavian than Russian, and is staged by Peter Gill with great precision and grace. I think it will be a huge success—and ruin ours. Because this is Chekhov the way the English like it, not particularly funny and not very passionate. The deflationary comedy that our rehearsals have revealed in nearly every line is not there at all. But it is intensely moving.

Monday 9 January
Goodbye to the Barbican penthouse today. No regrets, but lots of comic memories, and a few tender ones. We shall feel the difference, as my mother always says.

The actors in our *Cherry Orchard* are fascinated I was at Hammersmith on Saturday. I keep saying it is brilliant, but very wrong in my view, and not funny. Our cast are obsessively jumpy about it though. I don't *think* I'm showing that I am too. The fact is that it's David and Goliath. And we know who's Goliath.

Back tonight to the new flat, also in the Barbican. Chaos. Too much furniture, too big furniture. It's a very small flat.

Wednesday 11 January
Dinner with Peggy and Trevor: very pleasant and relaxing. Trevor said he's

signed on with the RSC for another seven years, with a sabbatical next year and up to four months away every year if he wants it. Lucky bugger. I felt my heart breaking. He has arranged his life well and I have arranged mine badly. He says that if the Barbican crucifies the RSC, as the South Bank is crucifying us, he wants to be able to get out. Wise man. Theatre is about people not buildings. Buildings are fine, they give you opportunity, a foundation, but they are the second priority, not the first. At the moment our building demands everything.

Peggy goes to India to make a film in a week or two: seventy years old and making her first visit to India. Acting keeps you young.

Friday 13 January

The notices for Peter Gill's Hammersmith *Cherry Orchard* are pretty good. We are indeed on a bad wicket with ours, because the gentle pathos of his production is hailed as what Chekhov is about.

Looked in at the Cottesloe to see how *The Hunchback of Notre Dame* was going. Riotous audience; riotous success. Apparently last night a woman objected to the 'Bums and Tits' song on the grounds that it was male chauvinism. She sang instead 'Bums and Pricks', and they all joined in. Thank God Victor Mishcon wasn't there.

Tuesday 17 January

Various meetings and home relatively early. In bed by 11 pm, but dragged out of it by the phone down the other end of the flat: Harold Pinter in fine order—but then he's a night bird and not, like me, an early-morning one. He said he'd thought about cutting the bad language in *No Man's Land* in the coming television production but was resolved to stick out. He wasn't cutting anything. He also said I would receive the second draft of his new play for my private eyes next week.

Thursday 19 January

Off to Granada's rehearsal rooms to start making the television of *No Man's Land*. John Gielgud asked, 'Any cuts?' 'Not as far as I know,' I said. Derek Grainger[1] then told us how Granada had decided to fight this one. They had an excellent record of standing up to the IBA, and even if it took a long time they were going to see this masterpiece done unchanged. At which point Ralph muttered, 'What about the American sales? Is it worth losing all that lovely money for the sake of saying "fuck"?'

The actors remembered the play remarkably well. There was a little bit of 'Weren't you sitting then, Johnny?' 'No, I think *you* were sitting, Ralph.' But generally it was very good. John said how wonderful it was to have a free

---

[1] The television producer.

afternoon in London. He isn't really enjoying the country, I think: he's a town rat, as Ralph has always observed.

The whole morning had a sort of party atmosphere, very like when *The Homecoming* was filmed at Shepperton. It's the pleasure generated by re-meeting a great text—and happy memories. I keep wondering about Harold's new play which hasn't arrived yet.

Hard afternoon on *The Cherry Orchard*. Ranevskaya seems to me more and more the greatest portrayal in classic drama of quintessential woman. She's so emotional, so instinctive, so changeable—so everything. Each character in the play lives by his or her dogmas, or tries to, whether it be Lophakin with his love of development, or Trofimov with his love of abstract progress, or Pishchik with his hope that something will turn up. But all their systems are ruined by the heavy dose of humanity which Ranesvskaya supplies. I think that is Chekhov's main obsession—that people are unpredictable and deny systems, dogmas, religions.

Saturday 21 January
Watched *The Last Picture Show*, Peter Bogdanovitch's movie, on television. Nostalgia for the fifties, and a bloody fine film. A small Texas town, where everybody knows who's having everybody else. Petting in the front of the car, sweaters off and breasts a-swinging, but nothing to be touched lower down because of the danger. The pre-pill age. Suspenders and stocking tops. The end of the cinema in the small town—and the end of an era. The Korean war, ducktail haircuts, and an older, sweeter kind of popular music. Each generation making the same mistakes, going through the same agonies. It's very sad. And I enjoyed it enormously.

Sunday 22 January
Today, Bernard Levin in *The Sunday Times* gives the Hammersmith *Cherry Orchard* the greatest notice you've ever read. But more to the point, he says the National Theatre is doing the play next month and they'll be bloody lucky if they are anything like as good. Christ!

Much trouble with the old folk at home. Auntie says she has only death to look forward to and she's such a burden to us all; Mother says she can't sleep for worry and what is to become of us; and with my marriage break-up looming over me I feel like I can't describe. . . .

Monday 23 January
Not a very good day on *Cherry Orchard*. How can I get my courage back? I admire this play more than any other I have directed. I think I feel it, I think I know it, God knows I was prepared. Yet when I am in rehearsal I lack freedom. If I am honest I haven't felt real creative freedom now for over two years. Is it that I'm trying too hard, or has my creative talent gone, leaving

me with nothing but a technique which I apply meticulously and aridly? I suppose everybody has bad patches, but the empty sheet of paper or the empty canvas seem a more enviable situation than a group of expectant actors looking unavailingly to me.

Wednesday 25 January
Last night of *Volpone*. Packed house, cheering. It's been a good run. Paul promised to keep in touch. I said I hoped he found what he wanted while he's away from us, and he said if only he knew what he wanted. I said I knew he'd find it whatever it was.

Friday 27 January
Home bearing a great pile of scripts for the weekend. Chief of them is Harold Pinter's new play. It is called *Betrayal*. . . .

Saturday 28 January
Read *Betrayal* early this morning. It is a bleak and disturbing piece about infidelities. There are plenty of laughs, and impeccable style, but my God the prospect is chilling.

Harold has been obsessed with time ever since he wrote *Landscape*; and working on Proust[1] confirmed that in him. *Betrayal* begins at the end, with a crisis-ridden heartbreaking scene, and ends seven years earlier, at the beginning of the affair. It weaves a very cunning web, and the metaphorical structure is extraordinary.

Sunday 29 January
Wrote a letter of resignation to Max Rayne, tore it up, moped and moodied and generally wondered what the hell I was doing. I can't resign now because it will be defeat. But I want to. And I certainly don't want to do *Macbeth*. Is it cowardice? Or is it the reality of George Devine's speech to me all those years ago—'When you feel the walls coming in on you, get out.' I got out of Stratford and I suppose have regretted it ever since somewhere deep inside me. The trouble is I feel a failure at the moment and that will make me one. You make your own luck in this profession.

Wednesday 1 February
Had a long talk with Ben Kingsley late tonight about the nature of Trofimov, who he's playing. Chekhov couldn't create the person he wanted—the revolutionary chucked out of universities—because of the censorship. But the original audience must have known the secret life of Trofimov: there is a still ferocity about his keenest beliefs. There is also in the character a ridiculous rhetoric, which is Chekhov making fun of the serious man, as he always does.

[1] Writing the screenplay of *A la Recherche du temps perdu*.

Thursday 2 February
Cherry Orchard all day. I gave six hours of notes without stopping, so by the time we came to the first preview tonight—not a bad one—my head was spinning. I don't mean I kept the company for six hours, but I was searching people out for that length of time, and talking to them with the intensity that all personal encounters between the director and the actors need at this stage. You get absolutely sucked dry.

Monday 6 February
Came to work this morning to find coloured graffiti daubed all over the front windows of the theatre. Not anti-us, just anti-Vanessa Redgrave, film producers, show business.

Another long day on *Cherry Orchard*. Saw John Russell Brown at lunchtime, and he worried me by not understanding what the production was getting at. He obviously saw it as old fashioned Chekhov, shy of emotion, whereas I am trying to do something I haven't seen done before: preserve the independence of the characters from each other, reveal their egotistical objectives, and allow the comedy to develop from their selfishness, from the fact that they don't change tone because of what's just been said or felt by somebody else. I *know* this approach is right. It is the comedy of the short stories. And at every point it rings true to the text of the play. I shall just have to make it clearer.

Yvonne Mitchell too found this production not as she imagined Chekhov. I suppose people do own masterpieces in their own minds, appropriate them in some way, and therefore get disturbed when their preconceptions aren't satisfied.

Some letters in from the preview audiences. Several people have been worried by the present-day connotations of 'Silly billy,' spoken by Firs, because Mike Yarwood says this each Saturday night as part of his television impersonation of Denis Healey. But I think Michael Frayn's translation of the play gives here a good English equivalent of Chekhov's phrase.

Tuesday 7 February
The Minister, Lord Donaldson, to lunch. . . . He has all the charm of the Old Etonian, but the politicians' habit of never looking you straight in the eye, and changing quickly from one subject to another. The clichés designed to draw you out abound. 'Tell me if I am wrong. . . .', 'It seems to me, and of course I am no expert on this matter. . . .'. Our meeting established some of the old rapport that was between us in Covent Garden days[1]. His message to me was hang on; help with money is coming, but not this year and probably not next. So it seems we must learn to live with our deficit, at least for the time being.

[1] Donaldson was on the Board of Directors of the Royal Opera House when Hall was Co-Director there.

Wednesday 8 February

Met a lady from Warsaw who has been playing Madame Ranevskaya for two years. She, through an interpreter, informed us that the Poles all wept about the cherry orchard being sold, and applauded references to freedom. She was obviously in shock from our production, theirs being, from all she said, much more sentimental. The Slavs own Chekhov as we own Shakespeare. It must have staggered her to see us at work.

Thursday 9 February

That tree cutting in *Cherry Orchard* is the most difficult sound in drama — particularly if you want it as it would be heard *inside* the house. At last night's preview we had people chopping logs at the back of the stalls, hidden behind the raised sections of the auditorium. It just disturbed the audience. Crazy.

Saturday 11 February

I read with pleasure David Holbrook's just published novel called *A Play of Passion*. It's about a grammar school boy growing up in Norwich in the early part of the war and, most remarkably, it has an unfictionalised account of Nugent Monck and the Maddermarket Theatre which he ran. I remember going there, I suspect it was in 1951 just after Christmas in my second year at Cambridge. I wrote to him and asked if I could come and watch, sweep the stage, do anything. So I was asked to this wonderful Elizabethan house, full of shiny old furniture, and stayed the night. Monck I remember as a hideous little man who giggled a great deal. There was no play on. What stays with me most is a feeling of stepping back into the past. This was the kind of amateur, high-minded theatre that really belonged to William Poel. And it was all part of the freemasonry of the love that dared not speak its name.

Tuesday 14 February

First night of *The Cherry Orchard*. The cast seemed in high spirits but very nervous. I tried to say something of what their support had meant to me, and nearly, I regret to say, burst into tears. I think Albert and Dorothy noticed and they stayed behind to talk to me and say thank-you.

The atmosphere in the auditorium during the first act was as cold as could be. In the air was not—How is this *Cherry Orchard*? It was—Here is the latest disaster from the National Theatre because they can't possibly live up to the Riverside production. I am not dreaming this; it is not my paranoia; I have never known a more hostile house. It says much for the cast that by the second act they had gripped the audience and by the end had scored a bit of a triumph. My gratitude and admiration for them is boundless.

Wednesday 15 February
The notices actually are quite good and reflect that one has made the play funnier than normal and less 'moving'. Something has clearly happened, but the critics are not quite sure what.

Dinner with Albert. He just wouldn't give up *Macbeth*, which I desperately don't want to direct. 'Why worry,' he says, 'it's only a play? Let's continue our adventures. We have a fine company, a fine theatre, you know *Macbeth*, I know it, why be so intense about it?' Difficult to argue with, especially when we need it to add weight to the repertoire. And he did a lot to put my confidence back. It was worth staying up until 3.30 am. . . .

The real reason for doing *Macbeth* is, I'm afraid, this: Albert has stuck by me through thick and thin. If he wants me to direct the play, I must stick by him.

Friday 17 February
Emergency meeting of the heads of the backstage departments. They feel they are not consulted in time, and that they are asked to do impossible things which they nevertheless, somehow or other, get done. I promised them earlier consultation, more information, and if they said no we would take it as no and not expect them to work miracles. One of our carpenters said that nobody likes to say no to me. If it was the guv'nor's production he was given what he wanted. I said I must be said no to.

Sunday 19 February
Though Frank Marcus in the *Sunday Telegraph* thinks the production of *Cherry Orchard* is a triumph, there are ghastly notices from Levin and Cushman. I know the work is good, not my best, but good. Leave it at that, I say to myself, and don't worry: the production will live on.

Met Ralph, Mu and John at Euston and boarded the train for Manchester, where this week we shoot *No Man's Land* for Granada television. John was drawn, white and pensive; the 'flu has not left him. Ralph talked in high spirits and we shared a bottle of champagne. His jokes were constantly interrupted by a small boy travelling on his own who kept calling on us. He said his name was Moby. He was five years old and bored stiff. Ralph was able to do his W C Fields act, saying loudly 'I hate children' after Moby's third or fourth visit. He also discoursed on children in general, and said he could never play with his. He thought somehow it would demean them as much as himself to play bears with them; one had to be oneself.

He was in excellent form, but disappointed in his notices for Firs—particularly Levin's: very morose about it. Even the old hands get hurt by critics. Come to think of it, I suppose I'm an old hand myself now.

Friday 24 February
Manchester: Going past the Opera House today down to the television
studios I looked at the small car shops which still line the street. I suddenly
remembered 22 years ago being there on tour with *Summer Time*, a Ugo
Betti comedy I had directed, with Dirk Bogarde, Geraldine McEwan, Gwen
Ffrangçon-Davies, and Ronnie Barker in a small part. It was my first big
commercial production. It was packed on its pre-London tour, and in my
terms I was making a lot of money from my small percentage. So I went into
one of the shops and bought a bright blue Ford Prefect. My first new car.

Monday 27 February
To the Arts Council. I have lost count of the number of crisis meetings I have
attended there in the last 16 or 17 years on behalf of the RSC or the National.
As these things go, this one was quite cordial, though they said, of course,
that there was no more money. But the main object of our chat was an Arts
Council enquiry into our financial needs. Everybody is keen to have one. I
certainly want one in order to nail the myths and prejudices. Kenneth
Robinson said the problem for the National Theatre is that we are politically
very unpopular in many parts of government. He indicated to me privately
afterwards that a lot of this opprobrium is actually attached to me; not that
anybody knows me; it's just that I've been so much painted as The Tyrant
of the South Bank, throwing money around with happy abandon. Don't I
know it.

Tuesday 28 February
The subject of the supposed red-hot revelations in the coming John Elsom
National Theatre book is hotting up: the Watergate of the Theatre.... The
South Bank Show want me to go on television with Elsom and have a
confrontation. I don't think I should. I just don't know how aggressive to be
in that situation.
   Roy Shaw and Richard Hoggart to lunch. We talked about the political
situation I was in and how the Arts Council enquiry was going to be helpful.
Hoggart said anything that was wrong with the National Theatre in its
financial or political position (never mind the art) was associated with me. I
was a convenient sacrificial victim, and as a consequence I now had a bad
image. He said if he was in my position he would spend the three years my
contract still has to run to talk, write articles, go on television, and generally
throw my weight about. I know that's my nature, and I suppose it's right, but
to do so is a full time job, and I am pretty sick of it all.

Wednesday 1 March
Requests asking me to talk about the coming Elsom book on various
television and radio programmes are piling up. My attitude is that if the

programme wouldn't happen without me, I say no. If it's happening anyway, I say yes and shoot my mouth off. Anyway, I have decided to go into the attack. I rang Harold Evans[1] to say I would like to do a piece about the first two years of the National on the South Bank, for publication on Sunday week. He agreed.

Sunday 5 March
Beautiful spring day; crocuses out; a promise of daffodils. I stayed in bed most of the day. There was no hope of doing the *Sunday Times* article. I tried, but it didn't work.

Peter Brook rang late tonight. He loved *The Cherry Orchard*—and what is more important to me, saw how it is different to other productions. He spoke about how the absolute selfishness of each character produces the comedy. I was very pleased.

Thursday 9 March
Full company meeting. I talked about what we had achieved in our first two years on the South Bank and thanked them, and went on to outline the future. Then Albert rose and quite emotionally made a statement of solidarity and support for me. He said he felt I was very alone and very vulnerable, and he was at the National Theatre because he believed in it but most of all because he believed in me. This got a lot of applause and I felt much better. . . .

Friday, Saturday, Sunday, 10, 11, 12 March
In Wallingford for three days. Very tired. I thought a little about *Macbeth*, but not very productively, walked round *Così fan tutte*, and on Sunday actually did some real work on it. Most of the time I was drafting the *Sunday Times* article: 3,000 words. I am describing the National Theatre as having an Opposition, which is as inevitable as Opposition in government. It's a true point and one the public understand. But the article was very difficult to do and took me many hours because I was picking my way through a minefield. By the end of Sunday the first draft was nearly alright.

It's spring. I was able to sit outside and work in the sun.

Monday 13 March
Good associates' meeting tonight. Plans were discussed to give talks to school parties before their visit to a play rather than after. But that's really the job of the teachers. One fifteen-year-old coming to *Madras House* asked his teacher whether it was in colour.

---

[1] Editor of *The Sunday Times* 1967–82.

Peter Hall's Diaries

Tuesday 14 March
Managed to finish, polish and deliver the *Sunday Times* article. Then to Cambridge to stay at St Catharine's till Friday, seeing Jenny and Christopher. I arrived in my senior guest room late and went straight to bed. I want to try to clear my head here.

Wednesday 15 March
Cambridge: Lovely day, thousands of crocuses out, white in the spring sun. Christopher took me round the audio-visual lab where I was told he was the only one who knew how to use the equipment, and would make a director: fatherly pride. We walked round the Backs and through Trinity Library, one of the most beautiful buildings in the world.

It is a good moment to be in a place full of associations—and God knows Cambridge is full of associations for me: school and university. Here I feel the past in perspective. I am worried about many things; professionally and personally I continue to be a mess. But here I am able to let it all rest.

To Trinity Hall tonight with Christopher to see Jenny in *The Tempest*. I was pleased. She was true and well-spoken, though she still looks physically a little embarrassed on the stage. A lady who said she was at Perse School when I was, and that we'd known each other then, was at the performance. 'I still see Emma,' she told me. I felt as if I was moving into *No Man's Land*. I nearly said 'Emma who?' but thought I hadn't better. It dawned on me later that she was speaking of the girl I first loved, a little blonde. We were both nine or ten.

The students of Corpus have gone on strike because the governing body have refused permission for them to have their girlfriends stay overnight. I asked Jenny and Christopher if it is allowed in other colleges. Apparently it is, though at Newnham, where Jenny is, they ask that boyfriends stay only three nights in a week. Jenny says that on a door in her corridor there is a label saying 'Tamara and Tim'. Tim is at Pembroke but lives at Newnham. In my time, even tea at Girton was a big erotic treat. One of the porters at St Catharine's who was there when I was said to me that my generation were much happier with restrictions. I said we weren't. Well, we weren't.

Thursday 16 March
Cambridge: A couple of hours with John Andrews[1] in his rooms, while startled undergraduates came in and out for their exeats. Seductive scene. We were in an elegant setting looking out on a beautiful quadrangle sipping white wine and chatting of Shakespeare, Chekhov, Robert Gittings's new books on Hardy, etc. I had to remind myself that this Arcadian peace was

[1] Senior Tutor of St. Catharine's 1977–80, and an old friend of Hall's.

340

not the reality. A don's life is as busy and as bitchy as anybody else's I am sure.

John asked me how much longer I could continue to take the punishment I was getting at the National, both physically and mentally. I said not much longer; it wasn't worth it; most of all, now, I felt I wanted to teach, to pass something on. I suppose this feeling, probably false, afflicts everybody who possesses a craft, as they get older—Michel Saint-Denis, Peter Brook, and others have all expressed it at some time.

Spent twenty minutes in the Fitzwilliam Museum before it closed. Most of the pictures are in exactly the same places as they were over thirty years ago when I was a boy at school. I loved this museum then and I do now. I looked at William Nicholson's rather sentimental painting of the girl with the black cloche hat, huge eyes, and a knuckle showing through her torn glove, and burst into tears. I am in an extraordinarily emotional state. I keep losing control.

I went to call on Dadie Rylands[1], up that grand eighteenth-century staircase at King's, just to see if he was there. He wasn't. The green baize door was tightly locked. I remember going there for sherry with him 25 years ago. I had written him a postcard asking if I could talk to him about going into the theatre. Could he help? He replied with a postcard: 'My advice to those thinking of going into the theatre is the same as that of Mr Punch to those who are contemplating matrimony: don't. But come and see me all the same.' His kindly discouragement made me even more determined, and he got me a job ultimately as an assistant stage manager with Tennent's, but I refused it; by then I was directing at Windsor rep. I don't think he ever quite forgave me.

Back to my rooms. Jenny called, and we chatted about Leavis and why one should study literature at all. Two terms at Cambridge have made an enormous difference to her. She speaks confidently and with a full mind. She was off to a party tonight. I sat talking to Christopher until well after midnight.

I have to admit I would like to return here. But I haven't a good enough degree. That's where my reassurances to Christopher break down. 'Never mind,' I say to him, 'Just do well enough to stay here the full time.' But I didn't do well enough to come back. I was too busy directing plays.

Friday 17 March
The Sunday Times are not publishing my article this Sunday. Apparently they weren't prepared for it because I made the arrangement with Harold Evans who is away. But I think the real reason could be that there is a big and

[1] George Rylands, Fellow of King's College and retired University Lecturer in English Literature.

very laudatory profile of Trevor, marking his ten years at the RSC, in the colour magazine and they don't want two vast pieces on the theatre in one week. I am distressed that it isn't in, but distribution strikes are affecting the delivery of newspapers at the moment, so perhaps I am lucky.

Monday 20 March
Lunch with Harold Hobson at the Ivy. He has seen an advance copy of Elsom's book and is appalled by it. He's reviewing it for *Books and Bookmen*[1], and intends to write to the chairman of the Arts Council pointing out what a biased piece of work it is. He is in a rage.

Tuesday 21 March
A lunch at the Savoy for the arts people who advise the CBI about patronage. It was to mark a new future for private subsidy. I made the point strongly that private subsidy should help initiative, individuality, risk, newness—all the things that private enterprise is supposed to revere—not the umpteenth production of *A Midsummer Night's Dream* or the safe glamorous concert. But private subsidy usually plays it safe because it wants prestige. I hope the point was taken. There are to be awards to industry for arts subsidy. This could help.

Wednesday 22 March
Most of the afternoon spent with Edward Bond. He is like an engaging boy who has joined a secret gang. In his case the gang is Marxism. He actually asks each of the actors auditioning for his new play[2] what their politics are. Derek Thompson said he was right of Genghis Khan. Bond sniffily pointed out that this is not original.

Lark Rise[3] preview tonight. Much very fine work. And a beautiful environment by Bill[4] who is a bit of a genius—the whole Cottesloe ceiling has a sky stretched over it. But I have fears. The audience—modern invaders into a lovely evocation of an Oxfordshire village—are expected to stand or walk around for two and a half hours. I think unless Bill Bryden cuts half an hour out of it there will be a new crucifixion, but of members of the public. *The Passion*—for which there were no seats either—rides again.

Tuesday 28 March
Macbeth reading with the actors—the first time in twenty-five years that I have not been paralysed inside with fear on the first day of rehearsal. Is this a good or bad sign?

[1] In this review, Hobson described Elsom as 'a critic of great perception and considerable reputation, who has allowed himself to be run away with by prejudices and personal feelings ...'
[2] *The Woman*.
[3] A play by Keith Dewhurst from Flora Thompson's book, *Lark Rise to Candleford*.
[4] William Dudley, the designer.

Wednesday 29 March

I've taken my article away from *The Sunday Times*; *The Observer* want to use it.

Reviews of Elsom's book are due tomorrow but I think there's going to be another newspaper stoppage.

First night of *Lark Rise*. A success I think. Thank God Bill[1] and Keith Dewhurst have cut it; it's only about two hours five minutes now. The audience are left wanting more, instead of being utterly exhausted.

Thursday 30 March

Late morning the *Evening News* front page had banner headlines which screamed 'A NATIONAL DISASTER' and 'THEATRE CHIEF PETER HALL IS ACCUSED.' It looked as big as war with China. The story is mainly the result of an interview with Elsom about his book, which publishes today[2], and all it really says is that I am secretive about my salary, have the wrong style of leadership, and do plays which are successful and may hurt the rest of the theatre. It's a muddled piece. But the importance given to it—it fills the whole front page—and the effect it will have in the corridors of power upset me more than I can say.

Saturday 1 April

To Wallingford in the early evening. I finished reading Robert Gittings's first volume of biography on Thomas Hardy, *The Young Thomas Hardy*. I look forward eagerly to the second, *Hardy in Old Age*. The interesting thing about the first volume is the sense one has of everything leading to that glorious outburst of verse that Hardy flowered into in his seventies: a most extraordinary achievement. It's clear why though. The approach of death, and the acceptance of old age, after a lifetime of insecurity, inhibition and regret, aroused passion and anguish in him as strong as the normal poet suffers in adolescence. I can see no reason why old age shouldn't be as deep an experience as adolescence. Certainly Hardy became a great, great poet as an old man. The novels seem less good in my memory.

All this is really to divert myself. God, I am low. In a way it's my own confidence, my own awareness that people now probably regard me as some sort of freak, a failure that has been corrupted, that does all the damage.

Sunday 2 April

My article in *The Observer* looks good today, though they cut all the jokes, so it's a bit heavy. There was no *Sunday Times*, due to a strike, and no review

---

[1] Bryden.
[2] Called *The History of the National Theatre*, it covers the period from the first suggestion of the idea in 1848 to the royal opening of the building in 1976. The last five chapters deal with Hall and his regime, generally in very critical terms.

of Elsom's book. Sat outside in the spring sun feeling utterly defeated for all that.

John Gielgud rang this afternoon to pledge support, giggled a lot, and cheered me on. He said he'd read the whole of Elsom's book and really it wasn't as bad about me as was thought. I said it was the publicity surrounding it that was damaging.

Tuesday 4 April

Woke up this morning for the first time in weeks feeling confident and better. Perhaps it's because that bloody book is at last out. The boil has burst, and its been there for two years, for it's that length of time since Elsom first passed the typescript round and the contents became the common gossip of Fleet Street. Yvonne Mitchell is writing to our chairman asking for the Board's solidarity behind me. Peggy Ashcroft is rushing into print with a spirited defence. All this of course makes me feel better.

On the *Tonight* programme on television last night, the commentator said that Michael Blakemore had called me 'the megalomaniac of the South Bank'. But this, in fact, is what I wrote of myself as self-mockery in my *Observer* piece. I don't think Blakemore has ever called me that. Anyway, he is in a great rage at *Tonight*. Can it mean his bottle is going?

Wednesday 5 April

Edward Bond and Sebastian Graham-Jones, who is to be his assistant director on *The Woman*, had an enormous row today apparently because Bond attacked Sebastian for going to Harrow. Sebastian has a low flashpoint. Bond loves confrontation. God help us if, come the revolution, he were ever made Minister of Culture. We'd all be in the salt mines. Lawrence's great dictum, 'Never trust the artist, trust the tale', keeps running through my brain.

Thursday 6 April

David Hare told me a merry Bond story today. Edward was at the Vienna Burgtheater surrounded by earnest, sweating technicians giving their all. A dog got into the auditorium and scampered about. Edward said in a loud voice, 'Thank goodness for something human. . . .'

An extraordinary letter has been got up by the stage staff and sent to the *Evening News*: a spontaneous statement of support for me. Very encouraging.

Dinner at Peggy's with Trevor: a rather alcoholic, giggly evening. Trevor is tired, and fed up. He speaks of betrayals, sudden changes of plan, people reneging on contracts. In fact, the ordinary happenings in a theatre director's life. . . .

344

Friday 7 April
A quick lunch, then off to the *Brand* run-through in the Olivier. I am excited by Geoffrey Hill's version of Ibsen's text, and fascinated by the direction of Christopher[1]. The play though is exhausting and difficult to watch. It won't be commercial, and I think a lot of people may hate it. It's like a very long Bruckner symphony; you either like its spiritual strength and clarity, or you don't. There's no point in us trying to remedy this by turning it into something it isn't. We just have to keep our nerve.

Saturday 8 April
In last night's *Evening Standard* there was a paragraph or two reporting the words of a guide on one of the Thames pleasure boats. Each time the boat passes the National Theatre he describes it to the passengers through a loud-hailer as 'A monstrosity run by a pig called Peter Hall'. No doubt when my office window is open I shall hear this sweet sound floating through.

Monday 10 April
Had a drink with Richard Eyre who was in the theatre to see a preview of *Plenty*[2]. He is now at the BBC for a year and is in some ways relieved to have left the Nottingham Rep. Over the four or five years he directed it, he tried, he said, to run a popular theatre with new writing, and all he got was a few good notices in *The Guardian* and two hundred people a night looking bored. He couldn't believe the full house at *Plenty*. He asked me how many people it would play to in all. I said about forty to fifty thousand if the reviews were mediocre; seventy to eighty thousand if they were good.

Tuesday 11 April
Four people—friends of somebody on the stage staff—came into the Green Room last night drunk. One of them got abusive and was asked to leave by the barman. At about the same time a lady fainted in the Cottesloe, and when the police arrived automatically with the ambulance ordered for her they walked into a fight. The four men had pulled knives. Two of them were arrested, the others got away, and two of our security men, shaken and with stab wounds, are now in hospital, though their condition is not critical.

As a result, there was unrest in the theatre all day. Some think we should bar visitors from back stage. I don't. But we obviously have to tighten up security. This kind of violence is appalling, and thefts are running at a high rate. I just hope we don't have to become a barracks—just like most public buildings in New York.

[1] Morahan.
[2] A new play, written and directed by David Hare, in the Lyttelton Theatre.

Wednesday 12 April

Plenty first night. The actors were rather tight and tense and I've seen them do better. Drinks with the cast and friends afterwards: a feeling of anticlimax but many people excited by the play. David Hare suicidal with post-natal depression. He knows it didn't really go well.

The letter from the stage staff has been printed in the *Evening News*. I learn that the cause of it being written was my friend Brian Mitchell who worked the trap door in *Hamlet* and one of the tough guys. Waving the *Evening News* front page, he had asked Rosie Beattie[1] who this guy Elsom was, and his address, because he thought some of the lads should go round and see him. . . . Rosie guessed he must be joking. But out of this was born the letter. My stage staff friend is now thinking of turning his attentions to our vocal waterman, the guide on the pleasure boats. . . .

Thursday 13 April

Depressing to find rather ordinary notices for *Plenty* this morning. Well, worse than ordinary, patronising and dull. I believe it to be one of the important plays of the decade, and one day it will be seen to be so[2]. Kate Nelligan[3] is wretched and David Hare bitter, saying he is fed up with being pissed on. The reviews have shattered them because they know it's good. David reminds me so much of John Whiting in personality, in mordant humour, and in his ability to provoke hostility in audiences. Christ, he's a big talent. We shall nurse his play.

Friday 14 April

To the Minister this morning. Max, very jumpy, made a long speech about the crisis-ridden South Bank and our low morale. He used as an example of the latter the fact that he had run into Albert Finney the other day who (no doubt sensing his mood) asked him if it was still worth rehearsing *Macbeth*. That was a joke of course, I said.

Kenneth Robinson was very supportive. He kept on saying we were a huge success and that the emphasis at the moment must be to help us.

Sunday 16 April

There's a wonderful letter from Michael Blakemore's agent in *The Observer*. It says Michael resigned because the National was run by a committee, not because I was a dictator, and he is coming back to us to revive *Plunder*. It isn't, the letter goes on, that there has been any rapprochement—he just cares for the play.

---

[1] Rosemary Beattie, stage manager.
[2] In 1982 *Plenty*, with Kate Nelligan, opened in America, off-Broadway, to critical acclaim, and was then moved to Broadway.
[3] Who played Susan Traherne.

The *Plenty* Sunday notices are not good. Incredibly, Bernard Levin doesn't understand why it's called *Plenty*, nor why Stephen Moore is naked at the beginning. He just can't have listened to the text. The audience understand, why doesn't he?

Monday 17 April
Max has offered me a three-year extension to my contract, giving me another five and a half years from now. I think Max and Victor have discovered what a body of support I have in the theatre. I think also it is now clear that I have a great deal of support from the full Board.

Tuesday 18 April
News today that F R Leavis is dead. A terrible shock. I never actually met him, but I went to his lectures. They were the inspiration of my Cambridge years. He somehow inculcated a feeling that art was to do with better standards of life and better behaviour. The paradox is that all we students pretended we sped to his lectures to imbibe his humanism. In fact, we were enjoying his character assassinations. Strange that a great moralist could be so destructive about creative artists.

All the textual seriousness at the basis of Trevor's work and of mine comes from Leavis, and there is a vast band of us. Comical to think that Leavis hated the theatre and never went to it. He has had more influence on the contemporary theatre than any other critic.

Thursday 20 April
Quite a good morning on *Macbeth*. It begins to flicker into life. I spent most of the afternoon trying to sort out the cross-casting of soldiers, murderers, thanes, and attendants: the usual logistic nightmare of any Shakespeare play—who's in armour? who's in robes?

Then an infuriating hour-and-a-half with Robert Cushman, whom the *New York Times* has commissioned to write a piece about the disasters of the National. He waved in front of my eyes, and questioned me about, some long article he had got hold of which stated that I must go, that there was evidence of extravagance, and that the morale was very low among the company and staff, witness the strikes. He had also decided that Elsom's book was good, sober, scholarly and had been crushed by the NT's publicity machine. All of this made me very angry.

He ended by saying he was sure I was going to have a good year. I observed with my brightest smile that if I did it would be no thanks to him.

I don't think the *New York Times* will find the National Theatre in very good order. Cushman came in a prejudiced position already—to write an article about disaster—and he was not to be convinced there wasn't one.

Dashed to the Queen's Theatre to see Alan Bennett's play *The Old Country*. A fine first act which is a gradual unfolding to the audience that two retired people are living not near Aldershot but just outside Moscow. In the interval an English lady behind me was chatting away to a young American gentleman. 'How very difficult this play must be for you,' she said. 'These are retired people who live in the country, somewhere in Surrey or Sussex I suppose. They're having friends down for the weekend.' It had completely escaped her notice that the play was about defecting traitors in Russia. It is at such times that I despair. Are American producers right who assume that audiences leave their intelligence at home when they come to the theatre? My mistake—or is it my strength?—is that I have simply never believed that.

Friday 21 April

A heavy, grinding, but stimulating day on *Macbeth*. Nicky Henson[1] and Daniel Massey[2] suddenly knew exactly how to take the verse. They became inordinately excited, as actors do when they see new disciplines opening up which can strengthen them. We all left rehearsal with headaches.

Sunday 23 April

Finished *Jude the Obscure*. Disappointing. I find now that I cannot stand Hardy's language. There's something fanciful about it, a desire to write in big pretentious words when small ones would do. He's wonderful of course at country truth, and at the sudden swift ironical turn in a plot, but the actual prose irritates me. And it is a sick book. Behind it is certainly a fear and possibly a loathing of physical passion, of physical commitment. Paradoxically, the constraints upon a writer at that time enabled Hardy to deal with a woman scared of sex more fully than a writer now, who would have to go into Freudian detail. But the interesting thing is Hardy himself. Sexuality and marriage are here just objects of anguish.

Monday 24 April

Stayed in Wallingford. A blessed day. Hot sunshine. Skylarks. I sat outside and read through *Macbeth*, dozed in the sun, and went for a five mile walk over the hills and through the beech woods. Wonderful. How I would like to spend more time in the country.

---

[1] Who played Malcolm.   [2] Who played Macduff.

348

Tuesday 25 April
First night of *Brand*. Pretty magnificent. I feel that Michael Bryant[1] falls short of greatness, though this will come. But it's a superb production of a superb text.

Thursday 27 April
Brand notices fairly awful, and Wardle's review is simply not on. He says we stage massive plays—like *Brand*, *Tamburlaine*, and the uncut *Hamlet*—not out of any need but to do cultural block-busters. Nothing makes me angrier than critics imputing motives to artists when they cannot know what those motives are. A critic's job is to be interesting about why he or she likes or dislikes something.

To the Coliseum to see the Martinu opera *Julietta*. I cannot *stand*—and it gets worse and worse—the way many English singers pronounce their own language when they sing in it: exaggerated consonants and unreal vowels. It sounds so piss elegant. It may help the voice, but it produces a language nobody has ever spoken.

Some of the audience looked at me as if I was a kind of pariah of the art world. I suppose that will die down when the attacks on me in the media do.

Friday 28 April
Edward Bond is playing up. The way he goes on is amazingly at variance with the attitudes revealed in his plays. True, it is almost impossible to make any form of art without totalitarian behaviour. All the same, I think people in the theatre should be as humane and tolerant to each other as possible. Indulging yourself is not the answer, and that is what Edward is doing.

Monday 1 May
Dinsdale Landen told today a wonderful story of his days as assistant stage manager at Worthing. He was a walk-on when Wolfit was there as guest star, playing Othello, but was not told what to do until the dress rehearsal, at which the great man said it would be a very good idea for Othello to have a page who followed him everywhere. He handed Dinsdale a loin cloth, told him to black-up, and said he'd got the part. Dinsdale did not know the play and just went wherever Wolfit went, the complete dutiful page, always in attendance. But at one point he found himself in a scene in which he felt rather ill at ease; he had an instinct about it. Suddenly he heard the great man's voice roaring, 'Not in Desdemona's bedroom, you cunt.'

Tuesday 2 May
Finished reading Bryan Forbes's book *Ned's Girl*, the biography of Edith Evans. Bryan gave me a copy the other week. I don't know why I didn't buy

---

[1] In the name part.

it—a feeling perhaps that, much as I adored Edith, and worshipped her greatness, I didn't want to meet her again through a book. Not yet anyway. But I was wrong.

It does make her live again. And it does describe the extraordinary love story between her and her husband Guy. Most of their marriage they were apart. He tried to make good in oil in South America, and they were always, in a sense, separated by her career. Separation was part of their union. The letters from Guy printed in the book are passionate and beautiful. None of Edith's survives. But there she is, confident and mysterious, shy and arrogant, just like she was. In a way, I think she most of all wanted to be an ordinary person, uncursed with talent. She loved the fact that she was a cockney, loved being the lower middle-class daughter of a post office worker. I remember how pleased she was with me because I was a station master's son. . . .

Wednesday 3 May

Finished reading *Peter Pan*. I think it is marvellous. Somehow it rubs on every subconscious nerve, and gets to everyone who is, or remembers being, a child. I am sure it must be returned to reality and played by a little boy.

A loud and acrimonious session tonight with Edward Bond. We shouted at each other. Among other things, I said it was a disgrace that a man like him, who didn't believe in extras, in actors just standing around, who had declared that in *his* play they must be real people—the community, the proletariat, the soldiery—then couldn't be bothered to enthuse people into playing small parts, saying if they didn't want to do it, that was that. I also accused him of seeking confrontation.

It was heavy stuff and looks like the beginning of a series of nasty situations.

Wednesday 10 May

Some good *Macbeth* work this morning with Albert. He's responding wonderfully to the fragmented nature of the last part of the play, which moves quickly from a man whose every word is about fear to a man who has almost forgotten the taste of it. All afternoon on the cauldron scene. Big breakthrough: the witches should look foul but be played as ordinary women, talk fairly; and Macbeth should enter the cavern as if to a seduction. It works.

Richard Eyre for a drink. I asked him if he would join us next spring when he leaves the BBC. He is attracted but worried that he would be going straight from one settled job to another. As a by-the-way thought, he said the outside image of me as somebody withdrawn, cool, and a power-operator was not at all what he found me or what the actors who worked with me knew; he suggested I speak out more, say more, not be so politic.

Sunday 14 May
Read an article on John Nash, the painter, by Ronnie Blythe, with a reproduction of a painting of his of a Suffolk harvest which moved me to tears. What an ass I am.

Tuesday 16 May
Another really hard, sweating day on *Macbeth*. It lifts now and then, and certainly Dorothy[1] begins to play the mask and the face very well. The mask is the delicate, seductive lady, totally irresistible to Macbeth. Under the mask is the passionate, practical, ambitious, real woman—and there's not much of that. I think this is the way to get rid of the hard hectoring note, usually such a problem with Lady M's. I am weeding, focusing, editing, the stage of rehearsal I enjoy, providing the energy keeps up and one doesn't hit a seriously knotty problem, for at this point there's seldom time to sort it out.

A strange lunch with Irving Wardle at my request, as I wanted us to meet, rather than protest to him in a letter, about his review of *Brand* in which he had claimed that we stage the big plays merely for the sake of doing the big plays. I asked him how he could impute motives to us when he didn't know them? He answered that he felt a lack of conviction in the productions and it was the exigencies of daily journalism which had prevented him making that clear. I said amiably I couldn't accept the argument. If he didn't like the productions, that was fair enough, but he couldn't impute motives. In the end, he sort of agreed. He said it must be awful for me after having been a press hero of the sixties to be a press villain of the seventies. I said it was awful but made a change.

I don't think he had a good time, and I didn't enjoy myself much. All the usual things came out: why do Ayckbourn? why not do dangerous foreign plays? there didn't seem to be a coherent company. I think the truth is we have done so much, that few of the critics can see our work distinctly anymore. Food for thought for the future.

Saturday 20 May
Delightful lunch at the Garrick Club with Gielgud. Hardly anybody there: a somnolent Raymond Huntley, and a clubbable Kenny More. John very spry. He's delighted about his success in the Alain Resnais film *Providence* and said with giggles of pleasure that he did feel a little embarrassed having such good notices for a movie at the same time as Larry was getting such odd notices for his Harold Robbins picture, *The Betsy*.

Sunday 21 May
A strange day because everything seemed to conspire to be about one subject. I woke early and finished reading the second volume of Robert Gittings's magnificent biography of Thomas Hardy. What particularly inter-

[1] Tutin.

ested me was the awfulness of Hardy, especially as I have been thinking again lately how intriguing it is that the humanity of an artist's work is no guarantee that he is a decent human being. Many of them are monsters, and contradict the tenor of their own work. By late morning I thought I had a play in my head that someone might write. An old writer, a left wing prophet now in his dotage, falls in love passionately for the third time. His second wife, talented, humane, progressive, a fine person, feels she is going mad as she sees history repeating itself. The new girl is a Marxist who has imbibed much of her philosophy from the great man. The play is about the clash between the private shit and the public saint in the author, and the fact that the second wife should, if there were any justice in the world, have genius too; she doesn't.

Here is the oddness of the day. Soon after this had floated into my mind, Peter Shaffer rang to talk about his new play. It's about Salieri and Mozart, and specifically about Salieri's confession on his death-bed that he poisoned Mozart. But Peter says it's become a kind of detective story, and he's dissatisfied with it. What interests him now is to write a play about the uniqueness and irresponsibility of talent. Salieri was in many respects a good man. Yet he wrote rubbishy music. Mozart was an irresponsible, feckless man, a doubtful father, a doubtful husband, perhaps a shit, but a genius. I encouraged Peter to write on.

Went this afternoon to see *Providence*. Gielgud is superb. Not only is his acting subtle and rich but his feelings are so great, his passion is so enormous, that he suggests heterosexuality in a way I would never have believed possible for him. He plays a famous old author going through a drunken, pain-filled night. The film is his imaginings as he tries to think of a new piece of writing which will use his knowledge of his son, whom he believes hates him, his son's wife, and his bastard son. Once again I was in the middle of something that was looking at the artist, and his ruthless tendency to cannibalise his life and the people around him for his work.

I rang John and told him how wonderful I thought his performance. He said he was delighted because it was his first butch part....

Monday 22 May

Learnt this morning of trouble with Michael Annals[1]. On Friday and Saturday he was stamping and raging, saying he would not have one of the sets put on the stage at all, it was so badly painted. When told he wasn't seen last Thursday when he should have turned up to look at the state of this set on the paint frame, and that anyway we would get the painting right during Saturday, he shouted that that would be in overtime, and the National was a mismanaged theatre run by left-wing revolutionaries and he

[1] Designer of *Plunder*.

was going to report us to the Arts Council and to the media for wasting the tax payers' money—his.

Final run-through of *Macbeth* this morning. Albert is sporadically superb, Dorothy very deep and complex, but I don't know what the production's like. Rather ordinary I think. It's not wrong-headed; it just perhaps doesn't have a head at all.

I had to miss the last few minutes to lunch with Kenneth Robinson and Shirley Williams[1]. She's a charming lady but I wish she didn't look like a slightly spruced-up Girton don. Why can't you look smart *and* be committed? Kenneth Robinson was superb. He led me to make all my points and mentioned a number of times what a success our building was. She was very sympathetic about the press attacks. She said she knew it always hurt. I bet she knows.

So what did I glean from the lunch? That Kenneth is our friend, and understands we are a big problem that has to be solved. I think Shirley Williams is for us too. Anyway, I hope.

Tuesday 23 May
A curious, standing water day: the set for *Macbeth* going up, with John Bury pouring enough lights on to the stage to make it burst into flames. It gives me a certain puritan pleasure to see the *Tamburlaine* stage, a circle, in use for *Macbeth*, and scenery with *Hamlet* stamped on the back. Economy triumphant.

Wednesday 24 May
Macbeth technical rehearsal. It started at 10 am and finished at 11 pm. I had two half-hour breaks during the day, ran I should think over twenty miles round the auditorium, sweated a great deal, and worried a great deal. We didn't do the battle sequence properly because the music cues and the sound cues are all terrible. We couldn't fly Hecate. The truck stuck, rumbled, and groaned. The cauldron hadn't been properly designed. I am not sure about the kilts or their colours, and I think there is a certain heaviness about the whole proceedings from the costume point of view.

Saturday 27 May
First *Macbeth* preview. The hold on the audience was very tentative to begin with, and Albert was just walking through it at the start: dry and uninventive. But he played the last movement magnificently, and the company did a fine job in keeping the production going. They were like circus players under adversity. There were cheers at the end and one boo. But we got through it, and it wasn't a disaster. Now I must tidy it and give it a clear interpretative

---

[1] Secretary of State for Education and Science 1976–79.

stamp. I suppose the real truth is, I've tried to direct the play too plainly — perhaps because I didn't have a strong passion to do it.

Sunday 28 May

The reviews of the revival of *Tristan* at the Royal Opera House[1] are good, and some of them are extremely flattering about my original production; William Mann in yesterday's *Times* said it was very nearly the finest Wagner production he'd ever seen. But we don't believe notices, do we?

I enjoyed less John Osborne's malice against me—because I took off *Watch It Come Down* when the business for it fell—in his *Observer* review of Irving Wardle's book on Devine[2]. George, incidentally, has now become a Saint. He would have cackled.

Monday 29 May

A better *Macbeth* preview tonight, though I am still worried about Albert. He's back to his staccato delivery. And Dorothy is too breathy and fading. But the production won't be a disgrace: just a rather boring, plain man's guide.

Wednesday 31 May

Not a good day. I am in some despair over *Macbeth*. Although I made some progress today in getting Albert and Dorothy to create a relationship, it's still unjuicy, and somehow Albert is unspecific again, unfocused.

Meeting at lunchtime about the garden we are opening in memory of Lilian Baylis on one of the theatre's outside terraces. Victor in the chair: rotund prose. Rayne full of smiles. It's obviously going to be a ghastly occasion, with Larry promising to make a speech then cancelling at the last moment, and the press mocking us for only having a garden named after Baylis, not a theatre. God, how I hate such functions.

Thursday 1 June

Heavy day on *Macbeth*. Some progress here and there, but I'm sick at heart. Albert is not worried enough. Dorothy is *too* worried.

A pleasant lunch with Michael Billington. He had no idea the stages were still so unfinished and that we were working under such difficulties. He said he hoped for more risky plays from us and argued that they were the ones that were commercial. It's not really true.

Saturday 3 June and Sunday 4 June

Our big 'Whither the National Theatre?' weekend, with all-day meetings and a full turn-out of associates and administrative heads. There was a

---

[1] Hall's 1971 production of Wagner's *Tristan und Isolde*, revived by Elijah Moshinsky.
[2] *The Theatres of George Devine.*

common thread running through everybody's statements: the saturation policy—our attempt to do everything, to be everything to all men—must stop. We had wanted to give the NT to the Fringe, to the regional reps, to the great companies of the world; we had wanted to have a children's theatre, a training scheme, to help new writers, to held the deaf, the disabled—and so on and so on. Perhaps those attempts had anyway been only a kind of initial guilt for receiving such a glorious building. We'd felt we had to make it available to everybody. But we'd opened the doors, and then not been able to be fully hospitable, partly due to limitations of resources, whether in money or because many things weren't yet working properly, partly due to there not being enough of us, or enough aesthetic energy, to be that far-reaching. So we'd been constantly in positions of compromise.

We are a success with the public, and there is fierce loyalty from the actors. But our central policy so far has been to get the building effectively opened. And that's no policy for the future.

What happens next? I know what this theatre should be artistically. It should be central, particular and prejudiced; and a much better place in which to work.

Monday 5 June
Spoke to Ralph at lunchtime who moved from a kind of tired sad tone to his usual exuberant baroque style during the course of a five minute conversation. He said he rang Willie Douglas-Home, who was appearing in his own play *The Editor Regrets* on tour because the leading actor had been struck down. Ralph told him not to engage in acting—it was a dangerous business. Willie asked if it was usual to find that as you stood waiting to go on, your hands were wringing with sweat and you discovered there was no pocket in your trousers, so the sweat dripped down your thighs. 'Absolutely usual,' replied Ralph.

Tuesday 6 June
Team talk to the *Macbeth* cast before today's first night. I thanked them for their hard work and their spirit. I explained that they mustn't expect success—the play was too big for there to be any certainty of that—also, I was trying to go for the classic virtues, as I am now militantly classic, which is not popular at the moment when everybody expects to see Shakespeare directed from one single interpretative viewpoint. I don't believe in that any more, so there can be accusations of ordinariness or blankness. We must embrace these difficulties, I said. The company seemed to respond well.

Usual sweaty agony—smoking furiously in the back box—at the performance. But it was the best yet: tumultuous reception, enormous cheers. The company played with a great deal of bottle, energy, and spirit. But I dictate this in the middle of the night knowing we will be murdered. Why? Because we use only the vigour of the play and the richness of the text, and the critics are not familiar with this.

A thought occurred to me during the course of the evening. Part of the epic scale of the great dramas is the way they stretch the individual heroic actor to his limit. If you have played the first two thirds of Hamlet or Macbeth or Lear correctly, the tragic intensity of the last third is that much heightened because of the physical marathon you've already gone through, which leaves you calm and clear-headed. Each of the tragedies is a microcosm of a man's life, full of effort and then exhaustion. So is the actor's performance. It is a metaphor as potent for the life of the individual as the metaphor of the Globe Theatre is for the world itself.

Wednesday 7 June
The notices are as terrible as any I have ever had. They are malicious and mocking, and there's not one which has a point that makes me pause. The critics just now don't like me, nor the Olivier, nor *Macbeth*. I suppose they consider that we are in a favoured position, me particularly, and that I can do any play I like and think I'm a genius. If only they knew. I thought the notices would be bad, but not *this* bad. The only decent one is Felix Barker's in the *Evening News*.

Everybody at the theatre is shell-shocked, and there's a lot of anger in the company. After five minutes of blind anger myself, I settled down and got on with my job. It's the only way.

What do I myself think of the production? It is well-spoken, full of contradictions, and the play is revealed—all of it. Albert is patchy and also at times inspired; you pay for the bits that are wonderful with bits that are gabbled or incoherent. Dorothy is superb if, as yet, a little rhetorical. In two or three weeks' time they will both be masterly. I think I could have helped more with the costumes; they are too heavy. John Bury and I have become stuck in our *Wars of the Roses* realism. Since we are trying to do plays on text and feeling and the free attitude of the body, it had better be apparent what the body is doing. It's not if it is clad in thick blanket. This is my fault: I did not brief John well.

The production is, I believe, a failure with the critics because it is unfashionably simple, unfashionably contradictory, and because it's directed by me—and I am out of fashion too. Just face it and go on. I am upset. But not really upset. It's temporary....

I was anyway able to hold my head up this evening at the Royal Court. But it was one of the very worst that I have spent at the theatre. I went to see Robert Wilson's *I Was Sitting On My Patio This Guy Appeared I Thought I Was Hallucinating*. I suppose it's some three or four years ago that Peter Brook asked me if I'd ever seen Robert Wilson's work. I said no. Brook was amazed and sent his wrists into little pirouettes to explain that Wilson was a new thing in the theatre: painting that moved, Magritte that was alive; some of the performances went on all night and they were beautiful. Then Mike Kustow tried to raise the money to bring Wilson's *Einstein on the Beach* to the National but failed. I can't say after tonight's offering that I am sorry. This is emperor's new clothes theatre. And it is bullshit: aestheticism run riot.

In the first part of the production, a man, Wilson, in a wonderfully designed setting, camps about for forty minutes uttering fragments of speech. None of them is resonant, none lodges in the mind. They sound and feel like aimless clichés, and are accompanied by a piano soundtrack of banal, kitsch music. Wilson, 6ft 4in, white faced (of course) and with dark black carmine lips, speaks in a quiet undertone using a radio mike. All sound is amplified at a hushed level. The cueing of the music is impeccable. The lighting is beautiful. There is plenty of technique—but no substance.

After a few minutes' interval, which we spent in the dark, the piece begins again, this time with a lady by the name of Lucinda Childs. She inhabits different places in the room to Wilson because, well, gosh, isn't she a different person? But she says the same words. My horror when I realised we were going to hear all that drivel again (though this time accompanied not by a piano but by a clavicord) nearly drove me screaming from the theatre; but we were in the middle of a row.

How so-called progressives can think all this is anything but silly I do not know. It has no meaning, no weight, and no ambiguity. It is arty-farty. I was very angry.

Tuesday 8 June

Went, because I'd promised, to the Harlechs for his sixtieth birthday party: Princess Margaret with Roddy; Princess Alexandra; Roy Jenkins, Jacqueline Onassis (looking tense and wild-eyed), Sam Spiegel[1], and George Weidenfeld[2]—a dinner party of about thirty. I had Pam Harlech on one side and Lee Remick on the other. All the talk was of children and education. Then there was dancing in the tastefully-lit marquee. Apple trees had real apples wired onto them. Home soon after midnight, tired of people commiserating with me about *Macbeth* and the National Theatre. It was not a moment to go out into the Establishment.

Friday 9 June

First read-through of Edward Bond's *The Woman*, set during the Trojan wars. Edward said nothing before the reading and then, after it, said it wasn't a play about the past, but about now; much of the society around us

---

[1] The film producer.   [2] The publisher. Created Baron 1976.

had been produced by the Greeks, and in a way we still had many of their virtues and their contradictions.

Train to Cambridge, where Christopher met me, to see Jenny play Nina in *The Seagull*. It was done by the Fletcher Society: Chekhov in the old Corpus Christi court which housed Christopher Marlowe and John Fletcher. When we got to the last act something happened which made me very pleased. Jenny began acting. That bent double, 'please don't look at me because I'm rather shy' acting went. She dealt with the breakdown scene touchingly and truly and the audience response changed. They listened. I told her afterwards that I truly believe she can be an actress.

Monday 12 June
NATTKE are asking for a 35% increase and a four-day working week. I begged our negotiators not to have a strike while I am away directing *Così* at Glyndebourne, where, when I arrived there today to start rehearsals, the summer seemed gone and it was cold. Heard all the ensembles with Haitink, and we have a very strong, very young cast that I think will work well. Musically they are in a wonderful state of preparation. I would be overjoyed to be spending a month on Mozart if everything were peace in London.

Tuesday 13 June
Glyndebourne: Up soon after 6 am as usual, but a lost dog. Where's the routine? I don't have my newspapers; I don't have my room; I don't even have the piles of paper from the theatre. So I wandered about and read *Così* and went on revising the opera until mid-morning when John[1] and I went through sets and costumes. Then a meeting with the cast and Haitink. I told them we had to be serious, realistic, and do nothing which would make the women look fools or destroy credibility.

Thursday 15 June
Glyndebourne: *Così* is much the most difficult opera I have ever tackled; such a Chinese box of emotions, of actions and counter-actions, of realities and hypocrisies, that it is at the moment a towering and confusing journey. I am meditating giving up directing for a year. I think it's what I need. I feel wrung out, uncreative, and unresponsive.

Friday 16 June
Glyndebourne: Nonsense from the National. The repertoire planning seems to be in total chaos. What do I do? Ignore the whole thing as if I were on holiday and let them get on with it? I can't.

[1] Bury.

Much talk with Moran. I asked him his view of me and the National. He said he thought I must be tougher, leave others to administer, and get on with what was important to me—being an artist. Well, maybe. He said that in a sense it grieved him to think my best work was being done at Glyndebourne.

Saturday 17 June
Went to *Saturday Night Fever* this evening. It's a computer picture, expertly made, beautifully shot, and with a blazing star performance from a new young man—John Travolta. I think the computer was asked, 'If you wanted to remake in the late seventies an Astaire/Rogers film, with all its appeal, and particularly its appeal to the young, what would you do?' This movie is the answer. A feeling of manipulation pervades the whole affair—and of course it works on the audience. I think what depresses me is that up to quite recently I have always believed popular art in all its manifestations in history was popular because it had merit—in some sense it was good. The public's own vitality saw to that. But now this isn't so any more. Market research provides the right product, the public is manipulated: 1984 has come.

Tuesday 20 June
Trevor with me this evening. To my surprise he arrived early, a habit he is not noted for, and staggered into my office looking very thin and extremely pale. He's very tired, very fed up, wants to leave, feels he has to stay for the start of the Barbican; and then, when it's opened, what is he faced with? A still larger organisation, a more difficult industrial situation than at the Aldwych: all the problems that I have.

We both agreed we didn't any more want to head huge organisations—we wanted just a simple space and 25 actors. We feel that all priorities are wrong in the theatre at the moment. These monsters that we head are having to get bigger and bigger in order to justify their subsidies, and the bigger they get, the less clear they become as artistic enterprises. I ought to leave the National, Trevor ought to leave the RSC, and Brook, Trevor and I ought to start a theatre together. It is blindingly clear, right for the times, and true. How the hell are we going to do it? The system has often fucked-up the individual: Larry, Ralph, and John Burrell by the Old Vic in 1949; Michel[1], George[2], and Glen[3] the next year; John Neville by Nottingham—the line is endless. If Trevor and I walked out, would we be beyond the pale? Certainly with the Arts Council—then we wouldn't get money for our new work. Think, think. . . .

An exhilarating evening: we looked into the abyss.

[1] Saint-Denis.   [2] Devine.   [3] Byam Shaw.

Peter Hall's Diaries

Wednesday 21 June
A long and hard associates' meeting. Michael Hallifax had done one of his amazingly elaborate charts, all lines and dots, showing how a year's work could be scheduled. Harry Birtwistle waved the chart in the air and said, 'I know some people who could play this.'

Saturday 25 June
Glyndebourne: News from the National that Sebastian Graham-Jones wants to resign from *The Woman* as Bond's assistant on the production. This, quite ridiculously, threw me into a great state. It hit me when the adrenalin was low at the end of a *Così* rehearsal. I was deeply depressed and did nothing all evening. Well, I lie. I went and saw the last half of *The Magic Flute* and then drank too much with Moran.

Friday 30 June
Glyndebourne: I must note the first orchestral rehearsal of *Così* because of what Haitink—known affectionately to the orchestra as Clogs—is doing with the music. It is very, very delicate. He is achieving real piano, real pianissimo. The consequence is that the dreadful, energetic, hearty Mozart which some conductors get trapped into out of a desire to be theatrical is completely gone. Each new voice makes its mark, and the whole thing has a luminous quality which makes any ambiguity possible. His tempi are on the whole slow, but you actually hear the subtlety and grace of the score, and it's not lacking in wit. It's magnificent.

I had to make a speech to the singers about wearing hats. I told them that I'd not worked for months with John Bury on the design in order to have the cast arbitrarily discarding hats, coats, gloves, scarves, swords, etc, because it was easier to sing without them. If that was the way they felt we should do away with all the costumes, all the lights, and just make music. They looked surprised, but it had the desired effect. Hats were worn.

All telephone attempts to talk to Max Rayne over the last three days have failed, though I hear he was in the theatre wardrobe this afternoon getting kitted out for a fancy dress ball. He goes as Figaro, Arnold Goodman as Friar Tuck.

Saturday 1 July
Glyndebourne: I whiled away the time on the train here today by trying to get to grips with what the set should be for Harold's new play *Betrayal*. Late last night at the end of the associates' meeting, when I was talking to him, a sudden thought came to me: light white milky screens on a softly mirrored floor, the objects seen dimly—all images of the past. For this play, like Harold's *Silence*, is about memory and time. I think there's something there. But why did the idea come at that moment, literally as Harold asked me

what was the news on the *Betrayal* settings? I don't know. That is the terror of creative work. Ideas come or don't come. You don't know when, where, or why. You can't make yourself think of a good idea. I put the screens notion to John Bury on the bus from Lewes to the opera house this morning. He grumped, but I could see that a seed was sown.

To *The Magic Flute* this evening. Ben Luxon gives a masterly performance as Papageno, and there's superb orchestral playing. But this is David Hockney's *Flute*. By Christ, it is! His designs are over-decorative and very talented, with beautiful colours everywhere. But the characters aren't people; the costumes just make silly abstract patterns. The serpent though got big laughs, and is a charming creature who puffs smoke and flashes his eyes. The animals in fact are wonderful, with a nervous hedgehog and an angry glum lion. But what did it all mean?

I think *Flute* is a bugger anyway. The German text is pretentious and really no match for the score. But there is a spiritual side to the piece, and this production was just a high-camp fairy tale. The children, who saw it with me, enjoyed it very much, except Lucy thought the look of it was too modern. She's damned right.

Wednesday 5 July
Glyndebourne: Clogs let *Così* off the leash today and it began to dance a little. But it's still too lugubrious. I think the truth is that neither conductors nor singers believe the realistic human truth Mozart and da Ponte allow: that people can feel more than one thing at once, and can change from ridiculous posing to heartfelt passion in the flick of an eyelid. Performers and musicians *will* make transitions. Mozart doesn't. Just as you think the emotion in the scene is real, it becomes funny. And when you are convinced that it is farcical, suddenly the heart is wrung. *Così* requires great flexibility of its singers, and we have two at least who certainly have that—Maria Ewing[1] and Håkan Hagegård[2].

Saturday 8 July
Jacky and I drove to Denys Lasdun's beautiful country cottage for dinner. It is of course immaculately designed, but homely. The living room has a wonderful door knob on it, honest iron. From this developed a scene out of Alan Ayckbourn. A screw had come out. So four times, to the great architect's increasing rage, Sue Lasdun pulled the whole door knob off and it fell onto the boards with a resounding crash. Denys got pinker and pinker. He kept asking her to be careful and to jam it in. Later in the evening he pulled it off himself. To anyone familiar with the problems of the National, it was a rich pay off.

[1] Who played Dorabella.   [2] Who played Gugliemo.

Sunday 9 July
Glyndebourne: A warm and lovely evening for the opening of *Così*. On the whole I liked the performance: great grace, elegance and seriousness. The triumph though was Haitink's. I've never heard more delicate playing. He makes a specific Glyndebourne sound, rich yet fastidious. And his tempi tonight even notched up a little more vigour, a little more wit.

A huge ovation at the end. It is very evident the production works and that people are amazed to see *Così* done as a serious piece. But it could have been better if I'd pushed it further. The second act, where feigned love becomes real, could be deeper still.

Albert Finney and Diana Quick arrived late and had to be smuggled into a box. In the long interval, we picnicked at the top of the lake. Ralph[1] brought a huge basket of drink. Diana supplied a fantastic feast of Greek goodies—stuffed vine leaves and all the rest. It was Glyndebourne at its most hedonistic, and I would have enjoyed myself if it hadn't been a first night.

Monday 10 July
Back to the London horrors: hundreds of problems falling thick and fast. So I wanted to do everything all at once, and by the evening felt like a zombie.

Oh, the *Così* notices. I was less concerned about them than I have been for anything for years, I expect because I'm so fed up with the press and the critics. Anyway, they're very good. I met Philip[2] on the Glyndebourne lawns last night and he said he supposed the period was kind of Kate Greenaway. I said, Kate who? I really didn't know what he meant. William Mann finds it set in the nineteenth century, which it isn't, and at odds with the music made by Haitink. Sydney Edwards manages to write a rave review in the *Standard* without even mentioning the one undoubted star performance—that of Maria Ewing. But the notices are excellent, so the sun is out.

Wednesday 12 July
At the South Bank Board meeting this morning it was implied that the appalling lateness of the stage machinery and its inefficiency was in some way due to the National limiting the access of the technicians completing the job. I banged about a bit, and said we all knew this simply wasn't true. Ulrich then declared we should have foreseen that access would be particularly needed by the technicians at this final stage. I replied we should in that case have foreseen it at any time during the last three and a half years, for we were always being wrongly told the technicians were about to finish. From there I went on to suggest that the clean thing to do was for the South Bank Board to

[1] Richardson.   [2] Hope-Wallace of *The Guardian*. Died 1979.

362

close us down until the work was done. At this, Joe Lockwood thumped the table angrily and said, 'All right, we *will* close you down.' Ulrich asked how much it would cost. I said in loss of income between £30,000 to £40,000 per week, quite apart from any redundancy payments. We then began a long period of reconciliation which ended in us all kissing and making up. Max and Victor arrived late when all the fun was over and we were in a warm glow. Horace Cutler[1] said we'd had an excellent argument. Joe Lockwood said I'd been very rude to the Board (this of course with an Establishment grin) but all was now well. A good morning.

The set for *Betrayal* is huge, composite, and no good. Bury got angry and bearlike, thwacked his thighs, said the play was undesignable, the playwright hadn't thought of the director's and designer's difficulties, and were he and I supposed to do his work for him. So we talked again about the play, that it concerned memory and time, and the images should have mistiness, whiteness, and be of the past. He went away to think, and in a few hours had designed a beautiful set, which solves the play entirely from my point of view. It is like a sundial, but with everything opaque, light and specific; and a revolve gently brings new segments into place. It is a triumph. You don't need time to have ideas. You just need to have them.

Friday 14 July

Went through the Jasper Johns exhibition at the Hayward. The iconography of the sixties now looks old-fashioned and rather tatty. But I still like his bronze called *The Critic*: a pair of glasses with bared teeth showing in the eye sockets.

Harold came to the theatre to see the *Betrayal* set, which he adores. Afterwards he told a wonderful story of him and Antonia going to Glyndebourne. They were nearly there, 'bowling along in the old Merc', when Antonia decided it would be good to have a cup of tea from the thermos before they arrived, so they pulled up on a verge. The trouble was that this verge was faulty. On the other side was a ditch and the car fell into it. So there they sat, immovable, dinner-jacketed and floral-printed, near to Glyndebourne yet very far away. Came a tractor with a friendly farmer who pulled them out—'They are built like tanks, these Mercs,' said Harold. But once they were started again the same thing happened. The car fell in. The tractor was by now a dot on the horizon. Antonia found this very funny; Harold didn't. But by dint of power and effort they finally managed to get out. I remember the old Merc ten or twelve years ago nearly knocking down one of my gateposts at Stratford. Harold is not the most precise of drivers.

[1] Conservative Leader of the GLC 1977–81. Member of the NT Board 1975–82.

Sunday 16 July

Thanks to a strike there were no papers in Wallingford, but John Goodwin phoned and offered to read me the Sunday notices for *Così* which, he said, were marvellous. I said no—if you keep them at arm's length when they're bad, you must keep them at arm's length when they're good. John agreed, and said that good notices were like a glass of champagne, and lasted as long. Dead right. I will wait.

Monday 17 July

This afternoon Laurie Evans surprised me by saying how disgruntled Albert was at the National, how he had been overworked, abused, mishandled. It looks as if I'm at the end of a good relationship. But I am afraid I let Laurie have it. I told him how little I had wanted to do *Macbeth*, and how dishonourable I felt the accusations were. These things nearly always happen when a production doesn't succeed. I just try to write them off and start again. It's the only way in this business.

Total tiredness tonight, total deadness. All aspects of my life, professional and private, are in a God-awful mess. I wondered whether I wanted to go on living.

Tuesday 18 July

Have at last seen the *Sunday Times* review of *Così* by Desmond Shaw-Taylor. It is about the best notice I have ever received. This is what I specially like: 'A more rounded and beautiful musico-dramatic whole ... I have not yet encountered, either under Strauss at Munich, or even under Busch and Ebert in Glyndebourne's earliest years. What makes the production so peculiarly winning is that it captures the precise tone of the opera, by which I mean of course my notion of its precise tone.' Well, I couldn't ask for more than that. I don't, though, think it's earned. The approach to the piece is right, but the clarity of the execution could be better. Still, this is like a glass of champagne to me—but, as John Goodwin said, as lasting.

With Christopher[1] to David Mamet's play *American Buffalo* at the Cottesloe: an invigorating evening, wonderful writing. I know no one who has caught more precisely than Mamet the pathos of the dim and unverbal in their desperate attempts to express themselves with language which is dead and repetitive. They say 'fuck' every other word, because that is their only way of getting emphasis. It is pathetic and moving. A fine play, very funny, and beautifully directed by Bill Bryden. It was seamless.

---

[1] Hall's son.

Wednesday 19 July

All day at the Tory party's Council of the Arts. The conference didn't achieve anything of course, but how could it? It's perfectly clear what the arts want: not, as here, endless wranglings over policy—just more money. This would increase Britain's international status, and in some ways transform our country. I said that ringingly and brought the house down. It wasn't very hard, though, as the audience was almost entirely composed of interested parties.

I saw Margaret Thatcher there in true blue, blonde hair glinting, with that rapt, attentive expression of hers. And it crossed my thoughts that the chief attribute of a political leader now is that he or she must be able to go anywhere and not be out of place. Uncle Jim would be alright down a coal mine, in a factory, in a school, in a hospital, on the lawns of Buckingham Palace, or in a street barbecue in Brixton. Margaret Thatcher wouldn't. I doubt if she'll win.

I think a reason for this conference is that Norman St John Stevas[1] may have caught on to something which I am surprised the political parties didn't realise long ago: there are certainly no votes in the arts, but there is considerable media sympathy. Any party that promises money for the arts is liable to be treated sympathetically by heavyweight journalists. It might even cause *The Guardian* to smile at the Tory party, however coolly.

Friday 21 July

Much of the day watching rehearsals of *The Woman*. The big and pleasurable surprise is that it is magnificently staged. The use Bond has made of the Olivier is exemplary, and the visual emblems are superb. Good meeting with him afterwards: he was open to suggestion; no problem at all. I am optimistic. Great relief, for I had been expecting a terrible crisis.

Thursday 27 July

Very low this morning. I feel in utter despair over everything, and trapped. I do not know what to do, so I will do nothing and hope the walls will not close in.

Friday 28 July

Dinner with Michael Rudman[2]. We darted from one subject to another. He's very pragmatic and open. I think the plan I have for him to run the Lyttelton will work. Many jokes, and many choice items of gossip. Simon Jenkins[3] told him that in only two organisations do the staff ring up Fleet Street to give dirty information: one is the BBC, the other is the National.

---

[1] Then Shadow Spokesman on Science and the Arts.
[2] Artistic Director of Hampstead Theatre Club 1973–78.
[3] Editor of the *Evening Standard* 1976–78.

Wednesday 2 August

During Saturday night I developed a raging throat, blocked nose, and burning sinuses. I woke up unable to breathe or swallow. So I've had the unaccustomed experience of being off work for several days, and therefore did a lot of reading. Apart from getting through five plays, I finished Frank Tuohy's elegant book, *Yeats*. A quote of his: 'The arts are at their best when they are busy with battles that can never be won'. I also finished a biography of Henry Irving by Madeleine Bingham[1] whose main thesis is that his grand affair with Ellen Terry withered because he was a creature who lived in the theatre, whereas she was a creature who worked in the theatre but wanted to live outside. Irving's will power was extraordinary. He made himself into a great actor when everything was against him, and made a great theatre when he should have ended up a great booby. He had no capacity for ordinary life at all. Like many of us, he worked furiously in the theatre because he wished to avoid life.

Two novels went down too. Trollope's *The Warden*, which I suppose I've not looked at for 30 years, was one. He's the greatest demonstrator of humbug. I'm now going on to the rest of the Barchester novels. The other novel was Michael Frayn's very funny *Towards The End Of The Morning*.

I suddenly realised I must have been reading day and night for days. I have. I haven't slept. And I haven't wanted to be with myself or think.

Kon Fredericks is leaving at the end of this week—for personal reasons. We were all just congratulating ourselves on this news when the works committee's total rejection of our new pay offer came in. We seem set for our next round of industrial troubles, for we are constrained by the White Paper to keep within the new 5% limits, though I learnt tonight that Covent Garden is nevertheless sticking to its offer of 8% to Equity and the Musicians' Union.

Friday 4 August

First preview of *The Woman*. The first part was magnificent, but the second needs more work—the narrative is not clear—and Edward still hasn't cut: the evening went on until nearly 11 pm. But I was encouraged by what I saw. At the end Edward, surprisingly, asked me if I could give him a good amount of time tomorrow to talk about the problems.

Saturday 5 August

An excellent two-hour meeting with Edward. He nodded, endorsed, made notes, and said I'd been very helpful; no argument, no confrontation. I think, at last, there is the beginning of trust; only artistic trust, of course....

---

[1] *Henry Irving and the Victorian Theatre.*

Monday 7 August
The NATTKE negotiating committee won't come to the conference table tomorrow unless we make an offer of more than 5%. And there's a lot of muttering about overtime bans and industrial action. I think we're in for it.

Tuesday 8 August
Heard tonight that Nick de Jongh has written a front page piece for tomorrow's *Guardian* giving details of all the big changes we are about to make: Rudman's arrival to run the Lyttelton; Morahan and Bryden being given control of the Olivier—which, de Jongh is revealing, Bill Gaskill turned down; me running the Cottesloe to do experimental research. And apparently the article may give the charming impression that I am taking a back seat because I am clapped out and not wanting to do more major productions.

Wednesday 9 August
The *Guardian* story today produced a storm of press calls to us. Why so much interest? I suppose because of the front page treatment and the implication that I am retiring from the centre of the National's work and might even be going. But the evening papers were really quite up-beat. More than that, the *Evening News*—which in March, when the Elsom business was at its height, headed its front page 'National Disaster—Peter Hall Accused'—did an editorial saying what a splendid chap I was!

Thursday 10 August
Bill Gaskill strolled in to see me looking cheerful and flirtatious. He said he was all ready to phone me to see if the job offer was still open, when the *Evening News* rang him about the *Guardian* story, so he supposed it wasn't. I asked him what he meant. He said hadn't I asked him to run a company of his own, with his own actors, responsible for four or five plays a year, but consulting me about the repertoire? I said certainly, a year ago and at various times since. Bill then said he would like to accept, but probably it was too late.

What am I to do? The National desperately needs Bill and has to have him. I asked him to give me a little time.

Why this change of heart? Is it that Gaskill never really believed I would give him a company and allow him virtually complete freedom to run it? Or is it that now he knows what I'm about to do with other people, he's suddenly clear what he wants to do himself? I don't know. But it's deeply annoying and worrying when all our plans have been made in the belief he isn't coming. I must get him, though.

First night of *The Woman*. A wonderful performance. I have been very lucky on this one. Edward has directed it magnificently, the play is fine and clear, and Yvonne Bryceland[1] gives a marvellous, and true, performance.

Friday 11 August

The notices for *The Woman* are disappointing. What I don't understand is that the critics fail to recognise it as a major work, which it is by any standards, as well as one which most originally tries in modern terms to re-examine the myth of the Trojan wars. I remain convinced that it is a superb play superbly done.

Talked to Bill Bryden about Gaskill changing his mind. Someone's got to stand down to make way for him. Perhaps it had better be me in the Cottesloe, where Bryden could then continue instead of moving to run the Olivier with Morahan.

Spoke to Goodman to find out how Covent Garden is able to offer 8% increases despite the 5% limit set by the government White Paper. Goodman dodged it by saying that the pay policy was only a guideline, but even if it had the force of law, no one could make you withdraw an offer already proposed. So that is Covent Garden's loophole.

Saturday 12 August

Saw the film *Close Encounters of The Third Kind*. It's beautifully made, but the dialogue is mumbled and incoherent, and the production values large and glossy—myth-making by visuals rather than by the revelation of human behaviour. And it is slow, slow, slow. It seemed to be saying that there is some outside force or power which is trying to communicate, and when it does, human beings become part of it and remain in suspended time. So? I was baffled.

Read the proof copy of Harold Hobson's autobiography, *Indirect Journey*. It is elliptical, witty, ironic, also vain, and sometimes outrageous—like the man. But I found it sympathetic. Hobson has, after all, a great deal to be vain about. His life proves that men make their own luck. At key moments, when things were bad, he found unbelievable courage, took action, and always succeeded.

Monday 14 August

Lunch with Bill Bryden. He volunteered that he would prefer to stay in the Cottesloe. I think what bothers him now is that Gaskill will still not come and he, Bryden, will once more be asked to go to the Olivier.

[1] Who played Hecuba.

368

Went to the camera shop this afternoon to update my equipment. Shops are getting dreadful for me. I can't bear to be recognised, talked to, advised. I panic. It was a horrible experience.

Spoke to Kenneth Robinson and reiterated our problems with the union. This week is looking like a nightmare. Will anything be settled before I go to Scotland on Saturday?

Tuesday 15 August
Travelled to Glyndebourne thinking, thinking, thinking. We are a play short at the Lyttelton in January. And the plans for the Olivier are in disarray because of the Bill Gaskill situation. Can we, anyway, afford him? Is it really right to have him? Well, yes, it is. But it does hurt me to give up the Cottesloe, for running it is what, at this period of my life, I most want to do.

Thursday 17 August
I am satisfyingly now right into *Barchester Towers*. Trollope is so humorous, so wise, such a castigator of humbug. And really all his novels are about politics: the Pallisers overtly, and the Barchester novels metaphorically. They are not about the church or religion, but about human envy and greed and the struggle for power. And they are very, very, funny. I am delighting in Obadiah Slope—one of the most venal creeps in literature.

Rang John Barton to press him about Galsworthy's *Strife*, which I've asked him to direct. He said he loves it and would have done it, but the RSC has just decided to do a whole programme of Greek plays, including *The Oresteia*, which he is starting next year. My heart came into my mouth. He said he felt he had to tell me because Trevor had pointed out that *The Oresteia* had been on my list for years. 'But surely,' he added, 'it would be interesting for the two theatres to do the Greeks at the same time?' This, though, is idiocy. I am absolutely shattered. The hopes of four years go down the drain. I can't do it now. . . .

Bill Gaskill has agreed to come for three years, to be responsible for some five plays annually, to be an associate, to choose his own actors, but to develop his Olivier repertoire in relation to Chris Morahan's. This is excellent. We embraced.

Thinking later today, and more soberly, about my *Oresteia* decision, I reflected that if you just follow your own personal obsessions, the theatre you run is only as good as you are. When Tony Quayle was at Stratford, George Devine at the Court, and when I later was at the RSC, we all drew strength from the talents of others, talents that were allowed to develop because, in a sense, we allowed them to walk over us. I think we went wrong when we tried to do it all ourselves, to be supermen. Well, I've tried to be a superman over the last three years in the interests of opening this building in the face of villainous hostility from sections of the profession who have tried

369

to isolate me. Larry has not helped, nor has the Jonathan Miller/Michael Blakemore faction. But if I can bring a form of devolution to the National, then I may, paradoxically, be able to do what I want in it.

Friday 18 August
Losing *The Oresteia* plays on my mind though I try not to let it. I am stunned by John Barton, Trevor and the RSC. How can one's friends do that sort of thing, despite ours being a cut-throat, competitive business?

Saturday 19 August
With a few days holiday upon me I am thinking of the future: forty-seven years old, nearly forty-eight, and blessed, or cursed, with having done much of what I set out to do. So I mustn't just go on. I want to work less, earn less, have fewer possessions. I have been thrashing with the desperation of the insecure for twenty-five years, and I am no nearer making it now that when I came out of Cambridge, because one never really makes it. I have done some good work and some bad, but I have been worried lately about my increasing incapacity to find joy in what I do. I would like to slow down so that things can begin again. But have I the strength to run the National, and leave more of the work to the formidable team now round me? Can I learn to live again, instead of using my profession as a means of escape from life?

I would like to cultivate friends, to travel, to write. I want to teach, and I am sure it will come. But I have to get back my own self-respect first. I have, perhaps, twenty years ahead of me of interesting work. My God, I'm fortunate. Most men don't reach their ambitions until they are in their fifties. I reached mine in my thirties. But now I must get fit, live well, and cease to behave like a demented superman.

I have been asking myself what is my handwriting as a director? I suppose it's more tender, more human, and more romantic than I allow myself to be. There is something in Peter Wood's theory that I am a Romantic director, and that ever since *The Wars of the Roses* I have forced myself into a kind of political puritanism.

Don Giovanni was me; *Così fan tutte* was nearly me; bits of *The Tempest* were too, and bits of *The Cherry Orchard*. But my handwriting as a director is shaky at the moment.

I have never, I believe, been envious of others, or thought I was in a race which I had to win, to stop Brook or Gaskill or Nunn overtaking me. That never occurs to me. Maybe my hubris is to want to try everything—plays, films, operas, the harsh, the epic, the political, the comic—and perhaps that is just stupid.

I look forward to the future with anxiety. But also, for the first time in years, with excitement.

370

Sunday 20 August to Saturday 26 August
My holiday. I read no plays and thought very little about the NT. Amazingly, there was no communication from there; nothing at all: the first time that's happened to me in years.

On Saturday I flew to Glasgow, and from there to Campbeltown in a tiny aeroplane. The cottage we had rented was pleasant, thick-walled, but tiny. The five young children[1] and a puppy invigorated its rooms.

It rained a great deal, but the countryside was very beautiful. The cottage was on the estate of a Scottish farmhouse changed, about 1900 I should think, into a Charles Mackintosh version of what a Scottish stately home should be. We were all bidden up for drinks: huge rooms; a fire even in August; and magnificent views of Arran and the sea. The owner's dad's VC hangs over the fireplace—South Africa, 1900.

I went fishing often in the bay in a small boat with the boys. Edward was delighted to have his father with him, but I wasn't so delighted by the eagerness of the mackerel to be caught. You pop down a line with seven hooks and shortly afterwards pull in seven heaving creatures: not my idea of fishing. Christopher, who has fish fingers, caught 120 and delivered them to the startled lady of the house, who was up all night gutting them for mackerel paté.

I always forget how beautiful Scotland is. I love the space. And I actually love the rain. As I grow older, sunshine seems less attractive. Modest colours and subtle shades please me more.

I read compulsively all the time, in spite of the din of joyful children. I finished *Barchester Towers*, and got through most of an enormous biography, *Samuel Johnson*, by Walter Jackson Bate—Johnson's life was a magnificent tragedy. I slept, I walked. Realities were kept at bay, which was no bad thing.

On Saturday we drove back: 500 miles in twelve hours. Big breaks for meals, but tiring.

Monday 28 August
Finished *Samuel Johnson* today. It was the chief joy of the holiday. I loved Johnson as a young man but can't pretend I've read him a great deal in the last twenty-five years. What I loved, I suppose, was his commonsense understanding of Shakespeare, with no antiquarian or romantic nonsense, and his huge capacity for life. After he had died his friends called and found something they never forgot: 'the most awful sight of Dr Johnson *laid out on his bed, without life!*'

The same sense of incredulity was shared by everyone who knew him. This was especially true of those who knew something of his early life — walking the wet road to school at Market Bosworth, leaving for London

[1] Edward, Lucy, two cousins and a friend.

with David Garrick, writing (indeed inventing) the parliamentary debates in a garret room—as well as the Johnson who wrote *The Dictionary*, *The Vanity of Human Wishes*, and *The Rambler*; struggled against despair to bring out his edition of Shakespeare; looked after waifs and strays; ran the race with tiny John Paine; imitated the kangaroo; rolled down hills; wrote *The Lives of The Poets*; and became the greatest talker in the history of the English language.

Boswell said, when he heard in Edinburgh the news of Johnson's death, 'My feeling was just one large expanse of STUPOR. . . . I could not believe it. My imagination was not convinced.'

Johnson had touched a chord in these people and changed their lives in some profound way no one else had ever done. He had given them the most precious of all the gifts that one can give another, and that is hope. With all the odds against him, he had proved it was possible to get through this strange adventure of life, and to do it in a way that is a tribute to human nature.

Here are some treasures from the book:

Johnson: 'When once a man has made *celebrity* necessary to his happiness, he has put it in the power of the weakest and most timorous malignity, if not to take away his satisfaction, at least to withold it.'

Johnson: 'Fame is a shuttlecock. If it be struck only at one end of the room, it will soon fall to the ground. To keep it up, it must be struck at both ends.'

The centre of Johnson, according to the author, Bate: 'He was to face throughout his life—though it was naturally to prove an indispensible source of his greatness when kept in healthful interplay with other qualities—a fierce and exacting sense of self-demand.'

It must have been this insistent self-demand that brought on his two big breakdowns—one after he had to leave Oxford through lack of money, the other in his fifties when he was five years late with his edition of Shakespeare. What I found so moving was that at the time Mrs Thrale deserted him he was old and sick, with all his terror of death, yet he managed to die well.

Throughout his life he thought it was possible to make a new start. His diaries are full of resolutions. He continually wrote notes to himself resolving to get up early and work harder. But he lay in bed, year after year, until midday or after. Perhaps the opposite of acute self-demand is sloth: you can't have one without the other.

Wednesday 30 August

Dorothy Tutin came and talked to me about lighting in the Olivier. It's not that she feels unlit, it's just that she can't see the lights. 'Give me a light and I will look up to it,' she cried. The truth is that she prefers working in a proscenium theatre safely buried from the audience. And she likes bright lights because then she is dazzled and can't see the audience. So she's never going to be happy in the open-stage Olivier. But I love her, and I love her talent, and I think there's a basis of truth in her anxiety. It is not good for actors to spread themselves into darkness. It is unreal to them. Lights attract them like moths, make them stretch out, expand.

The most amazing event of the day was a conversation with Edward Bond. He said that he owed me an enormous debt, that he'd loved his time at the National, had found more professional expertise here than at any theatre in his experience, and that it had made him, he hoped, a better writer. He quite understood my anxiety about him directing, but he wasn't worried because he knew he always had me as a back-up. He had learnt how to deal with people, how to take care of them, or at least he thought he had. He was generous in his thanks, though shy and embarrassed. I was flabbergasted. But I do believe he means it. He said, 'If you write a line that you don't like, you can cross it out ferociously. You cannot do that to an actor or to a technician when they are offering their best.'

Thursday 31 August
A long and painful session with Dame Peg[1]. I told her all about *The Oresteia*, how I didn't think it was the way for the RSC to behave. She agreed, and begged me not to do anything hasty. Once again, she said, she was Peg-in-the-middle.

Friday 1 September
A hurtful conversation with John Barton on the telephone, which started well and ended badly. He said there could be no question but that my Greek work must open before his. But he also added that he was going to do his next year come what may. I asked him if this meant there might be only a couple of months gap. He answered, perhaps. I said I thought that was very damaging—to both companies. John said: 'You say it is damaging, I say it is not. There is a difference of opinion, and you should honour my project.' He then went on to say I was down, depressed, unconfident. I am afraid it's true: that's why I am so easily hurt. But it doesn't alter the fact that friends should not do this to each other. I am going to think this weekend, but I honestly believe *The Oresteia* is now dead as a project for me. That is heartbreaking but has to be faced.

Saturday 2 September
Saw Truffaut's *L'Argent de poche* on television. It's a bloody masterpiece: witty, funny and sad. It shows in varying degrees the oppression of children,

---

[1] Peggy Ashcroft.

either direct by beating them, or emotionally by blackmailing them or misunderstanding them. It's saying that an adult can always do something, and a child can't. But it wasn't heavy, not didactic. It was renewing and extraordinary. I would love to see it again, and I would love Edward to see it.

Tuesday 5 September
Talked to Harold who'd somehow managed to contact Sam Beckett to sound him out about directing *Godot* for us. Sam is impossible to find as he now only has a one-way telephone: he can ring out but no one can ring him. He sent his love; and messages that he was getting tired and old and at the end of his directing days. This hardly squares with the fact that he's off on Saturday to direct *Play* at the Schiller[1], doing a television in Stuttgart in January, and probably directing *Happy Days* at the Court in the summer with Billie Whitelaw.

He asked Harold why I wasn't directing *Godot* at the National. Harold said, because I was trying to take things easier. Sam then asked Harold why in that case *he* wasn't doing it. Harold answered that with another play coming up he couldn't. But he amplified this to me. He said he didn't feel he could get anything more out of *Godot* than he'd already seen in other productions—and as it was such a big influence on him, it wasn't something he could measure up to without new thoughts.

After various alarms and difficulties we settled today the contracts of Gaskill and of Rudman, so they will be joining us soon.

Thursday 7 September
First night of *The Philanderer*[2] in the Lyttelton. An attentive and responsive house throughout, and by the last act the actors were playing like masters. The production is a magnificent achievement by Chris[3]. Let's just hope the buggers don't ruin it tomorrow with rotten notices.

Friday 8 September
The Philanderer notices are all in all excellent. At last the critics are seeing what we're doing without their awareness of the long-running political problems of the National Theatre coming between them and the production.

Saturday, 9 September
To Wallingford this afternoon. The children were having a disco party, so there was loud music, swimming, barbecueing, and parents to chat to. They were, as usual, full of sympathy about the awful time I am having at the NT. . . . Thank God it was a warm evening with the sun shining.

[1] The Schillertheater, Berlin.   [2] By Shaw.   [3] Morahan.

Tuesday 12 September
Dozed to-night over a television film about the Spitfire and its ancestors, the Schneider Trophy seaplanes. Deep nostalgia; shades of my childhood. How I treasured those Dinky toy miniatures. What images for imagination they were. . . .

Wednesday 13 September
The South Bank Board meeting went on and on and on. I dozed at one point. It was like being at a dreadful play, dropping off, and when you wake the play is still as dreadful, still apparently at the same spot, and you don't know how long you have been asleep. The Board was making its case against Denys Lasdun and the contractors over the building delays. Arnold Goodman pointed out that history is full of instances of foolish Boards and Committees and Proprietors sueing architects or arraigning great artists, but history is always on the side of the artist.

Saw our short Dorothy Parker platform performance, *Men Seldom Make Passes*, well directed by Julia Pascal. I hate the publicity she's getting as a result of being a woman; it's so patronising to her sex. But, goodness, women directors can direct—just as birds can sing. . . .

Thursday 14 September
We all gathered this afternoon on one of the National's river terraces to open it as 'The Baylis Terrace', commemorating a great lady of the theatre. Larry had telexed two pages of impenetrable prose. Ralph, who performed the opening ceremony, couldn't speak it. Nor could I. So I had it roneoed and put into the programmes. Everything passed unexceptionally: Ralph made a few nostalgic jokes, the television cameras whirred, the brass band played.

I am reading Iris Murdoch's new novel *The Sea, The Sea*. It doesn't help me forget my worries. It's about a self-centred, neurotic theatre director who is haunted by his guilts, and his loves.

Tuesday 19 September
To Campden Hill Square for a *Betrayal* dinner before we begin rehearsing it. Lovely house, the Fraser mansion: for a book freak like me the walls are a constant seduction.

John Bury, Harold and I showed the set to the cast and chatted about the play. Michael Gambon[1] was all actor, taking refuge behind a non-comprehension which certainly isn't true. Dan Massey[2] was all intellectual, wondering whether he should go and spend a day in a publisher's office to understand the world inhabited by the character he plays, which baffled Harold. 'It's all in the play,' he said.

---

[1] Who played Jerry.   [2] Who played Robert.

Thursday 21 September

Awful cultural exchange meeting at the theatre with a Russian delegation. Speeches of welcome and presents. I feel more than usually sickened by all this bullshit now, in the light of the repressions.

Saturday 23 September

Went to the Buñuel movie I've been longing to see all year, *That Obscure Object Of Desire*. Classic shooting, flawless. Buñuel has such a relaxed certainty that you don't ever see a cut: the film seems to flow in great chapters. The story is an obvious one of a girl who is both nymphomaniac and holy virgin, tender and wilful. But the two actresses playing the parts are beautifully directed, and the whole work is wonderfully funny and elegant. I loved it.

Sunday 24 September

Walked in Hyde Park for two hours all alone. How wonderful (though I only ever want it to be brief) to have no one to talk to—no children, no one. It reminded me of just such an autumn afternoon there about twenty-five years ago. I remembered the smell of the leaves then, the equestrian statue leaping at the setting sun towards Kensington Palace, and the Round Pond with the mad old gentlemen dressed up as sailors with their radio-controlled model boats.

Today, I wandered about disguised in my dark glasses, overgrown hair and casual clothes. It was the first time for months I felt unrecognised. I saw the Henry Moore sculptures by the Serpentine Gallery, which were alive with children peeping through the Moore holes. A big slag of a girl with a beautiful bare bronzed back crawled over one of the great shapes. She and Moore were as one. He is the most sensual of sculptors and the years seem to increase his sensuality.

I wandered my way round to Paddington and met Edward off the train from Wallingford. Then we both went to a Chinese restaurant in Queensway, and home. He is miserable at going back to school, wants to live in Wallingford, have a dog, hates London. He's very nervous about school, his sports; his self-demand is colossal. Much comforting needed. But he slept finally through the night.

Monday 25 September

The composer, Peter Mennin, president of the Lincoln Center's Juilliard School, came to see me. Would I consider going to the Juilliard as head of training, linked possibly with a renewing of the Vivienne Beaumont Theatre, as soon as possible? I said I had another five years of contract with the National, and was therefore only in the middle of a kind of war which I had to win: I wouldn't want to leave until I felt I had done the job, and could

376

pass it on to others to develop, as I had at the RSC. That might take five years, might not. So the answer immediately was no. He is going to invite me over to New York in November to have a look round.

Wednesday 27 September
To *The Observer* for lunch; very much me against them. The host was Donald Trelford, the editor. Conor Cruise O'Brien presided. Many people there I knew—some I like, some I don't: Richard Findlater, an old friend; Robert Cushman; the witty and energetic Clive James. I had a go at this and that and rather enjoyed myself. Cushman got angry at one point. I said that drama critics reserved their tolerance for middle-brow, middle of the road entertainment, usually of a commercial nature. They were never tolerant about great talent that failed. He called for proof, for documentation.

There was a good deal of talk about whither the Arts Council; also about whether the 5% pay policy would hold. The view of their political and financial staff was that the Ford strike was going to be a long one simply because it was a regulator which would enforce a lower norm on the rest of the country. Maybe that's right. I believe if Callaghan stands up to the unions now, he will win a landslide victory.

First night of *The Double Dealer* in the Olivier. I do admire what Peter Wood[1] has done. He has turned what was a near disaster at the beginning of the previews into a remarkable account of the play. I think he's shown the heart of Congreve by not emphasizing the misanthropy and the bitterness —that's the mistake I would have made. I am full of admiration for him.

A word in the interval with Kenneth Robinson. He said that Shirley Williams had asked to see him about the National Theatre, and he told me not to worry too much. I had friends in high places and there was a growing understanding of our financial problems.

Thursday 28 September
The Double Dealer notices are a little picky but, on the whole, excellent.
To the young Vic to see Peter Brook's Paris troupe doing *Ubu*[2]. A joyous, wonderfully uplifting evening. What struck me most was the extraordinary energy level of the troupe. They play with the relaxed abandon and complete commitment of circus performers, spending physically in a way which most English actors don't think of doing. Brook is just the best.

But I wondered tonight how much longer the fashion for rough theatre in rough places with old bits of costumes and approximate props will last. It's ten years since Peter did his *Tempest* experiment at the Round House[3],

---

[1] Its director.   [2] By Alfred Jarry.
[3] A workshop project, incorporating mime, and experiments in sound and movement. The audience watched from cat-walks and scaffolding, which also served as the set; there were no formalised costumes or props.

and we've had ten years of rough work on the Fringe. It must be time for something new to stir.

Friday 29 September
Patience Collier, whilst rehearsing Charlotta in *The Cherry Orchard*[1] has, by willpower and by talent, become ten or fifteen years younger. And this is reflected in her appearance off stage, her speed of movement and her agility, even her jollity. I have never seen such an exercise of mind over matter.

Rehearsals of Harold's new play begin on Monday. I'm getting nervous.

Sunday 1 October
Read *Betrayal* again, ready for tomorrow, and discovered the central fact about the triangle. The marriage of Robert and Emma[2] is actually kept going by her secret affair with Jerry and by the friendship of the two men. Once the betrayals cease, the marriage is over.

Monday 2 October
The beginning of *Betrayal* rehearsals. Harold with us all day. This morning we read it—which was nervous and speedy and took little more than an hour—then all sat around and discussed the characters. It was another matter this afternoon: real work. Actors in the early days of rehearsal usually don't share or react to each other. They are private, preoccupied. But these three—perhaps because they know each other so well—began affecting each other from the word go. I am specially pleased with Mike Gambon. He's a real actor—unexpected, and subtle.

Home reasonably early—7.15. Edward still in a state about being back at school in London: he didn't sleep last night and didn't go to school today. Jenny said, 'Remember that Edward, like you and me, is a Pamment'. Christopher isn't, nor is Lucy.

Tuesday 3 October
Our production of *No Man's Land* on television tonight. Some of the television critics are continuing the myth that it is about nothing and that the actors don't know what they're talking about. Do they really think such work can be done without understanding? The play is logical, and absolutely clear.

To *Evita* this evening at the Prince Edward Theatre. It can only be a huge hit because it has three hit tunes. It elevates the appalling Evita, whom we love because she's a star, but hate because there's the trendy, radically-correct Che Guevara on the sidelines telling us what a monster she is. And

---

[1] To take over the part from Helen Ryan.   [2] Played by Penelope Wilton.

what has he to do with it anyway? He's just as big a monster as she is, just as big a star, corrupted by power.

There's no vitality in the piece. It's the cult of kitsch again, inert, calculating, camp, and morally questionable. I felt out of step with popular taste, which really worries me. . . .

Friday 6 October
One of those days with never a moment to draw breath from six in the morning until eleven at night. The postscript was a meeting with Ralph on the stairs as he came away from the theatre after playing in *The Double Dealer*[1]. 'I hear you're giving a press conference on Monday,' he said. 'Forgive me saying so, but you must be charming, open, warm, welcoming, and humble. No suspicion that you have been hurt. No suspicion that there have been any troubles. Promise me?' I promised.

Saturday 7 October
To St Paul's Church, Covent Garden, for Robert Shaw's memorial service. A beautiful, still day. There was a gathering of figures from the profession, plus friends and family. Robert has left eleven children, nine of whom are still at school.

Harold Pinter gave a short address, stressing Bob the writer, and read from the *Four Quartets*[2]; Donald Pleasance read from an account of Bob's school days written by Bob himself.

It was a fairly joyful occasion, serious but not sad. I had my usual bewilderment about our lack of ritual. We all huddled together in the autumn sunshine outside the church—Paul Scofield, Kenneth Haigh[3], Harold, and many, many others. We all wanted to be together in Bob's memory. But what could we, un-Christian as most of us are, do?

Off to the Riverside Studios to see *The Changeling*[4], beautifully staged by Peter Gill, precise and clear. But I had an impression of a not very talented cast dutifully following the conception of a quite brilliant director.

Sunday 8 October
My head was so full on Saturday with things I had to do this weekend that I had a very bad night, and was up before four today working away until past seven, when I went back to bed for an hour and a half.

Rang Peter Brook at Stratford to see how he was and wish him good fortune for the opening of *Antony and Cleopatra* on Tuesday. He was non-committal about the production; in fact, sounded a bit worried. We arranged to meet next Saturday when I go.

[1] As Lord Touchwood.   [2] By T S Eliot.   [3] The actor.
[4] By Middleton and Rowley.

379

He thought that bringing Gaskill and Rudman into the National to join the team of directors was a marvellous idea because I would be able to delegate more, and it would allow me more artistic freedom.

Phoned Edward Albee to talk about his new play, *Lady From Dubuque*. I said that because the characters were not concrete, not realistic, and because one didn't know where they came from or who they were, there was a great danger of pretension. I mentioned the couple in his *A Delicate Balance* as being realistic and yet having more resonance as the play progresses. Albee says this new play is the opposite way round: the characters start as metaphors and become real.

He asked how I was. I told him I had just signed on for another five years. 'The enemies didn't get you, then,' he said.

Monday 9 October

Had our press conference today announcing Gaskill and Morahan running two separate companies in the Olivier, Rudman running the Lyttelton, and Bryden continuing to run the Cottesloe. A terrifically large press turn-out, plus two television crews and representatives of all the main radio stations. There was a certain amount of pushing on what I would or would not be doing personally; I think it went alright though. I was very nervous, but concealed it. Pictures were taken on the terrace of the new team; then came three radio and two television interviews. I went straight from these into the annual general meeting of the Board.

Tuesday 10 October

The papers are good: quite factual and fair. Nicholas de Jongh in *The Guardian* points out that the changes were as foreshadowed by his paper in August—which since his story then was that I might be packing it in, and that Bill Gaskill was *not* coming, is wonderful cheek. . . .

A difficult day's rehearsal of *Betrayal*. Dan Massey is in a state about whether or not to stay with the play, or indeed with the National Theatre. Also it's his forty-fifth birthday. I like him, but he's even more emotional than most of us.

Wednesday 11 October

There's something funny about Peter's *Antony and Cleopatra* at Stratford. John Goodwin and John Bury both went to the opening and both independently have told me how bad, slow and heavy it was. Yet they are not destructive, and they both adore Brook. John Bury observed, 'I have never been so glad to see an asp.' The press is distinctly disappointed, though deeply respectful. So they bloody well should be.

A very long associates' meeting. Many riches. One was Harold's very funny speech of passionate horror at the shoddy way play scripts are duplicated in the script department—I suddenly and vividly felt his physical need as a writer for absolute clarity of layout and type. And Harry Birtwistle strongly maintained that despite the RSC's Greek plays we must still do *The Oresteia*.... but let's see.

Saturday 14 October

Antony is a terrible disappointment. I was looking forward to it so much. It's handsome and chic but by no means a revelation, more a clear, hard-edged interpretation constantly let down by its actors. And there are no broad strands of emotion to sustain you. But some things I shall remember always, and Peter has shown that, though the play is about big passions and big events, it can be done as a chamber production.

Dinner with him afterwards. He spoke of his unhappiness during rehearsals, adding that once actors begin to think that working is doing the director a favour, they are finished.

He said the problem of the English theatre at the moment was that there were no great causes; there were no obvious holes: new writing was done, the classics were constantly re-examined. But he pointed out a paradox. In the early sixties I had insisted that all the rotundly-speaking Shakespeare actors were also in modern plays to sharpen their sensibilities. And now everybody was good at realistic mumbling, but inexpert in Shakespeare.

Sunday 15 October

Christopher phoned to talk about his university project. I kept on trying to nudge him towards Eugene O'Neill, and late tonight found a chapter by Eric Bentley who sees O'Neill primarily as someone who was all the time trying to surpass and surmount his father, the famous actor. It's too simple an idea, but there could be some truth in it, and I thought it might fascinate Christopher. Then Jenny phoned to talk about Farquhar's *Man of Mode* which she's in at Cambridge. Then I tried to help Edward write an essay on the Duke of Montrose—about whom I know nothing. Then Lucy had to be encouraged with her piano practice. I felt like part of essential services.

Monday 16 October

Copy letters in this morning from the Minister to Max Rayne, and Max's reply. The Minister suggests Peter James[1] as a member of our Board. Max has replied that what we want is more money, not more members. But the

---

[1] At the time, Artistic Director of the Crucible Theatre, Sheffield. From 1981, Artistic Director of the Lyric Theatre, Hammersmith.

notion of appointing Peter James is an interesting precedent. Fellow theatre directors on theatre Boards? I don't think so.

Tuesday 17 October

Early this morning, my long-delayed and eagerly-looked-forward-to visit to the RSC's new theatre in the Barbican. I think it's beautiful. John Bury and I can be proud. And I am sad Joe[1] Chamberlin died before it was completed. It's perhaps a little on the wide side, but it has a homely, intimate atmosphere. It lacks the grandiloquence of the Olivier, and that I like. The only problem is that the theatre is buried in the whole bloody complex, and it's going to be a hell of a job to find it. There's no shop window so there'll be no passing trade. I think they may have a problem getting audiences to go there. But the theatre will be a marvellous place to stage plays in. They say it will open in the autumn of 1980. I'd guess the autumn of 1981 or spring of 1982[2].

Thursday 19 October

Excellent day on *Betrayal* rehearsals though fatigue is beginning to settle in my head and in my limbs. I forced myself and was therefore very tense. But the play starts to flare into life. The actors are now presenting their text— using it as a weapon. Mike Gambon particularly is becoming tough, growing beautifully. And I am more than ever impressed by Penny Wilton. She takes ideas fast, and uses them subtly—so that your suggestion comes back to you a hundred times better.

Friday 20 October

I ran nearly all *Betrayal* at rehearsal this afternoon. Penny Wilton is really amazing. I believe hers is the best woman's part Harold has ever written. It is the influence of Antonia. Up to now his women have been neurotic enigmas, Mona Lisas who never reveal their secrets. Now he's written an absolutely enchanting, vigorous, life-enhancing woman with a keen appetite for life, a good intellect, a marvellous sense of humour, and little sense of morality — though an honourable sense of what is possible, which perhaps does less harm because it hurts others less.

It is an advance for Harold, this play. The tension builds up at an enormous rate. It's not fanciful to think of Mozart. From my point of view there's the same precision of means, the same beauty, the same lyricism, and the same sudden descents into pain which are quickly over because of a healthy sense of the ridiculous. A strange comparison I know. But it's there.

---

[1] The nickname for Peter Chamberlin.
[2] The Barbican Theatre opened on 7 May 1982; the Barbican Centre itself was opened by the Queen on 3 March 1982.

Saturday 21 October

Read Howard Brenton's new play *The Romans in Britain*. It's very exciting, and shattering in its power. The sequence where Caesar and his hordes suddenly turn into modern British troops in Northern Ireland sent shivers down my back. It sounds an obvious parallel, and cheap, but it's not, and Howard takes no sides. But there is a lot of work on the play still to be done.

To Oxford tonight, unwillingly, to see the touring version of the *Così* I directed at Glyndebourne in the summer. Simon Rattle, who conducted, is too hectic, takes it all a bit too quickly, but God he got it played well. He's a theatre animal. It was a most amazing piece of work for a 23-year-old man. He will be a great Mozartian.

A packed house loved the production. But I didn't. The cast now prance in time to the music, turn together on certain bars, and the Albanians, for instance, now disguise themselves in order to be funny, not in order to win the wager and to get the women to love them. The underlying gravity of the production has entirely gone.

I took copious notes, resolving that I must allow my fury to abate, and then see what we can do about the revival next year. Cool it, cool it, I thought. I therefore intended to slip away at the end. But Stewart Trotter[1] was there, sure enough, in the foyer, waiting like a wicked pupil wanting to challenge his schoolmaster. What did I think? I said that certain performances were splendid, but I would like to talk to him at leisure about changes in tone and emphasis. He went mad. He said he knew I would hate it, and wanted to know precisely what I hated and why. So I said it was no longer serious; it was just funny. It certainly had nothing to do with my original production, and his brief was to recreate it. He declared that what he had done was true to the text, and right—mine wasn't.

Our conversation, in a rapidly emptying foyer, grew more and more heated. Stewart finally said that if this was my feeling about his work, he had no intention of reviving the opera next year[2]. I replied I thought he hadn't better, if what he'd said was the truth of his feelings about the piece. He swept off into the night.

Sunday 22 October

An extremely busy day. I went through the script of *The Romans in Britain* again and phoned Howard. I expressed general enthusiasm but some specific reservations. As it stands, he seems to me to be dealing largely with the obvious. We know that people are corrupt, we know that societies torture their prisoners, and we know there is deep and wounding trouble in Northern Ireland. But surely the historical process, the clash of cultures, the large eating the small, is richer than that?

---

[1] Director of the touring version.   [2] It was revived by Guus Mostart.

Peter Hall's Diaries

Monday 23 October
Marvellous essay in *The Listener* by J H Plumb called *The Culture Vultures*. It's about the cultured families in the small market town of Bury St Edmunds in the eighteenth century. They opened up a whole slice of social history with their books, their music, their conversations, and above all their touring theatres—all those beautiful small theatres, now most of them no more. The essay shows a vanished, elitist and highly desirable way of life of which one can easily be very envious.

Tuesday 24 October
Not a good day rehearsing *Betrayal*. Everything seems to have got smoothed out. It's calm, bland and boring; all tension has evaporated. But this happens, working with a Pinter play. Suddenly it goes. Until the actors are absolutely sure of their inner life and can play it passionately, their outer life, as expressed simply by what they say, can take over and appear insubstantial. The text is written to be supported by the immense strength of the feelings underneath. In fact, it disguises the feelings.

Wednesday 25 October
To Hammersmith tonight to see *The Ragged Trousered Philanthropists* presented by Joint Stock. It's the best production I've seen this year: most meticulous and extraordinary work by Bill Gaskill. Nothing is out of place, nothing is overdone. And I didn't know a single one of the actors.

It's twenty years since I read Robert Tressle's book, but it seems to me the first part of this play, by Stephen Lowe, is very faithful to Tressle, whereas the second is excessively militant and committed. It's the mood of the moment. Marxism is almost the only upbeat solution among intellectuals. Gradualism, compromise, organic growth, are all dirty words. But Bill is now without doubt a great, great director.

Quite apart from the brilliant standard of the staging, I found the evening moving because it finally exposed in all its heartrending inadequacy the romanticism of the revolutionary. Of course the bosses were corrupt and money-grabbing, or most of them. Of course house painters were exploited—my grandfather was one. He had to walk miles to his job. When it rained, he was laid off—there was no pay. And before he was sixty he was crippled with rheumatism and sciatica and never worked again. In my childhood, I always understood that his boss was a bastard. I am sure many families have a similar heritage of bitter memories.

The sadness at the heart of this wonderful evening is that the name of socialism is now sometimes used to stop freedom, stop contradiction. God preserve us from Tony Benn. Checks and balances, argument, are essential.

The play took me back to my simple socialist youth, when I believed the working man only had to inherit the earth and all would be well. How pathetic I look to myself now. And that is what I felt about a lot of the audience tonight. They were sitting there eagerly having their socialist convictions confirmed, their hopes massaged into ecstasy. Where was there a tiny question mark?

A cat-and-mouse game tonight with Peter Shaffer. He was full of his new play, provisionally called *Salieri*. He's now done the first draft, and he says the finished script will be with me in January. But the cat-and-mouse game was all about John Dexter[1]. Would Dexter direct *Salieri* at the National? Would I do it with Dexter? The tension was that Peter must know the subject matter of *Salieri* is very near to my heart. But I let him down once when I directed his *Battle of the Shrivings*, a failure, and I think Dexter is much better for Shaffer than I: sweet with sour, and plenty of bitch. Anyway, it sounds as if we shall get *Salieri*. Please God, I like it.

Friday 27 October
An early start looking at management papers suggesting a working pattern for the stage staff, which would go a long way to giving us complete flexibility between our three theatres. Of course in a year or two the stage staff will once more be demanding separate teams for each theatre[2], but that is the nature of industrial relations.

Then to Peter Wright's to have my eye looked at. It has, as I knew, got considerably worse: it's not the infection, but the build-up of fatty deposits in the leaking blood vessels. The vision in the right eye is now appalling. Wright said there is a laser beam technique which could help me. It would actually eradicate the blood vessels providing they were in the right place for such precise and dangerous treatment. I have to set aside a day for tests to see exactly where the leaks are. A bit depressing really. All I can be glad of is that the left eye is fine: super vision.

Then off round the corner for breakfast with Arnold Goodman who, looking like an oversized and genial Paddington Bear without his hat on, was lying in bed sipping coffee and wondering how to reach someone who had been libelled by the *New Statesman*—or at least Arnold thought he had. We chatted away amiably about events, proposals, the Minister —who is still, by the way, beavering away about us having Peter James on our Board. I intend to make an issue of this. What other theatre Board has a rival theatre director on it?

[1] Director of three of Shaffer's previous plays, all big successes: *Royal Hunt of the Sun*, *Black Comedy*, and *Equus*.
[2] It was this issue that had led to the strike in August 1976.

A good *Betrayal* rehearsal except for Dan Massey. He said he didn't know what he was doing; he was playing someone a million miles away from himself. Penny pointed out that this part she was playing was a million miles away from her too—for, after all, she wasn't off having an affair for seven years. She—in life Mrs Dan Massey—then turned to Harold and said *sotto voce*, 'But in view of all this perhaps I will.'

Monday 30 October

To the annual dinner of the Institute of Credit Management to reply to the toast to the guests, all because I was blackmailed into it by Kenneth Cork, an old friend[1].

The speeches were a mixed bag. Some fellow who works for Kellogg's Cornflakes gave an absolutely uproarious speech with a laugh a line. So I was brief and serious about the arts and democracy and the rights of the individual—both in business and in art. God, how boring I must have sounded. . . .

Kenneth told me how sorry he was that we had never actually worked together as RSC chairman and RSC director, though we'd planned the Barbican and got it going. 'What a couple of pirates we would have made,' he said. He thought I should diversify, get out of the theatre a bit, have hobbies, and was just the chap to join him on the board of directors of Ladbrokes. I said I'd be delighted. . . . I bet I never hear another thing.

Tuesday 31 October

A meeting this morning to talk about the company. A number of actors are leaving, some after a long period of work. I suppose that is inevitable now that we have new directors who must be able to express their own tastes. But I am sad, because with this company there's been surprisingly little unrest, misery or neurosis: a happy group in my experience.

A telephone call later that the stage staff had called on me to say they were taking strike action tomorrow if a more acceptable increase were not offered than the one in the draft of the new NATTKE contract we are negotiating. I believe the deputation asked to see me as an attempt to get me to intervene and overrule management. But at least it was courteous, and much better than the anarchic antics of the past. I think though we may not be able to avoid a strike.

Wednesday 1 November

This evening the stage staff walked out. The management had met with the NATTKE shop stewards in the afternoon and told them the maximum

---

[1] An RSC Governor during Hall's regime; and Chairman of the RSC Governors from 1975. Knighted 1978. Lord Mayor of London 1978–79.

increase—with all the productivity saving going to the men—the Department of Employment would allow us. The stewards indicated they would recommend it to the shop floor, but the shop floor would have none of it. They walked out. So tonight we were forced to cancel full houses in all three auditoriums. The usual council of war, but what can we do? Our hands are tied. And further sporadic strikes like today's are threatened for any time. What could debilitate a theatre more?

Bill Gaskill came to see me. He said he recognised two sides of himself. One was the star-lover who in the end would cry 'Send for Maggie Smith.' The other was the person who adored working with special actors, usually unknown. Which did I want? I said the second. He said so did he, but he wanted me to be under no misapprehensions.

He asked what would happen about today's strike, which he considers monstrous. All the men, he declared, should be sacked for unprofessional behaviour. He also said roundly that he didn't believe in unions. I enjoyed this from the socialist who has just directed the classic of English working class union life. No, that's not quite fair. He hates unions *now*. And he's bloody right.

Thursday 2 November

Harold speaking to me this morning: 'You know that fellow. Alan. Yes, Alan Ayres. The fellow in the press office. Well, he said to me he knew I didn't want to talk about *Betrayal*, give any interviews, make any comment. But what about a piece about our friendship, the relationship between you and me for twenty years or however long it is, fifteen years?' I said to him, 'Now look. My friendship with Peter is of no concern to anyone except Peter and me. And as for our working relationship, it's in our work. It's there to see. Others can see it. It's our own bloody business'.'

The men were back at work at nine this morning. But there is nothing more in the kitty, and there's a notice on the stage door notice board tonight from the stage staff saying that unless there is a dramatic improvement in our offer, there will be further strikes.

Letter from Trevor saying I am clear to do *The Oresteia* any time before next October. John Barton won't start work on his Greek project until after that date. So Trevor has fixed things for me. I am very grateful.

Friday 3 November

Lunchtime meeting with the NATTKE general secretary, John Wilson, and his colleagues. I put the arm on Wilson, saying that in some respects I was glad this unofficial action had happened, because it would demonstrate clearly how little control there was by the union of the work force. This got Wilson going: a letter from him was delivered this afternoon to all NATTKE members telling them to behave themselves.

Harold is very depressed, tense and moody. He said to me tonight that *Betrayal* is the best piece of work he and I had ever done together and it was about to be ruined. For if there were more sporadic strikes next week, and we were prevented from having the previews, the play wouldn't come to the boil at the right moment and all would be lost. I told him not to be silly, and I mean it. I don't believe we shall open on time, but we shall open, and it will be good.

Monday 6 November
Negotiations were put on the rails again this morning, and the stewards will recommend to the men tomorrow that there is no further unofficial action until next week. It's arguable that it will be easier for us to get a little more through by then because I think myself the whole 5% strategy of the government is going to collapse.

Tuesday 7 November
Studied the implications on my life of doing *The Oresteia* after all, and within the next eleven months. It means twenty weeks for rehearsal without a break. I must radically rearrange my schedule to find the time.

There is rumour of an imminent stage staff strike in the West End, as indeed there are imminent strikes everywhere. I don't mind a further disruption with us if we play it absolutely by the book, step by step, cleanly. And I believe that in a sense Jim Callaghan and Shirley Williams would welcome any consequent, temporary shutting down of the National Theatre. It would be a resounding public demonstration of the firmness of the pay code, for it would get tremendous media attention, yet wouldn't affect the mass of people.

The *Betrayal* set was on stage today. I think it can be very beautiful, but every aspect of it has to be textured and real; though a white world, it must not be abstract, nor arty. I must concentrate on this play to the exclusion of everything else for the next few days. We have something wonderful in our hands.

Thursday 9 November
Peter Stevens has been to the Department of Employment and we are not in a position to offer more than a fraction of what the men are demanding. There will be a strike. I cannot see how it is to be avoided. At least *Betrayal* has been allowed to hatch. For hatch it did tonight, before a tiny audience of the staff. They were a bit respectful, and the laughter was not what it should be, but I think it's going to work.

Friday 10 November
I could only rehearse *Betrayal* in the morning, because of an Arts Council meeting this afternoon which was fairly gloomy. They clearly are not going

to have enough money to meet what the building costs us even before we stage anything. I think we should bring public attention to the enormous cost of the building alone. The Arts Council will need to get new money expressly for it. They were, though, totally sympathetic for the very first time.

Despite further industrial action hanging over us, we managed a good first preview of *Betrayal*, but we have quite a way to go; Gambon has to grow in his passion and Penny in her emotion, and somehow I've got to make Dan more simple. Jacky said afterwards she thought it was a play which husbands and wives could not discuss together. I said I rather agreed but thought it was wonderful, and very accurate. 'You should know,' she replied.

Saturday 11 November
I didn't see this afternoon's preview of *Betrayal* but it was full. Ralph was there, so I phoned him. A beautiful play, he said, beautifully performed: never had the Pinter pauses meant more and been less pretentious; and he loved Gambon but wasn't convinced by the last scene, the beginning of the affair. 'We've all been in love,' he said. 'Love is a very big bomb. It must go off.'

Monday 13 November
This afternoon the entire NATTKE membership debated in the Olivier. It seems there was a three to one vote in favour of strike action against the 5% pay policy, and the management is to be given a week's notice before each action. It was the moderates apparently who called for this notice, so the public should not be too badly disrupted. But the membership as a whole were not told about the productivity saving going to the stage staff, nor that the stage staff are reserving the right to unofficial action on their own, no doubt to keep their power base.

Unofficial action means the union will be required to discipline the strikers. As they aren't likely to, we shall have to do it for them, and that may well lead to the building closing down, at least for quite a while. I actually think it could be the best thing. You can't make theatre under these cliff-hanger circumstances.

Tuesday 14 November
The awful thing about industrial action is the rancid atmosphere of distrust and gloom that it spreads around. People look at each other in a less than open way: there's a lot of misunderstanding, and a lot of suspicion—hardly an atmosphere in which to produce plays. So it was ironic in the circumstances to go to see the run-through in the Olivier of *Strife*[1]. The writing isn't quite up to the subject, but the play is beautifully crafted, certainly

---

[1] Galsworthy's play about a strike in a tinplate works.

captures the waste of industrial action, and it makes both sides heroic —there are no baddies. I found it wonderfully directed by Christopher[1], and wonderfully acted, particularly by Michael Bryant[2] and Andrew Cruickshank[3] as the chief protagonists. There was no time afterwards to discuss anything with Christopher. I had to get back to real industrial relations.

We have received notice of an unofficial strike next Monday.

In my heart of hearts I believe this building will have to close down. And if that's what happens, it happens. We haven't got the money to get near what the men are demanding, and I cannot let us slide into a Fleet Street situation. Otherwise, isn't it possible that in a couple of years' time, our NATTKE branch could decide to take unofficial action if they don't like the particular political content or meaning of a play? Just as printers in Fleet Street ban some cartoons or articles.

Harold is walking about like a sad zombie, wondering whether *Betrayal* is to open or not. I believe the National will never get anything of his again if this sort of thing is allowed to continue.

The preview today was guest night, so there were less laughs. But the play bit well and deeply, and this evening Dan Massey took it and gave a superb performance, right on target.

Afterwards, I had supper with the whole Mishcon family. I wanted to talk to Victor about our general industrial strategy. He backed me entirely that we should now play it by the book, and take the consequences. He was very amiable, hospitable, and helpful. And I must say his family are delightful. All the young Mishcons with their wives, laughing and joking away. It did make industrial relations slightly more bearable.

Wednesday 15 November

Not a day I shall forget. The stage staff met at lunchtime and we asked if the opening of *Betrayal* would go ahead this evening. They simply said wait and see. So the anxiety about whether everything would stop just as the curtain was to go up, or in mid-play, was added to the actors' usual first night tension, and mine, and Harold's.

Tomorrow morning we break off negotiations because of these continuing threats of unofficial action. Then the shit will really hit the fan. But at least tonight we managed to get through. And it went quite well considering the strain. To be frank, I was in no state to judge, and Harold was walking round saying he felt like a lump of lead.

So *Betrayal* has been born, not at all under the happiest circumstances. The tension on this first night was the most cruel of my experience. Rehearsing the play, though, has been wonderful. I have enjoyed it, really enjoyed it, and I've respected my own work again.

[1] Morahan.   [2] Who played David Roberts.   [3] Who played John Anthony.

Thursday 16 November
I woke with a raging headache, the living proof that one line in Harold's play is inaccurate—you *can*, in fact, get drunk on Corvo Bianco. The critics range from the patronising to the bad, and are now taking him to task for being *un*-enigmatic. They find the play small, inconsequential, and about a segment of society, upper middle class intellectuals—like themselves, incidentally—who are not worth writing or thinking about.

I spoke to Harold several times during the day. He seemed cheerful and supportive. The actors were furious, but very proud of their work. This evening Harold said categorically to the assembled cast: 'I want to make my position clear. And I shall put it on the table. I think it is a very good play, superbly done. That is all I have to say on the matter.'

We formally broke off negotiations with the union at a meeting this morning, but stressed that we were prepared to resume them if the threat of unofficial strike action was withdrawn.

Later John Wilson held a mass gathering of NATTKE members. As far as I gather from a variety of reports he spoke quite well, though, to begin with, in an atmosphere of considerable contempt—of union cards being torn up and being thrown at him and a lavatory roll arriving at his feet. But he did talk about the theatre's financial position, the crippling effect of loss of performances, and the problems facing us. By the end, there was an insistence that he ask us to re-open negotiations. We answered we were unable to do this unless the threat of unofficial action was withdrawn.

Friday 17 November
The backstage unrest in the London theatre is I hear being carefully orchestrated among the London stage hands. The commercial theatre is being taken on first as it can break the pay code and has. Then, with a broken pay code, the National is tackled next week, the Royal Opera House the week after, and the RSC the week after that. And all this is being supported by a lot of decent people who understandably want more than 5%.

By the end of the day our situation was this. NATTKE have taken a firm line. We have agreed to renegotiate with the general secretary—but not necessarily with anybody else. And on Monday there will be another one-day strike.

Sunday 19 November
The Sunday notices for *Betrayal* are even worse than the daily ones. More accusations of pin-head drama. They are wrong.

Monday 20 November
The strike happened. But it wasn't as hellish as most of us had imagined.

Peter Hall's Diaries

Diana Boddington—Bod—our great stage manager rang me at 6.50 am. She was already in the theatre. She gets there about 6 to 6.30 nearly every morning having been to church first for prayers; I often think she is a reincarnation of Lilian Baylis. She said the barrier on the public road round the theatre had been jammed down and everything was locked.

I was there by about 8.30 and walked through the picket lines. There were no comments and not many people, but evidence of all sorts of minor destructive behaviour, like the removal of the head sets of the telephone switchboard so that it couldn't operate.

Spent all day interviewing, with Derek Mitchell[1], people to take over the job of general administrator from Peter Stevens who is leaving to join the Shubert organisation in New York. Peter should have been with us too, but he was in charge of strike headquarters. I think a man called Michael Elliott was the best of the lot, but I suspect he will never come. There will be, Derek Mitchell guessed, a protracted flirtation with the National, but finally a refusal actually to get into bed—rather a return to the wifely embrace of his present company[2]—they make Kleenex—with whom he has a vast career ahead of him.

Associates' meeting tonight. Harold said he had risen above the daily paper critics, but when *all* the weekend critics had had a go too he began to wonder. Then came a pile of mail from people he respects, and from members of the public, all praising the play. So he concluded that the object was the same for them as for the critics; it depended from which point of view you were looking at it.

Tuesday 21 November
At nine this morning Terry Williams and his fellow gun[3] were in my office. They are the industrial trouble shooters Derek Mitchell has found for me. I always enjoy meeting real experts, and these two wasted no time on formalities, but sat down with their huge notepads and were scribbling and thinking at once. They said that usually when they were called in they could point to some moment when management had done the wrong thing. In their view we had made no mistakes so far. They also thought that unless we could get the government's permission to break the pay code, we were going to have to close—therefore we must close in good order with no possibility of being called hasty or reckless.

I think we now have our strategy right. If there were a third sporadic strike action, we would be justified in suspending, and I would get it through the Board. We are not like British Rail. We don't *have* to

[1] Member of the National Theatre Board from 1977. Knighted 1974.
[2] Kimberly-Clark Ltd.
[3] The Managing Director, and a Senior Consultant, of Productivity and Management Services Ltd.

happen. And I don't want us to happen in circumstances which ruin the plays.

Ugly atmosphere in the theatre today: those who weren't out on strike yesterday being sent to Coventry by those who were. About 150 were out—of a total membership of 400. Many disputes on the stage. Is something a prop, or is it scenery? Can it be blacked?

Wednesday 22 November
I am forty-eight. Lots of people wishing me many happy returns of the day. But I don't want to return to this day. The strain on all of us is beginning to tell. We're bloody tired.

Had a jokey birthday card from the stage staff. It was of Charles Laughton, with whom I'm often compared in looks, dealing with his mutiny on the *Bounty*. I put a little note of thanks on the stage door notice board and asked if the birthday card was official or unofficial. It stayed up less than five minutes.

Meetings this morning with Wilson. He undertakes to discipline his dissidents, but I imagine there will still be another strike next week. If so, we must begin to suspend and lay off. In the meantime we are back round the negotiating table trying to work out new productivity deals.

Thursday 23 November
Lunch with Bernard Levin. He told me many a hair-raising tale. He said there was one fellow, a militant member of a print union, who over the last twelve years must single-handedly have cost his company £9m to £11m in losses. This had broken a manager, who suffered a heart attack. But the militant fellow signed his farewell card, and was there at the leaving party.

Much talk about the imminent closure of *The Times* and *The Sunday Times*. I questioned Bernard about the 5%: did he believe it would hold? He said he had no idea, but clearly the National had to hold it, and so we would soon be going down the same road as *The Times*. I asked him what he thought Uncle Jim was doing in Downing Street. 'Hiding under the table,' said Levin.

Friday 24 November
The works committee have accepted our new proposals, or rather Wilson has. We might now have a few months peace. But as the stage staff are not getting anything substantially more, I'm certain they will begin maverick action again fairly soon.

To *Watership Down* with the children as a promised treat. Very disappointing. The book's wonder was its narrative power. . . . what happens next? . . . you *have* to keep reading. The film isn't like that at all; its been softened out—tasteful Disney—and Disney's strength is that he isn't tasteful. I still believe real rabbits in real countryside, with glove rabbits for the closeups would have been miraculous.

Wednesday 29 November
I have always felt that in public terms the National is existing on the right point of political and artistic balance if it's taken to task by the *Telegraph* for being too left-wing and condemned by *The Guardian* for being too right-wing. So I was really pleased today to see a jokily ironic leader in the *Telegraph* which ends with the sentence: 'Appropriately enough, the National Theatre—a fount of left-wingery—is the worst affected [by the industrial action of those its attitudes appear to support]. Exit fashionable, subsidised playwright pursued by a NATTKE.'

Final interviews this morning for Peter Stevens's successor as general administrator. Elliott came through as first choice.

In the evening, went across the river to the Vaudeville and saw Dave Allen: two and a half hours of stand-up comedy with never a word out of place, never a laugh missed, and an integrity which is quite amazing. He defends children, mocks God, tears apart the Bible, exposes prudery, with a comic ferocity which is much more sympathetic to me than that of Mort Sahl or Lenny Bruce. I felt not only refreshed but inspired. The man's a bloody wonder.

Thursday 30 November
First night of *Strife*. The last line of the play, when the strikers end up with exactly the same offer they started off with, and the union official says, 'That's the fun of it,' struck home. The atmosphere was electric. Afterwards at the party I got caught by some of the stage hands. Much talk. They are very injured that they've been selected by the press as the wild men. And they added: Why don't I talk to them more? Why don't I thank them more? I asked them why they went out on unofficial strike? I should also have told them what they did to the first night of *Betrayal*, but I forgot. What a fool. It was a friendly conversation but it depressed me. They don't want to think logically. They just want more money.

Friday 1 December
The *Strife* notices are good, but they are not the kind to put bottoms on seats, beautifully done though the production is. People may well feel they have enough of strikes in their lives, so who needs them in the theatre?

All morning at the eye hospital. I entered to see about 300 people sitting in dark spectacles or frosted ones all gazing into the unseen like characters from a Samuel Beckett play. I had the feeling I always have when I arrive at a hospital, that I am a sack of potatoes delivered to the wrong kitchen. I was passed from nurse to puzzled nurse, lists were checked, but I finally got to the right place. I sat in a kind of barber's chair for an hour while various drops were popped into my eye in order to make it dilate. I was trying to read Howard Brenton's play during this. A wonderful boffin surrounded by tape recorders, cameras, microscopes, quartz lights, television screens etc, photographed my eye and taped it simultaneously on video, whilst at the same moment another doctor injected various kinds of coloured dye into my bloodstream. They then proudly played my eye back to me. I returned to the theatre at lunchtime, bright ochre yellow in the face and feeling increasingly strange, which I was warned might happen. It wasn't until evening that I felt myself again.

Saturday 2 December
To Cambridge with Jacky, Edward and Lucy. A cold day, you could feel the Fens. But my heart always lightens when I go to this town.

We called on Jenny at Newnham and then went to lunch at the Arts Theatre restaurant where Christopher joined us. Peggy[1] and Dadie Rylands were there and we all met up for coffee. Dadie gave me a short sharp lecture on the perils of *The Oresteia*, saying what a foolish boy I could be unless properly guided. This treatment of me as a pupil highly diverted Christopher.

Dadie is now I suppose in his mid-seventies, and the last surviving member of the Bloomsbury Group. He is going a little deaf, but his vigour and wit are unimpaired, and he looks wonderful. It does not seem forty years ago that I, a boy at school, was seeing him play all the leading parts with the Marlowe Society: Macbeth, Oedipus, Antony. But, to be honest, heroic actor he was not. He was good at nutters. His best performances were Angelo in *Measure* and Ferdinand in *The Duchess of Malfi*. A wonderful teacher, he was a setter of standards, and someone who made us all appreciate the beat and structure of verse. The theatre could do with a little bit of him now.

Monday 4 December
Finished Ayckbourn's new play, *Sisterly Feelings*, standing in a taxi queue. Audible laughter shook me, to the consternation of those around. It was like reading the William books on the train to school as a boy.

Sisterly Feelings is brilliantly, wickedly funny, but the bleakness under-lying so much of Alan's view of life seems in a way to be increasing. The play is about decisions, the moment of choice, whether to change your life or not, and the consequent calamities and happinesses. It has four versions, four variations really, on that theme, but with the first and last scene always the same. At the end of the first, two sisters toss a coin to see which of them shall try to win the love of a very attractive man. A different sequence develops

[1] Ashcroft.

according to whoever wins the toss. Later, whichever lady has won the man has another moment of decision, wondering whether to stay with him or to go back to her original boyfriend.

To an *Observer* dinner at Lincoln's Inn. If the Establishment exists, it was there: Harold Macmillan, Henry Kissinger, Merlyn Rees, Harold Lever, newspaper editors, heads of television. Macmillan is very old now, bent double. Yet the voice and the mind are both sharp and clear. He got up in pain, and looked as if he could hardly talk. But his performance built in gradual crescendo as the adrenalin began to flow. He spoke like John of Gaunt. He warned that this was the most dangerous moment for freedom and democracy since 1936, and in many ways was a repeat of 1936. He pointed out that the Soviet empire was ready to roll over the little barrier of freedom which still surrounded the West, the American government was the weakest this century—and what were we all doing? Quarrelling about five per cents, about norms, about political niceties which might not exist soon because freedom itself would not exist.

It was chilling. It seemed exaggerated, but the old don't care. That's how they make us care.

It was difficult for anyone to follow this frail, manic performance. Kissinger burbled on, associating himself with Macmillan but with a very heavy middle European pessimism: no heroics, no grandeur, and no wit. He said one thing which turned me to ice and showed what a professional politician he is. It went something like this: 'The 1914–18 war was a disaster, not because of the millions of men who were killed, but because after it every nation had lost its integrity and its self-respect.' Not because of the millions of men who were killed?

A wonderful example of Whitehall English: Apparently the DES has secretly intimated next year's grant to the Arts Council in these words: 'The dangers of the figure being less are less than the chance of it being more.'

Wednesday 6 December

A fascinating couple of hours with Howard Brenton. I sounded him out about Bill Gaskill directing *The Romans in Britain*, but he wants me. He said Bill was too much of a writer himself, so with him you had to be in at the beginning of a project. I explained that I couldn't do it until after *The Oresteia*. He accepted that. I kept asking him what his attitude was in the play. Was he against the Romans? Was he pro the IRA? He's like a wonderful kindly saint, being tugged one way as well as the other. He believes, and the play is trying to say, that nations have to have empires in order to realise their potential, but out of that life must come death—the danger in the historical process is to hang on to the past; you must embrace the future. Well, is that enough for a play? He's a Marxist, but he keeps avoiding his own Marxism, keeps on contradicting it. Humanism keeps breaking in. I asked some pertinent questions (I thought) and he went away to rewrite.

Thursday 7 December
Hair cut, shopping. I still feel threatened when I go into a shop. There's a comic contrast between the quivering me at Russell and Bromleys, hoping to buy a new pair of shoes, and me sitting expansively at, for instance, today's BBC management lunch, talking art and politics.

This was the nice Aubrey Singer's rich lunch. He used to be head of BBC2 and is now enthusiastically running Radio. He's a crafty bugger, but a humorous and good man. Sir Frank Figgures, the chairman of the BBC's general advisory council, was there; and a Conservative MP, Julian Critchley, who—make no mistake—was the point of the lunch. He's the Tory party spokesman on broadcasting. Others of us—Maggie Drabble and I for art, Louis Benjamin, head of the Palladium empire, for commercial culture — were there to impress him. The BBC from Reith on has always spent a great deal of time and money lobbying the top people. We ought, I suppose, to do the same at the National.

Apparently the 5% pay code problem is about to hit the BBC, and they see no solution, but believe that by January they may easily be operating on just one channel.

I rather enjoyed myself. I love Broadcasting House now: the solid art deco of the thirties is looking most attractive.

Sunday 10 December
Perfect journey to New York for a week there, a working holiday. Lunch with Tony Harrison. Excellent talk about *The Oresteia*. We'd said it all before—the sexual basis to the whole thing, the need to have no solutions until we'd found solutions—but at least I made contact again with this strange northern martyr. He was returning to London tonight, then to Newcastle and his home, except he wasn't sure whether his wife would let him in. I believe all his agonising lately about whether or not he should go to America have been nothing to do with art, but all to do with a lady. Well, maybe that's a better reason. It usually is.

Tuesday 12 December
New York: I wandered about in the brisk cold window-shopping, and gazing at this city of contrasts: such luxury, such elegance, such beautiful modern buildings; and yet such poverty, such cheap unpleasant tat. In my extremely staid hotel there is a bookstall in the lobby at which a blue-rinsed lady presides over gum, candies, magazines and newspapers. I bought a soft porn magazine and saw an article entitled 'Tossing'. It's not, as one would think, about masturbation, but about sexual gratification in which, irrespective

of your sex, you have sexual pleasure from another person and then kick them out, denigrate them, or disappoint them, as speedily as possible. According to the article this is the new craze that's sweeping America — 'Tossing'. The sheer indifference to the individual and to human feeling is appalling. But that's typical of this town—as is also an extraordinary multi-racial excitement. You walk down a street and see every physical type, every colour, every creed. It's truly a melting-pot.

Peter Mennin and his wife gave a cocktail party tonight at their beautiful apartment on Park Avenue. Imagine the head of the Royal College having a penthouse in Mayfair! All were there: Joe Papp[1], Clive Barnes[2], the Board of the Lincoln Center's Juilliard School, etc, etc; Joan Fontaine was being bright, Moss Hart's widow was being brilliant. The rich, the rich. Why do I always feel such unease? I escaped to Peter Shaffer's and had a superb dinner there: dry crispy duck and exquisite vegetables which he had tenderly prepared. We talked about music, theatre, politics; about nothing really. Home late but happy. Peter says his play about Salieri will be with me by the end of January.

Wednesday 13 December
New York: Spent all day at the Juilliard. Though this is a school, they have a theatre as big as the Lyttelton and another as big as the Cottesloe, as well as a small recital hall and a large-ish one where orchestral concerts can be given. The place is luxurious and handsome, well-appointed and clean. I found it depressing to compare it with our own already run-down, ill-maintained South Bank building. It's partly the difference in money I suppose, and partly the fact that the English apparently no longer care about material surroundings. They even seem to take a positive pleasure in defiling them.

Thursday 14 December
New York: This evening I went to hear Rostropovitch conducting the New York Philharmonic in Tchaikovsky's Manfred Symphony. Christ, he pulls music about as a conductor in a way he wouldn't dream of doing as a soloist.

Friday 15 December
New York: To the Metropolitan Opera House to talk about Verdi's *Macbeth*, which I may be doing there in October 1982[3]. I must study the piece. I have turned it down three times. It was the first opera David Webster asked

---

[1] The American theatre producer and director who runs New York's Public Theatre.
[2] Dance and Drama Critic of the *New York Post* from 1977, previously the same with the *New York Times*.
[3] Hall's wildly controversial production of the opera opened at the Met in November 1982, with Sherrill Milnes as Macbeth and Renata Scotto as Lady Macbeth.

me to direct at Covent Garden in 1958 or 1959; and I have been asked to do it at La Scala and at Hamburg. Why do it at the Met? Well maybe I feel right for it now. I will think. I would sooner, though, do *Simon Boccanegra*, a major Verdi; *Macbeth* is only fitfully fine.

Saturday 16 December
From New York to Boston this morning to see the matinée of Arthur Kopit's *Wings*. Constance Cummings is magnificent; I have never seen her better. And it's a beautiful production by John Madden, a young English director who works here at Yale. I saw Connie afterwards. There seems to be hope she will come and do the play in the Cottesloe, which is what I want.

Returned to New York on the shuttle, had an early supper with Peter Shaffer, and then both of us off to see *Ballroom*, the new Michael Bennett show. It was acutely embarrassing. It's about middle-aged people who have either split from or lost their loved ones, and who go to the Starlight Ballroom in the Bronx to regain their youth and try to find new relationships. There was an unbelievable line. Our heroine, a grandmother who has been shyly working her way back into social life, is nominated as next year's Queen of the Ballroom. She discusses with the postman, with whom she has fallen in love, her chances of winning. The postman tells her she must be confident and she *will* win, for 'Queens are not elected; they are born.' Peter Shaffer looked at me. 'You can say that again,' he said.

Sunday 17 December
New York: Up early to pack. Arthur Kopit at the hotel at 8 am to ride with me to the airport. He was pleased I had liked *Wings* but a bit cagey about it coming to the Cottesloe, a theatre he doesn't know.

A really excellent flight: Concorde at its best. I ate, drank, relaxed, listened to music, and read the first volume of Dirk Bogarde's autobiography[1]—a beautiful remembering of a Sussex childhood, really lovely.

I enjoyed my week away. I had too much to do to be lonely. Yet there was not so much to do that I got exhausted. And I wasn't away *too* long.

Friday 22 December to Tuesday 26 December
It's all merged into one—this little Christmas saturnalia at Wallingford. Too much food, too much drink. Morecambe and Wise less good now they've moved to the commercial channel, and Harold Wilson fairly ghastly as the star guest on their show. Well, George Brown is advertising a cross channel ferry. Politics is now a branch of show business.

[1] Volume one, *A Postillion Struck by Lightning*; volume two, *Snakes and Ladders*.

Pleasures during the holiday: Fred Astaire; the chase sequence in *The French Connection*; a wonderful new cassette by Perlman and Ashkenazy of Beethoven's *Spring* Sonata for Violin and Piano; Muhammad Ali's fury at being caught by *This is Your Life* and the physical respect everyone pays him as the strongest and most potentially dangerous person in the tribe; having no papers; and above all finishing the two volumes of Dirk Bogarde's autobiography—magnificent stuff.

Wednesday 27 December
Back to London. A ghost town. Everyone still on holiday. But it came to life during the day—you could tell by the number of police cordons, sirens, and bomb scares.

Some talk about the NATTKE situation. Peter Stevens is convinced the present peace will last. But I think he's being an optimist. And I can't believe the BBC's settlement just before Christmas will do anything but damage our position. They are now allowed to pay more than 5% because their people are not given parity with the commercial sector. I imagine the danger of blacked out television screens at Christmas was just too big for any political party to contemplate. A closed National Theatre wouldn't bother them too much. I still think there's stormy water ahead.

Friday 29 December
A nice letter from Scofield saying I might have read in the paper he was doing *Othello* with Jonathan Miller, but he wasn't; he still wanted to do it with me.

Christopher came to the office to show me his curriculum vitae. God, I feel for him. It took me back twenty-five years. In my last year at Cambridge I wrote sixty-eight letters by hand to theatres and members of the profession. I received five replies.

Michael Elliott's contract with us arrived back from him, signed. I telephoned to wish him well.

Saturday 30 December
Very upset this morning by the honours list. Why the fuck have they not given Yvonne Mitchell anything? Donald Sinden has a CBE (which seems a bit mean), Bernard Miles is made a Lord, Olivia Newton John gets an MBE, so does Tommy Steele. Yvonne will certainly be dead by Easter of incurable cancer. She was strongly advocated for an honour. Some fool has made a rotten decision.

Michael Rudman has given me this poem by Yeats. It's called *The Fascination of What's Difficult*.

> The fascination of what's difficult
> Has dried the sap out of my veins, and rent

Below: Harrison Birtwistle.
Frank Herrmann

Bottom: Tony Harrison.
Frank Herrmann

Below right: *Oresteia* rehearsals: 'Treat
your mask with respect.'
Nobby Clark

Opposite top left: John Dexter.
Zoë Dominic

Opposite top right: John Schlesinger.
Nobby Clark

Opposite bottom left: Michael Bryant
(left) with Michael Bogdanov at rehearsal
of *The Romans in Britain*.
Laurence Burns

Opposite bottom right: Peter Wood.
Nick Thompson

Below: With Peter Shaffer (left) and John Bury at *Amadeus* rehearsals.
Nobby Clark

Opposite: With Janet Baker, rehearsing Glyndebourne.
Zoë Dominic

The National Theatre. Denys Lasdun's IBM building now stands on the river front between the NT and the London Weekend Television tower

Spontaneous joy and natural content
Out of my heart. There's something ails our colt
That must, as if it had not holy blood
Nor on Olympus leaped from cloud to cloud,
Shiver under the lash, strain, sweat and jolt
As though it dragged road metal. My curse on plays
That have to be set up in fifty ways,
On the day's war with every knave and dolt,
Theatre business, management of men.
I swear before the dawn comes round again
I'll find the stable and pull out the bolt.

Sunday 31 December and Monday 1 January
Very, very cold. On Monday afternoon I tramped for miles through the
Wallingford snow. I also read *The Oresteia* yet again—twice—and thought
and thought and thought. I now feel it might be arbitrary and boring to do it
with all men, partly because I was irritated on Friday by the company's
anxiously progressive questions about whether it was right for men to play
women? Of course it is. But there is an element of doubt in my mind. The
play's political progress from matriarchy through patriarchy to democracy is
something so violently sexual that we've got to make that work. Something
is stirring after this weekend, anyway.

1979

Thursday 4 January
The idea that Granada should televise a number of our productions discussed at a meeting today. There was a lot of goodwill, a lot of determination to make it work. The premise was: we must make good television, not good theatre. David Plowright proposed £10,000 a production. I said I wasn't going to get anything past our Board that was under £25,000, with Granada paying the costs. So he is going back to his people to see if they will come up with that kind of money.

Friday 5 January
I have been asked to take part in a television commercial which Times Newspapers are getting together. Seven or eight public figures are each to say in seven seconds why they miss *The Times*[1]. The fee is £1,000. I have refused. It will leak that we have each been paid a large fee, and seem we have been bought.

Sunday 7 January
Watched an American television film about Maria Callas. There was an extract from that great second act of *Tosca* at Covent Garden in 1963 between her and Tito Gobbi which showed me, when I saw it then, the best operatic acting I have ever witnessed. There were also pictures of her at Covent Garden in the late fifties, fat and plain. She afterwards lost eighty pounds in two years.

The thing that always impressed me about Callas was her total relaxation —the way she drew the music into herself. So it was sad and interesting to see the recording of her singing at her last concert at the Festival Hall. The voice was gone, and now there was tension in the face, the arms, the hands—she knew the voice was not doing the job.

Monday 8 January
Board meeting all afternoon. They are still not grasping the nettle of our financial predicament—that we are seriously and fundamentally under-subsidised because of the enormous expense of the building itself—still

---

[1] *The Times* was on strike from November 1978 to October 1979.

405

muttering about cutting our coat according to our cloth. The cloth now no longer covers our arse.

Betrayal seems to have found its audience and become a success. I told this to Harold, who is hiding in the Grand Hotel, Eastbourne, writing the film script of *The French Lieutenant's Woman*[1]. Antonia and he are on one of their writing jags.

I have been thinking about the cults of 'authentic' music and 'authentic' instruments, for I believe this is growing. I heard on Sunday Mozart's 27th piano concerto on a contemporary fortepiano—a sad little noise, but that's what he heard. But did he? It's not just the instruments that have changed but the sensibilities. We don't play Shakespeare with boys in female roles, and perhaps now I shouldn't play Aeschylus with all men. Nearly every age except ours has cheerfully cannibalised, adapted, rewritten, reorchestrated the masterpieces of the past. It could be a sign of our own lack of confidence that we often defend ourselves with historical accuracy.

Wednesday 10 January
To Scarborough today to see *Sisterly Feelings*. Settled in a comfortable warm hotel room. Then a walk over the snowy, slippery streets to Alan's new theatre, the Stephen Joseph Theatre-in-the-Round. Frosted light bulbs strung between trees lead you down a drive to a school where it is situated. Scarborough may have been deserted but the auditorium was packed for the great local event—a new Alan Ayckbourn play. I loved it. It is a joy to behold such craft, such perception, such absurdity.

Alan is a strange, shy creature: jovial, eyes darting all over the place or palely looking at his boots, never glancing at you if he can avoid it; a warm, careful man. He is very vulnerable, and always afraid of saying something serious and so being thought ridiculous. He pre-empts this by making himself ridiculous before we have the chance. He's always laughing at himself. When he gets to the gates of heaven he will tell the recording angel that he's come to the wrong place before the angel has a chance to open his mouth.

Thursday 11 January
Most of the afternoon on *Fidelio*[2]. I feel now that I am in Beethoven's secret world. Composers' fantasies fascinate me. Tippett's is a slim-hipped American world of gorgeous young men, of mother figures and magicians, everybody bound by a great commitment to the freedom of man, the freedom of speech, and the last movement of Beethoven's Ninth Symphony. Mozart, I know, lived out a fantasy of wanting to marry, to bed, to live with

[1] From the novel by John Fowles.　　[2] Hall's next production at Glyndebourne.

406

the two Weber sisters[1], probably at the same time; they haunt all his works, and reach a powerful sexual climax in *Così fan tutte*. Poor Beethoven, locked in a world of deafness, yearned for a wife to release him from the prison of his own skull, of his own deafness—there you have *Fidelio*.

But he never had a wife. And I doubt whether Mozart went to bed with those two sisters, not both at once anyway.

Friday 12 January
A most interesting thing about Beethoven seems to me the way he represented his age, and changed with his age, like Shakespeare. It's amazing to think how Shakespeare, at the beginning, summed up a country's early national pride; could change from that into the torture of Jacobean disillusionment; and from that into the resolutions of the last plays, which spiritually resolve everything. Beethoven, a child of the Enlightenment, a true revolutionary, excited but later betrayed by Napoleon, was all the while forging a heroic style which moved into ferocious disenchantment and ultimately a neo-baroque peace. Neither men were creatures of fashion, but they were extraordinarily responsive to their own times, and represent its altering face with astonishing accuracy.

Meetings about the union position. We have worked for two months on making productivity deals which the Ministry would uphold, but our latest offer was thrown out this week by the works committee. So now I think we've had it.

Saturday 13 January
The country is gradually coming to a standstill. There are to be two days of rail strikes, timed so that the system will be paralysed for a week but the men will lose only two days pay. We are a society of greed and anarchy: no honour, no responsibility, no pride. I sound like an old reactionary, which I'm not, but what we have now isn't socialism, it's fascism with those who have power injuring those who do not. A paradox: the Labour party, financed by the unions, is advocating restraint and I would think before long a wage freeze; the Conservative party, financed by big business, is advocating what the unions prefer, free collective bargaining. I suppose Callaghan's best hope is to stand up as well as possible to the buffets of the next few weeks and then point to the chaos and say that's what it would be like under Thatcher. The gamble is a high one. If he fails, the country comes to a standstill, and we get a sharp dose of Thatcher.

---

[1] Constanze, whom he had married, and Aloysia, whom he had previously loved.

A big lunch at Luigi's with Jenny and Christopher before they go back to Cambridge. Then I packed them off in a taxi to pick up their things from their Clapham flat. I returned somewhat sadly to Wallingford. But glad of my good relationship with the two of them.

Wednesday 17 January

John Mackendrick, that mad, unhappy, talented writer, whose play *Lavender Blue* we staged not long ago, committed suicide last night. I am appalled. Did its failure contribute to his unhappiness? I can never know, but I don't think so. He was hooked on unhappiness. I never heard him content about anything.

Thursday 18 January

A fair amount of pandemonium, as this was my last full day in the office before going to Toronto to open *Bedroom Farce*[1]. I don't want to go. I am fearful of the mess that's brewing up here with the stage staff.

Friday 19 January

Left London this morning on Concorde in gathering snow. An immigration officer at Toronto looked at my passport and asked, 'Do you really have to kneel down while she touches each shoulder with a sword?'

Marshall Young, the company manager, met me and we drove straight to the Park Plaza Hotel. Marshall is bruised from going round America with Peter O'Toole playing *Present Laughter* and *Uncle Vanya*. 'A naughty boy,' says Marshall. I believe it. But what a genius he was nineteen years ago[2].

I was sad to leave an embattled England about to seize up with strikes and come to a place which is clean, well-organised and efficient. God, the tattiness of England now. We seem to be presiding over the collapse of decency and integrity without the energy even to realise what's happening. News tonight that on Monday the London ambulance drivers go on strike and, for the first time, other emergency services too. It's not that I'm against strikes, but where is the law of contract? The unions abide by nothing, and members don't even have to abide by their unions. Bully boy, strong-arm tactics rule.

Saturday 20 January

Toronto: Our American producers had told me the opening, with the critics, was on Wednesday—and Monday and Tuesday were paid previews. But

---

[1] Hall's NT production was visiting there and Washington before a New York run in the spring.
[2] O'Toole created a big stir in 1960, playing Shylock and Petruchio under Hall's regime at Stratford.

wouldn't you know they're not. Monday is the opening night and the critics come then. There is no time for work. I am furious. Also, all our billing instructions have been ignored, so the town is full of posters without a single actor's name on them.

In the late afternoon Tim[1] and I and the production crew went to look at the theatre, the Royal Alexandra. Built in 1907, it has red plush, good sight-lines, beautiful acoustics. It reminds me of the Marigny in Paris where I used to watch Barrault. The architecture is different, but the atmosphere of opulence, of warmth and of a real place for people to communicate with each other is exciting.

The Royal Alexandra, and half of Toronto it seems, are owned by a strange, self-made potentate called Ed Mirvish[2]: a very rich and happy man. He met us at the theatre, then proudly took us, Citizen Kane-like, round an incredible collection of restaurants, all his. They are graced with hundreds of Tiffany lamps, odds and ends from fairgrounds, turn-of-the-century statues, stained glass windows, etc etc. On one floor they served steaks with mashed potatoes and peas; on another, seafood with mashed potatoes and peas; on another hamburgers with mashed potatoes and peas: six thousand meals a night.

Sunday 21 January
Toronto: Went in heavy snow to see Ingmar Bergman's film *Autumn Sonata*. Ingrid Bergman and Liv Ullman are superb in it. There is one scene I shall always remember. Ullman, the resentful downtrodden daughter dominated by her successful concert pianist mother, plays with deep feeling one of those mournful Chopin preludes. The mother then shows with cool professional arrogance how the piece should be played. As Ullman listens to the music the camera holds a shot on her for what seems minutes, and you see how she loves her mother, hates her, wants to kill her, wants to be mothered by her. It would take a novel to reveal what is shown you in this one scene. I love Bergman's work now: so simple, so few cuts. But finally I grew a little impatient. That Swedish wanking is becoming almost a joke. Everything is always so bleak and black. Spring exists, after all, and it isn't necessarily painful.

Monday 22 January
Toronto: The amount of irritating time-wasting that a director and a designer have to go through getting a play ready doesn't change with reputation, or with any kind of eminence. Salutary I suppose, for the ego. But the company are in such a good state they are easily directable and we made further discoveries in the play. Over the years they have grown, inevitably, to think more and more of it as a series of laughs. But it is also

[1] O'Brien, designer of *Bedroom Farce*.   [2] Who bought the Old Vic in August 1982.

about the fact that if you give yourself to somebody you are vulnerable. So it's safer not to give, but you are then lonely and unhappy.

Our dress rehearsal couldn't begin until 4.15 so we had time for nothing but a straight run through the play, and a two-hour break for the actors, before the first night. The auditorium was full of our producers—this show has almost more of them than actors: an illustration of how difficult it is these days to raise money.

Tuesday 23 January
Toronto: The notices are superb, absolute raves, the kind of enthusiasm which the English for some reason do not permit themselves. It looks as if we shall do capacity business for the month here.

Wednesday 24 January
Toronto: To the art gallery in the afternoon where I saw nothing much except the Henry Moores. But by Christ, they will do. There is one vast, beautifully proportioned white room with dark grey marble flooring. In this is a collection of monumental casts for some of his greatest works. They are all in white plaster, rough textures, but tinged with brown and green, I imagine from the casting processes they have been through. They look like huge ancient primeval bones. But they are sensuous—not like *dry* bones—so there is a feeling of life as well as of death. I have never before been made so completely aware visually that death produces life and life leads to death, the circle of being. I walked into this room, stared in amazement, and burst into tears. Absolute greatness, deep perception into the mysteries of what the bloody hell we are about, can do that to me. It's rare though. Thank God I was alone. Moore is to me one of the masters of all time.

Another wonderful experience. Tonight I went to Massey Hall, the home of the Toronto Symphony Orchestra, because they were playing Tippett's new Symphony No 4, Andrew Davis conducting. I think it's his finest symphony to date: energetic, violent, sensual, but accepting mortality. It linked very well in my heart with this afternoon. Both Tippett and Moore are peculiarly English talents. There's something mystic and lyrical in them.

Thursday 25 January
Limousined to Toronto airport, and then off to New York. Peter Shaffer's *Salieri*, now called *Amadeus*, was waiting for me at the hotel. I think it's potentially one of the most remarkable new plays I have ever read.

Salieri on his deathbed confesses to, and through the play enacts, a consuming hatred of Mozart who is drawn as wilful, immoral, bewilderingly talented. Salieri is the decent man, the classical man of music without dissonance, without chromaticism. Though able to give Mozart opportuni-

410

ties, he witholds them, destroys him, and is himself destroyed by Mozart's genius.

Peter's script is tougher, more precise, and more personal than anything he has done before. In one way, he is writing about how he sees himself and his uncertainties compared to, say, Sam Beckett. The *nature* of talent, of art, comes winging through.

Peter's usual obsession is there: to prove the existence of God and the nature of God. Here He is shown as selfish and uncaring, following His own needs, indifferent to the suffering of man.

The question in *Amadeus* is why does God bestow talent so indiscriminately? I had an absolute child's lust to direct it. John Dexter, though, has given Shaffer his greatest successes, and I want Dexter to stage *Amadeus* at the National. But he doesn't like the place—the new building, I mean. He's spent the last four years saying he will never work there. So it's going to be difficult.

I mustn't lose that play for our theatre whatever happens.

Friday 26 January
New York: Dinner with James Levine—the first time I'd met him—and Dexter[1] to talk about me doing some operas at the Met. Levine was late, so we had half an hour on the Shaffer play. Dexter said again that he hated the National, never felt comfortable in it, couldn't bring in the right actors because it would upset the ones that were there already, didn't like the ones that were, and anyway felt the National would put *Amadeus* in the wrong frame for Peter because everything we did got bad notices. I was determined not to get irritated, and asked him if he thought *Equus* had suffered by being done at the National, if he had earned less money because of directing it there. But he gave way on nothing. He seemed bent on making me enraged.

I really got on with James Levine. I know him to be a wonderful conductor, but I liked his personality, his wit, and his mind. Anyway, the Met definitely want me to do Verdi's *Macbeth* and *Boccanegra*, and possibly *Figaro*, spread over the next five years. It might be possible....

Sunday 28 January
Travelled home on Concorde. The Captain said proudly as we taxied along the tarmac that the journey had taken only three hours twenty-two minutes. We then spent the best part of another hour while they tried to find a set of steps by which we could leave the aeroplane. Good old Britain.

---

[1] Respectively, Music Director and (at the time) Director of Productions at the Metropolitan Opera House, New York.

Peter Hall's Diaries

Monday 29 January
The stage staff continue to go slow, and poor Bill Gaskill's Olivier previews of *A Fair Quarrel*[1] are threatened. I could have sympathy with the stage staff's re-action to our latest offer if they were low paid. But they earn about £140 a week for not too much work.

Board meeting this afternoon. I reported the news of the day—that Granada could let us have £25,000 per play, plus a small percentage of their sales revenue, for televising our productions[2].

Tuesday 30 January
The profession's annual tribal dance—the *Evening Standard*'s drama awards at the Savoy. Callaghan proposed the toast to the drama and made a clever speech. He pledged more support for the arts, but said we had to join him in his fight against inflation, otherwise we would all suffer. He looked well, relaxed, and calm. Considering he'd had a hairy cabinet meeting in the morning, and was off to question time in the afternoon, I admired his cool. Politicians are a different breed. And how about this for memory? I said Hello to him and he said he thought we'd first met in the early sixties; wasn't it when I was at the RSC? Indeed it was, when he was shadow chancellor and I persuaded him to issue a statement deploring the fact that the Tories were not giving *any* subsidy to the RSC. That had great political influence and we began to get a subsidy soon after.

A memorandum against Howard Brenton's *The Romans in Britain* script is in from Harold. It is about as strong as it could be. Actually, I am determined to get that play on. Responses so far are that Gaskill and Morahan like it; and Bryden and Rudman, plus of course Pinter, hate it. David Hare, though he thinks it's a considerable achievement, says it's not at all his view of sex.

Spoke to Shaffer. Dexter won't do *Amadeus* in the summer as we hoped; won't do it in the Lyttelton; might do it in the Olivier; and will anyway only do it when Jocelyn Herbert is free to design it.

Wednesday 31 January
There's a two to one majority against accepting our pay offer, though a third of the NATTKE membership didn't vote. John Wilson said he'd talked to various other general secretaries, taken soundings at the TUC, and everyone thought the militants at the National had no case at all. Pay was fair, even generous.

The gravediggers are on strike now, and in Liverpool there are so many stiffs in the freezer they may have to resort to burying them at sea.

[1] By Middleton and Rowley.
[2] Granada subsequently televised *Bedroom Farce*, *The Double Dealer*, and Maugham's *For Services Rendered*, all in 1980.

412

Thursday 1 February
An interesting hour with Michael Hastings. He's a talented writer and wants a commission to write a promising-sounding play. He went on about us not making a real effort to employ black actors. I asked him why he didn't write some black parts, then we would. He also said we had a strong prejudice against women directors. I asked him if there was a woman he'd like to direct his play. He said there wasn't.

Friday 2 February
At 2 pm we served notices of suspension on fourteen stage staff for refusing to work according to the agreement. Or we tried to, for they wouldn't come in to receive them. I was reminded of the section of dialogue in *No Man's Land*:
Hirst: Refusal can lead to dismissal.
Briggs: You can't dismiss me.
Hirst: Why not?
Briggs: Because I won't go.
The notices were finally sent to the men's homes by recorded delivery and copies left in their pigeon holes at the theatre.

The latest line by this evening was that the management was hell-bent on closing the theatre down, and the workers were going to try and keep it open. Extraordinary, the double-think. I met Brian Kent[1] in the Green Room loo. He's rather right-wing, and an Equity deputy. He said what a pity it was that when we were so near accord on the new NATTKE agreement the management had to take this course. He might just have noticed that the Olivier was shut tonight because of yet another sporadic strike, and that this was entirely the result of unofficial action, of not working according to the rules[2].

Sunday 4 February
Watched *The Voysey Inheritance* on television. What a magnificent play. Granville Barker is one of the masters of the theatre. How *can* it be that he was ignored during his lifetime; respected by intellectuals, but condemned by indifference from everybody else? Meantime the egocentric entertainer, G B Shaw, was attracting all the limelight. No wonder Barker went bitter.

Monday 5 February
Long NATTKE meeting this afternoon. Difficult to get clear reports but it sounded like a mess. Nobody was really interested in talking about our offer.

---

[1] The actor.
[2] The Olivier was also shut next day, Saturday, and as a consequence three previews of *A Fair Quarrel* were lost.

They wanted to debate the suspensions, and passed a resolution which supported the fourteen men in not accepting them[1]. There is though enormous backing within the organisation for the action we are taking, and I am determined to fight this one through. There's no point in working in a theatre which, because performances are continually threatened, treats actors as we have to treat them. It will rapidly become like most forms of industrial life, not capable of anything creative.

Wednesday 7 February

The country grows madder. By the end of the day British Leyland at Longbridge had walked out—all 19,000 of them. Strikes are really the blood sports of the seventies. And being a trade union secretary is one of the strangest sacrificial jobs of our century. What makes a man do it? He must be a masochist, and have an absolute hunger for power.

Thursday 8 February

Good directors' meeting this morning, though we kept skirting round two knotty problems—the opposition to *The Romans In Britain*, and now to *Amadeus*. As far as Shaffer's play is concerned, Bryden says it will be a hit; Rudman regards it as the longest record sleeve note he's ever read; Pinter hasn't pronounced; and Chris Morahan, although he has reservations, certainly thinks it should be done.

First night of *A Fair Quarrel*. It depressed me mightily. A late start, a cold house, few laughs, a long interval, and some of the actors are frankly not good enough. Well, this is the beginning of Bill's group so I must stick with him. But by the end of the evening I thought we had a large-scale flop on our hands.

To supper afterwards in the restaurant where Max Rayne was giving a big party. Yvonne was there, hauntingly beautiful, also Derek, haggard and thin—they are divorced but still friends—and Cordelia[2] looking young and cheerful. I missed Denys Lasdun, who had flu, and Sue Lasdun was rather reserved. I think the tension between the National Theatre Board and the South Bank Board is beginning to polarise our loyalties. The restaurant did its best for Max: lobster, good wines, and well presented.

Friday 9 February

I am in a bad state again: no sleep and indecision about my personal life gnawing away at my guts.

---

[1] The suspensions were subsequently withdrawn when the men agreed to return to normal working.
[2] Yvonne Mitchell, Derek Monsey, and their daughter.

The notices for *A Fair Quarrel* are mostly as I guessed they would be—though Jack Tinker adores it, Michael Billington thinks it's wonderful, so does John Barber. It *is* a marvellously clear production of a very difficult play, but the actors are not up to it. If they weren't Joint Stock actors, fashioned by the Fringe, we would have been murdered. So we have marks, but I would have thought no audiences.

Harold has sent me a letter he's had from David Mercer about *Betrayal*, calling the play a major work, and saying that, like all true originality, it is ahead of people's responses. Mercer also writes: 'It seems to me [that today's] pernicious disease is *too much shallow communication*. It really is true that only writers can redeem language from the depredations of all who exploit it. . . . '

Wednesday 14 February

I had the most appalling news today. There was a message that Cordelia Monsey wanted to speak to me urgently. I could think of only one thing: Yvonne had died. I picked up the phone and Cordelia said, 'You won't believe this—D died last night.' Apparently poor Derek had a sudden heart attack and died on the way to hospital in an ambulance. I went round. Yvonne was sitting looking haggard yet quite beautiful in her bed trying to work on the book she is writing about the Redgraves. She told me Derek suffered a most awful death. For half an hour he had been fighting for life. She had not been able to help him. They'd assured her, she said, that her going would be peaceful, she would have no discomfort, she would slip away, there would be no pain—not like D. All this was spoken with no sentiment, no pathos, no indulgence, no sense of drama. What a courageous and clear-eyed lady.

The funeral is at Golders Green crematorium on Monday. She is determined to go. She is also determined to try to finish the Redgrave book[1], though she says she only has a few weeks of life left now. She is living a tragedy with dignity and there is wonder in that.

Shattered by the events of the day. I was ashamed, in the face of the courage I've seen, that I make such a meal of my own problems.

Thursday 15 February

Off to Dr Janvrin. He gave me the worst wigging yet. He said I was nearly fifty, and simply mustn't continue to work at such pressure; I must discipline myself. But how can I change the habits of a lifetime?

Back to the theatre. A meeting with Bill Bryden and Eileen O'Casey[2]. Oscar Lewenstein has tied up O'Casey's six best plays for his centenary next year—for the princely sum of £200. So we've lost the chance of doing any.

[1] It was never completed.   [2] Sean O'Casey's widow.

Bill is bitterly disappointed. Eileen O'Casey is a dear lady, but this is altogether mad. She might at least have got more money.

Friday 16 February

Had a wonderful lunch with Harry Birtwistle. He talked with mounting enthusiasm about his choral work for *The Oresteia*. Instead of classical rallentandos or accelerandos, this new music compresses or extends its pulse by arithmetical progressions. He says it's very potent and, like a deliberately wrongly cut film, disturbs your expectations all the time.

Oh, I long to do *The Oresteia*. But it's a truly massive work, and I long also to have a reasonable home life. I have I think won the greatest battle of my life getting the National Theatre launched. Now I want to bloody well enjoy it.

Monday 19 February

Went to the first rehearsal, a read-through, of Simon Gray's *Close of Play*. It's mordant, grotesque, and dreadfully funny. I was moved to see Michael Redgrave there, Crocker-Harris to the life[1], sitting listening attentively to the other actors and gazing quizzically over his half glasses. This was one of my favourite actors in his prime. Now he is slow and gentle and ravaged by Parkinson's disease. It's a miracle this part exists to get him back onto the stage—a part with no words, the character in a wheelchair, but the face having to convey infinite feeling.

Harold[2] was in total black, smoking black cigarettes. Peggy[3] read with an invalid knee propped up in the air.

To Golders Green after lunch for Derek's funeral, taking Peggy with us. A bleak, cold day. Some difficulty finding the right chapel. Inside, a bad organ whined. Two young burly firemen, friends of Yvonne's sister Peggy[4], helped Yvonne into the church. They supported her under the elbows, lifting her virtually clear of the ground, and walked very slowly while she moved her feet. Once in the pew, she could not rise for the prayers or the hymns.

All round sat the old tigers of the Beaverbrook Press with whom Derek worked in the fifties and sixties: Charles Wintour, Milton Shulman, Robert Muller, Bernard Levin. Bernard read an extract from Socrates, the piece about death being either a beautiful long sleep without dreams, or the delightful possibility of meeting Homer and asking him questions. It was magnificent, and made people laugh. At the end, we went out through the side door by the altar, and there was the most lovely expanse of white snow

[1] Redgrave played Crocker-Harris, the schoolmaster, in the film version of Rattigan's play *The Browning Version*.
[2] Pinter, the play's director.   [3] Ashcroft.   [4] A Fire Officer in the GLC.

over the gardens. All of us gathered together, looked at the flowers, shivered uneasily, and said hello, everyone with very pious expressions. Shakespeare's gravedigger seemed to be present. One car park attendant said loudly to the other one, 'This is the only place in London where productivity never declines. It's always good business here whatever the weather.'

Priscilla Bowden, the American painter with whom Derek had been living happily in the States for some years, crossed the Atlantic for the funeral but immediately caught a bad virus and was too ill to be there. I've met her once but don't know her. Apparently she'd had a terrible row with Derek just before he returned to London. The next thing she heard was that her man was dead. She had not made it up with him.

Thursday 20 February

Long session with Bill Gaskill this morning. He asked me if he was living in fantasy land to think that he could ever do the big plays with the actors in his group. I said he had to give it time, and then he would find an Ian Holm or a David Warner emerging. So I strongly urged him to do company plays and not big star plays for the next year. Trouble is, there are not many company plays as such. Drama is about protagonists and therefore tends to need stars.

First night of *The Long Voyage Home*: beautifully acted, beautifully directed by Bill Bryden, beautifully set by Hayden Griffin—and written from the gut. Truly O'Neill is the greatest *bad* writer among world-league dramatists. His dialogue is a string of cliches, but what power and authenticity of emotion! It has that awful tension you feel in Dickens or in early films. Don't let it happen, don't let the inevitable tragedy occur, don't—in this evening's case—let the poor Swedish sailor who has saved his wages during two years of voyaging be made drunk, drugged and robbed. But he is.

Wednesday, 21 February

A very lively associates' meeting tonight. There was a long and hectic conversation about the Brenton script. Harry Birtwistle was most touchingly understanding about the experiments of creative people. He also stamped on those who were saying *The Romans in Britain* wasn't a good piece of work because it wasn't really what Howard wanted to write. Harry pointed out that this was a presumptuous remark because he *had* written it.

Friday, Saturday, Sunday, 23, 24, 25 February

I can't really write coherently about these three days; they have been total twilight zones. It's the thought of facing the family with the break-up. I spent the weekend in confusion, not sleeping, worrying about everything, and trying—stupidly—to work out ways of not hurting people.

417

Peter Hall's Diaries

Monday 26 February
Lunch with Bill Gaskill. He's recognised the hard fact that his present group is simply not good enough to do the work he wants to direct, so he must build another, but he believes it will take him until September to do it properly.

Shaffer phoned tonight to tell me he would be talking to various West End theatre managers this week about *Amadeus*. I blew up. Well, when I say I blew up I mean I remonstrated forcibly—I probably never blow up. I said I wasn't getting into any kind of auction situation. He and Dexter must decide either that they want us to do it or that they don't want us to do it.

The submission of our new NATTKE agreement was made this morning with no substantial increase. We await storms.

Tuesday 27 February
This was my big day. After all those years, I started *The Oresteia*. We talked to the actors—Harry Birtwistle, Tony Harrison and I—about methods of work, not about the Greeks or Greek dramas. Then we went through the play. Three main factors—the use of masks, the use of percussion, and the whole text being spoken by the actors to the audience, not to each other— were understood from the start. The cast were reading through simple cardboard masks, some of them wearing glasses on top of their masks.

Rang up Lindsay[1] and asked him if he'd like to direct *Godot*. He wouldn't. 'Has to be done with clowns,' he sighed wistfully, 'and of course we don't breed clowns like that in England, apart from Max Wall.'

Wednesday 28 February
A long alcoholic evening with Trevor. He believes the Barbican Theatre is going to be beautiful—intimate, and a great success as a space: the best modern theatre. So do I. . . .

Thursday 1 March
Oresteia rehearsals. I asked the actors to sit in a tight little circle with this thought. They were the Chorus of old men who had to go out and face a public meeting and explain the sacrifice of Iphigenia. How were they going to tell what happened? Was it treason, or was it necessary? Was it a crime which would brand the family for the rest of time, or was it an heroic act to start an heroic war? So they sat round and pondered and made the Chorus live, each fragment taken by a single voice, qualifying, arguing, contradicting. We then tried to turn that private anxiety into a public demonstration. But it became generalised, full of shit.

[1] Anderson.

418

The centre of the day was taken up with John Dexter and Peter Shaffer. They came for lunch. John fizzed, and talked nineteen to the dozen without ceasing. I sat and listened. Peter looked troubled. When Dexter went to the lavatory, he—Shaffer—gazed out at the Thames and murmured through gritted teeth, 'My dear, during these last few days every one of the hairs in my head has gone white.' Anyway, I don't think we did badly, for after two and half hours the only big worry seemed to be whether or not we could persuade Paul Scofield to play Salieri.

Michael Elliott became general administrator today officially. I am glad, for we need him. There's more and more sporadic trouble with the work-shops and the stage staff. Unofficial action hangs over us all the time. I am sure we are going to have a big strike.

Friday 2 March
An exciting day on *The Oresteia*, working nearly all the time on masks. A lot of the actors were very shaken by the problems. But I feel now that I know absolutely how I want the project to be, to look, to sound. I've rarely been so certain in my life. But I also know, having seen this Everest in very hard contours, that it's going to take me virtually the rest of the year to get up it.

Sunday 4 March
Lay in bed until well after noon feeling like a zombie. I tried to get my mind into some kind of order about my chaotic personal life, and despised myself for not being more forthright and decisive.

Monday 5 March
Another good day on *The Oresteia*. In the afternoon we read thirteen different versions of the Iphigenia chorus. These were by Milton, Swin-burne, Pope, various Romantic poets, Macneice, and the intellectuals of the thirties. All were totally unspeakable and undramatic. It is incredible to believe they came from the same original. They also had no consistent texture; the vocabulary was drawn from a ragbag of 'poetics'. Tony Harri-son's version emerged the clear victor. It is living, dramatic, and actable.

Wednesday 7 March
There was an overtime ban by the stage hands tonight so we were short-crewed for scene changes. They are certain to walk out when we take the hard line. That must come now. The time is right for blood-letting. Our political situation is good: the country is strike-ridden and fed up with it; and we have the Board's backing. If we give way this time we have no hope of averting a major strike in the autumn when we are negotiating the next year's NATTKE agreement.

Strange feeling at *Oresteia* rehearsals working on the mask techniques that Michel Saint-Denis taught me in the early sixties at Stratford. Michel learnt them from Copeau[1], and taught them to George Devine who passed them on to John Blatchley[2] and Bill Gaskill, and Bill in turn passed them on to Peter Gill and Keith Johnstone[3]. Some of my actors are therefore full of the same training that Michel gave me, and it has changed very little. Why? Because it is based on something that works in human terms. Where did Copeau get it from? The mimes of the nineteenth century perhaps. It's believed to go all the way back to the Commedia. No one will ever know. The theatre does not chronicle itself well.

These are the techniques we are following. Treat your mask with respect. Go with it. Do not talk with it on in your own voice. Hide its straps, its elastic. Believe in it. Study it first in your hand, then put it on without looking in the mirror, then look at yourself quickly in the mirror. Become what you see, it is no longer yourself, be the person the image suggests. This person is always in the early stages very childish, anarchic, frequently vulgar. But slowly, as with us over the last week, the masks grow up. Actors begin to search in their new faces for what is wise, what is balanced, sophisticated, intelligent. So some of them are today able to talk fragments of Tony Harrison's text with a certain degree of strength. It has of course been learnt beforehand. So it's not read. If you read in a mask you are a man reading a script, not an actor glancing at his text.

Thursday 8 March
Jenny's first national press notice this morning, a very good one in *The Guardian* for her performance in *The Trojan Women* at Cambridge. Proud father is proud. The achievements of one's children give more pleasure than any achievements of oneself. It's something built into the instincts I suppose.

Saturday 10 March
To Cambridge to see *The Trojan Women*. Christopher in fine form, and Jenny wreathed in rave reviews from the undergraduate press. She was indeed true and very authoritative. There was only one moment of false acting and afterwards she knew where it was without being told. She's developing very well.

---

[1] Jacques Copeau (1878–1949) the French manager and director, one of the leaders of the reaction against realism on stage. In 1931 he handed over direction of his company to Michel Saint-Denis, his nephew and assistant.
[2] The director. A founder member of the theatre school, Drama Centre, where he was an Associate Director 1963–80.
[3] The writer/director. Was an Associate Director at the Royal Court in the sixties. Later took up a drama-teaching post at the University of Calgary in Canada.

Monday 12 March
Peter Shaffer has now instructed Robbie Lantz, his agent, to go and see Dexter today and say (1) the play is to be done at the National, and (2) if Dexter will not do it reasonably soon with Paul Scofield and Simon Callow[1], Shaffer is not prepared to wait until he can. If Dexter then blows up and won't work with Peter, will I direct it? There's never been a play I wanted to direct more, and now I don't think I can do it, what with *The Oresteia* and *Othello*, plus *Betrayal* in America, all upon me.

Wednesday 14 March
News tonight that our stage staff are going on strike this week. We've told Wilson to try and keep them in. I hope to Christ they strike. We can't continue teetering on the precipice.

Thursday 15 March
At *Oresteia* rehearsals we did exercises with the rhythmic nature of Tony Harrison's text. I think more and more that rehearsals should be divided quite clearly between the learning of technique, and the creative process of the actor. We shouldn't confuse the two, and that is what we always do. We part teach, part impose, part encourage from the inner life of the actor. I would like to sort all that out. There's teaching technique, and there's trying to provoke imagination, but separate them, separate them. . . .

Friday 16 March
Today it seems the workshops have caught the stage staff sickness. An assistant stage manager asked the workshops for a tea towel as a prop. They wanted a working drawing with full specifications. It's Alice in Wonderland —or to be more mundane, working to rule!

Wilson wrote to the men this afternoon urging no unofficial action, and we issued letters warning them they would be fired if they walked out. But the stage staff met at 5.30 and then left the building on unofficial strike. The works committee have advised NATTKE members not to cross the picket lines. Three full houses tonight went down the drain. This is the big one.

Robbie Lantz has formally offered the National the rights of *Amadeus*, providing either John Dexter or I direct it before April next year. I am still trying for Dexter.

Saturday 17 March
At the theatre at ten this morning and stayed until after eleven at night. I don't know what I was doing, except that it felt as if I should be there.

[1] As Mozart.

Quite a number of people crossed the picket lines and came to work, the majority in fact. We decided this morning that we would send *For Services Rendered*[1] to Nottingham, where it is due to play next week, without sets, and with whatever props and costumes could be got out of the building. But when a van drove in to pick up as much as could be managed, the pickets threw bricks at the scene-dock doors, swore and cursed, threatened, said they would get the van, get its driver, follow him. Television cameras were everywhere, interviewing the pickets, interviewing Michael Elliott, and shooting sad or angry customers arriving for the performances and having their money returned.

Sunday 18 March

A lot of time thinking how we are going to hold out against this strike. We shall of course be asked to reinstate the men. But I feel we can't: a short term patch-up will do nothing. So a theatrical Grunwick is on the cards, and the misery will continue and get worse. Who though is going to try and make us take the men back? The Arts Council? That would be an unlikely stance for them. The Board? Possibly, but they'd be faced with a huge walk-out of management and directors. I think my position is stronger than I know.

I forgot to report a phone call I had with Hugh Jenkins yesterday. He mused that one had to think of ways of increasing the stage staff's sense of involvement: really they should be asked to take a curtain call at the end of the plays. I nearly split a blood vessel. I have in the past suggested that stage staff take curtain calls. They do not want to, and indicated they would need appearance money if they went in front of the audience.

To Yvonne Mitchell's this afternoon. Poor lady. She has only a few days left, and is pale, emaciated, her eyes huge, and just occasionally when she laughs, as she still does, one sees the old Yvonne. She is now on morphine, so there were long periods when she just lay quiet, in mid-sentence. But there were also times when the conversation flowed animatedly. She wanted to hear all about *The Oresteia* and I talked about the masks. She remembered her days with Michel Saint-Denis at the London Theatre Studio just before the war, and how the young actors always took the old and grotesque masks. . . . never the young or the beautiful. I stayed with her a couple of hours and then came home. I am heartbroken.

Monday 19 March

Very nasty intimidation going on all day. When the milk float crossed the picket line our peaceful pickets took out their screwdrivers and punctured scores of the little cardboard milk containers. The butcher had his burglar

---

[1] By Somerset Maugham. Directed by Michael Rudman. Nottingham was the first date in a long regional tour before the production opened in the Lyttelton in May.

alarm set off and the back door of his van forced open. Yolande Bird, who'd unwisely left her car in the theatre car park with an NT sticker on it, found that it had been completely smashed up, all windows broken, and her belongings taken. Michael Redgrave's taxi was stopped when he came to rehearse *Close of Play* and he, despite having Parkinson's disease and being hardly able to walk, had to hobble the length of the building to the stage door. Peggy Ashcroft's taxi *was* finally let through, but she can't walk at all at the moment because of her invalid knee.

Meanwhile *For Services Rendered* went on at Nottingham with no sets, no costumes, no wigs, and no props. We had decided to try to play *Strife* in the Olivier this-evening but we didn't because Peter Plouviez, general secretary of Equity, came round with John Barron, its president, and warned that this might inflame the situation. We have to take Equity with us. At an associates' meeting tonight Harold, speaking of the impossibility of my position as an Equity member, said: 'Peter Hall is, well, Peter Hall. I mean I've known him for twenty years. And that speaks for itself. He's Peter Hall. But he's not Moses.' The associates passed a resolution backing me however long the dispute takes to settle.

Wednesday 21 March
Our friendly brothers on the picket line have made some twenty allegations of our extravagance to the *Evening News*, all of them very wild. The *News* phoned us to answer these but then didn't wait for our reply, and ran the allegations, without our comments, as today's front page story[1].

I have been thinking that maybe I could try for a while to run the theatre with no stage hands, just using actors, bare stages, and good lights. In which case, the question of the eventual reinstatement of those outside, who are now joined by some of the workshop staff, would no longer apply. We would pay them off, pay redundancies. You can't produce a newspaper without printers, but you can certainly produce theatre without stagehands. Theatre essentially needs actors, a space, and an audience—that's all.

The day started with a talk to Max Rayne and Victor Mishcon. They suggested compromise, but I replied they would have to sack me if that meant reinstating the strikers. Michael Elliott, who is doing magnificently, made the same point. He said that in the next couple of months he would have to start negotiations for the next year's NATTKE agreement, and if there were a fudge-up now they would have to find themselves a new negotiator. Added to this, I have received quite a large number of letters from top staff and actors saying that if the men come back, they will go. Also a NATTKE meeting today of all the members still in the building, by far the

---

[1] The NT's replies to the allegations were printed on an inside page next day. Later, a complaint to the Press Council by the NT was upheld.

majority, made clear that most of them did not want the men outside in again. And we got unanimous support at a Board meeting in the evening for our intention to dismiss them, though there were many anxious faces.

Thursday 22 March

Peter Plouviez is doing us no good in the press. He is saying a solution could be reached, we are being intransigent, and it is foolish to think in this day and age that a trade union would consent to the dismissal of so many people.

I should have left tonight for Washington to see *Bedroom Farce* there before it opens in New York, but it wasn't possible. And all the plays to come on the South Bank, including my *Oresteia*, are, of course, nowhere.

I wonder if I shall survive all this. I mean I wonder whether I shall still be at the National in a year's time. Somehow I doubt it. I don't much care. I want to start again. But you can't go off to the seaside in the middle of a battle.

Today, though, I have had enough. Poor Yvonne is near her end, and I haven't even had time to go and see her.

Saturday 24 March

Concorde to New York and then on to Washington. As I sat waiting for the plane I had a phone message. Yvonne died in the night. I am glad. The torture has gone on long enough. But she has come through it with such courage and such gaiety and such an heroic refusal to make others suffer. What a fine, sad woman. . . .

In Washington I went to talk to the actors before the *Bedroom Farce* matinee. They were delighted to see me, truly delighted, particularly as they knew what it means to come away from London at this moment. All are in fair shape, except jumpy—Broadway next week. Alan[1] and I gave them notes, reassured them. Back to London tomorrow.

Sunday 25 March

Washington: Phoned London before I left to check how they are. Spoke to Michael Elliott. We have now agreed the main ground of our fight. It is to try and outlaw unofficial action which actually affects performances. For it busts our contract with the public. It takes years to build audience loyalty and a few hours to lose it.

Here, incidentally, an unofficial strike is known as wild cat action, and the management have the right to sue the union for allowing it. Would it were so in England. . . .

A good flight home; in bed and asleep by midnight.

---

[1] Ayckbourn.

Monday 26 March

Today John Wilson returned from his executive with, among others, the following quite unacceptable resolutions: that the men should be reinstated, and that we should go to ACAS to conciliate—he wouldn't, he said, go to arbitration, that would mean judgement. . . . Also, NATTKE asked us to call off the performance of *Strife* planned for the Olivier tonight[1]. They said it was gross provocation since we were so near conciliation. Are we? Anyway, we still played, and *Strife* was an extraordinary experience. One chair, no more, because only two propmen were working. But the actors did wonderfully, performing with the clarity of steel. There was total silence, total attention from the audience. Many friends and supporters were there: John Gielgud, Maggie Smith, and all the staff who care. It was a real knock-out evening. I'll never forget it.

Amazed to see an awful series in the *Daily Mail* of Larry revealing all: his tempestuous life with Vivien, how Ralph advised him to give up sex while learning his part because it increased the phosphates in the brain, and more stuff of that kind. Laurie Evans tells me Larry had no idea the articles were happening until he saw them trailed on Saturday. So they both spent the weekend trying to find out who wrote them and, unsuccessfully, to get an injunction. Apparently an American journalist was at a three-handed dinner in Venice when Larry, who was making a film there, got slightly pissed and chatted away about life and death and love. The journalist had a tape recorder hidden in his handbag. So the direct quotations are direct quotations; no question about it. Larry has therefore no redress. What a sickening business.

Tuesday 27 March

Yvonne's funeral. The location the same as for Derek only just over a month ago—the same chapel at Golders Green crematorium, and almost the same people there. Many friends: Michael Redgrave, Peggy Ashcroft, Paul Scofield, Dorothy Tutin, Janet Suzman, Robert Muller, Bernard Levin. The Rabbi read an appreciation of Yvonne written by Derek about her honesty, her generosity. It was good.

Every morning I tell my taxi driver that he will be challenged by the picket at the theatre and not to bother if he doesn't want to cross it. Mostly they say they don't care. This one did. He was stopped and asked for his support as a union member. He said he'd torn up his union card fifteen years ago; he didn't believe in unions. He was then asked as an individual if he would support the men in their fair fight against the corrupt management. Suddenly the taxi driver's cool broke. 'Get out of my way,' he shouted, 'I know

---

[1] As the start of performances in limited decor at low prices in all three auditoriums, which continued fairly regularly from this date until the strike ended.

most of your faces, you're all a lot of fucking mini-cab drivers.' The pickets melted away like fog in the sun, and we proceeded unhindered to the stage door.

It was difficult today to hold the artists together. Peter Wood wondered whether it was worth starting rehearsals of *Undiscovered Country*[1] on Monday week. I told him it was. And Harold worried about *Close of Play*; it should be previewing in the Lyttelton next week but of course it won't[2].

Wednesday 28 March

Peter Shaffer on the phone about *Amadeus*. I said I was putting pressure on Dexter to decide his dates by the end of the week. Shaffer: 'Well, more or less the end of the week. Give him a day or two more if you have to. I would never hold a pistol to John's head. At the moment I would use a pistol to blow his head off. But I wouldn't hold it to his head.'

Friday 30 March

The theatre staggers on. Two performances tonight: a workshop in the Cottesloe made up of extracts from its productions, given on a bare stage but in costume; and *The Double Dealer* in the Lyttelton bizarrely parading itself in the first act set of *For Services Rendered*.

I didn't enjoy what I saw.

Today two of our works committee went to Peter Kaltenreider[3] and accused him of smuggling food in. Well, they're eating their lunches. If they think food should not be smuggled in through unofficial pickets, they should be out there on the picket line, not eating the proceeds.

Spent a brief hour with *The Oresteia* company. They're still very excited by it, and working on, but miss having a director. I've not been able to go to rehearsals since the troubles began. They asked if the production would still be able to start previews at the end of April, as planned. I said it wouldn't, so they wondered how we can pick it up again. Over everybody and everything looms the question of whether the theatre's going to close down entirely for a long period. I have a sad feeling that once more *The Oresteia* will be aborted. . . .

Bedroom Farce is a big hit on Broadway; fantastic notices. I wish I could have been there.

Sunday 1 April

Many phone calls. Talked to Peggy who has to withdraw from rehearsals of *Close of Play*[4] because her knee is now needing an operation. Michael

---

[1] By Arthur Schnitzler, in a version by Tom Stoppard—the next opening in the Olivier.
[2] It eventually opened on 24 May.   [3] Head of NT Catering 1976–80.
[4] Her part, Daisy, was taken over by Annie Leon.

426

Hallifax reported from America that *Bedroom Farce* is expected to run for a couple of years—it will if the cast replacements we have to make are good[1]. When can I go? When indeed. . . ?

Monday 2 April
During today's finance and general purposes committee meeting Michael Elliott took them through our new proposal to NATTKE. They agreed it. An important part in effect outlaws unofficial action which interferes with performances. So by Christ, if we could get it accepted by the union we would have a workable basis for the future. But in the evening NATTKE turned down every point except the easy ones. Yet the strike is still not official.

Tuesday 3 April
Another fourteen hours of boxing with problems, trying to figure things out. What will the union do now? And more to the point, what will we do now?

Wednesday 4 April
Chris Morahan at a meeting today proposed we should close. He said that to ask people to begin rehearsing new work in this atmosphere was unrealistic. Privately I sympathise with him, but I couldn't admit it. Unless we persevere, plan ahead, and start new work, this theatre will die much more quickly than a band of strikers can kill it. We have to go on.

Michael Elliott had a question-and-answer session with everybody this evening. The mood was sober and depressed. But he managed superbly: very laid-back, very cool. There were remarks from those there about 'malaise' in the theatre. Well, there's certainly something like that among the stage staff and to an extent in the workshops, but I've never known a happier company of actors, a better group of electrics or sound technicians. Michael was accused of not trusting the officers of the union. 'That is what it amounts to,' he answered. Well, it is. What evidence have we got of discipline by them in the past?

A bad associates' meeting tonight, which we shouldn't have had: great solidarity, but we were all tired, and too much was drunk. Still, resolutions were passed, most of them sensible, and we are going to continue to keep the theatre open despite the bare or wrong settings in which we stage the plays.

Then we got into the question of the new work we're about to start, and everyone began to be the romantic artist again. Surely we'd have to have proper sets for that? Surely we could get them in? Surely we could ask people to cross demarcation lines?

But we have always played by the rule book. The men have always torn up the book. Once we tear up the book too, we are nowhere.

[1] American Equity allowed the NT cast to play only for twelve weeks.

Peter Hall's Diaries

Thursday 5 April
Today I nudged Victor Mishcon into making a most elegant solution to the deadlock we are in. But it was his solution, not mine. He proposed that we dismissed all the men outside but offered the union two alternative courses, either of which they could choose to take *after* the dismissal. One was that the dispute went to arbitration and we all undertook to abide by the findings. The other was that the men could be reinstated if they signed an undertaking saying they realised unofficial action was a breach of contract. A letter was then drafted making these points, and I ended the day at midnight by pushing it through the letterbox at the Kennington Road headquarters of NATTKE. A bloody good day's work. I think we're on the move.

Friday 6 April
At midday the whole work-force inside the theatre, including all Equity and NATTKE members, met in the Lyttelton auditorium. Michael Elliott read them out the letter, spelt out the alternatives. I told them what our future programme was to be and thanked them for going on under such difficulties. The news that everybody who was outside was to be dismissed was received in total silence. My heart was in my mouth. I thought that all the NATTKE membership might walk out and be on official strike within minutes. They didn't.

We heard later that after the union had received our letter, Len Murray told Wilson that if he couldn't get an official strike—and Wilson has admitted that he can't—he had to settle.

Marius Goring phoned me wondering if there was anything he could do to help within Equity. I'm amazed to find myself supported by the right. I prefer to think I'm an old-fashioned nineteenth-century radical, believing in democracy and in law, principles which, sure as eggs is eggs, are forgotten by the heavies and left-wing extremists outside our theatre who are blowing whistles, making catcalls, and deriding the audience as they try to come in.

The press has reported our move quite accurately but I think with some amazement. Anyone dismissing workers these days is asking for trouble. Well, we can't have more trouble than we've got.

Saturday 7 April
Late last night I saw a television programme on Sir Adrian Boult who is about to celebrate his ninetieth birthday. To watch him conduct is a joy: such precision, elegance and delicacy, a real aristocrat of music. I can't believe he's ninety. He looks the same as he did when I was a schoolboy. I remember during the war, when I was about fourteen, chasing him into the Cambridge Guildhall because I wanted his autograph. He was, I suspect, already late for the concert he was conducting. How irritated he must have been.

Sunday 8 April
Stephen Fay has told John Goodwin that what we're doing is a bloody triumph in the circumstances of industrial relations in this country at the moment. I wish there were a *Sunday Times* for him to write it in. . . .

Monday 9 April
The afternoon was enlivened by Gawn Grainger and Lynn Farleigh[1]. They told me they'd had a meeting with the strikers who said they trusted me and Bill Bundy[2] and why couldn't they, the strikers, have a talk with us to work something out? I had to explain that things had gone far beyond that. Oh God, the fair-minded liberal! There are Gawn and Lynn, listening earnestly to strikers who have torn up the rule book, wrecked our work, vandalised our property, and spread lies to the *Evening News*.

Meanwhile, British Leyland is juddering to a halt, a big engineering works at Peterborough is entirely barricaded out by pickets, airports are going to be disrupted by customs men, and BBC television is threatened with an unofficial blackout.

A drink tonight with Stephen Fay. He said that last Tuesday night agreement was reached at *The Times* on the new technology, then on Wednesday morning the unions welshed on it. If he had a paper to write in he would be reporting the election, going round the country with Margaret Thatcher. I asked him who will win. He said let's conduct a poll in this office. He asked Michael Elliott how he would vote. Elliott said that for the first time in his life he was going to vote Tory. He could not support a party that was allowing the corruption of trade unionism and the corruption of picketing. He also thought that as a management Labour couldn't manage anything. Stephen said he was going to vote Tory too, for the first time, because he felt we needed a corrective. I said I feared I would do the same. At this point Johnny Goodwin went into shock. He couldn't believe us. He said he wouldn't be able to vote because he'd be abroad—at which we chorused our derision—but he still felt Labour was the party of social justice. But it's not. It's now the party of sectional interest; the party that protects pressure groups and bully boys. Anyway, I shall be voting Tory. That is, if I can bring myself to do it when I actually go to the poll.

Tuesday 10 April
We are into the fourth week in which everything has been to do with this stupid and appalling dispute. If you reckon that that is what is happening all over the country, is it any wonder we are unproductive as a nation?

[1] Members of the NT company.
[2] As NT Technical Administrator 1977–80, he was in charge of stage staff. Is an NT Associate.

Board meeting with Victor in the chair. They on the whole were more hawkish than Michael and I, certainly more than Victor.

Thursday 12 April

Today was dominated by a poll of all the NATTKE staff whether or not to have a poll for an official strike. 82 voted for it, 153 against, which even included some of the men outside. The meeting was apparently fairly orderly. Wilson told Michael Elliott that this vote was exactly what he wanted. It would give him further power with his national executive. Well, I suppose it might. But I think more and more we are talking about the virility of the trade union movement. You don't in our society dismiss men. That executive will go on until it drops insisting the dismissals be lifted and the men reinstated; and is in effect—at least so far—siding with the law-breaking minority outside against a majority inside who have not broken the NATTKE agreement.

Don't know when I've felt so tired. I'd like to do some creative work for a change.

Sunday 15 April

Beautiful spring day, hot sun, and I was able to sit outside and think. Bernard Levin rang for a long chat. *The Times* and *Sunday Times* are going to close down completely, he fears. So, I still believe, might the National Theatre.

Gielgud's seventy-fifth birthday, and we talked. . . .

Monday 16 April

Sunny weather, and the strikers were playing frisbee in the road. Their huts, which could be said to be trespassing on our land, have now become a positive holiday camp. At the moment NATTKE's national executive is having its Easter break while the National Theatre loses a fortune. Only in England could an issue as serious as this be halted by a holiday.

Tuesday 17 April

I have been restless and tense all day. My heart is no longer in this shit heap. I don't see any hope of making theatre, which is precious, delicate, personal, and demands at least the integrity of doing your best, in an industrial battlefield like ours.

Wednesday 18 April

Bill Bundy isn't in today. Nobody seems to know whether it's because he thinks we are being too tough, or not tough enough. Poor Bill. He gets in a terrible state when choices have to be made; and he hates hurting people. He really cares for those men outside, and he's right to care for some of them.

A brief associates' meeting, bringing everybody up to date. The directors were very unhelpful about scenic compromise. It's always the same. An artist will accept no discipline except his own. He will not do something for long-term or communal reasons. Well, he will—but only if there is a genuine aesthetic passion to do it that way.

Board meeting. Max Rayne back from abroad.

Thursday 19 April

Problems of the day? Well, Bill Bundy came back. He looked really shaken. In some way, I believe, he thinks he is responsible for the strike. He isn't. He's been cracked wide open by these men.

Ralph[1] told me at lunch today that he drove in the other evening in his car, was stopped by a picket, and wound down his window expecting a comment or leaflet. 'Do you know this is an official picket,' said the man. 'Yes I do,' said Ralph in a totally unprovocative way. 'You silly old fucker,' observed the picket. This to a great actor who has provided more jobs for NATTKE members over the years than I have had hot dinners.

Friday 20 April

Negotiations at ACAS go on. It's a curious institution. One party is in one room, the other in another, and a mediator runs between them trying to get each to a point when they are prepared to face each other across a table.

Tonight we go into our sixth week of dispute. And tonight I should have been dress-rehearsing *The Oresteia*. Silly isn't it?

Sunday 22 April

Wet, damp, spring weather, but my favourite moment at Wallingford: daffodils; sharp bright green leaves; sparkling water. Every year I love it, and every year recently I have believed it is my last here. Well, this is.

One newspaper today gives the Conservatives a 20% lead, and another a 6% lead. I think people deliberately tell lies now to anyone who is researching anything.

Monday 23 April

I was able to look at progress on *The Oresteia* in my absence. The cast have made such strides, and can now speak the text with enormously sensual clarity in full mask. For the actors to have reached that, with no end result definitely in sight, is a most extraordinary tribute to their dedication. This huge work could be the most exciting thing I've ever been associated with. Or has it now gone forever? No, of course it hasn't. It's just paused.

[1] Richardson.

Tuesday 24 April

The sad winding-up of *The Oresteia* group. They did some more work for me this morning. But by the time I'd got back to them from a meeting they were playing cricket in the rehearsal room, a kind of release.

Marius Goring came into my office this evening looking like a character from some strange German film of the twenties. He had a glass of gin in one hand, a cigar clamped in his mouth, and wore a rather overlong black trench coat. He wanted me to see the text of a resolution that the Equity council had just passed. It said the NATTKE executive had had a very good proposal[1] from the National Theatre management and should accept it. Even more to the point, it called on Len Murray and the TUC to investigate. All this is extremely good.

Just now it looks as if we hold all the cards in our hands, so I'm off to New York in the morning to look after the recasting of *Bedroom Farce*. Whether I should go or not, I don't know. I just don't want that play to run down.

Wednesday 25 April

Off early to the airport. I saw David Frost entering the Concorde lounge as I peered through the potted palms, so I hid. I like David, and like talking to him, but the thought of jabbering all the way across the Atlantic was not something I could face today. I was met on arrival in New York and swept straight to the Algonquin Hotel. All this super organisation was rather spoilt by the fact that my 'suite' wasn't yet vacated. So I could do nothing except register, check my bag, and then—feeling like a visitor from another world—go off to the theatre. Business for *Bedroom Farce* is good but not spectacular. It hasn't taken off as the notices would have indicated. Why? Nobody knows. A very English comedy? No stars? Seats too expensive? It's raining? Anyway, they think it will build.

Thursday 26 April

New York: Auditions throughout the day to find American replacements for the present NT cast. I am struck by the difference to Britain. American actors seem so eager to please, desperate to work; they don't perhaps have the same sense of security as English actors. But it was a good day. By the end I thought we had a cast that was possibly very exciting. In the evening I went to see the play. The company acted it beautifully: plenty of laughs, but thankfully the seriousness was intact. I talked to them all afterwards. They were utterly miserable, as usual. I've never known a more paranoid group. Perhaps it's because to play Ayckbourn properly you have to dig deep, be

---

[1] The 5 April offer of re-engagement under certain terms, including an undertaking to accept that unofficial action was a breach of contract.

serious, and then get laughed at. It wounds the personality. Anyway, I was proud of them, even though they don't seem to be very proud of themselves.

Friday 27 April
New York: Gave the *Bedroom Farce* company lunch. Afterwards I strolled down Fifth Avenue to buy some shirts, thought of this and that, and for the first time in weeks felt a few moments of freedom. But as soon as I was back at the Algonquin, bearing my shopping bags, the air was thick with telephone calls from London. Wilson addressed our branch this afternoon. He asked everybody if there was no compassion for the men outside, and got told there wasn't, in no uncertain terms.

Up early tomorrow to catch the plane home.

Sunday 29 April
Bad news from Glyndebourne about the rehearsals of *Ulisse*[1]. The main machine, the great ski lift which is rigged up towards the audience, and which allows the sun chariot of the eagle and all the actual dynamic of the flying to happen, was over-winched, slowly buckled up, and collapsed on the stage. It is irreparable. So that's that. They will now be reduced to a production where the performers just go up and down vertically.

Monday 30 April
A much-vaunted 10,000-strong mass picket of the theatre promised for today was last night estimated as likely to be only 1,000, and in the event this morning turned out to be 40 people standing in the road. The pickets' huts too have gone. Yesterday the residents were slowly but methodically dismantling their shanty town, burning it up, and clearing the rubbish off the pavements. Today even the caravanette, bought with £200 supplied by NATTKE, was moved off our property. All this was no doubt because of restraint orders we got against the six ringleaders.

As I came in to the stage door I was handed another lovely leaflet: 'The management of the National, in spite of the radical content of some of the plays they present, is one of the most right-wing administrations in the industry. They must be defeated.'

We were told at the Board meeting this afternoon that the Arts Council was running out of money and therefore couldn't pay us the part of our grant which is due. That's because the DES cannot pay the Arts Council. It normally does this through a civil service computer in Darlington. But civil service computer staffs are on strike and no computerised cheques are being paid. When the Arts Council suggested to the DES that handwritten

---

[1] Hall's 1972 production of *Il Ritorno d'Ulisse in Patria*, which was being revived by Patrick Libby (associate Dave Heather).

433

cheques would be quite acceptable, they were told that that would be provocative, tantamount to strike-breaking. So we run out of money in about a week, and will have to raise a huge overdraft and send the bill for the interest to the Arts Council. Which they won't pay.

Not very good news from Glyndebourne. Elisabeth Söderström doesn't want to rehearse *Fidelio*[1] any more until I arrive. Well, I'm afraid she'll have to wait until things are more settled on the South Bank.

Tuesday 1 May

First night of *For Services Rendered*, in the Lyttelton. The actors played it well and I liked the evening: a beautifully paced production by Michael Rudman. I was embarrassed to see the Christies at the performance since I have now missed so many *Fidelio* rehearsals at Glyndebourne. Beethoven forgive me. I shall be sitting on the train on my way there early tomorrow swotting up the score like a schoolboy who hasn't done his prep. Well I *have* done it, but I haven't revised.

Still, tonight *For Services Rendered* had proper settings, so we are building up our theatre again. It's a beginning.

Wednesday 2 May

Off on the familiar train to Glyndebourne. I tried to get a little of my head filled with *Fidelio* on the journey, but it wasn't much good.

Söderström inventive, and anxious to find realistic business to take away from being an opera singer standing up there singing. The cast on their toes; props prepared; set finished—ideal working conditions. What a tragedy I can't enjoy it or do it better, for by five I was on the train again back to London.

Election tomorrow. I fear for the Tories getting in because it could make the way easier for Tony Benn in five years time; but I also fear if they don't, because our present decline into a land without opportunity will continue. So on balance, I am voting Tory. Just. But that's tomorrow....

Thursday 3 May

It wasn't at all difficult this morning to vote Tory. In fact it positively felt good: wanting change.... and we have to have change.

I arrived back at the theatre from Glyndebourne this evening and felt pounced on. I sensed from everybody that I wasn't giving leadership, being clear, reconstructing a shattered institution. So unless things tidy up I think I shall have to resign from *Fidelio*.

---

[1] Hall was due to be rehearsing the production then, with Söderström as Leonore/Fidelio.

The election was fascinating television tonight as always. I shall not forget Thorpe's tragic, clown's face as it was announced he'd lost his seat. He should never have stood: no man could survive those allegations.

Friday 4 May
Thatcher's in with a majority of over forty: a resounding victory, but a vote by the prosperous south against Labour rather than a positive vote for the Tories.

Saturday 5 May
Once more on the early train to Glyndebourne. A sluggish rehearsal. All the time I had the feeling that while Beethoven learnt the complexities of ensemble directly from Mozart, and is often supremely successful at having three or four characters uttering contradictory emotions at the same time, in exactly the same way as Mozart, he lacks his divine sense of economy. Beethoven always goes on just a little too long for the drama.

Sunday 6 May
The Sunday papers are full of portraits, character sketches, the childhood and the early career of Margaret Thatcher. They are not so harsh about her now. The press, for a while at least, like to be on the winning side.

No references to the NT strike, thank God. Perhaps it will now peter away into a non-event so that audiences start realising that they can come to our theatre once more.

Down to Glyndebourne early yet again. I was on edge all day, ready to see Moran Caplat after rehearsal to say I had to resign from *Fidelio*. Long agonising conversation. He begged me to go on, just to do a bit. Couldn't I come on Wednesday? Couldn't I come next weekend? And as usual, because of my enormous capacity for feeling guilty, he talked me round. But it will be a lousy piece of work; conventional. I'm too worried about things on the South Bank. Tomorrow at Glyndebourne it's the promised day's rehearsal with Frederica von Stade[1] on the revival of *Ulisse*. I could do without that. But with the set a buckled mass of metal, and so many of the effects gone for nothing, it's important to keep her happy. Well, I'm a bloody fool. . . .

Monday 7 May
At the end of an interview with Nicholas de Jongh printed in *The Guardian*, Norman St John Stevas, the new Minister for the Arts, is quoted as saying he is going to be in touch with the Board of the National Theatre to sort out our dispute. That's bad news. There is no dispute. It's over. We want to get on

[1] Who played Penelope.

now and build up the depleted stage staff with good men. Sorting out the dispute could mean bringing the strikers back.

Tuesday 8 May

News from New York: *Bedroom Farce* has five TONY nominations—for the best play, the best director, and for the performances of Michael Gough, Joan Hickson, and Susan Littler—very nice indeed, but where is recognition for Stephen Moore's superb performance[1]?

Dinner at Ray Leppard's who has hired a beautiful house in some marshes not too far from Glyndebourne. He still had time in the middle of a hectic rehearsal schedule to whip up home-made pâté, delicious chocolate sweets, and delicate turkey casseroles. There was also wonderful wine. He seems very happy, and gets nicer and nicer. Frederica von Stade, her husband, and the Christies were there. Frederica seems quite unspoilt; just as modest and dedicated as ever. She is much like Janet Baker. They both have a highly developed sense of their own goofiness—one Yorkshire, one American. But they both know very well the transformation that comes over them when they sing.

Wednesday 9 May

Woke at Glyndebourne in relative luxury and peace this morning. Cold, clear light, dawn chorus at full volume, breakfast served in bed in feudal style. Almost equally feudal though is the chilliness of the guest room and the antique one bar electric fire, circa 1938. The greatest joy is the enormous, enormous bath. It must be nearly seven feet long. I can actually stretch out in it.

I took a short walk round the gardens. The daffodils are wilting now, but a wonderful hard, bright green everywhere. It is that moment of spring which is quite ferocious and insistent with life.

A frustrating day of rehearsal because Anton de Ridder, the Florestan, was due back from Germany and didn't arrive. Blood pressure high all round.

Dozed a little on the train back to London. There, I talked to Bill Gaskill. He gradually wants to drift away, but direct the occasional play for us. He doesn't believe he can run a company in the Olivier and get the big audience attendances we require; his tastes are too eclectic. I asked him what he could do to help us out whilst we are recovering our battered programme. He said Brecht's *The Mother*. I knew he would. Well, you can't say he doesn't have integrity—if you believe, as he obviously does and I don't, that integrity is doing what you want for yourself. But it was still an amiable meeting.

---

[1] Who played respectively Ernest, Delia, Kate, and Trevor.

Tonight a dozen or so people demonstrated at the performance of *The Double Dealer*. They climbed on stage, and accused everyone there of being scabs. The actors were furious. So were the audience, the most furious among them being Simon Gray's wife Beryl. Simon made a reasonable point in answer to one of the demonstrators and was told by him to shut up and sit down. Simon's wife then hit the man—not a gentle slap, a full-armed belter which must have produced stars. I was terrified he was going to hit her back. Finally the police arrived, the performance continued, and the visitors went. But unfortunately they had achieved their aim, which was clearly to get publicity, and this had been planned well in advance. There was a lady there scribbling eagerly who just happened to be from *The Guardian*. I challenged her and she said she was coming to the play anyway—a likely story. And less than two minutes after the demonstration started ITN News were on the phone.

Thursday 10 May

Last night's disruption is big news. The whole of the *Evening News* front page is about it. We had just begun to build up audiences once more, just begun to get back to normal, now we will appear to the public to be in disarray again. I asked Ralph if he had ever known anything like our last two months in all his years in the theatre. 'Not really,' he said with that chuckle which sounds as if something wet has been thrown into a hot frying pan.

I had a letter from the pickets saying they disassociated themselves from the interruption last night. And Wilson has apparently confirmed to Plouviez that the dispute is all over[1]. I suppose the pickets will now fade into the distance. Well, we at least I think have demonstrated that unofficial strike action which halts performances is not on, either at the National or in any other theatre.

Friday 11 May

News came that quite a number of the seventy dismissed men wanted forms in order to re-apply for their jobs, so they were sent them. By mid-evening several forms were back. Perhaps the dismissed militants are hoping they can unite with the moderates inside the building in hatred of NATTKE—for the union has not of course given them strike pay; and—because, amazingly enough, it made the picket official but not the strike—they don't get social security payments either. This appalled me. But we must now be very careful about whom we re-employ.

---

[1] The number of performances lost by the strike was not significant because, as often as possible, the plays were staged in limited decor and at reduced prices. The loss of box office revenue due to the strike was estimated at about £250,000.

I appealed to Gaskill tonight to do a popular classic to help us out. All he will do is *The Mother*. For several hours I really didn't like him, though I am very fond of him. But he is now like a stubborn child. Why won't he help?

Sunday 13 May

I sat in the sun and read *The Mother* just to make sure I was being fair to Bill Gaskill. It is very sentimental, very romantic. It would have had honesty in the twenties as a piece of fervent propaganda, much like the Eisenstein films, but it won't do now. The workers in it are totally right, totally pure, totally Marxist. The bosses—whom you never see—are totally corrupt. I suppose Bill wants to direct it immediately after the strike as a sort of perverse way of reapplying left-wing values. If I thought the play was better, I might find that an interesting gesture, but it's naive in the extreme. It won't do.

Thursday 17 May

Glyndebourne: Piano dress rehearsal of *Fidelio* all day. The production doesn't commit any blunders, but has hardly any interpretive strength. It's agony, working on something you worship, without being able to give the best of yourself to it, however insignificant that may be. We finished the last scene in a riot of white costumes and flags, and I rushed for the six o'clock train back to London and the theatre where everything seems unnaturally quiet outside now the pickets have gone. This strike though will take months to get over. For example, *The Double Dealer*, from playing to full houses, is now playing to a few hundred people. Also, we are all 'post-war' and lack energy.

Friday 18 May

Glyndebourne: Bernard[1] had the first hour and a half of rehearsal with the orchestra alone. I listened with pleasure, and remembered his remark that getting the LPO into the pit at Glyndebourne was like squashing an elephant into a canary cage. It squashed quite well this morning, and this elephant can sing. We spent the rest of the day on the first act and then ran it completely. There was the usual reluctance to wear hats by one and all but we managed it, and Elisabeth worried me slightly by a kind of radiant sentimentality which began to creep over her performance. But I will crack that.

Lunch with David Dimbleby about a television programme I am to do with him in the summer. I reminisced about a telly series I took part in in the late fifties or early sixties called 'The Young Lions'. It included John Bloom and several others who disappeared peremptorily from the scene. Well, I am

---

[1] Haitink.

still here, though I wonder why at times. . . , Dimbleby is pleasant, talks as little as possible, listens, watches, gets an impression.

Sunday 20 May
Last night Moran almost imperceptibly but quite definitely put into my mind the thought that I might like to join the Glyndebourne team officially, be more than a regularly visiting director, when he retires in two or three years. Would I like that, I wonder: something small and of high standard, which could give me freedom as well? I don't know. All I do know is that things at the National must change, for me anyway.

Monday 21 May
The front page of the *Telegraph* this morning has a story about the permanent civil servants who work for the Arts Minister—naming particularly Walter Ulrich. There are statements that he has alienated the arts world by his arrogance. He certainly alienated me by his attempts to make me into a villain for moving in to the unfinished National Theatre and starting work in order to short cut the building delays. He believes, to my mind, that artists have their priorities wrong; they not tidy, and they are expensive. I think, though, Ulrich is misjudged. He was just allowed too much rope.

The Arts Council enquiry on the National Theatre, which we called for[1], is at last ready. It's excellent and was clearly politically justified. It says that we are under-financed, that the deficit that relates to the moving-in costs should be wiped out, brushes aside criticisms of our policy, and reminds the South Bank Board that the building is still not completed to specification.

A long talk with Michael Elliott. He is optimistic about the future. He believes we can now get on and work at full stretch, better funding will come, and labour relations will improve. I am not sure.

Tuesday 22 May
Glyndebourne: Had a talk with Elisabeth Söderström and she cried and cried. All her training has been to disguise the fact that on stage she is, in effect, addressing the audience. Much of what I do in opera is concerned with the open demonstration in performance that you *are* doing just that. Ensembles and arias need a frank 'telling' to the audience to have emotional force. That's been the tussle from day one and now it's coming home to roost. I said to her that if she played Fidelio as she has been, we would have merely a glamorous conventional figure. Why not be bold? That's what caused the tears. It also caused a very good first act. Moran thought it excellent and observed dryly that the best fucks are always after a good cry.

[1] See diary entry 27 February 1978.

Peter Hall's Diaries

Thursday 24 May
Rang Peter Shaffer, who was lying prostrate in his New York apartment, having written a letter to John Dexter telling him their working relationship was at an end. I think it is only a tiff.

Friday 25 May
Michael Elliott had a company meeting this morning to bring everybody up to date on the end of the strike. Andrew Cruickshank slightly upstaged him at the end. He said with ringing authority that all National Theatres had to have their strikes, their revolutions, in order to reach maturity.

Spoke to Robbie Lantz, who told me that Dexter has returned Shaffer's letter unopened, attaching a note to it saying they shouldn't be communicating by letter at this stage of their relationship.

Sunday 27 May
A Glyndebourne Sunday. Walked by the sea at Newhaven, the world full of anglers catching tiny fish and staring at the water.

The first night of *Fidelio*. Riotous reception, ecstatic. What did I think? Well, I think I have done it right, but not fully. It's on the way to something. I would like to do it again, at a time when I could enjoy it and be less jaundiced.

Monday 28 May
Nothing much happened today. I lay in bed, flattened: dizzy regularly, and very depressed—reaction I expect to the end of two long battles, the strike and *Fidelio*. Now I must begin again.

Wednesday 30 May
Glyndebourne: The dress rehearsal of *Ulisse*. It's all much better, much smoother. But there's an odd atmosphere here at the moment. I don't feel at ease—because of my absenteeism or because of my paranoia?—and I don't think they feel at ease with me.

Spent forty-five minutes late at night in a freezing phone box talking to John Dexter. He declared he wasn't going to give up *Amadeus* whatever Shaffer said. He had spent a lot of time on it, and made a lot of suggestions, and what was all this now about not being able to wait until he was free to do it. I said I could not any more be drawn into the argument; it was Peter's play, and he must decide what he wanted. So the farce goes on. Shaffer had now made things worse by putting it all on not being able to wait. If he would say to Dexter that he is definitely directing it, or definitely not directing it, and that is the author's final word, then we could proceed. I am sick of the whole thing. I am beginning to wish the play never came near us.

440

Thursday 31 May
David Hare to see me full of cheer. He says he and Howard Brenton had now decided that those epic plays of many self-contained short scenes that are so exciting to write and to act, actually burn at a lower level for the audience than plays that follow through. He also says he finds the theatre a clumsy form at the moment, all that getting characters in and out of doors and explaining why they are there. I told him we didn't have to explain anything. 'But there must be a story,' he cried. I agree.

A long and distressing morning with Bill Gaskill. He won't even remain an associate. So he has cost us a lot of time, a lot of money, and a lot of aggro. Well, he's wilful. . . .

Friday 1 June
I looked in on Bill Bryden's rehearsals of *Dispatches*, adapted from Michael Herr's book, at the Cottesloe. It's the second play about Vietnam I've been concerned with. The first was *US*[1]. Peter Brook and I were called to St James's Palace by Lord Cobbold, the then Lord Chamberlain, who asked whether we thought it right for a theatre that was publicly funded to do a play which criticised our allies and therefore endangered the Anglo-American relationship. I asked if he was censoring the play. He said he was only censoring unsavoury words and actions, but thought we should consider our position. I remember George Farmer, the new chairman of the RSC and quite powerful, was very helpful on getting the play eventually staged as conceived. But clearing the way had all been started earlier by Fordy[2]. He and I knew that Anthony Eden, the RSC president, who was pro the Americans in Vietnam, was going to resign, and Fordy, plotting with me, succeeded in encouraging him to do this before *US* happened.

Now, thirteen years later, in a very different set of circumstances, I am producing another play about Vietnam which accepts without argument that the war was a lunacy.

Sunday 3 June
A dull, restless, childless day—everybody away. Sunday *Fidelio* notices are good, as were the dailies, so I have got away with it. That's, I'm afraid, how I feel, for I didn't *use* Glyndebourne in the way it's meant to be used, nor did I enjoy myself.

Edward returned home tonight pea-green and exultant from his May week-end at Cambridge. Jenny and Christopher had given him a taste of everything: punk rock, tennis, cricket, film-making, drama, looking at the

---

[1] A production with songs collectively evolved by the RSC with the playwright Denis Cannan and the poet Adrian Mitchell. It was directed by Peter Brook in 1966, when Hall ran the RSC.
[2] Sir Fordham Flower, the previous Chairman.

colleges, punting to Granchester. 'It was,' he said, 'the best week-end of my life, and I am lucky to have two such friends.' I told him Cambridge wasn't usually like that. . . .

The other night Edward woke up hearing me saying loudly, 'I am fed up with that damn queen.' The next day at home there was a phone call from the Buckingham Palace switchboard which he answered. He asked me in some alarm if I was having a row with the Queen. I explained that the queen I meant was quite another kind.

Monday 4 June
A boring Board meeting this afternoon with very little that was new. The Arts Council I hear is rather disappointed with the result of the enquiry it set up into our affairs; not fruity enough.

Tuesday 5 June
Howard Brenton to lunch. He promises the re-written *Romans in Britain* in August. It was a slightly strained meeting. Perhaps he, an ardent socialist, is uneasy with me now that I am being characterised by the left as a strike-breaker.

Saw Jack Kroll who is doing a *Newsweek* interview on Larry Olivier and wanted some pointers from me. He told me the New York cocktail circuit is buzzing with rumours of the revelations Ken Tynan is going to make in his book on Larry[1]. Kroll said that when he was interviewing Olivier he made the mistake of mentioning Tynan. Olivier tightened up and was very frightening. I wonder what happened to that love affair, for love affair there was in the artistic sense. Tynan was a truly passionate devotee at the Court of Larry.

This afternoon the president of NATTKE, Jim Tattum, plus representatives of its executive and John Wilson, came to see Michael Elliott to talk about the men who had been dismissed. Surely we must take them back? Surely they were good fellows? Michael Elliott made sympathetic noises, but said we couldn't. They seemed satisfied and left. Brother Tattum did produce this gem though. He said the dismissed men were many of them long-serving members of the National Theatre and they must have been doing a good job or we would have got rid of them long ago. This from a union chief, who knows the consequences of any sacking, is really the curtain line on the whole farcical comedy of the strike.

Michael went this morning to a grant-aided theatre committee meeting. He brought back disturbing news of substantial wage increases to NATTKE being considered by ENO and the Royal Opera House.

[1] Tynan died in July 1980, before the book was finished.

Apparently ENO are thinking of a basic stagehand wage, for a four-day week with no additional responsibilities, of £9,000 a year. Michael declared forcibly to them that we hadn't been through our horrible strike in order for everybody else to go on as if nothing had happened. It *had* happened, and it had achieved something. Couldn't we now collectively point out to the unions that there is not a bottomless purse, and the only sensible increases, for the time being, are inflation-linked? Everybody at the meeting in theatre management agreed. But both ENO and Covent Garden said they had Boards who believe you have to keep open at all costs. I understand their dilemma, but they have surely got to be tougher.

Dexter told me this afternoon that if Shaffer were really dumping him from *Amadeus* he would not go gracefully, he would go with all guns blazing publicly.

Wednesday 6 June
First night of *Dispatches*. Bill Bryden has done something extraordinary. You feel actually involved in the shit and the curious glamour of war, the horror and the excitement. The idiom, the American nature of the play, is wonderfully caught, which would have been unthinkable for English actors to achieve twenty years ago. The language is shockingly real: a fuck in every other line. It's a long way from *Journey's End*[1]. It's also a long way from *US*.

Thursday 7 June
Euro-election day. No one seems to be taking any notice, but I am moved by it. I remember Europe tearing itself to pieces. Now we are voting to live together, democratically. That must be good. Why is nobody interested? Sheer, bloody indifference. For there are no real issues, though most people believe vaguely that it's bad for their pocket. Also, there aren't any stars. Barbara Castle is about the only person anyone's heard of who is seeking a seat.

Glyndebourne: The first rehearsal of *Così fan tutte*[2]. Bernard Haitink turned up like a prince and we spoke to the cast. I told them the seriousness of the piece. In the break I talked to Bozena Betley[3], who is Polish, about the Pope's current visit to Poland. She burst into tears. I've never got any emotion out of her before. She had seemed immune to anger, flattery, jokes, irritation; nothing moved her. But the Pope in Poland makes her cry. I suppose it's an equation of her extreme Catholicism with nationalism, and with freedom. There's a paradox there though. The Catholic church has

---

[1] A play about the First World War by R C Sherriff.
[2] Hall's 1978 production re-staged by Guus Mostart.
[3] Who played Fiordiligi, as she had in 1978.

been quite as dogmatic, mechanical and repressive in its life as Communism. Anyway, I got some real alarm and panic into Bozena in the dressing-up scene as a soldier—the desperation of a woman running away from passion.

Friday 8 June
Rang Shaffer. I said wouldn't it be better for all parties if John and he made it up and John did *Amadeus*. Peter went mad. He talked for three-quarters of an hour and said categorically that there was no way he could work with Dexter at the moment. I said, 'Wait until Tuesday when Robbie Lantz is here.' This is becoming a disaster: the whole thing.

The event of the day was the Queen's lunch at Buckingham Palace to honour the Japanese Princess Chichibu. As we arrived, the inner court of the palace was filled with about eight large coaches labelled 'Alf's Holidays, Birmingham'—the Queen was giving a reception for the Provincial World Cricket Club; there were three hundred cricketers drinking orange juice. Ours turned out to be a small party: thirty people. I was next to Princess Margaret. When the plates for the main course were arranged she said, 'Oh, not silver. They are too hot, they burn you. Then they go cold very quickly, and you will find your food is quickly turned into a soggy mess.'

Prince Charles was jolly and wanted to know all about the strike. The Queen was relaxed and in command, a very nice, sensible upper-class Mum, generous, fair, but taking no nonsense, and not at all shy, though I have seen her so before.

Princess Chichibu is about sixty, Anglophile and charming. All the Japanese ladies were in full Japanese rig, very beautiful—'But,' said she 'not practical in this day and age, particularly in airports, where sudden gusts of wind blow them over your head.'

Monday 11 June
A long associates' meeting. We talked of our feelings towards private subsidy. It is my view, and I carried the meeting with me after a good deal of argument, that we must not seek private subsidy to pay for our main stage productions. It would be easy, for instance, to get Paul Scofield's *Othello* sponsored. But I believe this would not only be betraying ourselves but the rest of the subsidised theatre and the Arts Council. Private subsidy should be used to help us expand into areas we otherwise couldn't afford to be in: children's theatre, very experimental writing, etc. It must not be encouraged to take over from the government the responsibility of supporting the basic work of theatres like ours. That is the mistake Covent Garden have made. They are now in a dangerous position, for without private subsidy they cannot finance new productions. The whole of their grant is spent on overheads.

Tuesday 12 June
Showed Robbie Lantz round the theatre and had a good chat. Dexter and Shaffer are back in business. Shaffer rang me late at night, rather shamefaced. But I said I was pleased, which half of me is. It's not my job to split up partnerships like that, but to save *Amadeus* if it looks threatened. What has happened is best for the National, best for the play, and best for the future. It just doesn't happen to be best for me.

After the television news I saw a wonderful amateur film shot by an RAF officer in 1943 in colour about Lancaster bombers going on a mission. So nostalgic. All those Brylcreemed hair-dos. The men had a one in three chance of surviving. How the hell do they look so calm, so confident? And how were they, within months, so efficient? The young man the film was about flew for many thousands of hours, right until the end of the war, yet survived, and has never flown since. He is now an elderly accountant in Northampton. There is a terrible wonder about war.

Wednesday 13 June
Great relief all round this morning that *Amadeus* is really on at last. So I couldn't believe it when the whole thing opened up again this afternoon. Dexter said to me on the phone that Shaffer was now asking for a firm commitment from him by tomorrow morning without having resolved an important issue, which is whether he should be granted a piece of Peter's receipts in the play, wherever and whenever it was performed. He asked me if on this issue I didn't, as a director, have sympathy with him. I said I didn't, and I don't. I am sure my productions of Pinter have had a big influence on the way he's done all over the world, perhaps too much. But I wouldn't, as a result, dream of asking Harold for a percentage of his receipts. His reply would be interesting if I did. . . . But Dexter said he would only commit to the play if and when this is worked out. So we are back to where we started. I must say I am amazed at his tenacity.

We left it that he will only do the play if a deal with Peter Shaffer can be established right away, and I was on the phone the whole bloody afternoon as a consequence. I wonder how many hours I have spent on this play? If anybody should be getting a share of the rights, I reckon it's me! Anyway late tonight, to my intense surprise, I heard from Robbie Lantz, that Peter was not going to give a percentage. It's off with Dexter. Shaffer then rang, but I said I will not be involved personally any more. He must finally make up his mind what he wants, then ask his agent to inform mine what the position is. I have decided not to talk either to Peter or Dexter until things are cleared up.

Thursday 14 June
Two and a half hours with Sally Beauman who is writing a book on the RSC[1].

[1] *The Royal Shakespeare Company. A History of Ten Decades*, published 1982.

It was a strange feeling, ploughing over all those past years. What an extraordinary tradition Stratford has. All through its existence it has been possible for it to be evolutionary; and from Anthony Quayle on, every director has appointed his own successor—Quayle appointed Glen Byam Shaw, who appointed me, who appointed Trevor. It's a total justification for the existence of an institution. It makes change possible without severe fractures.

Laurie Evans has received a telephone call formally asking that I direct *Amadeus*. Peter Shaffer then rang me, and there is no question that he has now made up his mind. The trouble is, Dexter arrives here tomorrow to do *As You Like It* for us. The fur will fly I am sure.

Friday 15 June

John Dexter arrived today and was all cordiality and co-operativeness, but when he asked me what the position was I could only say that Peter was not relenting and that I knew a telegram was on its way. Dexter said he hadn't received it. After much to-ing and fro-ing to try and trace it, he rang his agent in my office, with me sitting there, and it was read to him. Perhaps I was wrong, but I simply couldn't have told Dexter myself what was in it, though I knew. It was impossible for me. Putting myself in his position, how would I have felt if Harold had sent me such a telegram? Dexter was very upset and I was distraught all day. I spoke to Laurie who firmly said that I had been asked to do the play and that's all there was to it.

Saw a preview of *Undiscovered Country*. John Wood[1] magnificent in a wonderful production by Peter Wood. It's a fine, fine play, though it creaked a bit here and there, and needs cutting. But I am optimistic. It has that massive quality, like a good novel, that *Madras House* also had in the Olivier. What a dramatist Schnitzler is! 'Working on the play,' said Tom[2], 'I often felt as if I were driving up the M1 in a Triumph Stag and finding myself overtaken by a 1922 Bentley.'

Saturday 16 June

Christopher and Jenny appeared. Christopher much relieved; he has been awarded a two/two degree. He reminded me that that was what I got, and later I heard him on the telephone reminding his grandmother and grandfather that that was what I got.

Jenny is wondering whether to be an actress after all. She will blow hot and cold like this all her life, as I and her mother have done. Part of being in a dedicated profession is that you are always on the brink of giving it up—that is, unless you have a real creative talent, like a writer or a composer. They

---

[1] Who played Friedrich Hofreiter.   [2] Stoppard.

don't seem able to help themselves; they just do it. A great talent that makes something out of nothing is never uncertain. But I think directors are, and actors, and conductors.

Tuesday 19 June
New York: Sam Cohn[1] rang me and chatted on this and that. For directing *Amadeus* on Broadway, when the time comes, he thinks he can get me 10% of the profits, but maybe not 5% of the gross—Christ, I am already talking like this town. But if I am to do *Amadeus* here, it may be one of my last chances of making money, real money. On the other hand I am not at all convinced the play will be a big commercial hit. It doesn't have, like Shaffer's *Equus*, erotic stimulation in the name of morality. Many Americans may see it as just a play about some highbrow musician. But with the right star it could do well.

I watched with horror an evening of American television. There was an hour-long news programme, the chief part a shoot-up. I don't know how on earth the camera was there. Perhaps they staged it for the benefit of the photographer, which in New York seems just possible. The story was of a hold-up in a shop, and the shooting by the proprietor of one of the three intruders. We had close-ups of the man's glazed eyes, wounded body, and bloodied head. The announcer warned us we might find these scenes distasteful. By God, we did. Sam Peckinpah has nothing on this. Television makes actuality into entertainment; life imitates art. The news was followed by a programme in which married couples discussed their sex lives in rather coy and giggly terms. They were interviewed tucked up in their own bedrooms. The main interest seemed to be what turned you on, when, and why.

One should watch television here to understand what an insane, jungle society it is. I am beginning to like it—well, not like it, but be fascinated by it.

Wednesday 20 June
New York: Last night on television I watched a correspondent in Nicaragua, who had been stopped by a patrol, kneel and open his arms to show he was unarmed—he was then made to lie down flat on the road, kicked in the groin, and very casually shot. Dead. The cameras continued to roll. I found it one of the most disturbing things I have seen in my life.

All day with Peter Shaffer at his apartment. I made two statements to him, both heartfelt. One was that I am aware that for the last decade there has been a strange division in my work. In the straight theatre I have had a professional puritanism, a care not to let things rip. The other side of me has

---

[1] Hall's New York agent.

luxuriated in opera. Supported by music, I have sometimes, in *Don Giovanni* for instance, been able to release a passionate and real rhetoric. I believe *Amadeus* could bring the two things together again. The other thing I told him was this. For years I have been praying for a sincere radical right-wing play, and this is it, because *Amadeus* is about the uniqueness of talent, its refusal to be part of a system, its refusal to be other than selfish. It celebrates the individual and individuality with a Renaissance fervour.

Phoned Paul Scofield and told him *Amadeus* would be starting rehearsals in September. He was delighted and frightened. I think he will be our Salieri.

Took Suria Saint-Denis[1] to see *Sweeney Todd*[2]. This weird melodrama, armed with eight Tonies and a precisely calculated artiness, has all the titillation of Grand Guignol—when will he cut the first throat?—but none of the revulsion of real blood, real horror. It's titillation without orgasm, because that would offend the middle-class public. A vast set representing nineteenth-century London looks as if it is made for a wonderful chase upstairs and across walkways, but the chase never happens. The music is a derivative procession of tonic and dominant with camp rhythms and sudden double time, all with witty, witty lyrics: Gilbert and Sullivan out of Leonard Bernstein—no balls, New York chic. The production is beautifully done, expert, precise, and the cast work their hearts out. Angela Lansbury is tremendous making her meat pies—a grotesque Cockney, full of energy and life; and Len Cariou gives a ferocious, arresting central performance. But it's a dreadful show. At the end, all the singers accuse us of somehow being responsible for Sweeney. I'm not.

Thursday 21 June
New York: Good news this morning. *Undiscovered Country*, which opened at the National last night, had pretty good reviews. Can it be that we are turning the corner? Winning back our audience after the strike?

Friday 22 June
New York: All day rehearsing the new American cast of *Bedroom Farce*. They treat me like God, too much, do what I say and the work is speedy, if hard. But the very English idiom of Ayckbourn's play really is almost impossible for them. I feel as if I am encouraging them to wear funny hats.

Christopher graduated today at Cambridge. I wish I could have been there.

---

[1] Michel Saint-Denis's widow.
[2] By Stephen Sondheim, directed by Hal Prince. It subsequently opened in London at the Theatre Royal, Drury Lane.

Monday 25 June

New York: Lunch with the Shuberts and Sam Cohn to talk about a Broadway production of *Amadeus*. Who are the Shuberts? Well, I hardly know them, and can never remember their names which is stupid; I think of them as Bernie and Bernie. But they own, or run, half the American theatre. They took me off in a vast air-conditioned limousine—one of those long, hearse-like Cadillacs with tinted windows so that people can't see you inside—and I was given a tour round the Shubert empire. They are installing computers in all their box offices which will, they say, show an immediate print-out of how much has been taken, how much is being booked. The next step is obvious. You ask the computer what will be a hit. It will probably come up with *Sweeney Todd*, and be wrong.

There's a booth in Times Square where from 3 pm anyone can buy tickets at half-price for any Broadway show which has seats available that evening. It's a wonderful scheme for making theatre cheaper and more accessible. But the producers say it stops people buying in advance at full price; they wait to get tickets cheaply on the day. I don't believe this. Audiences make audiences. Anyway, a lot of *Bedroom Farce* tickets were available at the Times Square booth for the opening with the new cast tonight, so we got a good lively audience in at half-price, and that helped the play along.

Wednesday 27 June

A non-event day spent flying home. Most of the way over I read John Lahr's biography of Joe Orton, *Prick Up Your Ears*. It's an alarming book, showing the aggressive anarchy of Orton. There is a passage in it, quoted direct from his diary, about a time when he goes to a lavatory in North London to get sex and it becomes an unbelievable saturnalia: six men in a tiny loo. The stimulation of rough trade, of risk-taking, was I suppose half the sexual fun for that generation of homosexuals. But Orton was a miraculous writer. I still remember the sheer breathless pleasure I had when I first read *What The Butler Saw*. That play is surely one of the comic masterpieces of the century? Has to be.

Thursday 28 June

To Glyndebourne. Moran has a whole programme of work planned for me, up to and including 1984. *Traviata* perhaps, Britten's *Midsummer Night's Dream* and, best of all, *Coronation of Poppaea*[1]. I thought I was coming to the end with Glyndebourne. Now there seems to be a positive rush to get me to do more. If I leave the National in '83, I wouldn't mind Glyndebourne being my home, and moving around the world the rest of the year.

[1] By Monteverdi.

Friday 29 June

There are posters all round the South Bank asking the public and the profession to boycott the National Theatre. The strike was another Grunwick confrontation, say the posters, aimed at busting the unions. Good stuff.

Saturday 30 June

Something is beginning to emerge in John Bury's designs for the *Amadeus* set. If the audience is the future, and the acting area is 1823, the time Salieri recalls the events of the play, then the background must be of a memory of the end of the previous century—mirrors, rococo, a maze of entrances, the stage of the past. I love what the play is trying to do more and more, if that is possible. But at the moment it is much, much too long, and about too many things.

Sunday 1 July

To Glyndebourne to see *Così fan tutte*—it isn't the press night, which is next Thursday, but I wanted to go. In the compartment of the train sat a Frenchman who introduced himself as the London correspondent of *Le Monde* and immediately began an interview. I finally had to stop this by saying it was Sunday afternoon, and if he wished to interview me, he should write to the National and make a date. Gallic cheek!

I enjoyed *Così* very much. Guus Mostart is the first heavyweight director Glyndebourne has given me to restage one of my productions. He is absolutely faithful to the spirit of the opera, but has developed and changed sections within the lines of what I did originally. I still yearn though for a Despina who is big bottomed, big bellied, big breasted, and about thirty-eight; someone who can really teach those two girls about men—from experience.

Bozena's Fiordiligi is good. Released from the competition of Maria Ewing's Dorabella, she has taken part of the opera back to herself. Last year was the first time I have ever seen a *Così* that seemed to be about Dorabella.

Bernard was the surprise of the evening. He took the overture of the first scene at an absolutely sizzling tempo, and then dug deep into the emotion and horror of the second act. He was alight afterwards. He said, 'Let's have a meeting, let's have a talk. You must stay at Glyndebourne. Somewhere there must be peace from your madness.' Deep in my heart I agree. But I need to change my personal life so I can enjoy that peace.

Monday 2 July

Finance and general purposes committee meeting. Next year's draft budget approved. Michael Elliott had a visual display which he put up on a board. At one point, Max asked for information on a detail. Michael said, 'I hope you won't mind if I leave that for the moment. I want to get to the end of this presentation so that you can have a clear view of the whole picture.' That's the way to impress Max.

Tony Field swore that the two big opera houses have promised not to exceed 10% increases and were contemplating direct cuts next year. In other words, monetarism as a policy is going to be made to bite. I have sympathy for it as a corrective. Though the abuses of capitalism lead to dreadful inequalities in the underdog, the old Keynesian doctrines no longer work. We have to find something new.

The chairman forgot to congratulate us on producing excellent figures in a year when we sustained losses of over £250,000 because of the strike; so did Tony Field.

Tuesday 3 July
To *Lady from the Sea*, the Royal Exchange production, with Vanessa Redgrave, at the Round House. Since Thelma Holt took over as director, she has improved this theatre enormously. It is now an attractive in-the-round space for five hundred people; attractive, that is, if you like theatre-in-the-round. I don't. My heart sinks as soon as I see a scene where I know I will be looking at the back of an actor's neck for the next ten minutes.

The play though worked enormously well. But there was a camp set in which half the acting area was made up of water; a translation with no rhythm, no tang, full of phrases like 'don't you know' and 'as they say'; and, among the cast, no male sexuality in sight, not a ball around. These men, repressed and perverse as they are, must have passion.

The miracle of the evening was Vanessa. She played Ellida in a most wonderful way. Her face appeared naked of make-up, and naked of guile. You could see right through the skin to the emotions, the thoughts, the hopes, the fears underneath. But here's the paradox. What Vanessa says politically is, to me, insane, and I believe that to her lies *are* truth if they support her ideology. So how can she express such truth, such sincerity, such lack of hypocrisy, in her art? In life, which is true, she is false. In art, which is false, she is true.

It also didn't seem to matter to her that there were lack-lustre performances around her. She acted to the others as if they were what they ought to be. Part of her belief extended to them too. Mind you, I have never thought it mattered to Vanessa whom she was acting with. She is so shortsighted she can't see who it is anyway.

Wednesday 4 July
To the City of London Girls' School for Lucy's open day. I always find the charm of seeing small children performing wears off in about ten minutes. You also know that all parents in the audience have their eyes riveted only on their own nearest and dearest. Anyway, when Lucy sat down at the grand

piano in the music room, she entirely disappeared from view. But she played her Schubert Ecossaise well, apart from a breakdown in the middle, and had a big and deserved success playing the harp.

Back to the theatre and more grinding away on the budget. The problem is the Cottesloe which simply cannot sustain a full ensemble of actors and still have low seat prices. Bill Bryden has run the Cottesloe brilliantly, built an audience there, made it a necessary theatre. But in fact he has done it with a large permanent company which I should not really have allowed; not because I didn't want it, but because we didn't have the money.

Thursday 5 July

To the Globe tonight to see Alan Ayckbourn's *Joking Apart*, which is closing Saturday, his first flop in years. In the play, a lady and her husband —the people with flair, with success, who always fall right, look healthy, become wealthy, can do everything—are contrasted to the rest of us paranoid mortals who fail in their wake. Alan has conceived a wonderful central idea. But he hasn't actually fulfilled it. Nor is it a particularly convincing thought on human beings. No one is that untroubled, that successful. The miracle of the Chekhov monster ladies is that they are vulnerable too.

Friday 6 July

To the Peking opera at the Coliseum—an invigorating evening of pure theatre. It's naive, almost cartoon-like, and I do get tired of impossible acrobatics: once you have accepted a few times that they can't be done, and it is demonstrated that they can, all surprise goes. Much more subtle was a wonderful little play about a nun escaping in a boat. She and the boatman enact their journey through the rapids. They showed the most beautiful physical control and, with no boat actually there at all, told us more about riding in one than any film of the reality could do. There was also a short piece about two men in the dark at an inn, one sent to murder the other, played in full light. Every bit of the story, each character's reaction —amazement, puzzlement, fear—is presented to the audience. Although they are in the dark to each other, they are in the light to us—the basis of Shaffer's *Black Comedy*. If the performer makes the convention, the audience believe it.

Saturday 7 July

Wimbledon final. Borg, like all true champions, nearly lost—but then won. I am feeling very ill today. Ill in the head. And ill with a terrible cold. My sinus is screaming.

Monday 9 July
Nothing much to report except that I still feel ill, and also in great personal crisis. I shouldn't be at work, but if I stayed away I would feel more sorry for myself and become, if that is possible, more stupid.

Tuesday 10 July
Feel marginally better. Spent all day, 10 am to 6.30 pm, being filmed in an interview by David Dimbleby for television. He was very amiable and perceptive, but not provocative, and didn't bowl me any nasty ones, thank God. The only trouble was that the little alter ego who normally resides in my head, checking on what I am speaking, wondering what impression I am giving, and generally giving a little form and shape to the proceedings, seemed to be totally sedated by antibiotics. I literally cannot remember what I said.

Wednesday 11 July
To Wallingford for the parents' golden wedding anniversary. Masses of flowers arrived from relatives and friends. Aunty sat looking cross in the corner. 'It's a pity,' she declared, glaring at Dad, 'that all those (pointing at the flowers) are going to die.' She was also very stuffy about Aunty Elsie who had sent flowers as well, earlier, as Terry's All Gold Chocolates. 'I don't know why she had to send flowers when she had already come in with those chocolates,' she said. I haven't heard that expression 'come in' used in that way since I was a child in Suffolk.

Thursday 19 July
John Bury made one or two ominous noises tonight about our joint commitment to Glyndebourne. I think the great outside is beckoning him because of all his international trips and prizes. That's a little worrying. I would find it hard to contemplate a change after being with John so long.

A meeting with IBM about their new office building going up alongside us on the South Bank. It's vast, though only to be their London branch headquarters; their main home is in Portsmouth. By employing Denys Lasdun as architect they may have avoided any trouble about putting up a giant next door to the National Theatre.

They are an extraordinary corporation. Everybody clocks in, there are no unions, and no drink is allowed on the premises. They are paternalistic, efficient, and if you are an IBM man it is fine for you.

Today in the Commons they debated the return of hanging. There was a resounding vote against it. I felt relieved. I think there should be a death penalty for terrorism and treason. But not for the madness of murder.

Friday 20 July

A summit meeting at the Royal Opera House. We are to make representations to Mrs Thatcher about the 10% cuts proposed in the arts next year. These will, after inflation, amount to cuts of 20% to 25%, which could actually wreck everything that has been built up in the last twenty-five years.

Sunday 22 July

Arnold Goodman is drafting a letter to Mrs Thatcher from us, the RSC, and the two big opera companies about the proposed arts cuts. His point is that everybody who works in the subsidised theatre subsidises a little bit themselves. Except for the stage staff, this is true, and it's more than a little bit with some—Gielgud or Finney, for instance, work on half pay.

Amadeus, as I read and re-read it, gives me a mounting feeling of excitement. I am tussling with what we are going to do about the music, and spent all day browsing through my records. It sounds pretentious to say that I know nearly all of Mozart—there's a hell of a lot of it—but I played one piece which *is* new to me. It is his Masonic funeral music, a short piece, C minor, basset-horns, and a painful chromaticism which with other similarities, seems to pre-figure the anguish of *Tristan* all those years later. If ever I heard a piece of music about death, this is it; death which resolves surprisingly and magically in the very last chord into a long held C major. It's magnificent. I played it again and again.

Monday 23 July

Finance and general purposes committee meeting. The interest was Denys Lasdun's justification of the IBM building going up next door. If Denys was not a genius architect, he would be a genius advocate. You can see he is not compromising himself, but he is certainly compromising you. He argues that he is creating, in modern terms of course, a piece of Venice by the Thames. He isn't. He is creating a wonderful building for IBM, and the National Theatre loses out.

Thursday 26 July

Shocking and sad news. Sydney Edwards died suddenly last night: a massive heart attack. We will greatly feel the loss of him; so indeed will the *Evening Standard*.

The day was marked by death. At lunchtime Bill Bundy rushed into my office saying that our storeman, George Evans, who has been with the National from its inception at the Old Vic, and was at the Old Vic prior to that from 1947, had been killed in an accident at our scene stores in Maidstone. A pile of scenery moved across a lorry and crushed him. Bill and Sue had the nightmare task of going to tell the widow before the police arrived. She has been in the theatre all her life—a dresser, a wardrobe lady. She dressed Leslie[1] at the Aldwych in the early sixties.

I feel such anger at the sudden death of friends.

Sunday 29 July

All day working on Mozart and *Amadeus*, selecting little bits of music for the production. Music, like colour, is the most dangerous thing to put in the straight theatre. It generalises emotion, generates it easily, and ends by dissipating it. And my God, when it's Mozart.... You can't easily let *him* into a play.

Tuesday 31 July

A wonderful lunch with Ralph. I opened my heart to him a little—not in particulars but in generalities. He said he'd guessed I was unhappy, that there were personal problems. Couldn't I get away with a friend, a male friend? How I wish I could....

Wednesday 1 August

Up at five this morning to get to grips with the re-writes of *Amadeus*. They arrived last night. Structurally, Shaffer has done some fine things. We are cooking. He's bubbling with ideas, and full of energy (of course). Three hours of him exhaust me utterly.

Had lunch with Kenneth Robinson who was less gloomy about the future of the arts than are most of us. He thinks there's a chance things may get better in the new year. I wanted to know whether or not we should run for commercial sponsorship. I believe the Arts Council position can only be strengthened if our main work remains the responsibility of the government. He agreed. The sponsorship argument is too easy and lets the government off the hook.

First night of *As You Like It*, in the Olivier: slightly slow, slightly tense, but you feel the whole of the Elizabethan mind is being laid out before you. I have seen the play better performed, but never better directed. John Dexter has done wonderful things.

Thursday 2 August

The *As You Like It* notices are rather stuffy, and the critics seem surprised the play is three hours long. They have grown up in a convention where Shakespeare is hacked, whereas we have given the full text. It is a genuinely classic piece of work. I told John Dexter again this morning, before he flew back to America, how pleased I was with the production. But I am afraid it may not do business.

[1] Caron.

Lunch at the Arts Council with Roy Shaw. He talked of the gloom of Norman St John Stevas about next year's grants. But he, Roy, has been along this road before, and says that finally money trickles through towards the end of the year when the Treasury finds it has more in its pocket than it expected.

Friday 3 August
The last day before I'm away from the office for a month, visiting Vienna, Salzburg, and Edinburgh. Inevitably there was a multitude of things to do, things undone, things left half done. I was given a lovely present by Bill Bundy and Sue—a working steam model of Stephenson's *Rocket*. I still love trains.

A long talk to Arnold Goodman. He has finished his letter to Thatcher about the proposed arts cuts. It is the first shot in a long campaign, though I fear she will put it in the wastepaper basket with other screams of protest about facilities which are dwindling and which we have till now taken for granted. But I am determined to forget about the theatre and all its problems for the next four weeks.

Saturday 4 August
Stayed in bed in Wallingford a good deal of the morning, wondering what to do. The place has never looked more peaceful and reassuring. Then poor Jenny had to be put together again, confidence reinstated, after being fired from rehearsals of a student play, bound for the Edinburgh Festival, because of a disagreement with the director. And Edward is in a bad state about me going away tomorrow, my constant absences, my not being like other fathers, able to play with him. . . .

Finished reading a book on Terence Rattigan[1]. I suppose out of that brilliant playboy talent have come two important plays, *The Browning Version* and *The Deep Blue Sea*. The rest seem to me full of moral evasions. Perhaps any homosexual dramatist who, during a time of secrecy and blackmail, presented his own emotional life in his work as if he were a woman, suffered some terrible disability. Tennessee Williams was the most successful, but then he is woman right through. I think the problem with Rattigan was that even if he had had the opportunity for frankness, his whole repressed class background, the stiff upper lip of Harrow, would have made it impossible for him. Deception and restraint are at the very heart of that kind of Englishman. I suppose it's at the heart of me, heterosexual as I am.

Sunday 5 August
After various adventures in the hell of Heathrow, I eventually met up with Peter Shaffer and we flew to Vienna where, in the evening light, we took a beautiful walk round, wandering down the dilapidated little street where

[1] *Terence Rattigan, The Man and his Work*, by M Darlow and G Hodson.

Mozart died, which we found by chance—there's no record of the actual house, it's disappeared. *Amadeus* kept re-appearing in our conversation every ten minutes.

I hope I can enjoy these days, relax and decide my future. It's wonderful to be back in Vienna. Seven years ago I worked happily here at the Burgtheater directing Pinter's *Old Times*.

Monday 6 August
Vienna: Peter Shaffer and I had a heavy day as tourists. After visiting the bank and surprising ourselves at the appalling exchange rate, we looked at the tomb of the parents of the Habsburg of our play, Joseph II. It is an absurd lead bed in which the mother, Maria Theresa, the previous Empress, awakes in death with happiness to greet her Emperor, her husband—a grotesque and over-blown piece of theatricality with, by its foot, the plain brass coffin, about a twentieth the size, of their son. The guide seemed rather embarrassed by the simplicity Joseph had insisted on. Joseph changed the taste of the times.

Over a pleasant and productive lunch Peter and I discussed *Amadeus* all the time. Our main problem is the length of the first act—about half an hour has to come out of it—and the complexity of the second. I am pushing Shaffer to make the main theme of the play Salieri's contest with God. It's there but it needs clarification.

To Schönbrunn Palace in the afternoon. We tramped round it with about two thousand Japanese. I loved it again just the same. For all the vastness of the building, the rooms themselves are tiny, and the white and the gold decoration is exquisite, not vulgar, the whiteness not really white, the goldness not really gold. I was interested to see again how the people there lived, room opening out to room, the stoves fed by private backstairs corridors: a servant would never have had to enter to stoke them up. The garden is grandiloquent and inhuman, and I hate the hill with the prospect crowned by a very Germanic temple. But the palace itself is superb.

In the evening, wine and food and talk, talk, talk, mainly about the play, but I told Peter a little of my personal problems. He has to know, since we are going virtually to live together during the next few months, getting *Amadeus* to its opening.

Tuesday 7 August
Vienna: We went to the Bibliotheque Nationale, the most beautiful baroque building inside I have ever seen: wonderful proportions, warm walnut, extraordinary symmetry.

At 3 pm we left for Salzburg on something that called itself the Orient Express. How the grand are reduced: plastic cups, and commuters dropping in and out. Our hotel, which had been described to us as being on the outskirts, with sauna bath and swimming pool, had both, though only for dwarfs. The people were pleasant, and the rooms clean, but ours were right by the autobahn. The traffic noise was perpetual. A roar. It's not going to be a place where Peter and I can work.

Towards the end of the day we went into the town, took a drink in the square, watched a moon as dramatic as a theatre prop nudge its way round the castle, and agreed that Salzburg, despite being full of the over-rich, is still one of the most beautiful places on God's earth. It's preserved without being dead: absolutely exquisite. I am glad to be here. Tonight I reflected on the absurdity of my life, which seems much like an Iris Murdoch novel. I suppose it's appropriate I should be considering it in a town which is itself part of baroque theatre. . . .

Wednesday 8 August

Salzburg: We cannot stay in this hotel. Peter and I spent a silly morning surrounded by scripts and pieces of paper yelling the finer points of *Amadeus* at each other to make ourselves heard above the roar of the autobahn.

Lunch with Max Schell who afterwards gave us a lightning tour round, refusing to let us stop anywhere, and streaming forth information. He said he was returning a tour of Stratford-on-Avon I gave him in '65. Did I remember? Of course I didn't. We fought our way through the streets to Mozart's birthplace where we saw all the familiar pictures—familiar because they are reproduced everywhere—and looked at Mozart's own small forte-piano, a beautiful walnut affair. A lady played the D Minor Fantasia on it: lovely sound, much more capable of legato playing than I would have thought.

Thursday 9 August

Salzburg: This morning we left the hotel, entirely by the generosity of Max Schell. He gave us his lovely apartment, looking straight down the valley, because he was off to Venice. We had room to stamp about and talk. Our work today was to tidy the melodrama of the story. Salieri accuses God for not making him a genius, vows to serve Him, is betrayed by God, takes Him on, has a number of combats with Him, and is, as all men must be, finally defeated. This narrative is now I think clearer.

Friday 10 August

Salzburg: Today I slipped into Peter's mind a major suggestion about the character in *Amadeus* of the great singer Catharina Cavalieri, hoping he would rise to the bait. He did. I don't want to indicate from this that Peter is difficult, nor that I can only suggest things elliptically, but if I said them strongly his response would not be natural. He likes to take an idea gently, delicately, savour it and, if it has merit, allow it to live. I remember from directing his play *Shrivings* that with him the forceful statement is a recipe for disaster. Somehow one wants to keep his own creativity exuberant and surprising.

I shall never forget these days in Salzburg. It's pretty rum that my eyes have opened so late to the rococo as well as the baroque. I have loved Bach and Mozart since I was a child. Why couldn't I *see* the architecture which mirrors their music?

Working on *Amadeus* is a joy, the place is a joy, and the sense of being on the brink of a new life makes me both happy and sad.

Saturday 11 August

Salzburg: The first night of *Figaro* at the Grösses Festspielhaus, a hideous fascist place. How can you possibly stage Mozart in a theatre that seats over two thousand? There is no eye contact between the performers, and certainly no possibility of contact between performers and audience. So that essential private intimacy, the basis of all Mozart ensemble, when the performer can talk to the audience as if they were his one and only intimate friend, is simply impossible. I hated the whole thing: a rich and glossy audience (my seat cost about £50), a rich and glossy performance with very highly-paid singers, a sheen on the music, and no life in it at all. Maria Ewing was wonderfully lively as Cherubino—in fact she and Kiri[1] were the only good things in the evening.

Drinks afterwards with the agent, Basil Horsfield, in the Goldener Hirsch. Kiri and Maria are his clients. Kiri made a number of forays to the hotel's jewellery shop which seems to stay open all night. She kept reappearing every few minutes with a ring worth £40,000, or a necklace worth £50,000. She tried them on, paraded them for a giggle. Basil and his companion loved it all. Perhaps that's how a diva should behave.

Sunday 12 August

Salzburg: Went to *Jedermann*, the morality play which is performed in the original Max Reinhardt production every festival outside the cathedral. I had thought it would be interesting to see a Reinhardt production preserved since the twenties. I was wrong. It all looked old-fashioned and meaningless. Theatre should never be preserved.

Monday 13 August

Returned to London, and was diverted to read on the plane, in the New York *Herald Tribune*, that Miss Piggy has been banned from Iranian television during Ramadan because 'Moslems do not eat pork and consider pigs unclean.'

I was wanting to be back yet not wanting to be, because of the state of my

---

[1] Te Kanawa, who played the Countess.

home life. I have known I would feel guilt, but not guilt as bad as this. Like a time bomb also has been the coming of *Amadeus*, and my need to do it. You cannot direct a play unless you are decisive. And, pathetically, that is something I am not sure I am at the moment.

Wednesday 22 August
A long weekend at the Edinburgh festival. It was strange moving so quickly from the glossy prosperity of Salzburg to this hard Scottish city. Yet in some ways I prefer Edinburgh—it has a freedom, a lack of constraint, which seems good.

I saw the two productions of the Georgians (they do not like being called Russians), the Rustaveli company, who are the sensation of the festival. *Richard III* is a free-wheeling adaptation which I didn't much admire, though its vitality, and its life are unarguable. Their production of *The Caucasian Chalk Circle* I enjoyed much more. The boring socialist prologue is cut, and the whole thing is presented as a frank entertainment with a narrator and a piano player who are man and wife circus performers. Ramaz Chkhikvadze gave both Richard and Asdak: he is a great ham, but a great liver, and a great actor.

This company are much influenced by Brook in their freedom, their eclecticism, and their embracing of rough theatre. But I have never seen acting like this before. Actually it comes down to national temperament. The Georgians are Latin, emotional, sly, cool, very humorous. They don't stamp and roar. They are not intense, not cosmic, and they are certainly not Russian. They seem to mock everything, which I like.

I preferred *The Chalk Circle* simply because it released Brecht's wonderful fairy story as a popular entertainment. Ideology and politics were out of the window. *Richard III* was, I thought, a liberty, a cartoon: nothing to do with Shakespeare, his world, or his play.

Monday 27 August
Edinburgh: To the Degas exhibition. I loved that. It is small enough to enjoy, and so many masterpieces. Yet it's strange how the over-reproduced painting becomes such an artifact that when you see it in reality it seems impossible, unreal, and a bit disappointing. Then, in the evening, to Pollini playing Schubert and Schumann. I think I have never heard such a superb musician: clear, disciplined, passionate, without being careful. A master. He thinks with his fingers. He turns music from a sensual experience into a metaphysical one.

Dreadful news today. The IRA have murdered Lord Mountbatten, his grandson and, it is suspected, some of his family. They were all on holiday off Ireland in a fishing boat which was blown up. The papers speak of radio-controlled lobster pots. I feel sick.

Tuesday 28 August
Returned to London this afternoon: Christopher very anxious to see me about the crisis at home. He was magnificent and made me feel much, much better. He has become a wonderfully mature man, and put my heart back into some kind of strength.

Wednesday 29 August
Today things began to go wrong again. My father has asked me to do little enough in his life. Now he is asking—urging me most strenuously—not to break up the family. My mother is muttering that what you sow you reap.

Sunday 2 September
Listened to a wonderful radio programme of people recalling the day war was declared, exactly forty years ago. I remember it vividly. Neville Chamberlain broke the news on the radio as I shredded beans for my mother on the doorstep of 121 Blinco Grove, Cambridge. We all expected immediate air raids, and she and I were rather frightened. Father was on relief Sunday duty at some country station, we weren't sure where, so we went down to Cambridge station to ask, and they didn't know either. Then he came home, as he came home every day throughout the war. Most families, of course, had hideous separations, or worse. We had none. I suppose I must also count myself lucky to have lived through so many years of relative peace, whatever the horrors, the Vietnams, the terrorists.

Monday 3 September
Back to work, not wanting to, and tremulous. Masses of letters and documents to look at. But I didn't. Mainly I tried to keep calm for the beginning of rehearsals, with a superb cast[1], of *Amadeus*.

Tuesday 4 September
We started to put *Amadeus* on its feet, cutting and trimming. A whole passage, one of the things which first attracted me to it, is now questionable. It is where Salieri describes his reason for being a musician. Music, he says, has absolute standards: all other human activity is relative, but a note of music is either right or wrong. I think that passage must go. It is too weighty, over-written. It's always what seem at first to be the best lines, the best movie shots, the best stage effects, that are cut.

---

[1] The cast included: Felicity Kendal as Constanze; Simon Callow as Mozart; Andrew Cruickshank as Rosenberg; Basil Henson as von Strack; Philip Locke as Greybig; John Normington as Joseph II; Paul Scofield as Salieri; Nicholas Selby as van Swieten; and Dermot Crowley and Donald Gee as the 'Venticelli'.

Wednesday 5 September
Went on with the play, but in a desultory way. Cast excellent and vigorous; Shaffer inventive. It's I that am desultory.

Thursday 6 September
Still not getting going. Dragging myself to work and pushing myself in rehearsal. I stand and stare at the actors. I think, though, we have solved the great problem of the music. It must be distant, under speech; Mozart's music of course, but as if through slightly distorting glass. Harry Birtwistle says he can do it electronically. If we inject Mozart's music into the play fully, to then follow with speech is impossible.

I was also convinced today by the wisdom of John Bury's idea of dealing with the opera passages just by showing, front on, the faces of the stage audience, and by mere wisps of music, with in Act I a vast battering section of the C minor Mass to cause Salieri to collapse. But Mozart is such a dramatic, such an emotional composer that we have to be careful.

Friday 7 September
To Mr Wright in Harley Street very early. He told me that my right eye, as I knew, has worsened. The infection is nearly over the centre of the pupil now, which is why the sight is deteriorating so badly. He says I should have the laser beam treatment immediately, so I suppose I must.

We staggered through the first act of *Amadeus* in the morning. Even with cutting it runs an hour and fifty minutes, so this afternoon the blue pencils were out again. I want a big but *lean* play. Shaffer is being marvellous about cutting.

Saw *Betrayal* tonight for the first time in months and was very pleased with its assured understatement. It is not a play I can easily take at the moment because of its subject matter. But as far as pride in my own work is concerned, it was like a tonic.

Saturday 8 September
I must be careful that Simon[1] does not act Mozart too coarsely, despite the oafishness in the part. Mozart admired grace and precision in everything. For instance, he hated pianists who waved their heads about when they performed. His awfulness in the play must therefore be delicate.

Another thing to remember is that we now think of vigour, of free expression, as something spontaneous, not requiring technique. That is a chief virtue of the modern movement. But Mozart could have chosen to write in discords; Poussin could have made great splodges of paint on his

---

[1] Callow.

462

canvas. The point is that they, and all artists then, believed art was to do with discipline, form, grace, and above all technique.

Began reading Ronnie Blythe's new book about old age[1]. It's wonderful. For the first time in history most of us will spend twenty years 'old'. Ronnie's theme is that the old used to be respected because they were a rarity. Now they are an embarrassing commonplace, and that respect has gone.

My own feelings of despair reached a pitch today that I have not known since the early sixties. It's as if emotion is physically eating me up.

Sunday 9 September

The day was dominated by the fact that I was to make an address tonight at the commemorative performance for Yvonne Mitchell at the Apollo Theatre. I was in a bit of a state because, as tears come to me regularly and irrationally at the moment, I didn't know if I had the strength or the guts to speak in public about her. Well, I did, just. I said of course nothing like as much as I had prepared but, I hope, managed to express my feeling that all her many wonderful achievements were none of them quite as original and particular as the woman herself.

Tuesday 11 September

There was a big meeting today with the cast of *Close of Play* and Harold Pinter about their proposed visit to the Dublin Festival. Michael Gambon, John Standing, Anna Massey, Zena Walker, Annie Leon, the stage management, and several understudies have all refused to go because of the Mountbatten murder. But if you give in to terrorism, more terrorism occurs. A cancellation of the visit by us will be front page international news, and invite bombs to the South Bank. All the IRA ever wants is publicity. I am absolutely furious. Harold initially was against the visit too. But Dublin didn't murder Mountbatten. Criminals did. The best way to help matters is to go there.

Thursday 13 September

Another grey day of *Amadeus* rehearsals, for me at least. No juices flowing. Well, the only juices are tears, and I hope that these are masked by the dark glasses I'm now wearing. I love the play, the cast, the author. But I don't love me.

Paul did the first dozen or so pages without the book today. Miraculous. Still too thick and of course slow, but miraculous. As far as Felicity Kendal and Simon are concerned, I almost want them to change roles. I want Felicity to be coarse and common as Constanze, Simon to be refined.

The Dublin situation looks better. Annie Leon and Michael Gambon have decided they want to go.

[1] *The View in Winter.*

Monday 17 September
A problem of the play is that the audience at the end of Act I may object to Mozart simply because he is an anus-fixated, botty-smacking child. But that is not enough to weigh against his genius. It's his sheer insensitivity which has to be dramatised. When Salieri says at the end of Act I that Mozart is inhuman the audience must be with him.

Tuesday 18 September
The actors eat the play voraciously. They have appetite for it. They love it. And Shaffer is being wonderful in cutting, slicing, making it more tasty. I stand by, a self-indulgent chef whose mind is on things which have nothing to do with *Amadeus*.

A visit at the end of rehearsal from Patience Collier. She said she was glad to see me in such good spirits because she had watched David Dimbleby interviewing me on television and had found it uncharacteristic of me: low-key, depressed, and unnecessarily humble. She just wanted to check I am still the same chap she'd always known.

Went to a preview of *Death of a Salesman*[1] in the Lyttelton. The play has a lot of soft lines in it, and is quite dated. But Michael Rudman has directed against that, kept it hard, kept it rapid, and has really done a superb job. Warren Mitchell's performance[2] is something I shall never forget. One of the half-dozen great bits of totally assimilated character acting I have seen.

Thursday 20 September
A superb letter from Nigel Williams to Chris Morahan today. Williams has written a play for us, which we commissioned, called *Line 'Em*; marvellously vigorous language, but infantile politics. When many of us had read and considered it, Chris sent a polite letter to Williams saying what we weren't happy with. As it happened, none of us in our conversations had spoken of its political implications, only of its defects dramatically. But now Williams has written a wonderful, insulting letter saying that the turning-down of his play by the reactionary, right-wing, union-bashing National Theatre has given him a great deal of satisfaction. Whoops. . . .[3]

Friday 21 September
The *Death of a Salesman* notices are good.

Saw a rehearsal of *Richard III*, which opens in the Olivier soon. John Wood[4] is an extraordinary actor: eloquent, adroit, unbelievably energetic, and now beginning to scratch greatness. What I chiefly like about Chris

---

[1] By Arthur Miller.   [2] As Willy Loman.
[3] *Line 'Em* opened in the Cottesloe in August 1980, directed by Morahan.
[4] Who played Richard.

Morahan's production is a surrealistic nightmare quality. But it wants pushing much, much further, which I said to Chris tonight.

Sunday 23 September
The *Death of a Salesman* Sunday notices are wonderful. We are in business.

Friday 28 September
The first *Richard III* preview was promising, but cumbersome, and not a true nightmare. I don't want to be immodest, but every production of that play since it was part of the RSC's *Wars of The Roses* trilogy is somehow influenced by how it was done then. This is also set in metal; and half political. With John Wood it should be Punch and Judy, with a tragic twist at the end. There is very little of this at the moment, but John is electrifying. I am hopeful for him, but not for the whole. It falls between two stools.

Saturday 29 September
Spent two and a half hours this morning talking to Chris about *Richard III*. He was very open and accepted much of what I said, particularly my criticisms of the mis-scansions of the verse. How is it possible for actors to mis-scan Shakespeare? It's like limping, it's an abnormality. I was pleased in the afternoon to hear John Wood say to the company, "There can be no pauses in this early stuff, unless they are marked; there must be energy; you have to ride on the verse.' He does that alright, superbly.

Sunday 30 September
Much thinking about *Amadeus*. I feel now that it's important we do not present the story entirely through Salieri's eyes. There must be a tension between what the audience sees and what Salieri describes. A difficult balance to achieve.

Also, I am more and more interested in the fact that Mozart was not a revolutionary *artist*, but a *social* revolutionary in a feudal world. In many respects he was the first star, the first free-lance—after Handel in London, anyway. Artists at that time were servants, eating below the salt. But Mozart wanted to be a star, wanted to be recognised for his uniqueness, much more than Haydn or Schubert or Beethoven. He was revolutionary in that. He did not want to be just the servant of a nobleman.

Monday 1 October
At Moorfields Hospital. A hundred or so laser shots were fired into my right eye in order to seal off the burst blood vessel. It was not pleasant. I had to keep the eye still, and each shot gave a slight kick, sometimes a painful pin prick. The problem was wondering which one was going to hurt. There was

also a faint sizzle from time to time. Anyway, I believe this treatment may improve things. I should have had it done a year ago, but it seemed risky.

Found an exquisite picture of the interior of the Warsaw National Theatre in 1790. It's the best representation I have ever seen of the sort of candle-lit, crowded theatre that Mozart knew. It's an intimate, magical place, dark, romantic, and very, very sexy.

Tuesday 2 October

Shaffer describes the process we are going through with *Amadeus* as carving out a play with actors. 'It must be very strange for you,' he says, 'evolving a text with actors like this. You are used to a firm, hard, finished text. . .like Harold's.' Peter must have made far more money, be far more successful in a material sense, than Harold. Yet I sometimes think that in Peter's eyes Harold is *the* dramatist.

I happened to have dinner tonight with Pinter. 'You couldn't cut my plays like that,' he said. 'They are not long enough to start with. They would disappear.'

Thursday 4 October

First night of *Richard III*. Unfortunately John Wood was too virtuoso in the first act—speedy-talking, terrific energy, leaping on to the next line before he had finished the last—but, by Christ, he was in command of the second. He got it right on target and did it beautifully. The production is good: honest, straightforward, well-staged, well-spoken, though the costumes lack character and do not help many of the actors who seem a mass of wailing barons, all beige and undifferentiated. But Wood got cheered and the audience liked it. I wager the press didn't though.

The *Daily Mail* was taking photographs of the incoming audience, and insisted on a picture of Jacky and myself. . . . Bad timing. . . .I did not have a peaceful night.

Friday 5 October

Some wonderful notices for John Wood and some very bad ones. I smelt blood in the air, that side of the theatre I don't much like, when it enters the arena of a blood sport, like a bullfight: somebody has to win. Jack Tinker expressed this feeling in the *Daily Mail* by reporting that Wood bangs on the door of greatness and is not admitted. I think the truth is that he is the first actor since 1944 to have challenged Olivier in the part on his own ground. He hasn't unseated him, but he might next time. He told me at lunch-time he thought he had had a complete failure. I said, how could it be a complete failure when you can't get a ticket. The trouble with John is that he has a too acutely developed sense of history. He looks forward a hundred years, and wants to see his Richard III written there. I find this difficult to understand. I don't care very much what is written about me in the future. I won't be around. They will get it wrong anyway; they get it wrong now. One must just work. Some kind of mythology settles over any kind of public figure which may be true, may be false. It's what history needs at that particular moment. Playing Richard III in a theatre named Olivier was putting one's head right in the lion's mouth. I warned John he might get it bitten off. Well, he hasn't, he's just been wounded.

Sunday 7 October
Though I can still see them poking their heads over the horizon, my Black Dogs have at last receded. I suppose it's because I begin to know what I must do about my personal life.

Monday 8 October
Today I mentioned a new line or two to Paul for the *Amadeus* first act. He begged suddenly for no more lines. They were, he said, like nails going into his head...there was no time for more.

Chris is a little down, feeling he always gets bad notices. I told him, and meant it, that his *Richard III* is the finest first crack at Shakespeare I have seen in my life. I also pointed out to him that his productions of *State of Revolution* and *The Philanderer* could hardly be described as badly reviewed. And I actually think he's the best Shaw director in the country.

We have lost the IBM fight. The Fine Arts Commission even commend Danys Lasdun for having put the building so close to us. The very thing we are against, they are for, aesthetically. I think you have to get up very early in the morning to outbox Denys on a matter like this. Now there will be a commercial building twinning the public one next door for the rest of time: 'What is that building?' 'Oh, it's the National Theatre and the local headquarters of IBM.'

Dinner with Alan Ayckbourn. He is in a considerable state because of the failure of *Joking Apart*. It is strange to see one of the most talented, most prolific and, I should think, richest dramatists in the world a bundle of forty-year-old insecurity....

Tuesday 9 October
At the Western Ophthalmic Hospital this morning to have lasers fired into my eye again—much more painful and disturbing than last time. I was told there was very little possibility the eye would recover full sight.

Close of Play went off today to the Dublin Festival as scheduled. The cast have sensibly had second thoughts about their refusal a month ago to take the play there because of the Mountbatten murder.

Friday 12 October

The first *Amadeus* full run-through. Quite pleased with it. But the play is still far, far, too long: three hours of solid red meat. The principals did their stuff. They all have to play against their natural selves. Paul must not be too silky and smooth and general. Simon must not sweat as Mozart, there must be no tension in him, he must go for grace and containment. Felicity must not be twee, little me-ish, but earthy and comic. All three made big steps today along those paths. Shaffer continues to be most creative and enthusiastic; never a cross word.

Monday 15 October

Spoke to Paul about the harsh sour nature of Salieri as narrator. The essential thing is that he should show his brutal self nakedly to the audience, but put on a mask of courtesy and charm to the other characters on stage. Inevitably Paul was side-stepping the issue. I say inevitably because the first instinct of any actor, however great, is to be noble, upright, and charming to the audience. That is exactly what Paul must not be.

Thursday 18 October

Christopher[1] came to the *Amadeus* rehearsal on Tuesday, another run-through, and gave me a new pair of eyes. He found the play too flaccid, not manic enough, not Hoffmann-like[2] enough. I thought this was beginning to appear but clearly it hasn't done so sufficiently strongly. Unless it does, I see the possibility of a fairly conventional evening.

Friday 19 October

The company is in good fettle. There's an air of creativity about the place. But I still have an uneasy feeling the play is too bland and soft. Is that because of my work? Is it Shaffer's writing? Can we actually make it a furious Hoffmann-like fable? That's the challenge.

Dinner tonight with Peter[3] and Trevor. It was wonderful to be with old friends. Peter says he is disbanding his Paris group; they have been together long enough. Trevor wants to leave the RSC. I have had enough of the National. So we began again to go round the possibility of what we could do together. Trevor said that if the RSC aren't able to afford the Barbican, we might go there; or if they are, perhaps to the Aldwych. Our idea is to have only 15 actors, just the three of us as directors, and a tiny staff. God, how attractive. And what an explosion if it happened. Well, let's not be con-

---

[1] Morahan.
[2] Ernst Hoffmann, the German Romantic writer and composer; his talent for inventing bizarre and grotesque adventures in an exploration of the relationship between the natural and the supernatural inspired Offenbach's opera *The Tales of Hoffmann*.
[3] Brook.

ceited, the tiny theatre world of Britain would explode. But Trevor and I are fed up with the huge set-ups and monstrous battles. In a way we created them, but physically and emotionally we can't go on much longer. Modesty is the thing for us now: low running costs in life and in the theatre, with the money spent on specifics.

Who paid for the dinner, all fifty quids' worth? I did of course. That must stop. It was an evening of elation, though.

Monday 22 October

Am brooding on Brenton's script, *The Romans in Britain*. There was a full discussion about it at today's directors' meeting. Bill Bryden hates it. Rudman hates it. Christopher is trying to be statesmanlike about it. And I positively like it. So does John Russell Brown. The play is romantic of course, because Howard is a romantic. But I hear in it a passionate and violent voice trying to understand, and condemn, violence.

Last night of *Close of Play* so I went round to see the cast. Michael Redgrave in tears. I think he feels that this was his last time on the stage. He said to me, 'Do remember I can learn more than four words.' His illness has resulted in such a loss to us all.

Thursday 25 October

Amadeus technical rehearsal from 10.30 am to 11.30 pm, which I left only for half an hour during the supper break in the evening. This technical was like pushing a heavy tank up hill.

I haven't recorded that when I met Tony Field the other night he told me the background story to all these leaks that are going on about Arts Council business, among them one about the possible closure of the Royal Court and other theatres. He says confidential Arts Council papers have not only been distributed throughout Fleet Street, but tampered with beforehand, opinions changed, names changed. So someone is deliberately making anarchy.

Friday 26 October

First *Amadeus* preview. I have never known a situation when an audience rejected a play at a preview and later, after much more work had been done on it, were persuaded into accepting it. The first preview is the one where you know beyond doubt if the play actually works or doesn't. This one did, no question. It's still slightly muddled, slightly sentimental, slightly old-fashioned. But what I like about it is that it accepts the great theatrical gestures, and tells a story of the eighteenth century and the revolution in music. My feeling of relief at the end was enormous. I saw it with Lucy and Peter Shaffer. Lucy, aged ten, asked me in the interval if Mozart was really like that, not a very nice man. But after it was over she said it was very sad.

So the play had worked its basic trick upon her. You are made to dislike Mozart in the first act, and then your heart is broken by him in the second.

It is fascinating, the way audiences tell you things. After Mozart's first scene, when he blows fart noises with a virtuosity that delighted the public, Paul goes into a serious speech about hearing a wind serenade. It brought the house down. Amazingly, not an actor, not a stage manager, nor Peter Shaffer, nor I, have realised during rehearsal that that laugh was there. It must go.

Sunday 28 October
I think this morning I at last clarified the end of the play. From the moment he knows his behaviour has killed Mozart, Salieri wants to atone. Society doesn't let him. Instead, they pour distinctions upon him. So he tries to cut his throat, and leaves behind a false confession of poisoning Mozart. But he also tells the audience—and this is what I am misinterpreting and have never got right—that most men are mediocre. Why? The audience represents the future, and Salieri tells them that as they come to this earth and fail, as most men must fail, they now have a patron saint of mediocrity, silent Salieri, looking after their interests. Finally those on stage and those in the auditorium have to unite as Everyman.

Monday 29 October
The preview tonight was the best yet. And the end began to climb on to a tragic plane. There is still something too complicated there though; and I still feel a softness in the play itself—I haven't yet crystallized the hard centre. But *Amadeus* is working, and terrifically successful with the audience — which tonight was very starry. The most interesting reaction came from Milos Foreman[1]. He was extremely excited, and saw it as a great play, the first he had ever seen, about the problems of the creative artist in all ages. Producers, he said, still tear up scripts as Rosenberg tears up the score of *Figaro*, and still the creative man can do nothing except rail and blaspheme; originality is always attacked by the conventional; the people who are successful are not the innovators.

Tuesday 30 October
I have an uneasy feeling. *Amadeus* is lavish, right-wing, and celebrates the individual, or rather the unique importance of the individual artist. Unless we are extraordinarily lucky, and the actors have extraordinary command, it will not be liked by the press. I bet it. But it's been a tremendous experience.

---

[1] He was later to direct the film of *Amadeus*.

470

Technical work with John Bury who told me he had thought up a very good idea for the show as a proscenium production when and if we do it in New York. It has to be said that if John had not challenged my staging assumptions on the first day of rehearsals the design for the open stage of the Olivier would not have worked at all. I owe him a lot.

Wednesday 31 October
Am I getting nearer to the heart of this play or further away? I talked to Ralph, whom I had asked to come to see it at last night's preview. He said it left him unsatisfied. He was also a little shocked by the shit-talking presentation of Mozart in the first act, but I told him Mozart's letters were full of scatology. He was, though, invaluable on one thing—the haunting of Mozart when he is ill at the end. He said it was unclear. Was the figure real or not? That set me thinking. I have done the scene so that when the figure goes past Constanze she doesn't see him. And yet I expect the audience to think of him as real. Madness.

I gave notes this-afternoon, but there was a feeling in the air that the actors have now taken *Amadeus* away from me, are enjoying playing it to an audience, so would I please leave them alone. They are right too. The play has now come to its own life, good or bad.

Paul Scofield said his was the hardest part he had ever tackled in his life. Much harder than Lear because, as Salieri, he was always on stage and had such continuous and alarming changes of tone and concentration.

Friday 2 November
First night. It went well. The second act still does not move on to a tragic level, partly Peter's fault, partly mine. But there was a tumultuous reception: cheers, bravos, everyone delighted. Peter in a great gloom of depression at about two in the morning: a love affair finished—with his play and the people who staged it.

I gave him a first night present—or, rather, a first night surprise. Mozart had a little snuff-box with a painting on it of a haunted moonlit street. Small, indistinct figures move in the shadows. This is one of the central images Peter held in his mind during his composition of *Amadeus*. I got hold of a picture of it, had a slide made, and incorporated it tonight as a projection in the production. It looked very beautiful, and delighted Peter.

Sunday 4 November
Not much to say, except that I am in a twilight zone again. I tried to think, tried to rest, and wished—oh, I wished so much—that I was not me, or that my private life, and those I love, were happier.

Played a little piece of *Figaro* from the 1935 Fritz Busch Glyndebourne recording. Magic. Such wonderful tempi, elegance, and drive. Ghosts of the past.

Monday 5 November
Read the *Amadeus* notices on the train back to town from Wallingford. The actors, rightly, come out of them wonderfully. and they are better for Bury and me than I had feared. But they mostly don't actually see what Shaffer is driving at.

Tuesday 6 November
At the Western Ophthalmic Hospital again, for more lasers to be fired into my eye. This was much the most painful session I have had, and the smell of burning, real or imagined, haunted me for the rest of the day. I was told I may have to have a cornea graft, as the cornea was now distorted. I have resolved to be one-eyed instead.

Saw Max Rayne. He asked me if I was basking in my glory. I said no. He observed that the press hadn't really liked the play as a play and Arnold Goodman had hated it; even so, he said, I had done a superb job on the production, particularly the musical bits, but then that was my field wasn't it, opera.

I told him I would be going to New York next week to direct *Betrayal* on Broadway. He took it in his stride.

Wednesday 7 November
Lunch with Norman St John Stevas. He pumped me about Board members, and I pumped him about the future of the arts. I suggested he should stop pushing the idea that the arts must go to the private sector for additional funds. The private sector had no money, there was no tax relief, and the amount of time and energy we all spent in getting a few thousand pounds from that source would be better spent doing our jobs. We should be properly financed by the government and made to earn more money for ourselves. He seemed to quite like that.

Talked to Paul and said he could now add Salieri to his Thomas More[1] and King Lear, just as Larry could claim as his own Richard III, Henry V, and Archie Rice[2]—all performances where the actor and the part become one.

Friday 9 November
Dinner with John Barton, which I enjoyed. It's years since we had a quiet time together. It sounds to me as if his RSC production of *The Greeks*, which

---

[1] In Robert Bolt's *A Man for All Seasons*.   [2] In John Osborne's *The Entertainer*.

will open at the Aldwych in early February, is going to pre-empt *The Oresteia* for a year or two[1].

Amadeus was packed again: an atmosphere like a football match.

Saturday 10 November
Drove from London to Bedales with Lucy and Edward who may be going there, as did Jenny and Christopher. Then to Wallingford with them and Simon Brook[2] who loves the school. Had a ghostly experience at Bedales: I thought I saw Jenny and Christopher jumping out of the bushes to greet us as we arrived. Time flies.

Tuesday 13 November
Paul rang me this morning, as emotional as I have ever known him, to say thank you for *Amadeus*. He said what a wonderful place the National was now, what a good atmosphere, and how he loved working in it. This was very generous and kind of him.

The *Daily Express* called at the Barbican flat today and, in front of Lucy who was standing there, asked Jacky if she and I were breaking up. Lucy laughed. It seemed to satisfy them, for they left without asking more.

Wednesday 14 November
Off this morning to New York on Concorde. A merry plane load—John Schlesinger, Bryan Forbes, and Placido Domingo.

To the Algonquin and the inevitable umpteen phone calls. The hotel room seems to be full of brandy (which I don't drink) from various kindly well-wishers.

Thursday 15 November
New York: I already have rising claustrophobia from staying in this hotel. My room is hot and cupboard like. Anyway, we all met this morning, talked about *Betrayal*, and read it. But bringing the three principals[3] into one style is going to be a problem. We are rehearsing on the forty-fifth floor of the Minskoff building. I look at the actors with the whole of Manhattan spread out beyond them: Central Park, the lake, the West and East rivers. Very distracting: no kind of set to rehearse against.

A pleasant dinner with Antonia and Harold Pinter. But I feel disorientated.

[1] Hall's *Oresteia*—played in full masks with an all-male cast, and designed by Jocelyn Herbert—finally opened in the Olivier in November 1981, to excellent reviews.
[2] Peter and Natasha Brook's son.
[3] Blythe Danner as Emma, Raul Julia as Gerry, and Roy Scheider as Robert.

Peter Hall's Diaries

Sunday 18 November
New York: Good progress on *Betrayal*. But I can't throw off this lethargy. Dinner at Peter Shaffer's. He had said, 'Come by on Sunday night for a little spaghetti and wine.' In fact, we had a splendid meal, beautifully served. He was very tender and considerate. He has always been a friend, but since *Amadeus* there is something very close.

Monday 19 November
New York: Yesterday's *Sunday Times*, in its guide to what's on in the theatre, prints the following thumbnail report on *Amadeus*. It is by James Fenton, the paper's new drama critic: 'Appalling new play by author of *Equus*. . .plasticated production by Peter Hall. . .Paul Scofield mediocre as Salieri. . .Simon Callow and Felicity Kendal do their best as the Mozarts.' How can anyone describe Scofield as mediocre, even if they don't like him? Fenton's full review of *Amadeus* a week ago was a real butcher's job. He is starting his reign by playing the terrorist.

To a preview of Bob Fosse's film, *All That Jazz*, about a director/ choreographer who has a heart attack and dies. It's showbiz sensuality, life and glitter, surface pleasures, set against inevitable mortality: an obvious theme, obviously autobiographical, and there is much in it which is indulgent, brash, and coarse. But Roy Scheider is magnificent, and I always enjoy Fosse's courage and energy.

He was at the dinner afterwards—a small, watchful 52-year-old Norwegian/American: bitchy, but tenderly so, an absolute product of showbiz, loves actors, hoofers, vaudeville. He suspects, I think, that this film, all ten million dollars of it, is not going to be a great hit. But it's him.

Tuesday 20 November
New York: A slow rehearsal, but I was pleased to see a relationship of joy and humour developing between Raul and Blythe: it helps enormously if Gerry and Emma make each other laugh. A good day, but a heavy one.

Then to a dinner in honour of Harold and Antonia—the full Manhattan chic: money, shrieks, and a lot of high-dressed, expensive bitches, who themselves do very little, telling us who was in, who was out. There were some workers there though—among them, Sam Spiegel, Harold and Antonia, Jules Feiffer, and me. But the air was thick with the twitter of dilettantes. I left at eleven. I can't stand that side of New York.

Wednesday 21 November
New York: The three principal actors are eagerly eating up *Betrayal*. Very soon now I must hand it back to them so that they can create something for themselves. I think they will. But I myself feel that after the National

production it's imitation stuff: Americans desperately trying to be British. The skins don't fit.

Walter Kerr is back at the *New York Times*, but to give him more time to write his notices he is now allowed to go to previews. The *Times* is on the streets as early as half past eight in the evening, and at an opening last week Peter Shaffer said people were reading in the interval Kerr's damning review, written the previous night, and saying there was hardly any point in going back for the rest of the play because it was a flop. . . .

Thursday 22 November
New York: Out to Long Island for lunch with some rich aristocratic friends of Antonia's. Their house is beautiful. It was built in 1923, is very Scott Fitzgerald, and set in rolling park land. Inside, the art was stupendous: a beautiful picture of Monet's wife, a Degas bronze, Matisses, Cézannes, Renoirs galore. It is the sort of place that in England is only partly lived in, if at all, and visited by paying admission money.

My forty-ninth birthday. Sam Spiegel gave a party for me at his penthouse on Park Lane: fantastic wealth, two butlers, too much food. Antonia's daughter and a friend of hers were there. The friend was an English girl who greatly roused Harold's wrath by saying the Americans should not send troops to Iran[1]. He got very belligerent. The girl won.

Phoned Paul who said the receptions for *Amadeus* continue to be extraordinary, more enthusiastic than any he has known. Last night, he got so carried away during the climax of the play that at the attempted suicide he actually did cut his throat slightly, grazed it. He won't do that again. He nearly didn't do it *ever* again. The razor has cellotape round it but is still dangerous.

Friday 23 November
New York: Moved today to Peter Shaffer's apartment, where I live pleasantly in the sun room with the plants and the tropical fish.

To Stoppard's *Night and Day*. Tom and Peter Wood[2] have done an enormous amount of work on the play since I saw it in London[3], but I still find it about too many things, everything that is in Tom's head at the moment—freedom of the press, the abuse of freedom of the press, trade unionism, the abuse of trade unionism, the position of women, the third world. Somehow he has tried to make it into one play. It's four at least.

Sunday 25 November
Flew back to London. Smooth journey, and royally welcomed by the children when I arrived at the flat.

---

[1] At the time, sixty-two Americans were imprisoned in Iran by the Ayatollah Khomeini's regime, held as hostages against the return of the ex-Shah.
[2] Its director   [3] At the Phoenix Theatre.

The main news among my papers is that Toby Robertson has been fired from the Old Vic after all that work[1]. His old friend, Timothy West[2], his colleague and loyal supporter through all the years of Prospect, has taken his place. I am appalled. Toby was in China on tour with the company at the time. Clearly it's not safe to be out of the country. I must be careful. . . .

Monday 26 November
Board meeting. Max went on about production costs, but I asked if he and the Board were more concerned about a one per cent over-run on expenditure or a five-and-a-half per cent increase in income. Our receipts are phenomenal. Last week all three theatres played to absolute capacity.

Back to America tomorrow.

Tuesday 27 November
Edward is thirteen today, and at least I had the pleasure of being with him at breakfast before he went off to school and I left for Heathrow. He is one of the nicest people I know.

Off at 9.30 on Concorde, so I was in Shaffer's apartment in New York by 9.30, and at rehearsal by 10.30. I had slept on the plane so felt pretty good. Rehearsed well, but crashed out at 9 pm feeling very curious indeed.

Thursday 29 November
New York: Took Raul's suggestion of getting a speech and accent specialist from the Juilliard School to teach the actors to place their tongues round English. He is a cheerful young man called Tim Monich, early thirties, American, and with the finest ear I have ever encountered. He is Professor Higgins-like. He knew at once that Blythe came from south of Philadelphia, and told her she hadn't quite disguised it. Explaining to her how to pronounce the word 'country' he said, 'You have got to be more open on the "count".' Blythe said she would, to the best of her ability. He blushed.

But what depresses me is that he is teaching the actors virtually a foreign language, so the nuance, the element I love in a Pinter play, comes very late and crudely. The cast work well and hard, but I feel I am manufacturing something rather than creating it. Why did I do it? I suppose because of my devotion to Harold and to *Betrayal*.

News from London is that the general picture continues to be good, and the excellent box office business goes on. *Betrayal* there has won the best play award from the Society of West End Theatre Managers, and apparently

---

[1] From 1964 to 1979 he was Artistic Director of Prospect Theatre Company, which mainly toured, but from 1977 to 1981 made its base at the Old Vic and during that time was re-named the Old Vic Company.

[2] The actor; Artistic Director of the Old Vic Company from 1980 to 1981, when the company went into liquidation.

Harold in his acceptance speech said he was genuinely surprised, and thought only Michael Billington would have been more so. Billington wrote in his review that he wasn't interested in the sex lives of Hampstead intellectuals. He wanted social issues.

Sunday 2 December
New York: Saw Francis Ford Coppola's *Apocalypse Now*: an overwhelming experience; I loved it. The Vietnam war bit is a touch long, but the last half hour, which has been heavily criticised for its pretentiousness, is I think wonderfully eloquent and surreal about violence. It's a film which is very much of America now. And how something costing millions of dollars, and therefore needing to be popular, can be exactly that without betraying itself, without betraying its integrity, is the measure of Coppola's achievement.

Monday 10 December
New York: We are rehearsing at the New Amsterdam Theatre, 42nd Street, which was the glamorous night spot of the twenties and is now a decrepit, crumbling bit of art nouveau. Outside is like a battlefield: sirens, police whistles—not the sort of noises you want invading a Pinter pause. 42nd Street is the end of the world, Hieronymus Bosch.

Two things have been brought home to me in New York. First, the pace at which I work and live, and how necessary to that is the excellent support system I have at the NT, which allows every minute of my day to be as productive as possible. Second, how marvellously spoilt anyone is when actually directing a play at the NT. Here I shout, scream for props, furniture, this and that. They nod, but it almost never comes. At least our objective on the South Bank is to do the play as well as possible. Here it seems to be to save as many dollars as possible.

Tuesday 11 December
New York: I have been given advance, confidential, news from London of this year's *Evening Standard* drama awards. *Amadeus* has apparently been voted the best play, and Warren Mitchell, in *Death of a Salesman*, the best actor.

Saw a terrible show tonight called *Sugar Babies*, a burlesque of burlesque, with fan dancers, pigeons, comic dogs. But the reason I went was to see Mickey Rooney. He is a master. Whatever he does—hoofing, clowning, singing, gagging—he does it with a discretion and a vulnerability which is superb. He is a great clown, quite wonderful.

Tuesday 18 December
New York: The Shuberts are amazed. . . . Paul Scofield has said no to playing in *Amadeus* in New York. Chauffeur-driven limousines day and

night, a house in Connecticut, and a maximum of only five performances a week won't tempt him. He doesn't like New York life, never has, so simply won't do it; he wants to go on playing on the South Bank.

Tuesday 25 December
New York: I didn't go home for Christmas.

I have always kept this diary professional and un-personal, but now it's beginning to seem ridiculous if I cannot say—or will not say—what is in my heart. I am deeply in love with Maria Ewing, and have been with her here. We plan to make our life together in the new year when she will come to London[1].

Thursday 27 December
New York: For once, I took a night off from the play. But a fierce lady in the audience at *Bent*[2] accosted me during the evening. She said that American Equity were wrecking my work here by not letting me have British actors. 'Your cast simply can't act it,' she observed.

Bent is a Manhattan fag's fantasy—black leather and swastikas, sex in concentration camps. The plight of the homosexual in Nazi Germany was terrible. But this is salacious and sentimental. I'm told there are often people in the audience wearing pink triangles—the mark of the homosexual in concentration camps.

Friday 28 December
New York: Peter Shaffer, who has been made very sore and angry by James Fenton's savage attacks on him and *Amadeus*, was cheered a little today, but not enough, by hearing that the critics have given it the *Plays and Players'* award for the best play of the year. This follows the news that Paul, for Salieri, has got the Variety Club of Great Britain award for the year's best actor[3].

Monday 31 December
Walked through Times Square on New Year's Eve on my way to the theatre. I have never seen such a vision of hell: drunks lying on the pavements, junkies leaning against walls, policemen in plastic helmets with batons at the ready, noise, lights, madness, violence in the air.

---

[1] Hall married Maria Ewing, an American, in February 1982 in New York; they have a daughter, Rebecca.

[2] By Martin Sherman.

[3] In all, *Amadeus* won thirteen awards, including five Tonys, and earned nearly £500,000 for the NT as a result of its commercial life after leaving the Olivier. It transferred to Her Majesty's Theatre in June 1981, where it ran until October 1982. Another production of the play by Hall opened in New York in December 1980 and, at the time these diaries went to press, is still running there.

1980

Saturday 5 January
New York: Opening of *Betrayal*. The cast did well, but the idiom of the play is not theirs. I was directing something that was in some sense foreign to them, and it's not finally creative.

Monday 7 January
Flew home, and as I left it seemed we were a hit[1]. Walter Kerr's review is particularly good and intelligent.

Back in London, I had an impromptu late Christmas with presents in the evening with the children.

Wednesday 9 January
John Gielgud, who was to have played Lear for us in the Cottesloe and abroad, has now said no, in a welter of sorrow, mortification and disappointment. He just doesn't want to risk tackling it again after so many previous successes in the part. I understand. But it will cause hell at all the European dates we had scheduled for it, and with the Edinburgh festival where it was also due to go.

Thursday 10 January
Spent the morning at the Barbican Theatre with Peter Brook and Trevor. It is beautiful, and makes me feel very proud of the work John Bury and I did on its design. It's the best theatre for Shakespeare I have ever been in.

Friday 11 January
It is rumoured I am to get one of those *Evening Standard* statues as a special award, like George Devine, Olivier, and Daubeny had in the past. It's the kind of rumour one must never trust, and I despise myself for caring. But I do. It's warming to be recognised. And it would not be true to say I have grown completely hardened to being a target at the National, despite my belief that when the job stops drawing fire it's time to get out.

---

[1] The play ran in New York until the end of May. Later, a film version of *Betrayal* was made, directed by David Jones.

Wednesday 16 January

Since I returned from America I have seen *Uncle Vanya* at Hampstead[1], with Ian Holm back in the theatre after five years, and simply masterly as Astrov; the RSC's *Once in a Lifetime*[2], brilliantly directed by Trevor; and Chris Morahan's production of *The Wild Duck* in the Olivier. The critics have been criminally unfair to *The Wild Duck*. There are things wrong here and there, but Michael Bryant as Gregers is wonderful, Ralph as old Ekdal is definitive, and Eva Griffith as Hedvig is very true and touching. I had a marvellous time.

Saturday 19 January

To see Michael Bogdanov's adaptation of *The Ancient Mariner* at the Young Vic: a brilliant production by him—physical, spectacular, enthralling to young people. Sailors climbed up swinging ropes, and the albatross was stretched out towards the audience on a long bamboo pole moved around by a black, masked figure. Beautiful.

Jonathan Miller collected his ticket at the same time as I did; I cut him before he cut me, and he was embarrassed. His criticism of me has done me harm, more than Blakemore, for Miller talks well and is listened to by the media.

Lunch with Ralph. Two bottles of chianti were downed, one each. He gently and generously offered himself as father confessor. But though, as he knows, I am going through a big crisis in my private life I somehow found I could confess little. . . .

Sunday 20 January

To Glyndebourne. Brian Dickie[3] and Moran Caplat are proposing I become artistic director around 82–3. I think it depends on three things: on the general shape of my life; on Bernard Haitink staying as music director; and on the money. It would certainly excite me, and I could combine it with other work. Whatever happens, I feel very pleased at the offer.

Harold rang me tonight to tell me *Betrayal* played to $110,000 last week, is now a hit, and is expected to do even better.

Friday 25 January

Lunch with Warren Mitchell. I don't think I have ever met so insecure an actor, and that's saying a lot. He had a hard life as a beginner. But even when he became a big television star, playing Alf Garnett, he couldn't, he said, quite throw off his feelings of inadequacy. And now that he is giving an indisputably great performance in the theatre it seems he still can't quite believe in his own strength. Well, he *is* a great actor.

[1] Directed by Nancy Meckler.   [2] By George Kaufman and Moss Hart.
[3] At the time, Glyndebourne Opera Manager, and from 1981 General Administrator.

Saturday 26 January
To Wallingford for the weekend. Worked all the time, apart from a two-hour walk in the cold, still day across empty, frozen fields.

We are now agreed to do Howard Brenton's *The Romans in Britain*. I am mightily excited. It is likely to be directed by Bogdanov[1].

Laurie Evans tells me the *Evening Standard* special award is definitely coming to me. Two years ago the *Standard* was crucifying me, so I hope the presentation statue has a little blood on it.

Tuesday 29 January
Evening Standard drama awards day. It was held in the National Theatre. Many friends came (and many enemies too, no doubt). It was rather like a Christmas party that went on too long. I thought I knew what present I was going to get, but I wasn't absolutely sure, and when I actually got it, I had the usual feelings of distress. Why?

Speeches galore: Trevor Nunn lucid and funny; Alec McCowen and Diana Rigg acerbic; and everyone got at the Minister about grants, who blushed pink. Ralph made a wonderful contribution, a masterpiece of comic timing, about keeping the secret of who was to get the special award, and not letting the cat out of the bag. Princess Margaret then gave me my present, 'for twenty-five years of service to the theatre'. Every single award was for work done by people in the subsidised sector. That could never have happened twenty-five years ago.

So, all in all, now seems a suitable time to finish this diary, though it is strange to think it will no longer be there to relieve my feelings, record my doubts, and release my resentments. Shall I miss it? I think I shall. It's become a habit, like cleaning my teeth.

As far as the National Theatre is concerned we have reached the end of the beginning of the new building, and that's a good point to stop.

Twenty-five years of trying to do the same thing is really why I was given that statue. When I was just down from Cambridge, running the Arts Theatre, I wanted to develop a permanent group of actors, all growing together, learning together. I still do. Yet I am as far away from it as ever. Perhaps I shall be able to achieve it under the banner of the National; perhaps Trevor and Peter and I will do it somewhere else; perhaps it will never be done. But whatever my new professional life is, however different it feels, I don't suppose it will be much changed. The same battles recur, the same fights are necessary.

I don't believe life begins at fifty, but I mean to try and make it.

[1] It *was* directed by Michael Bogdanov, and opened in the Olivier in October 1980 to instant controversy, which developed into a celebrated legal case. Mrs Mary Whitehouse brought a prosecution against Bogdanov on the grounds that a part of the production—a scene showing the attempted homosexual rape of a druid by a Roman soldier—was obscene. The case came to trial at the Old Bailey on 15 March 1982, but ended three days later when the prosecution was dropped, and *nolle prosequi* entered on the record.

SIR PETER HALL'S
PRODUCTIONS UP TO 1983 INCLUDE:

1953	THE LETTER	Somerset Maugham	Theatre Royal, Windsor
1954	BLOOD WEDDING	Lorca	Arts, London
	THE IMPRESARIO FROM SMYRNA	Goldoni	Arts, London
	THE IMMORALIST	Gide	Arts, London
	LISTEN TO THE WIND (children's musical)	Vivian Ellis	Arts, London
1955	THE LESSON	Ionesco	Arts, London
	SOUTH	Julien Green	Arts, London
	MOURNING BECOMES ELECTRA	O'Neill	Arts, London
	WAITING FOR GODOT	Beckett	Arts, London
	THE BURNT FLOWER-BED	Ugo Betti	Arts, London
	SUMMERTIME	Ugo Betti	Apollo, London
1956	THE WALTZ OF THE TOREADORS	Anouilh	Arts, London
	GIGI	Colette	New, now Albery, London
	LOVE'S LABOUR'S LOST	Shakespeare	Stratford-on-Avon
	THE GATES OF SUMMER	John Whiting	New, Oxford
1957	CAMINO REAL	Tennessee Williams	Phoenix, London
	THE MOON AND SIXPENCE (opera)	John Gardner	Sadler's Wells
	CYMBELINE	Shakespeare	Stratford-on-Avon
	THE ROPE DANCERS	Morton Wishengrad	Cort Theatre, NY
1958	CAT ON A HOT TIN ROOF	Tennessee Williams	Comedy, London
	TWELFTH NIGHT	Shakespeare	Stratford-on-Avon
	BROUHAHA	George Tabori	Aldwych, London
	SHADOW OF HEROES	Robert Ardrey	Piccadilly, London
1959	MADAME DE...	Anouilh	Arts, London
	TRAVELLER WITHOUT LUGGAGE	Anouilh	Arts, London
	A MIDSUMMER NIGHT'S DREAM	Shakespeare	Stratford-on-Avon
	CORIOLANUS	Shakespeare	Stratford-on-Avon

485

	THE WRONG SIDE OF THE PARK	John Mortimer	Cambridge, London
1960	THE TWO GENTLEMEN OF VERONA	Shakespeare	Stratford-on-Avon
	TWELFTH NIGHT	Shakespeare	Stratford-on-Avon
	TROILUS AND CRESSIDA	Shakespeare	Stratford-on-Avon
1961	ONDINE	Giraudoux	RSC
	BECKET	Anouilh	RSC
	ROMEO AND JULIET	Shakespeare	RSC
1962	A MIDSUMMER NIGHT'S DREAM	Shakespeare	RSC
	THE COLLECTION	Pinter (who also co-directed)	RSC
	TROILUS AND CRESSIDA	Shakespeare	RSC
1963	THE WARS OF THE ROSES (a trilogy, adapted with John Barton from Henry VI Parts 1, 2, 3, & Richard III)	Shakespeare	RSC
1964	RICHARD II	Shakespeare	RSC
	HENRY IV, Parts 1 & 2	Shakespeare	RSC
	HENRY V	Shakespeare	RSC
	EH?	Henry Livings	RSC
1965	THE HOMECOMING	Pinter	RSC
	MOSES AND AARON (opera)	Schoenberg	Covent Garden
	HAMLET	Shakespeare	RSC
1966	THE GOVERNMENT INSPECTOR	Gogol	RSC
	THE MAGIC FLUTE (opera)	Mozart	Covent Garden
	STAIRCASE	Charles Wood	RSC
1967	MACBETH	Shakespeare	RSC
1969	A DELICATE BALANCE	Albee	RSC
	DUTCH UNCLE	Simon Gray	RSC
	LANDSCAPE & SILENCE	Pinter	RSC
1970	THE KNOT GARDEN (opera)	Tippett	Covent Garden
	LA CALISTO (opera)	Cavalli	Glyndebourne
	THE BATTLE OF SHRIVINGS	Shaffer	Lyric
1971	EUGENE ONEGIN (opera)	Tchaikovsky	Covent Garden
	OLD TIMES	Pinter	RSC
	TRISTAN UND ISOLDE (opera)	Wagner	Covent Garden
1972	ALL OVER	Albee	RSC
	ALTE ZEITEN	Pinter	Vienna
	IL RITORNO D'ULISSE (opera)	Monteverdi	Glyndebourne
	VIA GALACTICA (musical)	Galt MacDermot	New York
1973	THE MARRIAGE OF FIGARO (opera)	Mozart	Glyndebourne
	THE TEMPEST	Shakespeare	NT
1974	JOHN GABRIEL BORKMAN	Ibsen	NT
	HAPPY DAYS	Beckett	NT
1975	NO MAN'S LAND	Pinter	NT
	HAMLET	Shakespeare	NT
	JUDGEMENT	Barry Collins	NT
1976	TAMBURLAINE THE GREAT	Marlowe	NT

1977	BEDROOM FARCE	Ayckbourn (who also co-directed)	NT
	DON GIOVANNI (opera)	Mozart	Glyndebourne
	VOLPONE	Jonson	NT
	THE COUNTRY WIFE	Wycherley	NT
1978	COSI FAN TUTTE (opera)	Mozart	Glyndebourne
	THE CHERRY ORCHARD	Chekhov	NT
	MACBETH	Shakespeare	NT
	BETRAYAL	Pinter	NT
1979	FIDELIO (opera)	Beethoven	Glyndebourne
	AMADEUS	Shaffer	NT
1980	OTHELLO	Shakespeare	NT
1981	A MIDSUMMER NIGHT'S DREAM (opera)	Britten	Glyndebourne
	THE ORESTEIA	the trilogy by Aeschylus	NT
1982	ORFEO ET EURYDICE (opera)	Gluck	Glyndebourne
	THE IMPORTANCE OF BEING EARNEST	Wilde	NT
	MACBETH (opera)	Verdi	Metropolitan Opera House, NY
	OTHER PLACES	Pinter	NT
1983	DER RING DES NIBELUNGEN (opera)	Wagner	Bayreuth

The years given are those of a production's first stage performance. Any revivals, tours, or television versions are not listed.

FILMS: WORK IS A FOUR LETTER WORD (1968)
A MIDSUMMER NIGHT'S DREAM (1969)
THREE INTO TWO WON'T GO (1969)
PERFECT FRIDAY (1971)
THE HOMECOMING (1973)
AKENFIELD (1974)

487

INDEX

Nijinsky, Vaslav 201
Nixon, Richard 104
No Man's Land 119, 129, 168n, 340, 413
   design of, 135–6, 141, 146
   rehearsals of, 152, 154–9, 175, 332–3
   opening and reviews of, 159–60
   London run of, 189, 195, 207–8
   in Lyttleton Theatre 229, 233–4, 284
   in America, 268–9
   on TV, 337, 378
No More A-Roving 112
Normington, John 461n
North and South 51
Norton, Jim 190
Nottingham Playhouse 14, 40n, 100, 124n,
   155, 177, 312, 345, 359, 422–3
Nova 79
Nozze Di Figaro, Le 43, 46–7, 49, 52–3, 78,
   97, 294, 299, 411, 459, 470, 472
Nunn, Trevor 5, 15, 22–4, 50–3, 65–7, 69,
   111, 148, 168, 173, 182, 227n, 234, 262,
   286–7, 313–4, 331–2, 342, 344, 347, 418,
   446, 481, 483
   and NT/RSC amalgamation or association,
    8, 12–14, 20–1, 30–2, 34, 37–8, 40–5, 48,
    55–6, 58, 91
   productions by, 115–6, 302, 314–5, 482
   discussions with Hall on future, 136,
    166–7, 359, 468–9
   and NT/RSC relations, 209, 369–70,
    387

Oakes, Philip 191n
O'Brien, Conor Cruise 377
O'Brien, Edna 68, 255
O'Brien, Leslie 87, 194, 257, 275
O'Brien, Timothy 96, 98–9, 119, 130, 409
Observer, The 6, 55, 71n, 85, 93, 126, 133,
   186n, 187, 189, 191n, 218–9, 230, 255,
   263, 272, 343–4, 346, 354, 377, 396
O'Casey, Eileen 415–6
O'Casey, Sean 415
Occupations 155
Odeon 95
Offenbach Jacques 468n
O'Keefe, John 273n
Oklahoma 319
Old Country, The 348
Old Times 7, 10–1, 14, 158, 457
Old Vic Theatre 3, 9, 11n, 13, 15, 19, 29, 34,
   36, 45, 49, 65, 69, 78n, 79, 81–3, 86–9,
   92–3, 95n, 104–5, 107, 109, 121n, 128n,
   130, 132n, 142, 145–6, 149n, 151n, 153,
   155n, 156, 167, 173, 175, 180n, 183n,
   186, 195, 197, 208, 210, 212n, 213–7,
   234, 259n, 275, 359, 409n, 454, 476
Olivier 153

Olivier, Laurence 16, 23, 36, 46, 50–1, 53, 56,
   58–9, 63–9, 71, 75, 78–9, 83, 85, 87–9, 92,
   109, 122, 149, 153, 163, 176–8, 189, 209,
   217, 233–4, 244–5, 253, 273–5, 282, 294,
   300–1, 351, 354, 359, 370, 375, 425, 442,
   466, 481
   and Hall's succession to, 3–4, 6–9, 11–2, 15,
    17–8, 29–30, 33, 35, 38, 60–1
   and NT/RSC merger talks, 20, 24, 30–2, 34,
    40–4
   at Associates Meetings 81, 96, 110, 121
   last performance at Old Vic of, 86
   planned resignation of, 150, 178
   refuses to appear at Old Vic or South Bank,
    187, 210, 214, 242–3, 257–8
   and Royal Opening, 264–6
Olivier Theatre 15, 19, 130, 145, 156–7, 166,
   176, 199, 208–9, 215–6, 218, 220, 225,
   228–9, 231–5, 241–4, 247–50, 254–5,
   257–8, 259n, 260–1, 263n, 267–8, 271n,
   272, 273n, 279, 282, 286, 288, 290, 292,
   294–5, 299n, 302, 304, 306–7, 315, 318,
   331, 345, 356, 365, 367–9, 372–3, 377,
   380, 382, 389, 412–3, 423, 425, 426n, 436,
   455, 464, 467, 471, 473n, 478n,
   483n
Onassis, Jacqueline 357
Once in A Lifetime 482
Ondine 175
One Flew Over the Cuckoo's Nest 238
O'Neill, Eugene 381, 417
Open Space Theatre 124n
Open University 128, 185
Orchard, Julian 83
Oresteia, The 166n, 310, 395–6, 473n
   plans for and delays of, 49, 223, 237, 276,
    302, 388, 397, 401, 416
   and the RSC, 369–70, 373, 381, 387, 397,
    473
   rehearsals of, 418–22
   stopped by the strike, 424, 426, 431–2
Orgel, Stephen 57
Orient Express 457
Orton, Joe 449
Orwell, George 36
Orwell, Sonia 36, 39
Osborne, John 100, 227, 258, 317, 472n
   and *Watch It Come Down* 115, 168n, 206,
    213–5, 235–6, 354
Ostvedt, Dr. 99
Otello 227
Othello 110, 143, 224, 268, 295, 311, 349, 400,
   421, 444
Other Place, The 171
O'Toole, Peter 408
Otway, Thomas 301
Oxford University 372

501